Inside Hitler's Germany

Inside Hitler's Germany

A Documentary History of Life in the Third Reich

Benjamin C. Sax

University of Kansas

Dieter Kuntz

University of Kansas

D. C. Heath and Company
Lexington, Massachusetts   Toronto

Address editorial correspondence to:

D. C. Heath
125 Spring Street
Lexington, MA 02173

Cover: Fritz Hirschberger

Interior illustrations: p. 22, The Bettmann Archive; p. 60, The Bettmann Archive; p. 90, Popperfoto; p. 124, The National Archives; p. 158, Ullstein Bilderdienst; p. 184, The Bettmann Archive; p. 218, The Bettmann Archive; p. 239, The Bettmann Archive; p. 240, Bundesarchiv; p. 241, Bundesarchiv; p. 242, Bundesarchiv; p. 243, Culver Pictures, Inc.; p. 244, Bundesarchiv; p. 245, George Weidenfeld & Nicolson Limited; p. 246, Ullstein Bilderdienst; p. 247, Ullstein Bilderdienst; p. 248, Bundesarchiv; p. 249, George Weidenfeld & Nicholson Limited; p. 250, George Weidenfeld & Nicholson Limited; p. 251, Münchner Stadtmuseum; p. 252, Popperfoto; p. 274, Ullstein Bilderdienst; p. 302, UPI/Bettmann; p. 336, The National Archives; p. 366, Ullstein Bilderdienst; p. 396, Popperfoto; p. 426, Popperfoto; p. 458, Ullstein Bilderdienst.

Published simultaneously in Canada.

Printed in the United States of America.

International Standard Book Number: 0-669-25000-7

Library of Congress Catalog Number: 91-75369

10 9 8 7 6 5

About the Cover

Fritz Hirschberger was born in Dresden, Germany, in 1920 to Polish parents. He completed his studies in art and the humanities shortly after Hitler came to power, and was then arrested by the Gestapo and deported to Poland. A soldier in the Polish army, he fought and was imprisoned by first the Germans and then the Russians, but was released in the fall of 1941. After the war he went to London, where he studied painting for a year at the St. Martens Art Academy. He eventually came to New York with his wife, and since that time has lived in the United States.

Now a resident of California, he continues to paint. Since 1980 he has concentrated on the Holocaust. His personal feelings about the event are strong because his father was killed at Camp Dora, but beyond that he is concerned about the evidence of society's indifference since the war ended in 1945. His intent is to refocus the attention of people not personally connected to those events from the massive and anonymous numbers involved to the individual human beings who made up those numbers. If viewers can see just one sufferer and sense the horror of that one experience, they can better understand the impact of that one multiplied by millions. Thinking only of the large numbers dehumanizes the event and fosters indifference. We cannot respond as fully to the suffering of millions as easily as we can to the suffering of one or two individuals.

The painting on the cover, "Indifference," expresses this aim with great poignancy. The white face of the baby and the white hand of the boy draw the viewer into an emotional response that the other figures cannot. The viewer feels their fear and the danger and wishes to help; the effect is deeply moving. The poem "written" into the barbed wire of the fence is by Edmund Yashinski, a Polish Yiddish poet. Ironically, Yashinski survived the Holocaust only to die in prison in communist Poland after the defeat of the Nazis. It reads:

> Fear not your enemies for they can only kill you
> Fear not your friends for they can only betray you
> Fear only the indifferent who permit the killers and
> Betrayers to walk safely on earth.

Billie Ingram
Photo Editor

Preface

Our aim in editing *Inside Hitler's Germany* is to make available to students and scholars a collection of source material dealing with various aspects of the political and social history of the Third Reich. We have assembled 126 documents, many of them never previously published or translated. Moreover, we have sought to avoid presenting mere illustrative snippets. In the hope of encouraging further understanding of this crucial phase of twentieth-century history, we have either reproduced the entire original documents or provided extensive offerings from them.

Our principle of selection has been whenever possible to reproduce first-hand accounts representing the attitudes and reactions — the roles and options — of specific individuals and social groups. The secondary literature on Nazism is extensive, and scholars continue to make important contributions, but these accounts too often leave the student with little sense of the social conditions or the experiences of individuals inside Hitler's Germany.

In addition, we have also tried to integrate the history of politics and society with cultural history. Whereas documentary anthologies have concentrated upon political, diplomatic, and military aspects of the Third Reich, we present materials dealing with (1) the ideological content of Nazism and its appeal to various segments of the population, (2) the cultural and social policies of the regime, and (3) the attitudes and reactions of various individuals and groups toward the dictatorship. By emphasizing the interaction between Nazi ideology and the policies of the state, as well as between this ideology and its impact upon German society, we think we have made a contribution to the further understanding of the National Socialist phenomenon.

The immediate occasion for assembling this anthology was to provide students at the University of Kansas with more compelling materials for understanding life inside Nazi Germany. In manuscript, it has served for several years as the major text in a course with approximately two hundred students. As a teaching device, *Inside Hitler's Germany* has far exceeded our expectations. Exposure to primary materials stimulated students' interest in Nazism and led them into closer analysis of its nature and origin. Through the development of techniques of critical reading and the development of their own interpretive viewpoints, students came to a better understanding of the Nazi phenomenon in particular and of historical methods in general.

To provide contextual background necessary for the understanding of this material and to allow the volume to stand on its own as a history of the Third Reich, we have included extensive introductory sections. They can easily be enhanced by other readings or by lectures as the instructor sees fit.

We have organized the three Units of this documentary history both thematically and chronologically. Unit One (Chapters 1–5) deals with the political history of Germany from 1918 to 1938, traces the development of the Nazi party from the early 1920s through the seizure of power in 1933, and concludes with the consolidation of Hitler's dictatorship in the mid-1930s. The documents in this unit represent first-hand accounts of the party's development. They include such diverse sources as testimonials by early party members and reports by police observers who analyze the Nazi appeal to various groups within Germany. Other documents included here come from the archives of the Nazi party itself and have not been published before. In addition, regional Nazi party archives, which have only recently been made available to scholars, have also been exploited.

Unit Two (Chapters 6–10) deals with the ideology and social policies of National Socialism. These documents reveal the ideological foundations of Nazism, the attempts to translate ideology into practice, and the impact of these policies upon German society. Here, too, we selected documents that would both offer the viewpoints of individual participants and present the most accurate and reliable information possible. Of special interest are the observations made by members of the outlawed and underground Social Democratic Party of Germany (Sopade). These monthly reports to the socialist leadership located outside Germany yield remarkably candid assessments of Nazi policies toward workers and other social groups. These valuable documents have to date received little attention by scholars and are offered here in translation for the first time.

The documents in Unit Three (Chapters 11–15) take up the history of the main instruments of Nazi totalitarian rule. We examine in detail the development of the SS, its extensive use of police powers, and its central role in the racial policies of the Third Reich. The conditions of the Jews of Germany in the early 1930s, the development of various official and unofficial policies toward them, and the program and implementation of the Final Solution can here be seen both from the regime's and the victims' viewpoints. The last chapter of this unit deals with the crucial question of popular attitudes toward the national socialist dictatorship. A selection of subversive pamphlets and manifestoes, as well as various SS police reports concerning popular attitudes and opposition, fill out the picture of the various types and methods of resistance in the Third Reich.

To familiarize students with relevant geographical locations, chronological sequences, and important individuals and organizations, we have included several maps and charts, a chronological table, a list of names, and a glossary of terms.

Many people helped in the preparation of this volume. Our deep appreciation goes to Professor John F. Sweets, who made valuable comments on the introductory materials, and to Professor Carl Strikwerda, whose suggestions on its classroom use improved the selection of documents. We are especially grateful to Anne Kuntz and Lynne Shapiro for their support and tireless efforts in preparing the volume. For their encouragement and assistance in the early stages of this project, we thank the following people from the Division of Continuing Education at the University of Kansas: Nancy Colyer, Director of Independent Study; Barbara Watkins, Manager of Curriculum and Projects; Donna Butler, Managing Editor; and Paula Schumacher, Editorial Assistant. Special thanks go to the reviewers whose comments greatly assisted us in shaping the anthology: Professors David F. Crew, University of Texas; Stephen Fritz, East Tennessee State University; and Kees Gispen, University of Mississippi. Finally, we deeply appreciate those individuals who, either as freelancers or as staff members of D. C. Heath and Company, gave extraordinary assistance in the production of this collection: James Miller, acquisitions editor; Susan Brown and Bryan Woodhouse, production editors; Alwyn Velásquez, designer; Rachel Parks, copyeditor; Billie Ingram, photo editor; Efrem Weitzman and Claude Bishop, photo researchers; and Dick Tonachel, purchasing coordinator.

B. C. S.
D. K.

Contents

Chronology

1914	June 28	Assassination of the heir to the Austrian throne by Serbian nationalists.
	July 28	Austria-Hungary declares war on Serbia.
	August 1	Germany declares war on Russia.
	August 3	Germany declares war on France.
	August 4	Great Britain declares war on the German Empire.
1917	March 8	Revolution in Russia; abdication of Tsar Nicholas II.
	April 6	U.S.A. declares war on the German Empire.
	November 7	Bolshevik Revolution in Russia.
1918	March 3	Peace Treaty of Brest-Litovsk (Bolshevik Russia and German Empire).
	November 3–4	German sailors revolt in Kiel.
	November 7	Revolution in Bavaria.
	November 9	Philipp Scheidemann (a Social Democrat) proclaims the German Republic.
	November 10	Emperor William II flees to the Netherlands.
	November 11	Armistice ending World War I signed at Compiègne.
1919	January 5	Founding of the German Workers' Party in Munich.
	January 5–12	Spartacus uprising in Berlin.
	February 11	Friedrich Ebert elected Reich President by the National Assembly in Weimar.
	February 21	Murder of Kurt Eisner in Munich.
	April 4	Soviet Republic established in Bavaria.
	May 1–3	Communists crushed in Bavaria.
	June 28	Signing of the Treaty of Versailles.
	July 31	Adoption of the Weimar Constitution.
	September	Hitler joins the German Workers' Party as member number 7.

1920	February 24	"Twenty-five Point Program" adopted by German Workers' Party.
	March 13–17	Kapp Putsch attempted in Berlin.
1921	July 29	Hitler becomes chairman of the Nazi Party.
1923	January	Inflation begins.
	January 11	Occupation of the Ruhr industrial area by French and Belgian forces.
	November 8–9	Hitler's Beer Hall Putsch attempted in Munich.
	November 15	Inflation ended by introduction of the *Rentenmark*.
1924	February 26	Hitler's trial for treason begins.
	December 20	Hitler released from prison.
1925	February 24	Refounding of the NSDAP
	February 28	Friedrich Ebert, first President of the Weimar Republic, dies.
1927	March 10	Lifting of speaking ban on Hitler
1928	May 20	Reichstag elections. Nazis receive 810,000 votes (2.6 percent) and 12 seats in the 491-member Reichstag.
1929	January 6	Himmler appointed *Reichsführer* SS.
	October 3	Death of Foreign Minister Stresemann.
	October 25	"Black Friday" on New York Stock Market marks beginning of the world economic crisis.
1930	July 16	President Hindenburg invokes Article 48 of the Constitution. Rule by presidential decree begins.
	September 14	Reichstag elections. Nazis receive 6,409,600 votes (18.3 percent) and 107 seats in the 577-member Reichstag.
	December 31	Central Office for Race and Resettlement (RuSHA) established.
1932	January 27	Hitler addresses Rhineland industrialists and gets financial support.
	March 13	Presidential election. Hitler receives 11.5 million votes, Hindenburg 18.6 million.
	April 10	Presidential (run-off) election. Hitler receives 13.4 million votes; Hindenburg is elected with 19.25 million votes.
	May 30	Chancellor Brüning replaced by Papen, who forms a right-wing cabinet.
	July 31	Reichstag elections. Nazis receive 13,745,800 votes (37.4 percent), and 230 seats in the 608-member Reichstag. Nazis are now the single largest party.
	August 13	Hitler refuses vice-chancellor post in Papen cabinet.
	November 6	Reichstag elections. Nazi vote declines to 11,737,000 (33.1 percent) and 196 seats in the 584-member Reichstag.
	December 2	General Kurt von Schleicher appointed chancellor.
1933	January 4	Papen and Hitler meet secretly to discuss the formation of a new cabinet.
	January 23	Schleicher resigns.
	January 30	Hitler appointed chancellor, with Papen as vice-chancellor.

	February 27	Burning of the Reichstag building.
	February 28	Hitler acquires emergency powers through presidential decree; basic civil liberties suspended.
	March 5	Reichstag elections. Despite terror and coercion, Nazis fail to get majority, receiving 43.9 percent of the vote and 288 of 647 Reichstag members. German Nationalist Party adds its 52 seats, giving the coalition a slim majority.
	March 23	Reichstag accepts the Enabling Act.
	March 31	Beginning of *Gleichschaltung* of state governments.
	April 1	First nationally organized boycott of Jewish businesses and professional people.
	May 2	Dissolution of labor unions and creation of German Labor Front.
	May 10	Public burning of "un-German" books.
	July 14	NSDAP declared the only legal party.
	July 20	Concordat between the Reich and the Vatican.
	September 22	Creation of the Reich Chamber of Culture.
	October 14	Withdrawal from League of Nations. Beginning of rearmament.
1934	April 20	Himmler appointed head of the Prussian Gestapo.
	June 17	Papen's Marburg speech.
	June 30	Blood Purge.
	August 2	Death of President Hindenburg. Hitler assumes combined offices of President and Reich Chancellor. Armed forces swear loyalty.
1935	January 13	Saar district returns to Germany after plebiscite.
	March 16	Hitler denounces military restrictions imposed by Treaty of Versailles and begins conscription.
	June 18	Anglo-German Naval Treaty. Beginning of German naval rearmament.
	September 15	Nuremberg Laws deprive German Jews of rights.
1936	March 7	German troops occupy the Rhineland area demilitarized by the Treaty of Versailles.
	August 1	Opening of Olympic Games in Berlin.
	September 9	Inauguration of Four-Year Plan.
	October 25	German-Italian treaty (Rome-Berlin Axis).
1937	November 5	Hossbach Memorandum. Hitler outlines plans to dominate Europe.
1938	February 4	Dismissal of War Minister Blomberg and Army chief Fritsch.
	March 12	German troops enter Austria.
	April 10	Plebiscite confirms "reunification" of Austria with Germany (*Anschluss*).
	September 29	Conclusion of the Munich Conference; Sudetenland ceded to Germany.
	November 9	Crystal Night (pogrom against German Jews).

1939	March 15	German troops invade and occupy remainder of Czechoslovakia.
	August 23	German-Soviet Nonaggression Pact.
	September 1	Germany invades Poland.
	September 2	Britain and France declare war on Germany.
	September 27	Surrender of Warsaw. Central Office for Reich Security (RSHA) established.
	October	Führer decree on euthanasia program.
1940	February 12	First deportation of Jews from Germany.
	April 9	Germany invades Norway and Denmark.
	May 10	Germany invades the Netherlands, Belgium, Luxembourg, and France.
	June 22	Franco-German armistice signed at Compiègne.
	August 13	Battle of Britain begins.
	September 27	Tripartite Pact signed by Germany, Italy, and Japan.
1941	April 6	Germany invades Yugoslavia and Greece.
	June 22	Germany invades Soviet Union. *Einsatzgruppen* begin extermination of Jews in conquered eastern Europe.
	September 19	Jews in Germany forced to wear yellow star.
	December 11	Germany declares war on U.S.A.
1942	January 20	Wannsee Conference. ''Final Solution'' discussed; mass extermination of European Jews to begin.
	June 23	First gassings in Auschwitz.
	July 21–22	Beginning of deportation of Jews from Warsaw ghetto to Treblinka.
1943	January 31	German troops surrender at Stalingrad, signaling turning of tide against German forces on eastern front.
	February 18	Arrest of leaders of ''White Rose.'' Goebbels announces ''total war.''
	April 19	Uprising in Warsaw ghetto suppressed.
	July 24	Hamburg heavily bombed by Allies.
	July 25	Fall of Mussolini.
1944	June 6	Allied landing in northern France (''D-Day'').
	July 20	July Plot: Stauffenberg's attempt on Hitler's life and coup by conspirators fails.
	December 16	German counteroffensive in Ardennes begins; fails by January 1945.
1945	January 26	Auschwitz liberated by Soviet troops.
	February 13–14	Allied bombing of Dresden.
	April 30	Hitler commits suicide.
	May 7	German surrender signed.
	November 20	Opening of Nuremberg War Crimes trials.
1946	October 16	Executions of Nazi war criminals at Nuremberg.

Glossary

Anschluss   Incorporation of Austria into the Reich in 1938.

Beer Hall Putsch   Failed attempt by Hitler and his Nazi Party supporters to overthrow the national government on November 8–9, 1923.

Blitzkrieg   Lightning war. Military tactics emphasizing mobility and fluidity, which were employed by German forces in 1939–40 during invasions of Poland and France.

Blood Purge   Also called "Night of the Long Knives." Hitler's purging of the SA leadership and other perceived opponents and former enemies, through a campaign of assassinations during the night of June 30, 1934.

Blut und Boden   (Blood and Soil). Nazi propaganda phrase derived from racial theory, which emphasized the peasant's role as the backbone of the pure Aryan race.

Bund deutscher Mädel — BdM   (League of German Girls). The girls' branch of the Hitler Youth, organized along lines similar to the HJ.

Center Party   Political party dedicated to Catholic interests, but appealed to all social classes and had support in most areas of Germany.

Confessional Church   Protestant church organization established in April 1934 by theologians opposed to Nazi racial doctrine and attempts to nazify the Protestant church.

Deutsche Arbeiterpartei — DAP   (German Workers' Party). Original name of the Nazi Party; changed its name to NSDAP in 1920.

Deutsche Arbeitsfront — DAF   (German Labor Front). The monolithic organization that included all German factory workers under the leadership of Dr. Robert Ley. It replaced all other labor unions in the Reich.

Deutsche Demokratische Partei — DDP   (German Democratic Party). A liberal party that increasingly lost votes in the late 1920s and early 1930s.

Deutsche Volkspartei — DVP   (German People's Party). A right-of-center party in the Weimar Republic.

Deutschnationale Volkspartei — DNVP   (German National People's Party). A rightist party that joined coalitions with the Nazis.

Edelweiss Pirates   Working-class youths between the ages of 14 and 18 who rejected

Nazism and Hitler Youth participation; loosely organized in gangs that engaged in noncon-formist activities.

Einsatzgruppen (Special Task Groups) Special units recruited from the security police; given the task of suppressing all opposition in occupied territories; engaged in mass liquidation of Jews in eastern Europe.

Enabling Act (Law for the Removal of the Distress of People and Reich) Act passed by the Reichstag on March 24, 1933, that altered the Weimar Constitution, giving Hitler the right to issue laws without Reichstag approval.

Endlösung (Final Solution) Euphemism used by the Nazis for the extermination of the Jews of Europe.

Erbhofgesetz (Hereditary Farm Law). A law enacted in 1933, stipulating that medium-sized farms could not be mortgaged or divided and could be passed on only to a single heir.

Freikorps (Free Corps) Volunteer paramilitary units composed of veterans who were politically right wing and dedicated to fighting communism. They initially allowed the government to circumvent the manpower limitations imposed by the Treaty of Versailles.

Führer (The Leader) Title used by Hitler to reinforce his position of authority as head of the Nazi Party and later as head of the Third Reich.

Führerprinzip (Leadership Principle) Nazi concept of hierarchical party organization that emphasized discipline and a chain of command that culminated in the charismatic position of the Führer.

Gau (Region) Largest territorial unit of the Nazi organizational structure. The *Gaus* corres-ponded roughly to the Reichstag electoral regions.

Gauleiter (Regional leader) Chief Nazi Party official within the regional organization.

Geheime Staatspolizei — Gestapo (Secret State Police). Under the control of the SD, the Gestapo was the most important security organization of the Reich and one of the most effective organs of the totalitarian state. Its powers were extensive and independent of the legal system, and it established its own law courts, ostensibly to protect all Germans and defend them against all enemies.

General Government Nazi term for those parts of occupied Poland that were not directly incorporated into Germany.

Glaube und Schönheit (Faith and Beauty). Branch of the League of German Girls. Intended to train girls between 17 and 21 in the physical and spiritual ideals of Nazi womanhood.

Gleichschaltung (Coordination). Nazi policy that sought to bring all sectors of the state and society under the control of the regime.

Hitler Jugend — HJ (Hitler Youth). Nazi organization for boys between the ages of 10 and 18. Membership was made compulsory in 1939.

Kapp Putsch A right-wing attempt to overthrow the republican government in 1920; failed when the Left called a general strike.

Kommunistische Partei Deutschlands — KPD (German Communist Party). The KPD was outlawed in 1933 and its leaders arrested.

Kraft durch Freude — KdF (Strength Through Joy). Nazi recreation organization for workers. KdF programs included subsidized tourism, theater performances, concerts, exhibitions, sports, hiking, folk dancing, and adult-education courses.

Kriminalpolizei — Kripo (Criminal Police). Under the control of the Sipo, the Criminal Police handled criminal matters in the Reich.

Kristallnacht (Crystal Night). Nationwide pogrom against German Jews during the night of 9–10 November, 1938.

Lebensborn (Spring of Life). Program designed by Himmler to improve the racial stock of the German *Volk*. Women regarded as racially pure were encouraged to breed with selected SS men without the sanction of marriage.

Lebensraum (Living Space). A concept that emphasized the need for the territorial expansion of overpopulated Germany. Only through the acquisition of new lands to the east could adequate raw materials and foodstuffs for the allegedly superior German *Volk* be ensured.

Nationalpolitische Erziehungsanstalten — Napolas (National Political Education Institutions). High schools for training the future Nazi elite.

Nationalsozialistische Betriebszellenorganisation — NSBO (National Socialist Factory Cell Organization). Organization of Nazi industrial propaganda units in factories.

Nationalsozialistische Deutsche Arbeiterpartei — NSDAP (National Socialist German Workers' Party). The Nazi Party.

Nationalsozialistische Frauenschaft - - NSF (National Socialist Women's League). Women's auxiliary of the Nazi Party, founded to help women rear their children as good patriots.

Nationalsozialistischer Deutscher Studentenbund — NSDStB (National Socialist German Student Union) A Nazi organization devoted to promoting Nazi ideals among university students.

Nationalsozialistischer Lehrerbund — NSLB (National Socialist Teachers' Association). Nazi organization for all primary and secondary school teachers.

Nationalsozialistischer Rechtswahrerbund (National Socialist Lawyers' Association). Nazi organization of all practicing lawyers in the Third Reich.

Oberkommando des Heeres — OKH (High Command of the Army). Supreme command of the army.

Oberkommando der Wehrmacht — OKW (High Command of the Armed Forces). Top-level military command structure created by Hitler in February 1938.

Reichsarbeitsdienst — RAD (Reich Labor Service). Nazi institution that compelled all young German men between aged 18–25 to perform six months of manual labor in the service of the Reich. Most worked on farms or land-reclamation projects. The Labor Service was made compulsory for young women once the war began.

Reichsbanner (Reich Banner). Social Democrat former-servicemen's organization during the Weimar Republic. They were unarmed but marched in uniform and functioned much like a private army, similar to the Nazi SA.

Reichsbund Deutscher Beamten (National Association of German Civil Servants). A monolithic organization of civil servants under the control of the Nazi Party, consisting of over 1 million members. It replaced all earlier associations of civil servants.

Reichskulturkammer (Reich Chamber of Culture). Organization headed by Goebbels. Its aim was the nazification of all cultural activities in the Reich.

Reichsnährstand (Reich Food Corporation). Nazi agricultural organization headed by Richard-Walther Darré. Membership in the organization was compulsory for anyone connected with agriculture. It had the power to regulate prices and production.

Reichstag The German parliament throughout the imperial period and under the Weimar Republic. During the Third Reich, it occasionally met as a rubber-stamp organization.

Reichswehr (Defensive Land Forces). Name of the Weimar Republic's standing army of 100,000 men. In 1935 Hitler changed the name to *Wehrmacht* (Armed Forces — i.e., the army, air force and navy).

Schutzstaffeln — SS (Guard Squadrons). Organization in control of the various police forces in Germany and in conquered territories. It also included military units.

Sicherheitsdienst — SD (Security Service). The intelligence service of the SS under the leadership of Reinhard Heydrich. It was responsible for the security of Hitler, the Nazi Party, and the entire Third Reich. The SD consisted of several police forces, including the Security Police (Sipo) the Criminal Police (Kripo), the Central Office for Reich Security (RSHA), and the *Schupos* (urban police forces).

Sicherheitspolizei — Sipo (Security Police). The Security Police organization, consisting of the Gestapo and the Criminal Police under the control of Reinhard Heydrich.

Sopade (German Social Democratic Party in exile). The underground organization of the outlawed Social Democratic Party, headquartered in Prague, Czechoslovakia, until 1938 and in Paris until 1940.

Sozialdemokratische Partei Deutschlands — SPD (German Social Democratic Party). Socialist political party. One of the major parties in the Weimar Republic, it found itself unable to deal with the violence and political machinations of Hitler and the Nazi Party.

Sturmabteilung — SA (Stormtroopers). The early private army of Brown Shirts of the Nazi Party. It was originally organized to protect party leaders and oppose rival political parties. It declined in power and influence after the Blood Purge of 1934.

Swing Youth Non-conformist middle-class youths who defied the Nazi regime by embracing the culture of Germany's wartime enemies, England and America.

Volk All-inclusive concept of nation, people, and race. Since the early nineteenth century, the term had implied homogeneity and a superiority of German culture, and later increasingly came to be associated with theories of race and a sense of mission for the German people.

Völkischer Beobachter (People's Observer). Main daily newspaper of the Nazi Party.

Volksgemeinschaft (*Volk* Community) The image of a harmonized, racially pure community stressed by Nazi ideology, which led to a number of governmental policies in the Third Reich.

Wannsee Conference A meeting of Nazi Party and state officials in Berlin on January 20, 1942, during which the plans for the Final Solution were outlined.

White Rose A student organization opposed to Hitler and the Nazi regime. Its leaders were executed in 1943.

Biographical Sketches

Beck, Ludwig (1880–1944). Chief of the general staff of the German army, 1935–38; opposed Hitler's plans for war and resigned in August 1938. Leading figure in resistance, committed suicide July 20, 1944, after failure of plot to assassinate Hitler.

Blomberg, Werner von (1878–1946). Reich Minister of Defense, 1933–35; Reich Minister of War and Commander-in-Chief of the armed forces from 1935 to February 1938. His removal from office in 1938 did much to end the continuity of military influence exerted by the aristocratic conservative class. Blomberg died in an American prison in Nuremberg in 1946.

Bonhoeffer, Dietrich (1906–45). Protestant pastor and theologian. Became a member of the Confessional Church and a leading figure in the resistance. Arrested in 1943 and sent to a concentration camp after the failure of the July 1944 plot. Executed by the SS on April 9, 1945.

Bormann, Martin (1900–1945). Head of the Party Chancellery and private secretary to the Führer. Increasingly more powerful in the final days of the Third Reich because of his proximity to Hitler. At Nuremberg he was sentenced to death in absentia. Mystery still surrounds his fate. Rumors abound of his death (in a tank) at the hands of the Russians, of his suicide, and of his escape to South America. German courts pronounced him officially dead in April 1973, on the basis of skeletal remains found not far from Hitler's bunker in Berlin.

Brüning, Heinrich (1885–1970). Member of the Center Party and German Chancellor, 1930–32, during the years of growing financial crisis. Emigrated to the United States in 1934 and became a professor at Harvard.

Darré, Richard-Walther (1895–1953). Reich Farmers' Leader and Reich Food Minister, 1933–42. Chief of the Central Office for Race and Resettlement, 1931–38. At the Nuremberg trials, sentenced to five years in prison. Died of liver disease after his release.

Diels, Rudolf (1900–57). First chief of the Gestapo, 1933–34. Dismissed as District Council President of Hannover in 1940 for stopping arrests of Jews. Imprisoned by the Gestapo after the July 20, 1944, plot against Hitler. Died in a hunting accident in 1957.

Drexler, Anton (1884–1942). Co-founder of the German Workers' Party on January 5, 1919. Pushed out of the party's leadership by Hitler in 1921. Left the NSDAP in 1923, and never rejoined the Nazi movement.

Ebert, Friedrich (1871–1925). First President of the Weimar Republic. Member of the German Social Democratic Party.

Eichmann, Adolf (1906–62). SS Lieutenant-Colonel; chief of the office dealing with Jewish affairs and evacuation within the Central Office for Reich Security. Entrusted by Heydrich with implementation of the "Final Solution." Arrested after the war but escaped to Argentina. Tracked down by Israeli agents in 1960 and tried in Jerusalem. Executed in Israel in 1962.

Frank, Hans (1900–46). Director of the NSDAP's legal department. Governor-General of occupied Poland, 1933–45. Tried and executed in Nuremberg in 1946.

Frick, Hans (1900–46). Reich Minister of the Interior, 1933–43, a position he used to draft laws that sent Nazi opponents to concentration camps; also drafted the Nuremberg race laws. Tried and executed in Nuremberg in 1946.

Fritsch, Werner von (1880–1939). Commander-in-Chief of the German Army from 1934 to February 1938. Opposed Hitler's plans for war, and was forced to resign his position because of SS-fabricated charges of homosexual activity.

Galen, Count Clemens von (1878–1946). Cardinal Archbishop of Münster. Opposed Nazi race doctrines and the euthanasia program. Arrested by the Gestapo after the July 20, 1944, plot; survived concentration camp.

Goebbels, Joseph (1897–1945). *Gauleiter* of Berlin. Reich Minister of Public Enlightenment and Propaganda, 1933–45. Committed suicide along with his entire family on May 1, 1945.

Goering, Hermann (1893–1946). Commander-in-Chief of the Luftwaffe, Reichstag President, and Plenipotentiary for the Four-Year Plan. Instructed Heydrich to prepare a solution to the Jewish question. Captured by the U.S. Army in May 1945 and tried at Nuremberg. Sentenced to death by hanging but committed suicide in prison on October 15, 1946.

Groener, Wilhelm (1867–1939). First Quartermaster General, 1920–23. Pledged the support of the army to Ebert and the new government in order to defeat the threat of Bolshevik revolution.

Hassel, Ulrich von (1881–1944). Career diplomat; held several ambassadorial positions during the Weimar Republic and the Third Reich until 1938. Opposed to Hitler's foreign policy, and joined the resistance. Arrested after July 20, 1944, plot; tried and executed in September 1944.

Hess, Rudolf (1894–1987). Early member of the NSDAP; secretary to Hitler 1925–32; Deputy to the Führer, 1933–41; flew to Britain in May 1941 on a self-appointed peace mission and was interned for the duration of the war. Tried at Nuremberg and sentenced to life imprisonment. Committed suicide by strangling himself with an electrical cord in prison in Berlin in August 1987 at the age of ninety-three; for twenty-one years, he had been the sole remaining prisoner at Spandau prison.

Heydrich, Reinhard (1904–42). SS Lieutenant-General; Chief of the Security Service and Chief of the Central Office for Reich Security. Convened the Wannsee Conference and laid the groundwork for the "Final Solution." Assassinated by a Czech resistance organization in 1942. In retribution, the Nazis razed the Czech village of Lidice and executed all its male inhabitants.

Himmler, Heinrich (1900–45). Reich Leader of the SS, 1929–45; Chief of the German police, 1936–45. Because of his position as head of the SS and the police, he was probably the second most powerful man in Nazi Germany. He was a fanatical disciple of race theory and dedicated to the implementation of the "Final Solution." Following the German surrender, he tried to escape in disguise but was captured by British troops. Committed suicide on May 23, 1945, by swallowing a poison vial before he could be tried.

Hindenburg, Paul von (1847–1934). General Field Marshal and national hero during World War I. President of the Weimar Republic from 1925 until his death in 1934. Did not like Hitler but under the influence of conservative groups accepted him as chancellor.

Hitler, Adolf (1889–1945). Joined German Workers' Party in 1919; chairman of NSDAP in 1921; jailed during 1924 for treason; assumed the title of Führer (leader) of the party from 1925 on. He became chancellor in 1933 and Führer of Germany after Hindenburg's death in 1934; thereafter, he was the all-powerful dictator until he committed suicide in his underground bunker in Berlin on April 30, 1945.

Hoess, Rudolf (1900–47). SS Captain, Commandant of the extermination camp at Auschwitz, 1940–43. Prided himself on introducing poison gas into the extermination process. Arrested on March 2, 1946, and sentenced to death by a Polish tribunal in March 1947. Executed at Auschwitz on April 7, 1947.

Hugenberg, Alfred (1865–1951). German press and film tycoon. Reichstag member from 1920; Chairman of the German National People's Party, 1928–33. From 1929 to 1933, cooperated with Hitler in the hope of being able to use and control him; became Minister of Economics and Agriculture in Hitler's first cabinet. Thereafter was merely a member of the Reichstag, without political influence, until 1945.

Ley, Robert (1890–1945). Gauleiter of the NSDAP in the Rhineland; Reichstag member; Chief of the German Labor Front, 1933–45. Ley was a rabid antisemite who deified Hitler. Captured by American troops while trying to escape into the Alps. Committed suicide on October 24, 1945, while awaiting trial.

Ludendorff, Erich (1865–1937). Brilliant military tactician; Quartermaster General in World War I. Embittered by Germany's defeat, became involved in postwar right-wing politics; participated in the Beer Hall Putsch. His relations with Hitler cooled after 1925, although Ludendorff continued to espouse increasingly eccentric ideas directed against Jews, Jesuits, and Freemasons.

Niemöller, Martin (1892–1984). Protestant pastor and leader of the anti-Nazi Confessional Church. Enraged by Niemöller's sermons, Hitler ordered his arrest in 1937. Niemöller spent seven years in concentration camps in "protective custody," until liberated by Allied troops.

Ohlendorf, Otto (1908–51). Lawyer, economist, and early Nazi Party member; rose within the SD to the rank of major general. Commander of Einsatzgruppe D, 1941–42, in the Ukraine, where his units liquidated 90,000 Jews. Sentenced to death at Nuremberg in 1948; spent three years in prison before being hanged in 1951.

Papen, Franz von (1879–1969). Conservative Catholic politician who served as chancellor of Germany for six months in 1932. Helped negotiate the coalition between the Nazis and the conservative Nationalists, which brought Hitler to power. Served as Vice-Chancellor, 1933–34; ambassador to Turkey, 1939–44. Arrested at the end of the war, tried at

Nuremberg and acquitted; a German court reclassified him as a "Major Offender"; released in 1949.

Ribbentrop, Joachim von (1893–1946). Foreign Minister, 1938–45. Signed German-Soviet Nonaggression Pact, which cleared the way for Hitler's attack on Poland. Found guilty at Nuremberg trials, he was the first of the defendants to be executed.

Roehm, Ernst (1887–1934). Participant in the Beer Hall Putsch; Chief of Staff of the SA, 1931–34. Arrested on June 30, 1934, on Hitler's orders, Roehm was shot two days later by the SS, one of the major victims of the Blood Purge.

Rosenberg, Alfred (1893–1946). Editor-in-chief of the *Völkischer Beobachter*, and a leading Nazi ideologue and race theorist. As Reich Minister for the Eastern Occupied Territories, 1941–45, he supported Nazi subjugation of the "inferior" Slavic people, although he protested ineffectively the regime's extermination campaigns in those territories. He was hanged at Nuremberg in 1946.

Schacht, Hjalmar (1877–1970). Talented economist who helped end inflation in 1923. As a conservative nationalist, he supported the negotiations that made Hitler chancellor. As Minister of Economics, 1934–37, he became the financial architect of Nazi Germany. Became disenchanted with Nazism and established limited contact with the resistance; sent to a concentration camp after the failure of the July 20, 1944, plot. Schacht was freed by Americans but tried at Nuremberg and acquitted. Later he enjoyed a second successful career as financial advisor to developing countries.

Schirach, Baldur von (1907–74). Reich Youth Leader, 1931–1940; Governor of Vienna, 1940–45, where he was responsible for the deportation of 185,000 Jews. At the Nuremberg trials, he denounced Hitler and recognized that he had misled German youth. He was sentenced to twenty years' imprisonment.

Schleicher, Kurt von (1882–1934). Army officer and last Chancellor of the Weimar Republic, December 1932–January 1933. Tried to split the Nazi Party in late 1932 by offering Gregor Strasser the post of Vice-Chancellor. On June 30, 1934, during the Blood Purge, he was assassinated by the SS.

Schmitt, Carl (1888–1985). German jurist specializing in constitutional theory and the top legal theoretician of the Nazi Party during the early 1930s; Prussian State Councillor, 1933–36, and professor of law in Berlin until 1945. Defended the Blood Purge as a form of "administrative justice." Lost favor with the Party when the SS denounced his lukewarm anti-Semitism.

Scholl, Hans (1918–43) and Sophie (1921–43). Brother and sister, Catholic student leaders of the "White Rose" anti-Nazi movement. The Scholls printed and distributed leaflets at the University of Munich calling for the overthrow of the National Socialist regime. Both were arrested by the Gestapo, who broke Sophie's leg during interrogation; both were executed on February 22, 1943.

Seeckt, Hans von (1886–1936). General; Commander-in-Chief of the Reichswehr, 1920–26. Readily used the army to suppress threats from the left, but was more kindly disposed toward the right wing of German politics. Supported military training liaison with the Soviet Union. Became the chief military advisor to Chiang Kai-shek in China, 1934–35.

Speer, Albert (1905–81). Hitler's favorite architect during the mid-1930s. Designed the Reich Chancellery building in Berlin, and used lighting effects to orchestrate the Nazi Party rallies at Nuremberg. In 1942 he was named Minister of Armaments and Munitions, and greatly increased army production. Acknowledged his guilt for "war crimes" at the Nuremberg trials and received a twenty-year prison sentence.

Stauffenberg, Count Claus von (1907–44). Lieutenant-Colonel on the General Staff who became disillusioned with the war and with Hitler while serving on the Russian front. A key member of the resistance, he attempted to assassinate Hitler with a planted bomb on July 20, 1944. With the failure of the plot, Stauffenberg was shot after a hasty court-martial.

Strasser, Gregor (1892–1934). Early member of the NSDAP and leader of the Party's social-revolutionary wing. NSDAP Propaganda Leader, 1926–32, but resigned from the Party in December 1932 over policy differences with Hitler. Strasser was murdered by the Gestapo during the Blood Purge.

Streicher, Julius (1885–1946). Gauleiter of Franconia and founder of the violently antise-mitic journal *Der Stürmer* (The Attacker). Lost his party posts in 1940 because of a feud with Goering. Sentenced to death at the Nuremberg trials because of his activities inciting the extermination of the Jews.

Stresemann, Gustav (1878–1929). Leading member of the German People's Party. Chan-cellor of the Weimar Republic in 1923; Foreign Minister, 1923–29. Worked to establish better relations with the western powers, especially France, and endorsed the policy of fulfilling the obligations stipulated by the Treaty of Versailles.

Todt, Fritz (1891–1942). Inspector General of German Highways, 1933–42, charged with building the *Autobahn* network. Reich Minister for Armaments and Munitions, 1940–42. Chief of the Organization Todt, a construction unit for military projects, that used foreign workers, as well as prisoners of war and concentration camp inmates, for slave labor.

German territorial acquisitions before the outbreak of World War II (Saar, Austria, Sudetenland, Bohemia-Moravia, and Memeland).

Rhineland remilitarized by Germany, 1936.

EUROPE, 1923-1939

SWEDEN
FINLAND
NORWAY
ESTONIA
LATVIA
DENMARK
LITHUANIA
DANZIG
USSR
UNITED KINGDOM
EIRE
NETHERLANDS
GERMANY
POLAND
BELGIUM
LUX
CZECH
SAAR
AUSTRIA
HUNGARY
FRANCE
SWITZ
RUMANIA
ITALY
YUGOSLAVIA
BULGARIA
ALBANIA
GREECE
SPAIN
PORTUGAL
TURKEY
FRENCH NORTH AFRICA

N

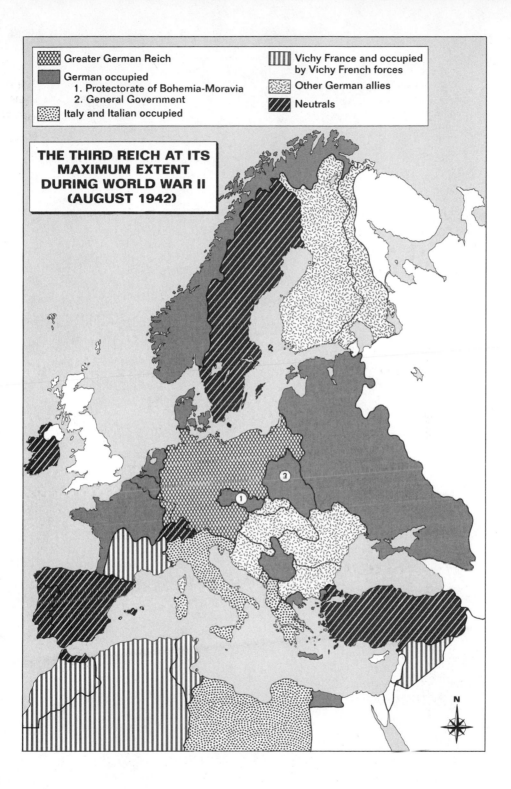

Greater German Reich

German occupied
  1. Protectorate of Bohemia-Moravia
  2. General Government

Italy and Italian occupied

Vichy France and occupied by Vichy French forces

Other German allies

Neutrals

THE THIRD REICH AT ITS MAXIMUM EXTENT DURING WORLD WAR II (AUGUST 1942)

Inside Hitler's Germany

Introduction

Whatever the final evaluation of National Socialism in the course of modern history, it will certainly be remembered for two things: its responsibility for bringing on the Second World War and its policy of genocide against the Jews and other peoples of Europe. The ultimate horror involved in the external war for *Lebensraum* in the East and the internal war against the Jews may be ultimately beyond our powers of full understanding; yet the attempt to explain these events historically, however insufficient for full comprehension, is a necessary first step. Historians have offered several frameworks for explaining the National Socialist phenomenon. Some have emphasized the particularities of the development of the German state and society in the late nineteenth and early twentieth centuries, which prepared the ground for the triumph of National Socialism, while others have pointed to the "totalitarian" nature of the Nazi regime, which shared certain structural features with the Soviet Union under Stalin. For still other historians, National Socialist ideology formed the essential foundation of the policies of the regime, whether the specifically Germanic features of this ideology or its common characteristics with other forms of fascism are stressed. Finally, National Socialism has been considered either as a rejection of modernity and an aberration within European history or as one of the best expressions of this modernity and the culmination of the civilization of the West.

In the following documentary history of National Socialism we do not speak to each of these interpretive schemes, although both the documents selected and the introductory material provide a starting point for exploring the various interpretative frameworks. Yet choices had to be made in presenting an open and full introduction to the National Socialist phenomenon. Historians have thoroughly studied both Nazi diplomacy and the conduct of World War II, and numerous published collections document these areas. We therefore emphasize life inside Hitler's Germany, restricting diplomatic and military considerations to the effect of these factors on conditions within the Third Reich. Whenever possible, we have chosen materials illustrating the experience of individual men and women from various social classes. We do not claim, however, that life in the Third Reich can be fully understood in either political or social terms. Rather, we aim to offer a wider perspective in our selection of the documentary material, one that synthesizes the political and the social with the ideological.

This documentary history comprises three thematic units, with each set of documents chronologically illustrating the various forms of power that constituted National Socialism. Unit I deals with the political history of Germany between 1918 and 1938, tracing the Nazi party's development from the 1920s through the seizure of power in 1933 to the establishment of Hitler's dictatorship in the mid-1930s.

1

Unit II then focuses on National Socialist ideology and its creation of the *Volk* community, with its dual aims of preparing for war and eliminating Jews from German society. The development of the dictatorship into the totalitarian regime of 1938–45 resulted from both the inner logic of the political consolidation and the full realization of the *Volksgemeinschaft* ideology. Unit III examines the main instrument of totalitarian rule, the SS, both within the internal governance of the Third Reich and in implementing the Final Solution. Whereas the documents in Unit I exemplify power in terms of revolutionary force and traditional political structures and Unit II examines it in terms of ideological and social policies, those in Unit III illustrate how power was realized in the police and the military — which was the essence of the totalitarian regime that was National Socialist Germany.

THE HITLER DICTATORSHIP

Hitler took over the reins of power from the Weimar Republic (1919–33) only after the parliamentary forms of government had collapsed. His assumption of the chancellorship ended three years of continual crisis from 1930 to 1933. Created out of the shambles of Germany's defeat in World War I, the Weimar Republic was by no means unique. For the countries and peoples of central and eastern Europe, the year 1918 marked not only the end of hostilities but also the beginning of national-democratic experiments in government. Within the space of a few months, international power relationships changed fundamentally, new states came into being, and the political and social relations within these states were irretrievably altered. The problems left unresolved by the war and by these new relations gave birth to authoritarian and dictatorial revolutionary movements throughout Europe. The constitutions of the nascent democracies stimulated the rise of antidemocratic yet extremely nationalistic dictatorships in many European states. In Russia and the new Baltic states, in Hungary, Poland, and the Balkan countries, in Italy, Germany, and Austria, and in Spain and Portugal, the new democracies were fragile from their origins, while both older sources of power and emerging mass movements called for restructuring the relationship between state and society. From one vantage point, the years between the wars saw a number of experiments in organizing society under strong state control; from another, they marked the end of the national-democratic forms of statehood developed in the nineteenth century. Of all the new democracies, only those of Finland and Czechoslovakia survived the 1920s.

Although the democracies of the interwar period tended to be weak and therefore easy prey for dictatorships, they did not inevitably succumb to fascism. Despite similarities with other states of central and Eastern Europe, Germany after World War I must be understood in light of its specific history. The seizure of the Weimar government by the National Socialist German Workers' Party and the organization of the Third Reich in Germany were intimately connected with the personality of Adolf Hitler and the almost magical hold he maintained over the German people. Yet beyond Hitler's talents and his charismatic appeal, events external to the development of the Nazi movement made the Party into a national political force. Economic, social, and political crises crowded the early 1920s, the time of the party's first successes, and they had telling psychological repercussions on the individuals who lived through them. The Nazis' emergence as a national movement in the early 1930s coincided with a second series of economic break-downs and political collapses. Hitler's appeal fitted a specific time and filled the specific needs of a large segment of the German population.

Two events in particular helped launch Hitler's career as the leader of a mass movement. One was the death of the influential conservative politician Gustav Stresemann on October 3, 1929, which ended the last and best attempt at forming a broadly based parliamentary coalition that would give stability to the Weimar Republic. The second event was the onslaught of the worst economic plight the modern world has known, which brought in its wake the dissolution of the German parliamentary system even before Hitler seized power in 1933. Growing unemploy-ment set in as early as 1928, but the crash of the New York stock market on Black Thursday (October 23, 1929), only three weeks after Stresemann's death, brought on a crisis. Germany was especially hard hit because its economic recovery depended largely on short-term credits that were now immediately withdrawn. Memories of the hyperinflation of 1923 had immediate political effects. The ensuing panic resulted in protests against the burden of reparations payments mandated by the Versailles Treaty, as well as against the Weimar government's seeming inability to deal with the worsening economic situation. The crisis manifested itself socially as a fear of proletarianization; politically and ideologically, it surfaced as extreme dread of a communist takeover. National Socialist propaganda — at once revisionist, anticapitalist, and anti-Marxist — seemed to offer the simplest and most persuasive solution to all these problems.

To be sure, the economic collapse offered the destructive forces of the antidemocratic extremists a major opening, but this alone cannot explain the fall of the Weimar Republic. The dire economic conditions brought on by the worldwide financial collapse do not by themselves explain why the crisis quickly took on social and political aspects and ultimately subverted the entire democratic system. What is of particular significance is the fact that in Germany (in contrast to Great Britain and the United States, which also experienced severe economic difficulties) the political parties, special interest groups, the army, and the public at large interpreted the economic crisis as a test of the democratic system itself. The combination of political inexperience, lack of familiarity with the workings of parliamentary government, and powerful residues of authoritarianism proved fatal.

The political developments that culminated in the triumph of National Socialism were by no means inevitable. In 1923, under similar circumstances, the enemies of the republic had been successfully repulsed by President Ebert. While the fact that the crisis of 1929–33 took a different course cannot be explained by economic factors alone neither can it be understood as a failure of democracy. The economic situation gave undue importance to demogogues like Hitler, but this fact alone did not ensure his success. He came to power only after the Republic had been overthrown from within. New political crises after Stresemann's death smoothed the road toward an extraparliamentary form of quasi dictatorship, which weakened the influence of the democratic parties and organizations in favor of the president, the army, and the bureaucracy and prepared the public for a dictatorial solution of its problems. With the diminishing of democratic responsibility after the change of government in 1930, and more particularly in 1932, which reduced political life to government by emergency decree, faith in democratic solutions eroded. The resultant power vacuum offered wide openings for the radicalism of both the Left and the Right.

The victory of National Socialism in January 1933 was followed by a rapid consolidation of the dictatorial system. By the summer of 1933, in fact, one-man and one-party rule had become the reality. The Party slogan promoting the National Socialist "legal revolution" provides the key to the character and development of the Nazi seizure of power. National Socialist propaganda emphasized that, although Hitler's takeover would mark the beginning of a revolution that would profoundly affect all aspects of life, it was a completely legal, constitutional process. The paradoxical notion of a "legal revolution" artificially linked two contradictory axioms of political action. This combination of the idea of a legal process with revolutionary aspirations was more than a mere propaganda ploy; it played a decisive role in masking the dictatorial coup in a legitimacy that made all legal, political, and even intellectual resistance difficult and even, in the opinion of many, unconstitutional. Moreover, the "legal revolution" enabled Hitler and his Party to take over the machinery of state intact, a fact vital to the success of Hitler's regime not only in 1933–34 but throughout the history of the Third Reich.

The Hitler state's harsh dictatorship had been established during the years 1933–37; the totalitarian regime — that is, the total control of society by the state — had yet to emerge. The source of the strength of National Socialism before the takeover was also the major weakness of this form of mass dictatorship once it came to power. Both its weakness and its strength lay in its constant need for revolutionary activity. National Socialism legitimized its unrestricted use of power by being ever dynamic, ever creative. As with most other forms of dictatorship, both ancient and modern, these demands would ultimately lead Hitler into a new phase of innovation, both at home and abroad.

The revolutionary side of National Socialism comes through most clearly in its perpetuating of constant change and innovation. The regime had to act in order to justify its own right to exist. Once he held firm control on the reins of government, Hitler undertook the economic, diplomatic, and military preparations for the war he knew he would soon begin. In these moves he was no longer bound by the strategy of the "legal revolution," which had brought him to power and guided his policies in the early years. The balancing of older principles of constitutional order and revolutionary innovation, and of the bureaucratic apparatus of the state and the unrestricted will of the Führer, was obviously a compromise clearly imposed by the practical political considerations of time and place. By the late 1930s, Hitler had no further use for such compromises. He could act without restriction; yet he had to continue to act in order to legitimize both the concentration of power in his own person and to justify to the German people their sacrifice of civil and political liberties. At the height of his power, action and will became the real principles of Hitler's power. The "legal revolution" was replaced by the "permanent revolution."

NATIONAL SOCIALIST IDEOLOGY
AND THE COMMUNITY OF RACE

Historians have too often dismissed National Socialist ideology as mere "window dressing," designed to cover the naked exercise of political and military power. To us it seems strange that anyone, let alone an entire nation (or at least a large segment of this nation), could come to believe in the bizarre mixture of ideas, prejudices, and passions that made up the ideology. National Socialist ideology included the cult of the personality of Hitler, the demands for Germany to reemerge as a major world power, and a racial theory that exalted the so-called Aryan race and denigrated Jews as a "parasitic" race. These components of the ideology led in the 1940s to Hitler's achieving absolute control over a totalitarian state structure, the launching of a war for *Lebensraum* in the East, and a governmental policy of exclusion and then elimination of Jews, first in Germany and then throughout most of the rest of Europe.

But although Hitler and the Nazi leadership probably always had these goals in mind, they were not implemented merely by forcing ideological concerns onto reality. Social and political action in general and the progress of National Socialism in particular are not so simple. Other, less negative and destructive aspects of Nazi ideology supplied the ideology with its grounds and meaning. The aim to reestablish communal bonds, to gain control over the often disastrous consequences of industrialization, and to reconstitute a national culture that would overcome class divisions provided these foundations. One cannot understand either how and why the Party won large-scale support among the German people or the economic and social policies of the Third Reich in the 1930s without acknowledging the positive side of Nazi ideology. National Socialism combined, sometimes illogically, both these positive and negative aspects. Emphasizing only the ideology's role in the attempt to rebuild a cultural community or reducing it to the military and genocidal policies of the Third Reich misses the meaning of the National Socialist phenomenon in modern history. Why the destructive side of Nazi ideology came to dominate the more positive aspects, even before the outbreak of war in 1939, is a crucial issue that the following collection of documents addresses.

Through recognizing these two sides of National Socialist ideology one can comprehend something of its contradictory nature. First of all, Nazism claimed to be a revolutionary doctrine, but unlike all other revolutionary ideologies of modern times, it was based on a return to the past. The movement both aimed to reform

5

German society in the future and called for a return to the more ordered, simpler forms of life of earlier times. Responding to the disruptions and chaos brought on by the industrial revolution and the subsequent shift from a primarily rural to a predominantly urban form of life for most Germans, National Socialism consciously appealed to the traditional values and agricultural life-styles of past ages. National Socialists sought Germany's reemergence as a major, if not *the* major, political and military power in the world, but they also wanted to subordinate the urban industrialized world which created the technology for such power, to that of the agrarian countryside.

Defined in this way, National Socialist ideology can be compared to other forms of fascism. National Socialism in Germany, Fascism in Italy, the Croix de Feu in France, and the Iron Guard in Romania, to mention only a few of the major forms, all shared nationalistic fervor as well as a belief in the need for a very strong state beyond parliamentary control and in the virtues of struggle and war. Aside from these common elements, each group took on its own national expression. Although the generic definition of fascism emphasizes the common elements that make it a unitary phenomenon, it is also the most diverse form of ideology. It possesses great unity of principle on an abstract level, but specific formulations varied widely from country to country in the interwar period. These variations are part of the nature of fascism. Yet even within a purely German perspective, National Socialism exhibited the diversity of ideas and symbols, theories, and popular prejudices that marked its origins. National Socialist ideology combined Social Darwinist thinking, which had a wide following in many countries in the late nineteenth and early twentieth centuries, with popular forms of antisemitism, which had assumed political and militant forms in southern Germany and Austria. It joined aspects of extreme German nationalism, which flourished among conservatives in politics and among Wagnerians in the arts, with ideas of the Superman and the value of struggle found in the antinationalist and anti-German philosopher Nietzsche.

The key to National Socialist thinking along these lines is contained in the notion of the *Volksgemeinschaft* — the folk community (*Gemeinschaft*) — that was to replace the atomized society (*Gesellschaft*) of industrial nations. The *Volksgemeinschaft* was a total community that regulated the entire life of the individuals within it. It was a mass society in which the equal participation of all individuals within the nation replaced the older divisions based on distinctions of birth or on class antagonism. But whereas the nation had developed over the course of centuries and had gained a political identity in the form of the nation-state in the recent past, National Socialism held as a basic tenet that the true foundations of the nation lay not in the legal and constitutional union of all its citizens but in the unity of all members of a common race. This definition of race radically restructured the community, redefining the place of politics as well as the relation of public and private life within it. It also provided a means of identifying all groups, such as the German Jews, who did not conform to this racial definition.

The end result was that National Socialist ideology called for a total cultural formation of German politics and society in which, in theory, the community — and in practice, the state — controlled every aspect of life. "Totalitarianism" was not just an ascription assigned to the Third Reich by others; it found its justification in National Socialist ideology itself.

The negative side of this creative effort led to the exclusion of all ideological opposition and all racial differences. All forms of socialism and communism fundamentally misunderstood the concept of the *Volk* and therefore had to be suppressed. But this suppression was not limited to socialists and communists within Germany. The conflict with communism was an ideological mission that went beyond a confrontation with the Soviet Union. National Socialism was a struggle against bolshevism in general. The enemies of National Socialism tended to become abstract in definition and in the pinpointing of their sources of power. Even more threatening than Marxism was the conception of the Jew in National Socialist ideology (although bolshevism and Judaism were often conflated). Against the image of the culture-building Aryan race there was the generic Jew as the culture-destroyer. In this sense, the Jew was not just a cultural parasite, as were other non-Aryan "races"; he aimed to undermine the very existence of the *Volk* community. The two races had been locked in a life-or-death struggle throughout history, and as contemporary culture revealed, the Jew appeared to be winning. National Socialist ideology identified the Jew as the source of all evil in the modern world.

Even this brief outline of National Socialist ideology makes clear that its particular jumble of "scientific" racism and popular prejudices, and its combination of cultural traditionalism and revolutionary militancy, arose from and spoke to a specific set of lower-middle-class fears. These fears were imagined, more than experienced, in the nonindustrialized areas of Bavaria and Austria. Whereas the anxieties aroused by the changing world of advanced industrial capitalism had become widespread throughout western and central Europe since the growth of impersonal urban life and the decline of older, more communal ways of existence, only in southern Germany and Austria were fears of impersonalization and the loss of class status combined with virulent antisemitism. Even before the rise of the Nazis there existed in Austria a form of politicized antisemitism that identified the Jews with capitalism and socialism and with modernism and the decline of traditional values. It was Hitler who joined antisemitism with a grand historical-cultural vision of cosmic proportions. Hitler was born an Austrian and had spent much of his early life in Vienna before moving to Munich, the capital of Bavaria, by the outbreak of the First World War. Throughout these decades, the central core of antisemitism remained the same. The "Jew" represented the modern world and all the evil with which it was associated in the minds of the shop owners and small-town dwellers of central Europe. This context clarifies the contradictory nature of National Socialism, a militant and revolutionary movement that would destroy all aspects of modern, industrial, urban, impersonal, atomized society for the sake of restoring an "Aryan" community in which all men and women would know their place, find meaning in their lives through dedication to the communal spirit, and return to a state of harmony, both between themselves and others and between the community and nature.

National Socialism translated the ideology of the *Volk* community into practice only in part, for most of its attempts along these lines resulted either in only partially successful policies or in outright failure. Only in the area of eliminating the Jews from national life did the Nazis fulfill their ideological mission. To build a racially pure community the regime had to sever, one by one, the relationships that tied the Jewish community to the surrounding population. The Nuremberg laws of 1935 systematically eliminated German Jews from public life and redefined their legal status within the community from that of citizens to that of subjects. By 1935, then, German Jews had been removed from the new racial community, but was this only the first step in the march to the physical destruction of the Jewish people? Did the systematic elimination of the Jews from German public life lead by the logic of the ideology itself to the Final Solution? Historians continue to debate whether the policy of genocide of 1942–45 was the inevitable extension of National Socialist ideology and the policies of the 1930s.

In many ways it would be misleading to downplay the importance of ideology in directing the policies of the regime. The persecution of the Jews was not merely another method of mobilizing the population as a function of the combative *Volksgemeinschaft*. Neither before nor after 1939 was it a matter solely of *realpolitik* or opportunism. Because many historians have misunderstood this persecution, the ideological obsession of Nazi leadership has not been taken seriously. But it is perhaps too simplistic to interpret the policy of genocide as the overarching goal or even as the logical extension of this ideology. Circumstances both within and beyond the control of the regime influenced when and how these ideological goals were to be achieved. In terms of the Final Solution of the Jewish Question, its timing and implementation were inexorably connected with both the political instability built into the regime's basic structure and the failure to win the war against the Soviet Union.

THE TOTALITARIAN STATE

Ideological considerations alone do not explain the outbreak of the war in 1939, and even less do they illuminate the methods and horrors involved in the Final Solution. Ideology had to be translated into actuality. The only areas in which National Socialism realized its ideological goals were in waging the most destructive war and in implementing the most systematic process of genocide known to history. Why was National Socialism most successful precisely in those areas of its ideology that were most destructive? Why could it build the new *Volksgemeinschaft* only by preparing the nation for war and by violently, and then criminally, eliminating all those who did not fit its definition of the racial community? Part of the answer to these questions lies in the fact that, according to Nazi ideology, the war for *Lebensraum* and the forcible removal of non-Aryans from the racial community were not negative features but rather the initial creative steps toward the full realization of the historic destiny of the German nation. Moreover, the ideology stressed the importance of struggle in itself as the proving ground for its racial principles.

Hitler eventually acted less for the sake of establishing the *Volk* community than for the purpose of acting, and acting became an end in itself. He did not devote his energies to the rationalization of the German economy or to the softening of the sharp class distinctions that continued to exist in the *Volksgemeinschaft*. Such a form of dictatorship contains dynamic elements generated by the popular appeal to the masses. The demand for dynamic leadership led to a tightening of the reins of power in 1937–38, and the accentuation of the more negative aspects of the ideology and, with time, resulted both in war and in the policy of genocide. National Socialism emphasized the drive to war and the necessity of eliminating the Jews because these aims provided Hitler with two arenas he could fully control and in which he could exercise his will in a spectacularly dynamic manner. Destruction was not just to be a means of achieving National Socialist goals. It was not just the first step to fulfillment of the communal ideal. Violence and war proved to be the essence of National Socialist ideology, which could only find itself in activity and could only act by destroying. By necessity, the Third Reich remained in a state of permanent improvisation, the condition both for its early success and for its final failure. It took both an inner dynamic within the ideology and the realignment of internal and external power relationships to bring this about. The war against both the Slavs and the Jews transformed Hitler's dictatorship into the totalitarian regime of the SS imperium.

If the Führer's power was omnipotent after 1937–38, abrogating all state and legal norms and sanctioning all deeds, the police powers of the state exercised this power through the *Schutzstaffel,* or SS. This organization not only took charge of the police forces of Germany and the extermination of the Jews but also became involved in the pacification of conquered territories and, to a large extent, the conduct of the war. The SS was not simply an outgrowth of the traditional police and military establishment of Germany. Although it co-opted all police functions and created many new ones of its own, the SS existed independently of the state apparatus and operated to effect the will of the Führer. To the SS was allotted all those political tasks to which Hitler was most deeply attached, including preserving his own power position and the regime's demographic policies, pacifying occupied territories, and persecuting or eliminating all actual or supposed opponents of National Socialist rule. Himmler, the head of the SS, saw himself as the instrument of the Führer and molded the SS accordingly. The SS reflected the pure ideological and executive expression of Hitler's will, which brooked no opposition from other governmental organizations, from the law, or even from moral norms. The history of the SS clearly indicates the dissolution of the dictatorship established in the mid-1930s and the creation of the totalitarian regime of the late 1930s and early 1940s.

Founded originally as a security group within the National Socialist Party and expanded after 1933 to engulf all the police authority of the state, the SS was eventually neither a party organization nor an organ of the state. As it enveloped more and more activities in the Third Reich, it systematically moved away from its Party affiliations and its legal place within the state apparatus. Hitler did not so much take over and exploit the organization of the state after 1937–38 as to simply dislodge those aspects of the state apparatus he wanted to use, freeing them from all restraints in order to carry out his designs more effectively. For the SS, the process was not one of coordination with the state but of expanded authority into an organization beyond both state and Party. The SS was completely loyal to Hitler alone and not to the state or the Party. It in fact became the only truly efficient force in the Third Reich. The SS, not the altered but more or less traditional machinery of government, effected the revolutionary practice of National Socialism.

The SS represented the "permanent revolution" of which National Socialism had always spoken. It laid claim to the total control of the people and the reshaping of their functions in the service of the new order. The National Socialist regime was totalitarian not only in its ideological goal to integrate the individual within the *Volk* but also in the reality of its system of terror, its most decisive characteristic. The police had the power, without any legal limitations, to take "preventive" action against persons suspected of at the most only possible opposition or infractions. The SS itself defined the policing authority it possessed, which ultimately encroached on every aspect of human life, and it took all necessary coercive measures to enforce its authority. The establishment of concentration camps, instruments of both reeducation and terror, and the resulting mass arrests and mass executions were simply consequences of this totalitarian authority. Total control of the entire population of the Third Reich was justified; not only did the people have to be protected, but they also had to be molded so as to fit into the *Volksgemeinschaft*. The SS appropriated complete control over the human material at its disposal both within the *Volk* community and, more horribly, over those who had to be eliminated from this community.

The organization of power within the Third Reich, the overthrow of all legal procedures, the secretive methods of administration, and the excessive use of force and terror as part of governmental policy had led to the creation of the SS as an independent political and military power neither restrained by the regular operations of the state nor confined by conscience. The SS therefore provided the practical political means by which the most excessive features of the ideology could be realized. As an extension of its police powers, the SS took charge of the regime's racial policies and eventually of the Final Solution. Himmler directed measures both to propagate pure Aryan stock and to remove all non-Aryans from the racial community. Various branches of the SS held responsibility for the administration, rounding up, and ultimate physical elimination of all "antisocial" groups. Besides Jews, other "nondesirables" such as Gypsies, homosexuals, and criminals of various types were sent to SS-run concentration camps, work camps, or death camps. This vast engine of destruction, bolstered by its all-pervasive police powers, made the SS an empire within an empire. The persecution and execution of these various groups marks the move from a semilegal system of dictatorship to the SS totalitarian state.

The following documentary history addresses the questions of how Hitler and the Nazi Party came to power, how they reshaped the German state and society, and how they conducted the most destructive war ever known and initiated horrendous policies of genocide against the Jews and other peoples of Europe. Selected to represent a wide range of personal experiences and attitudes, the texts enable us to understand what life was like inside Hitler's Germany.

Unit I

The Hitler Dictatorship:
The Origins and Development
of National Socialism, 1918–1938

A central issue in understanding National Socialism revolves around the questions of how power was organized and how the regime functioned during the twelve years of its rule. The internal organization of power in Germany between 1933 and 1945 did not remain the same from beginning to end. The more vicious aspects of the regime had emerged by the late 1930s and early 1940s, but they were balanced by other factors before 1937–38. What presented itself as the new governmental form of National Socialist Germany in the early 1930s was not a monolithic structure; rather, it was a type of power sharing between the Nazi mass movement and an older authoritarian state apparatus.

On August 20, 1934, Hitler proclaimed the Nazi Party's total victory over its opponents: "Beginning with the highest office of the Reich, through the entire administration down to the leadership of the smallest village, the German Reich today is in the hands of the National Socialist Party." And in fact, what mattered was not so much the Party's possession of all levels of government, which were never wholly under Nazi control, but that unchallenged leadership of both the state and society was in the hands of the National Socialists, subject to their manipulation and serving a regime focused entirely on the Führer. For the most part, however, the new regime brought anything but order and security, for National Socialist rule meant arbitrariness and internal chaos. Hitler himself tailored his proclamation of August 20 to this dual aspect of the consolidation of power: "The fight for governmental power has ceased as of this day. But the fight for our precious people continues." Competing sources of power had been successfully eliminated, but the in-gathering of the nation — the total unity of the people in the service of Hitler's goals — was not yet realized.

13

On a practical plane, power in the Third Reich before 1937–38 was based on a sharing of functions between the Party and the state, the Führer and the bureaucracy. This balancing process guaranteed some degree of legality and the continued operation of traditional governmental forms, which in part restrained the unchallenged rule of the Führer and restricted the full realization of the Party's revolutionary ideology. The Führer's will was beyond legality, penal codes, or constitutional sanctions; it was by definition beyond all restrictions and norms associated with the idea of a state. By 1938 the regime Hitler had established was in fact antithetical to the very idea of the state; it was the immediate expression of the Führer and as such reserved to itself complete freedom of action and decision making.

Hitler moved to consolidate his position as sole leader within the state, thereby enhancing the tendency toward one-man, nondemocratic rule already inherent in the governmental system. Hitler essentially retained and only slightly altered the structures of the state bureaucracy and judiciary, whose organization went back beyond the Weimar Republic (1919–33) to the German Empire (1871–1918). But the progress toward dictatorship between 1933 and 1938 specifically resulted from the way Hitler had "overthrown" the Weimar Republic. The republic was not destroyed through a revolutionary act that destroyed older forms of government and completely reestablished a new one; rather, Hitler and his allies among the conservative opponents of the republic took over the government by extraordinary but still for the most part constitutional means. This fact points to the two predominant factors that led to Hitler's assumption of power in 1933: (1) the severe crisis over the distribution of power in Weimar Germany which destroyed the parliamentary system in 1930 (that is, three years before Hitler became chancellor); and (2) the development of loose yet pervasive forms of control within the Nazi Party which allowed it to grow from a small cadre of loyal followers to a mass party. In other words, the deployment of power in Nazi Germany, both in its dictatorial and its totalitarian phases, cannot be understood without a grasp of the instability of the democratic institutions during the Weimar Republic as well as the development of National Socialism from a handful of revolutionary extremists to a mass and (by and large) middle-class party.

One of the main reasons for the triumph of National Socialism was the failure of other political parties to stabilize republican structures. In 1929 the Social Democratic Party, the largest single party, had resumed its stance of nonparticipation with other parliamentary groups. When the two wings of the Grand Coalition were unable to master the art of political compromise in the spring of 1930, parliamentary democracy ceased to function. Moreover, an early consequence of the economic collapse was the weakening of the labor unions, one of the props of the democratic system. The unions lost influence and control over the rapidly growing numbers of unemployed. Their membership declined, their economic power dwindled, and the weapon of the strike became blunted as the idle labor force increased. In order to express their dissatisfaction, the workers increasingly turned to the German Communist Party. This move to the left was mirrored by a move on the part of middle-class coalition partners, particularly the German People's Party, to the right. The polarization of political sentiment had severe implications for parliamentary politics.

A previous crisis, the early years of the Weimar Republic from the Treaty of Versailles (1919) to the occupation of the Ruhr and the hyperinflation (1923), saw the origins of the Nationalsozialistische Deutsche Arbeiterpartei, or NSDAP (National Socialist German Workers' Party). The first phase of the development of the NSDAP ended with the abortive Beer Hall Putsch staged in Munich on November 8–9, 1923, and Hitler's imprisonment for treason against the republic. His release in 1924 marked the beginning of a new stage of growth and a new organizational arrangement for the Party, but it was only in 1928–29 that National Socialism became a nationwide political organization with mass appeal. Until the NSDAP entered electoral politics in the late 1920s, it had not been concerned with winning victories at the polls. Like other extreme rightist parties (but more effectively than most), the Party concentrated its efforts on agitation and organization. It minimized political activity in the limited sense of channeled participation in the republican system, considering itself in permanent opposition to the parliamentary forms of the Weimar Republic. The NSDAP did not aim to be a political party in any usual sense of the term but rather a movement, above politics, the goal of which was to rescue Germany from both the Weimar Constitution and the Versailles Treaty.

The tremendous growth of the NSDAP and its emergence as a mass party are illuminated by an examination of National Socialism's connection with the middle class. The NSDAP had few supporters among factory workers and the trade unions. Despite its claims to be a workers' party, and although Otto Strasser had made some attempt to develop the Party along these lines, the NSDAP never attracted a wide following among the industrial workers of Germany. Only in 1928 did the effort begin in earnest to win over the growing number of unemployed workers. This campaign proved somewhat more successful than earlier ones. By contrast, however, the NSDAP made significant inroads among agricultural workers. Although initially the party was a petit bourgeois, semisocialist grievance movement that had little contact with the peasantry or agricultural issues, its antisemitic and anticapitalist pronouncements nonetheless appealed to the agrarian sector, especially as the antimodernist strain became more developed in the unstable markets of the 1920s.

But not only to the peasants did the National Socialists make their promises of being all things to all people. It was the urban middle class, in the broad sense of the term, that made the NSDAP into a mass party and carried it into an influential position in the Reichstag (parliament) in the 1930s. The panic of the middle class, which began with the outbreak of the economic crisis in 1929, was sharpened by the fact that it felt threatened not only economically but also socially. The violent reaction that drove many of its members to the extreme right arose out of a general desire for security in the face of yet another wave of catastrophic inflation. After remaining apolitical and isolated from the workings of the republic since its inception, this group reacted in a markedly political fashion to the new crisis, turning to the simple solutions offered by the National Socialists. The success of the NSDAP's appeal to the middle class begun in 1929 was closely connected with the frequently invoked anticapitalist sentiment of the petit bourgeoisie. What its members wanted was not socialism but protection of small property owners against the growing incursions of big business. The middle class, contrary to Marxist expectations, did not come over to the ideology of socialism. Faced with a choice between the extreme Left and the extreme Right, between international communism and ultranationalism, the middle class solidly selected the latter.

The makers of National Socialist propaganda knew how to operate flexibly and attractively without ignoring the pro-union, anticapitalist sentiment of those middle-class workers toward whom the appeal of the "workers' party" was initially directed. The growth of the National Socialist German Workers' Party in the early years depended almost exclusively on Hitler's ability as a mass agitator. He effectively manipulated the elaborate rite of the mass meeting so that his speech was the high point. The crowd was warmed up to a fever pitch well before his appearance. Martial music and songs, mass demonstrations and flags, the recitation of radical slogans and chanting built up to the climactic arrival of the Führer, when all these emotions would burst forth. The main themes of the speeches rolled on in almost monotonous repetition: the campaign against the Versailles Treaty, the denigration of Marxism and international capitalism, the attacks against the Weimar Constitution and the leaders of the republic, and ever and always the vilification of the Jews, who were blamed for every evil that had befallen Germany and the world. Hitler's speeches would not have had such effect if he had not combined a note of high seriousness, the destiny of the German nation, with popular oratory, hurling biting sarcasm against all his enemies. Hitler's ability to set forth the holy mission of the Nazi Party along with utterly scathing denunciations of real and perceived foes, all within the context of a mass gathering, separated him from the other members of the Nazi elite. Neither the coarser Streicher nor the more intellectual Goebbels was able to master mass oratory to anywhere near the same degree of effectiveness.

Hitler also knew how to articulate what his listeners wanted to hear. He could put into words — or better yet, easily remembered slogans — what they half-consciously desired and felt. He expressed and reinforced their unsure longings and deep-seated prejudices and thereby created in them a deeply satisfying sense of awakened self-awareness and belief in a set of certainties and truths that those outside the Party refused to recognize. Such leadership and oratory did not require a developed personality or a cultivated intellect. Indeed, the malleable features of Hitler's personality allowed him to feel what his audiences felt. In front of a crowd, he moved and was moved by his audience till he in fact became greater than a mere individual and his words took on a truth that they would not otherwise have had. This common bond between Hitler and the masses formed the source of his personal power. He came from a background of psychological and emotional dislocation, from a world of crumbling truths and values, and he, like many Germans, had felt adrift in the uncertain postwar world. With the crystallization of his ideas into a full-blown ideology and the growing self-awareness of a successful agitator, Hitler increasingly discovered his own mission and meaning in life, which he then transferred so successfully to the German people.

With its appeal to the national idealism of the middle classes, Nazi ideology spoke to ideals of social integration and national pride. National Socialism's dynamism and appeal did not lie in a class-oriented view of the world; on the contrary, it emphasized unity, bringing new strength and identity by overcoming diverse interests and antagonistic positions. Although in actual practice the NSDAP appealed only to a small section of middle-class Germans and its leaders criticized both working-class political parties and large-scale capitalists, National Socialist ideology glossed over such class divisions in the name of the integrated *Volk* community, in which all groups would find satisfaction in their place within the newly founded national life. For his part, Hitler devoted himself fully to addressing the ills facing Germany and issuing the call to action that would overcome these problems. His ability to turn Germans' latent anxieties over the state of the nation into a few easy-to-remember slogans made him the unerring Führer. The dual struggle, for example, of right-minded Germans against decadent foreign peoples as well as of "idealistic" members of the nation against both capitalist materialism and socialism proclaimed the primacy of national spirit over economic practicality. Hitler was thus not so much a leader guiding his people through difficult times or a revolutionary teacher instructing them in new ways of thinking as the catalyst of a particular mass process. Hitler took the problems of the republic and the deep anxieties felt by the German people and offered simplistic solutions and grand visions of the future. He was at once the anonymous exponent of popular anxiety and the single individual figure who could marshal and concentrate this anxiety, making it an extremely potent political force. The NSDAP could not possibly fulfill all the promises it had made to the heterogeneous groups it aimed to attract between 1928 and 1933, but when the dictatorship was firmly established, it no longer needed to do so.

Out of the confusing welter of political and personal factors leading to Hitler's assumption of the chancellorship of the republic, one fact emerges clearly: in the course of the negotiations with President Hindenburg and his political ally Franz von Papen, Hitler demanded that, as head of a presidential cabinet, he too must be granted extraordinary dictatorial emergency power. He gained legitimacy, not as the leader of a parliamentary coalition, but through this authoritarian loophole in the Weimar Constitution. Of all the possible means of taking over the state, his using the constitutional provisions of Article 48 both gave him the chancellorship and allowed him to rule in the months after his appointment. On January 30, 1933, the new chancellor found himself in a position to reap the fruits of his successful strategy, swearing formal allegiance to a constitution he immediately set about to destroy. The power thus seized by legal means could now be extended by the strategies of revolution and of overtaking, eliminating, and leveling all political, social, and intellectual safeguards and counterforces.

Once in power, Hitler needed another slogan to propound the policy of tightening control over the state and society: the call for "permanent revolution," the total remaking of German economic, social, and political life. The central policy of permanent revolution was *Gleichschaltung*, the "coordination" of the party and the state. This goal was never fully realized, but in trying to achieve it the Führer effected decisive shifts that placed all power in his hands. In practice *Gleichschaltung* meant the elimination of all remnants of democratic constitutionalism and the complete subordination of the state apparatus to Hitler. It established the form the dictatorship would assume until 1937–38 and laid the foundations for the totalitarian state that followed.

The Third Reich was officially founded on March 21, 1933, in a gigantic display at Potsdam. At the tomb of Frederick the Great and on the anniversary of the convocation of Bismarck's Reichstag in 1871, Hitler repeated his pledges of loyalty to the Constitution which so impressed the middle class, the civil servants, and the army. But in reality the oaths he took only served to deflect attention away from the terrorist methods he employed to secure his political domination. Only two days after the show at Potsdam, the veils lifted and the reality of National Socialist rule stood revealed. Hitler pushed through the Reichstag the so-called Enabling Act or "law for relieving the distress of the people of the Reich," which gave to the cabinet full legislative and budgetary powers, including the right to initiate constitutional amendments, for a period of four years. The Enabling Act thus called for complete abdication of power by the Reichstag. The Communist Party had already been eliminated as a political threat through the passage of the Reichstag Fire Decree. The bourgeois parties, from the German People's Party to the Catholic Center Party to the German Democratic Party, had been so intimidated by the pressures of accomplished facts of the previous two months and so impressed by the appeals to ultranationalism that they felt they could not withhold their agreement. Only the Social Democratic Party held out, but in vain. The Reichstag, by a vote of 441 to 84, made Hitler dictator. The Enabling Act alone gave Hitler the power to rule. Although supplemented by laws passed in 1937, 1941, and 1943, it remained the centerpiece of his consolidation of power. Since no new constitution was ever written, this emergency decree, which suspended the Weimar Constitution, shaped the entire constitutional history of the Third Reich.

The parliamentary system was therefore crushed, including even its claim to remain a force within the new system. The Liberals and the Center Party were probably motivated by the hope that the Enabling Act would bring the regime back from government by presidential decree and reestablish legislative rule. But precisely the opposite occurred. The passage of the Enabling Act only furthered the legal revolution, allowing the National Socialists to work in apparently constitutional ways to achieve a position of uncontested rule and giving sanction to the blatantly unconstitutional, terrorist tactics the NSDAP had been using all along. While providing Hitler with the legal means of consolidating and expanding his power, it eliminated all bases of any real opposition to the government.

The rapidity with which the new rulers overwhelmed the political Left, which astonished even themselves, stemmed from the Left's own self-delusion. The reasons for this collapse arc manifold. Because of their refusal to take hold of the reins of government in 1930 and their capitulation before Franz von Papen's coup in Prussia, the largest state within the federated national state, the Social Democrats found themselves excluded from the political arena even before 1933. The Nazi ploy of legal revolution proved very successful. The Socialists could not call for the overthrow of what looked like a constitutionally valid government. They consoled themselves that a coup against NSDAP rule was imminent — a coup that never, of course, materialized. The Communist Party, for its part, had not let any opportunity to stir up civil strife and weaken democratic defenses slip. The Communists in fact seemed more interested in attacking the Social Democrats than in stopping the Nazi takeover. They even cooperated with the National Socialists in helping to destroy the Social Democrats, justifying their incongruous yet typical cooperation on the calculation that, with the overthrow of the republic, Germany would become ripe for communist revolution. Like the Social Democratic leaders, they saw in National Socialism the last stages of collapsing capitalism. Hitler feared a well-organized general strike, but the Social Democratic Party, the labor unions, and the Communist Party showed a misplaced faith in legality; they believed their primary task was to keep their organizations from being outlawed. They thus became victims of their own strategy. In its own way, the Left sacrificed itself to the Marxist thesis that Nazism was merely counterrevolutionary.

The sort of pseudolegal sanctions with which the regime adorned its authoritarian moves clothed the creation of the one-party state, which put the final seal on the National Socialist seizure of power. The elimination of the political Left had been an irregular act, even though it was done by a decree of July 7, which ousted the Social Democrats from all state legislatures and municipal governments, "for the protection of the state." The Law Against the New Formation of Parties culminated the antiparliamentary moves, proclaiming in terse language the National Socialist one-party state and severely penalizing all other political activity. The law violated not only the provisions of the Constitution but the Enabling Act as well. With the Enabling Act stripped of yet another restriction, the state of emergency became a permanent condition, for now the fiction that legal opposition and parliamentary controls still existed could no longer be maintained. As in all modern dictatorships, elections functioned to confirm one-party voting lists or approve authoritarian decisions that had already been reached.

The death of President Hindenburg on August 2, 1934, appropriately symbolized the end of the period of takeover. More than just an image of the continuity between traditional constitutional authority and the new National Socialist regime, Hindenburg continued to pose a potential threat to the new order through his special relation with the army. With Hindenburg's death Hitler assumed the powers of the presidency while abolishing the office itself through a plebiscite. The entire state structure now served only Hitler. His total control was further institutionalized when the army took an oath of loyalty to the person of the Führer and tolerated his usurpation of the presidential office. This decisive act rested on the mutuality of interests between Hitler and the army, which thus permitted itself to be made an accomplice of Hitler's deeds.

It was of crucial significance that the Nazis' rise to power in the years 1933–34 oscillated between making a revolution and halting one. The structure of power and the allocation of authority that developed in the first phase did not result from any clear concepts or united action. Ideological considerations were not set aside, however; rather, the often vague tenets of National Socialist ideology provided a framework allowing flexible, changeable strategies and tactics in specific circumstances. This organized chaos stemmed from the Party revolution from below, the expansion of the central state dictatorship from above, and the often more or less spontaneous coordination and adjustment in social and public life outside politics. In other words, it issued from neither the simple implementation of ideology nor the accidental accrual of power derived from successfully exploiting chance opportunities. Both ideology and opportunism played their parts. The end of this stormy early phase with the establishment of the absolute power of the Führer in the summer of 1934 interrupted the internal shaping of the Reich, which was still a long way from being complete, and blocked the revolutionary tendencies within the party, which had grown stronger from the middle of 1933. The fluidity of power relations in all their contradictory and overlapping patterns was more or less frozen at this moment.

This mingling of official state institutions with party organizations derived from the National Socialist movement made the boundaries between state, society, and party difficult to define and created a competitive partnership among them. Just as the mass movement of the NSDAP had already begun to infiltrate the state through the Party's entry into local and municipal governments as well as public life in general by setting up numerous auxiliary organizations, offices, and associations, so the process of coordination in 1933–34 constituted a still more intensive form of fusion and confrontation between National Socialists and the old leadership forces in state and society. The speed and smoothness with which this coordination for the most part took place clarify certain essential features of the National Socialist state: very often the transition was more a matter of readjustment than a revolutionary upheaval. But the shift also resulted in the incorporation of a significant proportion of National Socialist membership into traditional structures and associations of state and society. Coordination signified that social forces were often contained at the price of dilution and further softening and splitting up of the National Socialist movement.

Hitler's relationship to both state and Party organizations is a point of debate among historians. One group (the intentionalists) stresses that he did not aim to tighten his hold on the reins of power, hoping instead to maintain his freedom to maneuver. Other historians (the structuralists) emphasize Hitler's inability or unwillingness to take over such control. Whatever Hitler's position in relation to the structures of power, the dictatorship of 1933–37 still recognized some limitations of constitutional form and legal norms whereas the totalitarian regime of 1938–45 supplanted the constitutional power of the state with the will of the Führer. The revolutionary core of National Socialism lay in this link between mass movement and one-man rule, which dissolved all intermediary agencies of law, politics, and even morality.

Both necessity and method guided the development of this structure. Alternately confronting and collaborating with established forces, the mass movement transformed itself into a governing organization. Both sides exerted pressure for collaboration, not least in the ministries and state administrations. Collaboration offered those nominally in charge of the state apparatus the possibility of recommending themselves to their new masters or of carrying out desired reforms with the help of the Party. Within the Party Hitler had long since made a practice of encouraging individual initiative, and he now applied this tactic in the realm of practical government by allowing experienced officials and administrators scope to effect measures for technical and economic management. The relatively loose and open-ended nature of the process of coordinating the party structure with the liberal middle-class and conservative groups in state and society lay the foundation for the success of the National Socialist takeover.

The following pages document the history of the Weimar Republic and the first five years of National Socialist rule. Chapter 1 deals with the organization of power in the Weimar Republic, whose political organization both continued that of the imperial regime and marked a break with it. Chapter 2 details the origins of National Socialism in the state of Bavaria in 1919 and Hitler's transformation of the NSDAP into a nationwide mass party in the course of 1928 and 1929. Chapter 3 focuses on the crisis of 1929–33 and the part played by Hitler and the Nazi Party. Chapter 4 addresses Hitler's consolidation of power in 1933–34, from his assumption of the chancellorship to the Roehm purge. Finally, Chapter 5 analyzes the form of dictatorship Hitler established in Germany before he turned to more aggressive national and diplomatic policies in 1937–38.

The runaway inflation of 1923 reached such astronomical proportions that German housewives used the utterly worthless currency to kindle household fires.

Chapter

1

The Ordeal of the Weimar Republic, 1919–1933

Born in a time of military defeat and revolution, the Weimar Republic experienced general domestic unrest and economic crisis in its first years of existence. It eventually collapsed in a second economic crisis brought on by the international economic collapse of the 1930s. Political and constitutional problems followed close on these economic difficulties. It is incorrect, however, to view the republic as doomed to failure from its very beginnings. The republic was not inherently weak, nor was its governmental system inappropriate for the German people. Once the initial shock of losing the First World War had passed and American economic aid had relieved the worst features of the reparations agreements of the Versailles Treaty, a series of working coalitions inaugurated a period of peace and stability between 1924 and 1930. Combinations of internal and external factors demarcated and defined the various phases of the Weimar Republic — the early chaotic years (1919–23); the relatively stable middle period, the "golden twenties" (1924–30); and the crisis-ridden final years (1930–33). The Weimar years cannot be dismissed as simply the backdrop to the rise of Nazism, nor the republican government as an unimportant parliamentary prelude to the dictatorship of Hitler.

The Weimar Republic replaced the German Empire, which went down to defeat in World War I. Although the new German Constitution ended the rule of the Kaiser and gave more power to the Reichstag, it did not break completely with these earlier political and social forms. The German imperial state had created a unique balance of forces within the state and society. Although the overarching structure changed during the Weimar Republic and again under Hitler, the forces themselves remained the same: (1) the parliamentary system and its political parties; (2) the federal, local, and municipal governmental structures; (3) the permanent structure of the national state — that is, the bureaucracy; (4) the judiciary; and (5) the army.

23

The imperial regime had united almost all ethnic Germans (with the exclusion of the Austrians) in a strong federal union in 1871. This unification was achieved less through the spontaneous rising of the people than through the diplomatic maneuvering and military success of Prussia, which along with Austria was the leading power among the various German states. Although all the major nations of continental Europe had developed from the seventeenth to the nineteenth centuries by organizing both large-scale standing armies and the state bureaucracies needed to support them, Prussia fostered more efficient forms of these structures, without the interference of other political or social forces. Besides the efficiency and organization of its army and bureaucracy, the activity of its monarchs made the originally small state of Prussia a major power. The chief architect of German unification was Otto von Bismarck, minister-president of Prussia and then after 1871 also chancellor of the Reich. Bismarck co-opted the democratic-national movements calling for unification and constructed a constitution that combined constitutional-parliamentary forms with authoritarian-bureaucratic ones. In the new federated Reich, Prussia continued to maintain a dominant position, both geographically and politically, over the other states (*Länder*) of the empire. By the beginning of the twentieth century, the German Empire was a world power, a leader in technology, science, and education — a nation-state proud of its cultural and historical traditions.

The constitutional monarchy of the Reich provided for both a national parliament (the Reichstag) and local state parliaments (*Landtage*), but their authority was severely limited by the power of the Kaiser and his chancellor. The parliamentary system therefore played an important yet limited role. Since unification had been imposed from above and represented in itself a compromise between the national-democratic tendencies of the early nineteenth century and the authoritarian-bureaucratic traditions of Prussia, the Kaiser and his chancellor were relatively free to conduct the affairs of state. For most Germans, with the exception of those who were members of leftist political parties, which called for more fully democratic forms, the combination of parliamentary and authoritarian forms was not thought to be inherently defective or in need of immediate reform.

Although not completely without accountability to the Reichstag, the chancellor and his cabinet ruled Germany and conducted its foreign policy at the sole discretion of the Kaiser. Through the Kaiser the chancellor also had charge of the state bureaucracy, the highly efficient and tightly organized structure that ran the day-to-day operations of government. Except in financial matters, the army too was independent of the Reichstag and under the direct control of the Kaiser and the chancellor. The independent standing and functioning of the judiciary were likewise a point of pride in the overall system.

Only military collapse and revolution made possible the breakdown of this state system and the establishment of another. The burdens of the conduct of World War I turned the quasi-parliamentary, quasi-authoritarian state into a military dictatorship under Generals Hindenburg and Ludendorff, and their eventual failure opened the way to democratic reforms. Military defeat, the uprising of sailors, soldiers, and workers, and the central government's lack of control led through a series of fortuitous events to the declaration of a republic on November 9, 1918. The so-called German revolution was a bloodless affair. When Kaiser Wilhelm II abdicated, the last imperial chancellor, Max von Baden, handed his office over to Friedrich Ebert, the leader of the Social Democratic Party. Ebert was selected because the Social Democrats, also known as the Majority Socialists, had gained a dominant position in the Reichstag in the last elections held before the outbreak of war in 1914.

To ensure stability and guarantee the orderly return of the troops from the front, Ebert had to contend against groups calling for more thoroughgoing political and social reforms. His major challenge then came not from the Right but from the far Left, especially from the Independent Social Democratic Party. At the end of the year, on December 30, 1918, most of the Independent Social Democrats formed the German Communist Party and staged in Berlin a rather amateurish attempt at revolution known as Spartacus Week (January 5–12, 1919). Since Ebert had come to an agreement with the army, the Ebert-Groener Pact, earlier in November and was not afraid to call in the aid of the *Freikorps,* the vigilante groups made up of former soldiers, this "second revolution" was quickly and bloodily put down.

Through these and other compromises with the traditional sources of authority, the basic problems of the empire persisted. The German revolution, the proclamation of the republic, and even the establishment of a more thoroughly parliamentary form of government under the Weimar Constitution (July 1919) took place amid a welter of revolutionary, reforming, and traditional forces. Authoritarian elements thun retained a role in the all-too-hastily improvised Weimar Republic. The older power structure, including an unreformed bureaucracy and an unrepentant army, survived within the new framework, which preserved the social, economic, and bureaucratic balance of power with only minor changes.

The resulting government was created through compromise. The six major parties that were to play a major role in national politics covered a wide spectrum from extreme conservatives to Communists. With the exception of the latter, they represented in renamed forms the only slightly reconstituted political groups of the German Empire. The desire for order and continuity found expression in the political alliance between the various middle-class parties and the Majority Socialists. No real reorientation or restructuring followed the collapse of leadership by the traditional, nonsocialist political elites. Instead, the democratic and socialist majority aligned themselves with the military and bureaucratic establishments, which knew how to exploit this connection without having to yield power.

As a result of the continuity of administration, which in the emergency situation during the winter of 1918–19 may have appeared essential, the relationships between the parliamentary government and on the one hand the military and on the other the bureaucracy, were never clarified during the entire history of the

Weimar Republic. In maintaining traditional sources of power, the bloodless revolution of November 1918 perpetuated authoritarian elements. Throughout the Weimar period, imperial precedents were constantly called on to support the formation of "above party" specialists' cabinets as well as to justify the predominance of the civil service and military in the presidential cabinets of the last years of the republic.

These factors could not but have a deleterious effect on the structure and vitality of a democratic Germany. Moreover, the sudden military defeat and the lack of full-scale parliamentary experience before the war left the country unprepared to establish workable democratic forms of government. The political alliance between the army and the bureaucracy halted revolutionary reform before the sociopolitical structures of power could be fundamentally remodeled. Finally, the desire for immediate restoration of order proved stronger than revolutionary or reformist ambitions, even though rushing to reestablish stability entailed rejecting vital aspects of democratization.

The problems the new republic faced were not entirely of its own making. However great the republic's difficulties in instituting a parliamentary system, these were secondary to the problems confronting it from outside. External factors, diplomatic and military as well as economic, would undermine the forces working for the stabilization of the republic and would eventually lead to its collapse from within. Since the defeat in 1918, German foreign policy was constrained by the Versailles Treaty, which decreed not only the reduction of German territory (by about 10 percent) and of the status of the Reich as a major power but also the imposition of severe economic measures against the nation. Versailles also compromised German sovereignty, limiting the size of the nation's army and navy and its control over its citizens.

The government's acquiescence to the terms of the Versailles Treaty led to counterrevolutionary activity from the Right. A variety of right-wing opponents of the republic, including Hitler and the National Socialists, concocted a whole mythology about why the war had been lost and the treaty accepted. Against the claim of the army leaders that they had been unable to continue the war, the Nazis declared that the Reichswehr was never defeated in the field but had been "stabbed in the back" by socialist politicians and Jews at home. A conspiracy of these groups led to the signing of the Versailles Treaty. The Right loudly decried the terms of the treaty. They were not only unjust, but they represented a betrayal of the German nation. In accepting the treaty the republic had committed an act of treason, and therefore everything Weimar stood for had to be uncompromisingly opposed. The fallacious yet powerful ideology of the NSDAP thus combined antidemocratic, antisocialist, and antisemitic elements to explain the rapid military, economic, social, and political decline of Germany.

The first serious political challenge from the Right came in the spring of 1920. One of the terms of the Versailles Treaty was that Germany reduce its armed forces by between 50,000 and 60,000 men, including members of the *Freikorps.*

To prevent this reduction, Captain Hermann Ehrhardt, a *Freikorps* leader, marched on Berlin on March 12–13 intending to overthrow the government. General von Lüttwitz, the commander of the army's Berlin district, proclaimed a new government with Wolfgang Kapp, a frustrated politician, at its head. The other Reichswehr divisions remained in an ambiguous position. Although called on by the government to suppress the coup, the army refused to do so; but it did not give its support to Kapp either. Confronted with this situation, the ministers of the Weimar government had few options. They finally decided to leave Berlin; the putsch seemed to have achieved instant success. Yet the Reich and the Prussian civil service refused to carry out the orders of the new government, and a general strike called by the official government and carried out by organized labor then completely shut down the capital. Without hope for further support, the putsch collapsed after only five days. Its leaders fled the country, and the Weimar government returned as quickly as it had left.

Besides the encouragement of right-wing opposition to the Weimar Republic, the worst feature of the Versailles Treaty for the German people was what was known as the war guilt clause. Article 231 identified Germany as the aggressor nation, which was therefore liable for reparations payments to the Allied countries for their losses in the war. This demand placed a tremendous economic burden on a state that had itself suffered massive devastation in the war. Although the actions of some German bankers also played a significant role in exacerbating the nation's financial problems, war reparations contributed to the devastating inflation of 1922–23 as well as to the economic crisis of 1929–33, when American loans, which had been extended to pay off the reparations, were withdrawn. This last crisis precipitated the political problems that brought on the final death agonies of the republic.

The confusion of the early years of the Weimar Republic reached a climax in 1923, when outside military intervention coincided with the severe economic plight of Germany. This external intervention began with the French occupation of the Ruhr industrial area, which was followed by a communist uprising in central Germany and an attempted nationalist coup in northern and southern Germany. With the onset of runaway inflation, which rapidly reached catastrophic proportions, the shaky edifice of the republic, the product of three years of laborious work, seemed near collapse. Looming over it all was the threat of either a military (rightist) or a communist (leftist) takeover. The Reichswehr and its commander in chief, General Hans von Seeckt, stood by the republic less out of concern for preserving democratic rule than from fear of a left-wing takeover and a preoccupation with securing the independent position of the army.

By August 1923 it was clear that the republic had weathered all these storms and would survive. With the exception of the passive Seeckt, the man most responsible for saving the republic and ensuring its stability both internally and in its relations with foreign powers was Gustav Stresemann of the German People's Party. Although he was chancellor for only a short time in 1923, Stresemann continued to serve as foreign minister until his death in 1929. His personality as well as his policies dominated the relatively peaceful years 1924–29. The general situation was favorable for the republic. Domestic crises and threats of overthrow seemed to have been mastered, the economy was recovering and making steady progress, and the unresolved problems with other nations were apparently on the way to being settled. Though the country may not have had large numbers of confirmed supporters of the republic, it looked as though a gradual acclimatization to the democratic system would in the course of time solidify and strengthen the government's political support.

The Stresemann era brought fresh hopes for the republic, yet causes for grave concern remained. Chief among them was the fact that in all the meetings of the Reichstag in 1924–28 the Social Democratic Party, the strongest single party in Germany, remained in opposition. By giving the government over to a weak middle-class alliance, the Social Democrats nurtured a fatal tendency toward minority cabinets. Not the least reason for this policy was their fear of losing voters to their Communist rivals if the latter were to join the government. Consequently the Social Democratic Party with its vast political power lost its political influence over the republic. This last fact — all the more urgent since the antirepublican Field Marshal Hindenburg and no longer the Social Democrat Ebert now presided over the government — along with the consequences of the international economic crisis, led the republic to the brink of collapse in 1929.

1. The Defeated Troops Come Home

The defeat of the German armed forces in 1918 came as a bitter realization for many patriotic Germans. Some in fact refused to believe that Germany had actually been defeated in battle, preferring instead to believe that the German military effort had been cut short by defeatists on the home front. Militarists and extreme nationalists argued that the Social Democrats and Jews had betrayed Germany and in effect "stabbed the army in the back."

For many young Germans hoping to make careers in military service, the collápse in 1918 was a double shock. The following excerpt from Ernst von Salomon's autobiographical novel *Die Geächteten* (The Outlaws), published in 1930, describes the bitterness, despair, and resentment felt by many who watched the army's return to a Germany in the throes of leftist revolution. Salomon was a young cadet in 1918, when he saw his hopes and ideals dashed. Such feelings led him and many others to join *Freikorps* (free corps) units, paramilitary freebooters

Excerpts from *Die Geächteten* by Ernst von Salomon (Berlin: Rowohlt Verlag GmbH., 1930), pp. 7–12, 19–20, 28–29, 33–34, 37–39, 83. Translated by Dieter Kuntz.

who volunteered to defend the Fatherland against bolshevism inside Germany as well as on its borders.

Salomon took part in the anticommunist fighting in Berlin in early 1919 and later was sentenced to a five-year jail term for complicity in the murder of Walther Rathenau, the head of the German delegation that signed the armistice in 1918. Salomon was not actively involved in the Third Reich, although he later worked as a scriptwriter for UFA, the German film company, producing work that won the approval of the Nazi regime.

The sky over the city seemed to be more red than usual. Unable to penetrate the November fog, the light from isolated lanterns colored the damp, saturated air and made the clouds appear heavy and milky. The streets were empty of people. The tormented, echoing sound of a trumpet could be heard in the distance. The clatter of drums rebounded threateningly against the rows of houses, making closed windows quake with fear, before finally being muffled by dark courtyards. . . . I sat shivering in my room while the eerie sound of the trumpets echoed through the streets. The silence of my room tormented me. I had placed on the table those things that were supposed to steady and support me. The picture of my father in uniform, taken at the beginning of the war; the pictures of friends and relatives who fell at the front; the field bandage; the curved hussar's saber; the shoulder straps; the French helmet; my brother's wallet, which had bullet holes and which was dotted by dark, dried blood; my grandfather's epaulets with the heavy tassels that were once silver but now had become blackish; a bundle of mildewed letters from the front — but I couldn't look at any of it, none of it. No, I could not look at it at all. It was all meaningless now. It had all been reminders of victories marked by flags draped from windows. Now there were no more victories; the flags had lost their purpose. Now, in this confusing moment, when all was going to pieces, when the way that had been mapped out for me was suddenly blocked, I uncomprehendingly stood face to face with a new and changed situation. . . .

I finally decided to go out into the street. Women stood, as usual, in long rows in front of the stores and engaged in animated conversation. . . . In the inner city, I decided to investigate the racket coming from one of the main streets. . . . A giant flag was being carried in front of a long procession. The flag was red. It hung wet and dreary from a long pole, and was like a blemish hanging over the quickly collected mob. I stood still and watched. . . .

. . . There they went, the warriors of the revolution. From this blackish swarm a red-hot flame was to spring? Was the dream of blood and barricades to become a reality? To capitulate to them was unthinkable. . . .

. . . Suddenly sailors appeared. Sailors sporting huge red sashes. They had rifles in hand and wore smiling faces under ribboned caps, and broad, chic, and elegant pants covered legs that set a lazy pace. "Our boys in blue!" That thought shot through my head, and I expected nauseous revulsion to climb into my throat, but it wasn't revulsion, it was fear. They had made the revolution: these young fellows with their determined faces; it was these coarse youths, linking arms with girls, and who moved along while singing, laughing, and hooting, and wearing fluttering neckties on their naked necks, and exhibiting self-confidence. . . .

[Several days later,] the terms of the armistice became known. I stood in the middle of a large mass of people in front of the newspaper building. There the news sheets were displayed with their glaring headlines. . . . At first I could not see anything, but someone in front of me laughed nervously and said that this was all nonsense; that this could not be true, and that Wilson would take care of this. But another silenced him with the remark that this certainly could not be expected of Wilson. Someone else exclaimed that the French had wanted this even at the beginning of the war. A woman cried hoarsely: "But that means that the French will come here." Then I was able to move to the front of the crowd and read. . . . My first reaction was anger toward the newspaper because it had printed these heinous, frosty, and laconic terms in an almost visually pleasing style with broad and portly letters. But then I felt as if the hunger, to which I had become accustomed, was tearing at the walls of my stomach. . . . At first I didn't understand. I forced myself to understand. I felt as though I needed to laugh. . . . I finally grasped the fact that the French would come here; that the French would march victoriously into our city. . . .

In mid-December our troops from the front marched into the city. It was only one division. They had come from the area around Verdun. Crowds gathered on the sidewalks. A few houses timidly displayed the [imperial] black-white-red flag. Many young girls and women were there, and several had brought baskets of flowers or small packages. More and more people gathered. . . . We stood and waited for the nation's best. Their efforts couldn't have been in vain. Could the casualties of war have been for nothing? That could not be the case; that was impossible. . . . Our field-grays had come home; our sparkling army that had done its duty to the best of its ability. It had won brilliant victories, but the luster of those victories now became unbearable — now that the war was lost, yet the army had not been defeated. The front had been held. . . .

The crowd then began to recover its nerve. The shouts of some sounded like a crackling from rusty throats. Here and there handkerchiefs were waved. . . . "Our heroes, our heroes!" . . . No flags. No sign of victory. When I saw these deathly serious faces; these hard, carved-from-wood faces; these eyes, which looked past the crowd as though they were strangers or hostile — yes, hostile — then I knew that it was all completely different from how we all had imagined it. . . . What did we know about the front; of our soldiers? Nothing, we knew nothing. O God, this was terrible. None of what they had told us was true. We had been lied to. . . . Suddenly it struck me. . . . These men who were marching past, with rifles on their shoulders and so distanced from all who were not of their own, did not really want to belong to us. . . . They did not belong to us, nor did they belong to the Reds. . . .

. . . I wondered if they hated the revolution? If they would march against it? If they, these workers, peasants, and students, would be able to reenter our world and become like us, with our sorrows, our needs, our struggles and our goals? . . . Then I realized that these men had found a close-knit camaraderie among themselves. The front and the war had become their home. . . .

. . . The war is over, but the warriors continue to march. . . . They will march for a different revolution. . . . There goes the last regiment of the division. . . . I don't notice the crowd anymore, I hear only the reverberating sounds of the soldiers' footsteps. . . . Appeals were made at street corners calling for volunteer units to help protect the eastern borders. I enlisted on the day after the entry of the troops into the city. I was accepted and was outfitted. I was now a soldier. . . .

. . . We were a band of fighters, intoxicated with all the passions of the world; full of lust and exultant in action. What we wanted we did not know, and what we knew we did not want. War, adventure, excitement, and destruction; an indefinable, tormenting force within our hearts drove us ever onward!

2. The Ebert-Groener Pact

On November 10, 1918, an agreement was concluded between Friedrich Ebert, the leader of the Social Democratic Party who the day before had become chancellor of the Reich, and Wilhelm Groener, who had just succeeded Ludendorff as quartermaster general and was second in command of the army. Groener had urged the Kaiser to abdicate and also later urged the republican government to accept the Versailles Treaty in the name of the Supreme Command. Many within the officer corps bitterly resented these actions.

The pact with Groener, however, had far-reaching implications for the subsequent relationship between the army and the government. Groener pledged

From William Groener, *Lebenserinnerungen* (Goettingen, 1957), reprinted in Wolfgang Michalka and Gottfried Niedhart, *Die Ungeliebte Republik* (Munich: Deutscher Taschenbuch Verlag, 1980), pp. 29–30. Translated by Dieter Kuntz. Reprinted by permission of Deutscher Taschenbuch Verlag, Germany.

the Army's support in establishing Ebert's new government, principally by offering to help check the threat of Bolshevism, if in return Ebert would keep the officer corps free from parliamentary interference and assist in limiting the activities of the soldiers' councils. This agreement allowed the Prussian authoritarian power base, the army, to retain its influence and actually established it as an almost autonomous force within the Weimar Republic. In his memoirs, Groener recalled his decision to ally with the government. Groener later became minister of defense and minister of the interior, and earned the wrath of the Nazis with a ban on the SA in 1932.

The collapse of the empire robbed the officers of the basis of their existence, of their focal point and orientation. They had to have a certain objective that validated their employment and could give them inner assurance. A sense of duty had to be reawakened, not only toward a certain form of government, but toward Germany in general. The fact that Hindenburg stayed at his post and took over the command of the entire army, a post the Kaiser had entrusted to him, made the transition possible and easier.

The officer corps, however, could only have cooperated with a government ready to take up the fight against radicalism and Bolshevism. Ebert was ready to do that, but he was only precariously maintaining himself at the helm and was close to being toppled by the Independent [Social Democrats] and the Liebknecht group [the Communists]. What could have been more obvious than to offer Ebert the support of the army and of the officer corps? I found Ebert to be of decent, reliable character, and to have the most politically farsighted head on his shoulders of any of the horde of party cronies surrounding him.

On the 10th of November [1918], Friedrich Naumann,[1] returning from a trip to the front, lingered at army headquarters, where I was to give him my thoughts on this matter. He endorsed the idea, and I urged him to influence Ebert in this general direction on his return home. During the course of the day, however, I began to realize I could not wait that long. In the evening I telephoned the Reich chancellery and informed Ebert that the army was at the government's disposal, but that the field marshal and the officer corps expected the government's support in maintaining order and discipline in the ranks of the army. The officer corps also expected the government to fight Bolshevism and was prepared for action for that purpose. Ebert accepted my proposal. From this point on we spoke every evening about necessary measures via a secret line between the Reich chancellery and the army command. The pact was tried and tested.

---

[1] Naumann was one of the leaders of the German Democratic Party, which was founded in November 1918, and was a vehement opponent of bolshevism (communism).

3. Revolution in Bavaria

The following account of the German revolution was written by Ernst Toller, an eyewitness to the chaotic events of early 1919 in Germany. Toller was a young poet and playwright who became actively involved in the revolutionary upheaval in Bavaria. He was a leading figure in the short-lived Bavarian Soviet Republic, which lasted for only a few weeks in April 1919. When troops sent by the Reich government in Berlin, supported by Bavarian *Freikorps* forces, crushed the revolution, Toller was captured and sentenced to a five-year prison term. The counterrevolutionary forces dealt ruthlessly with all suspected leftist revolutionaries, initiating a White Terror in Munich in which perhaps a thousand people lost their lives.

Toller presents a view of the revolutionary events in Bavaria from a left-wing perspective. His words reflect the disappointment of the artistic intelligentsia with the failure of the revolution and the shattering of their idealistic expectations. The defeat of the leftist revolutionaries in Bavaria was, however, an important victory for the Reich government, removing much of the threat posed by the Left to the Ebert government.

Toller, an avowed anti-fascist, was a victim of Nazi book burning after Hitler came to power. He emigrated to the United States, where he worked against Hitler. Apparently despondent over his and Germany's fate, he committed suicide in 1939 at the age of forty-five.

Germany's needs became ever more desperate. The bread got still worse, the milk still thinner; the farmers would have nothing to do with the towns, and would be hoarders came back empty-handed; the men at the front were incensed at the debauchery and gormandising at the base and at the misery at home. They had had enough. "Equal food and equal pay, and the Frenchies would soon be chased away," they sang.

For four years they had fought, on the Eastern front, on the Western front, in Asia, in Africa; for four years they had stood their ground in the rain and mud of Flanders, in the poisonous mists of the Wollunian swamps, in the scorching blaze of Mesopotamia.

During the night of October 3rd the Peace Note was despatched to President Wilson.

This unexpected bid for peace opened the eyes of the German people at last; they had had no idea of the impending catastrophe. So it was all for nothing — the millions of dead, the millions of wounded, the starvation at home. All for nothing.

The triumph of the bourgeois democracy which accompanied the move for peace aroused no interest; neither the Reichstag nor the people

Excerpted from *I Was a German* by Ernst Toller, trans. Edward Crankshaw (London: The Bodley Head, 1934) pp. 130–133, 136–139, 142, 145, 149–153, 161–162, 167, 184–189, 191.

opposed it. It came into being like ration cards, like turnip jam. And anyway what obvious changes did it make? The old, privileged electorate was abolished. Liebknecht and the other political prisoners were amnestied. But the Press was still censored; the right to hold meetings was still denied; the generals had still the ruling voice in public affairs; the ministers came from the old ruling caste. Scheidemann and Bauer,[1] the Social Democrats, were Secretaries of State. Excellencies. Good God!

The people thought only of peace. They had been thinking of war too long, believing in victory too long. Why hadn't they been told the truth? Why hadn't they been told when even the War Lords desponded? How could the people help despairing?

The men who ruled them, the men who had driven them for years on end with blind authority and had completely lost touch with them, had, indeed, noticed this anxiety, this tiredness, this despair; but they had no thought for anything but the Monarchy and danger to the Monarch. We can still save the Monarchy, they thought, if the Kaiser abdicates. The people consigned the Monarchy to hell; they had been lost to Wilhelm for a long, long time. The question was no longer Wilhelm or another Kaiser, but War or Peace.

The sailors of the Fleet, the Kaiser's own children, were the first to revolt. The High Seas Fleet was to have put to sea. The officers preferred "Death with honour to peace with ignominy." But the men, who had already begun to revolt in 1917, refused to put to sea. They drew the furnaces. Six hundred were arrested; the others abandoned their ships, stormed the prisons, and took possession of Kiel. The dockers joined them. The German Revolution had begun.

First Kiel, then Munich, then Hanover, Hamburg, the Rhineland, Berlin. On November 9th, 1918, the Berlin workers left the factories and marched in their thousands from North, South and East to the centre of the city. Old grey men, and women who had stood for years at the munition benches, men invalided out of the army, boys who had taken over their fathers' work. The processions were joined by men on leave, war-widows, wounded soldiers, students and solid citizens. No leader had arranged this uprising. The revolutionary leaders at the factories had reckoned on a later day. The Social Democratic Deputies were surprised and dismayed. They were even then discussing ways and means of saving the Monarchy with the Chancellor, Prince Max of Baden.

---

[1] Philipp Scheidemann (1865–1939), Social Democratic politician, was secretary of state in the cabinet of the government of Prince Max von Baden during October 1918, and subsequently held the position of Reichschancellor for four months during early 1919. Gustav Bauer (1870–1944), also a Social Democrat, was minister of labor during Scheidemann's term as chancellor, and subsequently became chancellor himself from June 1919 to March 1920.

The procession marched on in silence; there was no singing, no rejoicing. It came to a standstill before the gates of the Maikäfer Barracks. The gates were barred; rifles and machine-guns threatened from every window and loop-hole. Would the soldiers shoot?

But the men in field-grey were the brothers of these ragged, starving crowds. They flung down their weapons, the gates were opened, and the people streamed into the barracks and joined forces with the Kaiser's army.

The Imperial standard was hauled down and the Red Flag fluttered in its place. From the balcony of the Imperial palace Liebknecht proclaimed the German Socialist Republic.

The ruling powers gave in without a struggle, the officers surrendered. Only one officer in the whole of Germany, the captain of the *König*, remained loyal to his Kaiser and died for him. And the aristocracy? Prince Heinrich, the Kaiser's brother, sewed a red band on his sleeve and fled. The Bavarian Crown-Prince Rupprecht abandoned his troops. Wilhelm II fled to Holland. A pitiful *débâcle*, but dangerous for the people. They wanted peace, but what they got was power, which fell into their hands without a struggle. Would they learn to keep their power?

The Bavarians also were tired of war, and to their weariness was added the fear that the Italian troops might march on Bavaria after the collapse of Austria. The Bavarians had seen war in France and Russia; they remembered shell-churned trenches, devastated villages, a land laid waste. The old traditional hatred of the Prussians, the Hohenzollerns, reawoke. The Prussians could get on with the war as best they could by themselves. As for the Royal House of Wittelsbach, there was nothing more to be expected; the King, said the peasants, had got himself thoroughly tied up with Berlin; must have done, or he would have insisted on the farmers' rights before now; instead of which they weren't allowed to grind their own corn, and, just because the Prussian swine didn't mind bad beer, the Bavarians also had to swallow dish-water.

Eisner,[2] with uncanny acuteness, divined the mood of the country, and won over peasants and workers to his side to overthrow the Monarchy and resist the Social Democrats, who were then drawing up a new constitution.

Kiel was the beacon. On November 7th two hundred thousand people, led by Eisner and the blind farmer, Gandorfer, assembled in the

---

[2] Kurt Eisner was the Jewish leader of the Bavarian Independent Social Democratic Party, a left-wing socialist party. He headed a socialist republic in Bavaria from November 8, 1918, to February 21, 1919, when he was assassinated by a member of a right-wing organization.

Theresienwiese and marched on the city. The King fled and Bavaria was in the hands of the Revolutionaries. That night the Workers' and Soldiers' Councils elected Eisner President of the Bavarian Free State.

In mid-December I went to Berlin for the Congress of all Councils. Here at last, I thought, the political will of the German Revolution will make itself known. But what instability, what ignorance, what an utter lack of any will to power that Congress showed!

The German Congress of Councils voluntarily renounced all the power that the Revolution had thrust so unexpectedly into their hands. They threw it overboard and left the fate of the Republic to the chance results of a questionable election and an ignorant people. In every parliamentary Republic, the Congress decided, the ministers are responsible to the parliament; the People's Commissaries, therefore, must rule independently of the control and will of the Central Council. The Republic had passed its own death-sentence.

When Karl Liebknecht and Rosa Luxemburg,[3] the pioneers of the Revolution, tried to address the Congress, they were refused a hearing.

A month later the Spartacus rebellion broke out, against the will of Liebknecht and Rosa Luxemburg; and both were killed. "Shot while attempting to escape" ran the official report. The news reached me in Munich and I forced my way into a mass-meeting of the Social Democrats. "Liebknecht and Luxemburg have been murdered!" I shouted. The crowd, the deluded crowd, shouted back: "Serve them right! Why couldn't they leave well alone?"

In Bavaria the forces of reaction hindered the activities of the various Councils. They found allies among the Social Democrat ministers, and an armed Defence Corps was formed with the help of Auer. This Defence Corps was the first fruit of the counter-revolutionaries, forerunner of the *Orgesch,* of the *Stahlhelm,* of the *Einwohnerwehr,*[4] of the National-Socialist Storm Troops. The day was to come when they would turn on those who brought them into being. Side by side with the official Corps other

---

[3] Liebknecht and Luxemburg were leaders of the Spartacus Union, which became the German Communist Party in January 1919. This group attempted a coup in Berlin during early January 1919, prompting Ebert to rely on volunteer military forces to crush this threat from the extreme Left. Luxemburg and Liebknecht were subsequently murdered by members of these right-wing volunteer forces.

[4] The *Einwohnerwehr* (civil guards) were volunteer postwar semimilitary formations recruited from civilian ranks in various German cities in order to counter the communist threat. They were most prominent in Bavaria. The *Orgesch* (Organisation Escherich), named after its organizer, Dr. Georg Escherich, was a nationwide organization that attempted to unite the civil guards under Escherich's leadership. In essence, the Orgesch formed a reserve militia for the 100,000-man Reichswehr. The *Stahlhelm* (Steel Helmet) was a nationwide association of war veterans with antirepublican and strongly monarchist leanings. It had been formed in December 1918 for the purpose of defeating the leftist revolution.

unofficial corps grew up. A group of manufacturers financed a band of mercenaries; the officers of the old régime were in their element again, hatching plots to seize Government buildings; organising spy agencies and *Sprengkommandos*[5] and elaborate systems of defensive alarm. When they struck they would proclaim that they were saving the National Assembly from the Bolsheviks; actually their *Putsch* would mean the overthrow of the Republic. Their plans were betrayed to us, and the Workers' Council ordered me to disclose them to the Provisional National Council. The Defence Corps went on with its secret work, the results of which were soon to appear.

On February 21st, 1919, I returned to Bavaria. At one of the stations I heard a Swiss porter outside shouting excitedly, and in the carriage a German commercial traveller started cheering. I could not take in the words that were beating into my head; but at last I forced myself to realise — Kurt Eisner had been murdered.

The shot fired by Arco shook the whole Republic, and the people clamoured for revenge for Eisner's death. The Central Committee of the Workmen's, Peasants' and Soldiers' Councils took over the government, proclaimed a general strike and a state of siege throughout Bavaria. It convened the Congress of the Councils; and the working classes, disappointed by the inactivity of the Republic, demanded that their politicians should embrace the Revolution once and for all, crying that what had succeeded in Russia would also succeed in Bavaria, and that parliamentary government was a wash-out: the idea of a Soviet Republic had swept the masses.

Before the Bavarian Diet could start work the Augsburg workers, weary of revolutionary resolutions and proposals, sent a delegation to Munich to demand the proclamation of a Soviet Republic. The Government did not arrest these men for high treason, instead it listened to them peacably. The Social Democrat ministers lost their heads; in a frantic effort to retain office they were prepared to yield to all demands. One of them, President Hoffmann, was unavoidably absent; he wrote an anxious post card to the chairman of the Central Committee asking whether the Soviet Republic would pension former ministers.

The Communists remained aloof, distrusting the Social Democrats who, as so often before in this Revolution, were pursuing a shady game of their own, a dangerous game for the workers. Besides, they said, the workers were not yet ready, and without the support of North Germany

---

[5] *Sprengkommandos* (demolition units) were elite forces that specialized in attack tactics using explosives.

a Soviet Republic could not hope to last. But they should have said that earlier, in the days when they were frantically demanding a Soviet Republic and stigmatising as counter-revolutionary anybody who doubted its possibility. It is no good making pronouncements in which one does not believe, for dislike of the truth often leads to self-betrayal. And it is no good shrinking from reality when it happens to turn out a little different from what one had hoped.

The Independent Socialists hesitated. Had a revolutionary party the right to leave the people in the lurch? Revolutionary leaders should not blindly follow the whims of the masses; they should guard against making mistakes. But was this merely a whim? Wasn't it already a *fait accompli,* only the results of which we could influence? The party leaders advise, but it is the people who act. At that moment the Soviet Republic was already proclaimed in Würzburg, Augsburg, Fürth, Aschaffenburg, Lindau and Hof. We should long before this have enlightened the people as to the true balance of power in Germany; we had only ourselves to blame if they did not fully understand how things stood.

On the night of April 17th, 1919, the Central Committee delegates from the various Socialist parties, and from the Trade Unions and the Farmers' Union, assembled in the Wittelsbach Palace. The great rooms, where once maids-in-waiting and powdered lackeys had fawned attendance on their royal masters, now rang with the heavy tread of workmen, farmers and soldiers. Red Guards, couriers, and typists leaned out from the silk-curtained windows of the ex-Queen's bedroom.

The People's Commissaries were elected, and even here the ignorance, aimlessness, and general vagueness of the German Revolution was manifest. Men with diametrically opposed views on finance and economics were appointed to responsible positions, men whom nobody could expect to work together.

The first day of the Soviet Republic: a general holiday. Workers, self-conscious in their best clothes, crowded the fashionable streets, talking of last night's happenings. Heavy lorries crowded with soldiers patrolled the city, and the Red Flag streamed over the Wittelsbach Palace.

Work began in earnest. Edicts were issued, proclaiming the socialization of the Press, the arming of workmen and the institution of a Red Army, the State control of houses to alleviate the housing shortage, and the State regulation of food supplies.

The Munich garrison despatched representatives to the Central Committee, to declare their loyalty to the Republic. The men of the First Life Guards re-named their barracks after Karl Liebknecht. Even the old imperial lawyers and judges were unwilling to retire, and decided to stand by the Soviet, quite prepared to prosecute the enemies of the Revolution in the new Revolutionary Courts. All the church bells were set ringing for the Republic.

Only the Communists still opposed the Soviet. They summoned the workers to demonstrations and sent speakers to the barracks to prove that this Republic was not worthy of a soldier's defence.

Meanwhile President Hoffmann and the other ministers who had fled from Munich pulled themselves together; the Government formed by the Diet removed to Bamberg and called on Epp's army in Ohrdruf to protect them. They arrested supporters of the Soviet Republic and ruled all Northern Bavaria.

While the Revolutionaries were bickering amongst themselves in Munich their opponents in the North were uniting. Schneppenhorst, who only a week before had pledged his life in defence of the Soviet Republic, was forming an army to overthrow us. The internal strife in Munich had to be ended at once. The Central Council exhorted the Communists once again, pointing out that their co-operation was necessary to save the Revolution — parties apart. The Communists sent delegates to the Council, but they came too late.

The Soviet Republic was doomed. The inadequacy of its leaders, the opposition of the Communists, the secession of the Social Democrats, the disorganisation of the administration, the increasing food-shortage, the confusion among the armed forces — all these circumstances hastened collapse and gave power to the rapidly growing counter-revolutionary movement.

In my political inexperience I dared not reveal the true position in all its harshness to the workers.

But the politician's worst crime is silence. He must speak the truth, however unpalatable; the truth alone can spur on strength and will and reason.

This Soviet Republic was a failure, and the only thing to do with failures is to acknowledge them freely and discard them. Already the Soldiers' Councils were negotiating with the Social Democrats of their own accord. We had no time to lose: counter-revolutionary activity was striking at us from our midst.

Commissions were formed to reorganise the Red Army, to suppress counter-revolutionary activities, build up a proper economic fabric and regulate food supplies. The police were dismissed and the Red Guard took over their duties, commanded by the Communist, Eglhofer.

Eglhofer was one of the leaders of the naval mutiny at Kiel in the autumn of 1918. One in every ten of the sailors were sentenced to death, including Eglhofer, but the sentences were later commuted to penal servitude for life. The November Revolution brought freedom to them all. He lacked any organising capability, and chose his staff without the least discrimination.

On April 30th the streets were empty and deserted. Occasional individuals still crept furtively in or out of their houses; little detachments of Red Guards and armed workers still paraded the town; the Red Flag still fluttered from the roof of the War Ministry and the Wittelsbach Palace; alarm bells were still jangling from the church towers, scaring frightened women from the streets and market places. Only the children found any pleasure in all this; they delighted in the military cars tearing through the streets; and, imitating the grown-ups, played at being Revolutionaries, fought and conquered the enemy, captured towns and took prisoners, crying shrilly all the while "Hurrah for the Reds!" or "Down with the Whites!" They arrested counter-Revolutionaries and triumphantly locked them up in sheds and cellars. It was terrible to watch this childish play; but still more terrible was the reality.

In the last few days the Red Guard had been making frequent and indiscriminate arrests and we had to liberate their prisoners. I rang up the prisons; there should be no repetition of the acts of desperation which had characterised the Paris Communes if I could help it.

The men who had been sent to parley with Hoffmann came back with the news that the generals demanded the unconditional surrender of the town and of all the Revolutionary leaders. They knew perfectly well that the Factory Councils could not accept such terms.

Meanwhile, internal strife among the Revolutionaries had reached such a pitch that many of them dared not sleep in their own beds. Everybody distrusted everybody else; everybody saw an enemy in his neighbour.

At a meeting of the Factory Councils on April 26th the internal disagreements came to a head and resulted in open schism. The Factory Councils passed a vote of censure on the Government and formed a government of their own. But the Communists ordered the workers not to recognise this new Government, and the Communist Guard at the Wittelsbach Palace refused to lend its protection.

Thus two separate Governments were operating at once in Munich. The struggle between the opposing Revolutionary factions increased in fury from hour to hour.

The negotiations with Hoffmann's Government at Bamberg came to nothing; the generals who were now firmly in the saddle wanted no understanding.

That evening the Factory Councils sat for the last time, impotent in face of their fate. Their power was no more; the workers were overthrown, the Red Army in confusion. They ordered the people of Munich to lay down their arms and allow the Whites unimpeded entry into the city. The Revolution was defeated.

4. A New Constitution and a New Form of Government

On February 6, 1919, Friedrich Ebert, leader of the Social Democratic Party, gave the following speech to the National Assembly, which had convened in the city of Weimar for the purpose of providing Germany with a new constitution and a new form of government. His speech at once provides a portrait of the problems facing the Assembly and constitutes an appeal for moderation to the victorious Allies who were in the process of drafting a peace treaty. It also states Ebert's hope that Germany could be transformed from an imperialist power to a democratic nation.

Not all those assembled at Weimar shared Ebert's assessment of recent events or his hope for the future. The stenographer's report of the meeting illustrates the volatile emotions of the various political interests gathered at Weimar.

Named president of the new republic, Ebert served until February 1925, when he died in Berlin just a few months short of the scheduled end of his term. He guided the republic through a very difficult period, saving it from revolutions from both the Left and the Right.

Ladies and gentlemen of the Constitutional Assembly of the German nation, I greet you in the name of the Reich government. I particularly wish to extend my most heartfelt greetings to the women who for the first time appear in the national parliament on a basis of equal rights. The provisional government owes its mandate to the revolution; it will return it into the hands of the National Assembly. (*"Bravo!"*)

In the revolution the German people rebelled against an antiquated, collapsing despotism. (*Agreement from the left; fervent contradiction from the right.*)

As soon as the German people's right of self-determination is secured, we will return to the road of legality. Only on the broad highway of parliamentary debate and through the passing of resolutions will the urgent changes in the economic and social sphere be furthered, without condemning the economic life of the Reich. (*"Very true!" from the left.*)

For that reason the Reich government recognizes the National Assembly as the highest and only sovereignty in Germany. . . . We have lost the war. This fact is not a consequence of the revolution. (*"Very true!" from the left; fervent contradiction from the right.*)

Ladies and gentlemen, it was the imperial government of Prince Max von Baden which initiated the armistice that left us defenseless. (*Shouts.*)

From "Stenographische Berichte der Nationalversammlung," vol. 326, pp. 1ff., in *Die Deutsche Revolution* by Gerhard A. Ritter and Susanne Müller, eds. (Hamburg: Hoffman und Campe, 1975), pp. 205–210. Translated by Dieter Kuntz. Reprinted by permission of Dr. Gerhard A. Ritter and Dr. Susanne Müller.

Defeat and the need for foodstuffs have left us at the mercy of the enemy powers. Not only us, but our foes, too, have been left incredibly exhausted by the war. Out of this feeling of exhaustion among our foes springs their endeavor to seek compensation from the German *Volk*, and the spoliation notion is carried over to the peace process. These revenge and violation plans demand that we strongly protest. ("*Bravo!*")

The German people cannot for 20, 40, or 60 years be made the wage slave of other nations. The terrible misfortune of the war for all of Europe can only be made good again through the togetherness of the nations. In view of the wholesale misery on all sides the blame appears almost negligible. Nevertheless, the German *Volk* is determined to bring to accountability those proven to have had deliberate guilt or deliberate baseness. But one should not punish those who were victims themselves, victims of the war, victims of our earlier immaturity. According to their own testimony, why did our opponents fight? In order to annihilate "Kaiserism." It no longer exists, it is finished forever. The reality of the National Assembly itself is proof. They fought in order to destroy militarism. It has collapsed into ruin and will not rise again. (*Cheers from the Independent Social Democrats.*)

According to their festive proclamations, our enemies fought for justice, freedom, and a lasting peace. The terms of the armistice, however, have up to now been implemented in an outrageously hard and pitiless fashion. Alsace will, without further ado, be treated as a French territory. The election writs we issued for the National Assembly were illegally stopped. ("*Hear, hear!*" Shouts of "*Shame!*" and "*Boo!*")

The Germans are being driven out of the region. (*Again, boos from the Assembly.*)

German property is being confiscated. The occupied left-Rhine region is to be closed off and separated from the rest of Germany. The terms of the armistice, that no public securities are to be dissipated, they are attempting to expand incredibly into a general money economy enslavement of the German people. While we have long been hopelessly unable to renew the passage of arms, our 800,000 prisoners of war are still being held (*incensed shouts of "Boo!"*), and are endangered by mental collapse and forced labor. (*Again, incensed shouts.*)

These acts of old-style power politics do not exhibit the spirit of reconciliation. (*Ardent agreement.*)

The terms of the armistice were formulated so as to be imposed on the old Hohenzollern regime. How does one justify the fact that for the young socialist republic they are incessantly being intensified, despite all our efforts to come to terms with these imposed, oppressive obligations! We warn our foes not to press us to the limit. ("*Very right!*") . . .

want to join League [handwritten margin note]

Our free republic, the German people, desire nothing but to join the League of Nations as an equal partner and there, through diligence and ability, attain a position of respect. ("*Bravo!*")

Germany can still render much good service to the world. A German gave scientific socialism to the workers of the world. We are in the process of once again leading the world in socialism. . . . We cannot, however, forgo the unification of the whole German nation within the framework of one state. ("*Bravo!*") . . .

Our German-Austrian brothers have, in their National Assembly of November 12 of the previous year, already declared themselves to be part of the pan-German republic. (*Applause.*)

The German-Austrian National Assembly has now again, with passionate enthusiasm, sent us its greeting and expressed the hope that our and their National Assembly will succeed in restoring the bond which was torn apart by force in 1866. (*Renewed applause.*)

German-Austria must be united with the Motherland for all times. (*Fervent applause.*) . . .

History and tendencies, however, do inhibit the establishment of a tightly centralized unitary state. Many clans and many dialects are unified in Germany, but they must sound as one nation with one language. (*Fervent applause.*)

The demarcation line between national authority and clan [regional] authority may remain contested in particular instances. In general, however, we must all be in agreement that an unrestrained, uniform developmental possibility of our economic life, and the safeguarding of the future of our people can only be achieved by a solidly structured and unified Germany that is politically capable of action. . . . Ladies and gentlemen, the provisional government has assumed a very loathsome sovereignty. We were, in the true sense of the word, the bankruptcy trustees of the old regime ("*Very true!*" *from the Social Democrats*): all granaries, all storehouses were empty, all reserves ran low, credit was shaky, morale sank greatly. We were supported and aided by the central council of the workers' and soldiers' councils (*laughter from the right*) — supported and aided from the central council of the workers and soldiers' councils. (*Ardent agreement from the Social Democrats; unrest on the right.*)

image of trustees of old regime [handwritten margin note]

We gave our best efforts in fighting the dangers and misery of the transitional period. We did not forestall the National Assembly. But where time and need were pressing, we strove to fulfill the most urgent of the workers' demands. (*Shouts from the right.*)

Gentlemen, allow me this incidental remark: these continual interruptions truly evidence that you have learned preciously little during these difficult times Germany has had to endure during the last few months. (*Loud cheers and applause from the Social Democrats.*)

I will say it again: we did everything — and you (*turning to the right*) apparently don't even know what had to be done, ("*Exactly right!*" *from the Social Democrats*) in order to set economic activity in motion again. If the outcome fell short of our desires, then the circumstances preventing that must justly be appreciated. ("*Exactly right!*" *from the Social Democrats.*)

Many entrepreneurs who, spoiled by the large national market of the war economy and the high profits the old monarchic-military state granted them, have forgotten how to develop the necessary initiative. ("*Very good!*")

We therefore urgently appeal to entrepreneurs to do all within their power to promote the revitalization of production. On the other hand, we call on the proletariat to harness all its energy for work, for only that can save us. (*Fervent agreement from the Social Democrats. Shouts from the Independent Social Democrats.*) . . .

Socialism is, from our point of view, possible only when production observes a high level of working capacity. ("*Exactly right!*" *from the Social Democrats.*)

Socialism for us is organization, order, and solidarity ("*Exactly right!*" *from the Social Democrats*), not arbitrariness, selfishness, and destruction. (*Fervent agreement from the Social Democrats. Shouts from the Independent Social Democrats.*) . . .

The old state, too, would not have been able to avoid further expansion of the political economy in order to cover the incredible war debts. During a period of general distress there can be no room for private monopoly and effortless capital profit. ("*Very good!*" *from the Social Democrats.*)

We want to systematically eliminate profit in the areas where economic development has allowed the socialization of an industry to mature.

An uneasy future faces us. In spite of all that, we trust in the robust productive power of the German nation. The old foundations of German power have been broken forever. Prussian hegemony, the Hohenzollern army, and the politics of shining armor have been made impossible for our future. Just as the 9th of November, 1918, is connected with the 18th of March, 1848 (*shouting from the Independent Social Democrats*), so we here in Weimar must complete the transformation from imperialism to idealism, from a world power to intellectual greatness. The Wilhelmian era, geared toward external splendor, is characterized by the Lasallean[1] phrase, that the classical German thinkers and poets only flew over them like a flock of cranes. Now the spirit of Weimar, the spirit of the great philosophers and poets must again inspire our lives. (*Shouting from*

---

[1] Ferdinand Lassalle founded a working-class party in 1863, the German Workers' Union, which unlike later, more revolutionary parties, supported the state and sought to work within the system.

the Independent Social Democrats. "*Bravo!*" *from the German Democratic Party*.) . . .

That is how we want to approach our task, to have our goal solidly in focus, to safeguard the privileges of the German people, to anchor a strong democracy in Germany (*fervent applause from the left*.), and to inspire it with true socialist spirit and socialistic deeds. (*Renewed applause from the left.*)

We want to make the mission that Fichte[2] gave to the German nation come true: "We want to establish a nation of law and truthfulness, based on the equality of all that which possesses a human countenance." (*Tumultuous cheers and applause from the Social Democrats and the left.*)

5. The National Assembly Debate on the Treaty of Versailles

One of the most important decisions the National Assembly had to make was whether to accept or reject the terms of the peace treaty the Allies presented to the Germans. The Germans had received the terms with almost unanimous indignation and hoped at least to be able to amend several of the more objectionable clauses. The Allies, however, would tolerate no changes, threatening to resume hostilities unless the German government signed the treaty by June 23, 1919.

This issue created deep divisions within the first cabinet of the republic, led by Chancellor Scheidemann, which resulted in the cabinet's resignation. A new cabinet was formed on June 21, and on the following day arguments were presented in a meeting of the National Assembly. This debate of June 22, 1919, reflected the dilemma of the government and vividly illustrates the polarization of opinion both in the government and in Germany in general. The treaty was accepted by a vote of 237 to 138. The rightists maintained their opposition to the treaty for the remainder of Weimar's political life.

Bauer [Social Democratic Party, acting chancellor]: Ladies and gentlemen! The Reich president has entrusted me with the formation of a new

From *Deutsche Parlamentsdebatten,* vol. 2, 1919–33, ed. by D. Junker (Frankfurt, 1971), reprinted in Wolfgang Michalka and Gottfried Niedhart, *Die ungeliebte Republik* (Munich: Deutscher Taschenbuch Verlag, 1980), pp. 124–32. Translated by Dieter Kuntz. Reprinted by permission of Deutscher Taschenbuch, Germany.

[2] Johann Gottlieb Fichte, German philosopher (1762–1814), contributed to the stimulation of German nationalism through his writings and lectures. His "Addresses to the German Nation," delivered during Prussia's humiliation at the hands of Napoleon, called for the moral regeneration of the German people.

cabinet, to replace the Scheidemann government which has resigned. . . . The resignation of the cabinet resulted from its inability to reach an undivided position regarding the peace treaty that has been presented to us. . . . For each of us who were members of the former government it was a bitterly difficult matter to take a position between feelings of indignation and cold rage. And not less difficult was the decision to join this new government whose first and most pressing task it is to conclude this unjust peace. . . . We are here because of our sense of responsibility, aware that it is our damnable duty to try to salvage what can be salvaged. . . .

No matter how each one of us feels about the question of acceptance or rejection, we are all united about one thing: in strong criticism of this peace treaty (*"Very true!"*) to which we are being forced to affix our signatures! When this draft was first presented to us, it was greeted with a unanimous protest of indignation and rejection from our people. We defied disappointment and hoped for the indignation of the entire world. . . .

Rejection did not mean averting the treaty. (*"Very true!"* from the Social Democrats.) A no vote would only have meant a short delay of the yes vote. (*"Very true!"*) Our ability to resist has been broken; we do not have the capability to avert [signing]. . . . In the name of the national government, ladies and gentlemen, I ask you in view of the circumstances and pending ratification by the National Assembly, to sign the peace treaty laid before you! . . .

. . . The government of the German Republic pledges to fulfill the imposed conditions of the peace. The government, however, wishes during this solemn occasion to express its views quite clearly. . . . The imposed conditions exceed the limits of Germany's ability to comply. . . .

. . . Moreover, we emphatically declare that we cannot accept Article 231 of the peace treaty, which demands that Germany accept responsibility for singly intiating the war. (*Applause.*)

Gröber, delegate of the Center Party: Honored Assembly! The Center Party delegation of the National Assembly wishes to acknowledge the government's declaration. We accept this program and will support this government and accept [cabinet] participation. . . . We say we are prepared to accept the responsibility of fulfilling its terms as far as is humanly possible, but we do not recognize a responsibility for carrying out conditions that are impossible or intolerable. However, although these are oppressive and hardly fulfillable conditions and will have a detrimental effect on the German people, we must also take other facts into account.

First, the peace will shortly bring hundreds of thousands of prisoners back to German families. . . . Second, the peace will end starvation. . . . Third, only the peace will give us the possibility of economically rebuilding Germany. . . . Fourth, the peace also allows us to maintain our German unity. . . .

Schiffer, delegate of the DDP [German Democratic Party]: Contrary to the first two speakers, I wish to declare to this esteemed assembly, that the great majority of my political friends have decided to withhold their approval of the peace treaty laid before us. . . .

Count von Posadowsky, delegate of the DNVP [German National People's Party]: Our Fatherland finds itself in the most difficult hour of its history. The enemy stands before our gates, and in the country there are disconcerting signs of internal breakup. . . . We in our party are aware of the ramifications for our people which a rejection of the peace treaty will entail. (*"Very true!" from the right.*) The resultant harm, however, will only be temporary, but if we accept this treaty we will abandon countless generations of our people to misery. . . . For us, acceptance of the treaty is impossible for many reasons. . . . In addition to making Germany defenseless, there is also the matter of theft of our territory. . . .

Haase, delegate of the USPD [Independent Social Democratic Party]: We know that the peace treaty will bring incredible burdens for our people. . . . Nonetheless, we have no choice but to accept the treaty. Not only will rejection increase the harm, it will moreover mean sure ruin. (*Agreement from the Independent Social Democrats.*) Our people are in this desperate situation only because of the wicked warmongers and war extenders. . . .

Kahl, delegate of the DVP [German People's Party]: Gentlemen! The German People's Party unanimously rejects this peace. . . . We reject it because to accept it would mean the destruction of the German state. . . . We reject because we cannot justify the separation of precious segments of German earth, such as the eastern provinces, from the Motherland. . . . Yes, if only we had swords in our hands! (*Laughter from the Social Democrats.*) Then we would easily find a response! (*"Very true" from the right.*). . . .

6. The Terms of the Treaty of Versailles

On June 28, 1919, a solemn German delegation signed the Treaty of Versailles, which officially brought the Great War to a close. When the terms of the treaty were first presented to the German government on May 7 they were met with a

From *The Treaties of Peace*, 1919–1923, vol. 1 (New York: Carnegie Endowment for International Peace, 1924) pp. 84, 95, 101, 102, 105, 111–112, 123.

wave of indignation, sparking a ministerial crisis that culminated in the resignation of Chancellor Scheidemann, who charged that the Entente sought to make the German people a nation of "slaves and helots." The treaty had been composed by the victors, who had not allowed Germany to participate in drafting the terms. Most Germans felt that it was a rather harsh settlement and proposed negotiation on several points. The Allies, however, rejected the German proposals and threatened to resume hostilities unless the treaty was signed shortly. The German government had no choice but to accept since military resistance would have been hopeless.

Several provisions of the treaty were particularly hard for the Germans to swallow. Particularly repugnant was Article 231, the so-called war guilt clause, which forced the Germans to accept responsibility for all Allied damages caused "by the aggression of Germany." Germany was not to receive the full bill for reparations until 1921. Also irksome in German military circles were the clauses limiting the size of Germany's armed forces.

In German nationalist circles the treaty would be referred to as the *Diktat*, the dictated peace. It was seen as an unfair and humiliating treaty whose terms demanded amelioration. Revision of the Versailles Treaty became one of Adolf Hilter's favorite themes during his rise to power.

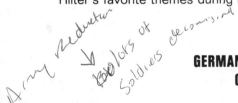

PART IV
GERMAN RIGHTS AND INTERESTS
OUTSIDE GERMANY

ARTICLE 119

Germany renounces in favour of the Principal Allied and Associated Powers all her rights and titles over her oversea possessions.

PART V
MILITARY, NAVAL AND AIR CLAUSES

In order to render possible the initiation of a general limitation of the armaments of all nations, Germany undertakes strictly to observe the military, naval and air clauses which follow.

ARTICLE 160

(1) By a date which must not be later than March 31, 1920, the German Army must not comprise more than seven divisions of infantry and three divisions of cavalry.

After that date the total number of effectives in the Army of the States constituting Germany must not exceed one hundred thousand men, including officers and establishments of depots. The Army shall be devoted exclusively to the maintenance of order within the territory and to the control of the frontiers.

The total effective strength of officers, including the personnel of staffs, whatever their composition, must not exceed four thousand.

ARTICLE 178

All measures of mobilisation or appertaining to mobilisation are forbidden.

In no case must formations, administrative services or General Staffs include supplementary cadres.

ARTICLE 180

—militarized Rhine land

All fortified works, fortresses and field works situated in German territory to the west of a line drawn fifty kilometres to the east of the Rhine shall be disarmed and dismantled.

ARTICLE 181

After the expiration of a period of two months from the coming into force of the present Treaty the German naval forces in commission must not exceed:

6 battleships of the *Deutschland* or *Lothringen* type,
6 light cruisers,
12 destroyers,
12 torpedo boats,

or an equal number of ships constructed to replace them as provided in Article 190.

No submarines are to be included.

All other warships, except where there is provision to the contrary in the present Treaty, must be placed in reserve or devoted to commercial purposes.

ARTICLE 183

After the expiration of a period of two months from the coming into force of the present Treaty, the total personnel of the German Navy, including the manning of the fleet, coast defences, signal stations, administration and other land services, must not exceed fifteen thousand, including officers and men of all grades and corps.

The total strength of officers and warrant officers must not exceed fifteen hundred.

Within two months from the coming into force of the present Treaty the personnel in excess of the above strength shall be demobilised.

No naval or military corps or reserve force in connection with the Navy may be organised in Germany without being included in the above strength.

ARTICLE 198

The armed forces of Germany must not include any military or naval air forces.

ARTICLE 199

Within two months from the coming into force of the present Treaty the personnel of air forces on the rolls of the German land and sea forces shall be demobilised.

ARTICLE 201

During the six months following the coming into force of the present Treaty, the manufacture and importation of aircraft, parts of aircraft, engines for aircraft, and parts of engines for aircraft, shall be forbidden in all German territory.

PART VIII
REPARATION

SECTION I

GENERAL PROVISIONS

ARTICLE 231

Sole guilty party
reparations

way of
detaining
the blame

The Allied and Associated Governments affirm and Germany accepts the responsibility of Germany and her allies for causing all the loss and damage to which the Allied and Associated Governments and their nationals have been subjected as a consequence of the war imposed upon them by the aggression of Germany and her allies.

7. The Runaway Inflation of 1923

Intimately related to foreign affairs, the economic problems facing the government in 1923 seemed insurmountable. Reparations payments to the Allies and the French occupation of the Ruhr Valley had added to the inflationary spiral which

Excerpt from *Confessions of the Old Wizard* by Hjalmar Schacht, trans. Diana Pyke (Boston: Houghton Mifflin Company, 1956), pp. 162–64, 168–69. Copyright © 1956 by Houghton Mifflin Company. Reprinted by permission of Houghton Mifflin Company.

reached fantastic proportions by November. If one person can be credited with ending this disastrous inflation, it was Hjalmar Schacht, who served as Reich currency commissioner in the Finance Ministry during late 1923 and established the Rentenmark, which formed the basis of a new currency. In December of 1923 he was appointed president of the Reichsbank, a post he retained until 1930. An ardent nationalist and monarchist at heart, Schacht also served under Hitler as minister of economics from 1934 to 1937. The following selection is from his autobiography, entitled *Confessions of the Old Wizard*, written in 1953, in which Schacht recounts the measures taken to stabilize the economy in 1923.

In the summer of 1923 the inflation misery in Germany reached its climax. Five years after the end of World War I found Germany in the grip of a fever that threatened to undermine her last vestige of strength. In Saxony, Thuringia and Bavaria riots broke out everywhere. Hitler was tub-thumping in the South. The Communist-Social-Democratic Zeigner Government in Saxony gave the Red Terror a free hand. In Hamburg street riots raged all day and fifteen policemen and sixty-five civilians were killed. The danger of a Communist upheaval was imminent. . . .

Everyone was agreed that the Communist peril could be averted provided the fight against the French Occupation of the Ruhr were ended (this being the principal cause of the rapid inflationary progress) and a stabilized currency established. For three years the most widely different plans for stabilization had been under discussion without coming to any definite decision. The Stresemann cabinet finally resolved to put an end to the Ruhr dispute and concentrate on an attempt to stabilize the national currency.

Stresemann's political merit in this late summer of 1923 cannot be overestimated. He wasted no time on theoretical propositions. His aim was to create such a position in internal affairs as would ensure a sufficient majority in favor of stabilization. Furthermore he succeeded in enlisting Allied interest and co-operation to establish order in German financial and economic affairs. This co-operation led to the convening of the group of international experts which met in January 1924 and has become famous under the title of the Dawes Committee.

Success depended on the ability to achieve a union of Right and Left in a joint monetary policy. In this connection the political Right, which had particularly strong ties with agriculture, played an outstanding part.

Agriculture had so far derived considerable benefit from the inflation in so far as the latter had enabled farmers to repay their debts with the debased currency, because the German law supports the principle that mark equals mark. This meant that debts which had been incurred in gold marks could be paid by means of equal nominal amounts in debased paper marks. In addition, the agricultural community used their paper marks to purchase as quickly as possible all kinds of useful machinery and furniture — and many useless things as well. That was the period in which grand pianos were to be found in the most unmusical households.

The agricultural circles felt themselves to be masters of the political situation, though, from a political point of view, they were no friends of Stresemann whose seat was far removed from them on the Liberal benches in the Reichstag. But Stresemann knew how to capture them.

He gave his blessing to a currency plan put forward by the Conservative German-Nationalist member Helfferich,[1] a plan which provided for a so-called Roggenmark (Rye mark). Several big undertakings had already conceived and adopted the idea of issuing bonds payable not in paper money but in kind (a ton of coal, a hundreweight of potash). Helfferich went further: he issued tokens for one hundred marks which were payable with a certain quantity of rye and remained valid for that quantity. It could not, of course, be described as a stable currency for the price of rye varied according to consumption and harvest, but the differences in value did keep within the bounds of the highest and lowest prices for rye.

Helfferich endeavored to exploit the Roggenmark plan to the advantage of his party by entrusting the issue of the tokens not to the Reichsbank but to a central bank institution shortly to be established and whose administrative force would be chosen for the most part from among agricultural groups. It is easy to understand that these groups would have acquired a strong influence in German economic affairs.

Naturally the idea met with stormy opposition from the Left. After much argument a compromise was reached in the shape of the so-called Rentenmark. In theory this Rentenmark was to be equal to the gold mark, but would be covered by a cautionary mortgage on the whole of German landed property, so that any given sum in Rentenmarks could be exchanged at any time for a like sum in mortgage bonds. Even this was obviously no guarantee for stability of value, for such a mortgage bond would fetch only fluctuating prices on the Stock Exchange. In the meantime something had to be done.

Under pressure of this "had to" Stresemann succeeded in obtaining a two thirds majority in the Reichstag which gave the government full power to decide as it saw fit in currency matters. So the Rentenmark became law. A special Rentenbank was founded; but the Reichsbank also came into the picture, for the distribution and loaning of Rentenmarks was entrusted to the board of the latter. Such was the situation when I was called upon to carry out the currency reform in a practical manner.

A few days elapsed before the necessary Rentenmark bills were printed. In the meantime the devaluation of the paper mark progressed rapidly. All previous efforts to establish a fixed price for the dollar on

---

[1] Karl Helfferich, Reichstag deputy and member of the National People's Party, had a reputation as an archreactionary but was also a very talented banker and economist.

Exchange had failed. For weeks on end only a percentage of the foreign currencies bespoken by business circles could be covered, and then at the rate momentarily fixed by the Reichsbank. Against this, however, all foreign currencies, particularly the dollar, fetched far higher prices in black-market dealings. The Reichsbank had no choice but to participate in this increase for the first few days. On November 20, 1923, the official rate was four trillion two hundred billion marks (4,200,000,000,000) for one dollar. . . .

The official rate of Exchange remained at 4.2 trillion while during the last week in November the dollar fetched up to twelve trillion marks in the black market.

In the course of those November weeks Germany was in a curious position with three separate currencies, so to speak, existing side by side — the paper mark, the Rentenmark and — theoretically — the old gold mark, which it was my aim to reintroduce in practice through the Reichsbank.

Two enemies of stabilization remained to be defeated — the black market and the emergency money issued by many public corporations and private businesses. This emergency money was on an equal footing with the paper mark, and so long as the former could be paid into the Reichsbank stabilization was not possible. In this instance there was no question of the Reichsbank exercising control over money that was issued: the emergency money was foisted upon it from outside. The time had come to put an end to the system. . . .

8. Article 48 of the Weimar Constitution: The Power to Govern by Emergency Decree

The Weimar Constitution attempted to establish the basis of democratic government in Germany at both the national and the state levels. The Constitution included a bill of rights which safeguarded personal as well as political freedoms. A parliamentary form of government was established through a system of proportional representation. Ultimately, however, the system proved to be politically impractical because splinter parties were able to gain seats in the Reichstag, making it extremely difficult to form strong, effective coalition governments. The Reichstag was the supreme authority under the Constitution since it could enact legislation. The President, however, also had important powers, such as the authority to govern by emergency decree in order to safeguard public order during a crisis situation. Article 48 of the Constitution gave the president these powers, which Ebert invoked to protect the republic and thereby save democracy in Germany.

From E. R. Huber, *Dokumente der Novemberrevolution und der Weimarer Republik, 1918–1932* (Stuttgart: Kohlhammer, 1966), p. 94. Translated by Dieter Kuntz.

From 1930 on, Germany's economic difficulties created continual parliamentary crises that prevented the Reichstag from fulfilling its responsibilities. The imprecise wording of Article 48 allowed the president to determine what constituted a threat to public order. By passing the Reichstag, the president's emergency decrees ruled the nation. Hitler would later make full use of Article 48 to consolidate his own position.

[handwritten: fear of Communism + red takeover]

[handwritten: what are these? Are they laid out]

ARTICLE 48

If a land [region] does not fulfill the obligations incumbent upon it according to the Reich constitution or the Reich laws, the Reich president can urge its compliance with the help of armed force.

The Reich president can, if the public safety and order of the German Reich are seriously disturbed or endangered, take such measures as are deemed necessary to restore public safety and order; if need be, he may intervene with the help of the armed forces. For this purpose he may temporarily suspend, either partially or wholly, the fundamental rights established in Articles 114, 115, 117, 118, 123, 124, and 153. . . .

[handwritten: –What determines public safety?]
[handwritten: – too much leeway]
[handwritten: – Suspending Rights]

9. Parliamentary Paralysis, 1930

The economic crisis that engulfed Germany in the aftermath of the U.S. stock market crash in 1929 was preceded by a gradual recession. This economic downturn, apparent since late 1927, brought about declining production, rising unemployment, and declining tax receipts for the government, while at the same time the demand on limited unemployment insurance funds dramatically increased. These economic problems soon spilled over into the political arena, primarily because of disagreement between the partners of the Grand Coalition government over the issue of unemployment insurance payments. Because of opposing interests and party loyalties, a compromise solution could not be reached, and the coalition of the Social Democratic Party, German Democratic Party, Center Party, Bavarian People's Party, and German People's Party fell apart in March of 1930. Parliamentary government was from then on paralyzed because of competing group interests that would not compromise even when it was in the national interest to do so.

From Herbert Michaelis and Ernst Schraepler (eds.), *Ursachen und Folgen vom deutschen Zusammenbruch 1918 und 1945* (Berlin: Dokumenten-Verlag Dr. Herbert Wendler, 1958), vol.8, pp. 21–35. Translated by Dieter Kuntz.

From April 1930 on, government functioned not through democratic parliamentary resolutions but rather through the so-called presidential system, which was predicated on the extension of the president's powers under Article 48 of the Weimar Constitution. This article gave the president emergency powers in time of crisis to restore law and order. Because the Reichstag was stalemated, Article 48 enabled the chancellor to enact governmental measures solely through presidential decree. Parliamentary democracy, in effect, came to an end in 1930.

The following documents illustrate the parliamentary paralysis that had set in by 1930. In a governmental declaration of April 1, excerpts from which are reprinted below, Chancellor Brüning made clear his intention to implement his policy of fiscal austerity, with or without the approval of the Reichstag. Brüning threatened to employ "every constitutional means" in order to achieve his ends. This implied threat to invoke Article 48 was received with alarm in the Reichstag, where the Social Democrats in particular warned of the dire consequences for democracy in Germany. The Reichstag debates that followed Brüning's declaration demonstrated the attitudes of Germany's political parties, evidencing all too clearly that disagreements made effective coalitions impossible and that the extremist parties were in no mood for cooperation but were instead determined to oppose the government so as to hasten its collapse.

> *Governmental declaration by Chancellor Brüning (Center Party) of April 1, 1930*: In accordance with the recommendation of the Reich president the new cabinet is not bound to any [parliamentary] coalition, although the political authority of this honored house could not be overlooked in the formation of the cabinet. The cabinet has been formed for the purpose of resolving as expeditiously as possible those problems that are widely regarded as crucial to the survival of the Reich. This will be the final attempt to resolve these problems through this Reichstag. . . . The government is able and determined to employ every constitutional means at its disposal in order to achieve its ends.
>
> *Reichstag speech of SPD* [Social Democratic Party] *delegate Breitscheid, April 2, 1930*: . . . I now turn to the most important point of the governments' declaration. The chancellor wants to put his program into effect through this, I think you must agree, rather motley collection of cabinet members. He says that he will do this, or attempt to do this "with all constitutional means." We have no illusions about what Mr. Brüning understands by "constitutional means." He clearly enough is flirting with Article 48. . . . As to the question of whether or not public security and order are threatened enough to justify the application of Article 48, we must flatly answer no. . . . I am convinced that Mr. Brüning and his closest associates believe that because of circumstances they realistically have no choice but to apply Article 48. But I am equally convinced that they have associates who have different intentions; people for whom the application of Article

48 in this instance is only a beginning — a beginning leading to the establishment of a dictatorship. . . .

Reichstag speech of KPD [Communist Party] *delegate Pieck of April 2, 1930:* A new government presented itself yesterday, not coincidentally on April 1 [April Fool's Day]. . . . We Communists call on the working masses to vigorously oppose this middle-class capitalist-dictatorship government; this government that will rob the masses and enrich the property-owning classes. We demand the resignation of this government. We demand the dissolution of the Reichstag and new elections so that the masses will have the opportunity to voice their judgment at the ballot box. . . . The Communists will gain the strength to topple capitalism and will set the dictatorship of the proletariat against the dictatorship of the capitalists. This will pave the way for the realization of socialism. . . .

Reichstag speech of DNVP [German National People's Party] *delegate Hugenberg of April 3, 1930:* . . . The governmental declaration by the new cabinet has not in the least assuaged the lack of confidence the German Nationalist delegation has in the composition of the Bruening government. The serious differences of opinion over foreign affairs, as well as over internal matters and economic policies, which existed between the German National People's Party and the [previous] Müller-Curtius-Severing government continue to characterize our relationship with the new government. . . .

Reichstag speech of NSDAP delegate Feder of July 18, 1930: . . . No one within the government, nor from among any of the parties supporting the government, has dared to point out the real cause of all our misery: the Dawes and Young plans. There is a straight line leading directly from the Marxists' stab in the back in the year 1918 to the armistice and the disgraceful peace of Versailles, to the conferences at Spa, Brussels, Ostende, Genoa, Geneva, and London, to the Dawes Plan agreements. . . . Mr. Brüning should not take shelter behind the world economic crisis. What has caused our misery is the ineffectiveness of German politics over the course of the last twelve years. . . .

10. The Hunger Chancellor Stands by His Policies

Heinrich Brüning, leader of the Center Party, became chancellor in 1930. For the next two years he struggled with Germany's growing economic and political woes.

From Wolfgang Michalka and Gottfried Niedhart, *Die Ungeliebte Republik* (Munich: Deutscher Taschenbuch Verlag, 1980), pp. 323–25. Translated by Dieter Kuntz. Reprinted by permission of Deutscher Taschenbuch Verlag, Germany.

He felt that the answer to the problems of economic depression, unemployment, and political division lay in fiscal reform in a program of increased taxation and reduced government spending. His speeches to the nation called for sacrifices from all. The program was not popular with the German people, many of whom were daily joining the ranks of the unemployed. It was not long before Brüning became known as the Hunger Chancellor.

Brüning had hoped to gain a center-right majority government in the Reichstag elections of 1930. When this plan did not materialize, he fell back on President Hindenburg's precedent of using Article 48 to govern by decree. Yet even such emergency measures did not bring much relief from the economic misery, and soon Hindenburg became discontented with Brüning. Brüning resigned as chancellor on May 29, 1932, one day after delivering the following speech in which he defended his policies to the members of the foreign press. After Hitler seized power, Brüning emigrated to the United States.

The fundamental problem occupying our attention literally almost day and night is the problem of unemployment. This vexation of mankind is acute in the entire world, but it has here in Germany taken on an incredibly oppressive gravity. You are aware of the numbers engulfed by this material and moral poverty. Six million unemployed, whose lot is shared by an equal number of family members; in short, one-fifth of our entire population! Of these six million unemployed, two million (or one-third) are under the age of twenty-five. They are unemployed at a time in their lives when physical strength and determination are seeking release in work. From among these two million, one million are under the age of twenty-one. One million young people who face life without a job; people who cannot find employment just at the time when they have reached maturity, and are able to think and act independently; just then are they confronted with an insurmountable obstacle. . . .

Is it any wonder that radicalism is welling in the hearts of these young people? Is it any wonder that they base hope of a better future on the downfall and destruction of the present system? . . .

. . . You all know that the cost of work-providing measures of the so-called productive work relief amounts to much more by far than even the pure unemployment payments. . . . Despite the temptation to make the necessary money available for these programs, the national government has refrained from employing artificial means, which in the long term would be counterproductive. These measures would lead to an unstoppable devaluation of the mark. The nation would not be able to survive a second inflation, but would sink into chaos from which recovery would not be possible. It follows that all we can do then is to take a path that will not bring on inflation, will not endanger the German currency, but will provide work for the unemployed, thereby protecting them from spiritual and moral destruction. Aside from what the Reich government can distribute in terms of public works projects and other internal measures, resettlement and volunteer labor service will also come under special consideration.

One thing, however, must be remembered: Germany cannot solve this problem alone. . . . The world economic crisis must be eliminated or at least softened somewhat, because salvation can come only through the joint actions of all. The first precondition is the restoration of confidence. This has often been repeated by all those who have closely examined this matter. Confidence can only be restored by finding solutions to the well-known political problem. . . .

11. Commerce Grinds to a Halt

The annual report for the year 1932 of the Chamber of Industry and Commerce in the Rhineland city of Mainz noted a continued steady decline in the national and local economy. By 1932, according to the report's findings, commercial activity in the Mainz region had practically come to a standstill as a result of a general lack of public confidence in economic recovery. The report pointed to the burdens on municipal government and the strain on local finances created by this situation.

CITY OF MAINZ CHAMBER OF COMMERCE AND INDUSTRY, ANNUAL REPORT FOR 1931

The year 1931 saw a further rapid decline of the German economy. This downward trend has been in evidence since 1927. . . . No more needs to be said about the desperate condition of the German economy. No further proof is required than the findings of the report issued by the Geneva committee of experts, which determined that one-third of the economy and those individuals dependent on it is lying idle, the unemployment figures have reached new, undreamed-of highs, and the number of business failures and shutdowns is growing day by day. . . .

ANNUAL REPORT FOR 1932

The catastrophically low level of the German economy which we detailed in the previous annual report persisted during the first half of this reporting year as well. The fourth presidential emergency decree of December 8 [1931] did make the attempt to slow the further decline of the economy,

From *Rhein-Mainische Wirtschafts-Zeitung* 14 (1933) No. 1., in *Die Machtergreifung der Nationalsozialisten 1933 in Mainz* (City of Mainz, 1983), p. 58. Translated by Dieter Kuntz. Reprinted by permission of Dr. Anton Maria Keim.

but it soon became clear that the planned artificial and far-reaching encroachment on natural economic relationships could not produce the desired result. The concerns over this encroachment, which we emphatically expressed in our last report, have since proved well founded. Existing contractual agreements in all areas of the market, be it in the area of housing, money and interest, or salaries and wages, were all loosened and changed, while good faith was not taken into account. As a result a considerable insecurity has taken hold not only in the economic sphere, but among the entire population in general. All initiatives falter because of despondent attitudes, and commerce appears to have come to a standstill altogether. This critical situation has been intensified by the failure to solve the reparations problem. . . .

The situation in the field of public finances continues to be of concern. The situation at the community level is hopeless. [Local government finances] bear the main brunt of unemployment, since over the course of time more and more unemployed individuals drift from unemployment insurance to public crisis relief and finally into general welfare recipient status. It is of the utmost urgency to relieve the local communities of this pressure by coordinating the entire system of unemployment relief. The economy in general would stand to benefit from the restoration of the financial health of local communities. . . .

→ need of mass employment

– susceptible to propaganda

logic of constitutional insecurity

Bruning's plan is tax & cut is spending leads to × decline in national local economy is inability to provide stability

During Hitler's early years as leader of the NSDAP, he was fond of wearing traditional Bavarian clothing. The style is reflective of the Party's roots in local politics. Here Hitler appears in *Lederhosen*.

Chapter

2

Hitler and the Rise of the Nazi Party, 1919–1929

The beginnings of the National Socialist Party were meager enough. At a conference January 2–5, 1919, Anton Drexler, together with twenty-five fellow workmen from the railroad shops in Munich, founded the German Workers' Party. Like many other groups in postwar Munich, it was nationalistic, anti-Versailles, and antisemitic, blaming the recent disorders brought on by the loss of the war, the civil unrest in Bavaria, and the Treaty of Versailles on a "Jewish conspiracy." The German Workers' Party, however, differed from other nationalistic right-wing groups in one important respect: whereas such better-known organizations as the Thule Society, with its racial theories and elitism, continued to be a small conspiratorial party, the German Workers' Party was from the outset a popular and even socialist party, open to all who wanted to join. Here lies the source of National Socialism's later success as a mass movement. It needed only a man with the organizational ability and the gift for propaganda to realize the potential power of combining extreme nationalism and antisemitism with a mass party organization. For the National Socialists, this man was Adolf Hitler.

Hitler first attended a meeting of the German Workers' Party on September 12, 1919, and soon afterward became a regular member. He quickly rose to take a place on its executive board as well as to become the Party's "propaganda chairman." In this position, Hitler immediately set to work to refashion the small debating society into a political combat organization and a force to be dealt with in Bavarian politics. The key to Hitler's success both within the Party and without was the mass meeting. His unerring exploitation of crowd psychology allowed him to consolidate his dictatorial position within the Party and at the same time expand its popular base. By recruiting ex-soldiers, *Freikorps* members, and younger men from the lower middle class, Hitler wrested the Party from its original founders and shifted it from its working-class origins. Through constant activity, by the summer of 1921 Hitler was the unchallenged head of the Party, with the title of Führer. In the same year he renamed the Party the National Socialist German Workers' Party (NSDAP) to distinguish it from parties with a more socialist ideology.

That Hitler's superior power as an orator and agitator was crucial in his attaining the leading position within the Party is evident from the early years. Only with Hitler as an attraction did the small German Workers' Party burst into the spotlight in a series of mass meetings held in the spring of 1920. Indeed, in the forty-six meetings staged by the Party between November 1919 and November 1920, Hitler appeared thirty-one times as the main speaker. Besides his political agitation, Hitler also pushed the Party out of obscurity with the creation of the Sturmabteilung (SA). Originally founded to provide an armed guard for Party meetings, the Storm Troopers or Brown Shirts grew into a large and violent force, guaranteeing the proper atmosphere at NSDAP gatherings by helping to whip up the crowd and attacking all opponents of the Nazis. Probably the existence of this military arm of the Party more than the NSDAP's political power led the general state commissioner, Gustav von Kahr, to look to Hitler in the autumn of 1923 to join him in forging an alliance of nationalist groups. The attempted coup of November 8–9, 1923, in Munich was both a tactical and a strategic mistake on Hitler's part. The so-called Beer Hall Putsch was poorly planned and ineptly carried out. At the last moment, Kahr removed his support, leaving Hitler and former general Ludendorff to execute the coup. It was easily suppressed and its leaders arrested. Ludendorff was released, but Hitler stood trial for treason. He turned defeat into rhetorical victory, however, as he gained further recognition by converting his trial into a public condemnation of the Weimar republic and all it stood for. Still, this victory had only limited practical success since the failure of the putsch resulted in the near-total dissolution of the party that Hitler had been building up for the past three years.

By 1924 the world Hitler returned to from Landsberg Prison had changed. The chaotic conditions of the postwar years, which had bolstered the success of NSDAP agitation, had been succeeded by the relative stability of the middle period of the Weimar Republic. The lack of a crisis atmosphere presented the Party with new problems. The NSDAP had been outlawed as a result of the failed putsch, and Hitler himself was barred from public speaking in almost all German states. Party membership declined drastically, and the Party organization seemed to be shattered. But this dismal situation within the Party, which Hitler made no effort to alter while he was still in prison, gave him a chance at a new start in 1925.

Hitler made several significant decisions regarding political strategy in 1925. First, he resolved that henceforth the NSDAP would act alone and no longer in alliance with other nationalist parties. Collaboration with these groups, he realized, tended to deplete rather than increase the strength of the Party. Cooperation had led only to political and ideological compromise. With this decision, Hitler was able to consolidate his position as the Party's undisputed leader. More significant, Hitler aimed to stop calling for the overthrow of the Weimar government, instead mapping out a strategy for working within the legal and constitutional framework of the republic. By maneuvering within the constitutional system, Hitler hoped to move the National Socialists into a position from which they could overthrow the republic from within in the policy of "legal revolution."

The political reorganization of the Party was part of Hitler's strategy. Although Hitler was prohibited from speaking in public for three years, he devoted himself with even greater intensity than before to the restructuring of the Party. He established the Political Organization as its central political wing, which became the framework for the future full-fledged political party and even shadow government, with "ministries" for different departments. In 1926 a *Reichsleitung* (Reich directorate) with secretary, treasurer, secretary-general, and several subcommittees was formed. The Reich directorate initially had twenty-five employees and three automobiles. The apparatus grew quickly; departments of foreign affairs, the press, industrial relations, agriculture, the economy, the interior, justice, science, and labor formed a miniature government. In addition, institutes on National Socialist issues like the notion of race and culture and of propaganda began to play an increasingly important part in party affairs. Later that year, the groundwork was laid for still more party auxiliaries: the *Gliederungen* (formations) such as the Hitler Youth, the National Socialist German Students' League, the National Socialist Law Officers' League, the National Socialist Physicians' League and the National Socialist Women's League. Through these new organizations the NSDAP moved toward total inclusion of its supporters within the party structure.

Besides the major organizational committees at the center, the party developed a host of other pseudogovernmental offices. The country was broken down into regions, or *Gaue,* that corresponded roughly with the nation's electoral divisions; each of these was divided into districts, or *Kreise,* and these in turn into local groups, or *Ortsgruppen.* The leaders of these various groups were the hard core of the Party who were responsible for spreading the Nazi message to the entire nation. Hitler used the expansion of the Party network for the further solidification of his control over every leader and employee of the NSDAP. He determined their remuneration, their eligibility for Party office, the Party's electoral candidates, and the personnel and financial policies of the regional offices. The leadership of Munich was conclusive and total, and Hitler's position was unchallenged.

The scheme of reorganization also extended to the SA. Hitler believed that the era of combat was over and that the debacle of 1923 had resulted from the faulty coordination of political and military aims. It was time to assert the superiority of the PO over the SA. In reorganizing the NSDAP, Hitler was determined not to permit the SA to function any longer as a relatively independent armed force under its own leadership. He broke with Roehm over this issue in 1925, after which Roehm resigned from the party and Franz Pfeffer von Salomon became the new leader of the SA. Hitler's aim was clearly to subordinate the SA, which was to become the fighting organization of the PO, conducting the political struggle without weapons. Although in practice it did not entirely renounce violence, the SA served above all to organize disciplined public demonstrations. Despite the reforms under Pfeffer, tensions between the SA and the PO continued. The primacy claimed by the leaders of the PO conflicted with the Storm Troopers' feelings that they were the real fighting troops of the movement and its most effective part.

Hitler aimed in his vast reorganization of the Party to expand the NSDAP from a provincial, putschist party within Bavaria into a nationwide political force. The spread of the Party and the SA was essentially achieved from below through the initiative of local organization leaders. Characteristically, regional groups were formed only if they had acceptable leaders willing to submit without qualm to the Party's command structure. Such arrangements were justified by appeal to the vague notion of the *Führerprinzip,* or leadership principle, through which leaders "naturally" emerged from the group. Once established, the groups sought confirmation by the supreme Führer himself. All levels of this new and greatly augmented organization gave their allegiance directly to Hitler. Even with this loose, decentralized framework, Hitler no longer feared any serious internal challenge to his absolute rule. Whoever founded a regional branch of the NSDAP or won through to the leadership position was generally recognized as regional leader or *Gauleiter.* Confirmation by Party headquarters or by Hitler, though obligatory, was in most instances a mere formality.

In this respect, Hitler showed virtually unlimited patience toward shady practices, denunciations, and corruption within various units of the Party. Before 1928 it was not rare for local regional leaders to be elected by members of their groups. Hitler did not formally veto this democratic procedure until 1929. Notwithstanding their dependence on Hitler and the party's Munich headquarters, the regional leaders enjoyed considerable freedom of operation, with a relatively strong popular and organizational power base. Individual initiative and their own claims to leadership roles played an essential part among these tough, long-serving Party leaders. It therefore proved extremely difficult, and indeed often impossible, to organize the Party more systematically and hierarchically when, after 1930, its mass growth demanded a tighter organization. This problem of control remained burdensome down to 1933.

The restructuring of the Party was a major reason for its success in expanding beyond the borders of Bavaria into all parts of Germany, in transforming the quasi-political and quasi-military groups of the early days into a loosely arranged yet hierarchical organization that would eventually emerge as a true mass movement. Hitler developed from this large number of nominally united groups, each professing allegiance to his person, a broad-based and popularly oriented Party. Appealing to all layers of the population and loyal to one man alone through a network of overlapping and all-inclusive local groups, the NSDAP became a powerful political force in the late 1920s. The capstone of the entire structure which held it all together was the Führer.

Yet despite the Party's expansion into a national organization in the mid-1920s, the NSDAP grew slowly. Initially, the new strategy and organization did not make much difference. Since the national political and economic situation had stabilized in the course of 1924, the radical Right found few popular issues. The mass agitation tactics of the earlier period no longer worked. The public activities of the NSDAP met with a long series of failures and setbacks. By the end of 1925, the Party had only 27,000 members, compared with the 55,000 of 1923. Eventually, however, the reorganization of the Party paid off. In 1926, Party membership doubled; in 1927, it tripled; and in 1928, four times the number of members of the year before were recruited. Even with these increases, however, the NSDAP continued to be a minor political force. But if the number of Party members rose slowly during the stable years of the republic, its rate of growth in both membership and popular support was tremendous after 1929. Party membership reached nearly a million, and the Reichstag election of September 1930 gave the NSDAP 6.5 million votes (18.3 percent of the total), compared to only 800,000 votes in 1928. The period 1928–33 marks the third phase in the development of the NSDAP, in which the Party moved into the national political arena with sufficient force to maneuver for itself.

The reasons for this increase in the Party's strength are not difficult to discover. With the worsening economic situation and the threat of another bout of radical inflation, the National Socialist position again became influential among many Germans. In other words, the cause of the increase in popular support for the Nazis lay outside the Party's control, in the international economic crisis and its social and political effects on Germany. Nonetheless, the reorganization of the Party and its changed political strategy allowed it to capitalize on the crisis situation. By 1928 the one-million-strong NSDAP, unlike the putschist Party of 1923, controlled local and state organizations in all parts of Germany. When economic and political storms beset the republic after 1929, the NSDAP stood ready to branch out into a mass movement.

As unemployment rose from 1,368,000 to 6,014,000 in 1932, the Nazis began to find support in areas they never expected and in numbers they never anticipated. During the mid-1920s the NSDAP had received most of its support from zealous patriots, fanatical antisemites, and social misfits. Once the depression had set in, the Party began to appeal to a much wider audience. Ultranationalism and Nazi leadership seemed to hold out the promise of salvation to unemployed workers, to agricultural laborers and small farmers who had been hard hit by the fall of prices, to industrialists whose markets disappeared, and to other economic groups. Hitler tailored the content of his message for specific audiences. If antisemitism would not be popular with an individual group, it was dropped; if it was a popular issue, it was played up all the more. Such directed appeals were especially popular with lower middle-class audiences — members of that social group whose lives

NSDAP Membership Statistics, 1925–29: Percentages of Members of NSDAP Chapters by Social Class and Occupational Subgroup in Various German Towns

Class	Occupational Subgroup	(A) Hamburg Mar. 1925[a]	(B) Barmen [Apr. 1925][b]	(C) Langerfeld Nov. 1925[c]	(D) Mülheim Nov. 1925[d]	(E) Brunswick 1925–26[e]	(F) Mettmann Feb. 1926[f]	(G) Starnberg July 1927[g]	(H) Königsberg [1928][h]	(I) Königsberg June 1929[i]
Lower	1. Unskilled workers	17.9	10.7	27.0	15.6	13.3	28.6	14.8	5.6	2.5
	2. Skilled (craft) workers	13.8	28.7	27.0	28.9	13.9	14.3	21.1	22.7	21.4
	3. Other skilled workers	1.9	4.9	2.7	6.7	2.3	3.6	11.1	4.7	3.8
Subtotal		33.6	44.3	56.8	51.1	29.5	46.4	47.0	33.0	27.7
Lower middle	4. Master craftsmen	7.9	16.4	16.2	15.6	8.0	7.1	12.2	13.1	12.4
	5. Nonacademic professionals	0	0.8	2.7	2.2	2.3	0	0	3.9	1.7
	6. Lower employees	14.2	17.2	0	17.8	19.5	32.1	7.4	14.2	20.0
	7. Lower civil servants	8.5	2.5	5.4	2.2	11.7	7.1	11.1	5.6	6.7
	8. Merchants	30.2	17.2	13.5	11.1	15.6	0	0	14.2	18.3
	9. Farmers	0	0.8	0	0	7.8	3.6	0	4.3	0.8
Subtotal		60.8	54.9	37.8	48.9	64.9	50.0	30.7	55.3	59.9
Elite	10. Managers	0.9	0	0	0	1.6	0	0	0	0.4
	11. Higher civil servants	0.9	0	0	0	0	0	14.8	0.9	0.8
	12. Academic professionals	3.8	0	2.7	0	2.3	0	3.7	1.3	2.1
	13. Students	0	0.8	2.7	0	0.8	3.6	0	7.8	7.9
	14. Entrepreneurs	0	0	0	0	0.8	0	3.7	1.7	1.3
Subtotal		5.6	0.8	5.4	0	5.5	3.6	22.2	11.7	12.5
Percent (total)		100	100	100	100	100	100	100	100	100
Frequency (N)		106	122	37	45	128	28	27	232	240

Source: From *The Nazi Party: A Social Profile of Members and Leaders, 1919–1945* by Michael H. Kater (Cambridge, MA: 1983), pp. 250–251. Reprinted by permission of Harvard University Press.

a NSDAP in Hamburg after refounding of Party, February–March 1925. Percentages calculated on the basis of information in NSDAP Hamburg membership list, appended to letter, Klant to Amann, Hamburg, March 11, 1925, BA, Schumacher/201. Also see *The Infancy of Nazism: The Memoirs of Ex-Gauleiter Albert Krebs, 1923–1933*, ed. William S. Allen (New York, 1976), p. 65.

b NSDAP in Barmen after refounding of Party, April 1925. Percentages calculated on the basis of information in NSDAP Barmen membership list (April 1925), HSAD, RW 23, NSDAP/Gauleitung Ruhr.

c NSDAP in Langerfeld by November 1925. Percentages calculated on the basis of information in NSDAP Langerfeld membership list, November 18, 1925, HSAD, RW 23, NSDAP/Gauleitung Ruhr.

d NSDAP in Mülheim-Ruhr by November 1925. Percentages calculated on the basis of information in NSDAP Mülheim membership list, November 23, 1925, HSAD, RW 23, NSDAP/Gauleitung Ruhr.

e NSDAP in Brunswick, 1925–26. Percentages calculated on the basis of information in Kurt Schmalz, *Nationalsozialisten ringen um Braunschweig* (Brunswick, 1934), pp. 225–229. Personal details pertaining to 128 out of the 150 members listed in Schmalz's book were found in the NSDAP Master File of the Berlin Document Center and statistically processed.

f NSDAP in Mettmann by February 1926. Percentages calculated on the basis of information in NSDAP Mettmann membership list, February 28, 1926, HSAD, RW 23, NSDAP/Gauleitung Ruhr.

g NSDAP in Starnberg by July 1927. Percentages calculated on the basis of information in Franz Buchner, *Kamerad! Halt aus! Aus der Geschichte des Kreises Starnberg der NSDAP* (Munich, 1938), pp. 159–160.

h NSDAP in the city of Königsberg by 1929. Percentages calculated on the basis of information in NSDAP Königsberg City membership list, [1928], SAG, SF 6818, GA/33.

i NSDAP in Königsberg and surroundings by June 1929. Percentages calculated on the basis of information in NSDAP Greater Königsberg membership list, June 18, 1929, SAG, SF 6818, GA/33.

were severely affected by worsening economic conditions. They did not have the financial reserves of the upper classes, nor could they fall back on the social and political associations of the workers, who, though they suffered most directly from the economic crisis, had both union organizations and the appeal of socialist or communist ideology to resist the Nazis' appeals. Hitler had least trouble in persuading the members of this class to believe that Jews, plutocrats, and socialists were the cause of all their woes, and that only a Nazi victory at the polls and the end of the Weimar Republic could save them.

12. An Early Speech by Hitler

Adolf Hitler's favorite themes in speeches he gave during his rise to power centered on the injustice of the Treaty of Versailles and the inefficiency of the Weimar government, and its "treasonous" attitude with its policy of fulfilling the treaty's terms. Bavarian police agents frequently attended meetings of political organizations in an effort to monitor their activities. The next selection comes from a police report on one of Hitler's early speeches, delivered in December 1922 in Munich. On this occasion Hitler spoke at a small "discussion evening" at one of the Party's favorite haunts, and as usual highlighted the government's policy toward the Allies, which he saw as "dishonorable."

Today one cannot call anyone a bandit because of the possibility of that individual being or having been a ministerial official; one clashes easily with these protective "laws." In the old days everyone knew . . . the ministerial officials, and knew that they were beyond reproach. If one of them was charged with something, the whole cabinet was dissolved. Today if a ministerial official is charged with sugar swindle, larceny, usury, and fraudulant tax declaration, he simply stays [in office]. In the old days subtle means sufficed, today it is necessary to use the "eye for an eye" approach. The government does what the Entente wants, even if it is dishonorable; the only thing the government fears is the possibility of arousing opposition among the people. (Evidently National Socialist agitation has not changed since [Chancellor] Wirth's resignation and Cuno's assumption of office!).

The insults to the Entente commission in Stettin, Ingolstadt, and

From *Nationalsozialistische Deutsche Arbeiter-Partei, Hauptarchiv, 1919–45* (Stanford, CA: Hoover Institution on War, Revolution, and Peace), H. A. reel 64, folder 1477 (NSDAP discussion evening in the Café Neumayr). Translated by Dieter Kuntz.

Passau were harmless in comparison to the French outrages committed in the Rhineland. For the most trifling affront to the commission we had to pay 2 billion marks. The Rhine is the grave of many German workers, women, and children; 17,000 marks is what the widow of a murdered German worker is to receive from Germany on the command of France. (Noteworthy here is the consistently anti-French attitude of the National Socialists!)

Not far off is the moment when the republic will have totally mismanaged and ruined itself; at best two years remain; I long for this moment. . . . The republic proved that it was incompetent when the French came into our land. Where French bayonettes have been, there one finds no more people saying "never again war."

At the head of government we need legally trained people. I would gladly trust Herr Friedrich Ebert [the president of the Weimar Republic] to restore a mattress, but rebuild the German people — that he cannot do.

The only party one can depend on is the National Socialists. The Nationalists yearned for ministerial seats; the People's Party is full of Jews and is to be compared to the DDP [German Democratic Party]; the DDP is worth as much as the SPD [Social Democratic Party] and is totally full of Jews. The Center [Catholic Center Party] goes hand in hand with the SPD.

The SPD elects as its leaders the dumbest people and those most useless to their professions. In these people they have the most compliant tools, they need only a few slogans — furthermore, they carry a reference book to every meeting with which they face the military man, the middle class man, and so on. Aside from that, Social Democratic successes are attributable only to a propaganda of lies. . . .

I thank God that the black-white-red flag [of imperial Germany] was the true representative of greatness and victory. It fluttered victoriously in East and West, in Asia, and over almost all oceans. The black-red-gold Entente flag [of the republic] is the true sign of the present.

We National Socialists are truly progressive. One describes a movement as reactionary if it leads us back to worse times. Imperial Germany brought us forward — it was progressive; the republic is reactionary — compare today's high cost of living.

We therefore yearn for revolution, because it is progressive.

We demand a referendum on the Constitution.

The government fears the results of such a referendum; that is why it will not allow one to be held.

We live in dangerous times, we are drifting closer to Bolshevism. We need a strong man, and the National Socialists will provide him.

Others create the best advertisement for us. We won many new members because of the ban on the party in Prussia. . . .

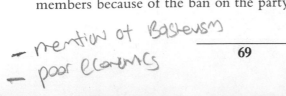

13. An Important Propaganda Tool: The Public Meeting

As the NSDAP expanded its network of local groups, organizational and procedural problems began to mount. Security at meetings was a major concern, and clashes with political opponents not infrequently disrupted meetings. Aside from the propaganda value of holding public meetings, the Party needed the revenue generated by admission fees. Good speakers like Hitler could easily attract one or two thousand curious potential supporters. This circular, entitled Anweisung zur Ortsgruppengründung (Instructions for the Establishment of Local Groups) and issued to local NSDAP groups in 1922, established strict guidelines that were intended to ensure the success of the Nazis' public meetings.

PROPAGANDA MEETINGS

The first propaganda meeting must be especially well prepared, otherwise it will not be successful.

Therefore, it is fundamentally better to have no meeting than an ill-prepared one. . . .

One should, for the first time . . . a too-large hall. Better to have a small, fully packed hall tha . . . half full or even conspicuously empty. . . .

AN EXAMPLE

The start of the meeting is set f⟨ ⟩ The doors to the hall will open at seven ⟨ ⟩ ittee along with assistants has already be⟨ ⟩ stributing leaflets, propaganda materials ⟨ ⟩ , readying the cash register, and prepa⟨ ⟩ ed on the podium]. It finishes its arr⟨ ⟩ e the hall opening can proceed smoc⟨ ⟩ box are women; controlling the e⟨ ⟩ ed be. A steward's committee allo⟨ ⟩ in such a fashion that party memb⟨ ⟩ und the podium as much as po⟨ ⟩ ponents sitting together as a bl⟨ ⟩ meeting chairman steps to the podium an⟨ ⟩ the bell; he greets first of all the gathering, secon⟨ ⟩ nd after briefly describing the purpose of the meeting turns ⟨ ⟩ to him.

During the speaker's talk the meeting chairman will see t⟨ ⟩ at there is order in the hall, that is, he will ring the bell in case of commotion

From Albrecht Tyrell, *Führer Befiehl* (Düsseldorf: Droste Verlag, 1969), pp. 42–44. Translated by Dieter Kuntz. Reprinted by permission of Droste Verlag, Dusseldorf, Germany.

and admonish hecklers to cease their interruptions and to wait until the discussion period to voice their opinions.

If an opponent calls for a point of order, the chairman will put the motion to a vote:

1. The first vote will determine whether or not the assembly wants the proposed motion to come to a vote.
2. If the assembly desires to have the motion come to a vote, the chairman will then conduct the voting.

Motions which in one way or another challenge house authority and rules are not to be voted on but are to be curtly rejected by the chairman. These would, for example, include motions calling for an end to the meeting, abbreviation of the speaker's allotted time, and so forth. If the party's power resource in the hall is sufficiently large, those causing a disturbance are to be sharply warned and, if the activity is repeated, ruthlessly removed from the hall. Disturbers of the peace who must be forcibly removed are to be dealt with in a manner that will once and for all make them lose any desire to disturb a National Socialist meeting.

If a Sturmabteilung [Storm Trooper] unit sent by Munich headquarters is present in the hall, the leader of the SA will supervise the maintenance of order.

The leader of the SA must report to the chairman at the beginning of the meeting and must come to an understanding with him.

The SA leaders receive their instructions from party headquarters.

If the speaker has finished his speech, the meeting chairman thanks him for his talk and exhorts the assembly to

1. take these words to heart and to act accordingly, and
2. after a short break of five minutes participate in the discussion. . . .

The meeting chairman will determine the speaking time per individual, depending on the time available and the number of announced speakers. It may not be under five minutes and should not be over fifteen minutes. If no opponents announce their intention to speak, supporters should not be allowed to speak either so that the effect of the main speaker's talk is not weakened.

Here the chairman must rely on instinct to do the right thing.

Once the discussion is finished, the main speaker will again be given the floor by the chairman in order to make closing remarks.

During the discussion itself, the chairman must see to it that the individual speakers stick to the point and above all else not offend or insult the assembly. In such cases the respective discussion speaker should basically be ruled out of order.

After closing the meeting, which is scheduled early if possible, the chairman calls for people to join the movement and entreats those who are willing to fill out the admission papers immediately.

14. The Party Program

On February 24, 1920, in the first public meeting of the German Workers' Party (as the NSDAP was known prior to its name change in April the same year), Adolf Hitler presented the "program" of the Party — a twenty-five-point statement Gottfried Feder, Anton Drexler (the founder of the German Workers' Party), and he had jointly formulated. The program reflected the Party's mixture of nationalist and socialist ideas. In fact, Point 17 proved to be something of an embarrassment to Hitler during the late 1920s when the Party began to gain supporters in agricultural areas: Many peasants wondered if the talk of "confiscation [of land] without compensation" meant the loss of private property. Hitler tried to assuage these fears by explaining that this point of the program was directed only at Jewish land speculators.

The National Socialist German Workers' Party at a great mass-meeting on February 25th, 1920, in the Hofbräuhaus-Festsaal in Munich announced their Programme to the world.

In section 2 of the Constitution of our Party this Programme is declared to be inalterable.

THE PROGRAMME

The Programme of the German Workers' Party is limited as to period. The leaders have no intention, once the aims announced in it have been achieved, of setting up fresh ones, merely in order to increase the discontent of the masses artificially, and so ensure the continued existence of the Party.

1. We demand the union of all Germans to form a Great Germany on the basis of the right of the self-determination enjoyed by nations.

2. We demand equality of rights for the German People in its dealings with other nations, and abolition of the Peace Treaties of Versailles and St. Germain.

3. We demand land and territory (colonies) for the nourishment of our people and for settling our superfluous population.

4. None but members of the nation may be citizens of the State. None but those of German blood, whatever their creed, may be members of the nation. No Jew, therefore, may be a member of the nation.

5. Anyone who is not a citizen of the State may live in Germany only as a guest and must be regarded as being subject to foreign laws.

6. The right of voting on the State's government and legislation is to be enjoyed by the citizen of the State alone. We demand therefore that all

From Gottfried Feder, "The Programme of the Party of Hitler," trans. F. T. S. Dugdale, in U.S. Department of State, *National Socialism: Basic Principles* (Washington, D.C.: U.S. Government Printing Office, 1943), pp. 222–25.

official appointments, of whatever kind, whether in the Reich, in the country, or in the smaller localities, shall be granted to citizens of the State alone.

We oppose the corrupting custom of Parliament of filling posts merely with a view to party considerations, and without reference to character or capability.

7. We demand that the State shall make it its first duty to promote the industry and livelihood of citizens of the State. If it is not possible to nourish the entire population of the State, foreign nationals (non-citizens of the State) must be excluded from the Reich.

8. All non-German immigration must be prevented. We demand that all non-Germans, who entered Germany subsequent to August 2nd, 1914, shall be required forthwith to depart from the Reich.

9. All citizens of the State shall be equal as regards rights and duties.

10. It must be the first duty of each citizen of the State to work with his mind or with his body. The activities of the individual may not clash with the interests of the whole, but must proceed within the frame of the community and be for the general good.

We demand therefore:

11. Abolition of incomes unearned by work.

ABOLITION OF THE THRALDOM OF INTEREST

12. In view of the enormous sacrifice of life and property demanded of a nation by every war, personal enrichment due to a war must be regarded as a crime against the nation. We demand therefore ruthless confiscation of all war gains.

13. We demand nationalization of all businesses which have been up to the present formed into companies (Trusts).

14. We demand that the profits from wholesale trade shall be shared out.

15. We demand extensive development of provision for old age.

16. We demand creation and maintenance of a healthy middle class, immediate communalisation of wholesale business premises, and their lease at a cheap rate to small traders, and that extreme consideration shall be shown to all small purveyors to the State, district authorities and smaller localities.

17. We demand land-reform suitable to our national requirements, passing of a law for confiscation without compensation of land for communal purposes; abolition of interest on land loans, and prevention of all speculation in land.

18. We demand ruthless prosecution of those whose activities are injurious to the common interest. Sordid criminals against the nation, usurers, profiteers, etc. must be punished with death, whatever their creed or race.

19. We demand that the Roman Law, which serves the materialistic world order, shall be replaced by a legal system for all Germany.

20. With the aim of opening to every capable and industrious German the possibility of higher education and of thus obtaining advancement, the State must consider a thorough re-construction of our national system of education. The curriculum of all educational establishments must be brought into line with the requirements of practical life. Comprehension of the State idea (State sociology) must be the school objective, beginning with the first dawn of intelligence in the pupil. We demand development of the gifted children of poor parents, whatever their class or occupation, at the expense of the State.

21. The State must see to raising the standard of health in the nation by protecting mothers and infants, prohibiting child labour, increasing bodily efficiency by obligatory gymnastics and sports laid down by law, and by extensive support of clubs engaged in the bodily development of the young.

22. We demand abolition of a paid army and formation of a national army.

23. We demand legal warfare against conscious political lying and its dissemination in the Press. In order to facilitate creation of a German national Press we demand:

(a) that all editors of newspapers and their assistants, employing the German language, must be members of the nation;

(b) that special permission from the State shall be necessary before non-German newspapers may appear. These are not necessarily printed in the German language;

(c) that non-Germans shall be prohibited by law from participation financially in or influencing German newspapers, and that the penalty for contravention of the law shall be suppression of any such newspaper, and immediate deportation of the non-German concerned in it.

It must be forbidden to publish papers which do not conduce to the national welfare. We demand legal prosecution of all tendencies in art and literature of a kind likely to disintegrate our life as a nation, and the suppression of institutions which militate against the requirements above-mentioned.

24. We demand liberty for all religious denominations in the State, so far as they are not a danger to it and do not militate against the moral feelings of the German race.

The Party, as such, stands for positive Christianity, but does not bind itself in the matter of creed to any particular confession. It combats the Jewish-materialist spirit within us and without us, and is convinced that our nation can only achieve permanent health from within on the principle:

THE COMMON INTEREST BEFORE SELF

25. That all the fore-going may be realised we demand the creation of a strong central power of the State. Unquestioned authority of the

politically centralized Parliament over the entire Reich and its organizations; and formation of Chambers for classes and occupations for the purpose of carrying out the general laws promulgated by the Reich in the various States of the confederation.

The leaders of the Party swear to go straight forward — if necessary to sacrifice their lives — in securing fulfilment of the foregoing Points.
Munich, February 24th, 1920.

15. The Beer Hall Putsch and Hitler's Trial

During the evening of November 8 and the morning of November 9, 1923, Hitler and his supporters staged an unsuccessful bid for power in Germany, launched in alliance with other right-wing nationalist groups from a Munich beer hall where Party meetings were often held. The right-wing Bavarian government had earlier in the fall itself entertained the idea of overthrowing the Berlin government. By November, however, the mood had changed, and the army under General von Seeckt appeared less inclined to sanction a coup from the Right (as had been the case in 1920) because of the fear that civil war would ensue. Hitler's paramilitary forces, however, expected action. It was in this atmosphere that Hitler attempted to coerce the leaders of the Bavarian government into supporting his march on Berlin. On the evening of November 8, Bavarian government officials were meeting with influential figures from the economic sector and leaders of local volunteer paramilitary associations in the Bürgerbräukeller, a Munich beer hall. Hitler, fearing that the Bavarian government, headed by General State Commissioner Gustav von Kahr, was planning the overthrow of the Berlin government, felt forced to undertake an action of his own — otherwise his plans to overthrow Berlin would come too late. Hitler stormed into the beer hall and proclaimed the establishment of a new government headed by himself but which also included current Bavarian officials. The Bavarian officials at first consented but later reneged on their promises of support and blocked Hitler's path. On the morning of the ninth, Bavarian police opened fire on Hitler and his followers as they marched through Munich in an effort to gain popular support.

Hitler was subsequently arrested and tried on charges of treason. Although the putsch was at first glance a failure, Hitler used his trial to catapult himself into national prominence. He denied that he had committed treason, claiming that he was a true patriot and that the real criminals were those who had signed the

From Ludwig Voggenreiter, *Der Hitler Prozess; Das Fanal zum Erwachen Deutschlands,* in U.S. Chief of Counsel for the Prosecution of Axis Criminality, *Nazi Conspiracy and Aggression* (Washington, D.C.: U.S. Government Printing Office, 1946), vol. 5, doc. no. 2404-PS, pp. 73–76.

shameful Versailles Treaty — that is, the officials of the Weimar government. He was sentenced to five years' imprisonment, though he served only nine months.

The following document consists of excerpts from Hitler's speech in his own defense, which was recounted in a book by Ludwig Voggenreiter entitled *Der Hitler Prozess* (The Hitler Trial), published in 1934, after the Nazis seized power. The excerpts were later used as evidence at the Nuremberg trials to illustrate the range of criminal activity engaged in by the Nazi Party.

May it please the Court!

. . . The Marxist movement is destroying the foundation of all human cultural life. Wherever this movement breaks through, it must destroy human culture. The future of Germany means: destruction of Marxism. Either Marxism poisons the people, their Germany is ruined or the poison is going to be eliminated, — then Germany can recover again, not before that. For us, Germany will be saved on that day on which the last Marxist has either been converted or broken.

We will fight spiritually for one who is willing to fight with the weapons of the spirit; we have the fist for the one who is willing to fight with the fist.

When we recognized that the territory of the Ruhr would be lost, our movement arrived at a big point of discord with the Bourgeois world. The National Socialist movement recognized clearly that the territory of the Ruhr would be lost if the people would not wake up from its lethargy. World politics are not made with the palm branch, but with the sword. But the Reich too must be governed by National Socialists.

A few weeks later, there was the Ruhr uprising and with that German unity broke down. Since then I did not go to Corps Area Headquarters [Wehr-Kreis-Kommando] anymore because I regarded all other discussions as completely useless.

But our movement has not been founded to gain seats in parliament and daily attendance fees; our movement was founded to turn Germany's fate in her twelfth hour.

As we had declared at numerous public meetings, that our leaders would not, like those of the Communists did, stand in the rear in the critical hours, our leaders marched in front. On Ludendorff's[1] right side

---

[1] General Erich Ludendorff had won fame in the Great War for his heroism on the eastern front. Disappointed and bitter over Germany's defeat and humiliation at Versailles, he subsequently embraced right-wing nationalist ideas and joined Hitler's Putsch attempt on November 9.

Dr. Weber[2] marched, on his left, I and Scheubner-Richter[3] and the other gentlemen. We were permitted to pass by the cordon of troops blocking the Ludwig Bridge, who wept bitter tears, were deeply moved and all gone to pieces. People who had attached themselves to the columns, yelled from the rear, that the guys should be knocked down. We yelled that there was no reason to harm these people. We marched on to the Marienplatz. The rifles were not loaded. The enthusiasm was indescribable. I had to tell myself: The people are behind us, they no longer can be consoled by ridiculous resolutions. The people want a reckoning with the November criminals,[4] as far as it still has a sense of honor and human dignity and not for slavery. In front of the Royal Residence a weak police cordon let us pass through. Then there was a short hesitation in front, and a shot was fired. I had the impression that it was no pistol shot but a rifle or carbine bullet. Shortly afterwards a volley was fired. I had the feeling that a bullet struck in my left side. Scheubner-Richter fell, I with him. At this occasion my arm was dislocated and I suffered another injury while falling.

I only was down for a few seconds and tried at once to get up. Another shot was fired, out of the little street to the rear of the Preysing Palace. Around me there were bodies. In front of us were State Police, rifles cocked. Farther in the rear there were armored cars. My men were 70 to 80 meters in back of me. A big gentleman in a black overcoat was laying half covered on the ground, soiled with blood. I was convinced that he was Ludendorff. There were a few more shots fired from inside the Royal Residence and from the little street near the Preysing Palace, and maybe also a few wild shots fired by our men. From the circle near the Rentamt, I drove out of town. I intended to be driven back the same night.

A few days later, at Uffing, we found out that I had suffered a fracture of the joint and a fracture of the collarbone. During those days I was all broken down by pains of body and soul, if only because I believed that Ludendorff was dead. I obtained the first newspapers at Landsberg. There I read the statement about a breach of my pledged word, that I had pledged my word to Mr. von Kahr never to undertake anything without informing

---

[2] The veterinarian Dr. Friedrich Weber was the leader of *Bund Oberland,* a Bavarian patriotic paramilitary association that in 1923 had joined forces with the Nazis and several other rightist groups.

[3] Max Erwin von Scheubner-Richter, a former diplomat, established the connection between Hitler and Ludendorff. He was the only leading National Socialist killed during the Putsch.

[4] "November criminals" refers to those Germans who were responsible for concluding the armistice with the Entente on November 11, 1918. Primarily implicated were the Social Democrats, but the extreme Right employed the term to include as well the other political parties who supported the Socialists in the "Weimer Coalition," and who accepted the Versailles Treaty.

him, that I had given this pledge still on the evening of November 6th. There I stood as a perfect scoundrel without honor. That is the lowest thing to do; that man, who worked together with us the whole time, stepped up with such lies against us now, when we could not defend ourselves and, to an extent, were broken down in spirit. I never gave such a pledge to Mr. von Kahr. I have said, I am standing behind you loyally, I will do nothing against you. Finally I said: "If you are not going to make up your mind, then I will not consider myself obligated as far as my decisions are concerned." When this campaign of slander continued in the course of the next few days and one after the other was brought in to Landsberg, whose only guilt was to have adhered to our movement, then I resolved to defend myself and to resist until the last breath. I did not enter this court to deny anything or to reject my responsibility. I protest against the attempt that Herr von Kriebel[5] tries to assume the responsibility, be it only for the military preparations. I bear the responsibility all alone, but I declare one thing: I am no criminal because of that and I do not feel as if I would be a criminal. I cannot plead guilty, but I do confess the act. There is no such thing as high treason against the traitors of 1918. It is impossible that I should have committed high treason, for this cannot be implicit in the action of November 8th and 9th, but only in the intentions and the actions during all the previous months. But if I really should have committed high treason, then I am surprised not to see those gentlemen here at my side, against whom the prosecutor would be obliged to file indictments; those who willed together with us the same action, discussed and prepared things down to the smallest detail, things which may be described in particular at a closed session later. I do not consider myself as a man who committed high treason, but as a German, who wanted the best for his people.

As far as the fight against Berlin is concerned, the gentlemen Kahr, Lossow[6] and Seisser[7] planned that too, but seemingly in the federal sense.

In contrast to that, I, from the beginning took the following point of view: The fight against Berlin will never be carried on by clothing it in a defense of strictly Bavarian rights, but the people expect that Bavaria will advocate a *general German right* in this fight, and by leading all of Germany will succeed in attaining fulfillment of her wishes for her very own state. . . .

---

[5] Hermann Kriebel was a retired colonel and a member of Weber's *Bund Oberland*. He served as military leader of the *Kampfbund* (Fighting Association), an alliance between the Nazis and four other patriotic right-wing paramilitary associations.

[6] General Otto von Lossow was the military commander of Bavaria and an ally of State Commissioner Kahr.

[7] Colonel Hans von Seisser was chief of the Bavarian State Police.

---

16. The Reorganization of the NSDAP

Released from prison in December 1924, Hitler immediately took steps to reassert his position at the head of the National Socialist movement, which had fragmented into rival factions during his imprisonment. On February 26, 1925, he issued a set of guidelines to his supporters which established the party's organizational ground rules. Though he quickly reestablished control over the south German districts, but it was not until the summer of 1926 that he was able to assert himself over the north German National Socialists led by Gregor Strasser and Joseph Goebbels. The guidelines for reorganization were designed to avoid the absorption into the Party of groups of supporters who might not entirely subordinate themselves to Hitler. The *Führerprinzip,* or leadership principle, is evident in the wording, which emphasizes obedience and a chain of command culminating in the one Führer.

FUNDAMENTAL GUIDELINES FOR THE RECONSTITUTION OF THE NATIONAL SOCIALIST GERMAN WORKERS' PARTY

(a) The new party acknowledges in its guiding principles and program, the guidelines of the old Nat. Soc. DAP dissolved on November 9, 1923.

The fight will be conducted according to the same tactical guidelines.

Organization will be implemented corresponding to the stipulations and provisions of the association's law on the basis of the old statutes. Changes in statutes and program can be effected only through a general membership meeting.

(b) Membership in the new party can only occur through new admission.

Admittance certificates will be issued by party headquarters, membership books likewise.

Acceptance [into the party] of existing associations en bloc can take place only if within the sphere of action of the association to be taken over there exists no splintering into diverse groups.

The en bloc acceptance of such associations can only come about on the basis of an express authorization by the first chairman of the party. The discussions regarding this are to be conducted with him personally. In this instance, too, the entire membership is to be newly admitted, but the applications of the same may be handled by their existing local group leadership, and so on.

In all other cases there can be no joining of our party by another group en bloc; instead, members will be accepted only individually.

From *Völkischer Beobachter,* February 26, 1925. Translated by Dieter Kuntz.

"Conditions" will not be granted in any form on entry into the new party, whether leaders or members.

Otherwise, new admissions will be dealt with according to the guidelines under the old statutes.

The leadership of the new movement will place less value on immediately gathering a great number, and will attempt instead to secure the internal unity of the movement and its organization from the ground up.

Those who are not prepared to subordinate themselves to the duly elected leaders do not fit into the framework of the NSDAP and should therefore keep clear of it.

(c) The membership books will be uniformly distributed to the entire movement. Every member is under the command of party headquarters, which will then call for the formation of individual local groups, insofar as no solidly organized sections are already in place as a result of the en bloc admissions of associations.

Integration into regional or other subsections will proceed according to natural development. Governing this will not be the Reichstag electoral district divisions, but rather the questions of practicality of propaganda as well as the available leadership material.

Prerequisite for the establishment of sizable subsections is always: first the leader, then the organization, and not the reverse. Fundamentally the following is to be observed: organization is not an end in itself, but a means to an end. It should make possible only the politically inflammatory struggle of the movement, and should create for enlightenment purposes those organizational prerequisites that are absolutely necessary.

The best organization is not the one that engages the largest mediation apparatus between leadership and individual members, but is instead the one that makes this connection in the shortest time possible. The organization must finally develop naturally and should not be artificially inflated.

As important as the role of time is in the deliverance of the Fatherland, so unimportant are years in the consolidation of a movement whose strength some day will be sufficient for the greatest events.

(d) The rebuilding of the SA will proceed on the basis that was standard until February 1923.

Its organization must be in accordance with the association's laws. Armed groups or formations are not to be admitted into the SA. Whoever, contrary to directives, carries arms or attempts to store them in warehouses will immediately be expelled from the SA and the party.

Any division that, contrary to headquarter's directives, organizes public processions or takes part in such will immediately be dissolved. The leader of the same will be expelled from the SA and the party.

Party headquarters can detect in such undertakings or endeavours the intention, through provocation, to put proof into the hands of the authorities for further persecution of the movement. Therefore, headquarters will view any such instigator as a deliberate and possibly even paid provocateur and informer, who will for that reason be ruthlessly reported.

The purpose of the new SA remains as it was prior to February 1923: hardening of the bodies of our youth, educating toward discipline and devotion for the great common ideal, training in the stewardship and enlightenment [propaganda] service of the movement.

(e) The political and demagogical struggle of the new movement will, according to the guidelines of the old movement, be conducted uniformly. The movement's program as well as the guidelines issued by headquarters are decisive here.

Any disunion in the fight is to be avoided.

The entire energy of the movement is to be directed toward the most dreaded enemy of the German people: Judaism and Marxism, as well as their allied or supporting parties, Center and Democrats.

17. An Accountant Recalls His Involvement in Party Activities

Gaining adherents for National Socialism was not easy during the middle years of the 1920s. In the period from 1925 to 1928 the Weimar Republic enjoyed relative economic stability and a measure of political tranquility, making it more difficult to find listeners for the party's negative propaganda. During these years the Nazi Party greatly expanded its organizational network and succeeded in gradually enlarging its membership as well. By 1927, the Party had regained the level of support it had had in 1923, and by 1928 it had gone well past that. The Party was able to attract adherents, primarily from the urban middle and lower middle class, and not until 1930 was it able to broaden its appeal and reach significant numbers within other segments of German society.

In 1937 the Nazis asked their early adherents (those who had joined the party during the "years of struggle," that is, before 1933) to write down their recollections of the formative days of the Party. Approximately one hundred members responded, sending brief political memoirs to the Party's archive in Munich. Written by an accountant who worked in a "red"-dominated factory in the industrial sector of the southern Rhineland, the following document is one of these accounts. Notice what the author says about the age and political experience of his early Nazi colleagues.

From *Nationalsozialistische Deutsche Arbeiter-Partei, Hauptarchiv 1919–45* (Stanford, CA: Hoover Institution on War, Revolution, and Peace), H. A. reel 26, folder 514 (Kampferlebnisse Adolf C., 1937). Translated by Dieter Kuntz.

MY EXPERIENCES IN THE STRUGGLE FOR THE FÜHRER AND FOR A NEW FATHER-LAND OF HONOR, FREEDOM, AND SOCIAL JUSTICE, 1925–33

1. HOW I WAS TRANSFORMED FROM A SUPPORTER OF ADOLF HITLER TO A COMRADE IN ARMS

In the workshops and offices of many large machine factories of the Reich, I became acquainted with Marxism and democracy in both party and labor unions as early as 1904. After the war, once I became aware of the shameful, treasonous action committed by the SPD [Social Democratic Party], Center, Democrats, and so forth against Germany, I instinctively fought against Marxism and its procurers wherever I possibly could. Even in my youth I was antisemitically predisposed and frequently paid for it with house detention because I did not tolerate the impudence and provocations of the Jewish boys. . . .

I also saw how Jewry was increasing its influence within the labor unions and the parties of November [i.e., of the coalition government] and how many Jews impudently and unscrupulously made their way into prominent public positions where they put on airs. Slowly I began to realize that this could not have been the reason for fighting the World War.

Through the ranting and raving of the newspapers of the parties supporting the [political] system, I learned that a man had risen in Munich whom they found to be annoying, and whose activity and new party became extremely troublesome to them. . . .

1922—23 I lived in a small village in the Catholic region near Ellwang. The only Catholic newspaper of that region delighted in tearing this new party and its leader to shreds. That was reason enough for me to connect with what this man wanted. Inflation raced through the land and ruined me, like many others.

As of January 1924 I lived in Ludwigsburg and from August 1924 on in Zuffenhausen, and was better able to follow the proceedings of the people's court of justice in Munich. The manly bearing of Adolf Hitler prompted me to seek out like-minded individuals. At first I made the acquaintance of a young lady who accordingly supplied me with the requisite literature, and who later also procured the *Völkischer Beobachter* for me. Only then did I get a true picture of the events in Munich and thereby became a fervent follower of Adolf Hitler.

On July 1, 1925, the Interallied Rhineland Commission [the highest occupational authority] had lifted the previous ban on the NSDAP as a political party. Several days later, when the party invited its supporters to gather for a public meeting in the Johannisgarten [a public hall], I was certain that the moment had arrived for me to become a part of this movement. I arrived early in the hall and seated myself so that I could have an overview of the entire room. JEWS NOT ALLOWED TO ENTER proclaimed a sign at the entrance, but nonetheless the Jewish "Behind-the-Front Fighter League"[1] of Neustadt had taken seats in the back of the hall. . . .

The leaders of almost all political parties and their most loyal supporters had filled the hall with approximately 450 opponents, — especially strong were the Communists . . . and the SPD . . . as well as the Center. . . .

No sooner had the young NSDAP local group leader, Hans G., opened the meeting, than it all began: the Marxist chieftains demanded a point of order. G. declares that only he can call that and that those who will not remain quiet can, on the basis of house rules, be removed from the hall. All hell breaks loose from within the ranks of the opponents as the evening's speaker began. The one and a half dozen National Socialists desperately resisted the attempt to disrupt the meeting. The Reichsbanner[2] leader, S., with the help of several cronies, attempted to shove Dr. W. [the speaker] away from the podium. Because of this chaos, G. had to close the meeting. . . .

From my vantage point I was able to observe quite well how continual contact was maintained between Jews and the Marxist party leaders through their go-betweens.

My resolve was firm: not merely supporter, but comrade in arms you must become in order to combat this corrupt Jewish system. At that instant I went to the NSDAP headquarters and declared my intention to become a member. . . . That is how I went from being a supporter of Adolf Hitler to fanatical comrade in arms, which I will remain as long as I live.

2. MY FIRST FIVE YEARS OF STRUGGLE IN NEUSTADT, 1925–30

A long period of untiring, nerve-shattering work and stubborn, fanatical struggle began for my comrades and myself. Family life did not exist anymore. I rejected everything that was associated with middle-class clubs. The struggle for the Führer and my job occupied my entire existence.

Ridiculed, laughed at, and scorned by former "friends"; likewise shunned and regarded as abnormal by my closest relatives; those were the immediate consequences. From the day of my entry into the party, there began a boycott of my father's and brothers' business by Jews and their cohorts which reached even into so-called German-Nationalist circles. Adding to this was the age difference that existed between me and my comrades which amounted to more than ten or fifteen years, and which

---

[1] The author is mocking the Red Front Fighters' League, the communists' paramilitary organization.

[2] The *Reichsbanner* was the unarmed but uniformed paramilitary organization of the Social Democratic Party, composed primarily of former servicemen.

my former friends and acquaintances pointed to as evidence of my stupidity and the inexperience of my comrades.

We began to collect and weld together the few faithful into a local group. Each and every one had to propagandize and persuade; we fought for every single individual with passionate, fanatical zeal. We established ties with other local groups and helped organize new locals in order to protect our meetings. It did not take long for our meetings to grow. They were no longer able to disrupt our meetings, although the attitude of many within the establishment police force was exceedingly deplorable in those days. We held meetings in the vicinity of Neustadt especially in the smaller towns, and on many Sundays I had to pay for the travel costs and provisions out of my own pocket because as speaker for the party I had to have a protection force for the meetings in order to have success. . . .

The first public meeting of the NSDAP in the town of Lambrecht occurred during this period. As the approximately twenty-five-man SA squad of the Neustadt local group marched into the hall, it was already heavily filled with opponents. The Marxists had brought in their heavy cannon — the Reichsbanner leader Schuhmacher from Ludwigshafen. Our now deceased party member K. Faber spoke first, dealing with [Foreign Minister] Stresemann's politics of illusion. I was supposed to make closing remarks. During the discussion period, Schuhmacher stepped up and railed in the most vile manner until finally a brawl broke out. Everything that was not nailed down was used as a missile: beer bottles, glasses, ashtrays, even the pieces of an entire oven were torn off and hurled at us. . . . We barricaded ourselves behind a table and threw everything that had been hurled our way back, toward the mob that was jamming the exit and howling and shrieking. . . .

During working hours I found myself employed as workshop accountant in the reddest factory in Mannheim. For eight years prior to the revolution, I was the only one, of about a one-thousand-man labor force, who openly and without reserve wore the party insignia. I had to endure much in those days. I was hated by those of different political views, ridiculed and mocked by intellectuals, shunned by all, then later feared, fought, slandered, and denounced. . . . It was worse than hell sometimes . . . but nothing was able to turn me away from an intractable belief in the Führer and ultimate victory. . . .

18. The Government's Assessment of the Nazi Party

The national as well as regional governments kept a close watch on the activities of the Nazi Party after its reorganization. The document that follows is the Weimar government's assessment of the NSDAP's aims and conduct in 1927. The government was still concerned lest the Party had not, after all, abandoned its earlier method of attaining power via revolutionary means. Noteworthy in the report is the mention of the Party's attempt to win favor with the working class, which was hindered because certain ideological tenets that appealed to workers tended to alienate the lower middle class. The government's overview of the development of the Hitler Youth shows that this organization was still in its infancy, and that many regional governmental authorities hitherto probably knew very little about its national organizational structure.

The National Socialist German Workers' Party has in the last few months continued its very active recruiting and propaganda work wherever there are large local groups. It maintains an extraordinarily brisk schedule of meetings and endeavors, through its public appearances, to attract the interest of the populace. In its press as well as in the speeches of many of its leaders is reflected a recent intensification rather than a moderation of the party's radical tone. The party openly identifies itself as revolutionary, and Hitler's remark at the party rally in Nuremberg, "Those on whom heaven bestowed the greatest portion of strength of action, also received power and sovereignty," clearly shows that the National Socialists do not count on coming to power legally, that is, through the winning of an electoral majority, but look to other means. The goal of the party is a National Socialist dictatorship under Hitler. This is often bluntly stated in meetings. Very characteristic is a remark by Dr. Goebbels, who in one of the party's discussion evenings in Munich (on June 20) casually remarked during critical comment on the *Stahlhelm* in Berlin that if he (Goebbels) could parade through Berlin with 120,000 men, like the *Stahlhelm,* he would not, like its leadership, give an assurance of a peaceable departure. He is positive that 120,000 National Socialists would not depart from Berlin in the same manner in which they arrived.

In their meetings in the industrial areas and in large cities, National Socialist speakers have lately conspicuously sought to woo the Communist elements among those attending their meetings. They emphasize the social-revolutionary nature of their party and seek to convince Communist workers that they will find the National Socialists better able to represent their interests than the "international" and "Judaized" Communists.

The result of these attempts has varied. In some cases it has led to meeting brawls and free-for-alls, while it has nonetheless undoubtedly had a certain propaganda effect. Lately it is increasingly being observed that Communist workers are going over to the National Socialists and are even assuming positions as functionaries. On the other hand, this obvious interest in Communist thought could be found objectionable by many lower middle-class adherents of National Socialism, and have the effect

From Ernst Deuerlein, *Der Aufstieg der NSDAP in Augenzeugenberichten* (Düsseldorf: Karl Rauch Verlag, 1969), pp. 286–89. Translated by Dieter Kuntz. Reprinted by permission of Karl Rauch Verlag.

of alienating them from the party. Numerically great successes have not been achieved by the National Socialists' attempts to recruit KPD [German Communist Party] adherents. However, these events do point out the progressively increasing radicalization of the National Socialist Party.

Noteworthy in this connection is the frequent debate a point in the National Socialist program has caused — namely, the demand for profit sharing by the worker. In the *National Socialist Letters* (Volume 1, July 1927) Gregor Strasser writes: "We have no doubt that our National Socialism will break this privilege of property and that the freeing of the worker will also be extended to sharing in profits, sharing in property, and sharing in output." The party has placed this demand in the foreground whenever it is attempting to attract new supporters from the working population.

The NSDAP is also attempting, now as before, to further develop its Storm Troopers. Headquarters is exerting pressure on all larger local groups who have not yet established such a unit, to set one up. The party sees the organization of the SA, now as before, as the backbone of the entire movement. On the occasion of the party rally in Nuremberg it was evident that the party, wherever it appears publicly, places great value on impressing the general public with the strength of its organization, displaying this through parades of uniformed SA members accompanied by flags, standards, and bands.

Noteworthy also is the fact that the NSDAP has lately established a farm employment agency. Until now primarily agricultural workers have been procured and sent to central Germany. The stipulation has been made that the prospects be members of the SA. An announcement by organization department leaders of May 7, 1927, regarding the engagement of agricultural workers in a rural district stated that hired SA comrades are subject to the directions and control of the organization's departmental leadership, which also takes care of room and board as well as the drawing up of the employment contract. The commitment must be of at least six months' duration. . . .

At the party rally in Nuremberg the proposal to establish National Socialist trade unions was debated. Whether such foundings have hitherto been undertaken is not known. . . .

The Hitler Youth was founded in the spring of 1925 in Saxony under the name Pan-German Youth Movement by the student Kurt Gruber of Plauen, who still serves as national leader today. This organization was from its beginnings to be regarded as a youth organization of the National Socialist German Workers' Party. In the spring of 1926 the organization adopted the name National Socialist Youth Movement. After the National Socialist Party rally in Nuremberg in August 1926, the organization carried the name Hitler Youth and spread its groups throughout the Reich. From this point on Gruber had the title National Leader of the Hitler Youth. Approximately 80 youth groups existed as of November 1926. In December 1926 a Hitler Youth national leadership conference took place in Weimar, which was attended by 55 representatives. The Hitler Youth is subordinate to the supervision of the highest Storm Trooper leader, Captain von Pfeffer. The national business manager is Max Undeutsch in Plauen. The members of the Hitler Youth are closely connected to the local leadership of the National Socialist Sturmabteilung. In Berlin, just as in Cologne, because of the ban on National Socialist local groups, the Hitler Youth locals too were prohibited. The National Socialist German Workers' Party rally in Nuremberg also found Hitler Youth members in attendance in large numbers (about 300). The members of the Hitler Youth wear the same uniform as the National Socialist Storm Troopers. The Hitler Youth publishes a monthly journal entitled *Hitler Youth*. The business office of this journal is located in Markneukirchen at the home of Bernhard Weller. This journal is obligatory and must be subscribed to by all members. (Price per issue is 15 Pfennig.)

19. The Nazis in Parliament

Although the NSDAP had since the Beer Hall Putsch opted for parliamentary tactics in its effort to acquire political power, the Party had a unique conception of what this approach entailed. It meant taking part in elections, but it did not mean that the Party intended to help make parliamentary democracy effective. It also did not mean that the Party's young activists would not engage in violent street battles with members of opposing political parties. As Joseph Goebbels, the Party's *Gauleiter* (regional leader) of Berlin-Brandenburg and future Reichstag member (elected in 1928) proclaimed, the intent was to paralyze the Weimar government.

Goebbels edited a weekly newspaper, *Der Angriff* (The Assault), in which he published the following article in April 1928, just prior to the party's first opportunity to participate in a national parliamentary election. The NSDAP did not fare well in that election, garnering only 2.6 percent of the total vote. Goebbels quite clearly states his contempt for the Reichstag in this article, which the Party republished in 1936 along with other writings by Goebbels.

WHAT DO WE WANT IN THE REICHSTAG?

We are an antiparliamentary party that rejects with good cause the Weimar Constitution and the republican institutions it has ushered in. We are opponents of a falsified democracy. . . . We see in today's system of majority vote and organized irresponsibility the main cause of our constantly increasing decay. What then do we want in the Reichstag?

From Joseph Goebbels, *Der Angriff: Aufsätze aus der Kampfzeit* (Munich: Franz Eher Verlag, 1936), pp. 71–73. Translated by Dieter Kuntz.

We are going into the Reichstag in order to equip ourselves in the arsenal of democracy with its own weapons. We will become Reichstag delegates in order to paralyze the Weimar way of thinking with its own assistance. If democracy is so stupid as to provide us with free [rail] tickets and allowances for this bearish task, then that is its own business. We are not going to give ourselves a headache over it. For us, any legal means with which we can revolutionize today's situation is justified.

If we succeed in this election [of May 1928] in sending sixty to seventy agitators and organizers into the various parliaments, then the state itself will in the future outfit and pay for our fighting apparatus. . . . Do any of you believe that when we march into the plenum of the house that we will immediately drink a toast to brotherhood with Philipp Scheidemann? Do you take us for such miserable revolutionaries that you are afraid that . . . we will forget our historic mission?

Mussolini, too, entered parliament. In spite of that, he marched on Rome not long afterward with his Black Shirts. The Communists, too, sit in the Reichstag. But nobody is so naive as to believe that they want to realistically and positively cooperate. Moreover, if we do not succeed this time in winning immunity for our most dangerous men, then they will all sooner or later sit behind bars. Will this happen if they acquire [parliamentary] immunity? Surely, and it no doubt will happen at the very moment when democracy, as a last measure of self-defense, will be forced to unveil itself, at that moment when it punches itself in the face and publicly establishes a capitalistic dictatorship which it normally practices covertly. But it will be some time before that comes, and until then the immune champions of our beliefs will have enough time and opportunity to widen the battle front so that the throttling and silencing of their public sermon will not proceed as noiselessly as democracy would like it to.

Another matter: The agitators from our party regularly spend six to eight hundred marks per month on travel — and are stabilizing the republic in the process. Would it not then be only fair for the Republic to compensate us for these travel expenses with free [rail] travel tickets? Who among you is in favor of us continuing to throw our own pennies into the jaws of the Jewish Dawes-railroad, whilst the Republic is truly aching to help us?

Do you think that this is the beginning of a compromise? Do you believe that we, who have stood before you hundreds and thousands of times and preached to you about believing in a new Germany; we, who dozens of times laughingly risked our lives against the red mob, brawling our way through, with your help, and against all opposition of official as well as unofficial character; do you think that we, who refuse to capitulate neither to terror nor to the commands of any authority — would surrender our weapons purely for a free [rail] ticket?

If all we wanted was merely to become [Reichstag] delegates then we wouldn't be National Socialists, but would, I suppose, be German

Nationalists or Social Democrats. They have the most mandates to distribute, and one doesn't ever have to risk one's life for them; as far as being able to compete with the intellectual luminaries of that party — well, we have plenty of brain power for that.

We do not come begging for votes. We demand conviction, sacrifice, enthusiasm! The vote is merely a device which helps us as well as you. We will set foot on the marble floor of parliament with hard strides, and will bring with us the revolutionary will of the multitude from which destiny has spawned us. We don't give a damn about cooperating with a stinking dung heap. We are coming to clear the manure.

One should not assume that parliamentarianism will be our Damascus. We have bared our teeth to the enemy, from the podium of mass rallies to the gigantic marching demonstrations of our brown regiments. We will also bare our teeth within the sluggish and satiated atmosphere of a parliamentary plenum.

We come not as friends, nor as neutrals. We come as enemies! Like a wolf breaks into a herd of sheep, that is how we will come. You no longer have it all to yourselves! And you will surely have no joy once we are there!

The Nazi electoral breakthrough during the early 1930s owed much to the feverish propaganda efforts of the Storm Troopers. Here a confident Hitler inspects SA ranks in Thuringia after the Party scored gains there in local elections. (Later, official photographers took care not to draw attention to Hitler's relatively short stature.)

Chapter
3

The Triumph of National Socialism, 1929–1933

The NSDAP of 1928 was still a small though bureaucratically overdeveloped party. Its members were united less by political principles or ideological concerns than by loyalty to the Führer. Thanks to Hitler's victory over rivals, party members kept to the road of legality and pinned all their hopes on a new radicalization of the political climate. Hitler himself was interested primarily in foreign and revisionist policies, which offered the best chance for breaking into the stabilized political life of the republic. The opportunity came with the renewed intensification of the debate over reparations payments in the summer of 1929. In July, Stresemann almost achieved another diplomatic success with the drafting of a new and far more realistic American policy on loans to Germany. The impatient nationalist movement was reformed for the first time since 1923 in a strong countermovement of German nationalists and National Socialists. Beyond representing mere opposition to the Young Plan for German payment of war reparations, right-wing groups took advantage of the rekindling of the dispute to attack the very structure of the republic itself. On July 9, 1929, these groups called for a national plebiscite against the plan. For the first time since 1923, Hitler countermanded his earlier decision and actively joined with other nationalist parties. This move effectively removed the NSDAP from its isolation as a radical splinter group and gave it a new identity as the most militant fighting organization within the socially influential, well-financed framework of the antirepublican Right, bringing the party into national consciousness in an unprecedented way and making it respectable. It finally lost the stigma of being an illegal, putschist party which it had carried since the early 1920s.

Through its alliance with other nationalist groups, the long-despised NSDAP thus gained not only social respectability but also financial backing and political

91

joining with other Groups broke isolation of NSDAP + brought it onto National Scene influence. Alfred Hugenberg, a wealthy and powerful industrialist and publisher who recently had been elected head of the German National People's Party, gave Hitler his full support. Suddenly the NSDAP found itself with undreamed-of propaganda and organizational resources. Hitler quickly sized up the situation and exploited all opportunities, soon becoming the strongest and loudest member of the newly formed "national opposition." No one was able to match the venom and ruthlessness of National Socialist propaganda. More radical than other groups in the alliance, the party saturated the German political climate with a biting indictment of the Weimar Republic, directing fears of the impending economic crisis into the channels of the party's Nazi ideology. While his self-confident partners in the right-wing nationalist alliance believed they could use Hitler for their own purposes and then discard him, they failed to understand either the man or the appeal of his movement. Hitler, the strongest and most dynamic leader of the extreme Right and having the best organization behind him, moved more and more into the spotlight as the leader of the opposition to Weimar and all that it represented.

Unlike Ebert in 1920–23, President Hindenburg, with his dislike of politics and especially of parliamentary politics, permitted himself to be pushed further and further toward authoritarianism, extraparliamentary experiments, and radical solutions to political problems. Beginning with the deadlock in the Reichstag and Chancellor Brüning's use of the extraordinary powers granted under Article 48 of the Weimar Constitution to form a working cabinet without parliamentary assent, Germany became the stage on which a procession of ambitious men sought to save the nation. The government reached a crisis of fatal significance when the president conceded the unworkability of German parliamentary democracy and with his conservative advisers developed concrete plans for restructuring the governmental system from above. Whereas Ebert had used Article 48 on its own, leaving the Reichstag with the power to undo his measures, Hindenburg used the article to refashion the government and dissolved the Reichstag at the same time. Hindenburg thus appropriated the unchallenged power to rule alone, appointing and dismissing chancellors at will.

The increased recourse to emergency decrees fundamentally altered the spirit of the Constitution. What was envisaged as a temporary exception became habitual, perverting the sense of the Constitution by giving the president the right to run the state for years without parliamentary approval. From 1930 on, Hindenburg met the worsening economic and political crisis by suspending the Reichstag and encouraging first Franz von Papen and then minister of defense General Kurt von Schleicher to experiment with authoritarian forms of rule. Such an attempt at patching together an effective government led Hindenburg to allow Hitler to become chancellor in the coalition government of January 1933.

It was Papen, however, who first actively sought NSDAP support. Although in his brief turn as chancellor in 1932 Papen aimed to restore an explicitly authoritarian state under a new constitution, which would have put an end to National

Socialist aspirations, he nevertheless played an important role in the ill-conceived effort to restrain the National Socialist revolution. To begin with, Papen immediately set about to win Hitler's cooperation. Toward this end he made a series of concessions that marked a break with Brüning's moderate authoritarian course. Papen rescinded the ban on the SA, which the Brüning government had insisted on in order to try to check the increasing incidents of violence in the streets. But Papen's move was more than a concession to the NSDAP; it was intrinsic to his central policy. He engineered a coup d'état in socialist-dominated Prussia in order to consolidate his authoritarian position within the state. He now sought a show of strength to break out of the political stalemate in which he found himself. His lifting the prohibition of the SA was a last-ditch attempt to bolster his falling reputation as savior of Germany. He hoped that a display of authoritarian self-confidence would be greeted with admiration, or at least fear, and thus help him win the respect and support of the people, the president, and the National Socialists alike.

Papen did not achieve the political stabilization of his authoritarian right-wing government, as the outcome of the Reichstag elections of July 31, 1932, indicated. Analysis of the election results shows to what extent an unresolved clash between three power blocs dominated the period after Brüning's ouster. The remnants of the democratic parties still maintained a potential negative force in the Reichstag; the Nazis and Communists also held positions of strength both outside parliament and within it and thus could prevent the formation of any democratic government; and Papen's authoritarian regime barely survived, though it could not remain in control with more than nine tenths of the electorate against it. No one group possessed enough power to gain control, yet each had just enough to prevent others from doing so.

The various groups tried to overcome the resultant paralysis — and, failing that, to exploit the situation for their own benefit. From the time of the July elections on, the conservative forces exerted greater and more unscrupulous pressure to include the NSDAP in the government. Only Hitler's mass party could give the necessary popular backing to any stable government. Influenced by the National Socialist electoral victory, Papen and Schleicher in early August renewed their efforts to persuade Hitler to join the government. But since they and particularly Hindenburg also insisted on considerable assurances from Hitler and offered him nothing more than the vice chancellorship, the upshot was another falling-out with the National Socialists. The Nazis of course had seen through Papen's plan of taming the NSDAP by including it in the government and thereby blunting its popular appeal while at the same time tapping its vote-getting potential. With this rupture and the inconclusive election results of November, Schleicher, who had been allied with Papen up to this point, withdrew his support for the government. At the last hour, Schleicher revealed that he possessed enough political realism to oppose the dangerously reactionary autocracy of Papen's design. Instead he held out to the president a newly formed coalition of various parties, including the Social Democrats.

The dramatic events of the weeks leading up to January 30, 1933, stemmed from individual decisions. Of course, the existing political situation and the body of problems encompassing the entire history and antecedents of the Weimar Republic produced and determined those decisions. Yet at this juncture not blind necessity but the actions of a small group of men governed the succession of events. When Schleicher's attempt to restore a more parliamentary form of government failed, Hindenburg again turned to Papen, who proposed a coalition government with Hitler as chancellor and himself as vice chancellor.

Here outlined are the immediate stages by which Hitler came to power. In the final months of the republic, individual acts took on historic importance: the raising of the ban of the SA, Brüning's resignation as chancellor, Hindenburg's turning his back on the democratic version of presidential rule, Papen's coup in Prussia and his frivolous dictatorial experiments, and finally Hitler's unexpected summons to the chancellorship at a time when the economic crisis had passed its nadir and the NSDAP was beginning to sustain electoral losses. Any attempt to reduce the interplay of decisions and developments between June 1932 and January 1933 to one common denominator would be an oversimplification. No doubt the intensification of the structural problems of the republic in the seemingly insurmountable power vacuum of 1932 made possible the rise of the National Socialists. But the irresponsible activities of the Papen-Hugenberg-Hindenburg camp dealt the final blow. This tiny minority, through its ambitious, overweening alliance with the antidemocratic mass movement of the Nazi Party, helped the National Socialists into positions of power which Hitler could never have captured on his own. Instead of the hoped-for restoration of merely authoritarian rule, there came a dictatorship that overwhelmed not only the Weimar Republic but also the proponents of a conservative third solution between democracy and dictatorship.

The NSDAP could not have accomplished its legal revolution by itself. It required the protection, or at least the good will, or middle-class and conservative forces in the government, armed forces, churches, commerce, and politics, which had also been the case in Munich before 1923. The Nazi Party thrived on the German people's desire for more decisive measures which was so easily aroused during crises as well as on the demand for a cure for the nation's ills. In this respect, it was less a revolutionary force than an opportunistic political party. In a time of economic and constitutional crisis, the NSDAP merely proved itself to be not only the popular enemy of socialism and communism but also the most effective organization agitating for the restoration of authoritarian forms of order in the state and society.

Voting Patterns, 1924–33

The graph illustrates the meteoric rise of the Nazi Party beginning in 1928 and shows as well the steady erosion of support for such parties as the German Democrats (DDP), who had no clear program, and the right-wing German National-

Electoral Statistics, 1924–33: Percentage of the Vote Received by the Parties.

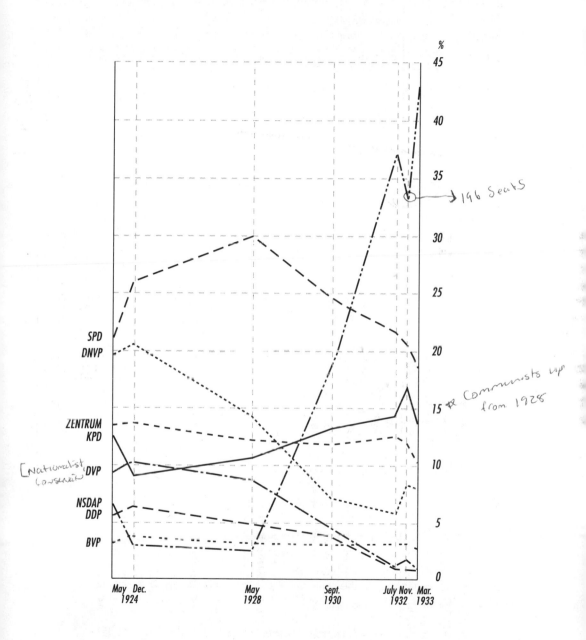

From *Das Ende der Parteien* by Erich Mathias and Rudolf Morsey, eds. (Düsseldorf: Droste Verlag GmbH, 1984), p. 779. Reprinted by permission of Droste Verlag, Düsseldorf, Germany.

New NSDAP Members, 1930–32
Percentages of NSDAP joiners in the Reich according to place of residence, and of NSDAP chapters in four communities, by social class and occupational subgroup, 1930–32

Class	Occupational Subgroup	(A) Reich Joiners 1930–32[a]	(B) City Joiners 1930–32[a]	(C) Small-town Joiners 1930–32[a]	(D) Country Joiners 1930–32[a]	(E) NSDAP Dt.-Kr., Kl. May 1931[b]	(F) NSDAP Pahres May 1932[c]	(G) NSADP Eutin May 1932[d]	(H) NSDAP Eltersdorf Jun. 1932[e]
Lower	1. Unskilled workers	15.4	12.6	9.9	18.2	22.8	23.5	12.4	13.3
	2. Skilled (craft) workers	18.1	15.0	18.4	19.5	25.5	22.4	22.0	21.2
	3. Other skilled workers	2.4	2.9	2.2	2.1	4.8	2.9	6.3	10.0
Subtotal		35.9	30.5	30.5	39.8	53.1	48.8	40.7	44.5
Lower middle	4. Master craftsmen	10.5	8.6	10.7	11.2	15.2	12.9	12.7	12.2
	5. Nonacademic professionals	4.2	7.0	5.1	2.7	2.1	0	0	0
	6. Lower employees	11.1	15.7	17.3	7.3	6.9	0	19.7	6.7
	7. Lower civil servants	4.6	5.4	6.1	3.7	4.1	0	3.3	0
	8. Merchants	11.9	16.3	16.3	8.7	4.1	2.9	12.0	13.3
	9. Farmers	12.6	1.0	4.2	20.4	11.0	32.4	1.4	20.0
Subtotal		54.9	54.0	59.6	54.0	43.4	48.2	49.1	52.2
Elite	10. Managers	0.9	2.3	1.0	0.3	0	0	0	0
	11. Higher civil servants	1.2	1.9	0.6	1.1	0	0	0	0
	12. Academic professionals	2.5	5.6	1.6	1.2	1.4	0	2.3	0
	13. Students	3.2	4.8	5.4	1.8	0.7	2.9	2.1	3.3
	14. Entrepreneurs	1.4	0.8	1.3	1.8	1.4	0	5.6	0
Subtotal		9.2	15.5	9.9	6.2	3.5	2.9	10.1	3.3
Percent (total)		100	100	100	100	100	100	100	100
Frequency (N)		1,954	516	313	1,125	145	34	426	30

Source: Michael H. Kater, *The Nazi Party: A Social Profile of Members and Leaders, 1919–1945* (Cambridge: Harvard University Press, 1983), pp. 250–51. Reprinted by permission of Harvard University Press.

[a] NSDAP joiners in Reich, 1930–1932. Columns B–D indicate the regional breakdown of Reich joiners given in column A. Percentage figures were calculated on the basis of information obtained for a subsample part of a larger sample (1925–1945), and drawn systematically from the NSDAP Master File in the Berlin Document Center. See Michael H. Kater, "Quantifizierung und NS-Geschichte: Methodologische Überlegungen über Grenzen und Möglichkeiten einer EDV-Analyse der NSDAP-Sozialstruktur von 1925 bis 1945," *Geschichte und Gesellschaft*, 3 (1977), 453–484; and the Introduction to this book at n. 47. The hypothesis of statistical independence and place of residence was rejected ($\chi^2 = 47.C18$; $df = 4$; $C = 0.153$; $P < 0.001$).

[b] NSDAP chapter in Deutsch-Krone and Klausdorf (East Prussia) by May 1931. Percentages calculated on the basis of information in (combined) NSDAP Deutsch-Krone and Klausdorf membership list, May 28, 1931, IfZ, MA-1217/207.

[c] NSDAP chapter in Pahres (Franconia) by May 1932. Percentages calculated on the basis of information in NSDAP Pahres membership list, May 1, 1932, appended to letter, Ortsgruppe Pahres to Kreisleitung Neustad:-Aisch, July 20, 1942, SAN, 503/96.

[d] NSDAP chapter in Eutin (Schleswig-Holstein) by May 1932. Percentages calculated on the basis of data in Lawrence D. Stokes, "The Social Composition of the Nazi Party in Eutin, 1925–32," *International Review of Social History*, 23 (1978), Part I, 6.

[e] NSDAP chapter in Eltersdorf (Franconia) by June 1932. Percentages calculated on the basis of information in NSDAP Eltersdorf membership list, June 1, 1932, appended to memorandum Ortsgruppenleiter, Etersdorf June 19, 1942, SAN, 503/96.

⊗ middle is overrepresented

ists and German People's parties (DNVP and DVP respectively). Many voters who formerly cast ballots for these parties switched to the Nazis. The Catholic Center Party (Zentrum) and Bavarian People's Party (BVP) maintained their electorate, as did the German Communist Party (KPD), which gained votes at the expense of the Social Democratic Party (SPD).

20. Nazi Propaganda Tactics

The organizational structure of the NSDAP included a propaganda department headed at the national level by Joseph Goebbels from 1929 on. Each *Gau*, or region, also had its own propaganda department, as did all lower levels of the party's organizational structure. Propaganda directives and local informational reports were relayed along this chain of command. Nazi propaganda offices were as a result quite adept at tailoring themes or slogans to local audiences and made effective use of posters and pamphlets from the Reich Propaganda Office, which supplied particular messages. The party also employed trained orators who were well versed on specific topics. Just in the sheer volume of propaganda activity, the Nazis could not be outdone. They literally saturated targeted regions with rallies just prior to elections. These tactics produced remarkable results in the Reichstag election of September 1930, making the NSDAP a party of mass appeal. The report of May 1930 of the Prussian Ministry of the Interior, which monitored the activities of political parties, describes some of the Nazis' tactics.

. . . The rapid and steady growth of the National Socialist movement is due primarily to the catastrophic worsening of the economic condition of large segments of the population. Gaining more adherents is the perception that only a fundamentally different political and economic basis can check this development. Since the economic situation is the result of the lost war and its financial ramifications, the propaganda of the National Socialists is gaining more and more support. They call for a fundamental elimination of the "tribute obligations" to foreign countries and want to reach this goal by changing the domestic political power relationships in favor of a National Socialist regime in the form of a "third Reich." It is primarily economic despair that is winning followers for National Socialism because these groups see a radical change as their only hope. . . .

It is noteworthy that the majority of the supporters of National Socialism come especially from those segments of the population which have been hardest hit by the present economic distress. Included are, on the one hand, those who have been affected by the misery of the agricultural

From Niedersächsisches Staatsarchiv Hannover, Hann. 80, Hann. II, nr. 777, in Herbert Michaelis and Ernst Schraepler (eds.), *Ursachen und Folgen vom deutschen Zusammenbruch 1918 und 1945* (Berlin: Dokumenten-Verlag Dr. Herbert Wendler, 1958), vol. 8, pp. 328–33. Translated by Dieter Kuntz.

situation as well as, on the other hand, the gradually slipping middle class comprised of small scale businessmen in small towns which has suffered from the high cost of credit and the competition of large businesses. Included too are salaried personnel who have already lost their jobs, or for whom unemployment threatens. And finally also included is the new, young academic talent — that is, students and university scholars who because of the economic situation have lost all hope of making a living in the future. Added to this lately is a not inconsiderable number of lower- and middle-ranking officials, especially from administrative offices . . . such as the postal service, the railroad administration, the revenue service, as well as from the ranks of teachers. In contrast to the working class, which in this situation tends more toward communism, these groups are seeking to avoid at all cost sinking to the level of the "proletariat," and consequently see their salvation embodied by the other, "non-Marxist" radicalism — National Socialism. . . .

Added to this is the important factor of the type and scope of the party's propaganda. Selected districts are veritably inundated and worked-over with propaganda operations consisting of methodically and skillfully prepared written and verbal appeals as well as a schedule of meetings, all of which in terms of sheer activity cannot in the least be matched by any other party or political movement.

Hardly a day passes when there are not several meetings held in even very narrowly defined local areas. Carefully organized propaganda headquarters in the individual districts see to it that speakers and topics are in tune with local conditions and economic circumstances. The party's Reichstag and Landtag [regional parliament] delegates as well as a great number of other party speakers are on the road continually, developing and expanding these agitation tactics. Through systematic training courses, correspondence courses, and recently through the NSDAP speaker-training school established on July 1, 1929, such agitators are trained for this task over a period of months and even years. If they prove to be qualified they receive official recognition from the party and are given a contract to give at least thirty speeches during an eight-month period, for which they are granted an incentive fee of 20 Reichsmark per evening in addition to expenses.

Rhetorical skills are combined with lecture topics carefully selected to suit the particular audience, which in the rural areas and in small towns is mainly interested in economic matters. This, according to our observations, ensures that meeting halls are almost invariably overcrowded with approving listeners. Meetings with an audience of between one thousand and five thousand people are a daily occurrence in the bigger cities. . . . At these events the government's entire internal and foreign policy is attacked in a demagogical style that does not shy away even from falsification, distortion, and slander. They are abusive and contemptuous of the government and blame it for the economic crisis. . . .

This propaganda is backed up almost everywhere by the simultaneous appearance of SA people, who, on bicycles or on trucks — some belonging to the party — go to the individual meetings in an area and merely through being there give a speaker considerable support, help fill the hall itself, act as a protective force for the meeting, and in the end also act as a coercive force in that they allow no one to interject or contradict the speaker, which more or less makes it impossible for anyone to make counterarguments. By their public appearance they directly and indirectly help advertise the meeting, and thereby support the speaker's propaganda, entice sympathizers and the curious, and ultimately through their organization of parades in uniform they win supporters locally, primarily from among the younger generation.

On such occasions the network of local groups is expanded as far as possible, or at least trusted individuals are recruited in order to lay the groundwork for the expansion of the movement through intensive, pervasive word-of-mouth propaganda. Frequently such propaganda squads remain in a certain place for several days and attempt to inspire support for the Party from the local population by staging a variety of events such as concerts, sports festivals, military marching spectacles, as well as even closed-rank church attendance in suitable towns. In other towns a propaganda speaker from elsewhere will be stationed for a certain length of time; with a car at his disposal, he will then systematically travel through the surrounding area. National Socialist theater groups also travel from town to town, serving the same purpose. . . .

21. The Targets of Nazi Propaganda

The Reichstag elections of 1930 propelled the Nazi Party into national prominence and made it a party of mass appeal by 1932. The economic crisis fueled by the stock market crash of 1929 in the United States had by 1930 created three million unemployed in Germany. Many Germans remembered the economic chaos of 1923 and feared a repetition. The Nazis increased their support among the middle classes because of their fear of unemployment and the possibility of a communist revolution. Workers, too, became more radicalized because as a group they accounted for the greatest percentage of the unemployed, but they tended to lean toward the German Communist Party. Nonetheless, the Nazis did not concede the workers to the leftist parties.

The police and regional governments closely monitored the activities of political parties and attempted to assess the public attitudes. The first document below is

From F. J. Heyen (ed.), *Nationalsozialismus im Alltag: Quellen zur Geschicte des Nationalsozialismus* im *Raum Mainz-Koblenz-Trier* (Boppard, West Germany: H. Boldt Verlag, 1967), pp. 21–29, 49–53. Translated by Dieter Kuntz. Reprinted by permission of Landesarchiv, Rheinland-Pfalz.

a police report from the Mosel Valley, filed in 1930, which details Nazi propaganda tactics in this agricultural area. Vintners, like other farmers, were hard hit by the depressed economy, and many turned to the NSDAP for help.

In February 1931 the district council president of Koblenz compiled the second document, a report indicating the tremendous gains made by the Nazis during the first year of the economic crisis. It also testifies to the Nazis' energetic propaganda efforts and their continued attempts to gain worker support.

POLICE REPORT FROM THE MOSEL VALLEY, APRIL 1930

From the region Trier-Traben-Trarbach: The political attitudes of the vintners is being shaped by the economic situation. In all towns the same opinions are being expressed: "If only the sale of wines could be increased, then everything would be all right." In Catholic regions, the Center Party has until now had the most support, while in the Protestant areas it has been the German Nationalist Party. The Center has lost many supporters, even in the Catholic areas, because it is alleged to have cooperated too much with the Social Democrats, and also because it voted in favor of the Young Plan. . . .

The National Socialists are taking advantage of the discordant attitude among vintners, and are using their demagogical tactics. Until now, however, they have not had much success in the area between Trier and Bernkastel. They are attracting a strong following in Protestant areas. Lately they have even gained significant influence in Catholic villages. Vintners are, like the people of the hill country, easily influenced. They uncritically believe in the message of the National Socialists. The NSDAP is very systematic in its agitation tactics. They first test the mood of the population and then shape their propaganda meetings accordingly. Their tactics are basically the same everywhere: opposition to taxes and higher salaries for government officials, and opposition to the Young Plan. Many older vintners . . . regard the NSDAP propaganda as mere child's play and feel that the German Nationalists have more influence than the NSDAP. Younger people, however, are easily won over to the ideas of the NSDAP. Many are hesitant to become party members because of the high membership dues. But the National Socialist idea has taken root in the minds of many who are convinced that only the NSDAP has a way out of the present plight. . . .

The success of the National Socialists in various towns is not as impressive as the National Socialists portray it. Their success is limited, at least in the towns between Trier and Trarbach, solely to gains among young people, who like the "military" flavor of National Socialist events, although these youths are politically immature and themselves lack rhetorical talents. The National Socialists are forced to bring in suitable party speakers from elsewhere. Nonetheless, the gains they are making among youths are noteworthy. . . .

REPORT OF THE DISTRICT COUNCIL PRESIDENT OF THE KOBLENZ REGION TO THE SENIOR COUNCIL PRESIDENT OF THE RHINE REGION, FEBRUARY 14, 1931

Whereas the NSDAP attracted 14,589 votes out of a total of 360,397 valid votes cast during the municipal elections in the fall of 1929, their vote total in the Reichstag election of September 14, 1930, rose to 56,699 out of 389,565 cast. Naturally, based on this electoral success, the NSDAP wanted to encourage even greater interest among these newly gained voters for the party, and sought to win them by expanding the party organization. Beyond that, they attempted to attract new voters from among groups that now noticed the party because of its electoral success.

All of this explains the fact that the NSDAP continued its propaganda in the same fashion even after the Reichstag elections, whereas the moderate political parties only rarely engaged in public activity. . . . The main content of the National Socialist propaganda exhausts itself again and again in struggle against Marxism, Social Democracy, the parties of the middle (especially the Center) the political goings-on in today's state, financial mismanagement, the Young Plan, and the scaling back of high salaries.

The NSDAP always emphasizes that the constitutional changes it plans to undertake will be strictly legal. This, they maintain, will not be overly difficult to accomplish, given a further large gain in Reichstag delegates in the next election, which they feel will take place yet this year. On the whole, National Socialist speakers repeatedly emphasize that it will all come to a head this year. . . .

It is noteworthy that the NSDAP is now with increased intensity attempting to gain influence in working-class circles. They are doing this by organizing National Socialist factory cells. . . . The members of the NSDAP are not to quit the liberal trade unions, but are instead to undermine the liberal unions by working for the National Socialist cause and building their own union cells. Only when an adequate number of workers has been won for National Socialism are they all to switch over to the "National Trade Union." . . .

22. The Meaning of the Electoral Breakthrough in 1930

The Nazis had expected to do well in the Reichstag elections of September 14, 1930, but the results stunned even Hitler. The NSDAP increased its voting support

From *Völkischer Beobachter*, September 18, 1930. Translated by Dieter Kuntz.

from 800,000 in 1928 to 6.5 million, or 18.3 percent of the total vote. This victory gave the Nazis 107 seats in the Reichstag, making it the second largest delegation, whereas previously the party had been represented by a small but noisy twelve-member delegation.

Two days later the NSDAP held a mass meeting in the Circus Krone building in Munich which featured Hitler as the main speaker. Brimming with confidence, he declared to the assembly that the Nazis' success in the election was just a first step toward the twin goals of removing all vestiges of the humiliation of November 1918 and effecting a "revolution of the German soul." Hitler's speech was printed in the NSDAP's newspaper, the *Völkischer Beobachter.*

We have won a great, hard-fought victory. The National Socialist movement can state that the greatest difficulty is behind us, because we do not regard the struggle itself to be the most difficult thing, but rather see the perceived hopelessness of the struggle as the most difficult thing we had to overcome. What was hardest during this time was that all our ambitions and intentions went for naught because no one listened to us. What we wanted was irrelevant in those days, and what we hoped for was of no consequence at all. The fact is that fundamentally no one understood our hopes, no one came to know our aspirations, no one even took notice of us. . . .

The battle we have been waging for almost eleven years is not a political battle for our goals but is instead a battle to eliminate those forces and powers that are blocking the realization of these goals, and who do not at all want to see those things we are fighting for realized, namely the resurgence of Germany. They wish instead to continue their policy of November 1918 and to humble Germany even more until she collapses altogether. . . .

Many years ago a vile idea took root in the minds of many. This idea basically had one goal: Germany's position as a powerful state should be destroyed and the German people should not become a political power factor! A foreign race, enmeshed in international interests, tried to take over the leadership of our people and had as its goal the collapse of the German state and German people. First they killed the spirit, and with the loss of spirit our people became enslaved. Political bondage was tolerated and was transformed into economic slavery. This translated into misery for millions of individuals. But the misery of these millions will prompt the uprising, meaning that the people will now begin to listen. The spirit of resistance is the inevitable result of this collapse, just as this collapse is the result of this system [the Weimar government], and this system is the inevitable result of the wish to come to this end. And so the cycle is complete.

Now the question is raised: What does this resistance want to accomplish? And what do these men want who use the great misery of the people — our opponents are quite right about that — when they make

103

their appeal to conscience, to honor, to political reason, and so on? What do these men want? What is their goal? Do they want to form a new government? No, it would be absurd to think that such a narrow goal could make good the damages. . . .

. . . Parliament is for us not the goal, but the means to an end. We are not a parliamentary party out of conviction; that would be a misinterpretation. We are a parliamentary party out of compulsion and out of necessity. The compulsion is dictated by the Constitution. The Constitution forces us to employ these tactics. But the Constitution does not compel us to aim for a certain goal; it merely specifies which path to take. It prescribes a method, and we — I repeat this again today — will take the legal, constitutional path. We are taking the path specified by the Constitution in order to reach the goals outlined by us. No constitution can forever prescribe the essence of a goal, especially not when this essence is identical to the right to existence of a people. . . .

We want to resurrect the values of our people, to free their values from tumors and deformities and raise them to a commanding level. We want to ground these basic values, these racial values, in logic to base them solidly on reason. This will mean the elimination of democracy and of the parliamentary system. We want these values of the German people, of the German race, to reach this highest level. This can be achieved by taking proper care of these values. This stewardship can only be based on logic, reason, and human insight and experience, and this insight and experience leads us on the road toward authority of the personality. . . .

From purity of race, strength of character and personal authority, and a fighting spirit spring those values that alone can allow a people to look with hope toward the future. These are the preconditions for the kind of life the people desire. Only after this has been established can those things be established which today's political parties long to create: prosperity, individual happiness, family life, and so forth. . . .

And so the victory which we have achieved is nothing more than a new weapon for the battle. In the legal fencing room [the Reichstag] of our current history stand 107 men. These 107 men will prove that we National Socialists can not only rouse and sway the masses, but that we are able to participate in the foil fencing that goes on in this hall. In this hall we will confidently take advantage of all opportunities that can bring us closer to our goal, but from this hall we will uninterruptedly emphasize and proclaim that this in itself is not our goal. We are not fighting for representative mandates; we are, however, capturing them so that we someday liberate the German people. . . .

Our victory today has enabled us to be noticed by the general public not only in Germany, but also far across our people's borders, because we can no longer be overlooked. First it is necessary to see properly; then the German people will slowly realize their mistakes, and such foolishness as we are currently experiencing will seem unthinkable within a few years. Everyone will know, not only in Germany but elsewhere, what the National Socialists want.

But it is also clear that this victory, which has not in the least realized our goal but has only provided us with new opportunities to energetically stride toward it, does not mean that we will rest. On the contrary, what a Prussian general once said about having to pursue the opponent to the last breath of man and horse applies to political life as well. Our opponents can be assured that we will not rest during this battle until we have reached our goal. This goal is not called upheaval or *putsch*; it is revolution of the German soul, conquest of the German people. The reckoning with the seducers we will leave to the sovereign German people.

We only want to be able to guarantee that our people will then bestow on themselves a constitution that will make another November 1918 impossible in the future, that should make impossible a repeat of the sorrow, grief, poverty, and misery that resulted from November 1918. . . .

23. Hitler's Pledge of Legality

Several days after the September 1930 Reichstag election, Hitler made a public appearance in Leipzig at the sensational trial of three army officers who had been charged with conducting subversive activities. The three were accused of having NSDAP connections and proselytizing for the Nazis among the ranks of the army. The defense based its case on establishing the innocuous nature of the NSDAP. Hitler was asked to testify and explain the methods and goals of his party.

Hitler gave his testimony on September 25, 1930, the third day of the trial, and, just as in 1924, used the opportunity to convey his political aims to the national press. He answered the court's questions about the party's position on legality with the assurance that his movement had "no need of force," and that he would use legal, constitutional means to bring about his conceived Third Reich. Revolution meant a "national revolution," which, Hitler maintained, meant diplomatic reversal of the Treaty of Versailles. He also hinted, however, that once power was "constitutionally" theirs, the Nazis would deal harshly with those responsible for November 1918. Violence was in effect cloaked in legality.

The witness, Adolf Hitler testified that he was born on 20 April 1889 in Braunau on the Inn, without citizenship.

President: You have been invited to testify at the request of Dr. Frank to give evidence that the NSDAP is striving to attain its goal by purely

From *Frankfurter Zeitung*, September 26, 1930, in Office of the United States Chief of Counsel for the Prosecution of Axis Criminality, *Nazi Conspiracy and Aggression* (Washington, D.C.: U.S. Government Printing Office, 1946), vol. 5, doc. no. 2512-PS, pp. 246–51.

legal means, does not intend to take violent action against the Constitution or Government neither encourages its members or supporters to violent action against Constitution or Government or even to prepare for this, even in 1923. I ask you to describe in broad outline the evolution of the Nazi Party.

You are to consider this matter objectively. You are not here to defend the existence of the Party. No one has attacked you. You should confine your statements and facts to actual evidence. You will be obliged as a witness to swear this on oath. (*Then the President referred the witness to Art. 55 of the Penal Law, whereby he might refuse to give evidence if he would as a result jeopardize himself or place himself in danger of criminal proceedings.*)

Hitler: I fought on the Westfront as a German soldier in the fall of 1918. At that time I already saw the collapse coming. This resulted because all political organizations were suffering from the same sickness. There are in general three phenomena which always reappear at such times, when the country is declining and which have slowly disintegrated the German people also. The nonutilization of our own national strength brought about by the general international attitude.

President: I believe that the witness is wandering from the point. Will you please describe the formation of the Party.

Hitler: I wanted first of all to depict the three main points, because they will show the type of struggle we are waging.

President: If you think this necessary, please proceed.

Hitler: The second factor is the setting aside of all authority and the third the pacifist spirit, the pandering to corrupt influences and the international feeling in general. It is obvious that the only kind of movement which could rise above this debacle is one which makes a determined stand against these aspects. But this can only be a new movement in consideration of the fact that all the old Parties were bound in theory to fight for freedom, when in actual fact since 1918, mob rule has prevailed. We had to take up the struggle fanatically for everything German [Deutschtum] and if necessary defend this spirit; thus our two-fold organization. That is where our Protection Detachments [Schutz-abteilungen] originated. They were exclusively for the purpose of pro-tecting the Party propaganda, but not to fight against the State. I have been a soldier so long that I know it is impossible to allow a Party Organization to fight against the disciplined organization of the Armed Forces, or against the *Freikorps* and police. When meetings are dis-turbed and disrupted, only then does the State step in and dissolve the gathering. But in this way those attempting the disturbance achieve their aim. In the beginning therefore it was only possible to carry on at all, if one took one's own steps against such a pantomime. That was the sole purpose of our Sturmabteilungen [SA]. It is obvious that a movement of many thousands of people cannot be judged on the statements of individuals.

(*The President then drew the attention of the Court to the Happenings in Munich in 1923*)

Hitler: I don't know whether I may speak about them.

President: I believe the Public is fully informed today of these occurrences. You, witness were sentenced on 1 April 1924 to five years confinement in a fortress for high treason. Furthermore it was also said at the Party Rally [Parteitag] in Nuremberg in September 1923 that the Party was a fighting organization and that force would certainly be used.

Hitler: At that time, the SA were going to be changed into a military organization. I myself did not make them into soliders, they were forced into being soldiers. [Nicht ich habe damals die Abteilungen in die Kasernen hineingefuehrt sondern sie sind hineingefuehrt worden] The situation was such that the latent state of war between the Reich and Bavaria had to break out. But I asserted in 1925 that the happenings in 1923 must be completely forgotten and that the movement must be led back to its basic aims. I published a decree completely prohibiting arms for the SA. On no account were they to assume a military character. Rather should all the SA serve exclusively to protect the movement from other Parties. All military exercises were forbidden and if a platoon was in possession of arms and one single one of them had a weapon in his possession without a license then these platoons were dissolved and their members expelled. I did everything to prevent the organization from assuming any kind of military character. This was particularly difficult at a time when one tried to equal the Fascists as best one could, and because of the inward pleasure it gives the German people, to carry a gun. I have always expressed the opinion that any attempt to replace the Reichswehr would be senseless. (*In an excited voice:*) We are none of us interested in replacing the Reichswehr, I have only one wish, that the German Reich and the German people imbibe a new spirit.

(*As the witness became more and more excited, the President warned him to discontinue this public propaganda and to confine himself to actual evidence.*)

Hitler: Naturally a movement which aspires to take over the State will bring to the forefront the idea of being able to defend oneself.

> We want to make sure once and for all that out of the present German Reichswehr a great German Peoples Army is formed.

There are thousands of young men in the Reichswehr of the same opinion. But that does not mean the replacement (of the Reichswehr). Nevertheless we regard the realization of this conception as the first essential for the future of Germany.

President: You could hardly attempt to carry our these ideals, purely by legal means. There is something else inferred in your program even if it is only between the lines.

Hitler: It would not be possible to lead such a great organization as ours, if we wanted to issue secret directives in addition to our public announcements. It would also be impossible after it had been publicly announced that no military exercises were to be carried out, nevertheless to carry out these. On questions of this kind only my orders are valid. All my political opponents and the State can control my speeches and directives. But above all this my basic principle holds good: if a (party) regulation conflicts with the Law, it is not to be carried out. I am even now punishing the failure to comply with my orders. Countless Party members have been expelled for this reason; among them Otto Strasser.

> Otto Strasser actually toyed with the idea of revolution. I never declared myself in agreement with this.

(The President then put statements to the debate, which had been made by the NSDAP author Reinhold Muchow. In these it was said that those countries with older constitutions had already had their revolution. But that Germany was on the threshold of a revolution and that this imminent revolution could only be National Socialist.)

Hitler: I think Mr. Muchow only wanted to illustrate a general spiritual movement. But I may assure you that if the Nazi movement's struggle is successful, then there will be a Nazi Court of Law too, the November 1918 revolution will be atoned, and there'll be some heads chopped off. *(Cheers from the gallery; the President asked that the applause be discontinued and said: We are in Court and are here to seriously dispense justice.)*

President (to the witness Hitler): What do you mean by the expression "German National Revolution"?

Hitler: The expression "National Revolution" should always be considered in a purely political sense. For the Nazis it is simply an uprising by the oppressed German people of today.

President: Do you mean independent movement, or one instigated by a Party?

Hitler: Naturally a movement will always represent an uprising, but it does not need to prepare it by illegal means. If we were to have two or three elections today, the Nazi movement would have the majority in the Reichstag and would prepare the Nazi revolution then.

President: You mean the spiritual (revolution)? And if we understand something different by this, you will say "We can't do anything about that."

Hitler: Germany is being strangled by Peace Treaties. All German legislation today is nothing more than an attempt to foist the Peace Treaty onto the German people. The Nazis do not consider the Treaty as a

[handwritten margin note: Violence towards those who signed Versailles Treaty]

law, but as something forced upon us. We do not want future generations, who are completely innocent, to be encumbered by this. When
we fight this with all the means at our disposal, then we are on the way
to a revolution.

President: Even by illegal means?

Hitler: I will declare here and now, that when we have become powerful
[gesiegt haben] then we will fight against the Treaty with all the means
at our disposal, even those which are illegal from the world's point of
view.

(*The President then referred to another pamphlet by Helmuth Brückner,
in which it says "Reform is only a half measure, revolution goes all the way."*)

Hitler: The German National People's Party is an opposition party just as
we are. But the German National People's Party is a reform party. The
Nazi movement sees as the core of the State, that which is summed up
in the term "people" (*Volk*). Therefore we cannot be compared with
other Parties. But it cannot therefore be said, because we used other
methods — therefore by force — Our propaganda is the spiritual revo-
lutionizing of the German people. This change is at least as gigantic as
that brought about by the Marxist ideology. It is a completely new
world. Our movement has no need of force. The time will come when
the German nation will get to know our ideas. Then 35 million Germans
will stand behind me. Whether we take over the Government today or
form an opposition is immaterial to us. The next election will increase
the number of Nazis in the Reichstag from 107–200. There will come
a time when people will be glad that there is such a movement, the
members of which are now trembling before the Court. Our opponents
are interested in representing our movement as anti-state, because they
know our goal is to be attained by legal means. Nevertheless they realize
that our movement must lead to a complete change of State.

President: What relation does this bear to the so-called Third Reich?

Hitler: We honor the memory of the old German Empire, we have fought
for it. But this State had an inner weakness from the very beginning.
Out of it came the present Germany. It is the embodiment of Democracy
and Internationalism. This second State wants to leave the German
people no men behind, who will defend their rights before the world.
We hope, therefore, for a new Reich in which all institutions —
beginning with the organization of the State itself down to those which
serve to maintain the national life [*Volkstum*] — will lead the people
towards a splendid future. It is only natural that this Third Reich will
quarrel with the decadent forces of today. Consequently the attempts
by our opponents to designate our methods as illegal and to attribute
to us a trend which we do not have. He who maintains that isolated
quotations are proof of a point of view, which he cannot construe from
regulations and Party orders, will find a thousand possibilities for this.

I have in our movement countless millions of people, whose hearts bleed for Germany. These young men, themselves fighters, are pushed about, come before the Court, although they had only the best intentions. They are struck down and hounded by the "red" mobs. That these people make statements, which are not in accordance with the spirit of the movement, is understandable because of their youth.

President: How do you imagine the setting up of a Third Reich?

Hitler: This term only describes the basis of the struggle but not the objective. We will enter the legal organizations and will make our Party a decisive factor in this way. But when we do possess constitutional rights then we will form the State in the manner which we consider to be the right one.

President: This too by constitutional means?

Hitler: Yes.

24. Hitler Appeals for Support from German Industrialists

The many public meetings of the NSDAP brought revenue into the party treasury, as did membership dues and newspaper sales. Nonetheless, financial mismanagement at the local and regional level often resulted in less money being funneled to headquarters in Munich than desired.

Hitler was consequently eager to expand the party's base of support in the wealthiest segments of society. This was not easy because to most industrialists and bankers the party represented a radical fringe of German politics. In an effort to assuage the fears of big business and win financial favor, Hitler made a two-and-a-half-hour speech to the members of the Industry Club in Düsseldorf. He had been invited to speak to the club by Fritz Thyssen, a steel magnate who was also a member and financial supporter of the NSDAP. In this speech given in January 1932, Hitler portrayed his movement as anticommunist and protective of big business and private property. Although he received "tumultuous" applause, the hoped-for financial support did not materialize.

If to-day the National Socialist Movement is regarded amongst widespread circles in Germany as being hostile to our business life, I believe the reason for this view is to be found in the fact that we adopted towards the events which determined the development leading to our present position an attitude which differed from that of all the other organizations which are of any importance in our public life. Even now our outlook differs in many points from that of our opponents.

From Norman Baynes, ed., *The Speeches of Adolf Hitler* (New York: Fertig, 1969), pp. 177–78, 826–29. Reprinted by permission of the Royal Institute of International Affairs, London.

Our conviction is that our present distress has not its final and deepest cause in general world-happenings which would therefore from the outset more or less exclude any possibility for a single people to better its position. If it were true that the cause of distress in Germany is to be found solely in a so-called world-crisis from which none can escape — a world-crisis on the course of which we as a people could naturally exercise no influence or at best only an infinitesimal influence — then we should be forced to characterize Germany's future as hopeless. . . .

I regard it as of the first importance to break once and for all with the view that our destiny is conditioned by world-events. It is not true that our distress has its final cause in a world-crisis, in a world-catastrophe: the true view is that we have reached a state of general crisis, because from the first certain mistakes were made. . . .

If I speak to you to-day it is not to ask for your votes or to induce you on my account to do this or that for the Party. No, I am here to expound a point of view, and I am convinced that the victory of this point of view would mean the only possible starting-point for a German recovery; it is indeed the last item standing to the credit of the German people. I hear it said so often by our opponents, "You, too, will be unable to master the present crisis." Supposing, gentlemen, that they are right, what would that mean? It would mean that we should be facing a ghastly period and that we should have to meet it with no other defences than a purely materialistic outlook on every side. And then the distress would, simply in its material aspect, be a thousandfold harder to bear, if one had failed to restore to the people any ideal whatsoever.

People say to me so often: "You are only the drummer of national Germany." And supposing that I were only the drummer? It would to-day be a far more statesmanlike achievement to drum once more into this German people a new faith than gradually to squander the only faith they have. Take the case of a fortress, imagine that it is reduced to extreme privations: as long as the garrison sees a possible salvation, believes in it, hopes for it, so long they can bear the reduced ration. But take from the hearts of men their last belief in the possibility of salvation, in a better future — take that completely from them, and you will see how these men suddenly regard their reduced rations as the most important thing in life. The more you bring it home to their consciousness that they are only objects for men to bargain with, that they are only prisoners of world-politics, the more will they, like all prisoners, concentrate their thoughts on purely material interests. On the other hand, the more you bring back a people into the sphere of faith, of ideals, the more will it cease to regard material distress as the one and only thing which counts. And the weightiest evidence for the truth of that statement is our own German people. We would not ever forget that the German people waged wars of religion for 150 years with prodigious devotion, that hundreds of thousands of men once left their plot of land, their property, and their belongings simply for an ideal, simply for a conviction. We would never forget that during those 150 years there was no trace of even an ounce of material interests. Then you will understand how mighty is the force of an idea, of an ideal. Only so can you comprehend how it is that in our Movement today hundreds of thousands of young men are prepared at the risk of their lives to withstand our opponents. I know quite well, gentlemen, that when National Socialists march through the streets and suddenly in the evening there arise a tumult and commotion, then the *bourgeois* draws back the window-curtain, looks out, and says: Once more my night's rest disturbed: no more sleep for me. Why must the Nazis always be so provocative and run about the place at night? Gentlemen, if everyone thought like that, then no one's sleep at nights would be disturbed, it is true, but then the *bourgeois* today could not venture into the street. If everyone thought in that way, if these young folk had no ideal to move them and drive them forward, then certainly they would gladly be rid of these nocturnal fights. But remember that it means sacrifice when to-day many hundred thousands of SA. and SS. men of the National Socialist Movement every day have to mount on their lorries, protect meetings, undertake marches, sacrifice themselves night after night and then come back in the grey dawn either to workshop and factory or as unemployed to take the pittance of the dole: it means sacrifice when from the little which they possess they have further to buy their uniforms, their shirts, their badges, yes, and even pay their own fares. Believe me, there is already in all this the force of an ideal — a great ideal! And if the whole German nation to-day had the same faith in its vocation as these hundred thousands, if the whole nation possessed this idealism, Germany would stand in the eyes of the world otherwise than she stands now! (*Loud applause.*) For our situation in the world in its fatal effects is but the result of our own underestimate of German strength. (*Very true!*) Only when we have once more changed this fatal valuation of ourselves can Germany take advantage of the political possibilities which, if we look far enough into the future, can place German life once more upon a natural and secure basis — and that means either new living-space [*Lebensraum*] and the development of a great internal market or protection of German economic life against the world without and utilization of all the concentrated strength of Germany. The labour resources of our people, the capacities, we have them already: no one can deny that we are industrious. But we must first refashion the political pre-conditions: without that, industry and capacity, diligence and economy are in the last resort of no avail, for an oppressed nation will not be able to spend on its own welfare even the fruits of its own economy but must sacrifice them on the alter of exactions and of tribute.

And so in contrast to our own official Government I cannot see any hope for the resurrection of Germany if we regard the foreign politics of Germany as the primary factor: the primary necessity is the restoration of a sound national German body-politic armed to strike. In order to realize this end I founded thirteen years ago the National Socialist Movement: that Movement I have led during the last twelve years, and I hope that one day it will accomplish this task and that, as the fairest result of its struggle, it will leave behind it a German body-politic completely renewed internally, intolerant of anyone who sins against the nation and its interests, intolerant against anyone who will not acknowledge its vital interests or who opposes them, intolerant and pitiless against anyone who shall attempt once more to destroy or disintegrate this body-politic, and yet ready for friendship and peace with anyone who has a wish for peace and friendship. (*Long and tumultuous applause.*)

25. The Presidential Election of 1932: Hindenburg or Hitler?

Hindenburg's term as president expired in March of 1932. The field marshal did not want to run for a second term and entered the campaign reluctantly, persuaded by supporters that he was the only possible candidate who could prevent the election of Hitler, the candidate of the surging Nazi Party. The moderate Weimar parties (including the Social Democrats) supported Hindenburg because he represented the best hope of preserving democracy. This portent was ominous for the future of the Weimar Republic because Hindenburg was not a republican at heart and at the advanced age of eighty-four was showing signs of the onset of senility. The German Nationalists and the Communist Party also entered candidates, but the race was clearly between Hitler and Hindenburg. The dilemma of which candidate to choose is the subject of the following article by Otto Braun, the Social Democratic prime minister of the state of Prussia. The article was first published in the Social Democrats' newspaper, *Vorwärts* (Forward), in March 1932.

On the 13th of March the voters are to elect to the office of Reich president an individual who through his character and his activities must guarantee that he will administer the highest office that the German people can bestow, in a manner loyal to the republican Constitution, true to his oath, for the welfare of the whole German nation, and that he will never misuse the power bestowed upon him. Ebert, the first German Reich president, has no doubt proved that a Social Democrat can guarantee this to the

From *The Political Education of Arnold Brecht: An Autobiography, 1884–1970* (Princeton: Princeton University Press, 1970), pp. 333–34. Copyright © 1970 by Princeton University Press. Reprinted by permission. First paragraph of selection translated from *Vorwärts* of March 10, 1932, by Dieter Kuntz.

German people. And if even the remotest prospect existed that a Social Democratic candidate could secure a majority of the votes next Sunday, or in an eventual second ballot receive even a relative plurality, then a candidate could have been nominated and supported. This prospect, however, unfortunately does not exist. The insane politics of the Communists have precluded the election of a Social Democrat, for the Communists have confused a considerable number of the working masses who have been worn down by the economic misery and are being encouraged to pursue a phantom.

Hindenburg or Hitler? Between these two the voters have to choose. Can that choice be difficult? Look at them! Hitler, this prototype of political adventurer, whose demagogic agitation, fed from dark financial sources, has gathered around him all despairing, hopeless people, as well as those who out of capitalistic lust for profits, reactionary habits of thinking, or political stupidity are deadly hostile to our present popular form of government, and who has won their support for his nebulous Third Reich, which promises to everyone everything he wants, to each at the cost of the others.

Facing him, Hindenburg: embodiment of calm firmness, manly loyalty, and devotion to the fulfillment of his duties toward the entire nation; whose life lies clear before everyone's eyes; who has shown, and by no means least so during his seven years as President, that all those can rely on him who want to deliver Germany from chaotic conditions and to lead us upward out of our economic misery, in peaceful cooperation of all classes bound together in a common fate. . . .

Although my world view and my political standpoint separate me from Hindenburg by a deep chasm, human values, all too often neglected in political life, have built a bridge across it uniting us in the desire, each according to his conviction, to promote the welfare of the people. I have come to know the President as a man on whose word one can rely, a man of pure intentions and mature [abgeklärtem] judgment, filled with a Kantian sense of duty, which has caused him once more to place himself at the German people's disposal and to assume the heavy responsibilities of his office in spite of his age and his comprehensible yearning for rest.

Just because, true to his oath, he has stood by the people as defender of the Constitution they [the National Socialists] now pursue him with their venomous hatred, showering him with abuse and calumnies. That is why I stay by him. I vote for Hindenburg and I call on the millions who voted for me seven years ago, and beyond them on all those who have confidence in me and my policy: Do the same, defeat Hitler, elect Hindenburg.

26. The Brüning Government on the Verge of Collapse

Chancellor Brüning had not been able to solve the republic's economic problems during his two years in office and had lost more and more support because of his budget-tightening deflationary policies. Hindenburg too had lost confidence in him and was ready to look for a replacement. The fall of the Brüning government was anticipated with particular relish by Goebbels and the Nazis. Goebbels's diary entries from April and May of 1932, excerpts of which are printed below, also reveal the backstage political machinations that became commonplace during the crisis years of the Weimar government.

April 14th, 1932

In the afternoon towards five o'clock the SA is prohibited throughout the Reich. Groener has launched his bolt. But perhaps it will prove his own undoing.

We are informed that Schleicher does not agree with his action. Just as I am about to leave, the police begin taking over the Party building in Berlin. My heart fails me. One stroke of the pen ruins the work of years! So that is the way we, the representatives of young Germany, are to be treated!

Leave for Altona. Here prohibition of the SA has already been effected. But the spirit of the Party has not suffered in the least. On the contrary, everyone is furious.

Prohibitions can only ruin weak parties. They stimulate and heighten the fighting power of strong ones.

Schleswig-Holstein is entirely ours. In the morning, on my way back, I read the comments of the Press on the SA prohibition. They are fairly cool. The Nationalist Press seems to have doubts on the subject. . . .

'Phone call from a well-known lady, a friend of General Schleicher's. The General wants to resign. But perhaps this is only camouflage.

We hold a council with our lawyers and resolve to bring an action against the Reich. But all this is by the way. The chief thing is to come off victorious in the struggle in Prussia.

April 23rd, 1932

In the evening the results come through. An amazing victory for us! We have obtained one hundred and sixty mandates,[1] and have thus become

From Joseph Goebbels, *My Part in Germany's Fight* (London: Hurst and Blackett, 1935), pp. 76, 78, 82–88, 92–95, 98–99.

---

[1] The Nazis won 162 seats in the Prussian *Landtag*. They had formerly held only 9.

the strongest party in the country. In Prussia alone eight millions of voters have declared for us. The Nationalists only managed to obtain thirty odd mandates. The negligible parties have been defeated. The Centre has more or less preserved its average. The Socialists have had a bad knock, and the Communists are out of it compared to us. The former Coalition[2] is in a hopeless minority. The so-called Nationalists (Conservative) are (even in coalition with Centre and *bourgeois* parties) nine mandates short of the quorum able to constitute a Government. Something must happen now. We *must* shortly come to power, otherwise our victory will be a Pyrrhic one.

Late at night I drive to the Sportpalast dog-tired. The crowd there is in a frenzy of joy. I speak a few words, and then they let me go home.

'Phone to the Leader who is in Munich. In Bavaria, in Hamburg and Württemberg the situation is the same. But in Anhalt our figures suffice for the formation of a Government. Now we must have our wits about us, and keep our heads screwed on particularly tight. This is the time to test what sort of stuff one is made of.

April 25th, 1932
Issue new orders to the District Leaders. The Party must be overhauled within a month to be ready for every eventuality. But for us to make any sudden bid is out of the question at present. I instance the Peasant Wars.[3] The German Rising must not risk being drowned in blood.

The SA organization remains, of course. But it is much more difficult now to maintain discipline and internal order. We have to be on the alert.

Ring up the Leader at Munich and detail affairs. He will come to Berlin as soon as things are a bit more in shape.

The questionable business of attempting to form coalitions begins. I hope it will not be long spun out.

April 26th, 1932
The Press is very reserved. We have a difficult decision to make. Coalition with the Centre and Power, or opposition to the Centre minus the Power. From a parliamentary point of view, nothing can be achieved without the Centre — neither in Prussia nor in the Reich. This has to be thoroughly thought over.

---

[2] Goebbels here refers to the "Weimar coalition," composed of Social Democrats, the Catholic Center Party, and Democrats.

[3] A peasant insurrection in Germany in 1525, in which peasants demanded the abolition of serfdom, was crushed by the forces of the princes and feudal lords. The peasants lost not only the war but all their remaining rights as well, and became politically ineffective for centuries following. Goebbels feared that a similar fate awaited the Nazis if they acted prematurely.

April 29th, 1932
The Leader pays us a visit in the evening, and we talk things over. He is strongly against the idea of coalition with the Centre. That is satisfactory, anyway, even if as yet we do not see a way out of the difficulties. He who adheres firmly to the position he has once taken up will finally succeed. The prelates can be left in suspense for a little while. It will only tend to sober them.

May 3rd, 1932
. . . The Berlin Jews are making a fuss about the "Officers — Camarilla" and their intrigues against Brüning and Groener. So things are starting up already. We are really glad of it. The Party must absolutely hold its tongue. We must appear quite disinterested. Too much chatter always tends to put the wind-up again.

May 4th, 1932
In Munich I hold a few conferences, and then am off to the mountains.

A report comes from Berlin that some of Hitler's mines are beginning to explode. That is A1, and we rub our hands with satisfaction. The first to be blown up must be Groener, and after him Brüning.

On the way to Berchtesgaden[4] we meet with storm and rain. High up on the mountains with the Leader we feel at home again.

May 6th, 1932
On Friday morning papers come from Berlin. They are full of fault-finding and guesswork. We do not let them disturb our peace, but go on sunning ourselves here, until a sudden 'phone call puts an end to this idyll. The bomb has exploded. The Minister of Economy has tendered his resignation, and Groener and Brüning are tottering to their fall. So that's the end of things here. The Leader must return to Berlin immediately. On the way we scheme out daring things. We are guests of the Leader for an hour at Munich, and leave for Berlin by the night train.

We hold tremendous private confabulations in sleepers; how little the conductor dreams what they are all about!

May 8th, 1932
On Saturday the delegates come and give us some information. The Leader has an important interview with Schleicher in the presence of a few gentlemen of the President's immediate circle.

All goes well. The Leader has spoken decisively. Brüning's fall is expected shortly. The President of the Reich will withdraw his confidence in him.

---

[4] Berchtesgaden is a German town in southeast Bavaria, famous as a winter resort. Hitler maintained an estate in the mountains there.

The plan is to constitute a Presidential Cabinet. The Reichstag will be dissolved. Repressive enactments are to be cancelled. We shall be free to go ahead as we like, and mean to outdo ourselves in regard to propaganda.

We require a week for preparation. The election campaign must be sharp and short. We shall employ squadrons of aeroplanes to work one province after the other. This at least is our intention. How odd it seems that nobody as yet has the slightest prevision; least of all Brüning himself. We are immensely keyed up, but doubtful still. If things turn out according to expectations our agents, headed by the Chief of Staff Roehm, have acquitted themselves in a masterly manner.

May 12th, 1932
In the evening the long-expected news comes through that Groener has resigned as Minister of the Reichswehr. That is the first result. He stumbled into his own trap, and we have tightly closed it.

The President of the Reich leaves for Neudeck. The great crisis is adjourned until next week. A respite for Brüning. I wonder if he will make use of it.

The Council sides with Loebe in the question of the prorogation of Parliament. The House dissolves until June. We shall see to it that it will not reopen. The parliamentary parties will be made to pay dearly for these sharp practices. I write an article roundly attacking the whole Cabinet.

One studies the Press minutely, for it is possible to detect between the lines how the opponents estimate their own chances. We have a slight advantage. . . . Groener's downfall is thought to be the beginning of the end. Late at night I give the Leader a description of the whole thing. He is extremely satisfied.

May 18th, 1932
Back in Berlin. The feeling of Whitsun is still in the air. For Brüning alone winter seems to have arrived. His position is becoming untenable. And the amusing part of it is that he does not seem to notice the fact. We've only to peg away! His Cabinet shrinks visibly, and he can find no substitutes for his losses. Nobody cares to espouse a hopeless cause. The rats flee from the sinking ship.

The organization in Berlin is recommissioned. The *Angriff*[5] has a good standing. That is reassuring. I decide on the policy once more with the editorial staff. The next steps to be taken in the district are discussed from the point of view of organization and propaganda. We are prepared for everything. Brüning is being severely attacked by our Press and Propaganda. Fall he must, whatever the cost.

---

[5] *Der Angriff* (The Attack) was a Nazi newspaper founded by Goebbels, given to sensationalism.

He is being secretly undermined. He is already completely isolated. He is anxiously looking for collaborators. "My kingdom for a Cabinet Minister!" General Schleicher has declined to accept the Reichswehr Ministry. From the Strasser side a sort of guerrilla warfare is in process. But we lay counter-mines. It is not at all easy to attain to power. Once it is ours, however, we can congratulate ourselves that we have deserved it. I accidentally and indirectly hear that Strasser intends to have a word with Brüning. That would be quite like him. We succeed in scotching the possibility!

Our mice are busily at work gnawing through the last supports of Brüning's position. The Press is groping in the dark. One fine day the whole building will crash.

Delightful May weather. The Leader has arrived in Berlin. I shall supply him with a few items of valuable information. Especially in the Strasser matter.

May 19th, 1932

The Leader has seen through everything long ago. He will intervene just at the right moment. Emissaries from General Schleicher; they are already drawing up the list of Ministers. A matter of no great importance: it has only to do with the transition period. Our Faction of the Prussian Diet assembles at the Hotel Prinz Albrecht. The Leader speaks with remarkable confidence.

In the Hamburg Party paper an ill-timed attack has been made on Schleicher. That is Strasser — that means the D.H.V.,[6] alias Trade Unions, alias Brüning. The person responsible will be expelled from the Party.

It is amusing to note how the Jewish Press, generally so well informed, is groping in the dark. It still believes we are hob-nobbing with the "Centre." Harmless idiots!

The Strasser clique is double-crossing us through the Parties and Trade Unions.

We have to keep a sharp look-out lest harm befall the Party.

The Leader makes a short trip to Idar, where he is speaking. But he will soon be back in Berlin.

May 24th, 1932

The Prussian Diet is opened. Through our confidential agents we are assured that we stand a good chance. Saturday will see the end of Brüning. Secretary of State, Meissner, leaves for Neudeck. Now we must hope for the best. The list of Ministers is more or less settled: Von Papen, Prime

---

[6] The Deutscher Handlungsgehilfen Verband was Germany's largest union of shop and office workers. It was nonpolitical.

Minister; Von Neurath, Minister of Foreign Affairs, and then a list of unfamiliar names. The main point as far as we are concerned is that the Reichstag is dissolved. Everything else can be arranged. The Prussian question can only be solved in this way.

May 30th, 1932
The bomb has exploded. Brüning has presented the resignation of the entire Cabinet to the President, at noon. The System has begun to crumble. The President has accepted the resignation. I at once ring up the Leader. Now he must immediately return to Berlin.

Discuss the situation at a great district and Press conference. The watchword [one party slogan or another] is given. Everybody overjoyed.

Go as far as Nauen to meet the Leader, who is coming up from Mecklenburg. The news of Brüning's downfall came through just as I was dictating the last article against him. So I could bid him farewell at once.

Meet the Leader at Nauen. The President wishes to see him in the course of the afternoon. I get into his car and give him a good all-round summary. We are enormously delighted. The whole country is relieved.

In Berlin we study the Press. Then the Leader goes on to see the President. In the evening I speak at the district meeting at the Tennishallen. They are overcrowded, and closed by the police. What a welcome! The party members of long standing are transported with enthusiasm. I speak for two hours and outline the situation.

Pay our SA at Wilmersdorf a short visit. The Leader is already waiting for me at home. The conference with the President went off well. The SA prohibition is going to be cancelled. Uniforms are to be allowed again. The Reichstag is going to be dissolved. That is of first importance.

Von Papen is likely to be appointed Chancellor, but that is neither here nor there. The Poll! the Poll! It's the people we want. We are all entirely satisfied.

27. Goebbels Reflects on the Seizure of Power

Adolf Hitler became chancellor of Germany at a time when the Nazi Party's political fortunes had apparently ebbed. The NSDAP had lost thirty-four seats in the November 1932 Reichstag elections as a result of a drop in votes for the party from the high of 37.2 percent in July of 1932 to 33.0 percent. Because of the high cost of financing frequent electoral campaigns, the party also had serious financial problems. It looked very much as though the Nazis would not be able to come to power after all — at least not through the electoral route. At this point, however,

From Joseph Goebbels, *My Part in Germany's Fight* (London: Hurst and Blackett, 1935), pp. 234–37.

Hitler received help from a small group of backstage intriguers who attempted to use the Nazis to further their own ambitions. This group was headed by former Chancellor Franz von Papen and included several other conservatives who deluded themselves into thinking that Hitler could be manipulated if they were to join with the Nazis in a coalition government. Hindenburg was finally swayed by this argument and ultimately agreed to make Hitler chancellor, even though he personally detested Hitler.

Appointed propaganda leader of the NSDAP in 1929, Joseph Goebbels had been extremely effective in organizing the Nazis' electoral campaigns, particularly during 1932, when the party reached its zenith in popular support. He was personally quite devoted to Hitler, seeming almost to idolize him, as entries in his diary suggest (for example, "Adolf Hitler, I love you!"). On the day of Hitler's appointment as chancellor of Germany, Goebbels felt nothing short of exhilaration as he recorded his thoughts.

January 29th, 1933

The Leader is in the midst of everlasting conferences. I make a final sally in an article: "The Road clear at last"!

In the afternoon, whilst we are having coffee with the Leader, Goering suddenly comes and reports everything to be A1. Tomorrow, the Leader is to be appointed Chancellor. One of our principal conditions is the dissolution of the Reichstag, as the Leader is unable to go on working with it as at present constituted. The Nationalists resist this with might and main. Their motives are more than obvious. This is surely Goering's happiest hour. And he is right. He has diplomatically and cleverly prepared the ground for the Leader in nerve-racking negotiations for months, or even years. His prudence, endurance, and above all, his firmness of character and loyalty to the Leader were genuine, strong and admirable. His face was turned to stone when, in the very thick of the fight, his beloved wife was torn from his side by death. But he did not flinch a second. Seriously and firmly he went on his way, a steadfast and devout shield-bearer to the Leader.

How often have he and I been together during the past years, and revived each other's courage! How often have our spirits been raised and fortified by our love of the Leader and by the untiring work for the common cause! Although our spheres of action were often wide apart we have each grown to respect and esteem the other's personality and accomplishments as loyal comrades whom neither distress nor crisis could sever.

This upright soldier with the heart of a child has always remained true to himself; and now he confronts the Leader and brings him the greatest piece of news of his life! We are quite unable to speak for some minutes; then we rise and solemnly shake hands.

A wordless vow to our Leader! As it has been, so it shall remain! The world will witness in us and through us, a splendid example of loyalty to the Leader, and an instance of the most beautiful companionship that *can* bind men together.

So be it!

In a talk with the Leader it is settled that I am to remain free of office till the end of the election campaign, so as to be able freely to carry on the election work. I have therefore a good opportunity to offer a last great proof of my ardour in this cause.

We are at home and are just about to leave for the Ausstellungshallen, to see the great (riding) exhibition there, when news is brought to us of a last dangerous move planned by our adversaries. We must keep our heads. One does not know if it is merely a threat, or something really serious, or just childishness. I inform the Leader at once, also Goering, both of whom are waiting in the next room. Goering at once informs Herr von Papen. Nothing is left undone to safeguard the following day.

We sit up till five o'clock in the morning, are ready for everything, and have considered the thing from all angles. The Leader paces up and down the room. A few hours' sleep and the decisive hour will strike.

The great hour has struck!

January 30th, 1933

It seems like a dream. The Wilhelmstrasse[1] is ours. The Leader is already working in Chancellory. We stand in the window upstairs, watching hundreds and thousands of people march past the aged President of the Reich and the young Chancellor in the flaming torchlight, shouting their joy and gratitude.

At noon we are all at the Kaiserhof, waiting. The Leader is with the President of the Reich. The inward excitement almost takes our breath away. In the street the crowd stands silently waiting between the Kaiserhof and the Chancellory. What is happening there? We are torn between doubt, hope, joy and despair. We have been deceived too often to be able whole-heartedly to believe in the great miracle.

Chief-of-Staff Roehm stands at the window the whole time, watching the door of the Chancellory from which the Leader must emerge. We shall be able to judge by his face if the interview was happy.

Torturing hours of waiting! At last a car draws up in front of the entrance. The crowd cheers. They seem to feel that a great change is taking place or has aready begun.

The Leader is coming.

A few moments later he is with us. He says nothing, and we all remain silent also. His eyes are full of tears. It has come! The Leader is appointed

---

[1] The Wilhelmstrasse was the street in Berlin where the chancellery was located. The name was a synonym for the German government.

Chancellor. He has already been sworn in by the President of the Reich. The final decision has been made. Germany is at a turning-point in her history.

All of us are dumb with emotion. Everyone clasps the Leader's hand; it would seem as if our old pact of loyalty were renewed at this moment.

Wonderful, how simple the Leader is in his greatness, and how great in his simplicity.

Outside the Kaiserhof the masses are in a wild uproar. In the meantime Hitler's appointment has become public. The thousands soon become tens of thousands. An endless stream of people floods the Wilhelmstrasse.

The day passes like a dream. Everything is like a fairy tale. Slowly the evening closes in over the Capital of the Reich. At seven o'clock Berlin resembles a swarming bee-hive. And then the torchlight procession begins./Endlessly, endlessly, from seven o'clock in the evening until one o'clock in the morning crowds march by the Chancellory. Storm Troopers, Hitler youths, civilians, men, women, fathers with their children held up high to see the Leader's window. Indescribable enthusiasm fills the streets. A few yards from the Chancellory, the President of the Reich stands at his window, a towering, dignified, heroic figure, invested with a touch of old-time marvel. Now and then with his cane he beats time to the military marches. Hundreds and thousands and hundreds of thousands march past our windows in never-ending, uniform rhythm|

The rising of a nation!

Germany has awakened!

In a spontaneous explosion of joy the people espouse the German Revolution.

What goes on within our hearts is indescribable. One feels like crying and laughing at the same time.

The everlasting stream of cheering people flows on and on and on. The tree-tops at the Wilhelmplatz in front of the Chancellory are swarming with boys who cheer the Leader in shrill ear-splitting chorus.

His people acclaim him!

For the first time the German people in demonstration is being broadcast. We speak for the first time over all German transmitters. I can say nothing, but that we are happy beyond words, and that we shall go on working.

When the jubilating defiles at last show some sign of coming to an end, long after midnight, ten thousand people still stand in front of the Chancellory and sing the "Horst-Wessel-Lied." I deliver a short address to the masses and close with three cheers for Hindenburg and the Leader. This miraculous night ends in a frenzy of enthusiasm.

| At length the square is empty. We close the windows and are surrounded by absolute silence. The Leader lays his hands on my shoulders in silence.\

Arrive home at three o'clock.

[handwritten margin notes: "like a great King out of fairy tale"; "a religious moment, view of politics that transcend rational discourse + debate"]

Nazi desire to restructure German culture prompted the regime to
encourage public burnings at universities of the works of authors
considered to be "un-German." Book burnings presaged the Nazis'
anti-intellectual cultural policies and drew adverse publicity abroad.

Chapter
4

Gleichschaltung:
The Coordination
of Party and State, 1933–1934

The official policy name *Gleichschaltung* denoted the permanent revolution by which Hitler brought all sectors of the state and society under Nazi control. Three stages made up this process of "coordination." First, an increase of executive power and the elimination of all potential sources of opposition were achieved through intensifying the power inherent in presidential rule and by liquidating the constitutional pluralistic state and replacing it with a one-party regime. The second stage brought the state bureaucracy and the federal structure as well as other organizations under central authority. The third phase neutralized the power of the SA and the army, the two remaining forces outside Hitler's immediate control.

Immediately on his appointment as chancellor, Hitler persuaded Hindenburg to dissolve the Reichstag once again. A recalcitrant parliament was suspended for seven decisive weeks, and the state continued to be ruled by emergency decrees. On this pseudolegal basis, freedom of the press was harshly curtailed (February 4), Prussia brought into line (February 6), basic rights repealed (February 28), and the states that still resisted National Socialist takeovers subjugated. In each instance the regime used political pressure and terror in combination with the power of the emergency decree to achieve its end. The Reichstag Fire Decree of February 28 suspended those sections of the Constitution which guaranteed civil and individual rights and authorized the government to use any methods, including house searches and arrests, to guard against "Communist acts of violence endangering the state." Armed with this decree, truckloads of Storm Troopers

125

rolled through the streets of German cities arresting Communists, Social Democrats, and the leaders of the liberal parties. The government radio station poured out a constant stream of revelations about communist conspiracies against the state. Yet when elections were held for the new Reichstag on March 5, 1933, the NSDAP did not gain a clear majority. The Nazis received 44 percent of the vote, giving them 288 seats in the Reichstag. In other words, 56 percent of the electorate held out against Hitler. Still, the Nazis had a working majority of 52 percent of the seats in the Reichstag since their allies, the German Nationalists, had won 52 positions.

With political control at the center guaranteed, *Gleichschaltung* then aimed at the separate states of the Reich. In March and April the new regime abolished the historical and constitutional rights of the states, dismissed their governments, and appointed Reich governors responsible solely to the national government. The Law for the Reconstitution of the Reich completed the process thus begun on the first anniversary of Hitler's assumption of power by formally transferring the states' sovereignty to the central government and putting their governors under the authority of the Ministry of the Interior. This move belies the claim that Hitler's actions were entirely constitutional. Since the Nazi takeover of the various states could not be achieved by parliamentary means, the National Socialists resorted to revolutionary, putschist methods to apply pressure from "the people" while at the same time providing pseudolegal protection for these tactics. The interplay of a stage-managed revolution from above and a manipulated revolution from below effected the takeover.

The second stage of *Gleichschaltung* (April–May) involved appropriating the bureaucratic structure of the state, purging all civil servants and members of the judiciary unfriendly to the NSDAP, merging the SS with the police forces, and smashing the trade unions and all professional organizations. Hitler first moved against the civil service. Because of the shortage of qualified personnel among the National Socialists, party members initially filled only key positions while the cooperation of the incumbent civil servants was won through promises and threats. The new rulers could rely on opportunism as well as bureaucratic susceptibility to nonparliamentary, hierarchical rule by a nondemocratic administrative state to secure the allegiance of the civil service. Although the state apparatus remained largely non–National Socialist despite numerous "March casualties," Hitler could depend on its continued smooth functioning by combining the appeal to the nationalist and antidemocratic, authoritarian tradition of German officialdom with the promise that the party and the state would form the twin pillars of the Third Reich. Rigid control of the party and support of the civil servants' faith in status and order were the foundations of the solution offered by the new order in 1933–34 under the slogan "unity of party and state."

The realities of power politics invaded the relatively independent realm of the state bureaucracies with the first civil service decree. After the prelude of the purge in Prussia and the Reich, the notorious Law for the Restoration of the

Professional Civil Service was passed on April 7, 1933. The euphemistic name is typical of National Socialist laws, whose positive designations rarely gave an inkling of the terrible practices they instituted. Like many other pieces of legislation of the period, the civil service law retroactively legalized a wide range of arbitrary and violent acts. Followed by numerous amendments and implementation decrees, the law made it possible to dismiss employees, even in violation of existing laws, if they did not possess the requisite "suitability," were not of "Aryan descent" (with the initial exception of war veterans), or "on the basis of their former political activities did not offer the assurance that they supported the national state without reservations." "For reasons of administrative efficiency," additional regulations under this law could be passed "outside regular legal channels." These arbitrary regulations showed that the true purpose of the law was not the restoration of the civil service but rather its intimidation and political leveling. The nonlegal state of emergency dominated the reconstruction of the machinery of government, regardless of existing restrictions. The dual existence of party and state by no means signified that a counterweight to National Socialist rule had been preserved; rather, the dictatorship gained a degree of support through these pseudolegal tactics which Party rule alone could never have achieved. The civil service legislation was also the vehicle by which anti-Semitism was first incorporated into an officially mandated tenet of law. Even a person who had only one grandparent of Jewish origin was held to be "non-Aryan." National Socialist policy was as unscrupulous in its use of these regulations of dubious legal validity as in its acceptance of pseudoscientific race theory, with its confused mixture of religious, socioeconomic, political, and biological "proofs."

The incursions of NSDAP control were especially serious in the judiciary. There the purge along political and racial lines ensnared lawyers as well as judges. Both had been among the pillars of the Weimar Republic. The passage of the Law on the Admission to the Practice of Law, also on April 7, restricted the freedom of the legal profession. Through the law's "Aryan articles" and the arbitrary imposition of prohibitions, the rights of a citizen defending himself against encroachment by the state could be violated even more profoundly than was already the case under the state of emergency and political terror. On the heels of this legislation came the coordination of lawyers in the Nazi-controlled German Law Front and the Academy for German Law. The chief of these associations, Hans Frank, the National Socialist legal luminary of the early days, was appointed to the position of Reich Commissar for the Coordination of Justice in the States and for the Renewal of Jurisprudence. The new structures aimed to put the law at the service of National Socialism on the principle of broadly interpreted "healthy folk emotions" and of the catch phrase "right is what's good for the people." Efforts to preserve justice were undoubtedly made in the twelve-year rule of the Third Reich. Hitler singled out lawyers as a group as guilty of undue "objectivity," and in fact the duality of Party and state was most evident in the field of law. But at the same time this duality formed the basis for the sort of legally justified dictatorial terrorism which found its strongest expression in the creation of special courts and people's courts and in the thousands of jail terms and death sentences meted out to "traitors and saboteurs."

The police agencies of the party and above all of the SS stood outside all judicial control; they were thus in a position to translate political orders into the terrorist justice of the concentration camps, leaving the victims no recourse to legal process. This impurity began in the first days of the seizure of power with the establishment of SA camps for political opponents of the Nazis. Even if a court showed compassion, political victims were at the mercy of this "second track" of official justice. Release from prison was frequently followed by transfer to a concentration camp. In the course of time, the dual system of a formal state governed by law and a "decree state" of officially sanctioned arbitrary power was subsumed by the totalitarian police-state of 1938–45. In this final phase, the last remnants of legal, objective procedure disappeared, and citizens became the defenseless pawns of the summary justice of SS terror.

Simultaneously with the mobilization of power came that "engagement" of the population through the infiltration and "alignment" of organizations and the creation of all-inclusive monopoly organizations in the economic sector. Police and SA units attacked the trade unions on May 2, 1933, and their leaders were arrested and their funds seized. Ten days later all their property was attached. On June 24, the League of Christian Unions of Germany was crushed in the same way. To replace the unions, the German Labor Front was created under the leadership of Robert Ley. This body, which eventually embraced all gainfully employed persons outside the civil service, served no genuine economic or political function and had nothing to do with the regulation of wages or the improvement of working conditions. The Labor Front administered the taxation of the working class and performed certain tasks of stewardship and defining rules of labor, but its essential job was to keep labor in an atomized and powerless condition and to extirpate the last traces of Marxism from the labor movement.

Gleichschaltung did not stop with these organizations. The policy extended to a host of professional agencies. The Reich Press Law of October 4, 1933, stipulated that all newspaper editors must be German citizens, Aryan, and not married to Jews. It further laid down censorship laws of the utmost rigidity. The radio was already a state monopoly and had become a mere voice of the Party. The Propaganda Ministry controlled all aspects of the film industry, including production. The most conspicuous result of this control of the mass media was that their intellectual level fell to abysmal depths, their dullness apparent even to the most loyal Nazi. *Gleichschaltung* also applied to education. All teachers, at whatever level, were subject to the racial laws and had to take an oath of allegiance to Hitler. The subjects and content of their courses and the books they could use were prescribed.

By September 1933, a bare nine months after assuming office, Hitler had taken over the state apparatus, ending pluralistic parliamentary democracy, and had begun a program of incorporating all areas of life into the National Socialist revolution. The first two phases of *Gleichschaltung* were completed. Yet two important sources of potential opposition still remained outside Hitler's direct control in the fall of 1933: the army and the SA. Although the army would continue to be in many ways beyond Hitler's control until 1938, it was made sufficiently innocuous and removed from direct political involvement by the summer of 1934. Hitler appeased the army by eliminating the SA, the only section of the NSDAP which threatened the power and independence of the Reichswehr's traditional position. Thus by moving against the last vestige of independence within the Party structure, Hitler also brought the army into alignment with the permanent revolution.

The position of the army resembled that of the state bureaucracy. The Reichswehr represented a source of power outside direct control by the Reichstag and, like the civil service, had no respect for parliamentary government. The National Socialist takeover would probably not have been possible had it not been for the deep gulf separating the army from the republic. Many of the higher-ranking members of the army wanted to end the close cooperation between the Reichswehr and the state which was inaugurated during Hindenburg's presidency and which reached a climax after 1930 with the army's direct participation in extraparliamentary governments. In line with this situation, Hitler initially seemed to defer to the army's desire for separation from politics and for independence of action. In the course of its own seizure of power, the National Socialist regime sought to push the army back into a more limited, purely military realm and to exclude it from policy-making decisions. The vacillations between acquiescence and resistance eventually revealed the lack of both power and leadership within the army. Under the dictatorship, and especially under the totalitarian state, its claims to independence and neutrality turned out to be illusory. Once Hitler had decided to use the army, he repeatedly interfered with its command structure. After the ouster of Generals Blomberg and Fritsch, Hitler transformed the army into a mere tool of the National Socialist war and extermination policies.

The sham independence of the army was only underscored in the spring of 1934. Although its leaders thought they could maintain an equal partnership with the NSDAP and force Hitler to emasculate the SA, Hitler used the opportunity to wipe out the only source of opposition left within his own party and to confirm his monopoly of power within the state to such a degree that even the army could no longer oppose him. The so-called Night of the Long Knives (June 30, 1934), which saw the elimination of the SA as a semi-independent force within the Party and the execution of its leader, Ernst Roehm, provided Hitler with the opportunity to realize the ideal of total leadership within the first eighteen months of his rule. The army gave its tacit agreement to the purge in the mistaken belief that the elimination of the SA would assure the army of complete control of military affairs. Consciously played up in various quarters, particularly by Goering and Himmler, the old tensions between the SA and the army came to a head once more in the spring of 1934. The myth was created and spread so effectively that even Hitler believed Roehm was planning a *putsch*.

The importance of the purge does not lie so much in its causes as its methods and consequences. In legitimizing the event, Hitler quite openly claimed the right to rid himself of his opponents without either legal investigation or trial. Earlier purges, even when bloody, had been seen as necessary but temporary by-products of revolution; now, however, murder committed by the government was incorporated into official policy. After the purge the law of July 3, 1934, formally "legalized" the crimes after the event in one terse sentence: "The measures taken on June 30 and July 1 and 2 to strike down the treasonous attacks are justifiable acts of self-defense by the state." Hindenburg's last significant act as president was to sign this law. In itself it marked the ultimate moral bankruptcy of the conservative position in the face of the new right-wing dictatorship. The legalization of terror more clearly than anything else revealed the true nature of National Socialist rule.

28. The New Chancellor Issues an Appeal to the German People

Two days after becoming chancellor, Hitler delivered a radio address to the German people in which he vowed to raise the nation from the fourteen years of "ruin" under the Weimar government, which he characterized as being influenced by Marxism. He warned of the threat of Bolshevism, promising to "declare a merciless war" against this political "nihilism" in a foreshadowing of the campaign against leftist parties which followed in several weeks. Although he mentioned four-year plans, his pledge to rebuild Germany offered only vague generalities.

> More than fourteen years have passed since that unholy day when, deluded by domestic and foreign promises, the German people forgot the most treasured assets of its past, of the Reich, and of its honor and liberty.
>
> Since that day of treason the Almighty has withheld his blessing from our people.
>
> Discord and hatred came onto the scene. Millions of the best German men and women from all walks of life watched with great grief as the unity of the German nation broke apart and dissolved in a tangle of egotistical political opinions, economic interests, and ideological differences.
>
> As has been the case so often in our history, Germany since the revolution is a picture of heartbreaking disunity. We did not receive the promised equality and fraternity, but we did lose our freedom. The collapse of the spirit and purpose of the unity of our people in domestic affairs was followed by the decline of our political position in the world.
>
> Passionately inspired were the German people as they went to war in 1914, without any feeling of guilt [for the start of the war], and filled with

[handwritten margin notes: "Imply God framed on treaty of Versailles" and "Call to nationalism"]

From *Völkischer Beobachter*, February 2, 1932. Translated by Dieter Kuntz.

the need and desire to defend the threatened Reich and the freedom and very existence of the German people. But we can now see in the disastrous fate that has befallen us since November 1918 only the result of our internal collapse. Since then the rest of the world has been no less shaken by great crises.

The historical balance of power, which at one time contributed in no small measure to the understanding of the need for internal unity of the nation, with all the resultant beneficial economic consequences, no longer exists. The insane notion of victor and vanquished has destroyed the trust between nations and has thereby also ruined the world economy.

The misery of our people is dreadful. Added to the millions of unemployed, starving industrial workers was the subsequent impoverishment of craftsmen and the entire middle class. If this ruinous condition culminates by engulfing farmers, then we will be in the midst of a catastrophe of incalculable consequences.

Not only will the Reich disintegrate, but it will also mean the ruination of a two-thousand-year inheritance of the loftiest values of man's culture and civilization. Threatening signs of this collapse are all around us. With unprecedented will and determination have the Communists employed their insane methods in order to poison and absolutely demoralize a shaken and uprooted people. . . .

Fourteen years of Marxism have brought Germany into ruin, but one year of Bolshevism would completely destroy Germany. The most beautiful and richest cultural area of the world would be turned into an expanse of ruin and chaos. Even the suffering of the last decade and a half would not compare with the misery of a Europe in whose heart the red flag of destruction has been raised.

The thousands of wounded and the countless dead this domestic war has already cost Germany should be the warning signal of an impending storm.

In these hours of overwhelming difficulties and concern for the future of the German nation, the aged leader of the World War has once again called on us men of the national parties and associations to fight under his leadership. Just as we were once at the front, now on the home front we must be united and loyal in order to save the Reich.

Because the honorable Herr Reich President has high-mindedly extended his hand to us so that we may work together, we, the national leaders, make a solemn vow before God, our conscience, and the German people to fulfill the mission entrusted to us, the national government, with steadfastness and perseverence.

The heritage we have assumed is an awesome one. The task we must fulfill is the most difficult one that has faced German statesmen in living memory. Faith in us is, however, unlimited, because we believe in our people and their everlasting values. Peasants, workers, and the middle class must work together to lay the foundation of our new Reich.

131

stability

*protect
Christianity*

*— disregard
Classes
to
restore
unity*

The national government sees as its first and foremost task the restoration of the unity of spirit and will of our people. It will preserve and
protect the fundamentals on which the strength of our nation rests. It will
preserve and protect Christianity, which is the basis of our system of
morality, and the family, which is the germination cell of the body of the
people and the state. It will disregard social rankings and classes in order
to restore to our people its consciousness of national and political unity
and the responsibilities that entails. It will use reverence for our great and
glorious past and pride in our ancient traditions as a basis for the education
of German youth. In this way it will declare a merciless war upon spiritual,
political, and cultural nihilism. Germany shall not and will not sink into
anarchistic communism.

In place of turbulent instinct, the government will instill national
discipline as the guiding principle of our lives. In so doing, the government
will devote careful attention to those areas that represent the true strength
and energy of our nation.

The national government will undertake the great task of the reorganization of the economy of our people through two great four-year plans:
rescue of the German farmer to ensure the means of feeding the nation
and thereby guaranteeing its existence; rescue of the German worker
through a mighty and comprehensive attack on unemployment.

In fourteen years the November parties[1] have ruined the German
agricultural class. In fourteen years they have created an army of millions
of unemployed.

*Goal
of
4 yrs,
full
employment*

The national government will with an iron determination and tena-
cious perseverence accomplish the following goal: within four years the
German farmer must be relieved of his misery. Within four years unemployment must be conquered. This basic requirement also holds true for
the rest of industry.

The national government will combine this monumental task of
cleansing our economy with the task of cleansing the Reich, the states,
and the local communities in administrative and fiscal matters. Only in
this way will the idea of a federated existence of the Reich become a
reality.

Socialism →

At the cornerstones of this program are the ideas of labor service duty
and land settlement. Concern for the guarantee of daily bread will be
combined with the fulfillment of our social responsibility toward illness
and old age.

In the thriftiness of the administration, in the promotion of work, in
the preservation of the peasant community, as well as by engaging the

---

[1] Hitler is referring to the politicians and political parties who formed the Weimar's
coalition government in the aftermath of the armistice of November 1918.

[handwritten margin note: economic stability]

initiative of the individual lie the best guarantees for avoiding experiments that could endanger our monetary standard.

In its foreign policy, the national government regards its highest mission to be the safeguarding of the right to life of our people and therefore to regain the freedom of our people. As it is determined to end the chaotic conditions inside Germany, it will cooperate with other nations in order to establish a state of equal value and equal rights within the community of nations. It is aware of its great responsibility to represent this free and equal people in its quest to maintain and strengthen peace, which the world is more in need of today than ever before. Let us hope that others will understand and cooperate so that this deeply sincere wish will be realized for the sake of Europe and indeed of the world.

As great as our love is for our army, which is the bearer of our weapons and a symbol of our great past, we would nonetheless be happy if the world through a limitation of armaments would never again make it necessary for us to increase our own weapons.

If Germany is to experience this political and economic reascendancy and conscientiously fulfill its obligations toward other nations, one crucial fact becomes clear: we must overcome the communist decomposition of Germany.

We, the men of this government, feel ourselves accountable to German history for the reconstruction of an ordered body politic and must therefore once and for all eliminate the insanity of classes and class warfare. We do not envision one class, but all the German people, the millions of farmers, workers, and bourgeois, who will either together overcome the troubles of these times or succumb to them together.

We are determined, true to our oath, and in view of the inability of the present Reichstag, to accomplish this goal and to entrust the German people themselves with its accomplishment.

Reich President General Field Marshal von Hindenburg has called on us to employ our courage in order to bring about the re-ascendancy of the nation.

We appeal therefore to the German people to support this act of conciliation.

The government of this national resurgence will work, and the people will work. It was not responsible for the fourteen years of decay of the German nation, but it will lead the nation back to the top. It is determined to make good in four years all of the damage that was done in the previous fourteen. . . .

German people, give us four years' time and then put us on trial and judge us. . . .

29. The Reichstag Fire Decree

On February 27, 1933, the Reichstag building was badly damaged by fire. The cause of the fire remains a mystery even now, but the Nazis blamed the blaze on the Communists and charged that it was a signal for the beginning of a communist revolution. Hitler used the situation to persuade Hindenburg to issue a Decree for the Protection of People and State on February 28. Known as the Reichstag Fire Decree, it established the basis for the creation of a police state by enabling the Nazis to curtail constitutional rights such as freedom of the press and the right to assemble. Armed with this decree, the Nazis rounded up Communists, Social Democrats, and other opponents.

DECREE OF THE REICH PRESIDENT FOR THE PROTECTION OF THE PEOPLE AND STATE OF 28 FEBRUARY 1933

In virtue of Section 48 (2) of the German constitution, the following is decreed as a defensive measure against Communist acts of violence, endangering the state:

ARTICLE 1

Restricts Rights

Sections 114, 115, 117, 118, 123, 124, and 153 of the Constitution of the German Reich are suspended until further notice. Thus, restrictions on personal liberty, on the right of free expression of opinion, including freedom of the press, on the right of assembly and the right of association, and violations of the privacy of postal, telegraphic, and telephonic communications, and warrants for house-searches, orders for confiscations as well as restrictions on property, are also permissible beyond the legal limits otherwise prescribed.

ARTICLE 2

If in a state the measures necessary for the restoration of public security and order are not taken, the Reich Government may temporarily take over the powers of the highest state authority.

From Office of the United States Chief of Counsel for the Prosecution of Axis Criminality; *Nazi Conspiracy and Aggression* (Washington, D.C.: U.S. Government Printing Office, 1946), vol. 3, doc. no. 1390-PS, pp. 968–70.

ARTICLE 3

According to orders decreed on the basis of Article 2, by the Reich Government, the authorities of states and provinces [*Gemeindeverbände*], if concerned, have to abide thereby.

ARTICLE 4

Whoever provokes, or appeals for or incites to the disobedience of the orders given out by the supreme state authorities or the authorities subject to them for the execution of this decree, or the orders given by the Reich Government according to Article 2, is punishable — insofar as the deed is not covered by other decrees with more severe punishments — with imprisonment of not less than one month, or with a fine from 150 up to 15,000 Reichsmarks.

Whoever endangers human life by violating Article 1, is to be punished by sentence to a penitentiary, under mitigating circumstances with imprisonment of not less than six months and, when violation causes the death of a person, with death, under mitigating circumstances with a penitentiary sentence of not less than two years. In addition the sentence may include confiscation of property.

Whoever provokes or incites to an act contrary to public welfare is to be punished with a penitentiary sentence, under mitigating circumstances, with imprisonment of not less than three months.

ARTICLE 5

The crimes which under the Criminal Code are punishable with penitentiary for life are to be punished with death: i.e., in Sections 81 (high treason), 229 (poisoning), 306 (arson), 311 (properties), 324 (general poisoning).

Insofar as a more severe punishment has not been previously provided for, the following are punishable with death or with life imprisonment or with imprisonment not to exceed 15 years:

1. Anyone who undertakes to kill the Reich President or a member or a commissioner of the Reich Government or of a state government, or provokes to such a killing, or agrees to commit it, or accepts such an offer, or conspires with another for such a murder;
2. Anyone who under Section 115 (2) of the Criminal Code (serious rioting) or of Section 125 (2) of the Criminal Code (serious disturbance of the peace) commits the act with arms or cooperates consciously and intentionally with an armed person;
3. Anyone who commits a kidnapping under Section 239 of the Criminal Code with the intention of making use of the kidnapped person as a hostage in the political struggle.

135

This decree enters in force on the day of its promulgation.

Berlin, 28 February 1933

> *The Reich President*
> VON HINDENBURG
> *The Reich Chancellor*
> ADOLF HITLER
> *The Reich Minister of the Interior*
> FRICK
> *The Reich Minister of Justice*
> DR. GÜRTNER

30. The Enabling Act

On March 24, 1933, the Nazi regime issued the Enabling Act, officially named the Law for the Removal of the Distress of People and Reich, which had been approved one day earlier in the Reichstag by a vote of 444 to 94. The vote was achieved through intimidation, threats, and promises to the Catholic Center Party that it would retain religious rights. The Communists had already been rounded up as subversives. Only the Social Democrats voted against the measure. This act altered the Weimar Constitution, legalized the National Socialist revolution, and provided the foundation for the establishment of the totalitarian regime. Through the cabinet, Hitler could issue laws without the consent of the Reichstag. He thus succeeded in destroying parliamentary democracy.

The Reichstag has resolved the following law, which is, with the approval of the National Council, herewith promulgated, after it has been established that the requirements have been satisfied for legislation altering the Constitution.

ARTICLE 1

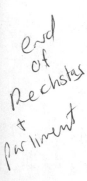

National laws can be enacted by the National Cabinet as well as in accordance with the procedure established in the Constitution. This applies also to the laws referred to in article 85, paragraph 2, and in article 87 of the Constitution.

ARTICLE 2

The national laws enacted by the National Cabinet may deviate from the Constitution so far as they do not affect the position of the Reichstag and National Council. The powers of the President remain undisturbed.

From U.S. Department of State, *National Socialism: Basic Principles* (Washington, D.C.: U.S. Government Printing Office, 1943), pp. 106–7.

ARTICLE 3

The national laws enacted by the National Cabinet are prepared by the Chancellor and published in the *Reichsgesetzblatt*. They come into effect, unless otherwise specified, upon the day following their publication. Articles 68 to 77 of the Constitution do not apply to the laws enacted by the National Cabinet.

No democracy Rule by decree

ARTICLE 4

Treaties of the Reich with foreign states which concern matters of national legislation do not require the consent of the bodies participating in legislation. The National Cabinet is empowered to issue the necessary provisions for the execution of these treaties.

ARTICLE 5

This law becomes effective on the day of publication. It becomes invalid on April 1, 1937; it further becomes invalid when the present National Cabinet is replaced by another.

Berlin, March 24, 1933

> *Reich President*
> VON HINDENBURG
> *Reich Chancellor*
> ADOLF HITLER
> *Reich Minister of the Interior*
> FRICK
> *Reich Minister of Foreign Affairs*
> BARON VON NEURATH
> *Reich Minister of Finance*
> COUNT SCHWERIN VON KROSIGK

31. A Violent Complement to the Legal Revolution

Although the Nazis claimed that they had effected a legal, bloodless revolution, in fact considerable violence accompanied the Nazi seizure of power throughout Germany. The takeover of state and local government was achieved under the guise of restoring "order" within the various states. On the basis of the emergency decree, the Nazi minister of the interior Wilhelm Frick dispatched Reich police

From Office of the United States Chief of Counsel for the Prosecution of Axis Criminality, *Nazi Conspiracy and Aggression* (Washington, D.C.: U.S. Government Printing Office, 1946), vol. 5, doc. no. 2544-PS, pp. 288–90.

commissioners to various states not only to assume control of the police but also to pressure resignations from legally constituted state governments and engineer the formation of Nazi governments to take their place.

SA and SS units were appointed as special police auxiliaries for the purpose of helping to "restore" order. Armed with the legal trappings of power, the SA and SS vented their frustration on their political opponents during much of 1933. In testifying for the prosecution during the Nuremberg war-crimes trials, Rudolf Diels, the first head of the Gestapo, discussed the tactics and the excesses of these organizations functioning beyond the constraint of legal institutions. For his part, Diels became caught in a power struggle between Himmler and Goering and was dismissed as Gestapo chief in 1934. He subsequently held local government positions.

I, Rudolf Diels, 45 years of age, testify under oath as follows: When Hitler became Chancellor of the Reich on January 30th 1933, I was a Superior Government Councillor [Oberregierungsrat] in the police section of the Prussian Ministry of Interior. There I was in the section: Political Police. Therefore I know the happenings within the police, as they occurred during the time after Hitler's seizure of power, from my own experience.

When Hitler became Chancellor of the Reich, Hermann Goering became provisional [Kommissarischer] Prussian Minister of the Interior and thereby my superior. As such he was the head of the centralized Prussian police administration. This organization constituted the strongest power [Machtfaktor] aside from the army.

The perfectly primitive Nazi conception of the conduct of a state was, that one had to annihilate or render harmless all adversaries or suspected adversaries. The inferiority complex of the Nazis towards everything they did not know, e.g. legal institutions, experts and so on has much to do with that.

As for that, it was a natural matter for the new Nazi Government and the party, which had come into power, to annihilate their adversaries by all possible means. These actions started after the Reichstag fire. They were executed by various party groups, especially by the SA; for such criminal purposes the government also tried to make the most of certain official government agencies. The methods applied were as follows: Human beings, who deprived of their freedom [were] subjected to severe bodily mistreatment or killed. These illegal detentions [Freiheitsberaubungen] took place in camps, often old military barracks, storm-troop quarters or fortresses. Later on these places became known as concentration camps, such as Oranienburg, near Berlin, Lichtenburg, Papenburg, Dachau in Bavaria, Columbiahouse Berlin, etc.

During this period of time, numerous politicians, deputies, writers, doctors, lawyers and other personalities of leading circles were arrested illegally, tortured and killed. Among the killed, there were the Social Democrat Stelling, Ernst Heilmann, the former Police President of Altona

Otto Eggerstedt, the communist Schehr from the Ruhr territory, and numerous parties and denominations, amongst them Conservatives, Democrats, Catholics, Jews, Communists and Pacifists.

These murders were camouflaged by the expression: "shot while trying to escape" or "resisting arrest" or similar things. Approximately 5[00]–700 people perished during this first wave of terror (from March until October 1933 approximately).

I myself and co-workers, old civil servants, Not-Nazis, tried to resist this wave of terror.

There was no legal possibility left any more, to undertake anything in order to stop these illegal arrests, because the Reich Cabinet had suspended Civil Rights by decree of February 28th 1933. On account of this fact, it was also impossible for the inmates of the concentration camps to appeal to any court. Such a state of affairs had never existed before, not even during extraordinary times. The word "protective custody" as used at that time for concentration camps etc. was an irony. There were a few cases of real protective custody, in which I put people behind safe walls, in order to protect them against terrible excesses.

The number of illegal cases attained an ever-increasing extent. When Heinrich Himmler took over the reins of power as the highest Chief of police in Prussia under Goering, these actions were really organized by the State proper. The first, great, state-organized terror project under his leadership was the blood purge of June 30th, 1934, at that time SA leaders, Generals, leading Catholics and others were murdered. He also arrested people again, who had been released from concentrations camps before that time. This at a time, when actually a certain tranquillity in the country had set in already.

Read by myself, approved, signed and sworn to:

[signed] RUDOLF DIELS

32. The *Gleichschaltung* of the Civil Service

The Nazis attempted to coordinate the government bureaucracy with the Law for the Restoration of the Professional Civil Service of April 7, 1933, which legalized the purging of members of the government bureaucracy, including not only judges but also teachers and professors, who had democratic or leftist sentiments or were of non-Aryan descent.

From Office of the United States Chief of Counsel for the Prosecution of Axis Criminality, *Nazi Conspiracy and Aggression* (Washington, D.C.: U.S. Government Printing Office, 1946), vol. 3, doc. no. 1397-PS, pp. 981–83; vol. 5, doc. no. 2867-PS, pp. 527–28.

LAW FOR THE RESTORATION OF THE PROFESSIONAL CIVIL SERVICE, APRIL 7, 1933

ARTICLE 3

1. Officials, who are of non-Aryan descent, are to be retired; insofar as honorary officials are concerned, they are to be removed from official status.

2. Section 1 is not in effect for officials who were already officials since 1 August 1914, or who fought during the World War at the front for the German Reich or who fought for its allies or whose fathers or sons were killed in the World War. The Reichsminister of the Interior can permit further exceptions in understanding with the appropriate special minister or the highest authorities of the federal states in the case of officials abroad.

[handwritten margin note: exemption for those who served before 1914 d were in the war]

[handwritten note: Gets rid of Leftists]

ARTICLE 4

Officials, whose former political activity does not offer a guarantee that they at all times without reservation act in the interest of the national state can be dismissed from service. For a period of 3 months after dismissal they are accorded their former salary. From this time on they receive ¾ of their pension and corresponding survivor's benefits.

THIRD DECREE RELATING TO THE IMPLEMENTATION OF THE LAW FOR THE RESTORATION OF THE PROFESSIONAL CIVIL SERVICE OF MAY 1933

Pursuant to Section 17 of the Law for the Restoration of the Professional Civil Services of 7 April 1933 (Reichsgesetzbl. I, page 175) the following is decreed:
To Section 2:

2.

A person who has been active in Communist affairs is to be dismissed, even if he does not belong any more to the Communist party, its auxiliary or substitute organizations. The so-called National-Communist Movement ("Black Front") is also considered as communist.

3.

1. A civil servant possesses for his career the prescribed training if upon taking up his official duties as a civil servant he has fulfilled certain requirements set by law, decree or administrative regulation.

2. A civil servant possesses for his career the usual training if he upon taking up his official duties has fulfilled those requirements which have been considered as a rule sufficient for his career.

3. A civil servant is otherwise qualified for his career:

(a) as a political official if on the basis of his position and activity in public life or on the basis of his experiences and the uprightness of his convictions and dealings he appears suited to be entrusted with office and who by the blameless conduct of the office has given proof that he is qualified.

(b) as a non-political official, if he on the basis of his earlier theoretical or practical activity as well as on the ground of the uprightness of his convictions and dealings upon taking over the office demonstrated a special aptitude and by the blameless conduct of the office has proven that he is qualified.

33. The *Gleichschaltung* of the Judicial System

The German judicial system was systematically purged and molded into a compliant and loyal body that interpreted laws according to National Socialist principles. The following deposition of a district court judge made before the military tribunal at Nuremberg in November 1945 illustrates how the regime influenced the administration of justice.

Dr. Hans Anschütz, at present District Court Director [*Landgerichtsdirektor*] at Heidelberg, after having been duly sworn, deposes as follows:

I was born in 1901 in Heidelberg, the son of university professor Dr. Gerhard Anschütz. After attending high schools [Gymnasien] in Berlin-Grunewald and Heidelberg, I studied law, and according to my inclination became a judge. Until 1933 I was employed as public prosecutor at Heidelberg, then I was transferred as Judge of a Local Court [Amtsgerichtsrat] and later Judge of the District Court [Landgerichtsrat] at Offenburg [Baden]. I was dismissed from service in the armed forces in 1944, because the father of my wife was a Jew, and for the same reason I could no longer be employed as a judge; I was assigned to the War Damages Office [*Kriegsschaedenamt*] at Mannheim. At present I am engaged again in my old profession as District Court Director [*Landgerichtsdirektor*] at Heidelberg.

In the attached statements on the problem of "National Socialism and Justice" I have recorded the experience which I was able to acquire during the last twelve years as a judge.

From Office of the United States Chief of Counsel for the Prosecution of Axis Criminality, *Nazi Conspiracy and Aggression* (Washington, D.C.: U.S. Government Printing Office, 1946), vol. 5, doc. no. 1964-PS, pp. 673–76.

STATEMENTS ON THE PROBLEM
"NATIONAL SOCIALISM AND JUSTICE"

It was a matter of course that a totalitarian system like that of National Socialism could not make an exception of the administration of justice in the extension of its power. The "coordination" or "elimination" of the administration of justice was achieved gradually but purposefully.

1. Immediately after the seizure of power those judges who were undesirable for political or racial reasons were eliminated or demoted from leading positions to unimportant ones; in particular they were eliminated from criminal courts. For this purpose they used the "Law Concerning the Reconstruction of the Professional Civil Service" of 7 April 1933, which did away with the principle that judges could not be removed or demoted and thereby destroyed the guarantees of the independence of justice.

2. Subsequently, the system of spying upon and supervising the political opinions of each citizen, which permeated the entire public and private life in Germany, was, of course, also extended to judges. This spy system eventually reached the point of open attacks and defamatory statements in the press; this was done particularly in the newspapers "Der Stürmer" and "Das Schwarze Korps," which took delight in distorting reports of trials and in naming those judges who had imposed sentences which the party considered intolerable. The political power of these papers, or rather those persons who were behind them, namely, Streicher and Himmler, was so great that not even the Reich Minister of Justice succeeded in having them publish corrections of trial reports which were demonstrably untrue.

3. Finally, the German Civil Service Code of 26 January 1937 (effective as of 1 July 1937) placed judges on the same level with all other public officials. Article 71 of this Code made it possible to retire any official who "indicated that he was no longer prepared to intercede at all times for the National Socialist State."

4. But while even the German Civil Service Code made certain exceptions for judges (Article 171 prohibited the retirement of judges solely because of the contents of decisions made by them), Hitler, in the Reichstag meeting of 26 April 1942 had the Reichstag confer upon him the "right" to dismiss judges even without regard to vested rights, if he thought it necessary. This Reichstag speech of Hitler's really constituted a signal testimonial to the German judge because it showed that Hitler had reasons to be discontent with the administration of justice in that it had not been sufficiently subservient to the party.

5. After the issuance of the German Civil Service Code, strong pressure was brought to bear upon all officials, including judges, to join the NSDAP or not to reject requests to join; otherwise there existed the danger that they might be retired or dismissed. But once a party member,

a judge was under party discipline and party jurisdiction which dominated his entire life as official and as private person.

6. In addition to these measures concerning judges, the party resorted to measures which might be characterized as the "undermining of regular jurisdiction" and the "establishment of special jurisdiction."

Until the end of 1933, the Supreme Court [*Reichsgericht*] was the highest German tribunal with jurisdiction over cases of treason and high treason. For that reason, the Reichstag fire trial still came before the Supreme Court. As is well known, it ended with the acquittal of most of the accused, whom the regime had hoped to see convicted as members of the Communist party. After this trial, the Supreme Court was deprived of its jurisdiction in matters of treason and high treason. This was transferred by law of 28 April 1934 to the newly created People's Court [*Volksgerichtshof*], which consisted of only two professional judges (even these, of course, were selected primarily because of political considerations) and five higher party functionaries. Thus, this court offered a guarantee that the law would be applied exclusively in accordance with the principles of the NSDAP.

Even prior to this, the law of 21 March 1933 had created Special Courts [*Sondergericht*] for the trial of political crimes. Their members were appointed at first by the Governing Council [*Präsidium*] of the District Court in whose district the Special Court was established, and later by the Appeal Court President [*Oberlandesgerichtspräsident*]. Actually, only party members were made judges of the Special Courts.

The power of these Special Courts was increased in the interest of the party, first, since it was up to the public prosecutor to decide whether to bring a case before the ordinary court or the Special Court, and second, by reason of the fact that not every German attorney but only those especially admitted attorneys could act as defense counsel before the Special Courts, and finally, by the virtue of the fact that there was no appeal from the decisions of the Special Courts.

7. A further means of influencing judges was contained in the institution of "Judges' Letters." In these letters, which were issued by the Reich Ministry of Justice and destined for internal distribution only, law cases were commented upon as illustrative of good or bad examples; while no names of judges were contained in them, they did name the respective courts and thus exercised pressure upon the judges.

Under the slogan of "Directed Justice," finally, they used pressure upon judges by having the District Attorney [*Oberstaatsanwalt*] in important criminal cases which might also include non-political matters, inform the presiding judge prior to the trial of the punishment which would be sought and point out that this sentence would be expected of him.

8. The strongest interference with the administration of justice, however, developed increasingly after 1933 "outside of" [neben] the adminis-

tration of justice. The police, under the command of the Reichsführer SS, arrested persons who were *persona non grata* for political or even for other reasons without judicial procedure (and, indeed, without any procedure at all) and detained them in prisons and concentration camps. In political cases, it was the rule rather than the exception that accused persons who had been acquitted by the court were taken immediately after trial into "protective custody" by the police and thus disappeared into concentration camps.

9. Finally, the party sabotaged the administration of justice by failing to execute sentences imposed upon "old fighters" or otherwise specially favored party comrades and by nullifying the sentences through the arbitrary exercise of the right of pardon.

10. The foregoing list of attempts to influence justice is, of course, by no means complete.

[signed] DR. HANS ANSCHÜTZ

34. The *Gleichschaltung* of Culture

On March 13, 1933, Hitler appointed Joseph Goebbels to the position of minister for public enlightenment and propaganda, giving him complete control over the communications media as well as over the film industry, theater, and the arts. This coordination of German cultural life allowed Hitler to infuse the arts with the *völkisch* ideal and enabled him to eliminate opponents from culturally influential positions.

The following excerpt from the memoirs of a left-wing Nazi opponent provides a firsthand view of the effects of cultural *Gleichschaltung*. The author derides the "illiterate revolver journalists" of the Nazi press.

How right my friends were who had advised me to be on my guard — a warning I then, as well as years later, cast to the wind despite wiser insight at times — I only began to realize when one evening two very unfriendly civilians, who identified themselves as state police [Gestapo] officials, snooped through every last scrap of paper in my desk and closets. Their efforts, however, were fruitless, since my farsighted friends had already gotten everything they deemed dangerous out of harm's way.

But what were these "dangerous items"? Did I possess highly treasonous documents? Had I taken part in political conspiracies? No! On the contrary, I had lived on the fringe of political reality. But just this — this

From Walter Thomas (Andermann; pseud.), *Bis der Vorhang fiel* (Dortmund: Schwalvenberg Verlag, 1977), pp. 20–21. Translated by Dieter Kuntz. Reprinted by permission of Karl Schwalvenberg Verlag GmbH.

inclination not to perceive oneself to be merely a cell within a great state organism, but rather to lead an individual existence responsible only to oneself — from now on was considered a crime, an individualism inimical to the community [*gemeinschaftsfeindlich*], as was proclaimed to us in speeches and demagogical newspaper articles.

Man no longer had claim to himself! The question of how the self prepares and deals with life and death, with God and the devil — the primal question which everyone who has come to consider the questionability and finiteness of his existence imposes on himself daily — because it was of an individualizing, community-threatening nature, abruptly became classified in the category of subversive problem-posing. The great standardizing and stamping-in machine of the state was in full swing. Through summary procedure it made ready-made citizens of those who outrageously believed that they had a right to their own lives — or crushed them underfoot as if they were only unusable waste.

Yes, the machine raged! One heard its unwavering uniform rhythm in the farthest corners. We felt the floor beneath our feet gradually giving way. Friends wound up in jail. Others fled across borders. Others took their own lives. And through the streets "with calm and firm stride" marched the brown batallions.

For quite some time I had been working for a newspaper that, because of its left-radical tendencies, the brown usurpers regarded as a stronghold of their foes. As was to be expected, one day brown mercenaries occupied the editor's office and printing shop. Through a power play that was later legalized, they took possession of the enterprise. The political editors were taken into custody and their positions were filled by illiterate revolver journalists from their own party press. The others were subjected to a painstaking examination of their political acceptability.

It came to pass that I too was one day ordered to appear before one of these new arbiters of power. His head, puffed up by victory celebrations, sat like a tomato on top of his brown costume. A leather holster lay on the desk. This was the new editor in chief.

He hissed at me: "Have you written political articles?" On my answering that I had restricted my work to novellas and reporting on the arts, he shoved an article entitled "Cultural Autarchy" toward me. In it nationalist-racist cultural apologists were characterized as narrow-minded idiots. It was signed by me.

"You probably thought that we would not come to power? Otherwise you would not have written such things a few weeks before the revolution. I could now have you disposed of. But I want to give you a chance. . . ."

That is how I and several other editors were accepted. They needed us. At the same time they monitored our every step. They waited for the day when they would be able to man our positions with people from their own ranks, reliable pen-pushers who could artfully manipulate the vocabulary of their official propaganda. . . .

145

35. The *Gleichschaltung* of Local Government

During March and April 1933 the Nazis had established control over state governments but had not yet penetrated into the administrations of many smaller rural
communities. In fact, the total *Gleichschaltung* of local government never did occur;
40 percent of German towns and cities were governed by mayors who were not
Party members. The following document is a newspaper account of the process
involved in "coordinating" local government in the rural communities of the Lübeck
region in northern Germany. The newspaper was an organ of the German National
People's Party.

On the 5th and 6th of October [1933] elections took place for the offices
of mayor and deputy mayor in the rural communities of the Lübeck
region. Present during this process were district council president Böhm-
cker and [National Socialist] regional leader Capelle. The district council
president personally claimed the chairmanship of the municipal councils
and nominated candidates, who were then unanimously elected. Those
elected were long-time party members, almost without exception, who
prior to the seizure of power had stood in the front ranks of the party's
struggle. The newly composed city councils that met for the first time are
made up of old and reliable National Socialists. The brown shirts worn by
the members gave the councils even outwardly an appearance of solidarity.

The district council president took the opportunity to address the new
mayors and council members and to issue policy guidelines. . . . [He]
emphasized that from now on the leadership principle [*Führerprinzip*]
would be in effect in all communities. This axiom, which has dominated
national administration since the revolution, must now be applied to the
municipalities. The mayor now was to have unchallenged authority within
his community. He also, however, must bear sole responsibility; he can
no longer hide behind anonymous municipal council resolutions. It was
not without reason that he emphasized the importance of putting old
fighters in positions of authority within the communities. This was the
best way to ensure that they would be able to actively apply their energy
and proven political experience in the interests of their respective communities. Today it is not enough for a mayor to carry out his duties in a
bureaucratic, businesslike manner, while strictly observing the eight-hour
day. No, today a major must utilize all his resources to develop initiatives
without regard to personal advantage and without self-indulgence. He
must work in the interests of the community. He can, of course, be
effective only if he has and can retain close ties to the people. It was also

From Lawrence Stokes, ed., *Anzeiger für das Fürstentum Lübeck,* October 8, 1933, in Lawrence D. Stokes, ed., *Kleinstadt und Nationalsozialismus: Ausgewählte Dokumente zur Geschichte von Eutin, 1918–1945.* (Neumünster: Karl Wachholtz Verlag, 1984) pp. 488–89. Translated by Dieter Kuntz. Reprinted by permission.

for this reason that old party members were selected who were close to the people and who had earned their trust. Like-minded individuals have been selected to stand at their side in the municipal councils. But the activities of the councils will be more advisory in nature, given the dictates of the leadership principle. . . .

36. Nazi Accomplishments After Six Months in Power

By the summer of 1933, the Nazis had largely completed the coordination of German social and political institutions. By July 14, the NSDAP constituted the only political party in Germany, and peasants, workers, and professionals had seen their former organizations replaced by Nazi ones. *Gleichschaltung* had been comparatively easy, taking only six months to complete. Goebbels, who had been made minister for public enlightenment and propaganda, gloated about the regime's accomplishments after six months in power in a radio address to the German people on July 17, 1933, in which he proudly proclaimed that Hitler's government had effected a National Socialist "revolution" that "reconstructed" Germany. He justified the purging of the civil service with the claim that it was necessary to remove those who lacked "moral qualifications," maintaining that the multiparty system had to be eradicated in order to free Germany of divisive political interests and "unify the whole German people." Goebbels's words also contained a warning to the "Bolshevik" elements within his own party — those restless SA members who were not content to see the revolution end.

My fellow countrymen and countrywomen! Adolf Hitler has now been in power for almost half a year. Last Friday the Reich cabinet he heads, in an extended meeting lasting from eleven o'clock in the morning until midnight, discussed and adopted the final urgent law proposals, thereby bringing the first part of our domestic reconstruction to a preliminary conclusion. Of course, there are still those in our country who are not teachable, and who think that not much has changed since the 30th of January. One look at the whole picture — at the accomplishments of the national government, at the mood of the country, and along with it at the still-growing trust of the people in Hitler and his co-workers — will easily belie the words of these external know-it-alls.

One does not have to exaggerate to maintain that the Hitler Cabinet during these past six months has implemented more in political deeds

From Joseph Goebbels, *Signale der neuen Zeit* (Munich: Zentralverlag der NSDAP, 1934), pp. 183–90. Translated by Dieter Kuntz.

than all other previous administrations during the past fourteen years of German collapse and German shame.

The speed of the National Socialist revolution in accomplishing its tasks has been breathtaking. The worthless values of [Weimar's] November politicians have been wiped out by an unmatched force and a powerful blow, replaced by the new values of National Socialist ideology. Things that a year ago seemed paradoxical today seem almost trivial. What had formerly been thought to be impossible has long since become reality, and the wrongs of the state and public life to which the German people had almost resigned themselves have been almost totally removed.

The multiparty state is now finally a thing of the past and will never again rise from the dead. The special interest groups of parliamentarianism have either been dissolved by the state or they have ended their existence of their own volition. No one sheds a tear for them, because they established justification for their very existence on the basis of class differences.

The National Socialist movement emerged victorious through its own power. It is the basis of the strong central authority, which is centered in the person of Hitler, and with which he and his colleagues will solve the most difficult historical problems which face our era and our generation. . . .

. . . It may well be that some who came before us had understood those problems, and knew the ways and means with which to solve them. But the critical factor is always whether or not one has the power to implement them and whether one has the real opportunity of bringing together the disparate forces of public life and unite them into a common denominator.

That Hitler was able to overcome the multiparty state and unify the whole German people into one will and a readiness for action is, perhaps, the greatest historic accomplishment of the past six months. In order to measure the accomplishments of these six months, one must remember that at the time of his appointment the Communists still raged, the SPD still did its dirty work, the bourgeois parties were still neither alive nor dead, and furthermore, that the disciples of Moscow are today in concentration camps and the representatives of the Second [Socialist] International are in exile in Prague and Paris, that no one speaks of the bourgeois parties anymore, and that National Socialism has become the accepted and binding concept of life in the German state.

A government without a solid, loyal, and responsible bureaucracy will not endure over time. Therefore the cabinet had to pass laws making it possible to cleanse the civil service of all those elements that had crept into it in the last fourteen years, mainly because of their party affiliations, but who lacked all competence and moral qualifications for their high office. This action involved some difficulty, but it was necessary to be hard in order to see the great reconstruction work of this administration through to its conclusion. The purge of unworthy individuals from the civil service has not yet ended, but here too we will soon realize this goal and be able to establish the general order, security, and stability that are so urgently needed.

Revolutions are not goals, but only means to an end. The goal is the maintenance of the life of our people and the continuation of our national race. Revolutions that lead to anarchy do not deserve the name. True revolutions destroy only that which must be destroyed, they do not destroy everything but seek to create room for the new and the necessary. This government is keeping a watchful eye on those camouflaged Bolshevik elements who speak of a second revolution at a time when the people and nation are preparing to secure and expand the results of our revolution for the next century. . . .

Hitler began our revolution at exactly the right moment. Now that we hold full political power in the state we no longer need to consolidate our position through force because it is legally ours. . . .

Just before we came to power, our opponents shrieked: "A half a year at the helm of government and you will be lost." The more cunning ones among them even thought they should put us to the test so as to make us innocuous for all time. We do not know if they still think that way. The German people have put us to the test, but only our enemies have been rendered innocuous.

The entire nation has put its faith in Hitler. Never before in German history has a government been able to claim that it represents the people as he has. The government can be tough if it is necessary to demonstrate our principles to our opponents. It can be tender and magnanimous when it needs to bring back into the great community of the German people [*deutsche Volksgemeinschaft*] those who have been led astray or those who still doubt.

The government knows that it needs the people if it wants to reach its goal. On behalf of the people it has begun a large-scale plan of war against unemployment, the sickness of our time. It has shown courage and bravery in this and, through an unparalleled expenditure of energy, has already succeeded in reducing the dizzying number of unemployed by two million in the space of six months. Here lies the central problem of our work. Even though there is a danger that one or the other well-meant theory might not work, all energies of the government and the people must for the present and the future be focused on this great task. If we succeed in solving this problem — as we must — we will win the gratitude of the entire people, and no one will ask afterward if we adequately took into account professorial and illusionary thoughts. Doors to factories are not reopened by a multitude of theories, but only through serious work, conscientious preparation, and boldly conceived yet sensible planning. It is the task of the government to proceed with initiative and a guiding hand, and it expects the tireless and trusting support of the entire population.

The government has succeeded in lightening the burden of taxation while decreeing no new burdens, and yet has not lessened its efforts on behalf of the poor and the poorest. It knows very well that there is still great misery in Germany, but it has a clear conscience because it has left no stone unturned in order to ease the misery and put people back to work. It does not believe it wise to try to solve the problem by giving alms to the starving, but rather by creating work so that everyone can again earn his daily bread through his own labor.

The entire world, too, will have to recognize the determination with which this government went about its task. Hitler has a genuine desire for peace in the world. He solemnly proclaimed this in his speech to the German Reichstag [May 17, 1933]. Our youthful Germany has no intention of provoking others or of causing disorder. Even if the world does not yet understand us, it should at least respect the dispassionate matter-of-factness with which we are attempting to solve our own problems, without begging other states for help and without acting like dupes in order to parade our troubles before the world. The justifiable pride with which we are attempting to take care of our own troubles at home will in the long run not fail to make a deep and lasting impression on honorable people of other nations. . . .

. . . There is no more imposing picture than the one of this nation, which not long ago was bleeding from a thousand wounds, but which has now taken its fate into its own hands and is trying to put an end to the misery of the times! For this the German people have earned the deeply felt gratitude of the government, a thank-you that I here and now wish to bring to you in the name of the Führer. The German people deserve it, for they will work for their freedom and for their bread. Because of their indomitable will to live, they will become masters of their fate. They must only work together and use their own resources.

Courage and self-confidence are required if the nation is to continue what it has achieved in the previous six months. With loyal and disciplined support of the Führer's work, and with a positive attitude in spite of the magnitude of this urgent task, we will solve this difficult problem. Then we will be better able to express our thanks to the venerable field marshal and president for the noble-minded resolve and deep wisdom with which he has blessedly held his hand over us; we will express our thanks in a way mere words simply cannot do: through the deeds of all classes and professions, united as one people who can again enjoy the honor and respect of the entire world.

37. Papen's Marburg Speech: The Nationalists' Challenge

Franz von Papen, the former German chancellor, was one of the chief figures involved in the intrigue that brought Hitler to power. In January 1933 he suggested the renewal of the alliance between the Nazis and the conservative German National People's Party in order to form a new right-wing coalition government. Such an alliance was acceptable to the Nazis because their electoral appeal had seemingly crested short of the party's gaining a majority in the Reichstag. Germany's conservative elite of industrial giants, landed aristocrats, and high government bureaucrats and army officers were for their part ready to accept Hitler because his party had popular support that might be harnessed in order to restore authoritarian government and save Germany from communism.

The coalition gave Hitler the chancellor's office, Papen became vice chancellor, and most other cabinet posts went to Nationalists. Papen persuaded Hindenburg to accept this new arrangement, confidently assuring the president that he could control and tame Hitler and the Nazis. Papen and his political allies, however, later found that they had underestimated Hitler as he easily outmaneuvered the opportunist Nationalists. The Nationalists in the cabinet were reduced to political impotence as Hitler's power grew but hoped to restore the monarchy after Hindenburg's death in order to stave off a Nazi dictatorship.

Papen voiced the concerns of the conservative elite in a speech at the University of Marburg on June 17, 1934. He was highly critical of Nazi policies and one-party domination and called for greater political freedom, restoration of a just legal system, and a return to principles based on Christian conservatism.

Goebbels suppressed dissemination of Papen's remarks. The speech enraged Hitler, who now determined to crush the "worm" Papen and the conservatives' threat to his power. Edgar Jung, who had written the speech for Papen, was murdered by the Nazis during the Blood Purge two weeks later.

We know that rumors and whispering propaganda must be brought out from the darkness where they have taken refuge. Frank and manly discussion is better for the German people than, for instance, a press without an outlet, described by the Minister for Propaganda "as no longer having a face." This deficiency undoubtedly exists. The function of the press should be to inform the Government where deficiencies have crept in, where corruption has settled down, where grave mistakes have been committed, where incapable men are in the wrong places, where offenses are committed against the spirit of the German revolution. An anonymous or secret information service, however well organized it may be, can never be a substitute for this task of the press. For the newspaper editor is responsible

From the International Military Tribunal, Nuremberg, 1945–46, *Trial of the Major War Criminals* (Nuremberg: International Military Tribunal, 1948), vol. 16, pp. 290–95.

to the law and to his conscience, whereas anonymous news sources are not subject to control and are exposed to the danger of Byzantinism. When, therefore, the proper organs of public opinion do not shed sufficient light into the mysterious darkness, which at present seems to have fallen upon the German public, the statesman himself must intervene and call matters by their right names. . . .

It is a matter of historical truth that the necessity for a fundamental change of course was recognized and urged even by those who shunned the path of revolution through a mass party. A claim for revolutionary or nationalist monopoly by a certain group, therefore, seems to be exaggerated, quite apart from the fact that it disturbs the community. . . .

All of life cannot be organized; otherwise it becomes mechanized. The State is organization; life is growth. . . .

Domination by a single party replacing the majority party system, which rightly has disappeared, appears to me historically as a transitional stage, justified only as long as the safeguarding of the new political change demands it and until the new process of personal selection begins to function. . . .

But one should not confuse the religious State, which is based upon an active belief in God, with a secular State in which earthly values replace such belief and are embellished with religious honors. . . .

Certainly the outward respect for religious belief is an improvement on the disrespectful attitude produced by a degenerate rationalism. But we should not forget that real religion is a link with God, and not substitutes such as have been introduced into the consciousness of nations especially by Karl Marx's materialistic conception of history. If wide circles of people, from this same viewpoint of the totalitarian State and the complete amalgamation of the nation, demand a uniform religious foundation, they should not forget that we should be happy to have such a foundation in the Christian faith. . . .

It is my conviction that the Christian doctrine clearly represents the religious form of all occidental thinking and that with the reawakening of religious forces the German people also will be permeated anew by the Christian spirit, a spirit the profundity of which is almost forgotten by a humanity that has lived through the nineteenth century. A struggle is approaching the decision as to whether the new Reich of the Germans will be Christian or is to be lost in sectarianism and half-religious materialism. . . .

But once a revolution has been completed, the Government only represents the people as a whole and is never the champion of individual groups. . . .

It is not permissible, therefore, to dismiss the intellect with the catchword of "intellectualism." Deficient or primitive intellects do not justify us in waging war against intellectualism. And when we complain frequently today about those of us who are 150 percent Nazis, then we mean those intellectuals without a foundation, people who would like to deny the right of existence to scientists of world fame just because they are not Party members. . . .

Nor should the objection be made that intellectuals lack the vitality necessary for the leaders of a people. True spirit is so vital that it sacrifices itself for its conviction. The mistaking of brutality for vitality would reveal a worship of force which would be dangerous to a people. . . .

. . . They oppose equality before the law, which they criticize as liberal degeneration, whereas in reality it is the prerequisite for any fair judgment. These people suppress that pillar of the State which always — and not only in liberal times — was called justice. Their attacks are directed against the security and freedom of the private sphere of life which the German has won in centuries of hardest struggle. . . .

. . . Great men are not made by propaganda, but rather grow through their deeds and are recognized by history. Even Byzantinism cannot make us believe that these laws do not exist. . . .

. . . But we must have no illusions regarding the biological and psychological limits of education. Coercion, too, ends at the will for self-expression of the true personality. Reactions to coercion are dangerous. As an old soldier I know that the most rigid discipline must be balanced by certain liberties. Even the good soldier who submitted willingly to unconditional authority counted his days of service, because the need for freedom is rooted in human nature. The application of military discipline to the whole life of a people must remain within limits compatible with human nature. . . .

. . . The Movement must come to a standstill sometime; a solid social structure must sometime come into existence which is held together by an impartial administration of justice and by an undisputed governmental power. Nothing can be achieved by means of everlasting dynamics. Germany must not go adrift on uncharted seas toward unknown shores. . . .

The Government is well informed on all the self-interest, lack of character, want of truth, unchivalrous conduct, and arrogance trying to rear its head under cover of the German revolution. It is also not deceived about the fact that the rich store of confidence bestowed upon it by the German people is threatened. If we want a close connection with and a close association among the people, we must not underestimate the good sense of the people; we must return their confidence and not try to hold them everlastingly in bondage. The German people know that their situation is serious, they feel the economic distress, they are perfectly aware of the shortcoming of many laws born of emergency; they have a keen feeling for violence and injustice; they smile at clumsy attempts to deceive them by false optimism. No organization and no propaganda, however good, will in the long run be able to preserve confidence. I therefore viewed the wave of propaganda against the so-called foolish

[handwritten margin note: shot at Hitler]

critics from a different angle than many others did. Confidence and readiness to co-operate cannot be won by provocation, especially of youth, nor by threats against helpless segments of the people, but only by discussion with the people with trust on both sides. The people know what great sacrifices are expected from them. They will bear them and follow the Führer in unflinching loyalty, if they are allowed to have their part in the planning and in the work, if every word of criticism is not taken for ill will, and if despairing patriots are not branded as enemies of the State. . . .

[handwritten margin note: Criticism of Hitler & Nazi's Crack-down]

38. General von Schleicher: A Victim of the Blood Purge

The radicalism of the SA had troubled Hitler since the seizure of power, and by the spring of 1934 the Führer was ready to put an end to the threat of a "second revolution," which leading elements of that organization were calling for. Ernst Roehm, chief of the SA, advocated continuation of the Nazi revolution in a more socialist direction. This kind of rhetoric alienated conservatives and industrialists, whose support Hitler still needed. Additionally, Roehm alienated the army with his plans of combining the SA and the Reichswehr into a new "people's army" under his command. Hitler saw the support of the army as vital to his future plans and determined to act against the SA.

During the night of June 30, 1934, Hitler not only unleashed an assassination campaign against the SA leadership but used the opportunity to settle old scores with enemies past and present. The SS carried out the assignment, murdering hundreds of individuals in the Night of the Long Knives.

Among those falling victim to Nazi retribution was General Kurt von Schleicher, the last chancellor of the Weimar Republic, who had attempted to divide the Nazis in late 1932 by offering Gregor Strasser the vice chancellorship. The Nazis announced over the radio on July 1 that Schleicher had conspired with treasonous elements of the SA and had been shot while resisting arrest. The Potsdam (Berlin) district attorney's office conducted an initial investigation into the matter but was ordered to halt its activities because the Gestapo had jurisdiction in cases with "political overtones."

The following two documents suggest that the official Nazi version of events was a fabrication and that Schleicher was in fact murdered. The first consists of

From Hans Rothfels and Theodor Eschenburg, eds., "Dokumentation: Zur Ermordung des Generals Schleicher," *Vierteljahrshefte für Zeitgeschichte,* 1 (January 1953), pp. 85–86, 92–95. Translated by Dieter Kuntz. Reprinted by permission of R. Oldenbourg Verlag, Munich.

the statement given by Schleicher's cook to police on the scene in the initial investigation, whereas the second document is a reconstruction of events made in 1952 by an investigating official in the district attorney's office.

TESTIMONY OF MISS MARIE GÜRTEL, BORN MAY 1, 1881, AT KRIMITTEN, EAST PRUSSIA

. . . I have been employed as cook for General von Schleicher since May 1929. Today during the noon hour, possibly around 12:30, I was looking through the window toward the street, where I spotted two gentlemen. I asked what they wanted, to which they replied that they "had to see General von Schleicher." I then set in motion the gate-opening mechanism to the garden entrance gate, whereupon the two gentlemen approached the main door to the residence, where they again rang the bell and requested entrance. I opened the door, whereupon one of the two gentlemen inquired if General von Schleicher were at home. I answered that General von Schleicher had gone out for a walk. After a considerable amount of questioning one of the gentlemen demanded in a very sharp tone to be admitted to General von Schleicher. The gentleman showed me a square-shaped badge, of which I took no notice, and urged me to admit him. The gentleman kept insisting more and more, and then advised me to tell the truth, otherwise I would be in trouble, or something like that. I replied that "I would go and see!" I then made my way into the general's study, while being followed by the stranger. Once we had arrived at the study, the stranger stood close behind me and asked Herr von Schleicher, who was sitting in a chair at the desk working, if he were General von Schleicher. The general said yes and turned his body in order to see the man who had asked the question. At that very moment shots rang out. I do not know what happened then, because I was terrified; I screamed and ran out of the room. I ran through the house, confused, and wanted only to reach the garden. In the winter garden I again came upon the perpetrator [who had shot the general], but I do not know where he went after that. Frau von Schleicher had been sitting by the radio in General von Schleicher's study. When I afterward again went back to the room I found Frau von Schleicher and the general, both shot and lying on the floor. I cannot provide an accurate description of the murderer, because I was too flustered. I do not think that I would recognize him if I were to encounter him again.

NOTES CONCERNING THE MURDER OF GENERAL VON SCHLEICHER

(Recorded in 1952 by ministerial counsellor Dr. Grützner, the junior barrister in the district attorney's office who in 1934 functioned as the official in charge of the judicial inquiry into deaths.)

After arriving at police headquarters I discovered that the department was in a state of alert. . . . I was not immediately able to ascertain the cause for the alert. After some deliberations, the homicide squad . . . finally left for Neu-Babelsberg [the scene of the crime]. On the way Criminal Police Commissioner Schwenzer informed me "confidentially" that, on Hitler's orders, Roehm had been arrested because of his treasonous connections to representatives of a foreign power. Furthermore, it was suspected that General von Schleicher had been working with Roehm. One had to assume that General von Schleicher had committed suicide.

On arriving at the scene, Attorney-General Tetzlaff entrusted me with the criminal investigation, which I conducted from the standpoint of the two possibilities that surfaced during my earlier conversation with Criminal Police Commissioner Schwenzer: (1) Did General von Schleicher commit suicide? (2) Was there evidence of General von Schleicher's involvement in Roehm's possible treasonous activities? I was able to determine quite quickly and positively the answer to the first question: suicide was not the case; instead, based on the factual evidence in conjunction with the testimony of the chauffeur and the cook of General von Schleicher, it could only be a question of murder. . . .

. . . I had a long conversation with Attorney-General Tetzlaff about the motive for the murder. . . . As far as we were concerned, there were only two possibilities. First, that General von Schleicher was murdered by Roehm's henchmen because they suspected that Schleicher had betrayed them. Or, on the other hand, that the same bunch that had taken steps against Roehm . . . had then also taken the opportunity to eliminate Schleicher. Attorney-General Tetzlaff then expressly cautioned me at the end of our conversation that I should not mention this second possible motive, which he held to be the more likely, even though we were both fairly confident that the perpetrators could only have come from the ranks of the SS. . . . The official press release from party headquarters had said that Schleicher committed suicide, but this was changed during the course of the afternoon to read that Schleicher had been shot in self-defense. . . .

39. Public Reaction to the Purge

The regime had eliminated many of its opponents as well as "revolutionaries" within the ranks of the party with the Blood Purge of June 1934, but as is evident from the following Gestapo report of July 5, not all malcontents had been silenced. The police were particularly concerned about the effect of Papen's speech at Marburg University.

From Herbert Michaelis and Ernst Schraepler, eds., *Ursachen und Folgen, vom deutschen Zusammenbruch 1918 und 1945* (Berlin: Dokumenten-Verlag, Dr. Herbert Wendler, 1958), vol. 10, pp. 201–02. Translated by Dieter Kuntz.

STATE POLICE, KASSEL, TO GESTAPO, BERLIN, JULY 5, 1934

1. PUBLIC MOOD

The political tension of the last few weeks and the public's sense of crisis have cleared up due to the Führer's resolute action against the traitorous leadership of the SA. In public one now hears only laudatory and enthusiastic comments about the Führer. The SA as well as the entire nation is firmly behind him. No incidents have been reported in this district. The situation is now totally calm. A few individuals, including some SS members, have made derogatory remarks about the SA in order to cloud the comradely relationship. Leaders of both SA and SS have stepped in [to end this].

2. THE FIGHT AGAINST MALCONTENTS

One hears grumbling not only from enemies of the state, but it is also very pronounced in the ranks of the Party. In the fight against alarmists, almost the opposite of what we set out to do has been accomplished. Six to eight weeks ago there was hardly any talk of grumblers and rumor-mongers. Now, however, the grumbling is in high gear because of the many malcontents. Large groups of the population which hitherto had been unaffected by rumors and grumbling, and which had been loyal to the Party and state, have been drawn into the ranks of the grumblers. . . . All oppositional elements have been given fresh impetus by Vice Chancellor von Papen's Marburg speech. . . . The speech is widely known. It has confidentially become known that reactionary circles have circulated typewritten copies of the speech. An investigation into this matter has not yielded any information.

3. PARTY AND STATE

The relationship between administrative departments, Party offices, and the state police continue to be good. Many Party members, however, are suspicious of state authorities. The friction between SA members and police officers has nonetheless begun to disappear recently. Difficulties have continued in isolated cases. Here the fault lies partly with police and constabularies who frequently lack the requisite aptitude, while Party and SA members also are to blame because they cannot adjust to the fact that the authorities are no longer our enemies but are instead officials of the Third Reich. . . .

The carefully orchestrated rallies staged in the historic city of Nuremberg were designed to demonstrate the Party's position of leadership in the state after 1933, and served to create an atmosphere of a united *Volksgemeinschaft*. The adulation from hundreds of thousands reinforced Hitler's image as Führer.

The Hitler State, 1934–1938

When President Hindenburg died on August 2, 1934, the offices of president and chancellor were amalgamated, the president's powers were transferred to the Führer and chancellor, Adolf Hitler, and the title Reich president was abolished. Hitler wished to be addressed both in official and unofficial correspondence simply as Führer and Reich Chancellor. This dual title signifies the structure of power in the new Third Reich. On one level Hitler was chancellor, the head of the supposed cabinet of the parliamentary government, but he unconstitutionally added to this position the powers of the presidential office. Combining the offices of the president and chancellor represented more than a step in the process of accumulating governmental positions and authority; it displayed a basic disregard for the Weimar Constitution and all constitutional authority whatsoever. The institutions of the state could be taken over, reformed, amalgamated, or abolished at will according to the wishes of the Führer and the demands of the moment. Hitler's legitimate claim to act in this way derived from a second and more important source of his power. By officially designating himself Führer, he asserted that his authority to act in affairs of state rested on something beyond what his constitutionally grounded offices allowed. Hitler laid claim to a power overriding and transcending that of the state (which carried with it the obligation of adhering to the limits imposed by governmental machinery and practice), the basis of which was his mission before history, the will of the Führer as a revelation of the German people's destiny, and the "oath-bound community" formed by the National Socialist movement. The appropriation of power which was the underlying significance of the title Führer thus allowed him to reshape the state at will. The title also represented the fluidity of Party and state relationships which came to dominate National Socialist Germany from 1934 to 1938.

[handwritten margin note: Presidency abolished on Hindenburg death]

159

Neither in the state nor in the Party, nor in their "coordinated" control over society, was National Socialist Germany yet a totalitarian regime. The duality of state and Party continued in the one-party state until 1937–38. Within the state, even though the process of *Gleichschaltung* effectively eliminated all sources of opposition, many older and efficient administrations still run by civil servants coexisted with various new National Socialist organizations and personnel. The combination of old and new was also a feature at the level of state and municipal government. The various states of Germany were turned into so many principalities in which as many as three different ruling bodies frequently claimed primacy. The relationship between the Party and the state remained tangled there as well, as evidenced by the hostile rivalry between separate state and Party offices at the local, district, and regional level on the one hand and the assumption of both government and Party positions by single individuals at the state and department level on the other. Instead of simplifying the administration, the expansion of the principle of one-man and one-party rule served only to complicate jurisdictional relations. It soon became apparent that friction, waste, and duplication resulted, this not merely from the upheavals of the seizure of power but were endemic to the entire system of National Socialist rule.

In fact, this largely conscious technique of rule fulfilled an important function, particularly during the takeover phase but continuing until the late 1930s. The approach facilitated the recruitment of technicians who were assured of the continuation of the existing order. Their satisfaction over their continued importance in the new system blinded them to the fact that this guarantee granted them only relative freedom, which could be rescinded at any time, and that the Führer, in command of the tools of coercion and terror, had the decisive voice on all vital questions. Alongside the surviving system of law and justice, therefore, the system of protective custody, the Gestapo, and the concentration camps developed beyond the reach of the courts.

This relationship between the state and the Party was also the key to Hitler's personal power. Hitler refrained from complete fusion of Party and state since the balance had to be regulated from time to time through Hitler's personal intervention, and the rivalry between the agencies enhanced his own power as Führer. Until 1938 the National Socialist regime could be described as a semi-authoritarian, semipopulist form of government which tended to strengthen the central powers of the state but still contained dynamic elements of a mass Party. The Führer alone stood above the confusion of jurisdictions and chains of command. On him rested almost all hopes, those of National Socialists and non–National Socialists alike, and this focus tied them to the regime. The rivalries between party officials, the conflicts between state and Party, the fights between the army and the SA, and the squabbles between administrative departments all constantly reaffirmed the omnipotent position of the supreme arbiter. By playing one against the other and apparently supporting each, Hitler not only preserved but strengthened his position of power. As in the early years of struggle, he manipulated this principle of making all dependent on him with remarkable virtuosity.

Among the reasons for the success of National Socialism in the time of both struggle and the consolidation of power was the tremendously important part played by the near-religious veneration of the Führer. The organizational structure and popular dynamism of the movement were based almost completely on this principle. In the center, of course, stood the figure of Adolf Hitler. Without this particular image of the Leader which he quite consciously cultivated after 1924, the entire National Socialist phenomenon, both as a political movement and as a revolutionary seizure and consolidation of power, would not have been possible. In addition, Hitler knew that force or even terror was acceptable to the German people only under the guise of legality, which he maintained even when it was no longer necessary. Through the loose organization of the Party and the state he established a political structure that was open at the bottom to admit many and allowed for competition among both agencies and personalities. The structure not only gave individuals the room to maneuver for position but also directed their ambitions against one another and not against the Führer. While a more hierarchically organized system would have been more efficient, it would have allowed power structures to solidify and thereby enabled individuals to challenge Hitler's rule. In the last analysis this loose system gave Hitler just what he desired, the uncontested position of sole ruler. In a modern state, which from necessity tends to bureaucratic routinization and rigidity, this systemless system gave Hitler both the system and free initiative within it.

40. The Omnipotent Führer

The Nazis transformed a parliamentary democracy into a personal dictatorship in the space of a few months. The contrast in governmental systems was one of extremes. Carl Schmitt, an expert on constitutional law and professor of law at the University of Berlin from 1933 to 1945, had been a critic of the Weimar Constitution, joined the NSDAP in 1933, and subsequently became the foremost legal theoretician of the Hitler state. By 1936, however, he had fallen out of favor with the regime because his attitudes toward racial theory were thought to be only lukewarm. Writing during the 1950s, Schmitt reflected on the constitutional aspects of authority and the delegation of power in the Hitler state, concluding that the Führer had created a "personal regime."

From Carl Schmitt, *Verfassungsrechtliche Aufsätze aus den Jahren 1924–54* (Berlin: Dunker und Humblot Verlag, 1958), pp. 431–32. Translated by Dieter Kuntz. Reprinted by permission of Dunker and Humblot GmbH.

[margin note: Hitler sole with power, access was a problem]

Because of the concentration of power in Hitler's hands, which was carried to an extreme, access to him [the Führer] became one of the most important problems of internal politics in the German Reich. Such a concentration of total power in a single human being — who insisted on ruling a modern industrial state of 70 million people, even down to the smallest detail, and on conducting a modern total war personally, down to issuing detailed individual orders — exceeds all known examples of a "personal regime," including those of Napoleon III and Wilhelm II. Correspondingly, the significance of being quite close to the leader was greater than in any previous regime. Hitler's chauffeurs became high officials of the regime; they received the rank of *Gruppenführer*, that is, the rank of a general, a rank not bestowed on the personal coachmen of Napoleon III or the chauffeurs of Wilhelm II. A *Gauleiter* who was able to gain access to Hitler was politically more important than a Reich minister who did not see his chief of state for years. The idea of an orderly and calculable distribution of responsibilities ends here. . . .

Hitler's personal position of power implied a colossal claim to omnipotence and to omniscience. The omnipotence did, to a large extent, exist. In contrast, the omniscience was pure fiction. Therefore, the first practical question was who would feed the omnipotent Führer the information on which he could formulate his decisions and his decrees, and who would select from the incoming mass [of letters and petitions] what was or was not to be submitted to him. The second question dealt with who should pass on orders and decisions to those carrying them out, a question that is of special importance because there were no clearly defined forms for the so-called Führer directives, and the orders were frequently very brief and abrupt. . . .

[margin note: The higher Hitler went the less contact was available]

The higher Hitler rose, and with him all those who had access to him or were in personal contact with him, the lower sank the Reich ministers who did not belong to this privileged group. Many were reduced to being mere civil servants. The Reich cabinet did not meet after 1937. Between the top level of political power and the previous highest posts, which were sinking, a vacuum developed which had to be filled through the creation of new "superministerial" structures, that is, through those corresponding to the extremely personal character of Hitler's use of power. Those filling these positions could, for all practical matters, not be authorities in the sense of a national and functionally developed jurisdictional hierarchy, but could only be highly personal staffs, regardless of the particular name under which they functioned. Usually, and in a certain sense typically, the term *chancellery* emerged. . . .

41. The Führer Principle

The "leadership principle," established early in the development of National Socialism, became the structural principle of Party organization prior to the seizure of
power, emphasizing discipline and a chain of command, all culminating in the
charismatic position of the Führer. After the seizure of power, the regime continued
to apply this concept to the Party's political organization. The proliferation of
Party agencies, however, created competency conflicts and outright institutional
confusion. In 1936 Robert Ley, chief of the Party's political organization, issued
guidelines in the *Organization Book of the NSDAP* spelling out how the system
was supposed to function in theory.

The Party was created by the Führer out of the realization that if our
people were to live and advance towards an era of prosperity they had to
be led according to an ideology suitable for our race. They must have as
supporters men above average, that means, men who surpass others in
self-control, discipline, efficiency, and greater judgment. The party will
therefore always constitute a minority, the order of the National Socialist
ideology which comprises the leading elements of our people.

Therefore the party comprises only fighters, at all times prepared to
assume and to give everything for the furtherance of the National Socialist
ideology. Men and women whose primary and most sacred duty is to
serve the people.

The NSDAP as the leading element of the German people control the
entire public life, from an organizational point of view, as well as from
that of affiliates, the organizations of the State administration, and so
forth.

In the long run it will be impossible to let leaders retain responsible
offices if they have not been recognized by the Party.

Furthermore, the party shall create the prerequisites for a systematic
selection of potential "Führers."

The reconstruction of the National Socialist organizational structure
itself is demonstrated by the observation of the following principles:

The Führerprinzip.
The subordination and coordination within the structure of the entire
    organization.
The regional unity.
The expression of the practical community thought.

From Office of the United States Chief of Counsel for the Prosecution of Axis Criminality,
Nazi Conspiracy and Aggression (Washington, D.C.: U.S. Government Printing Office,
1946), vol. 4, doc. no. 1809-PS, pp. 411–14.

I. FÜHRER PRINCIPLE [FÜHRERPRINZIP]

Party organization with H at top

The Führer Principle requires a pyramidal organization structure in its details as well as in its entirety.

The Führer is at the top.

He nominates the necessary leaders for the various spheres of work of the Reich's direction, the Party apparatus and the State administration.

Thus a clear picture of the tasks of the party is given.

The Party is the order of "Führers." It is furthermore responsible for the spiritual–ideological National Socialist direction of the German people. The right to organize people for their own sake emanates from these reasons.

This also justifies the subordination to the party of the organizations concerned with the welfare of the people, besides the inclusion of people in the affiliates of the party, the SA, SS, NSKK [Motor Corps], the Hitler Youth, the NS Women's League, the NS German Student Union and the NS German "Dozentenbund" [University lecturers association].

This is where the National Socialist Führer structure becomes more strongly apparent.

Every single affiliate is cared for by an office of the NSDAP.

The leadership of the individual affiliates is appointed by the Party.

The Reich Organization Leader [Reichsorganisationsleiter] of the NSDAP is simultaneously leader of the DAF [German Labor Front]. The NSBO [Factory Cell Organization] is the organization bearer of the DAF.

The Leader of the Central Office for Public Welfare also handles within the "Personal union" the National Socialist People's Welfare Organization and the Winter Relief.

The same applies to:

The Reich Justice Office [Reichsrechtsamt] for the NS "Rechtswahr-erbund,"

The Central Office for Public Health for the NS German Medical Association,

The Central Office for Educators for the NS Teachers Association,

The Central Office for Civil Servants for the German Association of Civil Servants,

The Central Office for War Victims for the NS War Victim Relief,

The Central Office for Technology for the NS Association of German Technology.

The Central Office for Race and Resettlement handles the National Association of Families with Numerous Children [Reichsbund der Kinderreichen], the NS Womanhood [Frauenschaft] and the Women's Work Association.

The Reich Office for Agrarian Politics of the NSDAP remains further-more in closest touch with the "Reichnährstand" [Reich Food Corporation] which is anchored in the State. Direct handling and personal contact of the leaders is also provided in this manner.

All attached affiliates, as well as the offices of the Party, have their foundation, in the same manner as in the Reich direction, in the sovereign territories, in the *Gaue* and furthermore in the districts [Kreise] and if required in the local groups of the NSDAP. This applies also to cells and blocks in the case of the NS Women's League, the DAF, and the NSV. The members of the attached affiliates will be included in local administrations, respectively district sectors or district comradeships which correspond geographically to local groups of the Party.

42. Nazi Leadership in Chaos

Otto Dietrich, Press Chief of the Third Reich from 1933 to 1945, had good opportunity to observe how the Führer state functioned in reality. He experienced first-hand this system of personal and institutional conflict which resulted in utter administrative chaos. While he was in a British internment camp immediately after the war, Dietrich composed an account of his relationship with Hitler, which was published posthumously in 1955. In his book, Dietrich made the claim that there was indeed purpose to the administrative tangle. He claimed that Hitler's position of authority was enhanced by "playing one off against the other."

In theory Hitler had built up an ideal Leader State. But in practice he created utter chaos in the leadership of the state. Before the eyes of his adherents he held up the mirage of a classless Leader State such as Plato had celebrated in his "Laws" as the highest possible form of the state. The Father of Philosophy described such a system as one which automatically brought forth out of the people the wise men to be their leaders, to whom the masses would voluntarily subordinate themselves. After two thousand years of human evolution and political experience the time seemed ripe to Hitler, and the people ready, to bring an experiment of this sort to fruition.

Hitler established his "folk-community" in Germany. At the same time he created a class of leaders who had, he said, risen by natural selection out of the political struggle on the domestic scene. He equipped these leaders with "authority over those below and responsibility to those above." On top of the heap he himself sat enthroned as absolute Leader responsible to no one. According to Hitler's planned "Constitution" the Leader was to be advised by a Senate appointed by himself. This Senate would then choose the Führer's eventual successor.

This "classless race-and-leader state" had been brought into being by revolution. Hitler wanted to ensure its continuance by setting up a functioning, permanent system for the selection of leaders. For this pur-

(handwritten margin note: Chaos brought on by Hitler's System)

From Otto Dietrich, *Hitler*, trans. Richard and Clara Winston (Chicago: Regnery Gateway Inc., 1955), pp. 112–19.

pose, all barriers of privilege were to be removed; the potential leaders seeking to rise above the broad masses of the people were not to be hampered by birth or economic condition. Competence alone was to be the qualification for leadership in this new state. The best youths of the nation were to be constantly recruited out of the people, were to join the leadership and grow into the pulsating life of the nation. Thus the state would be assured of both stability and progress. It would advance to the highest possible point of evolution. This system of perpetual renewal, of creative forces developing out of the society's own rhythm, was to constitute the best and most modern form of state, the most beneficial to the commonweal and at the same time the most just for each individual.

That was the "idea." In theory it was alluring and attracted many fine minds. But what was it like in practice?

In the twelve years of his rule Hitler created in the political leadership of Germany the greatest confusion that has ever existed in a civilized state. Instead of developing the hierarchy of leaders who were to stand at his side, checking his work, giving advice, and adjusting conflicts, he concentrated the leadership more and more exclusively within his own person. He permitted no other gods besides himself. The cult of personality he fostered was directed solely toward himself. He wanted no suggestions; he wanted only execution of his orders.

For centuries the conduct of government has been based upon the tried and tested principle of independent chiefs of different departments. But Hitler, wherever possible, eliminated this system and set up a series of dependent secretariats without authority. He did not appoint competent persons with independent responsibilities to important posts, persons who would then have borne their full share of the burden in the conduct of war and peace. Instead he set up mere executive arms who had to go to him for their exact instructions, who could do no more than carry out his orders.

For example, throughout the war Hitler never had the aid and support of a war minister or a commander-in-chief of the armed forces. In February 1938 he had dismissed the war minister and assumed those functions. In his place he appointed a chief of the OKW [*Oberkommands der Wehrmacht* — High Command of the Armed Forces] who was directly attached to himself. For the same reason he personally took over, in December 1941, the post of supreme commander of the army, although he certainly could not handle all the details of the commander's tasks. In August 1942 he transferred the leading post in the Army Personnel Office to one of his own adjutants. In this way he held the reins of the entire personnel organization of the army. Similarly, in May 1941 the administration of the Party was taken out of the hands of the independently responsible "Deputy of the Führer." Thereafter party affairs were handled bureaucratically by the "head of the Party Secretariat" (Bormann) who acted directly on Hitler's orders.

The strangest aspect of this leadership policy was the fact that in wartime the Reich had, to all practical purposes, no chief of government. As commander of the armed forces Hitler was unable to keep up with his duties as chancellor. He patently had no intention of submitting to Cabinet decisions. As I have already mentioned, throughout the war he did not call a single meeting of the Cabinet; his ministers therefore served no political functions whatsoever. He repeatedly stated that he was deliberately keeping himself free of all such "hampering" influences. The chancellor's business was conducted for him on a civil-service level by his "Chief of the Reich Chancery" (Lammers), to whom he assigned the rank of minister in order to facilitate his dealings with the members of the Cabinet. Hitler permitted a degree of independence only to the chiefs of those departments whose operations he did not feel he knew enough about. Among these were the air force (Goering) and the navy (Räder — Dönitz). He also allowed a certain freedom to the men of whom he felt absolutely sure, men who were completely devoted to him, like Goebbels (Propaganda), Ribbentrop (Foreign Policy) and Himmler (Police).

With his overwhelming need to dominate, Hitler could not permit the development of any other personality besides his. Instead of drawing to himself men of high character, rich experience and breadth of vision, he gave such persons a wide berth and made sure they had no chance to influence him. A miser unwilling to share his power, he consistently, cunningly and stubbornly isolated himself from the influence of all those whom he suspected of even the shadow of opposition to his will and his plans. Far from being the prisoner of his advisers, Hitler was rather the jealous guardian of his own rule. He surrounded his own autocratic dominion with impenetrable armor.

In addition, he systematically undermined the authority of all higher political organs in order to increase the absoluteness of his own power. He destroyed all clarity in the administration of government and established an utterly opaque network of overlapping authorities. It was almost a rule with Hitler to establish dual appointments and conflicting agencies.

By making Goering head of the Four-Year Plan Authority he gave him control of the entire German planned economy. But then at the same time he kept in office a rival minister of the economy (Schacht — Funk) whose functions were practically the same. Later on he added to these a minister for war production (Todt — Speer) who, just by the by, was engaged in a permanent feud with the OKW over problems of armament.

So long as Neurath was foreign minister Hitler handled his most important and most secret foreign affairs through the "Plenipotentiary of the Reich for Disarmament Questions" (Ribbentrop). When the latter became minister of foreign affairs, Neurath was appointed president of the nonexistent Privy Council. But in addition to the Foreign Office there was a "Foreign Policy Office" (Rosenberg) and a "Foreign Organization of the National Socialist Party" (Bohle). No one could possibly unravel their various jurisdictions in foreign affairs.

One day at Hitler's headquarters Ribbentrop persuaded the Führer to commit to him in writing the conduct of all propaganda intended for foreign consumption. Propaganda Minister Goebbels knew nothing at all about this. The morning of the following day movers, sent by the Foreign Office, appeared at Goebbels' various offices in Berlin to remove all the physical apparatus used for foreign propaganda. Goebbels' men barricaded themselves in their rooms, and the propaganda minister himself promptly telephoned to Hitler for help. Hitler, who had actually signed the order to Ribbentrop, ordered Goebbels to come at once by plane. When Goebbels arrived, he told him to sit down with Ribbentrop in a compartment of his special train and not to leave it until they had ironed out their dispute. Three hours later both men emerged redfaced and informed Hitler — as might have been expected — that they could not agree. Furious, Hitler withdrew and dictated a compromise which largely revoked his previous written order. In practice, however, Ribbentrop never adhered to this latter decision. Holding a facsimile of the first, rescinded order, down to the end of the war he continued to challenge the Propaganda Ministry's jurisdiction in all German missions abroad. Moreover, Ribbentrop had the obsession that all German authorities that had anything at all to do with foreign countries belonged under the Foreign Office. This fixed idea involved him in jurisdictional disputes with virtually all the ministries and *Oberste Reichsbehörden*, those "Supreme Reich Authorities" which existed side by side with the ministries. He even battled with the High Command of the Armed Forces. Hitler knew all about these squabbles. He frequently commented mockingly upon Ribbentrop's morbid ambitions, but in spite of all the complaints about the impossible situation he never intervened.

In 1933 Hitler assigned all press policy to the propaganda minister and appointed Goebbels Chief of the German Press Organization. But this did not stop him from installing a "Reich Head for the Press" (Amann, president of the Reich Press Chamber) under Goebbels and a "Reich Press Chief" (Dietrich). My official high-sounding title was "Press Chief of the Reich Government," but the title did not carry with it corresponding powers. My work was largely publicity and keeping Hitler informed on press matters. Since the Press Division of the Foreign Office dealt with foreign correspondents, and since the OKW during the war also claimed a considerable portion of the functions of the press officials, the jurisdictional disputes in this field were unending.

In the sphere of culture Goebbels and Rosenberg quarreled incessantly; in art Goering and Goebbels, Rosenberg and Buhler tilted against one another.

In the Party organization Ley and Bormann had the same radius of activities; in Party education Rosenberg and Ley were in competition.

[margin note: Conflicts from which Hitler benefitted]

In the armed forces the interests of army, Waffen-SS (Armed SS) and air force field divisions were inextricably confused and incompatible. Hitler had arbitrarily set up these organizations side by side.

Hitler divided the Reich Communications Ministry into Railroad and Post-Office departments, thereby creating an inexhaustible source of disputes.

In the sphere of justice he had a Minister of Justice and a Head of the German Legal Front (Gürtner and Frank) who feuded with one another.

He had a Labor Minister (Seldte), a Leader of the German Labor Front (Ley) and a Commissioner General for Manpower (Sauckel). In general education the field was divided between Rust (Minister of Education), Wächtler (National Socialist Teachers' Association), Axmann (Reich Youth Leader). Even in public health there were similar obscurities and crossing jurisdictions.

This is but a small sample of the utterly wild confusion of leadership. Everywhere in the Reich and in the occupied territories Hitler established the same conditions: dual appointments, special commissioners, a horde of officials with overlapping jurisdictions. I recall the pungent comment of Minister of Economy Funk in 1943, when he arranged a press release regarding a clarification of jurisdiction which Hitler had supposedly ordered. With biting irony he said to me over the telephone: "Consider what that means! Consider that for the first time in the history of the Third Reich we really have clear lines of jurisdiction and a distribution of spheres of operation!"

It was not negligence, not excessive tolerance and consideration which prompted Hitler, ordinarily so ready to cut across complexities, to create a tangle of struggles for position and conflicts of authority among the top men of the National Socialist State. There was a method in the madness. In this way Hitler had at his disposal two or three "chiefs" in every field, each with an extensive apparatus. He could ensure the execution of his plans by playing one man off against the other or showing preference to one rather than another. His method systematically disorganized the objective authority of the higher departments of government — so that he could push the authority of his own will to the point of despotic tyranny.

A further situation resulted from these jurisdictional squabbles. Each of the disputants naturally strove not only to maintain his own sphere of authority, but to enlarge it at the expense of the spheres of rivals. The scene was thus cluttered with numerous staffs and offices, each dependent upon a different chief, each employing large numbers of persons whose sole activity was to straighten out internal jurisdictional conflicts. A large number of persons were thus engaged in totally nonproductive work. The apparatus of government and Party, which has always been the breeding ground of human weaknesses, swelled beyond all proportion.

How fearfully such conditions destroyed that vital intangible, the

confidence of the people in their government! It is depressing to consider
how these internal conflicts paralyzed energies, hampered performances
and drained the strength of the nation during the war.

43. The Party and State Relationship

The Hitler state was never able to define the power relationship between state
bureaucracy and Party organizations. *Gleichschaltung* of the state bureaucracy had
eliminated only those members of the civil service who had democratic convictions.
Consequently, many members of the state bureaucracy who were not Party members continued to function at their old posts. Numerous Party positions were
established after the seizure of power which competed with state government
agencies, leading to conflicts between Party and state officials, and, ultimately,
administrative chaos. The following memorandum written in December 1935 by
the district council president of Bad Kreuznach in the Rhineland presents the
perspective of a state government official on this situation.

I have often reported that the lower-level party offices are still staffed by
thoroughly unqualified individuals. This is unfortunately still the case
today. I was, however, informed at the last meeting with the mayors
and police officials that the cooperation between party and government
officials has improved. In contrast to this, however, is the observation
from an extremely reliable source that the Party does not characterize the
cooperation with government officials as satisfactory. This is based on the
claim that government officials do not "toe the line" sufficiently. From
my point of view, the relationship between Party and state officials is
characterized by the fact that leading state officials, especially those in
public administration, have grown so accustomed to the continual med-
dling in their affairs by party officials that they put up with this in order
to avoid serious conflict. It is, however, not a healthy situation when
in the interest of maintaining a good relationship and for the sake of
appearances, state officials always give in. This is often detrimental to the
business at hand. After serving the district for almost three years now, I
feel compelled to say quite bluntly that the duality of Party and state
functions in administrative matters is intolerable in the long run, and is
capable of jeopardizing the development of our program. This view of
things is not mine alone but is shared by longtime party members who
have for many years held leading administrative positions. It is these

From F. J. Heyen ed., *Nationalsozialismus im Alltag: Quellen zur Geschichte des Nationalsozialismus im Raum Mainz-Koblenz-Trier* (Boppard, West Germany: H. Boldt Verlag, 1967), pp.
263–66. Translated by Dieter Kuntz. Reprinted by permission of Landesarchiv, Rheinland-
Pfalz.

people in particular who complain loudly to me that lower Party officials are apparently taking an example from the practices of higher Party officials, and have the notion that state officials are nothing more than agents who implement Party orders.

In fact, the Party's district leader has the attitude that: "there can be no other authority but his own within the Kreuznach district." Of course this maxim is taken even more seriously by local subordinate Party officials. It is frequently the case that grievances are contrived in order to have reasons for interfering in state business, so that state officials will feel that they are under Party supervision.

Although they do not have an adequately trained administrative apparatus, Party officials nonetheless handle administrative matters and make preliminary decisions that either have already been duly carried out by state officials or are still pending. In the end these are then entrusted to the care of state officials, who study them and make the necessary decisions. Until this happens, however, there is much duplication of work, and time and energy has been wasted. I am under the impression that in all of this the personal ambition of Party officials plays a leading role. Ambition leads Party officials to publicly, especially in the press, claim sole credit for work successfully accomplished by state officials, while for the mistakes they cause they gladly lay the blame at the feet of state officials. . . .

Moreover, the fact that in the appointment of city council members and mayors the deciding factor was not so much their personal qualifications as their membership in the Party leads one to surmise that from the beginning a personal dependence of community government offices toward Party offices was to be established. In actuality, it is true that mayors and council members generally feel that they are more under the command of the Party than of higher administrative offices. Not only has this created dissatisfaction among a large segment of the public, but it has led to frequent criticism of and opposition to city government offices, which in the end is detrimental to the National Socialist movement.

The endeavor on the part of the political leadership to make the staffing of high and low government administrative positions dependent on long-time Party membership, often goes so far as to exclude non–Party members and those Party members who joined after January 30, 1933, from those positions even if they have far better professional and moral qualities. A particularly striking case was the selection of the head of the area welfare office. From among a number of very capable applicants . . . an official was selected who was, to be sure, a longtime Party member, but who was neither professionally nor personally suited, as became evident when he was soon after arrested because of embezzlement during his previous appointment. It is inevitable that the public will come to believe that the Party has a mission to place Party members in public office without regard

[handwritten margin note: exclusion of non party members]

[handwritten margin note: party members in jobs they are not suited to]

to their qualifications and that in the end the Party is doing the same thing it fought against during the Weimar years. . . .

44. The Permanent Revolution

Goebbels had announced in his speech of July 17, 1933, that the National Socialist revolution was in effect over. The Party held full power in the state and, no longer needing to consolidate its position through force, would now begin to expand on the results of the revolution by building a *Volksgemeinschaft*, or folk community. But not until the activities of the "radicals" in the SA had been eliminated by the Blood Purge in the summer of 1934 can it be said that the violent first phase of the building of the Nazi state had indeed ended.

The National Socialists, however, did not discard the dynamic principle of revolution. In order to legitimize the Nazi state and their use of unrestricted power in setting up a totalitarian regime, the Nazis employed the concept of "permanent revolution." As long as there were Germans who were still recalcitrant, as long as "total unity" of the people had not been achieved, the Hitler state needed to continue its revolutionary activity. The regime justified its existence through perpetual action.

The scope of the regime's domestic activities is clearly demonstrated by a regional government memorandum from the Bad Kreuznach district in the Rhineland in December 1935. The report complains that the fever pitch spurred by the incredible number of party events was actually counterproductive.

The Party and its organizations were particularly active during the past month. Aside from the collection for the WHW [*Winterhilfswerk*, Winter Relief Organization], which is recognized in all circles as a really good measure, many felt that there was an overabundance of good being done at political meetings, social gatherings, various appeals, parents' evenings, cultural evenings, St. Nicholas and Christmas celebrations sponsored by the Party, the SA, the Hitler Youth, the BdM [*Bund deutscher Mädel*, League of German Girls], the NS Women's Organization, the Labor Service, the NS Chamber of Culture, and other organizations. Held almost simultaneously were special publicity campaigns and collections for the NSV [*Nationalsozialistische Volkswohlfahrt*, National Socialist People's Welfare Organization], the NS Women's League, the Labor Service, and so on. This glut of functions within a few weeks of Christmas was onerous for not only those people whose participation was expected, but also for those who were involved in the organization of such events.

From F. J. Heyen ed., *Nationalsozialismus im Alltag: Quellen zur Geschicte des Nationalsozialismus im Raum Mainz-Koblenz-Trier* (Boppard, West Germany: H. Boldt Verlag, 1969), pp. 290–94. Translated by Dieter Kuntz. Reprinted by permission of Landesarchiv, Rheinland-Pfalz.

If these events of the Party and its auxiliary organizations are to accomplish their purpose, which is to win over to the movement those still numerous segments of the population who are indifferent, then in my opinion it is psychologically and propagandistically ill advised to squeeze such an excessive number of events into such a short amount of time because inevitably the success of one event will come at the expense of another. Consequently not all events were able to register the hoped-for success. The promotion for the NSV in the rural areas has not had the anticipated result; that for the NS Women's League had only modest success, and then only among the women of Party members and officials.

As for the rest, it can be said that the pressure being exerted on people to a greater or lesser degree to join the various NS auxiliary organizations and economic and occupationally related organizations is meeting with increased criticism. In public one frequently hears: "we are organizing ourselves to death," or other comments charging that large numbers of organizations have been created only for the purpose of collecting dues payments. . . .

In earlier reports I repeatedly pointed out that the political attitudes of broad circles of the rural population are determined largely according to what the Party has tangibly accomplished at the community level. The great political successes of the Führer are no doubt understood to a certain degree by the average person, but they are not of lasting value when compared to local affairs and local conditions. One cannot, for example, expect a simple small-scale farmer to have unconditional faith in the National Socialist state if the local mayor, local farmers' leader, and local Party chairman are not harmoniously cooperating, but are instead obviously fighting one another and possibly fostering the creation of cliques and divisions among village inhabitants.

45. The Blomberg-Fritsch Crisis

In establishing the Nazi state, Hitler initially had to make some compromises in order to have the support of those elements essential to his conquest of power. Chief among these were the conservative forces of the army. Because such compromises had to be made, Nazi control of the state was never quite complete, and the army especially was not Nazified and managed to retain a considerable degree of independence after the seizure of power. By the end of 1937, however, Hitler was planning bold foreign policy moves and needed to increase his control over the military. During the Hossbach Conference of November 1937, at which Hitler outlined to his top military leaders his plans for future territorial expansion,

From Klaus-Jürgen Müller, *Armee und Drittes Reich, 1933–1939* (Paderborn, West Germany: F. Schöningh, 1987), pp. 244–47. Translated by Dieter Kuntz. Reprinted by permission of Verlag Ferdinand Schöningh.

Field Marshal von Blomberg and Colonel von Fritsch voiced their concerns about the practicability of the Führer's schemes. Both men were soon after relieved of their commands.

The initiative to purge the command structure of the armed forces did not come from Hitler, however. Hermann Goering, commander of the air force, and Heinrich Himmler, chief of the SS, also held resentments against Fritsch and Blomberg, who represented the traditional, elitist officer corps and who seemed to be blocking the expansion of both the SS and the air force. Himmler's police produced files containing personally damaging information about the two officers. Blomberg, who at the time was minister of defense and supreme commander of the armed forces, had recently married a woman who had been a registered prostitute; Fritsch, commander in chief of the army, was charged with having committed a homosexual offense, of which he was later vindicated. Both men had been disgraced, however, and were forced to resign in February 1938. Hitler made himself commander in chief of the armed forces, creating a new high command staffed by individuals loyal to the Führer.

The following document, Fritsch's recollections, written at the height of the crisis on February 1, 1938, illustrates Fritsch's relationship with Goering and with Himmler's SS and helps illuminate the motives of the purge of the army as well as the importance of this episode in establishing Hitler's control over the military.

. . . The year 1933 was characterized by the power aspirations of the SA. The SA wanted to take the place of the armed forces. . . . Although in 1933 the beginnings of the Luftwaffe were established, nothing was done for the army. On the contrary, all the steps so painstakingly taken to ensure the security of the borders were ruined through the intrigues of the SA. What manpower was available in the armed forces was employed mostly for the rapid training of SA people. The training of the army itself suffered.

Probably every discerning soldier shared my feeling that the SA wanted to take the place of the army, even though Blomberg or Reichenau again and again denied this. . . . On June 30, 1934, this period came to a close. In the meantime — contrary to the wishes of the Führer and Blomberg — I had on January 3, 1934, been appointed chief of the High Command of the army. This became effective as of February 1, 1934. My appointment was made possible only because of the strong insistence of Field Marshal von Hindenburg.

There I discovered that all was in ruins; that there was a severe confidence crisis within the High Command. Reichenau and the Party began their campaign against me on the day of my appointment. Quite possibly this had begun even earlier. Reichenau's motives are understandable. He had ambition to become chief of the army — and still wants to do so today.

The Party sees in me the man who not only opposed the aspirations of the SA, but who is also opposed to the infiltration of the Party's political maxims into the army. Irrespective of the fact that the foundation of today's army is and must be a National Socialist one, an infiltration of political infuence into the army cannot be tolerated. Such an influence would only bring about dissolution and disintegration.

On February 1, 1934, the Führer assigned me the following task: "Create an army of the largest size possible, but one with internal cohesion and unity, and train it to the fullest degree." I have worked since that time to complete this mission.

Reichenau's intrigues had the effect of making my relationship with Blomberg a strained one. I did not succeed during these years in developing the kind of trusting relationship I should have had with him. . . .

. . . I am not clear on just how the 30th of June 1934 evolved. I suspect, however, that Himmler and Reichenau were influential in shaping events. My relationship to the Party is characterized by the fact that my name, too, was included in the list read over the radio of individuals who had supposedly been shot.

In the fall of 1934 the party renewed and intensified its smear campaign against me. This was conducted primarily by the Gestapo and related offices. They succeeded in largely convincing Goering that I was planning a *putsch*. Himmler wanted to know if this *putsch* was to take place on the 10th of January 1935, or on another day in January. It was with this in mind that Blomberg extended invitations to the commanding generals and many other high-ranking officers for an evening social gathering. On the 10th, the first of the days in question, Himmler delivered a speech. I supposedly had incriminated myself by allegedly asking a professor, I think his name was Schmidt, to hold a lecture on the topic of state law at Tupitzufer on an upcoming day — Thursday, I believe. Goering maintained that this lecture was intended to show that a *putsch* was legal according to state law. This he said in the presence of ministerial officials and countless officers! . . . This person [Schmidt] was, and still is, totally unknown to me. I only mention this to show that they do not shy away from using anything at all against me, not even the most ridiculous things.

During the fall of 1934, the intrigues of the SS had created a great deal of excitement. The SS contended that the army was planning a *putsch*, while military circles were reporting that it was the SS that was preparing a coup. The Führer decided to order all leading party officials and many high-ranking officers to attend a meeting in the opera house on the evening of January 3, 1935. The Führer delivered a speech that was clearly a testimonial of loyalty to the army and its leader [Fritsch]. After the speech, the smear campaign of the SS let up somewhat. During the summer of 1935 it began anew. Especially revealing of the whole situation was the behavior of the SS Special Service troops at the military training area at

Altengrabow. There, for no particular reason, they hurled the most vile insults at the army and at myself. Although I succeeded in developing good and even trusting relationships with many Party officers in the following period, I was never able to do this with the SS. Seen from our point of view, this could be owing to the fact that there was hardly a higher-ranking officer who did not feel that he was being spied on by the SS. . . .

playing off SS + Army

In the end, it is the SS Special Service units that are being expanded, and that through their existence alone represent an antithesis to the army. They are living proof of the distrust of the army and its leadership.

Even though the army has some right to monitor the training of the SS Special Service, the fact is that this body of troops is being developed totally separately from and in deliberate opposition to the army. All units report that the attitude of the SS Special Service troops toward the army is quite cool, if not even negative. One cannot help but feel that the negative attitudes toward the army are being encouraged within the SS Special Service. Outwardly this negative attitude is evidenced by the fact that only rarely does an SS man salute an [army] officer.

As far as my relationship with Goering is concerned, it can be said that the establishment of unreserved trust is prevented because in his position as Prussian prime minister he is head of the Gestapo, the Security Service, and similar organizations whose activities are in no small way directed toward myself and the officer corps of the army. I regret this very much because a truly trusting relationship between Goering and myself would be useful. I am only now experiencing the result of the enmity of the SS toward me. Since they could not get the better of me through political means, they had to resort to the most dirty and vile means.

BARON VON FRITSCH

Unit II

National Socialist Ideology and the Community of Race

Most historians who study the Third Reich concentrate on Germany's involvement in the Second World War and the Nazis' attempt to exterminate the Jews of Europe — uncontestably the two most dire consequences of National Socialism. Yet understanding why the regime turned to these ends demands a familiarity with the ideas and ideals on which National Socialism was founded, not only with National Socialist ideology but also with the policies and programs instituted in order to realize that ideology. Although it was often simplified for propagandistic reasons, and although historians have often dismissed it as a mere facade masking the crude power politics of the regime, National Socialist ideology functioned as an ideal and a goal both for social policies implemented before the war and for political and military decisions made during the war. It also lay behind the policy of extermination of the Jews, the Final Solution. Not to recognize the importance of the ideology is to miss much of what constituted the reality of life inside Hitler's Germany.

Of all the major ideologies that have arisen in the modern world, the most internally contradictory is National Socialism. Perhaps the central contradiction within the Nazi ideology is its advocacy of a combination of revolution with the restoration of traditional society. It called for both the destruction of Western liberal principles and the rejection of all forms of Marxism. In this sense it stood in complete opposition to the principles of the Weimar Republic. Individual rights, a capitalist economy, and democratic political institutions, although not unchallenged in German history in the nineteenth and twentieth centuries, formed the basis of the Weimar Republic.

Unlike the revolutionary ideologies of liberalism and socialism, National Socialism did not demand creation in the name of a new future; rather, it called for a

177

return to past social forms through militant, revolutionary methods. The oxymoronic notion of a "conservative revolution" explains many of the contradictory principles of National Socialist ideology. Although founded on a "modern," "scientific" definition of race, it championed a traditional sense of communal organization that restructured the relationship of the individual to the group, of the economy to the national spirit, and of the whole to the will of the Führer. The natural inequality of the community of leaders and followers upheld by National Socialism confronted the Marxist ideal of the classless society; the nation was rededicated to its sacred soil against international communism; and the folk traditions of the racial group were united in the will of the Führer against the alienating forces of modern society.

The type of traditional society that the National Socialists hoped to form was the *Volksgemeinschaft*. According to National Socialist ideology, such a community would result from the creative activities of the German *Volk*. Unlike mere "society" (*Gesellschaft*), which had come to dominate modern industrial life with its impersonal structures and isolated individuals, the *Volk* community was integrated, personal, and organic — a national union in which each individual knew his place within the larger whole and in which every aspect of life furthered the good of the community. The notion of *Volk* had a mystical tone. It was at once "the people," "the nation," and "the race." In National Socialist theory a nation was defined in purely racial terms. The members of the Aryan race and thus of the German nation could be identified through modern racial science. The events of modern history had divided and diluted this racial group; Germans who lived outside the Reich in Austria, Czechoslovakia, and elsewhere had lost their racial identity through intermarriage with other groups. Moreover, the governmental structure of the Reich had developed in such a fashion that it no longer corresponded to the cultural needs of the people. Not just the weak and "false" political forms of the Weimar years but also the more impersonal operation of the bureaucracy and of public life generally under the imperial regime had to be reformed so as to express the needs of the *Volk* community. Within such a community not only would the diversity that is the basis of humanity be eliminated; but the reduction of all standards of value to biological inheritance would also deny human will and moral choice.

The mission of National Socialism was to reestablish the *Volk* community by bringing to full consciousness the awareness of race, blood, and soil among all Germans. At the heart of National Socialist ideology was the idea of creating the "new man" and the "new woman," of forming individuals with the strength of character, the awareness of race and soil, and the dedication to follow the Führer necessary to create the *Volk* community. National Socialism aimed to penetrate the very core of individual existence by constructing an organic society in which all people and organizations were "coordinated" under Party control, for the Party was the guardian of the *Volksgemeinschaft*. Class distinctions had to be broken down within the new community, and the very separation between occupational concerns and political existence and even between private and public life had to be overcome.

178

How did the National Socialists put these ideals into practice? The regime found many means of propagating its goals: through schools and universities, through various activities such as the annual Party rallies in Nuremberg, and through organizations such as the Hitler Youth and the League of German Girls. These meetings and organizations were not in themselves sufficient, however, to create a spirit of national community. Beyond these organizational means, mass suggestion pervaded every aspect of culture. As a call for "total culture," the ideology animated racial consciousness, supplanted the individual's feeling of isolation, and channeled his creative drives into promoting the mystique of blood and soil.

A series of National Socialist holidays redirected the attention of the German public toward the community and raised their level of participation within the *Volksgemeinschaft*. Most of these holiday celebrations included parades and mass meetings. Hitler believed that mass meetings allowed people to "step out of their workshops," where they felt small and distanced from others, and to become part of a body of "thousands and thousands of people with a like conviction." Alienation was to be exorcised, and the emotional unity of all stressed. The meetings were liturgical rites staged with close attention to detail and purpose. The National Socialists altered a number of traditional holidays. The Day of National Labor, the Nazi revamping of May Day labor celebrations, overshadowed all such occasions in mass participation. But instead of just praising industrial work, as most May 1 observances did, the Nazis added to the festival by honoring agricultural labor and paying tribute to the German soil as well. May Day festivities included felling maypoles, lighting bonfires, and choosing the King and Queen of the May. The next day the May Queen rode in a procession with folksingers, dance groups in regional costume, and garlanded carts symbolizing crafts, farming, or trade, and flanked by formations of members of the Party and the armed forces. The procession passed beneath triumphal arches adorned with the Party symbol, an eagle clutching a wreathed swastika. The second Sunday in May, Mothering Sunday, had its own observances, with crosses of honor awarded to prolific mothers in public ceremonies; in some regions, the party decorated houses in which mothers had given birth during the preceding year.

The Party invented new holidays, as well — festivals that supposedly looked back to primal Aryan rites and that celebrated the union of the *Volk* with the sacred soil of the Reich. Nocturnal bonfires into which wreaths commemorating war heroes or Party martyrs were tossed marked the Summer Solstice Celebration. After chanting hymns in praise of fire, the participants leaped across the flames. The ceremony concluded with a torchlight procession. There was also a Day of the Winter Solstice to observe the coming of winter. Finally, in autumn the Harvest Thanksgiving Day marked the end of the agricultural year.

Another array of holidays celebrated the history of the NSDAP: the Day of the Seizure of Power (January 30), the Day Commemorating the Foundation of the Party (February 24), and the National Day of Mourning (March 16). This last holiday, linked with the work of the Association for the Care of German War Cemeteries, had been observed before 1933. The NSDAP renamed it Heroes' Remembrance Day and then the Day of the Restoration of Military Sovereignty to commemorate both the reintroduction of conscription and the *Anschluss* (union) with Austria. Hitler's birthday (April 20) also became a major national holiday. Garlanded photographs of the Führer and houses liberally adorned with swastikas became part of the celebration. The focal point of the birthday festivities, the induction of new members into the Party's political leadership corps, included a nocturnal initiation rite lit by searchlights, pylons, and flaring torches and heralded by drumrolls, fanfares, massed choruses, and waving flags before the sternly classical backdrop of the Party's administrative building in the Königsplatz in Berlin. The ritual year reached a climax with the Party rally at Nuremberg in mid-September, which solemnized the allegorical "marriage" of the Party and the *Volk*. The sheer ostentation of the ceremonies in which crowds of up to one hundred thousand people bearing Nazi flags and banners marched past Hitler under a night sky illuminated by searchlights, dwarfed all other festivals in the Nazi calendar.

Not only occasionally, at these public ceremonies, but daily was the consciousness of belonging to a *Volk* community stirred. A series of ritualistic forms pried individual Germans loose from their accustomed ways of thinking about their place in society. In addition, parading columns — the ubiquitous marching groups of SA and SS men, which all bystanders were required to salute — gave a sense of the awakened *Volk* in the everyday world. The German greeting, *"Heil Hitler!,"* became the official form of salutation, both when meeting others and in writing; failure to use it was a punishable offense. Hitler's speeches and other events were broadcast on the radio. Cheap radios were offered for sale to families who could not otherwise afford them, and communal listening was obligatory in factories and offices. In restaurants and cafés, all noise had to be kept to a minimum during these radio addresses, and waiters had to stop serving. Uniforms, medals, songs, and ceremonies became part of the life of all Party members, conveying their sense of leading the *Volk* to the desired communal consciousness.

One of the main projects creating a new sense of the *Volk* was the Party's attempts to overcome class divisions and feelings of superiority among the traditional elites of Germany. A strongly anti-elitist and anti-intellectual drive surfaced early in the Third Reich. Both Hitler and Goebbels (the latter a failed writer himself) viewed intellectuals as lacking in character — people who had developed their minds but not the strength of their personalities. They were parasites on the community. Intellectuals, and especially university professors, had traditionally held an honored place in German society, and this stance attacked one of the most highly valued groups and one of the most cherished ideals of the nation. The regime required members of the intelligentsia to attend obligatory training camps to strengthen links with the *Volk,* and a period of national labor service — *Arbeitsdienst* — was inaugurated for university students, who were to learn the value of manual labor through participating in physical activities. Labor service was declared a condition for university admission in 1933.

The party instituted a number of organizations to awaken *Volk* consciousness and reform the social life of the individual. These groups included obligatory professional associations, all meticulously Aryan in their membership, for teachers, lawyers, and physicians. Journalists and artists were enrolled in national associations organized by the Propaganda Ministry. The all-embracing German Labor Front, headed by Dr. Robert Ley, replaced the proscribed trade unions. These organizations did not represent the interests of their members, but rather they directed and controlled all activities along lines conducive to the ideals and policies of the Party. No lawyer or doctor could practice without being a member of the appropriate organization; indeed, no one could work without the Party's official sanction. The individual was to serve the communal goals of the group, and the group the purposes of the entire community.

Formed under Goebbels to coordinate the cultural activities of the *Volksgemeinschaft*, the Reich Chamber of Culture encouraged "all forms of artistic creation or activity which are made public." Seven subordinate chambers — each with its own president and administrative apparatus, which was linked to the relevant department in Goebbels's ministry — oversaw literature, music, films, radio, theater, fine arts, and the press. Although the corporate structure was intended to give the appearance of self-government by artists, performers, and reporters themselves, in reality the chambers formed an integral part of the complex apparatus of cultural control, directed from a single source. Membership in one or another chamber was compulsory for all who made their living through the arts or the media, and denial of membership effectively silenced any undesired creative activity in the nation. Characteristically, however, Hitler did not give Goebbels uncontested control in the field of culture but balanced the ministry with another Party agency, the Office for the Supervision of Ideological Training and Education, whose chief, Alfred Rosenberg, a man of pronounced views about cultural uniformity, had since 1929 been waging war against all modern tendencies in art and letters. His Kampfbund für deutsche Kultur (League of Struggle for German Culture), which had been responsible for violent disruptions at exhibits of what was considered anti-Nazi and thus "degenerate" art, now became an executive arm, the "cultural SA," of the new Ideological Office of the NSDAP and was the force behind the book burnings, blacklists, and museum "cleansings" that were such prominent features of German cultural activity in the years after 1933.

The *Volksgemeinschaft* of National Socialist ideology called for a reformation of society. The artificial world of industrial society was to be radically restructured to incorporate the relationship between the *Volk* and the Reich. Men were to have complete dominance in all spheres, with farming, factory work, and pursuing a profession coordinated within the Party and the state and assuming a recognized status in the culture of the *Volk* community. The new German woman was to join the struggle to create the *Volksgemeinschaft,* but she was to do so by returning to her place in the kitchen and the nursery. Within the individual German family, the wife and mother was to return to her traditional roles: the comforter of her husband, the rearer of her children, and the nurturer of communal values. She was not to wear slacks or smoke cigarettes — two issues that continually vexed Party officials, including Hitler and Goebbels. In addition, she was not to follow modern trends in fashion, use cosmetics, or wear her hair in anything but a simple peasant style.

The position of agricultural versus industrial workers in the new order, however, remained problematic. On the one hand, National Socialist ideology proclaimed the peasant the highest representative of the union of blood and soil in the *Volk* community, but on the other hand, the Party was a "socialist" organization, concerned with the problems of urban laborers. Besides women, the honored group within the original National Socialist scheme were peasant farmers. On the land, where the German *Volk* had its inviolate being, the Nazis intended to rear a hardy nobility of pure Aryan stock. The idyllic agrarian image of Nazi ideology was that of the small-time peasant farmer, not the owner of vast estates east of the Elbe.

After the seizure of power in 1933, the NSDAP was faced for the first time with the need to define a clear policy for industrial workers. The party embraced a form of socialism, its leaders declared, but its ideology had little connection with international Marxism. Although other forms of socialism called for some degree of collective ownership, National Socialism did not. At the Berlin Auto Show of 1934, Hitler announced that the "free economy was contingent on its ability to work out its own problems." In other words, no economic system had priority in the Third Reich, but elements of all systems could be admitted as long as they were coordinated under state control. Between the alternatives of capitalism and socialism, National Socialism took a middle course, drawing from the principles of each. In an interview early in his rule, Hitler asserted that "National Socialism derives from each of the two camps the pure idea that characterizes it — national resolution from the bourgeois tradition, and vital, creative socialism from the teachings of Marxism. *Volksgemeinschaft:* this means the community of effective labor, it means the unity of all interests, it means the elimination of private citizenship and a mechanical, union-organized mass. . . ."

With its somewhat peculiar definition of socialism, the NSDAP engaged in a campaign to bring industrial workers into the *Volksgemeinschaft.* They were no longer to be considered the "lower class" but rather equal members of a racially defined community. The move to homogenize the still sharply defined German society naturally affected the aristocracy and the middle classes as well as the farmers of the Party's agrarian ideal. For the Nazis the term *bourgeois* denoted not so much a specific social class as a segment of history, the capitalist, democratic period preceding Hitler's takeover. Workers likewise were to perceive their past forms of class consciousness through their newfound sense of belonging to

182

the *Volk* community, and all members of that community were to acknowledge their equal status as fellow Germans, addressing them as *Kameraden,* ("comrades").

During the 1930s the Nazi dictatorship only partially realized National Socialist ideology, with its emphasis on reforming the community, restructuring the family and the place of women, and defining the role of the worker vis-à-vis that of the peasant. Women did not leave the labor force entirely and return to their traditional place in the family. Peasant farmers did not eventually fare better than large landowners in the Third Reich. And industrial workers, although in many ways better off in a material sense, lost all rights to organize and express their demands, independent of Party organizations. These failures resulted both from inner contradictions within the ideology itself and from the tremendous gap between National Socialist ideals and the realities of German society. In part at least, National Socialism was a response to the problems of urban industrialism, but the solutions it offered to these problems were overly simplistic. Nazi policy often ignored the great difficulties confronting modern industrial societies, and it therefore failed to create a *Volksgemeinschaft.* In all areas of life the ideology promised a new, organic community, but it in fact brought only greater state control and the complete subordination of social goals to the demands of a wartime economy. With the onset of war in the 1940s, the contradictions within National Socialism led to further contradictions between the social ideals of the ideology and the actual destructiveness of its activities.

Unit II is divided into five chapters. Chapter 6 deals with ideology, tracing its development and the redefinitions of race and racial history. Chapter 7 then takes up the discussion of the nature of National Socialism, focusing on the art produced in the Third Reich, which provides a window on the ideals and values propounded by the regime. Chapter 8 analyzes the various organizations and social policies initiated in order to translate these ideals into practice. Chapter 9, which evaluates the degree of success or failure these policies attained, deals with the effect that National Socialism had on German society. This theme is continued in Chapter 10, which examines education and youth organizations in the Third Reich and assesses the influence the ideology had on the young and how successful the Nazis were in redefining education along National Socialist lines.

Public ceremonies served to raise the consciousness of Germans of belonging to a racially pure *Volksgemeinschaft.* Here members of the League of German Girls celebrate a Nazified "May Day" with folk songs and traditional dances.

Chapter

6

National Socialist Ideology

Although others contributed to the full formulation of National Socialist ideology — the Social Darwinist academics Hans F. K. Günther and Ludwig Ferdinand Clauss, for example, along with the party ideologists Alfred Rosenberg and Joseph Goebbels — it was Hitler's worldview that gave the ideology its full theoretical explication as well as its militant edge. For Hitler the great issue of the twentieth century was not political or even military; rather, it was the life-and-death struggle of culture itself. Present-day culture, to Hitler, was both degenerate and stagnant, and it now faced total destruction, even the end of human life on earth. Saving human culture became Hitler's personal goal to which the NSDAP and later the Third Reich were the means.

Hitler prided himself on seeing, with a clarity that no one had before possessed, that the essence of any culture was an expression of race. The various races of the world, which the Social Darwinists had taught were in constant competition with one another, were not all equal. They could be ranked according to their culture-building abilities. Only one race, the Aryan, was culturally creative, able to establish and maintain cultural communities. Whether in conquering and creating a culture in India, founding the classical world of Greece and Rome, or in building the culture of the Germanic Middle Ages, the Aryan race had demonstrated its cultural generativity throughout history, striving for an ideal in an integrated, organic community in which the individual served the greater good of the whole. Most other races of mankind — the Mongoloid, the Negroid, and the Malayan — were at best merely cultural carriers. Incapable of creating their own forms of culture, they could only imitate Aryan culture and, through constant "reinfusions," maintain

185

something resembling true culture. In addition, one truly inferior, distinctive race could be identified — the "Jewish" race. Instead of building a common community for the good of all, the Jews were materialistic; they worked only for selfish reasons, which in turn atomized the community into competing classes and individuals; and they perverted the very notion of cultural community in the individualistic and class-divided society. The Jews could not even imitate Aryan creativity. They were parasites and, as twentieth-century conditions clearly indicated, threatened the very life of the Aryan community.

Hitler realized that no pure racial group existed in the modern world. The Nordic Aryans, which included the Germans, were, however, more racially healthy than any other group, because more racially pure Aryan individuals were supposedly to be found among them. The NSDAP therefore sought to preserve the purity of the race and save the culturally creative forces in the community. The first steps in pursuing this mission involved educating the German people in the proper understanding of race, taking over the state in order to convert it into a racial community, and eliminating the Jewish element from national life. To save the community from the dire conditions of the twentieth century, it was necessary to cultivate a new human type. The new person had to be able to see through the divergent and often culturally destructive values that dominated the modern world. In addition, he had to realize his or her nature as a cultural creator. This realization did not involve intellectual development; in fact, it called for just the opposite. The Jew was intelligent, especially good at viewing the world in rational terms and making it work for his individual ends. The new Aryan man, by contrast, was not "out for himself" but rather was dedicated to the good of the community. Through the ideals of self-sacrifice, service, and responsibility, he strove to build the community and purify the race. He did not approach this task in a theoretical or intellectual manner; instead, he knew instinctively what was right, or, as the National Socialists said, he thought "with his blood." He had the proper feeling when he worked for the good of the community. Compared with the rationalizing Jew, Hitler once remarked, the Aryan was a "blockhead."

In this worldview, the Jew represented the complete opposite of the Aryan. But it is important to point out that the image of the Jew that developed in Nazi ideology was based neither on a religious definition of Jewishness nor on the actual behavior of Jews past or present. This image was the product of popular antisemitism and the ideological necessity for an opposite, an "other," as the type diametrically opposed to the creative Aryan. In other words, the image of the Jew neither fitted the real historical development of the Jews of Europe nor was derived from an understanding of Jewish characteristics. Hitler himself recognized this fact when he spoke of the Jew as a "principle." Although rooted in the "science" of racial types, the image represented more a spiritual quality, a worldview unto itself, than a religious or national grouping. The image of the Jew was an amalgam of everything the Nazis disliked in the modern world, personifying all that they found repellent. But while the Jews aimed to destroy the Aryan cultural community, they were not alone in working their designs. "Judaizers," or "spiritual Jews," those non-Jews who were taken in by "Jewish" ideas and attitudes, were just as dangerous as "racially pure" Jews. By hoodwinking more creative individuals, the Jews had established the twin structures of the modern materialist world — that is, international finance capitalism and international socialism. In either system, both for the individual of modern capitalistic society and the class-conscious worker of the false communist community the ideals of the true cultural community and selfless striving for the good of the nation were destroyed. The evil genius of the Jews lay in their ability to create negative types of communities and then set them into competition with each other.

The Jews had also been tracking the creative center of Aryan culture in other ways. Through interbreeding with Aryans, they had diluted the racial purity of the *Volk*. This "mongrelization" had led to a long period of German national demoralization, which had culminated in the great catastrophes of the loss of the First World War as well as the military, political, moral, and cultural degeneration instituted with the establishment of the Weimar Republic. In some moods, Hitler viewed these events as the just retribution leveled at the German people for having forgotten their racial mission. The twentieth century would, however, bring about the final contest between the culture-building Aryans and the culture-destroying Jews. It was up to Hitler and the NSDAP to prepare Germany for this struggle and make sure that the Aryans would prevail, thereby reversing the trend of modern history toward liberalism, capitalism, class conflict, and socialism.

Although the Jews appeared to be winning the battle in historical time, as the events of the recent past indicated, there was another, larger dimension of time: the final conflict between Aryan and Jew would be a cosmic event. Measured by what Hitler called "racial time," the struggle did not span mere centuries or even millennia but the entire interglacial era. In the period between the last ice age and the next one, the human community would have to construct a culture that, though opposed to the forces of inorganic nature, could still work with them. On this cosmic level, the inorganic powers of nature, represented by the impinging forces of ice, were in eternal conflict with the creative forces of organic life. Individuals within atomized human societies would be inadequate to meet the challenges of the coming age of ice. Only a true community, organically unified in itself and tied to nature through each discrete human soul, would be able to survive in such a world; only the Aryan culture-builder could establish a community that did not resist the inorganic but cooperated with it in a true harmony of man and nature.

The society that Aryans would have to build in the future was similar to what they had built in the past, except that the new community would need conscious structuring and control. Through a series of community-uniting ceremonies and a constant barrage of propaganda, Hitler aimed to reawaken the self-sacrificing, communal Aryan spirit. The more natural, more emotional, more genuine character-istics of the Nordic Aryans would again be valued. The traditional German love of nature, a simple life-style, and good, honest fellowship were placed in opposition to the more rational, more artificial, more individualistic values of the Jewish-dominated present. The *Volk* were to be reunited in the face of both liberalism and socialist class consciousness. The love of the Nordic Aryan for the German soil was to be brought back to consciousness, and the unity between nature and man reestablished. This unity, which formed a mystical nexus of the blood (*Blut*), the people (*Volk*), and the soil (*Boden*) of the German Reich, found symbolic expression in the Party's colors of red (blood) and black (soil) as well as in the Nazi flag and the image of shovel and grain. The *Volk* community was not based on the legalistic relations of the modern democratic state, on the one hand; the notion of blood, or race, posited an organic relationship that went beyond the idea of citizenship, maintaining the racial ties of one individual to another and one generation to another. On the other hand, the new community would not be the workers' state proposed by international socialism, unconnected to the soil of a particular *Volk*. The racial foundation of the *Volk* was deeper, encompassing both individual and class. The NSDAP was only the vanguard and the state only the instrument of this cultural reawakening.

The *Volksgemeinschaft* encompassed all of life, and individuals gained fulfillment through it. No "eternal" criteria existed outside this highest good. The conception that law reflected a system of values transcending the Nazi worldview was condemned as "liberal," serving merely to fragment the nation. In the new definition of the state all power, and therefore all law, arose from the needs of the *Volk*, of which the Führer principle was the creative realization. The leadership structure was central to the government of the Third Reich and the organizational principles of the Party, and no sphere of life was held inviolate. Leader and followers, at every level of organizations and in all kinds of groups, were the poles around which the entire public life of Germany was to be reorganized. A new hierarchy, headed by the natural leaders of the people and no longer determined by such criteria as birth, wealth, or education, would emerge in the *Volk* community. The Nazis hated the old aristocracy and thought that the bourgeoisie had failed to unite the people. Leaders were to be culled from among those strong personalities who, regardless of background, had the will and power to actualize the *Volksgemeinschaft*. In Hitler's view, man's progress had derived from the activities not of the masses but of the individual leaders who directed the creative urges of the *Volk*. Hitler envisaged the government of the new community as a hierarchy of leadership: from the local leaders of the city block, through various intermediary units, all the way up to the Führer himself. Each leader was a miniature Führer, sharing the same dynamic character as Hitler himself and often having the word Führer in his official title. With the rejection of majority rule, leaders were appointed by those above them in the hierarchy. Yet the system did not simply impose dictatorship from above; Nazi theorists argued that it embodied a truly democratic principle of realizing the will of the *Volk*.

Just as the NSDAP was not a political organization but a "movement" in the cultural regeneration of the *Volk*, and the state was not an administrative structure but a means to the realization of the *Volksgemeinschaft,* so the position of the Führer was that of neither a mere Party official nor a simple post within the state. The position of the Führer was a special one in relation to the *Volk.* He recognized in his person the qualities that marked the true characteristics of the people. He also saw further than most individuals within the community. He could discern the present needs of the community because he had a special understanding of the past. Hitler alone grasped the essential nature of race in world history and, beyond this, the cosmic level of the eternal conflict between the Aryan and the Jew. He realized that modern society would not be able to meet the challenges of the coming age of ice. Not only because he had successfully become the leader of the Nazi party and had reached the chancellorship but also because of his keen, almost prophetic percipience about the future of the German people, Hitler was made the object of widespread adulation within the Third Reich. Beyond all legal relationships and constitutional arrangements, beyond all class divisions and social problems, Hitler was the living embodiment of the unity of the German *Volk,* individually and collectively, linking past, present, and future.

46. Hitler's *Mein Kampf:* Nation and Race

Although National Socialist ideology had its origins in a number of political, social, and biological theories of the nineteenth century, it took Adolf Hitler to weld these various elements into an overarching view of history and of Germany's place within it. Other Party theorists, such as Alfred Rosenberg, would make additions and work out the fine points of the ideology, but it was first and foremost Hitler's vision of the Aryan race and of the past, present, and future of Germany. His position as Führer was to some extent confirmed by his possession of this larger vision. Hitler worked out his ideas early, even before he joined the Nazi party, yet his early years in the Party as director of propaganda helped him develop them further. While imprisoned in Landsberg in 1923 he committed his ideas to print in his account of his life. The following chapter from *Mein Kampf* is perhaps the best short description of the main tenets of National Socialist ideology. The image of "the Jew" presented here is obviously not based on fact but in many ways represents the need of the ideology to find an "opposite" and a cause of cultural decline.

> There are some truths which are so obvious that for this very reason they are not seen or at least not recognized by ordinary people. They sometimes pass by such truisms as though blind and are most astonished when someone suddenly discovers what everyone really ought to know. Columbus's eggs lie around by the hundreds of thousands, but Columbuses are met with less frequently.

From Adolf Hitler, *Mein Kampf,* trans. Ralph Manheim (Boston: Houghton Mifflin, 1943, 1971), pp. 284–92, 295–303, 305–7, 327–29. Copyright © 1943 by Houghton Mifflin Company. Reprinted by permission of Houghton Mifflin Company. All rights reserved.

Thus men without exception wander about in the garden of Nature; they imagine that they know practically everything and yet with few exceptions pass blindly by one of the most patent principles of Nature's rule: the inner segregation of the species of all living beings on this earth.

Even the most superficial observation shows that Nature's restricted form of propagation and increase is an almost rigid basic law of all the innumerable forms of expression of her vital urge. Every animal mates only with a member of the same species. The titmouse seeks the titmouse, the finch the finch, the stork the stork, the field mouse the field mouse, the dormouse the dormouse, the wolf the she-wolf, etc.

Only unusual circumstances can change this, primarily the compulsion of captivity or any other cause that makes it impossible to mate within the same species. But then Nature begins to resist this with all possible means, and her most visible protest consists either in refusing further capacity for propagation to bastards or in limiting the fertility of later offspring; in most cases, however, she takes away the power of resistance to disease or hostile attacks.

This is only too natural.

Any crossing of two beings not at exactly the same level produces a medium between the level of the two parents. This means: the offspring will probably stand higher than the racially lower parent, but not as high as the higher one. Consequently, it will later succumb in the struggle against the higher level. Such mating is contrary to the will of Nature for a higher breeding of all life. The precondition for this does not lie in associating superior and inferior, but in the total victory of the former. The stronger must dominate and not blend with the weaker, thus sacrificing his own greatness. Only the born weakling can view this as cruel, but he after all is only a weak and limited man; for if this law did not prevail, any conceivable higher development of organic living beings would be unthinkable.

The consequence of this racial purity, universally valid in Nature, is not only the sharp outward delimitation of the various races, but their uniform character in themselves. The fox is always a fox, the goose a goose, the tiger a tiger, etc., and the difference can lie at most in the varying measure of force, strength, intelligence, dexterity, endurance, etc., of the individual specimens. But you will never find a fox who in his inner attitude might, for example, show humanitarian tendencies toward geese, as similarly there is no cat with a friendly inclination toward mice.

Therefore, here, too, the struggle among themselves arises less from inner aversion than from hunger and love. In both cases, Nature looks on calmly, with satisfaction, in fact. In the struggle for daily bread all those who are weak and sickly or less determined succumb, while the struggle of the males for the female grants the right or opportunity to propagate only to the healthiest. And struggle is always a means for improving a species' health and power of resistance and, therefore, a cause of its higher development.

If the process were different, all further and higher development would cease and the opposite would occur. For, since the inferior always predominates numerically over the best, if both had the same possibility of preserving life and propagating, the inferior would multiply so much more rapidly that in the end the best would inevitably be driven into the background, unless a correction of this state of affairs were undertaken. Nature does just this by subjecting the weaker part to such severe living conditions that by them alone the number is limited, and by not permitting the remainder to increase promiscuously, but making a new and ruthless choice according to strength and health.

No more than Nature desires the mating of weaker with stronger individuals, even less does she desire the blending of a higher with a lower race, since, if she did, her whole work of higher breeding, over perhaps hundreds of thousands of years, might be ruined with one blow.

Historical experience offers countless proofs of this. It shows with terrifying clarity that in every mingling of Aryan blood with that of lower peoples the result was the end of the cultured people. North America, whose population consists in by far the largest part of Germanic elements who mixed but little with the lower colored peoples, shows a different humanity and culture from Central and South America, where the predominantly Latin immigrants often mixed with the aborigines on a large scale. By this one example, we can clearly and distinctly recognize the effect of racial mixture. The Germanic inhabitant of the American continent, who has remained racially pure and unmixed, rose to be master of the continent; he will remain the master as long as he does not fall a victim to defilement of the blood.

The result of all racial crossing is therefore in brief always the following:

(a) Lowering of the level of the higher race;

(b) Physical and intellectual regression and hence the beginning of a slowly but surely progressing sickness.

To bring about such a development is, then, nothing else but to sin against the will of the eternal creator.

And as a sin this act is rewarded.

When man attempts to rebel against the iron logic of Nature, he comes into struggle with the principles to which he himself owes his existence as a man. And this attack must lead to his own doom.

Here, of course, we encounter the objection of the modern pacifist, as truly Jewish in its effrontery as it is stupid! "Man's rôle is to overcome Nature!"

Millions thoughtlessly parrot this Jewish nonsense and end up by really imagining that they themselves represent a kind of conqueror of Nature; though in this they dispose of no other weapon than an idea, and at that such a miserable one, that if it were true no world at all would be conceivable.

But quite aside from the fact that man has never yet conquered Nature in anything, but at most has caught hold of and tried to lift one or another corner of her immense gigantic veil of eternal riddles and secrets, that in reality he invents nothing but only discovers everything, that he does not dominate Nature, but has only risen on the basis of his knowledge of various laws and secrets of Nature to be lord over those other living creatures who lack this knowledge — quite aside from all this, an idea cannot overcome the preconditions for the development and being of humanity, since the idea itself depends only on man. Without human beings there is no human idea in this world, therefore, the idea as such is always conditioned by the presence of human beings and hence of all the laws which created the precondition for their existence. . . .

In actual fact the pacificist-humane idea is perfectly all right perhaps when the highest type of man has previously conquered and subjected the world to an extent that makes him the sole ruler of this earth. Then this idea lacks the power of producing evil effects in exact proportion as its practical application becomes rare and finally impossible. Therefore, first struggle and then we shall see what can be done. Otherwise mankind has passed the high point of its development and the end is not the domination of any ethical idea but barbarism and consequently chaos. At this point someone or other may laugh, but this planet once moved through the ether for millions of years without human beings and it can do so again some day if men forget that they owe their higher existence, not to the ideas of a few crazy ideologists, but to the knowledge and ruthless application of Nature's stern and rigid laws.

Everything we admire on this earth today — science and art, technology and inventions — is only the creative product of a few peoples and originally perhaps of *one* race. On them depends the existence of this whole culture. If they perish, the beauty of this earth will sink into the grave with them. . . .

All great cultures of the past perished only because the originally creative race died out from blood poisoning.

The ultimate cause of such a decline was their forgetting that all culture depends on men and not conversely; hence that to preserve a certain culture the man who creates it must be preserved. This preservation is bound up with the rigid law of necessity and the right to victory of the best and stronger in this world.

Those who want to live, let them fight, and those who do not want to fight in this world of eternal struggle do not deserve to live. . . .

It is idle to argue which race or races were the original representative of human culture and hence the real founders of all that we sum up under the word "humanity." It is simpler to raise this question with regard to the present, and here an easy, clear answer results. All the human culture, all the results of art, science, and technology that we see before us today, are almost exclusively the creative product of the Aryan. This very fact admits of the not unfounded inference that he alone was the founder of all higher humanity, therefore representing the prototype of all that we understand by the word "man." He is the Prometheus of mankind from whose bright forehead the divine spark of genius has sprung at all times, forever kindling anew that fire of knowledge which illumined the night of silent mysteries and thus caused man to climb the path to mastery over the other beings of this earth. Exclude him — and perhaps after a few thousand years darkness will again descend on the earth, human culture will pass, and the world turn to a desert.

If we were to divide mankind into three groups, the founders of culture, the bearers of culture, the destroyers of culture, only the Aryan could be considered as the representative of the first group. From him originate the foundations and walls of all human creation, and only the outward form and color are determined by the changing traits of character of the various peoples. He provides the mightiest building stones and plans for all human progress and only the execution corresponds to the nature of the varying men and races. In a few decades, for example, the entire east of Asia will possess a culture whose ultimate foundation will be Hellenic spirit and Germanic technology, just as much as in Europe. Only the *outward* form — in part at least — will bear the features of Asiatic character. It is not true, as some people think, that Japan adds European technology to its culture; no, European science and technology are trimmed with Japanese characteristics. The foundation of actual life is no longer the special Japanese culture, although it determines the color of life — because outwardly, in consequence of its inner difference, it is more conspicuous to the European — but the gigantic scientific-technical achievements of Europe and America; that is, of Aryan peoples. Only on the basis of these achievements can the Orient follow general human progress. They furnish the basis of the struggle for daily bread, create weapons and implements for it, and only the outward form is gradually adapted to Japanese character.

If beginning today all further Aryan influence on Japan should stop, assuming that Europe and America should perish, Japan's present rise in science and technology might continue for a short time; but even in a few years the well would dry up, the Japanese special character would gain, but the present culture would freeze and sink back into the slumber from which it was awakened seven decades ago by the wave of Aryan culture. Therefore, just as the present Japanese development owes its life to Aryan origin, long ago in the gray past foreign influence and foreign spirit awakened the Japanese culture of that time. The best proof of this is furnished by the fact of its subsequent sclerosis and total petrifaction. This can occur in a people only when the original creative racial nucleus has been lost, or if the external influence which furnished the impetus and the material for the first development in the cultural field was later lacking. But if it is established that a people receives the most essential basic materials of its culture from foreign races, that it assimilates and adapts them, and that then, if further external influence is lacking, it rigidifies again and again, such a race may be designated as *"culture-bearing,"* but never as *"culture-creating."* An examination of the various peoples from this standpoint points to the fact that practically none of them were originally *culture-founding,* but almost always *culture-bearing.*

Approximately the following picture of their development always results:

Aryan races — often absurdly small numerically — subject foreign peoples, and then, stimulated by the special living conditions of the new territory (fertility, climatic conditions, etc.) and assisted by the multitude of lower-type beings standing at their disposal as helpers, develop the intellectual and organizational capacities dormant within them. Often in a few millenniums or even centuries they create cultures which originally bear all the inner characteristics of their nature, adapted to the above-indicated special qualities of the soil and subjected beings. In the end, however, the conquerors transgress against the principle of blood purity, to which they had first adhered; they begin to mix with the subjugated inhabitants and thus end their own existence; for the fall of man in paradise has always been followed by his expulsion. . . .

The progress of humanity is like climbing an endless ladder; it is impossible to climb higher without first taking the lower steps. Thus, the Aryan had to take the road to which reality directed him and not the one that would appeal to the imagination of a modern pacifist. The road of reality is hard and difficult, but in the end it leads where our friend would like to bring humanity by dreaming, but unfortunately removes more than bringing it closer.

Hence it is no accident that the first cultures arose in places where the Aryan, in his encounters with lower peoples, subjugated them and bent them to his will. They then became the first technical instrument in the service of a developing culture.

Thus, the road which the Aryan had to take was clearly marked out. As a conqueror he subjected the lower beings and regulated their practical activity under his command, according to his will and for his aims. But in directing them to a useful, though arduous activity, he not only spared the life of those he subjected; perhaps he gave them a fate that was better than their previous so-called 'freedom.' As long as he ruthlessly upheld the master attitude, not only did he really remain master, but also the preserver and increaser of culture. For culture was based exclusively on his abilities and hence on his actual survival. As soon as the subjected people began to raise themselves up and probably approached the conqueror in language, the sharp dividing wall between master and servant fell. The Aryan gave up the purity of his blood and, therefore, lost his sojourn in the paradise which he had made for himself. He became submerged in the racial mixture, and gradually, more and more, lost his cultural capacity, until at last, not only mentally but also physically, he began to resemble the subjected aborigines more than his own ancestors. For a time he could live on the existing cultural benefits, but then petrifaction set in and he fell a prey to oblivion.

Thus cultures and empires collapsed to make place for new formations.

Blood mixture and the resultant drop in the racial level is the sole cause of the dying out of old cultures; for men do not perish as a result of lost wars, but by the loss of that force of resistance which is contained only in pure blood.

All who are not of good race in this world are chaff.

And all occurrences in world history are only the expression of the races' instinct of self-preservation, in the good or bad sense.

The question of the inner causes of the Aryan's importance can be answered to the effect that they are to be sought less in a natural instinct of self-preservation than in the special type of its expression. The will to live, subjectively viewed, is everywhere equal and different only in the form of its actual expression. In the most primitive living creatures the instinct of self-preservation does not go beyond concern for their own ego. Egoism, as we designate this urge, goes so far that it even embraces time; the moment itself claims everything, granting nothing to the coming hours. In this condition the animal lives only for himself, seeks food only for his present hunger, and fights only for his own life. As long as the instinct of self-preservation expresses itself in this way, every basis is lacking for the formation of a group, even the most primitive form of family. Even a community between male and female beyond pure mating, demands an extension of the instinct of self-preservation, since concern and struggle for the ego are now directed toward the second party; the male sometimes seeks food for the female, too, but for the most part both seek nourishment for the young. Nearly always one comes to the defense of the other, and thus the first, though infinitely simple, forms of a sense of sacrifice result. As soon as this sense extends beyond the narrow limits of the family, the basis for the formation of larger organisms and finally formal states is created.

In the lowest peoples of the earth this quality is present only to a very slight extent, so that often they do not go beyond the formation of the family. The greater the readiness to subordinate purely personal interests, the higher rises the ability to establish comprehensive communities.

This self-sacrificing will to give one's personal labor and if necessary one's own life for others is most strongly developed in the Aryan. The

Aryan is not greatest in his mental qualities as such, but in the extent of his willingness to put all his abilities in the service of the community. In him the instinct of self-preservation has reached the noblest form, since he willingly subordinates his own ego to the life of the community and, if the hour demands, even sacrifices it.

Not in his intellectual gifts lies the source of the Aryan's capacity for creating and building culture. If he had just this alone, he could only act destructively, in no case could he organize; for the innermost essence of all organization requires that the individual renounce putting forward his personal opinion and interests and sacrifice both in favor of a larger group. Only by way of this general community does he again recover his share. Now, for example, he no longer works directly for himself, but with his activity articulates himself with the community, not only for his own advantage, but for the advantage of all. The most wonderful elucidation of this attitude is provided by his word "work," by which he does not mean an activity for maintaining life in itself, but exclusively a creative effort that does not conflict with the interests of the community. Otherwise he designates human activity, in so far as it serves the instinct of self-preservation without consideration for his fellow men, as theft, usury, robbery, burglary, etc.

This state of mind, which subordinates the interests of the ego to the conservation of the community, is really the first premise for every truly human culture. From it alone can arise all the great works of mankind, which bring the founder little reward, but the richest blessings to posterity. Yes, from it alone can we understand how so many are able to bear up faithfully under a scanty life which imposes on them nothing but poverty and frugality, but gives the community the foundations of its existence. Every worker, every peasant, every inventor, official, etc., who works without ever being able to achieve any happiness or prosperity for himself, is a representative of this lofty idea, even if the deeper meaning of his activity remains hidden in him.

What applies to work as the foundation of human sustenance and all human progress is true to an even greater degree for the defense of man and his culture. In giving one's own life for the existence of the community lies the crown of all sense of sacrifice. It is this alone that prevents what human hands have built from being overthrown by human hands or destroyed by Nature.

Our own German language possesses a word which magnificently designates this kind of activity: *Pflichterfüllung* (fulfillment of duty); it means not to be self-sufficient but to serve the community.

The basic attitude from which such activity arises, we call — to distinguish it from egoism and selfishness — idealism. By this we understand only the individual's capacity to make sacrifices for the community, for his fellow men.

How necessary it is to keep realizing that idealism does not represent a superfluous expression of emotion, but that in truth it has been, is, and will be, the premise for what we designate as human culture, yes, that it alone created the concept of "man"! It is to this inner attitude that the Aryan owes his position in this world, and to it the world owes man; for it alone formed from pure spirit the creative force which, by a unique pairing of the brutal fist and the intellectual genius, created the monuments of human culture.

Without his idealistic attitude all, even the most dazzling faculties of the intellect, would remain mere intellect as such — outward appearance without inner value, and never creative force.

But, since true idealism is nothing but the subordination of the interests and life of the individual to the community, and this in turn is the precondition for the creation of organizational forms of all kinds, it corresponds in its innermost depths to the ultimate will of Nature. It alone leads men to voluntary recognition of the privilege of force and strength, and thus makes them into a dust particle of that order which shapes and forms the whole universe.

The purest idealism is unconsciously equivalent to the deepest knowledge. . . .

Especially, therefore, at times when the ideal attitude threatens to disappear, we can at once recognize a diminution of that force which forms the community and thus creates the premises of culture. As soon as egoism becomes the ruler of a people, the bands of order are loosened and in the chase after their own happiness men fall from heaven into a real hell.

Yes, even posterity forgets the men who have only served their own advantage and praises the heroes who have renounced their own happiness.

The mightiest counterpart to the Aryan is represented by the Jew. In hardly any people in the world is the instinct of self-preservation developed more strongly than in the so-called "chosen." Of this, the mere fact of the survival of this race may be considered the best proof. Where is the people which in the last two thousand years has been exposed to so slight changes of inner disposition, character, etc., as the Jewish people? What people, finally, has gone through greater upheavals than this one — and nevertheless issued from the mightiest catastrophes of mankind unchanged? What an infinitely tough will to live and preserve the species speaks from these facts!

The mental qualities of the Jew have been schooled in the course of many centuries. Today he passes as "smart," and this in a certain sense he has been at all times. But his intelligence is not the result of his own development, but of visual instruction through foreigners. For the human mind cannot climb to the top without steps; for every step upward he needs the foundation of the past, and this in the comprehensive sense in which it can be revealed only in general culture. All thinking is based only in small part on man's own knowledge, and mostly on the experience of the time that has preceded. The general cultural level provides the individual man, without his noticing it as a rule, with such a profusion of preliminary knowledge that, thus armed, he can more easily take further steps of his own. The boy of today, for example, grows up among a truly vast number of technical acquisitions of the last centuries, so that he takes for granted and no longer pays attention to much that a hundred years ago was a riddle to even the greatest minds, although for following and understanding our progress in the field in question it is of decisive importance to him. If a very genius from the twenties of the past century should suddenly leave his grave today, it would be harder for him even intellectually to find his way in the present era than for an average boy of fifteen today. For he would lack all the infinite preliminary education which our present contemporary unconsciously, so to speak, assimilates while growing up amidst the manifestations of our present general civilization.

Since the Jew — for reasons which will at once become apparent — was never in possession of a culture of his own, the foundations of his intellectual work were always provided by others. His intellect at all times developed through the cultural world surrounding him.

The reverse process never took place.

For if the Jewish people's instinct of self-preservation is not smaller but larger than that of other peoples, if his intellectual faculties can easily arouse the impression that they are equal to the intellectual gifts of other races, he lacks completely the most essential requirement for a cultured people, the idealistic attitude.

In the Jewish people the will to self-sacrifice does not go beyond the individual's naked instinct of self-preservation. Their apparently great sense of solidarity is based on the very primitive herd instinct that is seen in many other living creatures in this world. It is a noteworthy fact that the herd instinct leads to mutual support only as long as a common danger makes this seem useful or inevitable. The same pack of wolves which has just fallen on its prey together disintegrates when hunger abates into its individual beasts. The same is true of horses which try to defend themselves against an assailant in a body, but scatter again as soon as the danger is past.

It is similar with the Jew. His sense of sacrifice is only apparent. It exists only as long as the existence of the individual makes it absolutely necessary. However, as soon as the common enemy is conquered, the danger threatening all averted and the booty hidden, the apparent harmony of the Jews among themselves ceases, again making way for their old causal tendencies. The Jew is only united when a common danger forces him to be or a common booty entices him; if these two grounds are lacking, the qualities of the crassest egoism come into their own, and in the twinkling of an eye the united people turns into a horde of rats, fighting bloodily among themselves.

If the Jews were alone in this world, they would stifle in filth and offal; they would try to get ahead of one another in hate-filled struggle and exterminate one another, in so far as the absolute absence of all sense of self-sacrifice, expressing itself in their cowardice, did not turn battle into comedy here too.

So it is absolutely wrong to infer any ideal sense of sacrifice in the Jews from the fact that they stand together in struggle, or, better expressed, in the plundering of their fellow men.

Here again the Jew is led by nothing but the naked egoism of the individual.

That is why the Jewish state — which should be the living organism for preserving and increasing a race — is completely unlimited as to territory. For a state formation to have a definite spatial setting always presupposes an idealistic attitude on the part of the state-race, and especially a correct interpretation of the concept of work. In the exact measure in which this attitude is lacking, any attempt at forming, even of preserving, a spatially delimited state fails. And thus the basis on which alone culture can arise is lacking.

Hence the Jewish people, despite all apparent intellectual qualities, is without any true culture, and especially without any culture of its own. For what sham culture the Jew today possesses is the property of other peoples, and for the most part it is ruined in his hands.

In judging the Jewish people's attitude on the question of human culture, the most essential characteristic we must always bear in mind is that there has never been a Jewish art and accordingly there is none today either; that above all the two queens of all the arts, architecture and music, owe nothing original to the Jews. What they do accomplish in the field of art is either patchwork or intellectual theft. Thus, the Jew lacks those qualities which distinguish the races that are creative and hence culturally blessed.

To what an extent the Jew takes over foreign culture, imitating or rather ruining it, can be seen from the fact that he is mostly found in the art which seems to require least original invention, the art of acting. But even here, in reality, he is only a "juggler," or rather an ape; for even here he lacks the last touch that is required for real greatness; even here he is not the creative genius, but a superficial imitator, and all the twists and tricks that he uses are powerless to conceal the inner lifelessness of his creative gift. Here the Jewish press most lovingly helps him along by raising such a roar of hosannahs about even the most mediocre bungler, just so long as he is a Jew, that the rest of the world actually ends up by thinking that they have an artist before them, while in truth it is only a pitiful comedian.

No, the Jew possesses no culture-creating force of any sort, since the idealism, without which there is no true higher development of man, is not present in him and never was present. Hence his intellect will never have a constructive effect, but will be destructive, and in very rare cases perhaps will at most be stimulating, but then as the prototype of the "force which always wants evil and nevertheless creates good."[1] Not through him does any progress of mankind occur, but in spite of him. . . .

The Jew's life as a parasite in the body of other nations and states explains a characteristic which once caused Schopenhauer, as has already been mentioned, to call him the "great master in lying." Existence impels the Jew to lie, and to lie perpetually, just as it compels the inhabitants of the northern countries to wear warm clothing.

His life within other peoples can only endure for any length of time if he succeeds in arousing the opinion that he is not a people but a "religious community," though of a special sort.

And this is the first great lie.

In order to carry on his existence as a parasite on other peoples, he is forced to deny his inner nature. The more intelligent the individual Jew is, the more he will succeed in this deception. Indeed, things can go so far that large parts of the host people will end by seriously believing that the Jew is really a Frenchman or an Englishman, a German or an Italian, though of a special religious faith. Especially state authorities, which always seem animated by the historical fraction of wisdom, most easily fall a victim to this infinite deception. Independent thinking sometimes seems to these circles a true sin against holy advancement, so that we may not be surprised if even today a Bavarian state ministry, for example, still has not the faintest idea that the Jews are members of a *people* and not of a *"religion"* though a glance at the Jew's own newspapers should indicate this even to the most modest mind. The *Jewish Echo* is not yet an official organ, of course, and consequently is unauthoritative as far as the intelligence of one of these government potentates is concerned.

The Jew has always been a people with definite racial characteristics and never a religion; only in order to get ahead he early sought for a means which could distract unpleasant attention from his person. And what would have been more expedient and at the same time more innocent than the "embezzled" concept of a religious community? For here, too, everything is borrowed or rather stolen. Due to his own original special

---

[1] Goethe's *Faust,* lines 1336–1337: Mephistopheles to Faust.

nature, the Jew cannot possess a religious institution, if for no other reason because he lacks idealism in any form, and hence belief in a hereafter is absolutely foreign to him. And a religion in the Aryan sense cannot be imagined which lacks the conviction of survival after death in some form. Indeed, the Talmud is not a book to prepare a man for the hereafter, but only for a practical and profitable life in this world.

The Jewish religious doctrine consists primarily in prescriptions for keeping the blood of Jewry pure and for regulating the relation of Jews among themselves, but even more with the rest of the world; in other words, with non-Jews. But even here it is by no means ethical problems that are involved, but extremely modest economic ones. Concerning the moral value of Jewish religious instruction, there are today and have been at all times rather exhaustive studies (not by Jews; the drivel of the Jews themselves on the subject is, of course, adapted to its purpose) which make this kind of religion seem positively monstrous according to Aryan conceptions. The best characterization is provided by the product of this religious education, the Jew himself. His life is only of this world, and his spirit is inwardly as alien to true Christianity as his nature two thousand years previous was to the great founder of the new doctrine. Of course, the latter made no secret of his attitude toward the Jewish people, and when necessary he even took to the whip to drive from the temple of the Lord this adversary of all humanity, who then as always saw in religion nothing but an instrument for his business existence. In return, Christ was nailed to the cross, while our present-day party Christians debase themselves to begging for Jewish votes at elections and later try to arrange political swindles with atheistic Jewish parties — and this against their own nation.

On this first and greatest lie, that the Jews are not a race but a religion, more and more lies are based in necessary consequence. Among them is the lie with regard to the language of the Jew. For him it is not a means for expressing his thoughts, but a means for concealing them. When he speaks French, he thinks Jewish, and while he turns out German verses, in his life he only expresses the nature of his nationality. As long as the Jew has not become the master of the other peoples, he must speak their languages whether he likes it or not, but as soon as they became his slaves, they would all have to learn a universal language (Esperanto, for instance!) so that by this additional means the Jews could more easily dominate them!

If we pass all the causes of the German collapse in review, the ultimate and most decisive remains the failure to recognize the racial problem and especially the Jewish menace.

The defeats on the battlefield in August, 1918, would have been child's play to bear. They stood in no proportion to the victories of our people.

*Jews + Races
mixing
led to
defeat in
WWI*

It was not they that caused our downfall; no, it was brought about by that power which prepared these defeats by systematically over many decades robbing our people of the political and moral instincts and forces which alone make nations capable and hence worthy of existence.

In heedlessly ignoring the question of the preservation of the racial foundations of our nation, the old Reich disregarded the sole right which gives life in this world. Peoples which bastardize themselves, or let themselves be bastardized, sin against the will of eternal Providence, and when their ruin is encompassed by a stronger enemy it is not an injustice done to them, but only the restoration of justice. If a people no longer wants to respect the Nature-given qualities of its being which root in its blood, it has no further right to complain over the loss of its earthly existence.

Everything on this earth is capable of improvement. Every defeat can become the father of a subsequent victory, every lost war the cause of a later resurgence, every hardship the fertilization of human energy, and from every oppression the forces for a new spiritual rebirth can come — as long as the blood is preserved pure.

The lost purity of the blood alone destroys inner happiness forever, plunges man into the abyss for all time, and the consequences can never more be eliminated from body and spirit.

Only by examining and comparing all other problems of life in the light of this one question shall we see how absurdly petty they are by this standard. They are all limited in time — but the question of preserving or not preserving the purity of the blood will endure as long as there are men.

All really significant symptoms of decay of the pre-War period can in the last analysis be reduced to racial causes.

Whether we consider questions of general justice or cankers of economic life, symptoms of cultural decline or processes of political degeneration, questions of faulty schooling or the bad influence exerted on grown-ups by the press, etc., everywhere and always it is fundamentally the disregard of the racial needs of our own people or failure to see a foreign racial menace.

And that is why all attempts at reform, all works for social relief and political exertions, all economic expansion and every apparent increase of intellectual knowledge were futile as far as their results were concerned. The nation, and the organism which enables and preserves its life on this earth, the state, did not grow inwardly healthier, but obviously languished more and more. All the illusory prosperity of the old Reich could not hide its inner weakness, and every attempt really to strengthen the Reich failed again and again, due to disregarding the most important question.

It would be a mistake to believe that the adherents of the various political tendencies which were tinkering around on the German national body — yes, even a certain section of the leaders — were bad or malevolent men in themselves. Their activity was condemned to sterility only because the best of them saw at most the forms of our general disease and tried to combat them, but blindly ignored the virus. Anyone who systematically follows the old Reich's line of political development is bound to arrive, upon calm examination, at the realization that even at the time of the unification, hence the rise of the German nation, the inner decay was already in full swing, and that despite all apparent political successes and despite increasing economic wealth, the general situation was deteriorating from year to year. If nothing else, the elections for the Reichstag announced, with their outward swelling of the Marxist vote, the steadily approaching inward and hence also outward collapse. All the successes of the so-called bourgeois parties were worthless, not only because even with so-called bourgeois electoral victories they were unable to halt the numerical growth of the Marxist flood, but because they themselves above all now bore the ferments of decay in their own bodies. Without suspecting it, the bourgeois world itself was inwardly infected with the deadly poison of Marxist ideas and its resistance often sprang more from the competitor's envy of ambitious leaders than from a fundamental rejection of adversaries determined to fight to the utmost. In these long years there was only one who kept up an imperturbable, unflagging fight, and this was the *Jew*. His Star of David[2] rose higher and higher in proportion as our people's will for self-preservation vanished.

Therefore, in August, 1914, it was not a people resolved to attack which rushed to the battlefield; no, it was only the last flicker of the national instinct of self-preservation in face of the progressing pacifist-Marxist paralysis of our national body. Since even in these days of destiny, our people did not recognize the inner enemy, all outward resistance was in vain and Providence did not bestow her reward on the victorious sword, but followed the law of eternal retribution.

On the basis of this inner realization, there took form in our new movement the leading principles as well as the tendency, which in our conviction were alone capable, not only of halting the decline of the German people, but of creating the granite foundation upon which some day a state will rest which represents, not an alien mechanism of economic concerns and interests, but a national organism:

*A Germanic State of the
German Nation*

---

[2] Typical Hitlerian metaphor. The Star of David, it will be remembered, is not a star, but a shield.

47. Ideology and Racial Biology

National Socialist ideology was not simply a form of rhetoric to be manipulated for political ends. In various ways and with differing degrees of success, it was a blueprint for the regime's actual policies. This was true not only for the laws redefining the position of the Jews in the Third Reich and the war for *Lebensraum*, but also of the attempt to reconstitute German society in a *Volksgemeinschaft*. Because racial biology lay at the heart of the ideology, this "science" had to be further developed from its roots in nineteenth-century social Darwinism. Introduced into the curricula of the schools, the doctrine was established as the foundation of all education. The following selection from Paul Brohmer's *Biologieunterricht und völkische Erziehung* (The Teaching of Biology and Folk Education) outlines a program for introducing racial biology into the educational system.

From our pedagogical standpoint, which considers the task of the school to be the inculcation of *völkisch* thinking and volition, in opposition to the carrying-over of Darwinian ideas to the teaching of biology in schools, it can be objected that teaching these ideas will hardly serve this pedagogical aim. These teachings are, so to speak, international, since they examine all the countries of the world for the phenomena which the laws of the theory of descent supposedly predict. Thus, we find that textbooks deal with almost more foreign animals and plants than native ones; the selection is made on the basis of localities where the phenomena under consideration — mimesis, protective coloration, adaptation — can best be recognized. Thus the student learns all about the Indian meal moth, the walking-stick insect, the walking leaf, but not about the parasites which destroy the harvest in our own orchards or cause enormous losses in the fields of German agriculture. The student might be familiar with the Australian monotremes and marsupials, but know hardly anything about the animals and plants that are most frequently come upon in the fields and forests of the homeland.

Such knowledge may well be of use to the researcher, but not to the German who is not an expert in the field of biology. It is no exaggeration to assert that much of the subject matter of biology teaching is alien to life, the homeland, and the *Volk*. The reason for this aberrant development in the teaching of biology lies mainly in the fact that, owing to the tendencies of the time, the Darwinian ideas became the principal content of instruction in the schools. . . .

From Paul Brohmer, *Biologieunterricht und völkische Erziehung* (Frankfurt, 1933), in G. L. Mosse, ed., *Nazi Culture* (New York: Shocken Books, 1981), pp. 81–90. Reprinted by permission of Professor George L. Mosse, Weinstein-Bascom Professor of History, University of Wisconsin.

The inclusion of physiological viewpoints in the teaching of biology leads to a specific technical procedure, to an elaboration of biology as subject matter for the school based on instructive work-experience. In this sense there has already been a great improvement in the past few years. But this is not the essential problem. It is not just a question of improving the teaching procedure, but rather of transforming the content of our subject, of guiding the student to a new conception of nature! To accomplish this, teachings taken from physiology must be introduced. Consequently, this purpose is not served if a number of physiological experiments are carried out and interpreted as post-scripts or appendices, so to speak. Here, too, from the very beginning the student must be guided to an overall, total view, and not, say, to one that is encyclopedic. He should perceive and feel that behind the individual achievement there is a meaningful plan, that behind it stands the whole organism. Let us take, for example, an experiment showing the action of saliva in changing starch into sugar. This is not just a random interesting fact, but a real accomplishment, a process in the service of the preservation of the whole organism. Or, let us consider the process of seeing: the eye by itself is not able to produce any visual images but requires the cooperation of a number of organs. Thus, the act of seeing is also an accomplishment achieved by the entire organism.

These examples show us two ways in which physiology considers the whole: first, in that the accomplishment is in the service of the whole; second, in that it is achieved by the whole. Hence these two methods of observing an event from the standpoint of the whole organism are intimately connected: the conception that every occurrence is planned, as a part of the total accomplishment, and the conception of the organism as a totality, in which everything that occurs is conditioned and regulated by a meaningful plan. If we guide the student to this conception of nature as a unified totality by way of repeated concrete examples, we shall have helped to provide him, at least in this branch of biology, with a modern method of observation and he will have acquired the basis for an organic *völkisch*-based thinking. Naturally, this must also be done in the other branches of our subject. . . .

The importance of emphasizing physiological ideas in the teaching of botany and zoology is also to be found in the fact that the way for it is prepared by the new teaching of anthropology. The physiological processes in plants and animals with which the student becomes acquainted create a basis for an understanding of the corresponding processes in man. In the actual teaching of anthropology, however, a strong emphasis on physiology is necessary because it prepares the way for teaching hygiene, and it certainly is a task of this branch of instruction in biology to provide a guide for a rational way of life. Individual hygiene, again, is a prerequisite for racial hygiene, which is so important. Thus the study of physiology is likewise connected with this problem. It can be successfully utilized, however, only on the basis of a total view, which must be introduced into all branches of the teaching of biology. . . .

Introducing the student to this mode of observation is in the spirit of a *völkisch* education. On the basis of the elaboration of the laws of biology we turn to the emotional life of the student: he must come to see Germany as his "living space" and himself as a link in the German biotic community and the German destiny; and he must regard all Germans as his blood relations, his brothers. If we reach this goal, then all party and class divisions sink into nothingness, and more is accomplished for education in citizenship than is done by studying governmental and administrative structures.

For the very reason that the theory of the biotic community is so important for the development of biological knowledge and for education in organic *völkisch* thinking, it would be expedient to base the school curriculum on this idea. When we go into the free, open spaces we always come upon animals and plants in their specific living space in which they form biotic communities. It is not a mechanical system which orders the natural arrangement of organisms, but the living space. This living space not only presents an external frame of community but links its inhabitants to each other with indissoluble bonds. Whoever, in teaching the concept of the biotic community, utilizes it only as a principle of the organization of matter has not grasped the deeper meaning of bionomics. He stands, as it were, in front of a deep well of precious water and draws nothing from it although his companions are dying of thirst. Thus it is a question of opening up *völkisch* values to the students. . . .

Another change we must make in the teaching of biology if its cultural value is to be increased concerns the position of man in our discipline. In the usual textbooks, anthropology is treated as a supplement to biology; man is dealt with in somewhat more detail than any other mammal, but according to the same points of view. The only difference is that, on the basis of the knowledge of the structure and functioning of the organs, some rules on health may be offered, and it has been said that the teaching of anthropology should offer the student a guide to intelligent living. No doubt, anthropology should fulfill this task too. But all it does is promote knowledge as such; it does not add to the growth of the student's intellectual or religious culture. . . . Furthermore, knowledge as an individual accomplishment must be supplemented by a knowledge of a supra-individual character, because German man must not think only of himself, but should be cognizant of his duty to place himself in the service of the people.

Our aim is not merely that man be made the object of the study of nature, but that he should also be placed as subject in the biological consideration of nature. To be sure, everybody must have a certain fund of knowledge about the structure and function of his "body tools," and everybody should also know how to keep healthy. Hence we should welcome the methodological demand that the road to the teaching of anthropology should always be prepared by the teaching of biology. Consequently, it is possible in zoology to elaborate, for example, on the nature of digestion, breathing, etc., and then refer back to it in anthropology. The study of botany, too, offers many opportunities for preparing the way for anthropological knowledge. . . .

Beyond and above this, the place of man vis-à-vis nature must constantly be discussed in the teaching of biology. This is made easy precisely by arranging the subject matter, and the insights deriving from it, in terms of a biotic-community approach. We would start with — since our concept of biotic community is a broad one — the domain of "house and home." In it man is the master; he has taken into his household the animals and plants which he keeps either for his use or for his pleasure. He gives them shelter, food, and care; he has changed them through breeding and he holds their lives in his hands. Without him most of the organisms he keeps as domestic animals or indoor plants would perish. At this point we can discuss in an elementary way the attitude of man toward nature. In this biotic community we meet first and foremost the will to rule over nature, the viewpoint of utilitarianism, which is, however, accompanied by the joy in the beauty of the things of nature and love of nature itself. Similar discussions will come up in the study of biotic communities in the garden, field, and meadow.

It might be thought that with the "anthropological idea," as I should like to designate the emphasis on anthropology in biology teaching, our aim is to return to the anthropocentric point of view which has been justifiably attacked; or that we wish to foster a utilitarian pedagogy by discussing more thoroughly than was done in the past domestic animals, useful plants and their parasites, and eugenics from the viewpoint of the individual and the race. It is anthropocentric if it is assumed that nature has been created only for man. We decisively reject this attitude. According to our conception of nature, man is a link in the chain of living nature just as any other organism. On the other hand, it is a fact that man has made himself master of nature, and that he will increasingly aim to widen this mastery. The teaching of natural history must contribute to this. Thus its task is not merely to transmit theoretical knowledge, to foster joy in nature, to arouse love of one's homeland and one's country; it has, in addition, practical aims. One may call this utilitarian pedagogy if one so pleases. But in our view instruction in biology that does not take the problems of agriculture, forestry, gardening, and fishing into consideration is a failure; it is a form of teaching that is alien to the practical life of our people. School is not a research laboratory, but an institution which aims to educate Germans, and these should stand at their posts in the life of the German *Volk*. We are as far removed from a one-sided utilitarian viewpoint as we are from pedagogy that is alien to life. . . .

Still more important, it seems to me, is the fact that the task of biology teaching, briefly referred to above, can be fulfilled by an orientation toward the concept of the biotic community. It must be grasped here once more on the basis of another idea. We have said that the student must be led to the conception that Germany is his living space to which he is linked by the bond of blood. We have explained in detail that the bionomic approach teaches that the organisms within a living space are dependent on each other as well as dependent upon the whole, and that each link must perform an indispensable function in the total accomplishment. When this insight is applied to the human biotic community, when the future German racial-comrade feels himself to be a link in the German biotic community, and when he is imbued with the idea of the blood relationship of all Germans, then class differences and class hatred cannot take acute forms, as was often the case in the past due to a misunderstanding of the actual bond that unites all estates together. Once every German regards Germany as his living space and feels himself to be a link in the German biotic community, he will be fully conscious of the fact that every individual within the metabolism of the biotic community into which he was born must fulfill his own important task. Thus a supra-individualistic attitude is created which constitutes the best possible foundation for training in citizenship. Indeed, it can be said that it has achieved its deepest fulfillment once this attitude is transformed into action.

idea of unique tasks ?

Racial eugenics works in the same direction, namely, the education of the student in a national sense. Although it constitutes the finishing touch of biology teaching, its concepts should from the very beginning permeate all biological instruction in all types of schools, and not be left for discussion in anthropology, which concludes the study of biology. It should be repeatedly emphasized that the biological laws operative in animals and plants apply also to man; for example, that the knowledge acquired from studying the genetics of these organisms can, in a general way, be applied to man. Thus, the teaching of animal breeding and plant cultivation can effectively prepare the way for conceptions of racial biology. Naturally, a more systematic discussion of these questions will first take place in the teaching of anthropology.

It is not so much a matter of making the student knowledgeable on all questions of eugenics, but of creating motives for his action. Racial eugenics is particularly valuable for school because of its educational significance. If the emphasis on the ideology of the biotic community creates a feeling of belonging to our people and state, then racial eugenics creates the will to struggle, body and soul, for the growth and health of this biotic community.

Racial eugenics

This is also the place for discussing, from a biological viewpoint, the family as a value, and the improvement of the sense of family which has been sorely neglected by many modern pedagogues. The family, after all, is the smallest biotic community since it forms the germ cell of the state. If we take up these questions, the fields of individual hygiene and racial eugenics, of genetics and sex education, combine to form a meaningful unit, just as, generally, the teaching of biology, which in the past was fragmented into many unrelated individual fields, will be fused into a unified whole once our efforts achieve fruition. In these discussions on the family we are less concerned with the student's enlarging his knowledge and more with the aim that he be imbued with a sense of responsibility, that he begin to sense that the deepest meaning of human life is to grow beyond himself in his children, and that nothing he could leave to them would be more valuable than the German heritage which he has received from his ancestors, and that, through race mixing, he could taint and impair his progeny in a most unfavorable way.

Such ideas lead to an ethnology of the German people, which we mentioned earlier by way of a few pedagogical observations. All that remains to be discussed is at what stage it should be introduced. As we have explained, the way to it is already prepared in zoology and botany and it is concluded in the teaching of anthropology. Now a short remark on the goal of ethnology: the knowledge of physical and spiritual features of the individual races has little value if it does not lead to the firm will to fight against the racial deterioration of the German nation and if it does not imbue the student with the conviction that the fact of belonging to a race imposes a responsibility. . . .

The actual method of teaching racial eugenics of necessity will vary with the individual types of schools. Even the simplest village school may not pass over these problems. It can build upon the children's own radius of experience in the fields of animal breeding and plant cultivation. From this, simple rules of heredity can be deduced; these, however, do not need to involve cellular research and the theory of chromosomes. Children are familiar with symptoms of degeneration in animals and plants, and not much initiative is required to find such signs of degeneration and decline in man too. Thus a point of departure is created for introducing racial eugenics during instruction in zoology and botany. At suitable opportunities — this can also be done in the teaching of geography and history — such ideas will be elaborated further until they are most fully treated in the teaching of anthropology. Not one elementary-school pupil should leave school without having internalized the iron command that he is to bear part of the responsibility for the fate of his fatherland, without the awareness that he is only a link in the chain of his ancestors and descendants and the carrier of the future generation. The higher schools can devote more time to racial eugenics: the students in the later classes are more mature than those in the elementary and intermediate schools. Here, too, the way will be prepared in zoology and botany. Further, the teaching of history can be made very meaningful through racial eugenics, since we know that modern historians consider the cause of the collapse of the ancient world to lie in non-eugenic racial mixtures. . . .

When teaching the theory of family and race, as well as eugenics, it is methodologically important to stimulate independent activity on the part of the student to the greatest possible degree. It can be suggested that the student draw up a genealogical chart of his family as far back as he can go. In addition, he can be asked questions about the physical characteristics of his parents and other forebears as far as they can be determined (size, figure, shape of head and face, color of hair and eyes, form of nose, etc.), about their intellectual and characterological qualities, their special achievements (for example, rescues during the war, scientific or literary publications, compositions), their life span and cause of death. In given cases, deformities and hereditary diseases should also be reported. The number of children produced by the student's ancestors should be determined. This is the kind of material in which the student will be directly interested. But when explaining hereditary diseases the teacher must take care not to arouse feelings of inferiority or fear of such diseases in students who come from families with handicaps of a hereditary character. It also goes without saying that he is duty-bound to keep certain information confidential as far as the other students are concerned. In every class, then, there will be sufficient usable material which can serve as a basis for teaching in the afore-mentioned fields.

48. Protecting the Racial Stock of the *Volksgemeinschaft*

Besides altering education in a fundamental way, the introduction of racial science had direct consequences in reshaping society in the Third Reich. To preserve racial purity, the regime promulgated the Law for the Protection of Hereditary Health in July 1933. The following excerpt is taken from the *Textbook on Racial Science, Genetics, and Racial Policy*, by Dr. Steche (1937), a popular exposition of the regime's policy on heredity.

THE FIGHT AGAINST DEGENERATION

It is a great fortune, that the leadership of our people has not only recognized the danger of the situation, but also has made a strict decision to combat it. He who wants to live as a member of our community, is not only obliged to put all his efforts at the service of this community, but

From O. Steche, *Lehrbuch der Rassenkunde, Vererbungslehre, und Rassenpflege* (Leipzig, 1937), in U.S. Chief of Counsel for the Prosecution of Axis Criminality, *Nazi Conspiracy and Aggression* (Washington, D.C.: U.S. Government Printing Office, 1946), vol. 5, doc. no. 2442-PS, pp. 176–77.

also must make sacrifices. He must tolerate encroachments on his personal rights, if the need of the community demands it. It is one of the first duties of the community, to see to it, that the increase of those, inferior by heredity, is stopped. At our stage of culture, we cannot think of it of course, to expect them from our community, but we can easily see to it, that they are not propagated and give their inferior heritage to new generations. To prevent this, the law exists for the prevention of hereditarily unsound progeny. This gives the right to the national community, to exclude those men and women from propagation with whom it can be expected with certainty through knowledge of the heredity laws, that their offspring will to a great extent be physically, mentally and spiritually inferior.

*i.e.
mass
sterilization*

Costs of Welfare in Comparison to Average Earnings

The daily cost of a

Deaf mute	=	6.00 M
Cripple	=	6.00 M
Reform School inmate	–	4.85 M
Mentally Sick	=	4.50 M
Criminals	=	3.50 M

The daily earnings of a

Laborer	=	2.50 M
Employee	=	3.50 M
Civil Servant	=	4.00 M

Only comparatively simple medical intervention is necessary for that, which will not affect the well being and ability to live of the person at all. The law enumerates a whole series of hereditary diseases, in case of which the prevention of procreation can be carried out. Into this class belong in the first place serious physical disabilities such as hereditary blindness and deaf-muteness, but also a series of serious mental diseases, especially hereditary feeblemindness and idiocy. Of course, in every case, before such intervention is ordered by the state, all circumstances must be thoroughly examined by a court, appointed especially for the purpose.

These measures, of course, cannot show their results immediately, but in the course of many years, the health of the heritage of our people will improve, and the tremendous burden, which is placed today on the community by taking care of the inferior ones, will decrease more and more. Actually, today it is so, that the state spends more for the existence of these actually worthless compatriots, than the salary for the work of a healthy man, with which he must bring up a healthy family.

RACIAL HYGIENE

When choosing a mate, for marriage, we also take the obligation, to keep in mind the racial composition of our national substance. The six basic races, which we have learned to know previously, are so mixed in our national community and their participation in the construction of our culture cannot easily be separated, that we cannot easily put them against each other in strong contrast. We have previously seen that the Nordic race distinguishes itself by a special leadership talent and that it has certainly played an outstanding part in the development of our national substance. The result is that today, we have relatively many Nordic people among the leading strata of our people. If, therefore, an increase of these strata is helped along, the share of Nordic blood within, it will become a greater one. But it is very essential, that we avoid, as best as we can, the penetration of elements of alien races into our national body.

49. Sterilization of "Mentally Deficient" Children

To guarantee a healthy racial stock, undesirable elements had to be prevented from "breeding." The regime therefore issued laws for mandatory sterilization of, among others, persons deemed "mentally deficient" and so unfit for purposes of propagating the race. In the following document, instructors in schools for these deficient children were given the task of explaining to the children's parents the necessity for the state's laws on sterilization.

Informational guidelines for dealing with parents of children in special schools for deficient children, concerning measures for compliance with the sterilization laws.

1. All educational work of this nature must have as its motto: We want to convert the parents to the notion of sterilization. Therefore, all discussion about different attitudes toward the sterilization law must be eliminated from the beginning. He who is not inwardly convinced of the value of the law should refrain from all educational work. . . .

2. The notion of helping must come to the fore. The impression must never be created that sterilization is a punitive measure. The intelligent ones will realize it [sterilization] is a necessary offering to the altar of the Fatherland; to the less intelligent ones it must be represented as a welcome measure of help from the state.

Sterilization as help

From *Nationalsozialistische Deutsche Arbeiter-Partei, Hauptarchiv 1919–45* (Stanford, CA: Hoover Institution on War, Revolution, and Peace), H. A. reel 13, folder 245 (Sterilization Guidelines). Translated by Dieter Kuntz.

The teacher must never pose as the executor for the state. He is always to be a helper to the parents, someone who will protect them and their families from further problem children. Be also warned of misguided compassion; stress instead that the law is a blessing for the child to be sterilized as well as for the parents and the entire family, for the unborn generation, and for the entire national community [*Volksgemeinschaft*].

Of great benefit in this matter can be the participation in a course for race and hereditary biology sponsored by the Dresden Museum for Eugenics. Moreover, the existing literature can give everyone a reasonable immersion into the problems of eugenics.

3. Educational work during parental evenings as well as during other meetings can deal only with the most general matters and is to prepare the groundwork for the following necessary individual education. A partial list of such general topics includes:

1. Our problem children and what is to become of them.
2. A way for parents of children in schools for children to deal with the sexual needs of their children.
3. The demographic crisis and the economic distress of our nation will lead to the ruin of our people if we are unable to upgrade our breeding.
4. The sterilization law and its implementation statutes.
5. What is sterilization?
6. What is the difference between sterilization and castration?

During such general educational work one must avoid creating the impression that all these children are purely and simply to be sterilized. Parental questions are to be either answered in general terms or are to be directed toward individual consultation.

4. More important than the general educational work is the educational work done on an individual basis. Those wanting to do individualized educating must be familiar with the local environment. Home visits are therefore recommended.

5. Best suited for individualized education is the classroom teacher, but only if the teacher has a good relationship with the parental home and if he is not too young. In the two instances mentioned last, a previous teacher the child may have had, or the school principal, can substitute for the teacher.

6. Aside from familiarity with local conditions, it is necessary for the educator to know what sort of parents he is dealing with from a mental standpoint.

a. One might deal with parents who are intelligent enough to comprehend clearly the situation they and their problem children find themselves in, and who accordingly will grasp the meaning of their acquiescence. . . . These parents can be important helpers in the educational task if we can succeed in utilizing their contacts with parents in similar situations.

b. Other parents or guardians might be intelligent enough, but might at the same time be indifferent to the fate of their children (especially where girls are concerned, for they are easier to place than boys). What is called for here is the awakening of the conscience of the parent or guardian, while emphasizing parental responsibility toward the children and at the same time coolly and mathematically pushing the financial consequences of the child's future into the foreground.

c. Only ignorant parents are to be educated. But if ignorance is complicated by an emotional sentiment, such as the eternal hope that things will be better with the child and that "the [brain] nodule might still dissolve," or, in more serious cases, if stubborn resistance is encountered which cannot be altered even with reason, then the only recourse is to refer to the law. . . . The ideological and practical value of the new law must be pushed into the foreground. . . . It must also be stressed that it is no disgrace to have a feebleminded child because often it is fate. It is a disgrace, however, to knowingly bring new feebleminded children into the world. In this case the state must be more rational than the parents who cannot or will not understand this.

d. Are the parents themselves feebleminded? Then all will depend on somehow gaining their confidence, while overemphasizing the harmlessness of the proposed measure. . . .

50. The Euthanasia Program

Enforced sterilization was not the only measure for ensuring the purity of the race. As early as 1935, Hitler stated that if war came he would implement a policy of euthanasia or "mercy" killing for the incurably insane. Under pressure of war, he thought, resistance to such a policy, especially by the churches, would be lessened. By the autumn of 1939, procedures for euthanasia were accordingly put into operation, although even then the measures were implemented under top secrecy and with dubious official (that is legal) sanction. Hitler signed a decree in October 1939 charging Reich Leader Bouhler and Dr. Karl Brandt with responsibility for "expanding the authority of physicians, to be designated by name, to the end that patients considered incurable in the best available human judgment, after critical evaluation of their state of health, may be granted a merciful death." The various aspects of this policy, from initial selection of the subject-victims to transportation to incarceration and extermination, provided the model for the elimination of other "undesirable" elements in Germany and German-occupied Europe.

From Herbert Michaelis and Ernst Schraepler, eds., *Ursachen und Folgen vom deutschen Zusammenbruch 1918 und 1945* (Berlin: Dokumenten-Verlag Dr. Herbert Wendler, 1958), vol. 14, pp. 184–87. Translated by Dieter Kuntz.

Despite the attempt at secrecy, the churches of Germany did in fact discover and protest the regime's practice of euthanasia. The following document, dating from July 9, 1940, shows how the Lutheran church learned of the exterminations and of the policy behind it.

EVANGELICAL MEMORANDUM ON THE EXTERMINATION OF THE SO-CALLED UNWORTHY OF LIFE

During the course of the last few months it was observed in various districts of the Reich that a continuous procession of inmates from sanatariums and nursing homes was being transferred due to reasons of "economic planning." Some were transferred several times; after several weeks a death notice arrived in the home of relatives. The similarity of the measures and the similarity of the attendant circumstances eliminates all doubt that what is taking place here is a large-scale measure to remove thousands of people deemed "unworthy of life" from the face of the earth. Some are of the opinion that it is vital in the name of the defense of the Reich to do away with these useless eaters. Others are of the opinion that it is necessary in view of the regenerating process of the German people to exterminate as quickly as possible all those feebleminded and otherwise hopeless cases, as well as the abnormal, antisocial, and those unable to live within the community. It is estimated that more than one hundred thousand people are affected. An article by Professor Kranz in the April issue of the NS *Volksdienst* puts the number of those whom it is more than likely desirable to exterminate at one million. It is a matter that probably affects thousands of countrymen who have already been eliminated without a legal basis or who are on the verge of dying. It is urgently necessary to halt these measures as quickly as possible because the moral basis of the entire nation will otherwise be extremely shaken. The sanctity of human life is one of the keystones of every orderly state. If death is to be ordered, then valid laws must be the basis of such a measure. It is intolerable that sick people are continually, without conscientious medical testing, without any legal recourse, and even without the approval of relatives or legal representatives, being eliminated merely out of expediency.

The following facts have been observed: in October 1939, a circular letter from the Ministry of the Interior appeared at many sanatariums and nursing homes that were caring for the feebleminded, epileptics, and others. The letter stated that, in view of necessary economic planning and registration of sanatariums and nursing homes, the enclosed registration forms must be completed. . . . The instructional pamphlet listed the types of patients to be reported:

1. those who suffer from the illnesses or diseases listed below, and who cannot be given work in the sanatarium's workshop or who can only work at mechanized tasks. . . . The illnesses include: schizophrenia;

epilepsy (if exogenous, explain if this was due to a war injury or other causes); senility; those who have diseases not yielding to treatment, and all who are affected with syphilitic diseases; feeblemindedness, regardless of cause; encephalitis, Huntington's disease, or others with neurologically terminal conditions;

2. those who have been in an institution uninterruptedly for at least five years;
3. those in custody who are judged criminally insane;
4. those not in possession of German citizenship, or who are not of German or closely related blood, are to be listed along with indication of their race and citizenship. . . .

A letter from the National Ministry of Defense of January 20, 1940, moved up the date of the transfer of inmates from sanatariums and nursing homes. It was arranged that the patients would be transferred through large collective transports. The notification of next of kin was not desired. . . .

. . . Next the news surfaced in March 1940 from Württemberg, that of 13 epileptics who had been transferred from the Pfingstweide Institution to the Grafeneck Institution, four patients died after only three weeks. News of the deaths was relayed to the next of kin, usually about one to two weeks after the occurrence. The same wording was always used. The patients were said to have died suddenly due to influenza, pneumonia, or cerebral apoplexy [stroke], or the like. Because of epidemic control measures, it was necessary to cremate the corpses immediately and burn the clothing likewise. The urns were made available. . . .

In order to get to the bottom of just how many people perished in Grafeneck, I point out that the urn of Herr Heiner, who died on April 10, 1940, had the number A 498, whereas the urn of Max Dreisow, who died on May 12, 1940, had number A 1092; the urn of Else Lenne, who died on June 28, 1940, already had number A 3111. Since the entire sanatarium has only 100 beds, it can only mean that this is a matter of continually occurring deaths. Accordingly, during the 33 days from April 10, 1940, to May 12, 1940, 594 people died. This amounts to 18 deaths per day in a 100-bed institution. During the period from May 12 until June 28, 1940 — 47 days — a total of 2,019 people died; this averages out to 43 deaths daily in a 100-bed institution. This conclusion does not appear to be an impossibility since it has been reported that in a one- to two-month period 300 patients were transferred from Bedburg-Hau to Grafeneck; from Buch likewise several hundred; from Kuckenmühle approximately 150; and from institutions in Württemberg, a large but unknown number. . . .

What we are dealing with here is a conscious, planned action to exterminate all those who are mentally ill or are otherwise not seen as socially desirable. These are, however, by no means people who are complete imbeciles, who are not cognizant of their surroundings and are not fit for work; instead, observations have revealed that often they are people who for years led productive lives but who only later developed mental disturbances. When one remembers that the registration forms called for the inclusion of senile patients, it becomes clear that all aging people who are suffering from a mental or possibly physical affliction can befall the same fate. . . . Questions of the utmost concern arise here. . . .

As the first public building dedicated by the Third Reich, the House of German Art played a key role in Hitler's cultural revolution. Works were exhibited here that idealized the past and glorified the themes of "blood and soil."

Chapter

7

Art and the Ideal

The values fostered by National Socialist ideology, expressed in ideal form, were most clearly realized in art, especially in painting and literature. Although societies commonly give expression to their values in art, Hitler and the other founders of National Socialism argued that in truly creative cultures — that is to say, in Aryan cultures — the arts had an almost symbiotic relationship with the community, drawing their inspiration from the *Volk* and, in turn, returning to the community an ideal image of itself. The arts, then, had a special position within the ideology. They were no longer considered the work of isolated individuals or seen as reflecting internal developments within a genre; rather, they arose from and in turn served the greater purpose of building the racial community. More important, the arts were no longer viewed as a single, relatively minor aspect of the life of the individual and of the *Volk*; because the entire community embodied a creative effort, art was the leading expression of the essence of the community, pervading it through and through, calling out the true values of the individual and infusing him with the goals of the *Volksgemeinschaft*. In 1936 Hitler even went so far as to declare that "art is the only truly enduring investment of human labor." To Hitler, National Socialism was "a mighty cultural revolution" that would bring about the "new artistic renaissance of the Aryan man."

The cultural revolution or turning point came with the rejection of the art of the Weimar period. Whatever may be said about Germany's politics and its economic problems, the fourteen years of the Weimar Republic marked one of the most creative periods in the history of modern art. In literature, theater, film, painting, architecture, and domestic design, Germany took the lead among the cultural centers of Europe. A list of artists who worked in the republic would be extensive,

219

including some of the most influential people of the twentieth century, such as Thomas Mann in literature and Walter Gropius in architecture. This artistic flowering began even before the end of the First World War but gathered an intensity in the early 1920s that few eras ever witness. Although the artistic creativity of this early period in the Weimar was often rebellious and ecstatic, and sometimes just ridiculous and chaotic, it produced an age of experimentation with new forms and new subjects. What is generally referred to as the "new objectivity," which directed artistic talents into more socially useful but no less creative channels, superseded the expressionism of the early 1920s by the middle of the decade. To this movement we owe much of modern architecture, the design of household utensils, social realism in film, and a new understanding of the place of literature and theater in modern life.

Once in power, however, Hitler pronounced the prodigious cultural output of the ·Weimar as "fourteen years a junkyard." Hitler and other party members dismissed the creations of this period, with its ultramodern themes and styles, as "degenerate art," which more than anything else evidenced the decline of the *Volk* in the twentieth century. The new art, the art of the *Volksgemeinschaft*, was to be completely different. This art was to be a realization not of individual talents or of the inspirations of a lone genius, but of the collective expression of the *Volk*, channeled through the souls of individual creators. All the arts were to be built on popular taste. The people liked their paintings and literature to be simple and easily understood. And the *Volk*, as Hitler declared, did not like "problem art," nor did it care for the distortions of expressionism or the "socialist" tones of the "new objectivity."

Hitler's call for a "genuine German art" meant both a return to something old but also a turn to something new. The notion of an "external German art" was often invoked as the criterion for artistic production. As with the National Socialist revolution itself, the movement forward aimed to be a movement back to the past — the manufactured, sentimentalized, idealized past that so many Germans found comforting and reassuring but that had never existed.

Perhaps the single most important event in the history of German art under the Third Reich was the opening in Munich of the House of German Art on July 18, 1937. The art exhibition that accompanied it constituted an official statement of what was truly "German" in art. The museum itself, which replaced an earlier building that had burned in 1931, was new. Hitler's favorite architect at the time, Paul Ludwig Troost, was given the commission, and Hitler himself laid the cornerstone on October 15, 1933. But this was not just another public building or the ceremony just another official occasion for the Führer: it was the first public building dedicated under the Third Reich, and the fact that it was a museum of art was highly significant. As the catalogue (published at the museum's opening in 1937) pointed out, "It was a symbolic act that the Führer joyfully dedicated the first monumental structure of his government to German art." The ground-breaking ceremony indicated the place the Führer envisioned for art in the new cultural community. The fact that, in 1933, Germany still suffered from massive unemployment, and that there were many more pressing practical problems to be faced in the economy and in the running of the government as a whole, betokens just how exalted a position art held in the Third Reich. Despite the dilemmas confronting the regime, Hitler was proud "to lay the foundations for this new temple of honor to the goddess of art."

Four years later the Great German Art Exhibition of the House of German Art opened with much fanfare. Between 1937 and 1944 there were to be seven other exhibitions of this kind in Munich. But the exhibition of 1937 was the most important, because it set the tone for the others. The opening of the exhibition was surrounded by pomp and ceremony. Pageants designed around the theme of a "day of German art" took place. Participants wore historical costumes and formal dress, and models of German artworks were displayed. Hitler gave "cultural speeches," and the entire National Socialist leadership attended. In one speech, Hitler called attention to the obvious break that had occurred in the history of German art: "When we celebrated the laying of the cornerstone for this building four years ago, we were all aware that we had to lay not only the cornerstone for a new home but also the foundations for a new genuine German art. We had to bring about a turning point in the evolution of all our German cultural activities."

Both the style and content of the paintings as well as the manner in which they were exhibited show the extent to which the exhibition was meant to speak to popular tastes. One of the principles of the exhibition and, by extension, of all art in the Reich was that art was no longer to be the special domain of a wealthy or educated elite but rather to be by and for the *Volk*. All modernist or experimental styles were rejected outright. The movement toward abstraction in art, so pervasive since the 1920s, was replaced by obviously representational styles reminiscent of the art of the nineteenth century. In the Great German Art Exhibition, the works themselves were arranged primarily according to subject matter: landscapes; paintings of farmers, artisans, or animals; still lifes; portraits; nudes; group portraits; allegories, and so on. This method of grouping pictures according to content and not, as is customary in the twentieth century, according to artist, school, stylistic affinities, or other such categories, clearly indicates that the organizers of the exhibition were appealing to the masses. The proportions in which different themes were represented at the exhibition have been estimated as follows: landscapes 40 percent; "womanhood and manhood" 15.5 percent; animals 10 percent; farmers 7 percent; artisans 0.5 percent. National Socialist Germany was represented only by portraits of functionaries (1.5 percent) and by views of new public buildings (1.7 percent). Landscapes, nudes, and pictures of farmers dominated the exhibit, followed by portraits, still lifes, and paintings of animals and industrial subjects. As the first in the series, the exhibition of 1937 bore less of a National Socialist stamp

[handwritten margin note: Art was to be for all people]

than did later ones, which increasingly emphasized National Socialist iconography, war paintings, allegories, and armaments. But the later exhibits were also thematically oriented and adhered to the principle of organization by content.

The subject matter of a work of art therefore became the key element in evaluating its worth. As Hitler proclaimed, "Blood and race will again become the source of artistic inspiration." Landscape paintings, the most popular, expressed the close ties between the *Volk* and the soil of the Reich. These landscapes represented the Fatherland and the mystical union between the community and the earth. Related to these in theme were paintings of agrarian scenes — peasant farmers shown plowing, sowing, reaping, and gathering winter wood, portrayed against a background of earth and sky with their crops and animals around them. Paintings of these men and beasts — "sound by nature," according to Nazi ideology — represented closeness to the native soil, the restorative powers of the land, the protection of the race from impure stock, the force of deeply rooted tradition, and the blessings of labor, which formed the proper relationship of man to nature, of the organic to the inorganic. Portraits of simple rural artisans, ennobled by the discipline of manual work, also eulogized what the Nazis considered "healthy" activity. The German peasant, the driving force and purifier of the nation's history, symbolized the *Volk*. He embodied the substance of Germanness, evolving independently of older political forms, holding German uniqueness, German racial stock, and indeed all German history in his custody. The peasant was the cultural hero of the movement.

Family scenes and depictions of motherhood in particular made up another subject area. The family shaped and formed the new person that National Socialism sought. Character, as opposed to intellectual sophistication, lay at the core of the new person and the new racial community. Character was built more by home and family life than by educational institutions or even Party organizations. Central to themes of hearth and home, womanhood and, more specifically, motherhood inspired many artists' works. In Nazi ideology, motherhood took on a mystical, almost sacred, quality, for the mother participated in the natural order of things and was the creative origin of all life in the cultural community. Related in theme, depiction of the female nude as a physical being bursting with health expressed the biological value of the individual as the precondition of all creative and spiritual values. Such paintings portrayed perfect, beautifully shaped human types that represented the ideal far more than the real.

Modern themes were not entirely excluded. Paintings of highways, dams, and factories had a marked technological flavor, however, intended to manifest community spirit by glorifying engineering projects made possible only by the free cooperation of all the nation's groups under a united leadership. But although depictions of workers in such paintings broke from the themes of nature and motherhood, industrial laborers were represented in a traditional, straightforward style. Indeed, the message remained the same; such paintings extolled the unity of the *Volk*, in which every individual was dedicated to the life of the whole community.

As in officially sanctioned artworks, the traditional and the sentimental dominated literature. Josefa Berens-Totenhohl, one of the most popular and widely read authors of the Third Reich, wrote novels of peasant life which paid homage to the peasant's virtues and strength, his roots in the soil, and above all of the sacredness of family life. Purely sentimental novels like the immensely popular stories of Hedwig Courths-Mahler were not considered desirable reading because they did not contain ideological overtones and aimed solely to entertain their readers. Such themes combined with regionalism in a genre called the *Heimatroman*. The novelist and poetess Agnes Miegel had a literary horizon only as wide as the boundaries of East Prussia, her home province; Hermann Stehr, writing of Silesia, mixed literature and religion tinged with mysticism. Emil Strauss, a Swabian, was yet another regional writer in whose work life on the land assumed spiritual significance. Preaching a cult of hardihood, he juxtaposed an idyll of rustic serenity with the isolation of the asphalt of the big cities. In literature as in the other arts, the regime fostered that antimodern, anti-urban mood of the tradition-loving middle class that felt so threatened by dynamic industrial society.

More popular art forms, such as film, also upheld the values depicted in National Socialist art: family, motherhood, comradeship, character building, and the glory of war — all wrapped up in a covering of love of soil and race, concern for the destiny of the German people, and the mystery of the eternal Aryan. Although the state held a monopoly of the film industry, Goebbels, in charge of both production and censorship, allowed a wide variety of films to be made. About half of the 1,100 films produced during the Third Reich were either love stories or comedies, without any direct ideological bent. A quarter of the films were adventure stories, crime thrillers, or musicals; the last quarter consisted of historical, military, and overtly political subjects. But it is almost impossible to be exact on this point. Many films produced for entertainment on one level also carried political and ideological messages. Historical films always had some obvious or hidden correlation with the current political situation, and many domestic comedies, while not explicitly espousing National Socialist ideology, did not contradict one of its basic premises in praising love and marriage. On the one hand, Goebbels allowed a wide variety of films not overtly Nazi in content to be produced; but on the other, he did not permit any film that went against the basic ideology of the regime to be made.

The type of film that dealt with ideological issues in a clear-cut fashion, such as *Hans Westmar* (based on the real-life Nazi hero Horst Wessel) and *Hitlerjunge Quex* (a film biography of the young Hitler Youth martyr Heinz Norkus), was soon abandoned. Goebbels, who had once called for a Nazi cinema as powerful as the Soviet film *Battleship Potemkin*, soon realized that his own productions along this line were unsuccessful. (The stunning cinematographic achievements of Leni

Riefenstahl make something of an exception to this rule. Whatever her creative intentions, her filming of both the Party rally in Nuremberg in 1934, *The Triumph of the Will*, and the Berlin Olympics of 1936, *Olympia*, resulted in powerful pieces of propaganda. But they were produced without the support of Goebbels and under the direct sponsorship of Hitler.) Goebbels finally recognized the futility of his efforts to make the German film industry an organ of Nazi propaganda when he declared that "the SA's proper place is in the streets and not on the cinema screen."

Instead, Goebbels moved to less direct expressions of true Germanness. *Ohm Kruger*, for instance, dealt with British atrocities during the Boer War and the British obsession with material things, a value the film attributes to Queen Victoria as well as to the soldiers in the field. This acquisitiveness contrasts sharply with the nature of the God-fearing Boers, who, raising their crops and tending their cattle, formed a true *Volk*, bound to the soil of South Africa. "Führer-type" biographical films also flourished that did not necessarily deal with leaders as such but might center on any historical figure whose life provided an analogy with Hitler's. Thus the life stories of the alchemist Paracelsus, the poet Schiller, and the inventor Diesel exemplified the triumph of untutored genius over formal learning and of intuition over pedantic routine. Glorification of motherhood was also common in movies such as *Motherlove, The Second Mother, The Sin Against Life*, and *The Charitable Lie*. Wartime themes came into their own after 1939 with such films as *Stuka Pilot*. Films about the despair and anguish caused by the breakup of family life were extremely popular, as well. The two greatest box office hits of the Third Reich, *The Great Love* and *Request Concert*, both dealt with this theme of separation.

Most of the cultural endeavors the Nazis encouraged as a replacement for all that they silenced, expelled, or destroyed were of a quality so inferior as to be embarrassing. This was true not only of the high arts of painting and literature but also of such popular forms of entertainment as film. The regime did not simply impose a set of propaganda lines on the producers of art. They gave sufficient freedom for creativity but limited the scope in which such creativity could be expressed. The result was not a new, revolutionary form of art but something rather different. In both form and content the art produced during the Third Reich, not surprisingly, strongly resembled that of the nineteenth century. National Socialist ideology appealed primarily to the lower middle class, whose members felt more at home in the imagined world of the idealized nineteenth century, a world in which ties to the natural and the communal prevailed and which had not yet been subjected to the full force of industrialization and urbanization. What passed for National Socialist art reflected the aesthetic ideals of the culturally uneducated lower middle class, full of moral attitudinizing, mock heroics, and sentimentalized love of family and community, and emphasizing the special nature of the German soul and the sacredness of German soil.

51. Hitler's Speech Dedicating the House of German Art

The single most important event in the history of the arts under the Third Reich — one that shows the significance of the arts in National Socialist ideology — was the dedication of the House of German Art and the opening of an official exhibition in July 1937. The House of German Art was the first public building constructed under the Third Reich. The building was designed by Hitler's then-favorite architect, Paul Ludwig Troost, and Hitler himself laid the cornerstone on October 15, 1933. Despite the pressing practical problems facing the nation, art was nevertheless assigned a central place in the new *Volk* community. Hitler, who had taken an active role in judging what was to be included in the opening exhibition, gave the following speech at the dedication of the museum on July 18, 1937.

Four years ago, when the festive cornerstone-laying ceremonies for this structure took place, we were all aware that not only was a stone being laid in place for a building, but that the ground had to be prepared for a new and truly German art. It was imperative to bring about a turning point in the development of all German cultural activity. . . .

The collapse and general decline of Germany was, as we know, not only economic and political but, possibly to a greater extent, cultural. Moreover, these proceedings were not to be explained solely through the fact of a lost war. Such catastrophes have often affected states and peoples, and it has been these which have not infrequently been the stimulus for purification and, thereby, inner uplifting. That flood of slime and filth which the year 1918 vomited to the surface was not created by the loss of the war, but was instead only released by it. A body tainted inherently, through and through, discovered only through defeat the total extent of its own decomposition. . . .

Certainly the economic decline had naturally been felt the most because its effect alone was emphatically able to reach the awareness of the great masses. The political decline, on the other hand, was either flatly denied by countless Germans or at the least not recognized, while the cultural decline was neither seen nor understood by the majority of the people. It is noteworthy that during this time of general decline and collapse catchwords and phrases simultaneously began to make their triumphant appearance. . . . But the general distress, especially the misery of the millions of unemployed, could not be denied, and neither could the consequences for those affected be excused. It was therefore more difficult

From *Völkischer Beobachter*, July 19, 1937. Translated by Dieter Kuntz.

to hide the economic than the political collpase of the nation with catch-words or phrases.

In the political sphere for a time the democratic and Marxist phraseol-ogy of the November [i.e., Weimar] Republic, as well as continual refer-ences to various aspects of international solidarity and the effectiveness of international institutions, and so on, was able to veil from the German people the unparalleled decline and collapse. . . . Far more successful and, above all, far more enduring was the effect of these phrases and catchwords in the cultural field, where they created complete confusion concerning the essential character of culture in general and about German cultural life in particular. . . . In this sphere, more than in others, the Jews employed all means and devices that shape and guide public opinion. The Jews were especially clever in utilizing their control of the press and with the aid of so-called art critics were able not only to create confusion about the character and purpose of art but were also able to destroy generally sound perceptions. . . .

Art was said to be an experience of the international community, and thus all understanding of its essential association with a people was destroyed. Art was said to be associated with a particular age, so that there was no actual art of a people or of a race, but only an art form of a certain period. According to this theory the Greeks did not create Greek art, but instead it was the expression of a certain age. The same was said to be true of Rome. . . . So today there is no German, French, Japanese, or Chinese art, but there is only simply "modern" art. . . . According to such a theory art and artistry is put on the same level as the craftsmanship of our modern tailor shops and fashion studios, according to the principle of something different every year. One time Impressionism, then Futurism, Cubism, perhaps even Dadaism . . . If it were not so tragic, it would be almost comical to find out how many catchwords and phrases these so-called students of art used during recent years to describe and interpret their wretched creations.

It was sad to experience how these catchwords and this verbal non-sense created not only a general feeling of uncertainty in the appraisal of artistic achievement or endeavor but contributed to the intimidation of those who might otherwise have protested against this cultural Bolshe-vism. . . . And so, just as today clothes are judged not by their beauty but only according to whether or not they are modern, so are the old masters simply rejected because they are not modern and it is not fashion-able to admire them or to acquire their works.

But true art is and remains eternal, it does not follow the law of seasonal fashion assessment of works created in dress design studios. It merits appreciation because it is an eternal revelation arising from the depths of the essential character of a people. . . .

. . . But those whose works do not have eternal value do not like to speak of eternities. They prefer instead to dim the radiance of these giants who reach from out of the past into the future, in order that contemporaries might discover their own tiny flames. These lightweight smear artists are at best only the products of a day. Yesterday they did not exist, today they are modern, and the day after tomorrow they will be forgotten. These littlest producers of art were overjoyed by the Jewish discovery that art was connected to a certain period. Lacking all qualifications for eternal value, their art could now at least be the art of the present time. . .

It is these artistic dwarfs who themselves demand the greatest tolerance in the judgment of their own works, but who in turn are extremely intolerant in their valuation of the works of others, be they artists from the past or the present. Just as in politics, there was here, too, a conspiracy of incapacity and mediocrity against better works of the past, present, and the anticipated future. . . . These miserable art-critiquing windbags were always able to take advantage of the cowardice and insecurity of our so-called wealthy citizens because these nouveau-riche types were too uncultivated to pass their own judgment on art. . . . These types of art creators and art dealers loved nothing better than to play into each other's hands, and to characterize all those who saw through their scheme as "uncultivated philistines." But where the parvenu was concerned, the favored and surest method to counteract any latent doubts and resistance was to emphasize right from the beginning that the artwork in question was not easy for just anyone to understand and that because of that its price was set correspondingly high. These so-called art connoisseurs have grown rich by these methods, but no one understandably wants to be told by one of these types that he lacks appreciation for art, or does not have the money to pay for it. This type of buyer often judged the quality of a work simply by the amount of the price being asked for it. And when this nonsense was then also praised in obscure phrases, it became all the easier to come up with the money. In the end, one could still secretly hope that the thing that one did not understand oneself, one's neighbor most certainly would not understand either. . .

Here today I want to make the following declaration: until the seizure of power by National Socialism, there existed in Germany a so-called modern art; that is, as the word implies — almost every year there was a new one. National Socialist Germany, however, desires to have again a "German art," which, like all creative works of a people, should and will be an eternal one. When the cornerstone was laid for this building it signaled the beginning of the construction of a temple for art; not for a so-called modern art, but for an eternal German art; better yet: a House of Art for the German people, and not for an international art for the year 1937, '40, '50, or '60. Art is not dependent on an age but on a people. . . . Time changes, the years come and go . . . but the people are a constant point within the entire range of phenomena. . . . There can therefore be no standard of yesterday and today, of modern and unmodern, but only of "valueless" or "valuable," or of "eternal" or "transitory." . . . And therefore when I speak of German art — for which this House was built — what I want to see is the standard for that art in the German people, in their character and their life, in their feeling, their emotions, and in their development.

From the history of the development of our race we know that it is composed of a number of more or less distinct races that in the course of thousands of years, thanks to the formative influence of a certain outstanding racial kernel, produced that mixture we see before us in our people today. This force, which formed the people in time past and which still today continues to shape it, stems from the same Aryan branch of mankind we recognize not only as the carrier of our own civilization but of the earlier civilizations of the ancient world.

The way in which our race was composed has produced the many-sidedness of our own cultural development. . . . But nonetheless, we the German people, as the end result of this historical development, wish to have an art that corresponds to the ever-increasing homogeneity of our racial composition, and that would then in itself present the characteristics of unity and homogeneity. The question has often been posed, to define just what it means "to be German." Among all the many definitions that have been put forth, it appears to me that the most praiseworthy are those that have not attempted to arrive at a definition but have instead chosen to state a law. The most fitting law I would propose has already been expressed by a great German: "To be German is to be clear." What this means is that to be German is to be logical and above all, to be true. . . The deepest inner desire to have such a truly German art is reflected in this law of clarity, and has always been present in our people. It has inspired our great painters, our sculptors, our architects, our thinkers and poets, and above all our musicians. . . .

During the long years of planning the formation of a new Reich, I thought much about the tasks that would confront us in the cultural cleansing of the people's life, because Germany was to have not only a political and economic rebirth, but above all else, Germany was to undergo a cultural renaissance. . . .

. . . I was convinced, after our collapse, that a people that have stumbled and from then on have been trampled on by the whole world have all the greater duty consciously to assert their own value toward their oppressors. There can be no greater proof of the highest rights of a people to their own life than immortal cultural achievements. I was therefore always determined that if fate should one day give us power I would debate these issues with no one, but would make my own decisions. Because an understanding for such great tasks has not been granted to everyone. . . .

Among the countless plans that floated through my mind both during the war and in the period following the collapse was the thought of building in Munich, the city with the greatest tradition of cultural exhibits,

[handwritten margin note: Art must reflect unity & homogeneity of the German people]

a great new exhibition palace. This was needed in view of the totally undignified condition of the old building. Years ago I also thought about the location where this building now stands. . . . In 1931, the seizure of power by National Socialism still appeared to be in the distant future, and there was little prospect of reserving for the Third Reich the building of a new exhibition palace. For a time it actually did look as though the men of November wanted to create an art exhibit building in Munich which had very little in common with art, but which would have corresponded to the Bolshevik tenor of the times. Possibly some of you remember the plans that were drawn up during those days. . . . The intended building was difficult to define, and could easily have served as a Saxon yarn factory, a market hall of a town, or possibly even a train station or [an indoor] swimming pool . . . but the lack of resolve of my former political enemies [to carry out this project] gave me joy and provided the only hope that in the end the erection of the new building . . . might still fall to the Third Reich, and that it would become its first task. . . .

This new building we have conceived is, you will no doubt agree, of a truly bold and artistic design. It is so unique and so individual that it cannot be compared with anything else. . . . It is, I daresay, a true monument for this city and, beyond that, for German art. . . . This House that has arisen here possesses proper dignity and will enable the highest artistic achievements to present themselves to the German people. This House represents a turning point; it brings to an end the era of chaotic, incompetent architecture. This, the first of the new buildings, will take its place among the immortal achievements of our German artistic life.

But you understand now that it is not enough merely to provide the House . . . the exhibit itself must also bring about a turning point. . . . If I presume to make a judgment, speak my opinion, and act accordingly, I do this not just because of my outlook on German art, but I claim this right because of the contribution I myself have made to the restoration of German art. Because our present state, which I and my comrades in the struggle have created, has alone provided German art with the conditions for a new, vigorous flowering.

It was not Bolshevik art collectors or their literary henchmen who laid the foundation for a new art or even secured the continued existence of art in Germany. No, we were the ones who created this state and have since then provided vast sums for the encouragement of art. We have given art great new tasks. . . . I declare here and now that it is my irrevocable resolve that just as in the sphere of political bewilderment, I am going to make a clean sweep of phrases in the artistic life of Germany. "Works of art" which cannot be comprehended and are validated only through bombastic instructions for use . . . from now on will no longer be foisted upon the German people!

We are more interested in ability than in so-called intent. An artist who is counting on having his works displayed, in this House or anywhere else in Germany, must possess ability. Intent is something that is self-evident. These windbags have tried to make their works more palatable by representing them as expressions of a new age; but they need to be told that art does not create a new age, that it is the general life of peoples which fashions itself anew and therefore often seeks to express itself anew. . . . Men of letters are not the creators of new epochs; it is the fighters, those who truly shape and lead peoples, who make history. . . . Aside from that, it is either impudent effrontery or an inscrutable stupidity to exhibit to our own age works that might have been made ten or twenty thousand years ago by a man of the Stone Age. They talk of primitive art, but they forget that it is not the function of art to retreat backward from the level of development a people has already reached. The function of art can only be to symbolize the vitality of this development.

The new age of today is at work on a new human type. Tremendous efforts are being made in countless spheres of life in order to elevate our people, to make our men, boys, lads, girls, and women more healthy and thereby stronger and more beautiful. From this strength and beauty streams forth a new feeling of life, and a new joy in life. Never before was humanity in its external appearance and perceptions closer to the ancient world than it is today.

This type of human, which we saw last year during the Olympic games . . . exuding proud physical strength — this my good prehistoric art-stutterers — this is the "type" of the new age. But what do you manufacture? Deformed cripples and cretins, women who inspire only disgust, men who are more like wild beasts, children who, if they were alive, would be regarded as God's curse! . . . Let no one say that that is how these artists see things. From the pictures submitted for exhibition, I must assume that the eye of some men shows them things different from the way they really are. There really are men who can see in the shapes of our people only decayed cretins; who feel that meadows are blue, the heavens green, clouds sulphur-yellow. They like to say that they experience these things in this way.

I do not want to argue about whether or not they really experience this. But in the name of the German people I only want to prevent these pitiable unfortunates, who clearly suffer from defective vision, from attempting with their chatter to force on their contemporaries the results of their faulty observations, and indeed from presenting them as "art." Here there are only two possibilities open: either these so-called artists really do see things this way and believe in that which they create — and if so, one has to investigate how this defective vision arose — if it is a mechanical problem or if it came about through heredity. The first case would be pitiable, while the second would be a matter for the Ministry of the Interior, which would then deal with the problem of preventing the perpetuation of such horrid disorders. Or they themselves do not believe in the reality of such impressions, but are for different reasons attempting to annoy the nation with this humbug. If this is the case, then it is a matter for a criminal court.

This House, in any case, was not planned or built for the works of art incompetents or for maltreaters of art. A thousand workmen did not labor for four and a half years on this building only to have creations exhibited here by people who are lazy to excess and who spend but five hours bespattering a canvas, while hoping confidently that the boldness of the pricing would produce the desired effect and result in the hailing of the work as the most brilliant lightning-birth of a genius. No, the hard work of the builders of this House demands equally hard work from those who want to exhibit here. I do not care in the least if these pseudo-artists then are left to cackle over each other's eggs!

The artist does not create for the artist, but for the people! We will see to it that from here on the people will be called on to judge their own art. No one must say that the people have no appreciation for a truly valuable enrichment of its cultural life. Long before the critics did justice to the genius of a Richard Wagner he had the people on his side. For their part, however, during the last few years the people have had no affinity for the so-called modern art that was placed before them. The mass of the people moved through our art exhibits in a completely uninterested fashion or stayed away altogether. The people's healthy perceptions recognized that all these smearings of canvas were really the outcome of an impudent and unashamed arrogance or of a simply shocking lack of skill. Millions of people felt instinctively that these art-stammerings of the last few decades were more like the achievements that might have been produced by untalented children of from eight to ten years old and could under no circumstances be regarded as the expression of our own time or of the German future.

Since we know today that the development of millions of years repeats itself in every individual but is compressed into a few decades, we have the proof that an artistic creation that does not surpass the achievement of eight-year-old children is not "modern" or even "futuristic" but is, on the contrary, highly archaic. It probably is not as developed as the art of the Stone Age period, when people scratched pictures of their environment on the walls of caves. . . .

I know, therefore, that when the *Volk* passes through these galleries it will recognize in me its own spokesman and counselor . . . it will draw a sigh of relief and joyously express its agreement with this purification of art. And this is decisive, for an art that cannot count on the ready inner agreement of the broad, healthy mass of the people, but which must instead rely on the support of small, partially indifferent cliques, is intolerable. . . . We are convinced that the German people will again fully support and joyously appreciate the future truly great artists from within their ranks. . . .

This exhibition then is but a beginning. . . . But the opening of this exhibit is also the beginning of the end of the stultification of German art and the end of the cultural destruction of our people. . . . Many of our young artists will recognize the path they will have to take; they will draw inspiration from the greatness of the time in which we all live, and they will draw the courage to work hard and will in the end complete the task. And when a sacred conscientiousness at last comes into its own, then, I have no doubt, the Almighty will lift from this mass of decent creators of art, several individuals who will rise to the eternal star-covered heaven of immortal, God-favored artists of great ages. . . . We believe that especially today, when in so many spheres the highest individual achievements are standing the test, so also in the sphere of art will the highest value of personality again emerge to assert itself.

52. Culture in the Service of the Reich

The Reich Chamber of Culture was established in September 1933 under the direction of Joseph Goebbels to oversee cultural activities. The chamber was divided into seven subchambers for literature, music, film, theater, fine arts, radio, and the press. Through this organization, Goebbels controlled and guided Nazi cultural policy by imposing strict conformity and censorship. Chamber membership was compulsory for anyone working in one of the seven fields, but anyone judged lacking in suitable attributes could be excluded. These extracts from the 1937 *Handbuch der Reichskulturkammer* (Manual of the Reich Chamber of Culture) illustrate some of the intended functions of the subchambers.

THE NATURE AND FUNCTIONS OF THE REICH CHAMBER OF CREATIVE ART

The Reich Chamber of Creative Art was established as a professional body of public law on grounds of the law of the Reich Chamber of Culture. Membership in the Chamber is a prerequisite, for the members of the following professions, in practicing their professions:

Architects, interior decorators, horticulturists, sculptors, painters, engravers, commercial engravers, designers, fine art craftsmen, copyists, restorers of works of art, dealers in works of art and antiques, fine art publishers, dealers in prints.

Members of the Chamber must also be: all artists' associations, art associations, associations of fine art craftsmen, institutes for creative art and their faculties.

From U.S. Chief of Counsel for the Prosecution of Axis Criminality, *Nazi Conspiracy and Aggression* (Washington, D.C.: U.S. Government Printing Office, 1946), vol. 5, doc. no. 2529-PS, pp. 262–67.

The first problem confronting the Chamber following its establishment was to locate and organize all professionals required to join the Chamber and to unite them in an organization in conformity with the new principles. In the course of these measures, all former associations which were backed by some interests were discontinued without exception, and each member obligated to become a member of the Reich Chamber without fail.

[handwritten margin note: disband all Organization & (re-organize under Nazi Control)]

THE NATURE AND FUNCTIONS OF THE REICH CHAMBER OF MUSIC

The Reich Chamber of Music has been called upon to keep alive the fundamental thought to professional progress by organizing, with due consideration for the character and activities of the musician, the cultural, economical and legal conditions of the music profession or by protecting the existing conditions in such manner that music will be preserved for the German people as one of its most precious possessions.

THE NATURE AND FUNCTIONS OF THE REICH CHAMBER OF LITERATURE

The Reich Chamber of Literature comprises as members all persons who are connected with German literature, whether they are the authors of the original literature or just commercial dealers. It keeps the profession free from undesirable elements and the book market free from un-German books. . . .

. . . It is the function of the Reich Ministry for Popular Enlightenment and Propaganda (Department VIII) to exert political influence on German literature and especially to influence the policy of libraries. . . .

[handwritten margin note: propaganda through lit]

THE NATURE AND FUNCTIONS OF THE REICH CHAMBER OF MOTION PICTURES

The national socialistic State had to intervene at once in this field. It had to lift the motion pictures out of the sphere of influence of literalistic economic thinking, give them a sound economic foundation, and assign to them political and cultural missions to be fulfilled within the national socialistic state. . . .

. . . The great significance of the motion picture in pointing the way to our people towards the creation of a national will, requires of all those who are active in the motion picture industry to become bearers and conveyors of culture. It is one of the most important duties of the Reich Chamber of Motion Pictures to see to it that the entire motion picture profession will become cognizant of this mission.

[handwritten margin note: movies as prop]

THE NATURE AND FUNCTIONS OF THE REICH
CHAMBER OF BROADCASTING

. . . Another aspect, however, now steps conspicuously into the foreground in the field of broadcasting: Campaigning for broadcast reception! Until the time of the seizure of power by National Socialism, Germany had considerably fallen behind several great civilized nations in the number of its radio listeners. Causes for this backwardness undoubtedly were: inefficiency, lack of ability and above all lack of resourcefulness and aggressiveness on the part of the broadcasting authorities of the time of the Weimar Republic [Systemzeit]. National Socialism effected thorough changes in that respect, and in due recognition of the necessities, initiated a strong propaganda which appealed to the people. . . .

. . . It was inevitable that the Chamber had to become a factor in various aspects of the broadcasting economy, so that the goal of total dispersion of broadcasting among the German people could be as closely approached as possible. Department III — Economy and Technical Science — concerns itself with an immense number of problems arising in this connection. We mention the most important one: To plan the construction of apparatus. The following results to be mentioned here, among others: the creation of the "People's Receiver" [Volksempfänger], which because of its technical features and price level, started its triumphant career which has no comparison, in spite of all kinds of obstacles, with a total sale of $2\frac{1}{2}$ million pieces, thus contributing considerably to the attainment of the high number of listeners of today.

THE FOSTERING OF CULTURE OF COMMUNITIES
AND COMMUNITY SOCIETIES

The following is the total picture: the Reich sets up the principles guiding the policy on culture, and maintains model institutions. It is the communities which foster the local cultivation of arts, complemented and supported in many respects by the district and provincial associations. The administration and the patrons of art must work closely together. All is dominated, however, by the close alliance of the art and people which is convocated and stimulated by the cultural societies.

53. Art and National Education

The creation of a racial culture for the *Volksgemeinschaft* proved to be more difficult than imagined. On the one hand the various Party and government agencies involved with cultural policies squabbled among themselves, and on the other,

From *Deutschland-Berichte der Sozialdemokratischen Partei Deutschlands (Sopade) 1934–1940*, (Frankfurt: Verlag Petra Nettelbeck, 1980), 2 June (1935): 711–22. Translated by Dieter Kuntz.

acceptance of these activities was less than enthusiastic. The following report, written in 1935, from the underground organization of the Social Democratic Party, which had a keen interest in evaluating the popularity of the regime, indicates the limited success of many of the National Socialist cultural policies.

Considerable differences have existed for quite some time between the Reich Chamber of Culture and the NS Cultural Association. These differences have recently become more pronounced. During the last quarterly meeting of the National Association of German Writers, the representative of the Chamber of Culture poignantly declared that no competing organization would be tolerated. To which the representative of the NS Cultural Association replied that it was his cultural organization that was created by the party. Indicative of the differences between Goebbels and Rosenberg was Goebbels's rescheduling of National Theater Week to begin now in Hamburg instead of later in the fall. He did this in order to have a counterweight to the congress of the NS Cultural Association in Düsseldorf. It should be noted that Hitler went to Hamburg, but not to Düsseldorf.

Some time ago the regional congress of the NS Cultural Association took place. The large hall, which can accommodate 3,000 people, was only about one-quarter full. The organization Strength Through Joy [Kraft durch Freude, or KdF] was even invited to attend. No one representing that organization came, however, as they too are again feuding with the NS Cultural Association. The conflict between these two organizations stems from the fact that the KdF organizes its own theater productions. . . . The differences between the Reich Chamber of Culture and the NS Cultural Association can be traced to the various interests of party bigwigs. If one wants to isolate the essential difference between the two, one can perhaps say that the "old fighters," or the political realists, are at home in the Chamber of Culture; for these men art is an instrument of political power. In the NS Cultural Association, on the other hand, one finds the strong influence of Rosenberg and his irrational, mystical, racial ideology. The first are attempting to gain greater ties to the working class, while the latter group would like to remold Germany spiritually.

1. THEATER AND FILM

Berlin: An official of the Reich Chamber of Culture recently voiced his opinion unreservedly to a confidential circle of associates. In his judgment, the German theater is in a dreadful state. There are too many competing authorities trying to have their say, and consequently there is so much uncertainty that theater directors are hesitant to undertake original productions. Typical is the Frankfurt director who recently declared that for the next theater season he will stage no premiers at all but limit the fare instead to old, reliable pieces. The authorities are now trying to help the theater get back on its feet by luring the masses to the show through organizations like Strength Through Joy and offering cheap tickets (beginning at 50 Pfennig). With these low prices, however, it is hard to imagine that the theater can be operated on a financially sound basis. Because of the low gate receipts the actors are not paid well and the performances have been sinking accordingly. . . .

Silesia: The film of the party rally, *Triumph of the Will*, has proved to have very little appeal. Even though SA and SS members were eligible for 50 percent discounts, hardly any of them saw the film. There were also very few in attendance from the ranks of the political organization. The strongest contingent of movie-goers were the Sudeten Germans. The film ran for only three days. . . .

Lübeck area: The film theaters are frequented quite heavily. The favorite themes are foreign films and harmless entertainment films. Nazi films such as *Triumph of the Will* are being shunned. The "Week in the News" is also being avoided. Most people have developed the habit of coming to the theater only after the "Week in the News" has ended. Nazi parades and speeches are meeting with indifference. If Goering appears on the screen, a general snickering ensues. . . .

2. LITERATURE

The National Socialists are making desperate attempts to create a new workers' literature. They have been courting Marxist working-class poets especially. Several have, indeed, been coordinated [*gleichgeschaltet*], but they are generally regarded with contempt. With the other writers the Nazi efforts have been in vain. . . . Writers are often subject to the whims of National Socialist editors who arbitrarily change verses and allow no protest to be lodged — if one dared to do such a thing. . .

3. MUSIC

Southwestern Germany, especially Baden and the Palatinate, was in earlier days the land of working-class singing associations and musical bands. Since the revolution, however, these popularly rooted traditions are threatening to peter out. From Baden: Our musical bands have suffered since the Nazi seizure of power. They were requisitioned by countless NS organizations for all sorts of functions, while at the same time the Reich Chamber of Music made life difficult for them. The chamber stipulated that only musicians who have received identity cards from the chamber can officially play in public. . . .

4. NEWSPAPERS AND MAGAZINES

The difficulties in the newspaper business continue to persist. In the last few months a large number of regional enterprises have gone under, while others have been merged with National Socialist papers. . . . Rhineland-Westphalia: The Catholic press continues to be vital despite all kinds of bullying. Our new police president in Recklinghausen, who is a Streicher[1] supporter and previous SA leader, has unleashed a wave of aggression against Catholics and Jews. Newspapers have been attacked because they sometimes carry Jewish advertisements. The police president spoke to all public officials and demanded that they cancel their subscriptions to the Catholic press. He recommended instead Goering's *Nationalzeitung* (National Journal). Some officials, however, have in protest ordered instead the paper *Rote Erde* (Red Earth) from Dortmund, and many continue to subscribe to the Catholic paper despite the threat. . . .

---

[1] Julius Streicher, *Gauleiter* of Franconia, was editor of the violently antisemitic journal *Der Stürmer* (The Attacker).

NAZI POSTER ART

In addition to radio and film, political and propaganda posters offered the Nazis a popular medium for effectively and efficiently spreading their ideas. From the very early days of the Party after World War I to its expansion into a nation-wide political organization in the 1920s, garish red posters proclaimed the NSDAP message on city walls and kiosks. Although often tailored to specific audiences, even to industrial workers and farmers from whom the Nazis did not ordinarily receive support, the slogans on these posters were simple, direct, and repeated almost infinitely. Compared with the often wordy and visually confused campaign posters of most of their political opponents, these posters presented eye-catching color schemes, bold designs, and powerful symbols.

Hitler himself took great interest in all features of Nazi propaganda, including political posters. Even before he joined the Party, Hitler had produced a number of advertising posters during his Vienna years. In order to make some money and fancying himself an artist, he drew posters which declared the benefits to be derived from hair tonic, soap powder, and an antiperspirant named "Teddy." Upon entering the German Workers' Party, he took charge of recruitment and propaganda and became enthralled in designing Party emblems and insignia. Hitler established the swastika as the Party emblem, selected the Party colors of red and black as symbols of blood and soil, and searched through numerous images of eagles before choosing one appropriate for Party stationary. In designing posters, he also freely drew upon what he found impressive from other political parties, from the Italian Fascists to the Russian Communists. Nazi posters must have been effective, for they simply relied upon recognition of NSDAP symbols and designs to get their message across. Hitler's image itself became one of the most powerful representations of the Party and its call for a great leader. One of the most memorable posters of the 1932 presidential campaign simply represented Hitler's face against a solid black background with only the name "Hitler" written below.

With the consolidation of power in 1933 and 1934, the heightened atmosphere of the political campaigns of earlier years did not cease. Party propaganda merely shifted from politics to the *Volksgemeinschaft*. Posters encouraged Germans to join various local Party organizations, directed women to participate in a multitude of Party programs, and instructed children to apply to the Hitler Youth. There were posters that also celebrated the new integration of all segments of society into the *Volksgemeinschaft*. Farmers were told of festivals honoring agriculture, and industrial workers were informed of art exhibitions organized around the theme of the beauty of labor. The *Kraft durch Freude* program, in particular, created a number of effective posters. Government subsidized theatrical performances, vacation trips within Germany, and cruises to Norway and the Mediterranean were all announced in this fashion. The KdF car, the Volkswagen, in particular, was proclaimed through a number of powerfully designed posters. As with the visual arts and popular forms of entertainment, Nazi poster art of the 1930s and 1940s was not for the most part heavy-handedly propagandistic. Although the experimental, abstract, and modernistic tendencies of the 1920s were forbidden in favor of clear and "realistic" designs, these posters still exhibit a creative use of color and design.

The Nazis propagandized various NSDAP ideas and programs through posters. This popular means of communication was often attached to billboards such as the one here, which displays a viciously antisemitic image identifying the Jews with gross money-making schemes and bolshevism.

The Nazis first made effective use of posters in the political campaigns of the late 1920s and early 1930s. Here the image of a people suffering from the impact of the Great Depression are warned: "Our Last Hope — Hitler."

Nazi propaganda did not deemphasize political violence; rather, it stressed that combat against Communists and Social Democrats was necessary. This poster reads, "We Are Building the New Germany — Think of the Victims [who gave their lives for the cause] — Vote for National Socialists — List 1."

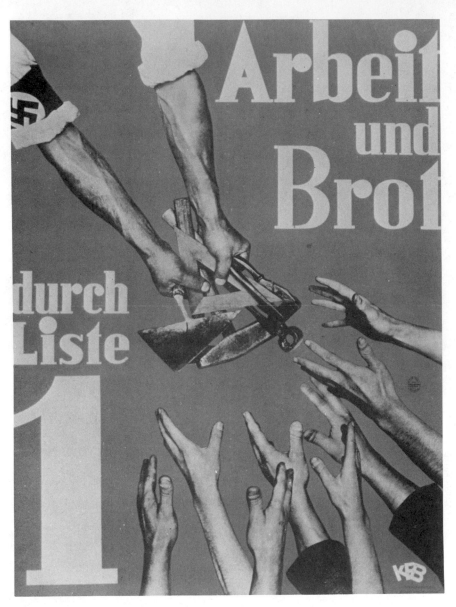

This poster demonstrates how Nazi propagandists effectively employed simple yet powerful images. It says, "Work and Bread — through List 1."

Throughout the 1920s, the Nazis made various though unsuccessful appeals to the working class of Germany, in order to lure them away from the Socialist and Communist parties. In an obvious reference to many workers' experience of the war, this poster directs, "Worker, Choose the Front-line Soldier — Hitler!"

Hitler had become so well known by the early 1930s that the NSDAP could simply use his image for political and propaganda purposes. This poster of his face against a solid black background is one of the most powerful of all such posters.

In a clear alignment of the Party to an idealized image of family life and values, this poster proclaims, "The NSDAP safeguards the *Volksgemeinschaft* — Comrades — If You Need Advice and Help — Turn to Local Party Organizations."

German workers and their families were also meant to feel a part of the *Volksgemeinschaft*. This poster announces an exhibition of German art dealing with the theme of work: "German *Volk* — German Work — Exhibition Berlin 1934 — Sponsor: Reichspresident von Hindenburg — Honorary President: Reichsminister Dr. Goebbels."

Farmers were one of the favored groups in Nazi ideology. They represented the traditional values of the *Volk*. Here a poster announces the celebration of the Third Reich's Day of the Farmer in the town of Goslar in 1935.

One of the most widely publicized programs in the *Kraft durch Freude* campaigns was the subsidized cruises to Norway and the Mediterranean. This poster proclaims, "You Too Can Now Travel" and provides ticket-purchasing information.

Although never fully realized, the program to supply cheap automobiles for the German public is effectively advertised in this poster: "Your KdF Car — Information Available at all KdF Offices."

Some of the most successful propaganda campaigns were aimed at young Germans, urging them to join the various components of the Hitler Youth. This powerful poster proclaims, "This Hand Leads the Reich — German Youth Follow It in the Ranks of the HJ [Hitler Youth]."

This poster from the war years simply announces a district meeting of the NSDAP, but the image is that of a German peasant woman working the land while the troops are fighting at the front. Although the poster suggests that all Germans need to help out in the war effort, it contradicts what Nazi ideology had propagandized during the 1930s — that a woman's place is not in the workplace but with her home and family.

Hitler lays the foundation stone of the Volkswagen factory at Wolfsburg in 1938. The Volkswagen program was launched amid much fanfare by the regime, which promised to provide even the poorest member of the *Volksgemeinschaft* with his own automobile.

Chapter
8

The *Volksgemeinschaft*

The means by which the Nazis translated party ideology into reality can best be understood through the ways in which the regime reshaped the lives of women, farmers, and workers within the Third Reich. Membership in the National Socialist Women's League "coordinated" the good German woman with the *Volk*. One of the mammoth units of the Third Reich and outstripped in membership only by the German Labor Front and the National Association of Civil Servants, the organization trained women in the proper functions of German womanhood. Its programs included teaching cooking techniques and inculcating eating schedules, providing suggestions on the use of leftovers, and giving guidance in the substitution of domestic for imported goods. In addition, members of the league held classes on mothering skills and domestic-economy courses for schoolgirls and others. During the war the scope of the group's activities widened. Members did Red Cross work, helped collect scrap metal and other items needed for the war effort, and aided servicemen and their families.

National Socialist agricultural policy was directed mainly toward peasant farmers. It designated some six hundred thousand medium-sized farms as *Erbhöfe*, which could not be mortgaged or sold and had to pass intact from father to eldest son. This policy preserved these family farms, but it also favored eldest sons at the expense of both parents and other siblings. The monetary grants that farmers received upon retirement were converted under this law into maintenance in kind for the improvement of the family farm. The immediate impact of this policy was to increase the size of the *Erbhöfe*. By 1938 the average acreage had nearly doubled — fifty-five acres, compared to thirty acres six years earlier. In this instance, at least, the German farmer was better off.

The policies of the regime toward industrial workers were often contradictory. All labor in the Third Reich was organized and coordinated through the German Labor Front, which replaced the various unions that had sided with the Social Democratic and Communist parties. Up to the time of the seizure of power, the unions had been the main organizations of German workers; they were forcibly dismantled early in 1933. But the Labor Front did not exactly adopt their role in representing workers' needs and demands. Under the Labor Front, workers lost their right to organize, their right to bargain collectively, their freedom to choose their occupation, and their freedom of movement. Such rights and freedoms were now considered unnecessary and disruptive to economic life in the new community. The German Labor Front would henceforward redefine and "protect" the position of workers within the *Volksgemeinschaft*.

The Factory Cell Organization represented the Labor Front on the level of the individual factory. The Law on the Organization of National Labor of January 1934 established the new form of factory organization, designating each factory a "shop community," a microcosm of the *Volksgemeinschaft* of which it formed a part, and separating factory workers into "leaders" and "followers," reflecting the "natural" structure of the larger community. Leaders were not necessarily the former owners but rather were to arise from the mass of owners and workers in yet another application of the *Führerprinzip*. In conjunction with advisory boards, these leaders were not so much to control the followers as to express their best interests and direct the entire shop community to a happier and more efficient existence as a unit within the *Volk* community.

Along with the attempt to make the factory over into a microcosm of the *Volksgemeinschaft* went the effort to clean up and improve factory buildings and workers' facilities. Better lighting, locker and shower rooms, subsidized canteens providing hot meals, and kindergartens were introduced. Under Albert Speer, initiating the Beauty of Labor program, green lawns replaced asphalt ground coverings, and flower gardens were planted and parks laid out so that workers could enjoy the outdoors during breaks. Athletic facilities gave workers a place to exercise and relax when not working. In some factories, chapels containing busts of Hitler were built. The shop community was no longer to be merely a place of work — a grimy factory from which workers fled once they had completed their shifts for the day — but a community in its own right, merging workers into a close-knit organization that reminded them of their unity with other workers and of the dignity of labor in the new cultural community. The shop community aimed to incorporate workers fully into the community of labor just as their family life established their relationship with the racial community.

The Beauty of Labor program formed only one part of a much larger campaign dedicated to improving the lives of industrial laborers in the *Volksgemeinschaft*. The much-publicized *"Kraft durch Freude"* ("Strength Through Joy"), or KdF, program attempted to bring workers into full participation in National Socialist life by subsidizing such activities as theater performances and concerts, exhibitions, films, dances, sports, hiking, folk-dancing groups, and adult education courses. Its most grandiose scheme, however, was a massive program of organized tourism. The number of vacation days with pay allotted to the individual worker almost doubled, rising from an average of three to eight days to one or two weeks. Travel holidays ranged from a week in the Harz Mountains to a week on the North Sea coast, to two weeks on Lake Constance, to a tour of Italy. Other vacation packages included trips to the Bavarian forest, the Rhône and Eiffel areas, and the Masurian Lakes. Ocean cruises to Norway or Madeira aboard one of two KdF-owned ocean liners were the most spectacular of these holidays. As part of the cruise ritual, all passengers — from the most exalted managing director to the lowliest worker — drew lots for the allocation of cabins.

The most lasting relic of the *"Kraft durch Freude"* movement was the development of the Volkswagen — the "people's automobile," also known as the KdF Wagen. The Volkswagen became an important symbol, for owning an automobile had been a distinctly upper middle-class prerogative. Now each worker would commonly own a car. (In actuality, during the years of the Third Reich no Volkswagen was delivered to workers who had subscribed for them. Manufacturing of consumer goods was placed on hold as the national economy was reoriented to war production.) The ideal of worker-owned automobiles still had its ideological effect, however. Ability to own a Volkswagen represented the integration of workers into the *Volksgemeinschaft*. The worker, declared Dr. Robert Ley, the head of the German Labor Front, "sees that we are serious about raising his social position. He sees that it is not the so-called educated classes whom we send out as representative of the new Germany, but himself, the German worker, whom we show to the world." At the KdF convention in Hamburg in 1938, Ley announced that "there are no longer classes in Germany. In the years to come, the worker will lose the last traces of inferiority feelings he may have inherited from the past." The cost of this new status and these new amenities was the state's total control and regimentation of workers' lives. "There are no more private citizens. The time when anybody could do or not do what he pleased is past."

54. Personality and the Conception of the *Völkisch* State

Nazi ideology defined the community in opposition to the individualistic society produced by liberal democracies on the one hand and the false sense of community promoted by the communists on the other. This community of the German people, the *Volksgemeinschaft*, was a tightly organized and clearly hierarchical unity. In

From Adolf Hitler, *Mein Kampf*, pp. 442–51. Copyright © 1943 by Houghton Mifflin Company, 1971. Reprinted by permission of Houghton Mifflin Company. All rights reserved.

the following selection from *Mein Kampf*, Hitler elaborates on this type of community, its foundations, its relation to the state, and the personality type it produces.

The *völkisch* National Socialist state sees its chief task in *educating and preserving the bearer of the state*. It is not sufficient to encourage the racial elements as such, to educate them and finally instruct them in the needs of practical life; the state must also adjust its own organization to this task.

It would be lunacy to try to estimate the value of man according to his race, thus declaring war on the Marxist idea that men are equal, unless we are determined to draw the ultimate consequences. And the ultimate consequence of recognizing the importance of blood — that is, of the racial foundation in general — is the transference of this estimation to the individual person. In general, I must evaluate peoples differently on the basis of the race they belong to, and the same applies to the individual men within a *Volksgemeinschaft*. The realization that peoples are not equal transfers itself to the individual man within a *Volksgemeinschaft*, in the sense that men's minds cannot be equal, since here, too, the blood components, though equal in their broad outlines, are, in particular cases, subject to thousands of the finest differentiations.

The first consequence of this realization might at the same time be called the cruder one: an attempt to promote in the most exemplary way those elements within the *Volksgemeinschaft* that have been recognized as especially valuable from the racial viewpoint and to provide for their special increase.

This task is cruder because it can be recognized and solved almost mechanically. It is more difficult to recognize among the whole people the minds that are most valuable in the intellectual and ideal sense, and to gain for them that influence which not only is the due of these superior minds, but which above all is beneficial to the nation. This sifting according to capacity and ability cannot be undertaken mechanically; it is a task which the struggle of daily life unceasingly performs.

A philosophy of life which endeavors to reject the democratic mass idea and give this earth to the best people — that is, the highest humanity — must logically obey the same aristocratic principle within this people and make sure that the leadership and the highest influence in this people fall to the best minds. Thus, it builds, not upon the idea of the majority, but upon the idea of personality.

Anyone who believes today that a *völkisch* National Socialist state must distinguish itself from other states only in a purely mechanical sense, by a superior construction of its economic life — that is, by a better balance between rich and poor, or giving broad sections of the population more right to influence the economic process, or by fairer wages by elimination of excessive wage differentials — has not gone beyond the most superficial aspect of the matter and has not the faintest idea of what we call a philosophy. All the things we have just mentioned offer not the slightest guaranty of continued existence, far less of any claim to greatness.

256

A people which did not go beyond these really superficial reforms would not obtain the least guaranty of victory in the general struggle of nations. A movement which finds the content of its mission only in such a general leveling, assuredly just as it may be, will truly bring about no great and profound, hence real, reform of existing conditions, since its entire activity does not, in the last analysis, go beyond externals, and does not give the people that inner armament which enables it, with almost inevitable certainty I might say, to overcome in the end those weaknesses from which we suffer today.

To understand this more easily, it may be expedient to cast one more glance at the real origins and causes of human cultural development.

The first step which outwardly and visibly removed man from the animal was that of invention. Invention itself is originally based on the finding of stratagems and ruses, the use of which facilitates the life struggle with other beings, and is sometimes the actual prerequisite for its favorable course. These most primitive inventions do not yet cause the personality to appear with sufficient distinctness, because, of course, they enter the consciousness of the future, or rather the present, human observer, only as a mass phenomenon. . . .

Man complements this first invention by a second: he learns to place other objects and also living creatures in the service of his own struggle for self-preservation; and thus begins man's real inventive activity which today is generally visible. These material inventions, starting with the use of stone as a weapon and leading to the domestication of beasts, giving man artificial fire, and so on up to the manifold and amazing inventions of our day, show the individual creator the more clearly, the closer the various inventions lie to the present day, or the more significant and incisive they are. At all events, we know that all the material inventions we see about us are the result of the creative power and ability of the individual personality. And all these inventions in the last analysis help to raise man more and more above the level of the animal world and finally to remove him from it. Thus, fundamentally, they serve the continuous process of higher human development. But the very same thing which once, in the form of the simplest ruse, facilitated the struggle for existence of the man hunting in the primeval forest, again contributes, in the shape of the most brilliant scientific knowledge of the present era, to alleviate mankind's struggle for existence and to forge its weapons for the struggles of the future. All human thought and invention, in their ultimate effects, primarily serve man's struggle for existence on this planet, even when the so-called practical use of an invention or a discovery or a profound scientific insight into the essence of things is not visible at the moment. All these things together, by contributing to raise man above the living creatures surrounding him, strengthen him and secure his position, so that in every respect he develops into the dominant being on this earth.

Thus, all inventions are the result of an individual's work. All these individuals, whether intentionally or unintentionally, are more or less great benefactors of all men. Their work subsequently gives millions, nay, billions of human creatures, instruments with which to facilitate and carry out their life struggle.

If in the origin of our present material culture we always find individuals in the form of inventors, complementing one another and one building upon another, we find the same in the practice and execution of the things devised and discovered by the inventors. For all productive processes in turn must in their origin be considered equivalent to inventions, hence dependent on the individual. Even purely theoretical intellectual work, which in particular cases is not measurable, yet is the premise for all further material inventions, appears as the exclusive product of the individual person. It is not the mass that invents and not the majority that organizes or thinks, but in all things only and always the individual man, the person.

A human community appears well organized only if it facilitates the labors of these creative forces in the most helpful way and applies them in a manner beneficial to all. The most valuable thing about the invention itself, whether it lie in the material field or in the world of ideas, is primarily the inventor as a personality. Therefore, to employ him in a way benefiting the totality is the first and highest task in the organization of a *Volksgemeinschaft*. Indeed, the organization itself must be a realization of this principle. Thus, also, it is redeemed from the curse of mechanism and becomes a living thing. *It must itself be an embodiment of the endeavor to place thinking individuals above the masses, thus subordinating the latter to the former.*

Consequently, the organization must not only not prevent the emergence of thinking individuals from the mass; on the contrary, it must in the highest degree make this possible and easy by the nature of its own being. In this it must proceed from the principle that the salvation of mankind has never lain in the masses, but in its creative minds, which must therefore really be regarded as benefactors of the human race. To assure them of the most decisive influence and facilitate their work is in the interest of the totality. Assuredly this interest is not satisfied, and is not served by the domination of the unintelligent or incompetent, in any case uninspired masses, but solely by the leadership of those to whom Nature has given special gifts for this purpose.

The selection of these minds, as said before, is primarily accomplished by the hard struggle for existence. Many break and perish, thus showing that they are not destined for the ultimate, and in the end only a few appear to be chosen. In the fields of thought, artistic creation, even, in fact, of economic life, this selective process is still going on today, though, especially in the latter field, it faces a grave obstacle. The administration of the state and likewise the power embodied in the organized military might of the nation are also dominated by these ideas. Here, too, the idea of personality is everywhere dominant — its authority downward and its responsibility toward the higher personality above. Only political life has today completely turned away from this most natural principle. While all human culture is solely the result of the individual's creative activity, everywhere, and particularly in the highest *leadership* of the *Volksgemeinschaft,* the *principle of the value of the majority* appears decisive, and from that high place begins to gradually poison all life; that is, in reality to dissolve it. The destructive effect of the Jew's activity in other national bodies is basically attributable only to his eternal efforts to undermine the position of the personality in the host-peoples and to replace it by the mass. Thus, the organizing principle of Aryan humanity is replaced by the destructive principle of the Jew. He becomes "a ferment of decomposition" among peoples and races, and in the broader sense a dissolver of human culture.

Marxism presents itself as the perfection of the Jew's attempt to exclude the pre-eminence of personality in all fields of human life and replace it by the numbers of the mass. To this, in the political sphere, corresponds the parliamentary form of government, which, from the smallest germ cells of the municipality up to the supreme leadership of the Reich, we see in such disastrous operation, and in the economic sphere, the system of a trade-union movement which does not serve the real interests of the workers, but exclusively the destructive purposes of the international world Jew. In precisely the measure in which the economy is withdrawn from the influence of the personality principle and instead exposed to the influences and effects of the masses, it must lose its efficacy in serving all and benefiting all, and gradually succumb to a sure retrogression. All the shop organizations which, instead of taking into account the interests of their employees, strive to gain influence on production, serve the same purpose. They injure collective achievement, and thus in reality injure individual achievement. For the satisfaction of the members of a national body does not in the long run occur exclusively through mere theoretical phrases, but by the goods of daily life that fall to the individual and the ultimate resultant conviction that a *Volksgemeinschaft* in the sum of its achievement guards the interests of individuals.

It is of no importance whether Marxism, on the basis of its mass theory, seems capable of taking over and carrying on the economy existing at the moment. Criticism with regard to the soundness or unsoundness of this principle is not settled by the proof of its capacity to *administer* the existing order for the future, but exclusively by the proof that it can itself *create* a higher culture. Marxism might a thousand times take over the existing economy and make it continue to work under its leadership, but even success in this activity would prove nothing in the face of the fact that it would not be in a position, by applying its principle *itself*, to create the same thing which today it takes over in a finished state.

Of this Marxism has furnished practical proof. Not only that it has nowhere been able to found and create a culture by itself; actually it has not been able to continue the existing ones in accordance with its principles, but after a brief time has been forced to return to the ideas embodied in the personality principle, in the form of *concessions;* — even in its own organization it cannot dispense with these principles.

The völkisch philosophy is basically distinguished from the Marxist philosophy by the fact that it not only recognizes the value of race, but with it the importance of the personality, which it therefore makes one of the pillars of its entire edifice. These are the factors which sustain its view of life.

If the National Socialist movement did not understand the fundamental importance of this basic realization, but instead were merely to perform superficial patchwork on the present-day state, or even adopt the mass standpoint as its own — then it would really constitute nothing but a party in competition with the Marxists; in that case, it would not possess the right to call itself a philosophy of life. If the social program of the movement consisted only in pushing aside the personality and replacing it by the masses, National Socialism itself would be corroded by the poison of Marxism, as is the case with our bourgeois parties.

The *völkisch* state must care for the welfare of its citizens by recognizing in all and everything the importance of the value of personality, thus in all fields preparing the way for that highest measure of productive performance which grants to the individual the highest measure of participation.

And accordingly, the *völkisch* state must free all leadership and especially the highest — that is, the political leadership — entirely from the parliamentary principle of majority rule — in other words, mass rule — and instead absolutely guarantee the right of the personality.

From this the following realization results:

The best state constitution and state form is that which, with the most unquestioned certainty, raises the best minds in the national community to leading position and leading influence.

But as, in economic life, the able men cannot be appointed from above, but must struggle through for themselves, and just as here the endless schooling, ranging from the smallest business to the largest enterprise, occurs spontaneously, with life alone giving the examinations, obviously political minds cannot be "discovered." Extraordinary geniuses permit of no consideration for normal mankind.

From the smallest community cell to the highest leadership of the entire Reich, the state must have the personality principle anchored in its organization.

There must be no majority decisions, but only responsible persons, and the word 'council' must be restored to its original meaning. Surely every man will have advisers by his side, but *the decision will be made by one man.*

The principle which made the Prussian army in its time into the most wonderful instrument of the German people must some day, in a transferred sense, become the principle of the construction of our whole state conception: *authority of every leader downward and responsibility upward*.

Even then it will not be possible to dispense with those corporations which today we designate as parliaments. But their councillors will then actually give counsel; responsibility, however, can and may be borne only by *one* man, and therefore only he alone may possess the authority and right to command.

Parliaments as such are necessary, because in them, above all, personalities to which special responsible tasks can later be entrusted have an opportunity gradually to rise up.

This gives the following picture:

The *völkisch* state, from the township up to the Reich leadership, has no representative body which decides anything by the majority, but only *advisory bodies* which stand at the side of the elected leader, receiving their share of work from him, and in turn if necessary assuming unlimited responsibility in certain fields, just as on a larger scale the leader or chairman of the various corporations himself possesses.

As a matter of principle, the *völkisch* state does not tolerate asking advice or opinions in special matters — say, of an economic nature — of men who, on the basis of their education and activity, can understand nothing of the subject. It, therefore, divides its representative bodies from the start into *political and professional chambers*.

In order to guarantee a profitable cooperation between the two, a special *senate* of the élite always stands over them.

In no chamber and in no senate does a vote ever take place. They are working institutions and not voting machines. The individual member has an advisory, but never a determining, voice. The latter is the exclusive privilege of the responsible chairman.

This principle — absolute responsibility unconditionally combined with absolute authority — will gradually breed an élite of leaders such as today, in this era of irresponsible parliamentarianism, is utterly inconceivable.

Thus, the political form of the nation will be brought into agreement with that law to which it owes its greatness in the cultural and economic field.

As regards the possibility of putting these ideas into practice, I beg you not to forget that the parliamentary principle of democratic majority rule has by no means always dominated mankind, but on the contrary is to be found only in brief periods of history, which are always epochs of the decay of peoples and states.

But it should not be believed that such a transformation can be accomplished by purely theoretical measures from above, since logically it may not even stop at the state constitution, but must permeate all other legislation, and indeed all civil life. Such a fundamental change can and will only take place through a movement which is itself constructed in the spirit of these ideas and hence bears the future state within itself.

Hence the National Socialist movement should today adapt itself entirely to these ideas and carry them to practical fruition within its own organization, so that some day it may not only show the state these same guiding principles, but can also place the completed body of its own state at its disposal.

55. The Role of Women in the *Volksgemeinschaft*

Women were to play an important part in the *Volksgemeinschaft*. In their privileged position as wives and mothers, they preserved the values of the community and protected the purity of the race. But these traditional roles ran against modern currents, which increasingly brought women out of the home and into the work force and public life in general. At the Nuremberg Party rally of 1934 Hitler defined the role of women in the new Germany.

If one says that man's world is the state, that his world is his struggle, his readiness to devote himself to the community, then one might be able to say that the world of woman is a smaller one. For her world is her husband, her family, her children, and her house. (*Ardent applause.*) But where would the larger world be if no one wanted to care for the smaller world? How could the larger world exist if there were no one to make the cares of the smaller world the essence of their lives? No, the larger world is built on this small world! . . .

. . . Providence has assigned woman the task of caring for this world of her own, and only from this can the man construct and mold his world. These two worlds are therefore never in conflict. They complement each other, they belong together, like man and woman belong together. (*Applause of several minutes.*). . .

We do not think it is proper if woman invades the world of the man and enters his territory; instead we think it is natural for these worlds to remain apart. One is characterized by strength of feeling, strength of soul! While the other requires strength of vision, toughness, determination, and willingness to sacrifice! . . .

. . . What man offers in heroism on the field of battle, woman equals with unending perseverance and sacrifice, with unending pain and suffering. Every child she brings into the world is a battle, a battle she wages for the existence of her people. (*Tremendous applause.*) And both must therefore mutually respect and value each other when they see that

From *Völkischer Beobachter*, September 9, 1934. Translated by Dieter Kuntz.

each performs the task that Nature and Providence have assigned. Out of this separation of functions there will necessarily come mutal respect.

It is not true, as Jewish intellectuals maintain, that respect depends on the overlapping of spheres of activity of the sexes; instead, respect demands that neither sex should attempt to do what rightly is in the other's sphere. In the final analysis, respect comes from each knowing that the other is doing everything necessary to maintain the whole relationship. (*Enthusiastic agreement.*)

. . . Woman is egotistical when it comes to maintaining her small world in order to enable the man to defend the larger world; and man is egotistical in the maintenance of the larger world, because it is inseparably linked with the other. We will protect ourselves against an intellectualism of the most corrupt kind which threatens to put asunder that which God hath joined. (*Ardent agreement.*)

Because she springs from the root of life, woman is also the most stable element in the preservation of a people. When all is said and done, it is she who has an infallible sense for what is necessary if a race is not to perish, because it will be her children who will be the first to be affected by that disaster. Man is often far too unstable mentally to immediately find his way to these fundamental truths. Only in good time and with a good education will man also know exactly what his task is.

We National Socialists have, accordingly, for many years protested against bringing woman into political life, a life that in our eyes is unworthy of her. A woman once said to me: "You must see to it that women go into parliament, because only they are capable of ennobling that institution." "I do not believe," I answered, "that man should try to ennoble something that is inherently bad. And the woman who becomes involved in the workings of parliament will not ennoble it, but will instead be dishonored by it. I would not want to leave something to woman which I intend to take away from man." (*Enthusiastic applause.*) My opponents thought that this [attitude] would prevent us from ever winning women to our movement. But we gained more than all the other parties together, and I know that we would have won over even the last German woman if she had only had the opportunity to study parliament and the degrading role played by women therein.

That is why we have incorporated the woman into the battle for the *Volksgemeinschaft* in the manner in which nature and providence have determined it. Our women's movement is for us not something that inscribes on its banner a program consisting of the fight against man but something that defines its program as the common fight of woman together with man. For the new National Socialist *Volksgemeinschaft* was established on a firm basis precisely because millions of women became our most loyal, fanatical fellow-combatants. (*Long-lasting applause.*) Fighting women who fought for life in its communal whole, in the service of the common task of maintaining life; fighting women who did not fix their gaze on rights that a Jewish intellectualism mirrors before their eyes, but rather on duties that Nature imposes on us collectively. (*Fervent applause*.)

If earlier liberal intellectual women's movements contained many, many points in their programs whose openings were based on so-called intellect, our National Socialist women's movement contains only one single point, and this point is called: the child; that tiny being that must be born and should grow strong, for whom the entire life struggle gains its meaning. . . .

What is the purpose of the whole human struggle? Why the sorrow and the grief? For an idea alone? Only for an idea? Only for a theory? No, it would not be worthwhile wandering through this temporal valley of tears. The only thing that allows us to surmount all this is our view from the present toward the future; from ourselves to those who will come after us. (*Loud approval*.) Several minutes earlier I spoke to the assembled youth. It is wonderful to be able to look on this golden youth; we know that they will one day be Germany, after we shall be no more. (*Enthusiastic cheers*.) Youth will maintain all that we create and construct. We work for our youth. This is what our struggle is all about.

Since we recognize this simple and elegant goal Nature has given us, the work of both sexes naturally finds its logical and proper engagement no longer in conflict but in the common struggle of real life. (*Thunderous applause*.)

56. The National Socialist Women's League

Like other sectors of society in the Third Reich, women were provided with an organization that would define their role in the new community and coordinate their activities within the state. Established in 1931, the National Socialist Women's League was not very active until after the seizure of power in 1933. Its main purpose was to bring other women's organizations into line with official ideology. The party issued the following guidelines for the league in 1933.

PRINCIPLES AND ORGANIZATIONAL GUIDELINES
OF THE NATIONAL SOCIALIST WOMEN'S LEAGUE

1. We want an awakening, a renewal, and a reeducation of women to equip them for their task as guardians of the nation's source of life: sexual life, marriage, motherhood and family, blood and race, and youth and nationhood. A woman's entire education, development, vocational

From *Nationalsozialistische Deutsche Arbeiter-Partei, Hauptarchiv 1919–45,* (Stanford, Calif.: Hoover Institution on War, Revolution and Peace), H. A. reel 13, folder 254 (National Socialist Women's League Guidelines). Translated by Dieter Kuntz.

pursuit, and position within *Volk* and state must be directed toward the physical and spiritual task of motherhood.

2. We recognize that the great transformational process of women's lives over the last fifty years, due to the machine age, has brought about a certain necessity, and we accept the education and official integration of the female work force in the interest of the nation, unless this prohibits them from performing their duty within the *Volk* in terms of marriage, family, and motherhood.

3. We reject the misguided direction of the democratic-liberalistic-international women's movement because they have not discovered new paths based on God and nationhood, and which are rooted in women's souls; instead they represent the point of view that women are competitive with [or equal to] men, and in the demands they have raised they have elevated temporary stopgap measures to the position of a fundamental principle. This has resulted in the creation of a womanhood that has misplaced its energies and that has not understood its task in Germany's time of need.

4. We want a movement for the revitalization of womanhood which will reawaken these profound female energies and will give women strength for their special tasks within the freedom movement, as well as strengthen them for their tasks in the future Germany.

5. We therefore demand and pursue the fight against the systematic debasement and destruction of women's honor and women's dignity, as well as against the moral corruption of youth.

6. On the other hand, we are raising the determination of German women which is rooted in God, nature, family, *Volk*, and Fatherland, as well as establishing our own women's cultural program that will find its shape within the Third Reich.

7. We therefore, with all our energy, take part in the freedom movement's struggle for internal political change and seek the establishment of the Third Reich through utmost propaganda even on the smallest level.

57. Mothering Sunday

Nazi population policies, attempting to encourage procreation of children in order to stem the falling birthrate, accordingly emphasized the role of the mother within the family. Women were assigned traditional domestic functions in the *Volksge-*

From *Anzeiger für den hankreis Eutin,* May 22, 1939, in Lawrence Stokes, ed., *Kleinstadt und Nationalsozialismus: Ausgewählte Dokumente zur Geschichte von Eutin, 1918–1945* (Neumünster: Karl Wachholtz Verlag, 1984), pp. 895–96. Translated by Dieter Kuntz.

meinschaft, but their role as mothers, whose purpose was to bear children who would ensure the continuation of the race, was considered pivotal. The regime instituted a campaign designed to encourage women to bear more children by publicly honoring particularly prolific mothers. Introduced in 1938, the German Mother's Cross was annually bestowed on mothers who had had four or more children. Those with eight or more received a gold cross. The second Sunday in May became Mothering Sunday, on which the Nazis awarded the honors to deserving mothers in local ceremonies. A newspaper from the nothern German city of Eutin described one such ceremony in 1939.

> Similar to ceremonies elsewhere in the German Fatherland, so too, here in Eutin, did the NSDAP local group yesterday commemorate Mothering Sunday with the bestowal of the Honor Cross from the Führer on German mothers over the age of sixty who have been blessed with a large number of offspring. After much painstaking and thoughtful preparation, the ceremony took place in the wonderfully decorated assembly room of the Palace Hotel. The mothers and their relatives were seated at the long rows of tables. Since many party and youth organization members were also in attendance, all seats in the room were taken. The festivities began with a musical number by the Hitler Youth orchestra. The BdM [Bund deutscher Mädel, or League of German Girls] girls then honored and congratulated the mothers, and presented them with bouquets of flowers. All then joined in singing a song, and after a poem had been recited, local group leader Langmaack read a few words from the Führer which expressed high esteem for the mother and the woman-citizen. All then again sang the song "Holy Fatherland," which was followed by the local group leader's ceremonial address.
>
> . . . On this solemn occasion he first greeted the older mothers and then all other guests, but especially those representing the Party and all its organizations, as well as the armed forces and other authorities. His words, which came from the heart and which were also taken to heart, brought forth all the emotions one feels when one hears the word "mother." Happy and thankful are those who still have the love of a mother's heart. Our mothers will always be our guiding stars. Just as man risks his life in battle, so too does the mother bravely and faithfully offer her life for the nation when she fulfills her sacred duty. Thousands of years ago the Teutons honored woman as a holy being. In their society the mother was the focal point of the people, because only through her was renewal and continuation of the people possible. . . . We must also be grateful to the mother because she is the source of strength of a nation. Today's mothers have experienced and seen much, and were called on to carry out tasks during the World War while their husbands, sons, and grandsons were fighting at the front. . . . The place of the mother as focal point of the nation had been undermined during the postwar period. Today Adolf Hitler has again restored the German mother to her noble and saintly

position in the heart of the people. Today the mother and her offspring are again honored. The mother is ready to give children to the Führer in the numbers our people need for survival. To offer herself for the sake of the nation so that the nation might have eternity, that is the life purpose of the German mother, and that is why we must return to the eternal laws of blood and race.

Thereafter the local group leader, in the name of the Führer, congratulated each mother and awarded her the Honor Cross. Each was visibly moved on receiving this honor. After a song by the choir . . . the local group leader again spoke and urged those present to remind others to apply early for further awards. . . . He further thanked all those involved for a successful ceremony, and after a salute to the Führer and the singing of party songs the official segment of the commemoration was concluded. . . .

58. The *Volksgemeinschaft* and the Farmer

German farmers, like women, held an honored position in National Socialist ideology. More than the factory work, farming expressed the deep tie between blood and soil that formed the foundation of the entire ideology. Emphasizing traditional values and idealizing antiurban modes of life, the Nazis singled out the peasant farmer as the agrarian ideal. The Party had also won considerable support from the agricultural sector of German society during the last years of the Weimar Republic through propaganda campaigns promising economic relief for the small and marginal farmer. In the following speech made to peasant farmers at a harvest festival in October 1933, Hitler reiterated the Party's commitment to improving their situation.

Liberalism and democratic Marxism may have disavowed the farmer, but the National Socialist revolution will stand by him because he is the safeguard of the present and the only guarantor of the future. We know that the ruin of the German farmer will mean the end of the German people. The purpose of our political struggle is not to win against or conquer foreign nations, but is concerned instead with the maintenance and security of our own people. We are therefore determined to stand up for the German farmer. We will not accept compromises or half measures. A glance at our population statistics shows us that the future of the nation even today depends exclusively on support from the farmer. Therefore, it is the task of the state leadership first and foremost, and with all means and under any circumstances, to support this group on whose existence the continuation or destruction of our people depends. The city dweller

From *Völkischer Beobachter*, October 2, 1933. Translated by Dieter Kuntz.

whose business goes under can always establish another; the farmer, once driven from his piece of soil, usually goes under permanently. . . .

We are establishing a new national community. No social class can exist without the aid and understanding of the others. We are making millions of city dwellers aware of the tremendous importance of the German farming community. They are prepared to make sacrifices for others. To lend aid to one another is a tremendous undertaking, and we are symbolically organizing it for the first time for the coming winter. What city and country together can sacrifice in order to save our needy countrymen will form a fund from which all will someday be able to draw. The solidarity between city and country and worker and farmer will thereby be demonstrated more mightily than what could be achieved by a thousand speeches. Providence will reward those who are sincere and undaunted. May this feeling of solidarity between city and country and between workers of the hand and of the head be increasingly strengthened until we can proudly realize a powerful oneness. We are one people. We want to be one nation! But we beseech the Almighty, in this hour of humility, to bless us also in the future in our endeavor to provide the daily bread.

59. The German Labor Front

Just as the National Socialist Women's League had to counter the demands of the contempory European women's movement, in the German Labor Front Nazi ideology contended against social trends affecting the working class in order to define its position within the *Volksgemeinschaft*. But unlike women, many German workers had been organized before the Nazi takeover, both in labor unions and in political parties such as the Marxist Social Democratic Party. At the time of the seizure of power, the Nazis outlawed the Social Democratic Party and destroyed its leadership, but they still had to take pains to convince the workers themselves of the falsity of Marxist ideology. National Socialist ideology emphasized that it was itself founded on both "nationalist" and "socialist" principles — that, in other words, it spoke to the concerns of workers as well as promoted the unity of the nation. The following article, written by a functionary of the German Labor Front, explains the status of the working class within the new national community. The *Nationalsozialistische Monatshefte* was a relatively popular monthly magazine that disseminated primarily Nazi ideology, because it was edited by Alfred Rosenberg, one of the party's chief racial theoreticians.

It is necessary for National Socialism to establish a new relationship between state, politics, the economy, and the individual working country-

From Max Frauendorfer, "Deutsche Arbeitsfront und Ständischer Aufbau," *Nationalsozialistische Monatshefte*, 54 (September, 1934): 817–22. Translated by Dieter Kuntz.

man, because only when these concepts can be grouped together in accordance with their significance for National Socialism can it then be expected that the harm done in past times in these areas can be redressed. . . .

It is the historic achievement of National Socialism to have brought about the synthesis of "national" and "social" elements of the German people. With these two concepts, two large groups under which our people have decayed during the last few decades are being renamed: two groups of German people who stood apart from each other as enemies and between whom lay an unbridgeable gap, despite the sincere intentions of individuals. These two fronts became increasingly more paralyzed, and the strength of the nation was sapped more and more through this internal struggle.

That is why the gathering of all forces became the basic prerequisite if the nation were to be guided toward a better future. National Socialism brought about the realization among the German people that the concepts "national" and "social" do not imply antagonism but are in reality dependent on one another, because a people can externally direct the national aspect only if it is healthy internally. But this inner health — and it must be the goal of every true socialism — can, on the other hand, be conceived of only if the nation is in the position to defend its *Lebensraum* against other peoples.

It was therefore only natural that the National Socialist movement complete the conquest of the nation by destroying Marxist ideology, by taking possession of the organizations that had previously been the germ cells of this ideology, and by seizing the other non–National Socialist associations, thereby ensuring victory for the new ideology. Aside from this ideological goal there was also the absolute determination to safeguard the basic rights of every working German and to protect existing assets from ultimate destruction, that is, in a much more successful manner than would ever have been possible under a Marxist or liberal ideology. It was necessary to counter the capitalistic, profit-oriented position with the same determination with which we drained the swamp of Marxist corruption.

These National Socialist beliefs found expression in the action of May 2, 1933, when the trade unions of both orientations (and in the ensuing period the associations of employers and employees also, the instruments of class warfare of these parties) were taken over by National Socialism. Taking their place was the organization uniting all workers, the German Labor Front. Led by the chief of staff of the political organization of the NSDAP and thereby equipped with the full authority of the party, the German Labor Front formed the broad basis of an organic reorganization of the German people. . . .

The basic tenets of this challenge have been realized through the German Labor Front. After the seizure of power, these tenets gained immense popularity as slogans for the reorganization of the social classes. Aside from a regional arrangement according to areas, districts, provinces,

269

and local groups, the millions within the German Labor Front are linked together through an arrangement of giant groups, which are connected through their common daily activity. These national associations, such as those for industry, commerce, crafts, transportation, liberal professions, and so on, include all working people within their respective fields, regardless of the nature of their personal activity. . . .

Through the development of the German Labor Front, the requirements have been met for the attainment of the two goals of National Socialism. In calling for regulation of the class system, National Socialism sought the prevention of class warfare and the possibility of leadership rising from the ranks of working Germans from various branches of the economy. . . .

The road taken by the German Labor Front guarantees that between the larger groups of our people — agriculture, industry, commerce, crafts, liberal professions, and so forth — the same degree of cooperation, based on the mutual recognition of the indispensability of the other, will be achieved, just as it exists in each field between business manager and employees. Clearly the significance of these classes goes well beyond pure economics if one considers that it is imperative to establish a German peasantry as well as a civilization based on craftsmen's skills, and to restore to the concept of a "German merchant's dignity" the value and meaning it once had. . . .

60. "Strength Through Joy"

Under the direction of Dr. Robert Ley, the leader of the German Labor Front, a campaign was launched in 1933 to improve the lot of workers. The resulting *"Kraft durch Freude,"* ("Strength Through Joy") or KdF, program aimed to create a new lifestyle for workers and their families by making available to them the amenities of middle-class life. Art exhibitions, theater performances, and film presentations were all organized for workers. Special KdF cruises were also sponsored. The KdF also inaugurated the production of an inexpensive automobile, which eventually became known as the Volkswagen. Because the regime readjusted production priorities, with the onset of the war, few automobiles were actually produced, but the basic "bug" design continued to be used. Also as part of KdF, the Beauty of Labor campaign created better working conditions in factories through improved lighting and ventilation and the installation of sports facilities. Four years after it was started, Ley reviewed the achievements of the KdF in the following speech.

The social rebuilding of Germany is unthinkable without the NS association "Strength Through Joy," and we are proud that the Führer himself

From *Völkischer Beobachter*, November 27, 1937. Translated by Dieter Kuntz.

has called it one of the greatest social organizations of all time. "Strength Through Joy" is not merely a leisure-time organization; it is a National Socialist community involved in creating a new life-style and in establishing the new social order. Beauty of Labor is a necessary component of Strength Through Joy; it forms the basis on which planned recreation must be established.

The improvements that were reported to this organization come to a total of 109 million marks this year. These funds were spent exclusively on factory improvements carried out in the spirit of "Beauty of Labor." But we can confidently state that the actual figure is much higher because today improvements are often not reported to us as they are commonly regarded as a matter of course. The total expenditures for Beauty of Labor come to approximately 600 million marks.

The campaign "Good Illumination — Good Light" conducted last year was repeated this year, and the success of this lighting campaign can be seen in the tremendous sales increase achieved by the electrical industry as a result of good modern lighting.

An equally great success was the campaign "Clean People — Tidy Factory." . . .

From the development of the workplace as the basis of communal life and communal culture, the road leads to the development of the time after working hours, leisure time. We not only want to expose you to the diverse number of possibilities of spending your leisure time, but we also want to direct you toward a meaningful life. . . .

The greatest activity was undertaken in the area of theater, which was even expanded this year. For the 1937–38 season, approximately 7,000 performances have been scheduled.

The Special Campaign for Reich Superhighways was expanded this year. During 1937 a total of 110,000 working comrades were registered and living in 550 work camps. In each of these camps we organized the showing of two or three movies a month. The grand total comes to 4,000 concerts and 3,000 entertainment evenings for the camps altogether.

Another newly established organization, founded this year, is the Soldier's Theater, which is part of "Strength Through Joy" but performs only in army garrisons and in places where the army is on maneuvers. This first Soldier's Theater was so successful that for the coming year a new series of similar theaters is planned.

A further important measure of our cultural-political theater activity is the Reich Theater Campaign of "Strength Through Joy," which is employed primarily in the border areas of the Reich.

The cultivation of concert activity in general was given a further boost this year. Aside from the master concerts, the factory concerts were also carefully cultivated. Here symphony orchestras as well as the factories' own orchestras were engaged.

The agency After Working Hours has to a large extent undertaken the task of carrying out art exhibitions in businesses and factories. Up to now, the total number of these exhibits comes to 1,273, of which 602 — almost half — were organized this year alone.

The grand total of all those participating in the cultural and entertainment events of the agency After Working Hours comes to a figure of roughly 34 million for this accounting year.

The activity of the German educational/cultural enterprise "Strength Through Joy" shows us to what extent the individual countryman today strives to coordinate himself with a National Socialist life-style. The number of countrymen who have become involved in Strength Through Joy since the inception of the educational/cultural activity totals 10,180,000.

Cultural activity in the area of music has been anchored in the Reich Music Chamber division Youth and *Volk* Music. The singing and musical associations directed by "Strength Through Joy," in cooperation with the Hitler Youth and other formations, held 4,400 "public singings" and other musical events during the past year. There were 800,000 German countrymen who witnessed these events. . . .

An area just as important as the proper use of leisure time is the promotion of bodily exercise. The past year signaled the introduction and energetic advancement of sports in the factory. With this, we tackled a new field of activity of immense proportions and meaning.

The continuing extension of the activity of the sports department and particularly the development of sports in the factory has led to a noticeable lack of qualified exercise instructors and exercise facilities. The number of available gymnasiums, sports fields, and swimming pools is insufficient, particularly in winter. The sports department of "Strength Through Joy" has therefore undertaken a large-scale training program for honorary exercise directors. On the other side of the coin, many factories have begun construction of their own sports facilities. Sports facilities at 900 factories are already finished and another 235 are currently being built. . . .

The crowning, so to speak, of the efforts of Strength Through Joy to provide dignified and meaningful utilization of the leisure time of German working people is the organization of vacations.

Nowhere in the world do people work so much and so diligently as here in Germany. Those that work, however, need equally complete rest and relaxation. The more you work, the better should be your vacation! Sensibly organized vacations are of great importance in maintaining the vitality and productivity of our people.

The KdF trips have become so popular with our people because all has been planned for them, even to the smallest detail. The KdF vacationer travels without cares. Each one has his place reserved on the train; his room and board, sightseeing, excursions — all have been prepared ahead of time.

The number of trip participants has this year again experienced a significant increase. The previous year saw the number of KdF travelers rise from three to six million, and this time we saw another increase of three million. This year, then, there were nine million KdF travelers. One-third of these have taken extended vacations of one to three weeks. Almost two million took part in KdF hikes and 180,000 have traveled to Norway, Madeira, or Italy aboard ships from our KdF fleet. This ship traffic dominates the harbors of Hamburg and Bremen and exceeds by far the total of all other cruise travel in all German harbors together.

We created something else new: what are called the Exchange-Trains. They are the fruit of our accord with Italy. . . . At the beginning of October, 425 *Dopolavora* [Italian workers] came across the border bound for Munich, Nuremberg, and Berlin. A short time later, a long express train with first- and second-class carriages left Berlin and took 425 workers from the Reich capital across the Brenner [Pass] to Rome and Florence. Two organizations with the same goal, "Strength Through Joy" and "*Dopolavora*," have found each other through their common activities and are now strengthening the political axis between Rome and Berlin because they are improving the practical relations between the peoples of the two nations.

For the last three years we have been traveling to Portugal as regularly as we have to Norway. It won't be long before our KdF fleet leaves Europe in search of different parts of the earth. As soon as next year we will visit Africa, where we will provide experiences for our German workers which will far surpass those hitherto. . . .

In Rügen we are constructing a giant KdF seaside swimming facility, which is looking more and more as though it will be the most beautiful seaside facility in the world. Four others are soon to be built.

This year we will begin construction of winter hostels in the mountains for the KdF vacationers in order to further winter vacations and winter sports, which are the healthiest and most beautiful one can imagine.

The village beautification activity, which was extended this year and in which more than 5,000 villages were involved, goes a long way in beautifying the overall image of German villages and, above all, improves housing conditions.

Everything we are creating has but one great goal: the formation of a just social order based on our racial ancestry and our German character, and the creation of the highest standard of living for our people. What the German people have accomplished in four years on poor soil and in limited space has no equal in the world. It was accomplished with unity of purpose in order to ensure the existence, future, and joy of life of the German people. . . .

Collective listening to important radio broadcasts was a typical feature of public life in Hitler's Germany. Work in offices and factories was suspended for the occasion. Here workers in the Rheinmetall-Borsigwerken (iron-works) in Berlin listen to a speech by Goering in 1939.

Chapter

9

German Society Under National Socialism

The reasons the Nazi regime never completed its total reformation of society are not hard to discover. The task of remodeling society, restructuring it entirely and restoring the idyllic conditions of the past, was in itself difficult if not impossible. But the major reason lies in the fact that National Socialist ideology embraced inner contradictions in its very essence. On the one hand, the Nazis promoted a return to a preindustrial, classless world of rural simplicity and functionally defined social groups. But on the other hand, they called for the transformation of Germany into a political and military power, second to none. The proposed war against the Slavs and the creation of Greater Germany demanded the development of such power. Germany had to enlarge its military apparatus to the highest potential, which in the modern world meant both military technology and the industrial complex to support it. The nation's military ambitions required more industrialization and urbanization, not less. This contradiction at the heart of the ideology not only affected National Socialist policies toward agriculture and labor but also defined the role of women and the overall organization of society within the Third Reich. The contradiction led to further difficulties when the ideology was applied in practice.

The officially sanctioned position of women in the Third Reich was in the home, and removing women from the labor market was one of the basic goals of the Party's social program from 1933 on. Before the Nazis came to power, the number of working women in Germany increased dramatically. Between 1907 and 1925, the number of women in the work force increased from 8.5 million to 11.5 million, whereas the population as a whole grew from 54.5 million to 62.4 million. The social position of women can also be measured in other ways. The Weimar

Constitution gave women the vote, and many prominent women assumed a vital role in national poltics. Women also formed a tenth of the membership of local elected bodies and a fifth of the student population.

Although the Nazis launched a campaign to restore married women to their "proper" place within the home and to maneuver them out of the work force, the program could not be carried out immediately. For the most part, only women in the professions were affected, not the main body of female workers. When the Nazis seized power, women were forced out of certain occupations. Married women doctors and civil servants were dismissed in early 1933. By 1935, the number of women teachers at female secondary schools had decreased by 15 percent. In the following academic year, women were no longer permitted to enter teacher-training programs. By this time, the number of women academics had declined from 59 to 37 in a total teaching body of 7,000. From June 1936 onward, women could no longer act as judges or public prosecutors. Female assistant judges and assistant teachers were gradually dismissed. Although women were not entirely displaced from the civil service, their numbers were greatly reduced. Positions in the social services continued to be open to them. Even as late as 1938, every tenth civil servant was a woman. Half of all agricultural workers were women. In 1933 women formed 37 percent of the total labor force in Germany.

The National Socialists launched a marriage-loan program soon after taking power, which offered loans to newly married women on condition of their not seeking employment. It was hoped that as a consequence of this program eight hundred thousand women would leave their jobs within the next four years. Although the proportion of women in the work force declined to 31 percent by 1937, the total number of working women actually increased. By 1939 there were 7 million white- and blue-collar women workers in Germany, approximately one-third of the total. They represented 25 percent of those employed in industry. In specific branches, their proportions were higher: two-thirds in clothing manufacture, one-half in the textile industry, and two-fifths in distribution and food production. Women also comprised two-fifths of all office workers and provided useful semiskilled and unskilled labor in the relatively new rubber and chemical industries. With the ever-growing demand for female labor, the government in 1937 rescinded its law that working women were disqualified from receiving marriage loans.

In 1941, when Germany finally placed its economy on a wartime footing, the regime redirected labor from such sectors as domestic services, catering, and retail distribution into more essential industries. At last, on January 27, 1943, after the defeat at Stalingrad, a total mobilization of female labor was attempted. The Reich's plenipotentiary for labor conscription called up 3 million women, aged seventeen to forty-five. Yet of the 3 million potential workers, only just over nine hundred thousand actually entered the work force full-time. One million were found to be unfit, over half a million were doubtful cases, and of the rest, just under half could be employed only part-time. By 1944, the 14.5 million female workers in Germany were likely to work up to fifty-six hours a week.

Despite Nazi rhetoric to the effect that a woman's place was in the kitchen and the nursery, women formed three-fifths of Germany's wartime labor force. Here as elsewhere, contradictions within the ideology were revealed once it was translated into actual policy. The intention of the conservative revolution to return women to the home had to be subordinated to other ideological goals — industrial expansion and war preparation. As a result, National Socialism did little to change the actual status of women.

As far as farmers in the Third Reich were concerned, the Law on the New Formation of German Peasantry of June 14, 1933, gave priority in the settlement of new lands to young farmers ineligible for the family inheritance. In all, the Third Reich created 20,748 new farms, but the Weimar Republic, which had no such loudly proclaimed policy on farming, had created nearly twice as many. In addition, whereas the number of small- and medium-sized farms increased from year to year under the Republic, it fell steadily throughout the Third Reich. Official funding allotments did not aid the resettlement policy. Investment planning deliberately reduced the volume of credit available for agriculture, and soaring land prices did the policy in. The price per acre, 643 marks in 1932, rose to 1,457 marks by 1938. Finally, other government agencies and policies tended to take over and relegate the resettlement policy to a minor role, and big business and the large landowners did everything possible to frustrate the program.

The Erbhofgesetz (Hereditary Farm Law) marked the high point achieved by the regime's ideological goal. By this act of July 1938, the Nazis came closest to institutionalizing a policy that supported the many family farms at the expense of the more economically efficient large estates. These estates were already being broken up before the Nazis came to power, and the law of 1938 completed the process. Yet even with this law, neither the large estates as economic units nor their ownership changed appreciably, and because most consisted largely of forest, the number of new homesteads did not rise significantly. But the policy had dire consequences for the peasant farmer. The Erbhof (hereditary farm) was to remain in the family. It could be neither sold nor mortgaged. For the time being, the land was attached to the farmer; for the future, however, the farmer was attached to the land. Though an official Nazi spokesman declared the policy to be a realization of "German socialism," in effect peasant farmers were almost returned to the status of medieval serfs who were tied to the land.

The government also introduced a set of laws to control both prices and the market in farm products. The purpose of the legislation was to achieve agricultural self-sufficiency for Germany. Grain imports declined from 6.2 million metric tons in the single year 1928 to 1.7 million metric tons in the four years from 1933 to 1937. Through all this, wheat production remained consistent. The 1930–35 annual average of 4.8 million metric tons still held at 4.6 million metric tons in 1937. During the same period, however, rye production fell from 7.8 million to 6.9 million metric tons. Total grain production also fell by over one million metric tons.

The prices of virtually all other agricultural products were also controlled. The

Law of the Reichsnährstand (National Food Corporation) of September 1933 was extended to all other agricultural production in 1934. National Socialist agricultural policy did not produce more grain for domestic consumption, but it did establish fixed prices and an internal monopoly for the farmers of the Third Reich.

The overall picture of agriculture in the Third Reich is not a favorable one. The short-term results showed an increase in the price index, but seen in the long run and in comparison with other sectors of the economy, there was both economic stagnation for farmers and a loss of real freedom. While wages and salaries increased in volume by 49 percent and profits in trade and industry by 88 percent, farm income grew by only 33 percent. Although 1933–35 saw the annual income of agricultural workers increase by 17 percent, income levels after 1935 leveled off and even declined. In the same period, average national income in all sectors of the economy continued to increase yearly at a rate of 6–12 percent.

These policies highlight the contradictory nature of National Socialist attitudes toward farmers. Both the limited applicability of many of the laws and the restricted opportunities for credit show how little the goal of reconstituting the German farmer as the backbone of the *Volksgemeinschaft* molded agricultural policies. In overall economic planning, this goal was secondary to the more immediate ideological intention of creating a modern industrial economy. Before 1939, peasant farmers did gain some security of land tenure, but at the cost of more work for smaller returns. Conditions were only slightly better for owners of middle-sized farms and large estates. In addition, the rural population of the Reich actually declined by about 2 percent. The ideal of the traditional German peasantry, which was to give cultural direction to the *Volk,* was never realized before the war and completely forgotten after 1939. If National Socialism set itself the goal of returning to a traditional agricultural society, it failed. As with the status of women, the pace of social development in an industrial society continued to run forward. The contradictory nature of Nazi ideology and policy becomes clear at this point. If, on the one hand, National Socialism called for a return to older social forms of organization, it also demanded that Germany be the leading European military power, which meant that it must secure its place as a leading industrial power as well. Modern industry leads to its own forms of social organization, further straining traditional society and its values.

With regard to industrial workers, National Socialism did not have a consistent policy. Through a series of contradictory statements, the ideology exhibited neither a favorable nor an unfavorable image of the worker. In practice, however, the regime established a highly controlled economy. Without ideological restrictions, efficiency was the guiding principle of industrial policy. In this sense, labor policy was subordinated to general economic planning, guided initially by the problems of unemployment and then by preparation for war. Through various public works and rearmament programs, the unemployment figures for 1933 of over 6 million were cut in half by 1934. By 1936 the employment level nearly reached that of the most prosperous years of the Weimar Republic. By the late 1930s, a marked labor scarcity prevailed in the Third Reich.

The organization of workers in the German Labor Front and the coordination of the Labor Front with the "shop communities" did less to benefit workers than to provide new forms of control for both the regime and the factory owners. The Law on the Organization of National Labor set up the shop communities and divided the work force into "leaders" and "followers," but in effect these were just new names for "owners" and "workers," and no reorganization of social relations occurred in the factories. The foremost beneficiaries of the new law were employers, not employees. The advisory councils were without legal status. Their members were forbidden to express opinions publicly or to represent the interests of the workers. Although the purpose of the shop community was to establish collective responsibility for working conditions and production schedules, the law limited and actually undercut this goal. Under certain circumstances, more could be demanded of workplace followers than the loyalty required by law. The leaders, freed from pressure from below, were answerable only to themselves. Above the entire system in each factory was the Reich Trustee of Labor. Directly responsible to the Ministry of Labor, he had the ultimate authority to set wages, regulate working conditions, determine vacation schedules, appoint members of the advisory council in cases in which elections were inconclusive, and approve large-scale dismissals of workers. The trustee guaranteed that the factory conformed to the demands of the regime.

Under Nazi policy, organized labor lost its rights: the right to organize, the right of collective bargaining, its freedom of movement, and its right of vocational choice. But National Socialism also provided labor with definite benefits. Industrial workers were again employed. In an economy characterized by a labor shortage, as in Germany in the late 1930s and early 1940s, workers' power to negotiate for better conditions was bound to improve, even without the acknowledged right of labor to organize in unions or express political opinions. Although wage rates did increase during the Third Reich, they are not the best indicators of the position of workers, for the regime controlled wages and prices and was obsessed with the fear of inflation. Nonetheless, it does seem that the living standards of workers improved a bit under the Third Reich. The ending of unemployment formed the leading goal of the regime's economic policy from 1933 on, and its success in this regard was for many workers the crucial experience of life in the Third Reich. Whatever else it might have meant, for the vast number of German workers, National Socialism provided them with jobs.

Paradoxically, the area of society the Nazis had given the least amount of honor in their ideology was the one for which they definitely can be said to have improved the lot of its members. Compared with the traditional *Hausfrau* and the independent German farmer, the industrial worker was not central to the social ideals of National Socialist ideology, yet it was this group that made actual social and economic advances under the Third Reich. For various reasons, the guiding economic policy of the National Socialist regime was one of full employment, which was reached even before preparations for war got under way. With the shortage of labor from the late 1930s on, real opportunities for advancement and general social improvement also arose. Although their right to organize on their own was denied, German workers achieved a greater sense of importance in society and even a certain equality with factory owners. Yet in the final analysis, these relative improvements were less the result of consistent policy decisions than of both the response to a fear of unemployment, which could threaten the stability of the regime, and the ineluctable economic planning demanded in a society preparing for war in a technological age.

61. New Career Opportunities for Women

During the war years 1939–45, women increasingly entered the labor force in all spheres of the economy. This trend obviously ran against the Nazis' ideological goal of returning women to their traditional roles of wife and mother. But even before the autumn of 1939, the recovery of the economy actually brought opportunities for women to embark on new careers, many of which were not in the traditional mode of female employment, as can be seen in this article written by a functionary of the Frauenschaft (National Socialist Women's League).

Selecting an occupation is today no longer a problem, in financial terms, for the young female job aspirant. Many opportunities are presenting themselves to allow one to attain an ample wage. Factory employment beckons because it requires no special previous experience and no long training period, yet it guarantees a certain degree of freedom of movement. Office work, too, allows much more freedom of movement than do domestic women's occupations and is, for that reason, a frequently chosen vocation. Yet every girl, after finishing school and before taking that crucial step into life, should first thoroughly weigh whether or not her talents and inclinations will be best utilized and satisfied sitting behind a machine in the factory hall or in an occupation we today call typically feminine because it cannot be performed by male labor. Let us now take a closer look at the critical female occupations (this is the term used today for those occupations that suffer from a constant labor shortage). These are the domestic servant, visiting nurse, hospital nurse, and farm housemaid, to name only those most needed. They all, however, have one thing in common: their pronounced biological importance. They are simply indispensable to the biological survival of our people. Without the domestic servant, baby nurse, community nurse, and visiting nurse, with their numerous branches of activity, mothers, especially those with many chil-

From *Völkischer Beobachter*, January 22, 1939. Translated by Dieter Kuntz.

dren, would be hard put. We continually need hundreds of thousands of helpful women's hands to assist the mothers who otherwise would not be able to fulfill their duty to the state. The above-mentioned occupations did not have such prestige in earlier times when the great economic and biological value of the household and domestic activity was not recognized. Today it is not only necessary but also honorable to dedicate oneself to one of these occupations. . . .

The enumeration of critical women's occupations would be incomplete if we did not also name a number of higher women's occupations that had not previously seen encouraging conditions but that now are also beginning to feel a shortage of young recruits. Here we must mention primarily the educational occupations; female primary school teachers especially are in short supply. The female trade school teacher is also an occupation that offers a good future. . . . Undoubtedly, training and preparation for the upper levels of the teaching profession will again become promising for especially talented girls, as here too the reserves are beginning to be depleted and sooner or later we will have to reckon with the replacement of male teachers by female teachers not only at high schools but at universities as well.

Equally justifiable is the great interest shown by talented female youth in medical careers because here too is a growing labor shortage. There is already a large demand for female laboratory collaborators, which explains the popularity of technical occupations such as the chemical engineer, metallurgist, technological assistant, and technical draftswoman among our rising female talent.

The commercial economy, pressured by circumstances, is also reaching deeper into the female labor pool, and evidence is beginning to appear which suggests that entire occupational categories that previously had been the domain of men are now open to women. . . . The scope of this demand for female labor over the next few decades is hard to predict. But this much is certain: whoever fails to give his daughter a solid, purposely directed education today is committing a sin in terms of the future, which will offer unexpected opportunities as well as make unexpected demands on the productive capacities of all our people regardless of sex.

62. Women and Total War

In the aftermath of the tremendous military defeat at Stalingrad in January 1943 and the subsequent need to reequip the army, mobilization of the economy was redoubled under the direction of Albert Speer. Some of the new measures aimed

From *Nationalsozialistische Deutsche Arbeiter-Partei, 1919–45* (Stanford, CA: Hoover Institution on War, Revolution and Peace), H.A. reel 50, folder 1181 (*Gauleiter* Reports). Translated by Dieter Kuntz.

at bringing hitherto untapped labor reserves into the war economy. Ideological goals were abandoned as women between the ages of seventeen and forty-five responded to the call to aid the war effort. However, the higher priority of the regime to mobilize its entire work force — even women — for war production severely compromised the attempt to reconstitute the German family through returning women to the home. The following excerpts from *Gauleiter* reports written in 1943 summarize the situation in various parts of the Reich.

GAULEITER REPORTS OF FEBRUARY 12, 1943

The new decree concerning the duty of men and women to report for total war mobilization has been received with satisfaction by the populace, particularly by those countrymen who have been working very hard for many years. This is unanimously expressed in the reports sent in by the various districts. . . .

The Hamburg district reports: "The industrial conscription decree is being met with approval by a large segment of the population. This measure is welcomed especially by those women who are already heavily burdened and have already been mobilized. . . ."

Everyone is convinced that the harnessing of all available energy, if applied and implemented fairly, will be of decisive significance for the extension of mobilization. The districts are demanding, therefore, that we accommodate ourselves fully to the circumstance of total war and endeavor to mobilize those countrymen who have previously been able to shirk any type of work.

Hamburg, among others, reports: "Expectations are being expressed that differing standards will not be applied. One hears again and again that it is very important that specifically those women from the upper echelons of the party, the state, the economy, and the army lead the way in setting a good example!" . . .

"If we again employ only half measures," writes the Sudetenland district, "and certain groups of women find it possible to evade mobilization, the result could be a development the consequences of which would be difficult to foretell. . . . In this regard it is absolutely necessary to point out the fact that we are already, in part, experiencing criticism of certain sections of the decree calling for total mobilization. The decree is said to be much too tender-hearted. The implementing statutes supposedly allow too much opportunity for some to slip through."

Several districts addressed this matter. . . .

The Warthegau district reports: "Some see a loophole in the provisions governing mobilization in that women who have one preschool child, or two children under the age of 14 years, and who live together under one roof, are not bound by the decree. Some are of the opinion that women who have female domestic servants will be better off than many mothers who, aside from their household, must also care for their children. A law is being demanded which for such cases would enlist either the housewives or the servants for service important to the war effort."

The Baden district reports: ". . . Women themselves judge the age limitation of 45 years to be too low. Everyone is concerned that the publicized exemption clauses offer too much opportunity for evasion. It is expected that physicians will experience a boom in business — providing the necessary documents to malingerers and slackers. The question of the future mobilization of the regiments of female domestic servants has also remained untouched. People are generally of the opinion that many housewives could manage their households without help. The so-called better class of people would not compromise their dignity by learning the practical aspects of the work of a German housewife. In university cities the aim is primarily directed at the many girls who are studying; the public rejects something like this in view of our situation of total war. . . . This same view is expressed over boarding schools, which today are being termed establishments for slackers. It is time that something drastic is done in this area. It is highly indecent to give strong and healthy girls the opportunity to shirk labor service or mobilization because of their studies, which cost the state more than they themselves are paying. . . ."

In summation it can be said that the supreme sacrifice of our men at Stalingrad has stirred the hearts of the homeland to the utmost and has brutally demonstrated to the positivistic labor force the necessity of total commitment. . . . It must unequivocally be pointed out that the further development of [work force] morale and the willingness to cooperate, and with it the ultimate victory, depends solely on the consistent and impartial implementation of this measure. When the populace sees that all arrangements, situations, and circumstances that are not consistent with the rigors of this war are to be ruthlessly eliminated, and when the war reaches the stage that it must reach in the eyes of all decent Germans, that is, when it becomes the personal concern of every single countryman, the assurance can be given that the total mobilization of all can be achieved on a halfway acceptable scale.

GAULEITER REPORTS OF APRIL 2, 1943

The work period of young girls employed in field service is seen as insufficient in several districts. Total war mobilization demands of every countryman the utmost productivity. It is therefore urgently necessary, at least for girls mobilized for agriculture, to institute a change in the work period.

The Baden district reports: "The Reich Labor Service for female youth continues to hold fast to its plan, sending the girls to the farms at 10 o'clock in the morning and bringing them back to the camp at 5 o'clock in the afternoon."

The Halle–Merseburg district reports: "In terms of the female Labor Service, the complaint is constantly heard that the actual help that is supposed to be given to the household or the farmstead is much too limited. . . . It has been proposed that we fully mobilize the girls of the Labor Service and give them at most one free afternoon for the purpose of schooling at camp. . . .

GAULEITER REPORTS OF APRIL 18
THROUGH MAY 1, 1943

The measures to mobilize the labor force have for the most part been completed. The incorporation of the newly acquired labor force into the factories, that is, their training and reeducation, has not given rise to any particular difficulties. The readiness and willingness of women, as far as we can discern from these reports, is generally acknowledged by the factory managers.

The Mosel district reports: "Women and girls are generally exhibiting a sincere devotion and joy toward their new activities. They have taken up their tasks with energy and love. Only in isolated instances was it necessary to intervene."

63. The Problems of Mobilizing
the Female Work Force

Although official National Socialist policy toward women changed with the outbreak of the war and the reverses on the eastern front, the regime continued to be ambivalent about bringing women into the work force. The following SS intelligence report of 1941 illustrates the failure of the mobilization policy and the resistance it met with from women who simply refused to show up for work.

Reports dealing with the frequent unwillingness to work on the part of women who previously have not been in the workforce have come in from Würzburg, Münster, Neustadt a.d.W. [an der Weinstrasse], Halle, Aachen, Dresden, Leipzig, Allenstein, Tilsit, Linz, Munich, Thorn, Karlsruhe, Augsburg, Düsseldorf, Oppeln, Innsbruck, Frankfurt/Main, Klagenfurt, Dortmund, Weimar, Braunschweig, Dessau, Bielefeld, and Frankfurt/Oder. Aside from isolated local successes, the reports all point to the fact that even after the previous speech by the Führer, the expected

From Wolfgang Michalka, ed., *Das Dritte Reich* (Munich: Deutscher Taschenbuch Verlag, 1985), vol. 2, pp. 281–82. Translated by Dieter Kuntz. Reprinted by permission of Deutscher Taschenbuch Verlag, Germany.

voluntary assumption of jobs has not materialized. The women in question apparently are awaiting a further appeal. . . .

Dresden, for instance, reports very meager success. Out of 1,250 women invited to a recruitment event, only 600 actually came. Out of these 600 only 120 actually declared themselves willing to work, and the majority of these probably would have preferred to take back their assent. . . . Leipzig reported that on May 8, 1941, the first and only woman registered with the employment office. . . . Dortmund reports that nowhere in the district was any kind of practical result achieved in terms of the voluntary mobilization of the female labor force. The report states, for instance, that work eagerness among women not previously in the labor force has seen no increase at all. Out of 223 mostly childless women who were summoned, only 17 consented to work — but only for part-time. Aachen reports that there seems to be a "wait and see" attitude among the populace as far as the mobilization of female labor is concerned. . . .

64. Agricultural Discontent

The Nazis had received much support from Germany's agricultural community during the years of economic depression prior to the seizure of power, and many farmers hoped that the new regime would ease their financial problems. The Nazis did undertake measures that they hoped would revitalize German agriculture and make Germany self-sufficient, but many policies failed to produce the desired results. Farm incomes did not keep pace with the growth in other sectors of the German economy, and farm workers continued their migration to cities and industrial jobs. Farm owners also became increasingly unhappy with government policies and, as this Koblenz Gestapo report of 1936 illustrates, voiced their displeasure over the regime's price control and production-quota policies.

SITUATION REPORT BY GESTAPO, KOBLENZ OFFICE, FOR THE MONTH OF FEBRUARY 1936

I characterized the peasants well enough in the previous situation report. There has been no improvement. When I summarize the findings of the reports, which are unanimous in their opinions, the farmer surfaces as the one member of society who is least enamored of National Socialism. The

From F. J. Heyen, ed., *Nationalsozialismus im Alltag: Quellen zur Geschichte des Nationalsozialismus im Raum Mainz-Koblenz-Trier* (Boppard: H. Boldt Verlag, 1967), pp. 166–67. Translated by Dieter Kuntz. Reprinted by permission of Landesarchiv, Rheinland-Pfalz.

peasant dealt with Jews

peasant is reserved during meetings; he rarely attends party events; press sales promotions have little success in peasant circles. On the other hand, it is the farmer who still does the most business with Jews. The reason can be found purely and simply in the peasant's almost complete lack of appreciation for the cardinal National Socialist dictum of "common need before individual greed."

In one of my previous situation reports I mentioned that there are towns and villages where the local farm leader is sometimes the only National Socialist. I should correct this report, because even this is not always the case. Recently a district president brought a case to my attention of a local peasant leader who refused to make a contribution to the NSV [Nationalsozialistische Volkswohlfahrt, National Socialist People's Welfare Organization], and who gave nothing at all during the latest one-pot meal collection. I pointed out earlier that in spite of everything, the peasant should not be regarded as a serious opponent of the state. This should not, however, lead us to underestimate his obstinate passivity.

I reported in the daily report of February 25, 1936, that the wife of Farmer A from the village explained to a police official, who was auditing milk deliveries, that for the time being it was not possible to make any milk deliveries. The son, who happened upon the scene, interjected: "You won't live long enough to see any milk deliveries from us." The official then suggested to the woman that milk deliveries should be made as long as fodder was available. To this the son again replied: "Then we'll sell the cow." This case is indicative of the attitude of many peasants, although not all express them publicly. . . .

It has also been determined that there is no particular fondness for the Reich Labor Service among peasants. A district president reported that in one month alone there were 50 applications from peasants' sons who were born in the year 1916 asking for exemption from the Labor Service. Many are of the opinion that the Labor Service is superfluous for the sons of peasants because they have already learned how to work in their fathers' businesses. Added to this is the fact that peasants have extremely strong religious ties. This allows the clerics of both denominations to acquire much influence and provides them with fertile ground for their agitation against the state.

65. Coercion of Farmers

By 1937 the agricultural situation had not improved and farmers were more dissatisfied than ever. The fear of communism, which the Nazis constantly portrayed

From *Deutschland-Berichte der Sozialdemokratischen Partei Deutschlands (Sopade), 1934–40* (Frankfurt: Verlag Petra Nettelbeck, 1980), August 1937, pp. 1098–99, 1104, 1106. Translated by Dieter Kuntz.

themselves as providing a bulwark against, forced farmers to compromise with the regime. The following report on agriculture by the Social Democratic underground organization in 1937 illustrates the effects of a "coercive economy" and the fear of land expropriation, which influenced farmers to resist leftist ideology.

The "production battle," or the attempt by the Hitler regime to attain self-sufficiency for Germany through the coercion of agricultural production, has not reached its goal but has instead led to growing difficulties in the supplying of cities with foodstuffs. This failure has forced the regime to intensify its measures of coercive economy and has thereby limited even further the right of the farmer to market his products freely. He can see that he is no longer master over his own estate, and that he must more and more follow the commands of the National Food Corporation bureaucracy. . . .

Greatest dissatisfaction can be found primarily among older farmers. They compare their present circumstance with the time before Hitler. They remember the great promises with which they were persuaded to vote for Hitler prior to the seizure of power. These promises have been largely unfulfilled. . . .

A report from Rhineland-Westphalia: "The control over agriculture has been increased tremendously. Officials of the National Food Corporation tell the farmer how much milk his cow has to produce, how many eggs his hen must lay, how many pounds of seed to deliver, how much wool his sheep has to produce, how many acres he should plant of what type of crops, how many potatoes and sugar-beet fields he must have, and how much he should harvest under what weather conditions."

A report from Bavaria: "I spoke to a farmer with a medium-sized farm, a former member of the German People's Party. He felt that the regime did bring certain advantages for farmers, especially for those who were heavily in debt and faced imminent forced sale of their property. The Hereditary Farm Law had its advantages as well as disadvantages, the same was true of the market regulations. [He felt that] many farmers could not really differentiate between advantages and disadvantages. They grumble constantly. Many are facing heavier financial pressure than before, while others are better off."

The regime's struggle against the Christian church has angered farmers even more than their economic misery. Farmers are deeply concerned over questions of religion. The farmers are not receptive to communist ideas, at least not the medium-size landowners. They fear that Bolshevism would take away their land. They prefer to try to compromise with the Nazis rather than have their property expropriated.

287

66. The Condition of the Working Class Under National Socialism

After the seizure of power, the Nazis quickly "coordinated" working-class organizations, destroying their trade unions and creating the German Labor Front in their place. In the following period, the Labor Front attempted to win working-class support for the regime and the idea of the *Volksgemeinschaft*. The attitudes of workers toward the regime, however, remained mixed. On the one hand, the regime had helped alleviate unemployment. Many workers, content simply to have jobs again, at least tolerated the regime. On the other hand, those workers who had formerly belonged to leftist political parties and had been staunch union supporters were not won over so easily, remaining skeptical of Nazi promises of a better standard of living. The following reports by the Social Democratic underground organization, dating from the year after the Nazi takeover, indicate the variety of reactions to the new regime among workers.

APRIL/MAY 1934

The reports from the Reich as yet do not provide a uniform picture. . . .

The following report is from southwestern Germany: "Judging by public attitudes, the regime seems to have the most support among workers. This is especially true for those who earlier had not been part of a political organization. . . . It also seems that workers submit more readily [than other social classes] to Nazi terror methods and allow themselves to be easily influenced."

A similar report from Berlin: "Large segments of the working class continue to submit [to the regime]. Faith in Hitler is remarkably strong. The circle of old [Social Democratic] party members is for the most part unshaken and refuses to accept Nazi ideology. . . ."

From northern Bavaria similar sentiments: "The mood among workers has changed abruptly. This is especially so among those large-income earners who were never satisfied with their pay; who were abusive toward Social Democracy and blamed it because they didn't earn more; who never came to a single meeting, and who had no money to spend for a party newspaper. These indifferent egotists actually thought they would effortlessly earn more under Hitler. Now they have got their surprise. They are the ones grumbling the loudest in the factories, because now they earn barely half of their former pay and must make contributions and pay membership dues. . . ."

From *Deutschland-Berichte der Sozialdemokratischen Partei Deutschlands (Sopade), 1934–40* (Frankfurt: Verlag Petra Nettelbeck, 1980), April/May, June/July 1934, pp. 29–31, 207–8. Translated by Dieter Kuntz.

A different angle sheds light on the situation in southern Bavaria: "A large segment of the work force is indifferent toward the Third Reich. The percentage of workers in this category is changing, however. Much has to do with the ability and quality of the NSBO [Nationalsozialistische Betriebszellenorganisation, National Socialist Factory Cell Organization] people. In general it can be said that in factories where solid union organizations existed earlier the workers have remained skeptical. It is also evident that underground activity will be difficult to get going here. The workers are indecisive; they are not sure of the goal nor of the path toward it. Many are also afraid of losing their jobs. A not inconsiderable number of those not 'coordinated' [gleichgeschaltet] are discouraged and resigned to their fate."

[handwritten margin note: Workers are unsure + indecisive]

Much more optimistic is a report from western Saxony: "The situation here has changed markedly since Christmas. The change is a very unfavorable one for the National Socialists. Within factories, at construction sites and other workplaces, there is now much discussion during breaks. One can surmise from this that the workers are basically opposed to the regime. Even [National Socialist] party members are expressing their dissatisfaction and disappointment. . . ."

[handwritten margin note: dissatisfaction]

A Berlin report analyzes the reasons for the more confident mood of the workers: "Workers today are not as afraid of unemployment. They do not have to fear losing their jobs from one day to the next because the regime, in its effort to provide work, is exerting heavy pressure on employers to retain even their surplus work force as long as possible. . . .

JUNE/JULY 1934

. . . The reports from the period of June 30 almost all express the opinion that of all segments of German society, the working class is most submissive toward the regime, and it is presenting the least opposition.

From East Saxony: The workers in the factories are, without exception, adopting a wait-and-see attitude toward the regime and do not believe the things the Nazis are prophesying. Doubts about the accuracy of the Marxist ideological basis surfaced during this past year amid the ranks of former low-level [Social Democratic] party functionaries. The reports of rapid dwindling of the masses of unemployed were not believed by all. Many are doubting the authenticity of the figures released publicly. In any case, the fact that it was possible to obtain large sums on credit, to create new jobs and new work projects without having serious difficulties surface during the first year has shaken the opinion of many who believed that the National Socialist economic program would collapse. . . .

The matter-of-fact way in which factory workers are accepting everything that is being thrust on them is frightening. They only grumble when the dozens of different collecting lists and the contribution collectors approach them. There is not even an inner resistance to the Hitler greeting.

accepting &
adopting
Nazi
rituals

The fact that one has to greet others by raising the hand is regarded as an insignificant act, as is participating in the May 1 events. The number of those who could have excluded themselves from the beginning could have been much higher. There is a fear throughout the ranks that one will have difficulties at work and possibly lose one's job. This fear induces the workers to act in a certain way. Moreover, these things are probably only demanded of the workers in order to gauge their response. I have encountered only a few who have said, "I can't stand this rubbish anymore, I'd rather sacrifice my job."

67. The Four-Year Plan

The stated main goal of the National Socialist movement was to create a *Volksgemeinschaft,* a more tightly controlled and communally coordinated society that would counter the impersonalizing and dehumanizing tendencies of the last two centuries. In many ways the ideology harked back to earlier and supposedly simpler times when values were commonly shared and individuals felt secure within the social whole. But to what extent did the Nazi leadership strive to achieve the goal of creating the *Volksgemeinschaft?* Or, to formulate the question more precisely, to what extent was the attempt to make Germany the major economic, political, and military power in Europe also an essential part of Nazi ideology, one that compromised and even contradicted the attempt to reconstruct German society in more traditional ways? In addition, Hitler often spoke of *Lebensraum* and the territorial expansion of Germany to the East, but the details of such a move were left vague in the late 1920s and early 1930s. The Four-Year Plan launched in the summer of 1936, however, was clearly intended to prepare the nation for war by 1940. The establishment of an up-to-date military in turn demanded that the economy be reorganized along the most efficient and modern lines. When this latter goal ran against the antimodern pronouncements of the ideology, the Party sacrificed its social and cultural goals. Hitler inaugurated the Four-Year Plan under the directorship of Hermann Goering. The following document is a condensed version of a memorandum prepared by Hitler in August 1936 that detailed Germany's military and economic problems and outlined future steps to correct these perceived deficiencies.

THE POLITICAL SITUATION

Politics consists of the conduct and course of the historical life struggle of nations. The aim of these struggles is the assertion of existence. . . .

From Wilhelm Treue, "Hitler's Denkschrift zum Vierjahresplan 1936," *Vierteljahrshefte für Zeitgeschichte,* 3 (April 1955): 204–11. Translated by Dieter Kuntz. Reprinted by permission of R. Oldenbourg Verlag, Munich.

Since the outbreak of the French Revolution the world has been drifting toward a new conflict at an ever-increasing tempo. The most extreme resolution of this conflict will be in bolshevism, whose essence and goal, however, lies in the elimination and replacement of the hitherto leading social classes of mankind to be brought about through internationally widespread Judaism.

Bolshevism as a threat

No state will be able to avoid or distance itself from this historic conflict. Since through its victory in Russia Marxism has established one of the largest empires in the world as a starting base for further operations, this question has become an ominous one. A democratic world ideologically torn faces a unified aggressive will founded on an authoritarian ideology.

The military power potential of this will of aggression is meanwhile increasing rapidly from year to year. . . .

Germany will, as always, continue to be regarded as the focal point of the Western world's confrontation with the Bolshevik threat. I do not regard this to be a pleasant mission but rather as a handicap and burden to our national life which has unfortunately resulted from our position in Europe. But we cannot escape this destiny. A victory of Bolshevism over Germany would not lead to a Versailles Treaty but would instead mean the final destruction, even the annihilation, of the German people.

The dimensions of such a catastrophe cannot be foreseen. Indeed, it cannot be foreseen whether densely populated Western Europe (including Germany), in the event of a Bolshevik debacle, could survive what would probably be the most gruesome catastrophe to befall mankind since the collapse of the states of antiquity. In the face of the necessity of defense against this danger, all other considerations must recede into the background because they have become completely irrelevant!

GERMANY'S DEFENSIVE CAPACITY

Germany's defensive capacity is based on several factors. First and foremost I would list the intrinsic value of the German people per se. The German people, under impeccable political leadership, a sound ideology, and a thorough military organization, certainly constitute the highest-quality resistance factor today's world can possess. Political leadership is ensured by the National Socialist Party, and ideological solidarity has, since the victory of National Socialism, been introduced to an extent never previously attained. On the basis of this concept we must strive constantly to harden and deepen it. This is the aim of the National Socialist education of our people.

People as key to defense

Military development is to be effected through the new army. The extent and pace of the military development of our resources cannot be too great or too rapid! It is a capital error to believe that there can be any negotiation on these points, or that any comparison can be made with other vital necessities. Even though the general pattern of life of a people should be a balanced one, it is nevertheless imperative that during particular times a certain shifting of the balance — to the detriment of other, less vital, tasks — must occur. If we do not succeed in developing the German armed forces within the shortest possible time into the foremost army in the world in terms of its training, raising of units, armaments, and above all also in spiritual education, then Germany will be lost!

GERMANY'S ECONOMIC SITUATION

We are overpopulated and cannot feed ourselves from our own resources. The solution ultimately lies in extending the living space of our people, that is, in extending the sources of its raw materials and foodstuffs. It is the task of the political leadership to solve this problem in days to come.

Temporary improvement can be brought about only within the framework of our present economy. To that end the following is to be noted:

Since the German nation's food supply needs will be increasingly dependent on imports, but since we must also in any case, at least in part, draw on certain raw materials from foreign countries, it is necessary to work with all means toward making this importation possible.

The increase of our own exports is theoretically possible, but unrealistic in practical terms. . . .

It is not enough to draw up every now and then raw material or foreign exchange balances, or to talk about a preparation of a war economy during peace time; it is instead essential to ensure peace time food supplies and, above all else, the means for the conduct of war; these things can be assured through human energy and activity. And I therefore set up the following program for a definitive solution of our essential needs:

1. Like the military and political rearmament or mobilization of our people, there must also be an economic mobilization, and it must indeed proceed with the same tempo, with the same determination, and if necessary even with the same ruthlessness. The interests of individual gentlemen will no longer matter in the future. There is only one interest, and that is the interest of the nation, and only one point of view, and that is that Germany must be brought to a position of political and economic self-sufficiency.

2. For this purpose, in every domain where it is possible to satisfy our needs through German production, we must save foreign currency in order to be able to apply it to those requirements that can only be met through imports.

3. With this in mind, German fuel production must now be increased at the fastest pace and must be completed within eighteen months. This task must be tackled and carried out with the same determination as the

waging of war because the future conduct of the war will depend on the completion of this task rather than on the stockpiling of gasoline.

4. It is equally obvious that we must organize and secure the mass production of synthetic rubber. . . .

5. The question of the cost of these raw materials is totally irrelevant because it is still better for us to produce in Germany expensive tires and be able to drive on them than to buy theoretically cheap tires for which the Economics Ministry cannot allocate foreign currency, which then, in view of the lack of raw materials, cannot be manufactured and therefore obviously cannot be driven. . . .

It is further necessary to increase to the utmost the German production of iron. . . .

It is further necessary to immediately prohibit the distillation of alcohol from potatoes. Fuel must be gotten from the ground and not from potatoes. . . .

It is further necessary to make our supplies of industrial fats independent of imports and to satisfy our needs from our own coal. This task has been solved chemically and is screaming to be completed. The German economy will either handle the new economic tasks or else it will reveal itself to be simply incompetent to survive further in this modern age during which a Soviet state is setting up a gigantic plan. But then it will not be Germany that will go under, but instead it will at most be a few industrialists.

It is further necessary to increase, at all costs, Germany's output of ores, and in particular to increase the production of light metals to the utmost in order thereby to produce a substitute for certain other metals.

In the end it is also necessary for rearmament to make use even now, whenever possible, of those materials that in case of war will and must replace high-grade metals. It is better to ponder and solve these problems during peacetime than to wait for the next war, and then while faced with a profusion of tasks to try first to undertake economic research and methodical tests!

Summarized briefly: I consider it necessary that from now on with iron determination we attain 100 percent self-sufficiency in all these areas so that we will not be dependent on foreign countries for these most important raw materials, and that thereby we will also be able to save the foreign currency we require during peacetime in order to import our foodstuffs. I would here like to stress that in these tasks I see the only true economic mobilization, not in the throttling of armament industries in peacetime in order to save and stockpile raw materials for war.

I do, however, find it necessary to undertake an immediate investigation into the outstanding debts in foreign currency owed to German business abroad. There is no doubt that behind this lies in part the contemptible intention to possess certain reserves abroad which are thus kept out of the domestic economy. In this I see a deliberate sabotage of our national self-assertion, that is, of the defense of the Reich, and for this reason I consider it necessary for the Reichstag to pass two laws:

1. A law that will mandate the death penalty for economic sabotage.
2. A law that will make Jewry in its entirety liable for all damages inflicted by individual specimens of that community of criminals on the German economy and thereby on the German people.

. . . Nearly four precious years have now gone by. There is no doubt that we could already today have achieved complete independence of foreign countries in the fields of fuel supplies, rubber supplies, and in part also of iron ore supplies. . . We have had enough time over the last four years to determine what we cannot do. It is now necessary to carry out what we are capable of doing.

I therefore set the following tasks: (1) the German army must be operational within four years, and (2) the German economy must be fit for war within four years.

[handwritten marginal note: Answering / Comry up / War]

68. Workers Adjust to National Socialism

The following document of December 1936 is an excerpt from a report of workers' groups to the executive committee of the Social Democratic Party of Germany in exile. Describing the political attitudes of workers in various industries, the report touches on the regime's more clumsy attempts to influence workers with Nazi propaganda.

Berlin, large-scale electrotechnical plant (work force over 5,000): The attitudes of our colleagues vary considerably. Aside from the large number of those who are indifferent, one finds many groups of politically aware workers who act without prearranged agreement and who have no well-defined principles, but who nonetheless make common cause with us. If, for example, there is a majority of former trade union or otherwise previously politically organized individuals in the three- to ten-member work crews, they will attempt to make life as difficult as possible for the one or two Nazis on the crew. . . . Our technique of branding as poor workers those who are politically undesirable is quite effective and not at all dangerous. Admittedly these are unscrupulous methods, but after all, the Nazis employed much worse tactics in dealing with us.

From *Deutschland-Berichte der Sozialdemokratischen Partei Deutschlands (Sopade), 1934–1940* (Frankfurt: Verlag Petra Nettelbeck, 1980), 3 (December 1936): 1565, 1567, 1580–82, 1588–89. Translated by Dieter Kuntz.

Osram: The present political views among the work force, which in earlier years was heavily Social Democratic, is approximately: 10 percent Nazis, 30 percent undecided, and 60 percent inclined toward a passive rejection [of the regime]. Political activism is rare, although discussions are conducted quite frequently within closed circles. . . .

National railroad repair shop: The work force consists of approximately 2,500 men, of whom about 10 percent are Nazis while the rest are divided evenly between those undecided and those who passively reject the regime. Dissatisfaction is widespread in the shop, but people are very timid! Interest in the Nuremberg party rally was next to nil. Sixty people were scheduled to go cost-free. They refused, however, on the grounds that last year it was cold and the food was bad.

At the Buderus Iron and Steelworks, in Wetzlar on the river Lahn, an act of passive resistance was carried out recently. Mandatory collections had been ordered, whereby the amount was simply deducted from the worker's pay. The factory management, moreover, had arbitrarily rescinded the function of the workers' council without first informing the work force of this measure. The several-hundred-man work force then went to work as usual, but refused to work. A portion of the work force even stayed home.

Automobile factory (location not given): The work force was very disgruntled over the fact that they had to remain at the workplace longer in order to hear a speech by the Führer. Many headed for the gates but were not allowed to leave. Some workers were even forcibly removed from the restrooms. The head official of the Nazi factory union got on a chair himself in order to see if people were hiding in the toilets. He then grabbed their arms and took them to the meeting hall.

A workers' council member (who proudly boasted that he could improve the circulation figures of the *Stürmer*) estimated that the work force was made up of approximately 50 percent Marxists, 25 percent Nazis, and another 25 percent of indifferent individuals.

Saxony: During a communal radio listening session of the previous speech by the Führer, several firms employed peculiar methods in order to force the workers to listen to the speech. At Tool Factory X the workers' dressing room was locked until the conclusion of the speech in order to prevent an early departure of the workers. . . .

Bavarian Motorworks (BMW), Munich: Since wages are still relatively high in comparison to other metal industries, the mood among workers is accordingly less bitter. One can, however, report that the National Socialists have nothing else that they can announce. Even though the workers do not express it publicly, one senses that the workers will never be conquered by National Socialism. All must, of course, yield to the present pressure, but whenever possible they show that they really have very little interest in all of Hitler's gibberish. This attitude was quite obvious during the last speech by the Führer, at which a communal radio listening had been ordered. . . . During the speech the workers conversed among themselves so that the factory SA had to intervene in order to restore quiet. . . . During the last third of the broadcast there occurred a lengthy round of applause over the loudspeaker, whereupon the workers immediately ran for the doors, demanding to be let out as the speech had apparently ended. The gate attendants were taken by surprise as a general race for the exits ensued. Yes, even windows were opened and people squeezed through them as though they were fugitives. . . . Even the Nazi supporters in the factory, of which there are still a few in every group, say that the broadcasts of the speeches in the factory do more harm than good for National Socialism.

Attempts to influence the workers

69. Attitudes of Workers During the War

The regime's efforts to win the working class continued to have mixed results. The Nazi mobilization of the economy placed greater demands on German workers, and threatened to undermine morale. The Security Service (SD) of the SS attempted to find the cause of reported poor morale and work discipline among the industrial labor force of Germany. The following SD analysis of the situation dates from April 22, 1941.

Countless reports continue to pour in which analyze the problem of poor morale in the labor force and which attempt to find its causes and ways to combat it. The consensus is that there has been no marked increase lately of cases of lack of discipline. Additionally, in relation to the total number of employed, there is no reason to speak of a bad attitude within the labor force. . . .

A number of reports do indicate that incidents of excessive and unjustifiable sick leave or simply unexcused absence from work are, in the case of certain individuals, more numerous especially before and after holidays. Aside from that, we continue to receive reports of insolent and presumptuous behavior. The reports list varying causes for this behavior. Frequently the personal attitudes of plant managers and their views of the sociopolitical concerns of their employees are cited as the primary factor for the large-scale disorder. . . .

Another reason that is cited for the poor morale in the workplace is the exertion caused by the mobilization of labor. Because of the labor

From Heinz Boberach, *Meldungen aus dem Reich* (Neuwied, 1965), pp. 135–38; reprinted in Wolfgang Michalka ed., *Das Dritte Reich* (Munich: Deutscher Taschenbuch Verlag, 1985), Vol. 2, *Weltmachtanspruch und nationaler Zusammenbruch, 1939–1945,* pp. 276–78. Translated by Dieter Kuntz. Reprinted by permission of Deutscher Taschenbuch Verlag, Germany.

shortage, it is said that every source of manpower is being recruited. . . . Whereas previously all those who did not perform satisfactorily at the workplace were simply dismissed, today, however, emphasis is placed on retaining all manpower as long as possible since the employers do not know if replacements can be found for those dismissed. Because of these conditions the workers have the attitude that they are indispensable. Those workers who have low standards to begin with then feel that they can do as they please at the workplace. . . .

Other factors that influence attitudes in the workplace are wages and demanding working conditions. A report from Würzburg determined that "the attitude of workers is in general somewhat depressed. The reasons for this lie in the taxing working conditions, which are marked by the length of the workday, difficulty in traveling to work for out-of-town workers, and problems with existing rations. . . .

70. The Realities of "Strength Through Joy"

Even the much-vaunted "Strength Through Joy" movement, which was intended to incorporate the working classes of Germany into full participation in the *Volksgemeinschaft,* seems to have met with less than unqualified success. Even before the outbreak of the war and the discontinuance of many KdF activities, the various programs failed to live up to expectations and were greeted with contempt by many participants. The following report by the Social Democrats in exile in April 1939 clearly indicates the problems.

Within the structure of the German Labor Front the subsidiary organization KdF has been given the task of "guiding the leisure time activities of the masses," that is, to influence and monitor their activities. At the last national conference of Strength Through Joy, which was held in Hamburg in June of 1938, Dr. Ley typically defined the purpose of KdF as "the quickest means of bringing National Socialism to the masses." If he meant that National Socialism — which is not a uniform whole but instead a conglomeration of different ideas and goals — is through KdF everywhere meeting the needs of the "broad masses" through travel and hiking, sports and games, theater, concert, film, and cabaret, then his remark was appropriate. It would, however, be erroneous to assume that KdF events are consciously perceived by the participants to be long-term manifestations of National Socialism and indicative of gains to be had. Since social life in all aspects has been monopolized by KdF, and since destitute sections

From *Deutschland-Berichte der Sozialdemokratischen Partei Deutschlands (Sopade), 1934–1940* (Frankfurt: Verlag Petra Nettelbeck, 1980), 6 (April 1939): 462–63, 468–69, 471–72, 474–77, 480, 486–89. Translated by Dieter Kuntz.

KdF → gift to workers

of the population really have no other possibility aside from the public enterprises of participating in cultural things, one tends to put up with KdF. The feeling that one is accepting a gift from the regime or acknowledging its legitimacy has gradually dwindled. This feeling had distanced many from KdF in the beginning. At best, one appreciates the organizational achievement. Otherwise most participants rationalize their involvement the following way: "The cost of KdF is being met by our membership fees to the German Labor Front. We would be stupid if we did not get our money's worth." Presently KdF is not enough to dissuade the growing discord or even to soften the criticism of prevailing conditions.

The travel activities of the KdF Department of Travel, Hiking, and Vacation, continue to figure most prominently in the public's awareness of KdF undertakings. KdF-Sports still has a lively following, whereas the four remaining "departments" of KdF — Communal Culture, Beauty of Labor, Armed Forces Clubs, and Village Beautification — have been pushed into the background with the passage of time. Since our last report a new project, the Volkswagen, has been created. . . .

The Department of Travel, Hiking, and Vacation has of all KdF departments the most funds at its disposal. It also has been delegated the largest share of propaganda work. Hiking activities are of little consequence to the department. Hiking has always been popular in Germany — long before Hitler. The regime had great difficulties in its attempt to destroy existing hiking clubs. This was attempted by threatening to initiate proceedings against the clubs as well as through the denial of travel price reductions. . . . At present there are 15,000 "hiking attendants" active in KdF service. As a rule they lead groups of 15 to 20 participants and have the task of combining their guide services with fervent political propaganda. Since hiking is most easily accomplished on an individual basis, however, one still finds that most hikers take to the roads alone and KdF hiking activities have not enjoyed the same popularity as those of the travel association.

People don't all join in

The travel association has accordingly received the most attention from the KdF leadership. Grand facilities have been created, and their own hotels, ships, and thermal baths and recreational swimming pools have been constructed. . . . A report from northern Germany details the spa at Rügen: ". . . I saw the KdF spa being built last summer. It is of monumental proportions. . . . It is one of the most effective advertisements for the Third Reich. However, nine-tenths of all German workers will probably see the spa only in pictures. . . ."

KdF vacation trips continue to be extremely popular. . . . In various factories, savings programs have been initiated which are intended to allow the workers the opportunity to go on a KdF trip. The premiums are 0.20 marks, and those who have seniority in the firm are primarily those who will benefit from the program. . . . Workers now avail themselves of trips within Germany. These are extraordinarly cheap and, because of the savings plan, everyone who otherwise might not be able to afford it is able to go. On the average, a fourteen-day trip costs 60 marks, all expenses included. The KdF trains are relatively comfortable, although they consist mostly of older railroad cars. Room and board is also relatively good. On the other hand, restaurant and hotel owners complain that they receive reimbursement from KdF only 6 to 9 months later. It has happened that communities on the Baltic Sea and in southern Germany have refused to accept any more KdF groups. . . .

. . . Trips abroad, although appearing to be inexpensive at first glance, are prohibitive for the worker under normal circumstances. If the factory does not partially or completely pick up the tab, most have to forego the trip.

[A Rhinelander's report of a KdF trip]: . . . Registration for a trip is seemingly made as difficult as possible by the bureaucracy involved. . . . The last day in the factory prior to the trip is a strenuous day of working off the backlog. There is hardly time to eat or change clothes. Exhausted, one races to the train station. There a train with the oldest of cars is waiting. . . . Tired, one tries to sleep. It doesn't work well. Some are lying in the baggage nets, while others have brought inflatable air mattresses and are sleeping in the aisles. . . . The hygienic conditions on KdF trains are appalling: no toilet paper, no water for rinsing; sometimes there is water for washing, but never any towels.

[A report from a Hamburg worker]: It was something to see the faces once the cabins were delegated on board ship. I was one of 18 assigned to a much too small room in the front section of the ship. . . . Steel walls, steel military bunk beds, no wardrobe. . . . I was glad nonetheless to have even such quarters. At least here there was air. Others were worse off — some in the middle or rear of the ship and in the lower decks were squeezed into small, hot, airless rooms with twenty people. . . . The food on board is primitive but sufficient. The handsome and artistically illustrated menu, which every traveler is allowed to take home as a souvenir, presents a plentiful and sumptuous food list bordering on luxury; but what is served in reality is more akin to the type and quality of fare found in a moderate pension.

Nonetheless, the package in its entirety seems to be a bargain, and many are under the impression that KdF is giving the workers a present. . . . I spoke afterward with a number of trip participants. All were impressed by the spectacular travel experience. Some, however, did not want to participate a second time under such primitive conditions. They felt very crowded among 1,900 to 2,300 people on a ship not equipped to handle such numbers. They criticized the fact that they were not able to go on land a single time, and criticized the fact that the trip had resulted in immense stress and exhaustion. Others, however, were full of praise,

Mixed reactions

and actually deluded themselves into thinking that the Führer had made them a present. . . .

The least amount that a German worker spends on a seven-day Norway cruise, including all extras, is 100 marks. Usually the cost is higher, averaging 15 marks a day. Anyone can figure out which segment of the public is generally represented on these Norway cruises. In Hitler's Germany, where the head of a family earns weekly 30 marks, a KdF ship is really no place for a working couple. These trips are almost without exception reserved for the preferred middle class. Yet Ley and the leading elements of the regime continue to maintain that the German worker is cruising the oceans of the world. . . .

During 1938, the KdF was given a new assignment: the marketing of the "Volkswagen." This Volkswagen is in the future to be produced at an annual rate of one million . . . and to be sold for the price of 990 marks. . . . The KdF car is intended to give its owner the feeling of climbing the social ladder — in spite of disproportionately low real wages. . . . Moreover, through the Volkswagen program the regime is hoping to effect a further "total organizing," registration, and standardization of the populace. It has been planned to create the position of "honorary supervisor of all KdF car owners" within each community. Among other things, he is supposed to organize weekend trips and secure cut-rate accommodations. This is a new step toward the total surveillance of the population — even during leisure time. . . .

. . . The following reports indicate approximately how the Volkswagen program is being received by the workers. Southwest Germany: The Volkswagen program is, for the time being, not taken seriously by the workers. All say that even if a worker could save the money to buy a car, he still would not have enough to maintain and drive it. . . . Saxony: The attitude of the populace toward the KdF car is not uniform. Most of the workers reject the idea. . . . Public officials and white-collar workers are enthusiastic. . . .

Central Germany: Most of the workers are laughing about the Volkswagen program. "There is hardly enough [money] for daily bread, let alone a car." Some are outraged over the entire publicity campaign. But others find that "in and of itself, the idea is not bad." A car for a thousand marks is a very enticing thing. . . .

Although these reports evidence much skepticism, one should not assume that the Volkswagen program is a propaganda blunder. Hitler knew what he was doing politically and propagandistically when he launched the program. The effectiveness of the propaganda campaign is attested — although obviously reluctantly — by the following report. . . .

Rhineland-Westphalia: . . . For a great many Germans the announcement of a people's car was a very great and pleasant surprise. A

Volkswagon program met with mixed reactions

veritable KdF-Wagen psychosis developed. For a long time the KdF-Wagen was the main topic of conversations among all classes of people in Germany. All other pressing problems — both domestic and in foreign policy — were for a time pushed into the background. The drabness of daily existence in Germany disappeared with these dreams of the future. Wherever in Germany the test cars of the new KdF-type would appear, they were immediately surrounded by people. The politician who promises that every man will have a car is a man of the masses if the masses believe his promises. As far as the KdF-Wagen is concerned, the German people believe Hitler's announcements.

Everybody in Germany knows that Hitler has his hobbies and pet ideas. And these he will carry through, even if it means that other far more important and urgent matters will go to the dogs. For example, every child in Germany knows that Hitler is crazy about cars and the Autobahn. If Hitler gets it into his head that every German worker should have his own car then Hitler will translate this into action with his usual fanatical obsession, and every German worker will get his car. Even if otherwise the most basic social demands of the workers cannot be realized.

The Nazis found some of their most enthusiastic supporters among the young. These members of the Hitler Youth exhibit the military values and physical attributes Hitler hoped to instill.

Chapter
10

Hitler Youth and Education

National Socialism energetically recruited the younger generation, among which the regime found the most malleable component of the German population, into the *Volksgemeinschaft*. The training of the young in National Socialist Germany composed a primary means of transforming ideology into practice. The major organization for the integration of young Germans into the *Volksgemeinschaft* was the Hitler Jugend (Hitler Youth) or HJ and its companion organization Bund Deutscher Mädel (League of German Girls), or BdM. These groups underwent an unprecedented growth from their rather modest beginnings, quickly becoming the largest organizations for young people ever known. By the end of 1932, membership in the Hitler Youth was just over one hundred thousand; within two years of the Nazi seizure of power, this figure increased by a factor of thirty-five. Until December 1936 the Hitler Youth claimed to be an entirely voluntary organization. After that date, however, membership in what was now known as State Youth became obligatory for young people. By the outbreak of the war, virtually every German boy between the ages of ten and eighteen was a member of the Hitler Youth.

The Hitler Youth emphasized physical ability, sports, and above all commitment to the person of Adolf Hitler and to the values of the *Volksgemeinschaft*. The youngest members, who belonged to the Jungvolk, consisted of ten- to fourteen-year-olds. A *Pimpf*, or child, completed his initiation only after he could recite a much condensed version of Nazi dogma and all the verses of the song "Horst Wessel" and had passed a map-reading exercise, participated in pseudo—war games, and collected waste paper, scrap metal, and the like. In addition, he had to undergo an athletic examination in which he was required to run 60 meters in

303

twelve seconds or less, complete a long jump of at least 2.75 meters, throw the shot put, and take part in a cross-country march lasting a day and a half. As a member of the Jungvolk the *Pimpf* learned such things as how to communicate in semaphore, repair bicycles, and lay telephone wire, and he was drilled in the use of small arms. At fourteen, he graduated to the core of the Hitler Youth where as a *Kern* he remained until the age of eighteen. These years were full of strenuous exercise, routine drills, and other forms of monotonous activity.

The League of German Girls was also composed of two divisions. Up to the age of fourteen a girl was a *Jungmädel*; between the ages of seventeen and twenty-one she could, if she wished, join an organization called *Glaube und Schön-heit* (Faith and Beauty). Because they tended to lose interest in organized activities in their middle teens, and the regime encouraged them to marry and raise a family, there was no Nazi organization for girls between the ages of fourteen and seventeen. The activities required of a *Jungmädel* were regular attendance at Girls' League clubs and sporting events as well as participation in organized outings and camping trips. The girls also had to learn about the Party — its early history and the vicissitudes of the Führer and his followers during the *Kampfzeit* (Time of Struggle) — and memorize all verses of "Horst Wessel" and the names of Hitler Youth martyrs. They were also instructed in history and geography as it related to the Aryan race: the significance of the Treaty of Versailles, facts about Aryan populations around the world, local history, German customs, and Teutonic sagas. Physical feats required of each girl included running 60 meters in twelve seconds or less, making at least a 2.5-meter long jump, throwing a ball at least 20 meters, somersaulting, walking a tightrope, marching along a two-hour route, and swimming 100 meters. The Girls' League attached special importance to "journeys." During Youth Hostel Weekend each *Jungmädel* had to take part in group activities and chores such as making beds and packing standard equipment. After the age of fourteen, membership in the Girls' League was no longer mandatory. Through a program of physical culture, health instruction, and domestic science, however, the Faith and Beauty movement continued to attract older girls and young women. This voluntary organization also emphasized fashion consciousness and cultivation of the National Socialist ideal of feminine beauty.

The Hitler Youth and the Girls' League had a considerable effect on the schooling of young people in Germany. The all-encompassing youth movements came to dominate the world of the adolescent, tending to replace both the school and the family as the most important influence in youngsters' lives. These organizations formed only one aspect of a general attack on intellectual endeavors. The anti-intellectual mood engendered by the Nazis' transformation of traditional values accelerated the teacher's loss of public esteem after 1933. The ideal implied in the notion of "thinking with the blood" made everyone equal when it came to questions of intelligence. Analogously, the regime boasted the self-esteem of students in relation to teachers. The head of the Hitler Youth, Baldur von Schirach, contrasted the image of a glowingly inspired youth marching forward to a new dawn to that of the pedantically stupid schoolmaster, the captive of the bourgeois past. Moreover, the program of the Hitler Youth appealed to the young in a more immediate way than classroom instruction ever could. Often physically exhausted because of their involvement in Hitler Youth activities, pupils were restless and unable to settle into the routine of schoolwork after the excitement of a match, an athletic competition, or a collection drive.

The place of physical training and sports in the curriculum was also readjusted under the Nazis. State policy increased the time allotted to physical education from two to three hours a day in 1936 and then to five in 1938. In addition, both the scope and the academic standing of such classes grew. Schools offered cross-country running, football, and boxing for the first time, and introduced physical-education examinations both for entrance and for graduation. Unsatisfactory performance in these classes constituted grounds for expulsion from school and for exclusion from further studies. Physical education instructors, responsible for training the character of their students, also advanced from the periphery of the teaching program to its very center.

While physical education moved to the center of the school curriculum, the importance of traditional subjects of study also shifted. History, German literature, and biology, taught with new National Socialist textbooks, became focal. In National Socialist biology, the "science" of race and heredity, pupils were trained to measure human skulls and classify them according to racial types. Racial biology also became the foundation for the study of history. The Nazi understanding of world history viewed racial competition, the "life struggle" of peoples, as the key to the past, and the racial qualities of various ethnic groups and nations constituted the main line of instruction. German history, too, was stressed, with its earlier phases construed to forecast the coming of the National Socialist regime. The history of the NSDAP, of course, took on major significance. Religious instruction, which held a traditional place in the curriculum, was increasingly downgraded and eventually replaced by special history courses on the Party's *Kampfzeit*.

Although the goals of the Hitler Youth and the traditional values of German education clearly diverged, surprisingly little disaffection existed between primary and secondary school teachers and the National Socialist regime; in fact, the teaching profession was one of the more politically loyal segments of the population. Ninety-seven percent of all teachers were enrolled in the National Socialist Teachers' Association, and of these, 32 percent belonged to the Nazi Party by 1936, a figure twice as large as that among, for instance, the National Association of Civil Servants. The regime also set up special camps for teachers to instruct them in proper National Socialist thinking. By 1938 two-thirds of the country's teaching force had attended a compulsory one-month training course at such camps, where the regimentation and physical activity tended to depersonalize participants. The goal of this training program was to make teachers, once they returned to school, feel closer to their students.

The Nazis also created several new types of elite schools to train the leaders

[handwritten margin note: Shift in educational system]

of Party, state, and *Volk*. The national political educational establishments (*Nationalpolitische Erziehungsanstalt*, or Napola) served as training grounds for future political and military leaders, whereas the Adolf Hitler schools aimed to nurture future political leaders. The Party orientation of Napola training became clear when in 1936 the schools passed to SS control. The curriculum of these schools resembled that of ordinary grammar schools, with political inclulcation in place of religious instruction. Great emphasis was also placed on such activities as boxing, war games, rowing, sailing, gliding, shooting, motorboat driving, and motorcycle riding. The classes, or "platoons," adhered to a communal routine of school life based on that of a military camp, complete with reveille sounded in the morning to rouse students to physical education drills before breakfast. Lessons were taken in the open air as often as possible. In his sixth year, each Napola student had to spend six to eight weeks doing farm work; in the seventh year, each spent the same period of time working in either a factory or a coal mine. It was often reported that the academic level of students at these schools fell well below that of students attending regular grammar schools.

The training of future leaders of the *Volk* was delegated to the Adolf Hitler schools, whose students were chosen by a process of "natural selection." Having been preselected during their second year in the *Jungvolk*, potential Adolf Hitler students were assessed according to racial qualities. Although physical appearance was a main criterion for initial selection, the evaluation of leadership potential was primary after acceptance. The Adolf Hitler schools dispensed with many features of normal school routine. Examinations, progress reports, and conduct marks were eliminated. Physical education and the building of character were the center of the curriculum; as in the Napolas, students' academic performance was markedly low. But instead of redressing the imbalance between intellectual and physical education to overcome this difficulty, the directors of these schools added still more physical-education courses.

But their low academic achievement scarcely hindered Adolf Hitler scholars, since universities were not necessarily the institutions for which they were destined. The ultimate goal of such students was enrollment in an *Ordensburg* (Castle of the Order), a finishing school that possessed the mystique of the medieval orders of chivalry. Each *Ordensburg* accommodated a thousand students (called *Junkers*) plus five hundred instructors, administrative staff members, and grooms. The curriculum accorded a dominant role to horseback riding, but students were also trained in sailing, gliding, skiing, mountaineering, and physical education as well as in war activities such as the use of live ammunition and trench digging. Once again, Party officials noticed the low intellectual ability of graduates but did nothing to alter the situation. Although they were presumably trained in the art of leadership, many graduates even failed to receive Wehrmacht commissions.

The elite of the Third Reich who did not enter this political leadership training program still went to traditional German universities. Hitler himself had nothing but contempt for the universities, but he did not give Reich Minister of Education

Bernhard Rust the authority to develop a consistent National Socialist policy toward them. Policy was therefore left to the mercies of the *Gauleiter*, whose approach to higher education was often even more primitive than that of the Führer. Although the universities had an ethos of their own and remained relatively free to govern themselves after the Nazi takeover, the process of "coordination" with the new regime was carried out with little difficulty. Members of the academic community were prone to view the rise of National Socialism as a renaissance of German life, and they often gave unsolicited support to Nazi measures that tended to destroy the very essence of university training and research. Aside from this voluntary process of coordination, the various faculties generally supported the Nazi purge of the universities. The turnover of academic personnel after the seizure of power was not drastic — the one thousand two hundred professors and instructors dismissed, mostly Jews, Social Democrats, liberals, and others who left under protest, made up barely a tenth of the university teaching force. Yet the consequences of the purge were disproportionally grave. Not only had the regime interfered with the freedom of the universities with no fear of opposition, but faculties also showed themselves willing to adapt to fit in with the new order, even at the cost of losing their best scholars and researchers. Jewish professors, for instance, constituted 12 percent of all German professors, and among them were numbered some of the world's most respected scholars and a quarter of Germany's Nobel Prize winners. Without doubt, the historically excellent German universities declined, and the lack of protest by the remaining faculty members indicates to what extent the regime was accepted.

The Nazis also ensured that the universities would henceforward become even more tightly wedded to National Socialist ideology. No one could assume an academic post without having attended a six-week political-indoctrination course at Lecturers' Association camp. To ideological training this camp added physical education courses, military drill, and endurance tests. One of the association's primary functions was to select and train university personnel. After 1933, moreover, universities lost control over admissions policy, and enrollment more and more came to be dominated by members of Nazi youth organizations.

The regime set up university student organizations to inculcate allegiance to National Socialist ideology. One attempt to enroll all male students in the SA failed, especially after the Roehm purge of 1934 and the diminished prestige of the Storm Troopers. Then followed an experiment in which freshmen underwent both military and political drills during a year-long obligatory residence in "comradeship houses." These efforts coincided with a drive to suppress student fraternities, which were officially disbanded but never entirely broken up. Because of their resilience, the plan for compulsory residence in comradeship houses was eventually replaced by a voluntary program. Once the residency in comradeship houses was made voluntary, they proved to be no different from the older fraternities, and coexisted with them.

This did not mean that most students escaped membership in some Nazi-affiliated organization. From 1933 on, all students were required to belong to the National Socialist German Students' Association (Nationalsozialistischer Deutscher Studentenbund, or NSDSTB), although one student out of every four did somehow manage to avoid the obligation. But it was impossible to evade membership in a *Fachschaft*, a group comprising all students studying the same subject. Such groups met twice a week for ideological lectures and physical-fitness training programs. A student needed 150 points to be awarded the university's sports achievement badge, without which he was barred from further studies unless he could produce a medical certificate. Defined in opposition to the liberal heritage of the universities, the *Fachschaft* stressed service to the *Volksgemeinschaft*. The "socialism" of National Socialism was taken to mean the absence of privileged individuals in the community; the value of the individual was determined by how well he served the *Volk*, and such service could not be based on intellectual achievement alone. Above all, he should not consider himself a member of a privileged caste within society because of his university training.

Through the training of young men and women, the Nazis procured a most impressionable group of individuals on whom to impose their ideas in the hope of creating the new men and women of the *Volksgemeinschaft*. This sense of community was to be instilled through service and obedience. The liberal ideal of the cultivated individual was to be replaced with an educational program based on the fellowship of battle and the building of character. "Character" in this sense did not refer to self-reliance and independence but a hardening of the individual for service to the *Volk* and obedience to the Führer, whereas "fellowship" meant a feeling of openness with the racial community in its battles against its enemies, however abstract they might be — "the Slav," for example, or "the Jewish principle." What National Socialist training produced, however, were duller and stupider, though healthier, individuals. By the late 1930s, the authorities became increasingly aware of the fact that while students, no longer able to think for themselves, would therefore not resist the regime, they were incapable of either providing political leadership in the future or contributing the intellectual and technical skills necessary for running a modern industrial society. They proved to be the most willing to sacrifice themselves to the principles of National Socialism. For our purposes, the life of young people in the Third Reich is a good area in which to evaluate the cultural policies of the regime.

71. Training the Youth of Germany

Although the Nazi leadership had to counter many of the trends that had shaped modern German society, in the youth of Germany it had a malleable element to mold at will. National Socialist attitudes toward the young in many ways clearly exhibited the ideals of the ideology and the goals of its policies. With its stress on racial characteristics, Nazi ideology stressed the importance of physical over intellectual education. The strength of a race came not from the mind but, as Hitler repeatedly said, from "thinking with the blood." The training and education of young people should proceed above all from the development of physical attributes. Physical strength and dexterity were to imbue German youth with a conviction of their superiority.

If as the first task of the state in the service and for the welfare of its nationality we recognize the preservation, care, and development of the best racial elements, it is natural that this care must not only extend to the birth of every little national and racial comrade, but that it must educate the young offspring to become a valuable link in the chain of future reproduction.

educate Youth to continue future

And as in general the precondition for spiritual achievement lies in the racial quality of the human material at hand, education in particular must first of all consider and promote physical health; for taken in the mass, a healthy, forceful spirit will be found only in a healthy and forceful body. The fact that geniuses are sometimes physically not very fit, or actually sick, is no argument against this. Here we have to do with exceptions which — as everywhere — only confirm the rule. But if the mass of a people consists of physical degenerates, from this swamp a really great spirit will very seldom arise. In any case his activity will not meet with great success. The degenerate rabble will either not understand him at all, or it will be so weakened in will that it can no longer follow the lofty flight of such an eagle.

Realizing this, the völkisch state must not adjust its entire educational work primarily to the inoculation of mere knowledge, but to the breeding of absolutely healthy bodies. The training of mental abilities is only secondary. And here again, first place must be taken by the development of character, especially the promotion of will-power and determination, combined with the training of joy in responsibility, and only in last place comes scientific schooling.

Body over Mind

Here the völkisch state must proceed from the assumption *that a man of little scientific education but physically healthy, with a good, firm character, imbued with the joy of determination and will-power, is more valuable for the national community than a clever weakling.* A people of scholars, if they are physically degenerate, weak-willed and cowardly pacifists, will not storm the heavens, indeed they will not even be able to safeguard their existence on this earth. In the hard struggle of destiny the man who knows least seldom succumbs, but always he who from his knowledge draws the weakest consequences and is most lamentable in transforming them into action. Here too, finally, a certain harmony must be present. *A decayed body is not made the least more aesthetic by a brilliant mind,* indeed the highest intellectual training could not be justified if its bearers were at the same

Strong over weak

time physically degenerate and crippled, weak-willed, wavering and cowardly individuals. What makes the Greek ideal of beauty a model is the wonderful combination of the most magnificent physical beauty with brilliant mind and noblest soul. . . .

Physical training in the völkisch state, therefore, is not an affair of the individual, and not even a matter which primarily regards the parents and only secondly or thirdly interests the community; it is a requirement for the self-preservation of the nationality, represented and protected by the state. Just as the state, as far as purely scientific education is concerned, even today interferes with the individual's right of self-determination and upholds the right of the totality toward him by subjecting the child to compulsory education without asking whether the parents want it or not — in far greater measure the völkisch state must some day enforce its authority against the individual's ignorance or lack of understanding in questions regarding the preservation of the nationality. It must so organize its educational work that the young bodies are treated expediently in their earliest childhood and obtain the necessary steeling for later life. It must above all prevent the rearing of a generation of hothouse plants.

This work of care and education must begin with the young mother. Just as it became possible in the course of careful work over a period of decades to achieve antiseptic cleanliness in childbirth and reduce puerperal fever to a few cases, it must and will be possible, by a thorough training of nurses and mothers themselves, to achieve a treatment of the child in his first years that will serve as an excellent basis for future development.

The school as such in a völkisch state must create infinitely more free time for physical training. It is not permissible to burden young brains with a ballast only a fraction of which they retain, as experience shows, not to mention the fact that as a rule it is unnecessary trifles that stick instead of essentials, since the young child cannot undertake a sensible sifting of the material that has been funneled into him. If today, even in the curriculum of the secondary schools, gymnastics gets barely two hours a week and participation in it is not even obligatory, but is left open to the individual, that is a gross incongruity compared to the purely mental training. Not a day should go by in which the young man does not receive one hour's physical training in the morning and one in the afternoon, covering every type of sport and gymnastics. And here one sport in particular must not be forgotten, which in the eyes of many "völkisch" minded people is considered vulgar and undignified: boxing. It is incredible what false opinions are widespread in "educated" circles. It is regarded as natural and honorable that a young man should learn to fence and proceed to fight duels right and left, but if he boxes, it is supposed to be vulgar! Why? There is no sport that so much as this one promotes the

[handwritten margin note: Physical training is a must, less superflous knowledge]

spirit of attack, demands lightning decisions, and trains the body in steel dexterity. It is no more vulgar for two young men to fight out a difference of opinion with their fists than with a piece of whetted iron. It is no less noble if a man who has been attacked defends himself against his assailant with his fists, instead of running away and yelling for a policeman. But above all, the young, healthy body must also learn to suffer blows. Of course this may seem wild to the eyes of our present spiritual fighters. But it is not the function of the völkisch state to breed a colony of peaceful aesthetes and physical degenerates. Not in the respectable shopkeeper or virtuous old maid does it see its ideal of humanity, but in the defiant embodiment of manly strength and in women who are able to bring men into the world.

And so sport does not exist only to make the individual strong, agile and bold; it should also toughen him and teach him to bear hardships.

If our entire intellectual upper crust had not been brought up so exclusively on upper-class etiquette; if instead they had learned boxing thoroughly, a German revolution of pimps, deserters, and such-like rabble would never have been possible; for what gave this revolution success was not the bold, courageous energy of the revolutionaries, but the cowardly, wretched indecision of those who led the state and were responsible for it. The fact is that our whole intellectual leadership had received only "intellectual" education and hence could not help but be defenseless the moment not intellectual weapons but the crowbar went into action on the opposing side. All this was possible only because as a matter of principle especially our higher educational system did not train men, but officials, engineers, technicians, chemists, jurists, journalists, and to keep these intellectuals from dying out, professors.

Our intellectual leadership always performed brilliant feats, while our leadership in the matter of will-power usually remained beneath all criticism.

Certainly it will not be possible to turn a man of basically cowardly disposition into a courageous man by education, but just as certainly a man who in himself is not cowardly will be paralyzed in the development of his qualities if due to deficiencies in his education he is from the very start inferior to his neighbor in physical strength and dexterity. To what extent the conviction of physical ability promotes a man's sense of courage, even arouses his spirit of attack, can best be judged by the example of the army. Here, too, essentially, we have to deal not solely with heroes but with the broad average. But the superior training of the German soldier in peacetime inoculated the whole gigantic organism with that suggestive faith in its own superiority to an extent which even our foes had not considered possible. For the immortal offensive spirit and offensive courage achieved in the long months of midsummer and autumn 1914 by the forward-sweeping German armies was the result of that untiring training which in the long, long years of peace obtained the most incredible achievement often out of frail bodies, and thus cultivated that self-confidence which was not lost even in the terror of the greatest battles.

Particularly our German people which today lies broken and defenseless, exposed to the kicks of all the world, needs that suggestive force that lies in self-confidence. This self-confidence must be inculcated in the young national comrade from childhood on. His whole education and training must be so ordered as to give him the conviction that he is absolutely superior to others. Through his physical strength and dexterity, he must recover his faith in the invincibility of his whole people. For what formerly led the German army to victory was the sum of the confidence which each individual had in himself and all together in their leadership. What will raise the German people up again is confidence in the possibility of regaining its freedom. And this conviction can only be the final product of the same feeling in millions of individuals.

Here, too, we must not deceive ourselves:

Immense was the collapse of our people, and the exertion needed to end this misery some day will have to be just as immense. Anyone who thinks that our present bourgeois education for peace and order will give our people the strength some day to smash the present world order, which means our doom, and to hurl the links of our slavery into the face of our enemies, is bitterly mistaken. Only by super-abundance of national will-power, thirst for freedom, and highest passion, will we compensate for what we formerly lacked.

72. The *Gleichschaltung* of Teachers

Teachers, too, had to be won over to the ideals of the new regime. As with all other sectors of German society, teachers were brought under the control of their own professional organization, the National Socialist Teachers' Association. In addition to their regular training as teachers, members of the Teachers' Association attended compulsory one-month training courses, which stressed Nazi ideology and physical education. Although as a group teachers had given unprecedented support to the Party, the following report shows that in 1934 the *Gleichschaltung* of educators had not yet been completed. The regime still had to weed out former political opponents and overcome the resistance of these educators who objected to its policies of political or racial indoctrination.

From *Nationalsozialistische Deutsche Arbeiter-Partei, Hauptarchiv 1919–45* (Stanford, CA: Hoover Institution on War, Revolution and Peace) H.A. reel 13, folder 246 (National Socialist Teachers' Association Report, March 1934). Translated by Dieter Kuntz.

PROGRESS REPORT OF THE
NATIONAL SOCIALIST TEACHERS' ASSOCIATION–SAXONY
FOR THE MONTH OF MARCH 1934

The majority of teachers appears to have been won over to National Socialism. The least amount of opposition to the NSLB [Nationalsozialistischer Lehrerbund, or National Socialist Teachers' Association] measures is provided by teachers who at one time belonged to the democratic or Marxist camp. On the other hand, working with those who have always been nationalistic and emphatically Christian is occasionally difficult. This was evident when we tried to persuade teachers to join the NS Public Welfare Organization. Even though in some areas up to 95 percent of the teachers have become members, we have found that in a few places we are still meeting resistance.

It can be determined, however, that a large proportion of teachers from all types of schools are actively supporting the National Civil Air Defense. Teachers were also numerically well represented at the huge SA parade in Dresden. Recently a great number of women teachers joined the NS Women's League. . . . The outfitting of schools in National Socialist terms is progressing. Busts, National Socialist wall decorations, and consecration of banners are repeatedly mentioned in incoming reports. . . .

The application of the leadership idea to the schools should automatically result in the selection of "leaders," or men, for the top school positions. Their character, their achievements, and their proven National Socialist conviction fully guarantee that the power and the political and instructional/educational responsibility lies in the best of hands.

Since the NSDAP national leadership takes the view that former Freemasons and members of orders are to be kept away from any party offices and since staff expert positions are to be filled only by old party members, it would be contrary to Adolf Hitler's sought-after fusion of party and state if former members of Freemasonry lodges that were once fought by the NSDAP and persons who, until the revolution, stood in the democratic or liberal camps were to be allowed to remain in school leadership positions, or even given considerably enhanced "leadership" authority and placed in positions superior to the old fighters of the party; they should be denied power even if, as Adolf Hitler explained in his Reichstag speech, "they endeavour, with 110 percent effort, to hinder or avoid answering questions as to their background and previous activity."

It would be desirable if school authorities would, when possible, refrain from transferring apprentice teachers who are actively working with youth, as otherwise the coalescence between the Hitler Youth and apprentice teachers could be jeopardized.

73. A German Elementary Reader

The following excerpt is from an elementary school reader used in the Third Reich. Relating an episode in the early life of Hitler, it is a highly fictionalized account of the Führer's vision of the future unification of Germany and Austria.

On the border between Bavaria and Austria lies the small town of Braunau, in which Adolf Hitler was born on 20 April 1889. Braunau belonged to Austria; Hitler's father was an Austrian customs official. There was a lot to see for the little boy at the border. However, he could not understand one thing; the same men lived on either side, they spoke the same language and they had the same appearance, however, on the other side of the River Inn another emperor ruled; here the eagle had two heads on the shield and over there only one. That was really strange.

The boy learned well in school. But he rather played around with the other boys in the meadows and forests. They liked to obey him, and he frequently was the gang leader in their games.

During history classes, his eyes shone with enthusiasm during the teaching periods. That was something for him, to hear about war and heroes. After he had been at home a long time, he still thought about everything he learned in school. Even today he remembers the history teacher with pleasure. He wanted to know more and more of Germany's past. He could not find out enough, and soon he was not satisfied anymore with what he heard in school. He searched for books and read them.

Then one day he found in his home a volume with the heading "The German-French war." He read it through and was glad that he was a boy and could also become a soldier one day. When reading and looking at the pictures, he thought a great deal and could not figure it out:

"Father, on these pictures there aren't any Austrian uniforms; how come?"

"We did not fight then."

"Why not?"

"We do not belong to Germany, but to Austria."

"But we are also Germans."

"Certainly — but not Reich Germans."

From now on this word would not leave him alone.

"I rather would belong to the German Reich," he answered his father then. The longing awoke in his young heart for one big Reich, which includes all Germans.

From U.S. Chief of Counsel for the Prosecution of Axis Criminality, *Nazi Conspiracy and Aggression* (Washington, D.C.: U.S. Government Printing Office, 1946), vol. 5, doc. no. 2443-PS, pp. 181–82.

74. Anti-Intellectualism Reconsidered

As the war took an increasingly unfavorable turn for the Germans, the failings of many National Socialist policies clearly emerged. The urgent need to reverse the Party's anti-intellectual stance is reflected in the notes taken by a recording secretary of a report presented by *Gauleiter* Dr. Scheel to the Party chancellery in 1944.

GAULEITER DR. SCHEEL SPEAKING ON THE SUBJECT OF UNIVERSITY AND STUDENT QUESTIONS

He expressed satisfaction with the fact that gradually a greater understanding is developing for the necessity of scientific studies. One has, unfortunately, come rather bitterly to feel the results of an underestimation and lack of support of research and science. It is in this area that gigantic confusion has been created which only now is slowly being cleared up.

The training of young talent for scientific studies must proceed in such a way that an ever greater number of those truly gifted must be located and encouraged from among the simpler classes of the *Volk*. . . .

The noticeably strong increase of female students is a result of the time of war; many girls are no longer able to marry and consequently seek an occupation.

The most difficult problem is that of leadership among the student body, particularly since such heavy war casualties have taken their toll (of 120 student leaders, 90 have already lost their lives).

One must appreciate the fact that the National Socialist revolution brought a radical change to the centuries-old traditions and idealistic ideas of students, and this will not be smoothed over from one day to the next. What is needed is time and sympathetic training within the community of like-minded National Socialist recruits. The student must be trained for the great achievements the *Volk* expects of him.

For the National Socialist German Students' Union, one of the most important tasks lies in politically and intellectually satisfying the needs of the young person. In the Hitler Youth, young people most often do not receive an answer to their ideological questions. We should, therefore, institute Hitler Youth Working Groups, which should be led by men of action. . . .

The social organization of the Reich student leadership, namely the National Student Welfare Organization,[1] has failed. Shaping the NS Ger-

From *Nationalsozialistische Deutsche Arbeiter-Partei, Hauptarchiv 1919–45* (Stanford, CA: Hoover Institution on War, Revolution and Peace) H.A. reel 50, folder 1181 (Party Chancellery Reports, September 1944). Translated by Dieter Kuntz.

---

[1] This organization provided assistance to Nazi students, especially to those deemed virtuous National Socialists.

man Student Union so that it can completely carry out its mission is a difficult task. The universities are a thing unto themselves and cannot so easily be given orders. Here we must seek success above all through persuasion and through intellectual influence.

Need intellectual influence

Unfortunately, so far the means have been lacking for university teachers to conduct their practical tasks. Individual industrial firms are contributing funds for research and the training of young talent many times over the amount the state makes available. Foreign countries have recognized the urgency of research and scientific development much more than we have, and consequently it will be difficult to catch up. For instance, there are said to be 5,000 physicists in Germany compared to well over 20,000 in the hostile states who are steadily working on important research projects. We must do all we can in order to attract qualified young talent again to the various scientific fields. . . .

must ↑ interest in intellectual pursuits

75. The Training of German Girls

The League of German Girls, the female branch of the National Socialist Youth Movement, paralleled the organization of the Hitler Youth. The girls in the league were groomed for their future role in the *Volksgemeinschaft* as good German wives and mothers. They were trained to function as the bearers of National Socialist ideology, but on a strictly nonpolitical basis. This selection, from an official publication of the Reich Youth Headquarters, deals with the political education of girls.

We are a political Organization of Girls and acknowledge herewith the task which has been set for us by the National Socialist State: to remain alert and ready for our duty and to help with all our strength in the building of a National Socialist *Volk*. Politics today means to us not only the consideration of daily political occurrences, but Politics means to us also the ideological, spiritual, and cultural forming of the entire German people in the sense of National Socialist Demands. Our educational work is determined by this great political task. It has to readjust itself continually to these demands. Then there will emerge from the community where such work is done the person who is the embodiment of our way, healthy and capable, inwardly strong and womanly, consciously German and consciously National Socialistic.

These recreation camps, where our community becomes closely cemented, are an essential expression of our way. Our chief work in the summer month is therefore consciously the holding of recreation camps

From U.S. Chief of Counsel for the Prosecution of Axis Criminality, *Nazi Conspiracy and Aggression* (Washington, D.C.: U.S. Government Printing Office, 1946), vol. 5, doc. no. 2439-PS, pp. 136–38.

in which our political education pattern takes shape. Recreation camps force a cementing of community. Girls from all walks of life, from over-populated cities as well as the wide open country, stand together under our flag for days and weeks, leaving behind all their ordinary interests in life — school and machine, lecture hall and household — and finding a vigorous and healthful life.

Political education in the recreation camp is not synonymous with scientific discussions, but is rather determined by the experiences shared by the camp community and is shaped accordingly. Our recreation camps are organized more loosely than the leadership schools [Führerinnenschulungen], but in spite of all fun, rigid discipline prevails. Our girls should really be able to leave their daily troubles and cares behind during this week to ten days.

Many who have not yet found us inwardly, acquaint themselves here with the life and the forms of the National Socialist League of Girls and become so attached to it that they cannot dissolve this bond upon their return to everyday life. . . .

Everything the girls experience here takes on a clear, visible pattern in their joint discussions, in which knowledge of their mission in our state, our educational pattern, and the National Socialist Ideology is imparted. During the domestic evenings [Heimabende] the work done during the forenoon, and the work of the Führer and his assistants, the work of the young creative forces in our ranks, is brought closer to them. During the forenoons devoted to reading, they acquaint themselves with the literature of National Socialism and so absorb lasting values. . . .

In clear recognition we created these recreation camps not only for the girls already in our ranks, but also for all the others. We want to do our work with a joyful sense of responsibility, with loyal performance of our duty, and with industry. In order not to become tired and sluggish under the burden of work which each working girl carries however, we need a time which permits quiet collection of strength — free time: Our recreation camps, in which the girls are schooled and prepared for their responsibility and duty to the people and the State, are a political necessity.

BORDERLAND

The circular which called us to camps stated: each junior girl leader will give a survey of the historical and native development of her subdistrict [Untergau] and will consider how she would work this out with junior girls [Jungmädel].

Each of us then realized anew how many living witnesses of ancient history, memorials, walls and bulwarks, legends, tales and jokes, songs and old customs are still alive in her subdistrict.

We had been in camps for three days now. We had penetrated deeper and deeper into National Socialist ideology, emphasized especially the cultural desire of National Socialism; we had discussed our junior girl activities and had worked on the arrangement of our home; we had sung, gone on a short trip, and participated in practical junior girl sports. Today in our domestic evening we want to hear something about Pomeranian customs and Pomeranian History.

After supper we march silently down to the sea. . . .

Our Pomeranian coast lies before our eyes. Now Traute, from the village of Leba up on the Polish border, tells us about the immensity of the shore and on the sea. . . .

Then she suddenly becomes serious: "In our subdistrict we have 200 kilometers of border. Consider what that means: 200 kilometers of border. The Versailles Treaty separates German soil from German soil, blocks our access to the nearest port, and cuts off traffic to the east. Our border city of Lauenburg is flooded with agricultural products. One farm after another in our country gets into great difficulties since, because of the demarcation of the border, there is no longer a market outlet for agricultural products. In Lauenburg itself the greatest amount of unemployment in Pomerania prevails. The Winter relief work tries to alleviate the worst conditions of misery and distress during the winter. Everything is shut down — the factories, the brickyards, and all large plants. These are the effects of the demarcation of the border on our Homeland. . . ."

"And the border itself; visualize a forest, through which a road leads to a railroad station. The road is neutral, the forest is German on the right and Polish on the left. I cannot tell you how one feels on this road; you would have to come and experience it all yourselves."

"But we know that we are on outpost duty there. You can rely on us." Traute is silent. We all get up, grasp each other's hand, and our song is solemn now: "Holy Fatherland, in danger thy sons will flock around thee. . . ." And then we stand around the flag and look silently toward the East.

76. A Former Girls' League Leader Reflects

This account by Melita Maschmann, a former leader of the League of German Girls, reveals the organization's appeal to young girls. Maschmann recounts the pleasures as well as the disappointments of her association with the league.

There must be many answers to the question — what caused young people to become National Socialists at that time. For people at a certain stage of adolescence the antagonism between the generations, taken in conjunction with Hitler's seizure of power, probably often played a part

From Melita Maschmann, *Account Rendered: A Dossier on My Former Self*, trans. Geoffrey Strachan (London: Abelard-Schumann, 1964), pp. 10, 12, 16, 18–19, 20, 22–23. Reprinted by permission of the Blackie Publishing Group, Glasgow and London.

in it. For me it turned the scale. I wanted to follow a different road from the conservative one prescribed for me by family tradition. In my parents' mouths the words "social" or "socialist" had a scornful ring. They used them when they waxed indignant over the hunchback dressmaker's desire to play an active part in politics. On January 30, 1933, she announced that a time was now at hand when servants would no longer have to eat off the kitchen table. My mother always treated her servants correctly but it would have seemed absurd to her to share their company at table.

Whenever I probe the reasons which drew me to join the Hitler Youth, I always come up against this one: I wanted to escape from my childish, narrow life and I wanted to attach myself to something that was great and fundamental. This longing I shared with countless others of my contemporaries.

It will be more difficult to explain how this impulse carried me forward through the twelve years up to 1945. The fact that I clung to National Socialism for so long is bound up with the experiences of my early childhood. It is noteworthy that while the "socialist" tendency expressed in the name of the movement attracted me because it strengthened me in my opposition to my conservative home, the nationalist tendency, in contrast to this, was meaningful to me just because it was in harmony with the spirit that had been drummed into me since my infancy. . . . But my own childhood experiences corresponded to those of a whole generation, which grew up at that time in right wing middle class surroundings, and from whose ranks much of the young leadership of the National Socialist movement and the army of the Third Reich was later drawn.

. . . My parents rejected the Weimar Republic. Both consciously and unconsciously they directed their children's attention towards those facts which were likely to discredit the new system. They themselves saw only the blunders and had no eyes for the desperate struggle of the men who were trying to save the Republic. Even the exceptional burgeoning of intellectual and artistic creativity in those years escaped their notice.

I believed the National Socialists when they promised to do away with unemployment and with it the poverty of six million people. I believed them when they said they would reunite the German nation, which had split into more than forty political parties, and overcome the consequences of the dictated peace of Versailles. And if my faith could only be based on hope in January 1933, it seemed soon enough to have deeds to point to.

. . . I therefore refused to join the League of Luise, and as my parents would not allow me to become a member of the Hitler Youth I joined secretly. Now began by own private "years of struggle." I made up for what my new comrades had achieved before 1933, when it had cost personal sacrifices to belong to the National Socialist Youth. But, if I may anticipate, what now awaited me was a bitter disappointment, the extent of which I dared not admit to myself. The evening meetings for which we met in a dark and grimy cellar were fatally lacking in interest.

The time was passed in paying subscriptions, drawing up countless lists and swotting up the words of songs, the linguistic poverty of which I was unable to ignore, although I made a great effort to do so. Discussions on political texts from, say, *Mein Kampf* quickly ended in general silence. . . .

I remember with more pleasure the weekend outings, with hikes, sports, campfires and youth hostelling. Occasionally there would be "field exercises" with neighbouring groups. If there was any rivalry between them the game often degenerated into a first class brawl. What kind of a picture these girls fighting over a flag would have presented to an outsider I prefer not to imagine.

But for me, not even the outings made up for the tedium of the remaining "duties." In my group I was the only girl attending a secondary school. The others were shop girls, office workers, dressmakers and servant girls. So my desire to be accepted into the community of "working youth" had been fulfilled. The fact that this fulfilment was a bitter disappointment I explained to myself thus: these girls came from the lower middle class and regarded the "wellborn daughters" I was trying to escape from with envy. They were not the real companions I was looking for; "young working girls" from factories. I understood that such girls had no militant class consciousness, and I wanted to struggle to woo them from communism on behalf of the *Volksgemeinschaft*.

. . . I was what they called a "March violet."[1] My secret entry into the Hitler Youth dated from March 1, 1933, and all the leading positions were occupied by the so called "Old Guard." I was prepared to respect and admire them without question, but in practice there were difficulties. I liked very few of them, and just because I was a March violet and a high school girl as well, they all looked down on me and made it clear to me that I was not one of them. They were sometimes painfully coarse and primitive, and corresponded — I was unhappy to observe — with the image of "proletarians" which my mother was wont to evoke.

It was then that I first consciously said to myself: Party leaders can make mistakes like everyone else; perhaps there are also rogues and charla-

---

[1] Early in 1933 there was a big increase in the Party membership. The new members were scornfully known as "March violets."

tans amongst them who have wormed their way into office because they are hungry for power or because they want to sap the movement from within. If they dream up such shameless lies, the people who are not well enough educated to be able to judge for themselves will fall for their nonsense. Anyone who observes this should not be silent about it. But one also has no right to turn one's back on the Party on account of such disillusionments. Gradually the spirit of truth will prevail over the lies. One must hold one's ground and fight where one stood.

In later years I must often have reflected similarly — very often indeed during the war. But I found one excuse, something like this: All decent, able bodied men are in the army now: the Party has to use the sixth or seventh best to keep afloat. I incurred the displeasure of my superiors several times, and was punished, for example by loss of rank, because I was guilty of disobedience. On each occasion it was connected with one particular problem which oppressed me: Should not National Socialism rather remain the affair of a small order of leadership recruited by rigorous selection? What would it become if every German were finally admitted into the order? A monstrous company of fellow-travellers.

My tendency to work towards the formation of an élite was contrary to the Party line. I suffered as a result of the disobedience to which this tendency tempted me, but I always returned to the hope that within a few generations we should succeed in educating every German to be a decent National Socialist. I wanted to share in the task of this educational work. For this reason I stayed in the Hitler Youth. I wanted to help create the *Volksgemeinschaft* in which people would live together as in one big family.

77. Attitudes of Youth Toward the Regime

The following reports to the Social Democratic Party in exile exhibit a wide spectrum of attitudes toward the Hitler Youth and the League of German Girls as well as toward the regime's ideology among the young people of Germany. Dating from 1934 and 1935, the excerpts indicate very mixed feelings about participation in these youth organizations before membership in them became compulsory.

MAY/JUNE 1934

Youth is, as before, still supportive of the regime. Young people find the new elements of drill, uniforms, and camping very exciting, and

From *Deutschland-Berichte der Sozialdemokratischen Partei Deutschlands (Sopade), 1934–1940* (Frankfurt: Verlag Petra Nettelbeck, 1980), 1 (May–June 1934): 117, 2 (June 1935): 684–87, 689, 692–93, 707–8. Translated by Dieter Kuntz.

Youths
Support
Regime

consequently school and the parental household are taking a back seat to these new aspects of the youthful community. A grand time is to be had, risk free. Many believe the persecution of Jews and Marxists will open doors to them for economic opportunity. The more enthusiastic they are, the easier their exams will be, or the better will be their chance of getting a professional position or a job. Peasant youths practically live in the Hitler Youth and SA. Even young workers are participating. They say: Maybe one day we will have socialism; the current attempt is merely a different path toward it; the previous system surely did not bring it about. *Volksgemeinschaft* is certainly better than being in the lowest social class.

JUNE 1935

. . . Is Hitler correct when he asserts again and again: We know that many older Germans reject us; but youth has been won over with body and soul? — This question will in time be answered by developments and will have much to do with the continued existence of the regime. That is why it is important to follow closely the activities of German youths and proceedings within schools, universities, the Hitler Youth, and the work place. Following are several general observations:

Bavaria: "The reports dealing with youth and its enthusiasm for the regime are not uniformly in agreement. Inasmuch as most of our colleagues [agents] detect tremendous support for the regime among the oncoming generation, some maintain that the sentiments among youth are diverse. It goes without saying that the Hitler Youth does its utmost to create enthusiasm, but among working-class youths one can hear much criticism. . . . Approximately one-third of those in our schools are not members of the Hitler Youth and must consequently attend school on Saturdays. In several classes the number of students in attendance has increased lately because parents feel that their children are better off there than to be constantly subjected to strenuous Hitler Youth drills. . . . An individual observer from Munich provides the following picture of the mood of the population: The nation [*Volk*] is not recognizable after two years of Hitler . . . the older generations are suffering from a lack of freedom. The same cannot be said of youth. Young people are full of heart and hope and are not disappointed because they still have expectations of the future. The growing self-confidence of youth is one of the fundamental characteristics of the new age. It is like this: the valuable segment of German youth is today in the ranks of the fascists. . . ."

Report from Rhineland-Westphalia: "Youth under the age of 18 makes no presuppositions. Youth no longer has tradition. This is one of the greatest dangers facing us. The Weimar political parties are nothing but criminal parties in their eyes. Youth, however, has only a very general relationship with the symbols of the National Socialist movement, but is not concerned with political problems. Youth is fond of Hitler, but cares not at all about Goering or Frick."

Youth hardly concerns itself with political ideas. The Labor Service is a keen opportunity as far as youth is concerned. The possibility of getting into the army represents the chance to escape from unemployment and to get out of reach of parents. . . . Report from southwestern Germany: "To youth in the secondary schools, the continuous force-feeding of National Socialism is having the same effect as the heavy emphasis on religious instruction in earlier decades. National Socialism is no longer a matter of youthful rebellion but has instead become the state-sponsored school curriculum. Consequently National Socialism has lost much of its appeal, especially since the suppression of political opponents and otherwise-oriented youth organizations. This is why today the frequent dodging of the Hitler Youth and its events, as well as the transgression of National Socialist prohibitions, has become a favorite game for youths who eagerly want to outfox the authorities. . . ."

The relationship between school and Hitler Youth is clarified in the following reports:

Rhineland-Westphalia: "The implementation of the national day of youth is still not a uniform matter. BdM [Bund deutscher Mädel, or League of German Girls] members, for instance, must now again attend school on Saturdays, whereas their leaders are not required to attend. Some of the teachers tried everything in order to force children into the Hitler Youth. In Arnsberg, for instance, Principal Eckelmann made vile threats to teachers because of the meager participation of students in the Hitler Youth. Consequently the teachers begged parents to send their kids in order to ward off punishment. Many among the children who previously had belonged to socialist or Catholic organizations refused nonetheless. . . . Many children are trying to avoid the onerous questions teachers pose concerning their home life. Many lie, while others wantonly try to trick their teachers. Many questions continue to be asked in the classroom about the situation at home. Teachers inquire whether or not one's father is a party member or is in the SA, the civil air defense, the NS People's Welfare Organization, or which newspapers are read at home. Children whose parents are avowed opponents of the Nazis answer yes many times simply because they are afraid. . . ."

The reports dealing with the Hitler Youth uniformly describe the brutalization and demoralization found in the organization. . . .

Rhineland-Westphalia: "In the rural areas as well as in industrial cities, one can see an increasing demoralization of youth. In the rural areas there has been a sharp decline in participation at Hitler Youth events. Many have resigned their membership, and membership dues are only infrequently paid. While at first uniforms and war games were quite appealing, the regimented routine is now regarded as burdensome by children. The power of authority which was bestowed upon some children has given rise to discontent and resistance. It is not unusual for a youthful group leader whose position of authority has gone to his head to receive a beating from his charges because he wanted to drill the already exhausted group even harder. . . .

In cities, a shocking morality can be found within the "state youth." Young girls between the ages of 14 and 20 are frequently lacking in moral standards altogether. In the town of Buer, 17 girls were kicked out of the BdM because they were pregnant. Mothers are puzzled over the unchecked moral conduct of their children. The constant bombardment of propaganda about racially pure offspring has resulted in unbridled sexual degeneracy. . . ."

Silesia: ". . . The neglect of morality within the Hitler Youth has reached frightening proportions. Lately two fourteen- and fifteen-year-old girls gave birth in our clinic. When they were asked to name the fathers, they were at a loss. When it was suggested that surely they knew with whom they had been intimate, they applied that they really didn't know the individuals because they had drawn lots. . . .

. . . Sympathy for the Hitler Youth has cooled noticeably among youths. . . . The relationship between Hitler Youth members and non-members differs considerably from school to school, and even classroom to classroom. There are girls' classes in which one finds only one person belonging to the BdM whereas others boast a two-thirds membership. As a rule, in the countryside almost all children are in the Hitler Youth. At the beginning teachers exerted considerable pressure on children to join the Hitler Youth. Children who did not join were branded as communist children and were ill treated by teachers and classmates. Now the picture has changed somewhat. Nonmembers are no longer ostracized by classmates and teachers no longer differentiate between them. Nonetheless, heavy pressure to join can still be felt. Not long ago a Hitler Youth recruitment week was held here, during which there was again heavy pressure on children. There are cases of nonfascist families, for instance, where children beg their parents to let them join merely because they want the pestering to stop. This can cause difficulties among siblings because the older children disdain the fickleness of their younger siblings. A young boy told his sister that if she joined the BdM, he would no longer consider her his sister. . . . Classroom instruction bears the heavy imprint of National Socialism. Most of the dictations and essays the children are expected to write have National Socialist themes as their subject matter. Written assignments dealing with Hitler, Goering, and other high-ranking party officials are common. Children are told to go to National Socialist films such as *Horst Westmar* and *Triumph of the Will* and then write essays about them. Sometimes they are given the assignment of listening to a Hitler speech on the radio and then writing about it. The effect this has on children is not uniform. . . ."

78. Parental Concerns About the Hitler Youth

Parents, too, did not unreservedly accept the Hitler Youth. This 1938 report of the underground Social Democratic Party displays the concern of parents both for the welfare of their children and for their own safety.

. . . Parental concerns about the physical overexertion and moral endangering of their children in the Hitler Youth are only one aspect of the overall problem of the relationship between youth and the parental home. National Socialist child-rearing methods have created these difficulties. The totalitarian demands of the Hitler Youth, the sense of authority and self-confidence, the mercenary spirit and fanaticism of these youths, have added so much to this problem that it approaches an unbearable intensity. This is true even within circles of what could be called 100 percent Nazis.

The national Hitler Youth leadership continually attempts to reassure parents, claiming that "the Reich youth leader understands the concerns of parents;" that the Reich leadership is very much opposed to "the independence of youth if this is detrimental to the natural reverence, respect, and love for parents." . . . But all these reassurances have not changed the fact that parental influence over youth continues to diminish, and that relationships within families grow more tense and hostile. The relationship between parents and youth is especially tragic in cases where the parents are not true Nazis or are even opponents of the regime. In such cases the government shows no consideration. Children denounce their parents — whereupon they lose jobs, positions, and are threatened with the loss of parental rights and personal freedom.

From *Deutschland-Berichte der Sozialdemokratischen Partei Deutschlands (Sopade), 1934–1940* (Frankfurt: Verlag Petra Nettelbeck, 1980), 5 (December 1938): 1400–1401. Translated by Dieter Kuntz.

Unit III

The Totalitarian State: War and the Final Solution, 1938–1945

The causes of Hitler's triumphs were also the causes of his failures. The same qualities that brought Hitler success both in the early years of the growth of the Party and in the seizure of power resulted in his diplomatic and military victories in the late 1930s and early 1940s as well. Besides his amateur's lack of stereotypical thinking on given subjects, Hitler quickly mastered another tactic that looked like intuitive genius. In any contest of will he upped the stakes to such a high level that his opponents were moved first to compromise and then to give in. But his inventiveness and his risk taking, which had served him so well up to 1941–42, were the source of his undoing. The fact that he compromised less and less after 1937 as he re-created the world in his own image is a measure of his blindness to reality, which increasingly encompassed him as time went on.

On December 10, 1941, with the war in Russia going against him, Hitler declared war on the United States. This act, more than anything else, revealed the Führer's helplessness in the face of developments over which he no longer had control. For him it was the realization of a long-desired dream of taking on the forces of international capitalism as well as of international communism. In the back of his mind he always held a global strategy of world conquest which called for a second war against the sea powers of Britain and the United States. But this conflict was to come only after Germany's continental position had been broadened and consolidated, and time and energy had been devoted to the construction of a navy. The fact that Hitler now welcomed the war with America when it had been prematurely forced upon him indicates the degree to which delusion and ideological obsession had overtaken him. Hitler was beginning to pay the price for ideological rigidity. At first the reversals brought an acceleration of Germany's military efforts and above all a brutal intensification of totalitarian rule. In the end, however, they resulted in a heightening of ideological concerns over which Hitler still had control, speeding up the destruction of Germany itself. Only complete military collapse ended his fantastic visions of total conquest.

National Socialism's two major goals were the achievement of *Lebensraum*, for which war was launched in 1939, and the establishment of the racially pure *Volksgemeinschaft* by an unassailable political regime. Begun in 1933, intensified in the mid-1930s, and extended throughout occupied Europe in the early 1940s, this latter policy was put into effect by the SS (*Schutzstaffel*). As time went on, the SS increasingly infiltrated and directed the conduct of the war as well. Charged with creating the racial community within greater Germany, this organization instituted such policies as the movement and elimination of undesirable peoples, the breeding of Aryan stock, and the policing of individuals within Germany and the occupied territories. The type of totalitarian regime that was the Third Reich can for the most part be identified with the aims and methods of the SS, whose origins, development, and all-embracing power present the best means of understanding the nature of the ideological stance and the destructive practices of National Socialism.

The SS originally grew out of the restructuring of the SA in the spring of 1925. Formed as a replacement for the Shocktroop Hitler, the SS initially drew its membership from the ranks of the SA, and the entire organization was administratively subordinate to it. The SS's role was to serve as a bodyguard for party leaders. The scope of its activities remained rather limited, even insignificant in the overall party system, until Himmler's appointment in January 1929 as Reichsführer SS. Under his direction, members of the SS came to view themselves as the Nazi elite and the main purpose of the organization the policing of other party members. Heinrich Himmler, who was instrumental in the overthrow of Roehm and the degradation of the SA in June 1934, also helped maneuver the SS into an independent position within the party. After the Blood Purge, the SS began to grow in stature as the central agency for the internal government of the Third Reich. It was eventually to take over all police functions within Germany and the occupied territories. It controlled the concentration camps, ran its own industries manned with slave labor, and fielded its own army, the Waffen SS, which fought alongside the Wehrmacht. The SS developed its own bureaucracy and quasi-governmental powers to such an extent that, in a regime that proclaimed total control over society, the SS became the highly centralized mechanism of this control within the Third Reich — an empire within an empire.

The heart of the SS state and the lifeblood of its strength was its unrestricted monopoly of police powers. The buildup of its powers began when the SS obtained control of the political police, the section of the German police force that dealt with antigovernment political activity, and it was in this sphere that, in the course of time, the SS reached its fullest development. There was good reason for this. Of all public institutions, the political police provided the greatest scope for secret processes, unauthorized executive measures, and deviations from legal norms. Once under way, the development of the police power of the SS involved both the centralization of all police forces and the "degovernmentalization" of the police.

The police powers of the SS eroded the last remnants of the legal system in Germany. In accordance with the decree of the Ministry of Justice of April 13, 1935, the Gestapo (Geheime Staatspolizei, or Secret State Police) could legally consign "undesirable" persons who had served their prison sentences to concentrations camps. In so doing the SS transformed permanent, "protective" custody into a positive act, justifying it as a measure both to guard the individual against public anger and to preserve the Volksgemeinschaft. In addition, governmental and police actions were exempt from court review, and as these came more and more to rest on political authority and leadership, the individual's right to protection under the law was also eroded. The Gestapo's freedom to act without legal restraint was the most evident aspect of the principle of "permanent revolution." Once an undertaking of the SS was deemed political and declared an "act of leadership," legal review was blocked. And only the interpretation of the respective National Socialist leaders determined what was in fact "political." The fact that, after September 1939, administrative actions were not subject to any review whatever sealed the development by which the dictatorial state blended into the totalitarian state. The transition from the older to the newer definition of police authority marked the shift from a semilegal, semiconstitutional state to an outright totalitarian police state.

The SS was not merely a police, surveillance, and paramilitary organization. Its main objective, from which it derived its "legitimate" use of force, was to create the racially pure Volksgemeinschaft. As the SS evolved from a police organization operating within an administrative whole to become an independent organization, it grew from being not so much a protective arm of that community as the political expression of the community. Whereas in all legally constituted states the police force forms only a part of the general administrative apparatus and the political police is merely one branch of the police force, these roles were reversed in the Third Reich. The political police became the active part of the political community, making all decisions of any political importance. The remainder of the police force was subordinate to the political police, functioning only as a uniformed executive and carrying out its directives. Yet the SS did not simply safeguard the new political order; in Himmler's words, it was also charged with "creating" the new order. Police power became creative power within the Third Reich, its protective role enlarged so as to allow it to make policy beyond the limits of legitimate state activity and to fuse the elements of the new racial community together.

The substitution of the indefinite, elastic, and wide-ranging principle of "prevention" for the protective role of the police removed all possible limitations on surveillance, persecution, and even extermination of potential enemies. The police could do anything in the name of the Volksgemeinschaft. Himmler's appointment

Evolution of SS marked shift from semilegal state to police state

as Reich Commissioner for the Strengthening of German Nationhood on October 7, 1939, substantially broadened his powers. A loosely worded decree charged him with bringing ethnic Germans back and resettling them within the Reich as well as excluding "nationally alien populations constituting a threat to the Reich and the *Volksgemeinschaft.*" The decree elevated Himmler above the army and the civilian administration, making him responsible only to Hitler, and he used this power to consolidate his own apparatus. Himmler's Office of the Reich Commissioner became a central office of the SS which, together with other central offices (such as the SS Economic and Administrative Central Office) and their numerous subdivisions, formed the executive head of the SS state.

Achieving security had been the original goal of the SS, and this aim only increased when it co-opted all other police forces in the state and no longer encountered legal restraints on its activity. Any measures could be taken in the name of security, which meant that those responsible for security could never feel satisfied that they had done everything conceivable to prevent disorder; as long as any possibility remained of taking further concrete action, they had not done their duty. This unlimited responsibility for security inevitably resulted in a reconstitution of the SS, transforming it from an organ of defense charged with protecting the existing order to an institution exercising tremendous political power for the establishment of a new cultural order.

Closely linked to this development was abuse of the principle of preventive measures. The aim to eliminate every potential danger replaced the notion of defense against actual visible danger. In light of the Führer's all-embracing authority, any spontaneous political initiative, even independent thoughts or scruples, constituted a source of danger. Mere suspicion of opposition or of lack of enthusiasm caused the police to act. Not only the Gestapo but also the Criminal Police Force held this distorted conception of the principle of preventive measures. These measures for suppressing crime, particularly as applied to malingerers or so-called antisocial persons, amounted in practice to ruling the lives of men and women in a manner entirely incompatible with human rights.

Preventive measures too often meant consignment to a concentration camp — considered not a punishment but an objective, protective measure only indirectly connected with the guilt or innocence of the victims. Established in March 1933, Dachau had always been operated by SS troops, which in the early days had worked with little systematization and a great deal of brutality. By June 1933, institutionalized terror, under Theodor Eicke, the new head of Dachau, replaced the chaotic approach. In detailed instructions Eicke explained that lashings were to be administered in the presence of guards and inmates; the death penalty was proposed for, among other things, inciting or spreading atrocity stories; punishments were to be administered with the greatest harshness and inflexibility but in an impersonal and disciplined fashion. By 1935 the SS and the camps operated entirely outside the legal system. The police system was now complete. The SS could arrest, sentence, and execute individuals without any interference

[handwritten margin note: Independence of S.S.]

or restraint. Independence, combined with bureaucratic systematization and uninhibited violence, characterized the SS imperium.

By 1934 the Nazis had eliminated all political opponents, but they then became increasingly obsessed with the abstract enemies of the German people: international Bolshevism and international Judaism. Seeing the enemy as an abstraction, the police carried on the struggle by abstract methods. If the enemy engaged in systematically perverting German character and spirit, the police similarly had to extend their countermeasures in order to protect German character and spirit. Here the regime's claim to total power over the disposal of its human material emerged with the greatest clarity. Police latitude for investigation had no limits; the police were empowered to take security and preventive measures against those merely suspected of opposing the regime or of committing a crime. It was this power that made the police an instrument of terror. The Gestapo's use of physical coercion and torture were not its primary objective, though it made good use of both; its aim was total control of the people, both in Germany and in the conquered countries.

[handwritten margin note: total control of the people]

Hitler's grand designs for postwar Europe accorded a prominent place to the SS in the administration of Greater Germany and the full realization of the ideological goals of the regime. In the decisive phase of the war effort, during the winter months of 1941–42, Hitler gave expression to these plans, envisaging a Germanic empire stretching from Norway to the Alps and from the Atlantic to the Black Sea, linked by a gigantic network of highways lined with SS defense settlements to secure the conquered territories. Comparable only to ancient Babylon or Rome, Berlin, renamed Germania, would overshadow London and Paris as a gigantic world capital. Leningrad, the symbol of Soviet resistance, was to be razed; the Crimea, once ruled by Goths, was to be turned into a Nordic cultural and recreational area and resettled by farmers from the southern Tirol. Russia itself was to become in part a vast army camp and in part an area in which Aryan "Reich peasants," racially selected from throughout Europe, were to be settled. All of eastern Europe was to become a huge colony, directly connected with the German heartland. The 180 million Russians, for their part, would die out. They were to be prohibited from procreating, and Russian schools were to be closed to prevent the development of an educated class and of resistance. The Russians were not "to learn more than at most the meaning of traffic signs" and, of course, enough German to understand orders. Hitler described this new order for eastern Europe in some detail. Once a year a group of "Kirghiz" were to be taken through the capital of the Reich in order to impress on them the power and grandeur of German monuments. If any difficulties arose, the populations of the cities would be rounded up and liquidated by a handful of bombs — "and the matter is settled." Nazi racial ideology, the system of slave labor, and National Socialist rule as a whole testified to the extent the regime realized these plans in the eastern territories. Himmler, to whom it fell to direct the SS program, executed Nazi policies with the pedantic care and intensity characteristic of the ideology from the start, even after it was patently obvious that the war was lost. National Socialist ideology constituted an absolute, which regardless of its effect on the progress of the war, determined Nazi policy even after the military situation was hopeless.

The persecution of the Jews of Germany between 1933 and 1941 most clearly exemplified the shift from the semilegal dictatorship to the totalitarian SS imperium. Until 1938 National Socialist policy toward the Jews included legal exclusion from the social and political community, an effort to force Jews to emigrate from Germany, and sporadic violence. With the coming of the war, the growing power of the SS corresponded with the systematic persecution of German Jews and Jews in the occupied territories, and to a large measure it depended on such persecution. The overt "solution" to the "Jewish Problem" of this period was concentration, and Jews from all over Europe were sent to concentration camps in the East. Although the actual decision to move to the Final Solution of physical extermination was probably arrived at as early as 1939, the systematic organization and the vast bureaucratic machinery of liquidation did not get under way until 1941–42.

On Hitler's accession to power in 1933, local bands of the SA and SS began a campaign of terrorism against Jews, invading their apartments, offices, and stores. Jewish lawyers, doctors, and other professionals were arrested. Most were later released after being tortured and forced to sign a statement saying that they had been treated well. In a characteristic tactic of National Socialist leaders, the Nazis did not accept responsibility for these acts of violence but blamed them on the Communists or the German people's alleged deep hatred of the Jews. They claimed not to have inaugurated but to have at most directed widespread antisemitism among the people.

The issuance of the first official government policy toward the Jews, however, belied this claim. In response to the campaign of "atrocities" Jews abroad were supposedly carrying out against the new regime, Hitler announced, as an act of reprisal, a boycott of all Jewish businesses to begin on April 1, 1933. That the boycott was not successful and that mass boycott meetings were not well attended indicates that antisemitic policies were not popular in Germany. The American consul in Leipzig wrote, "In fairness to the German people, it must be said that the boycott was unpopular with the working classes and with the educated sections of the middle classes." Many middle-class people disliked the violence and lack of restraint associated with the anti-Jewish campaign, particularly as it affected individual Jews. Yet still there was no popular protest. Many regarded these incidents as necessary or at least as an expedient in time of "national emergency." Major and minor acts of violence against Jews continued through 1934, aroused in part by relentless propaganda aimed at hardening anti-Jewish German opinion. The party systematically and without significant opposition pursued a policy calculated to destroy good feelings between Jewish and non-Jewish Germans. Party officials did not fail to pressure anyone who continued to have business dealings or even friendly social relations with Jews. Such boycotts worked effectively in villages and small towns, but in cities even Party members were often issued appeals, warnings, and threats from above to ensure the fulfillment of the desired goal.

With the invasion of Poland, which brought several million Polish Jews under Nazi rule, the concentration effort began in earnest. The war freed the regime of both the need to observe any tactical restraints and the fear of foreign intervention, opening the way to more radical solutions of the "Jewish Problem." No longer concerned with public opinion, either within or outside Germany, the regime now had carte blanche to institute National Socialist ideology. A number of *Einsatz* (special task groups) units of the SS moved in on the heels of the advancing army, ostensibly to secure the newly occupied territories by eliminating all enemies of the Wehrmacht and the German administration. In reality they engaged in the wholesale slaughter of Poles and the random killing of Jews. With the formation of the Waffen SS, these outrages increased in intensity from week to week, culminating in a number of mass executions after mid-October 1939.

The implementation of the methods and the coordination of various agencies that eventually brought the Final Solution into full-scale operation were the topics of the Wannsee Conference on January 20, 1942. Members of the Central Office for Reich Security, the Central Office for Race and Resettlement, the Security Police, Party headquarters, the Reich chancellery, the Ministry for the East, the Interior Ministry, the Ministry of Justice, the Office of the Four-Year Plan, the General Government (German occupied Poland), and the Reich Foreign Office attended this conference in a Berlin suburb. In other words, represented at the conference were all departments that would need to be involved in identifying, arresting, transporting, concentrating, and exterminating Jews in both Germany and all the conquered and satellite countries of Europe. The discussions focused on the stages of the process and on the various ways in which such mass executions could be carried out. Perhaps the most consequential outcome of the conference had to do with the use of Jewish labor. Whether or not to employ the condemned before liquidation always posed a difficulty for the SS. Himmler himself believed that exploiting such labor power would only slow up the ultimate goal of extermination. Those attending the conference decided otherwise, but it was clear that the reprieve given prisoners considered fit to work was to be brief.

The major problem discussed at the Wannsee Conference was the method of killing. *Einsatz* units had undertaken mass executions of Jews since the invasion of the Soviet Union began in June 1941, killing over a million victims by November of that year. There was talk at the conference of shipping Jews from all over Europe to Russia and having them dispatched by these "experienced" forces. Jews from the West had been transported to Minsk, Riga, and Kovno, but it was recognized that in the long run, the shooting of millions of people would create insurmountable problems. There would be too many witnesses, too many bodies, and too many soul-burdened members of the SS. Some of the deportees were consequently sent to the overcrowded ghettos of Poland, which were themselves soon dissolved. In several parts of the occupied Polish territory, the SS erected facilities for a more impersonal, more efficient, and more silent manner of doing away with large numbers of people. These units were the first of the extermination centers.

Himmler explained that the initial step in implementing the Final Solution would effect Hitler's wish "that the Altreich [prewar Germany] and the Protectorate [Bohemia] should be cleared of Jews from west to east." Those who had survived the first wave of murder in occupied Russia would be assigned to forced labor in ghettos and concentration camps until such time as the extermination centers were fully functioning. The concentration camps were to be revamped, and completely new "extermination camps" (*Vernichtungslager*) constructed.

More than the political programs and social policies designed to reconstitute Germany, even more than the outbreak and conduct of the war, the Final Solution shows National Socialist ideology in action. Although prefigured to only a limited degree in a small number of earlier attempts at genocide, the Final Solution is actually a uniquely twentieth-century phenomenon. The policy of exterminating the Jewish population of Europe can be explained only in part by pointing to the totalitarian state structure that planned it and the enormously powerful police apparatus that executed it, because the Final Solution is inconceivable without a certain definition of modern science and a high degree of technological capability.

Although today we clearly see racial science as a repulsive pseudo-science, the fact that the Nazis could appeal to scientific criteria of truth both to define racial characteristics and to justify excluding and then exterminating a segment of European society indicates how science could be manipulated in the service of the state and its ideology. Within the death camps themselves, science took on an even more sinister face. Himmler himself advocated the development of medical experimentation to advance Nazi racial theories, and the inmates of the camps provided an inexhaustible supply of "expendable" human subjects. In the name of research, Nazi doctors carried out hideous experiments in the use of X-ray and chemical methods of mass sterilization. It is even more horrendous that these experiments were not only crude and unsystematic but also senseless and useless.

For the Nazi leadership directly involved in the Final Solution, beginning with Himmler and Heydrich to Eichmann and the various camp commanders, the task of exterminating European Jewry was first and foremost a logistical and technological problem. Goering initially set the tone when he launched the policy of genocide in terms of the need for the "organizational, technical, and economic measures for the execution of the intended Final Solution of the Jewish question." They viewed the process as a logistical and technological problem of isolating and transporting millions of individuals, and temporarily housing and exploiting as slave labor a large number of them, with the intention of exterminating and removing all traces of the killing process while recovering all usable by-products, especially hair and gold teeth. Technological expertise in such enterprises was highly prized, and technological efficiency was the dominant value. The details of the extermination procedures were understood in the same manner. When the shooting of individual victims proved too slow and inefficient, group carbon-monoxide poisoning by trips in "death vans" was tried before the process of mass executions in gas chambers (shower-like facilities filled with hydrogen cyanide) was evolved.

Life in the camps was unbearable for those the Nazis did not or could not kill immediately. Rounded up by the Gestapo from their homes with little or no foreknowledge, cut off from their accustomed way of life, transported like cattle in sealed railway cars, those who survived were subjected to an instantaneous selection process in which those chosen for exploitation as slave labor were divided from those who were slated for immediate extermination. Families were broken up, husbands separated from wives, children from their parents. Those who were not immediately exterminated were forced to survive under inhuman conditions. Forced to work for incredibly long hours, stuffed into unheated barracks, with few or nonexistent toilet facilities, fed barely enough food to keep them alive, and subjected to constant work and constant beatings with the threat of imminent death hanging over their heads, inmates soon became dull and apathetic, emotionally unbalanced and argumentative. Added to these horrendous conditions, diseases spread rapidly through the camps, further torturing the inmates. The continual moaning and frequent cries of suffering humanity, and the overwhelming stench created by the general filth and the smell of burning corpses, were all-pervasive. Under these conditions, the average life expectancy was estimated at three months.

The chapters of Unit III focus on aspects of the history and activities of the SS. Chapter 11 deals with the causes and course of the Second World War, which provided the background for the growth of the SS and in many ways brought about its rise. Chapter 12 traces the history of the development of the SS and analyzes its various activities and organizations. Chapters 13 and 14 examine the evolution of National Socialist policy toward the Jews between 1933 and 1945, from the Nazis' initial attempts to remove Jews from public life to the nature and operation of the extermination centers. Finally, Chapter 15 discusses the resistance to the regime.

With the startlingly rapid conquest of France in June 1940, Hitler reached the peak of his career. He had avenged the German humiliation of 1918. Here he is in the midst of a three-hour tour of Paris.

Chapter
11

The 1939–1945 War

Hitler was always explicit about the goals he sought. His intention of "purifying" the *Volksgemeinschaft* of "foreign," "destructive" elements and realizing this racial community as a great military-political power formed two aspects of a single project. To Hitler these aims represented more than personal whims or a propagandistic blind behind which he could act as he saw fit; the historical destiny of the German people demanded their fulfillment. The first step in the Führer's task of leading the people in this mission was to eliminate all "non-Aryan" — that is, Jewish — components from the newly founded racial community; the second was to expand eastward through a war against the Slavs. These ideological goals, rather than the attempts to reconstitute German society, dominated the regime in the 1940s.

The timing and methods for reaching these ends were either never made public or announced only when they were already foregone conclusions, but preparations for each had been in the works for a long time. Beginning in 1933 but accelerating after 1935, these preparatory stages increasingly guided policy. Hitler never left any doubts that his regime embraced an expansive foreign policy. Whatever other ideological goals were intended, the policies of the mid- and late 1930s aimed directly at creating the military and psychological preconditions for war. The interlocking of foreign and domestic policy in some ways defined National Socialist totalitarianism, and the notion of the "permanent revolution" continued to play a vital role. Total rule demanded that a constant barrage hailing German diplomatic and military successes distract the public from the failures of domestic policies by holding out the hope for external expansion and, moreover, compensating the people for their loss of freedom by repeatedly reminding them of their historic mission. This constant movement led to the concentration of power in Hitler's hands and to changes in both foreign and domestic policies, but this same dynamism ultimately resulted in his and the nation's undoing.

The foreign policy of the Third Reich stemmed directly from its ideological principles. Not until 1935, however, after Hitler's consolidation of domestic power, did a more aggressive phase of Nazi foreign policy begin, although the regime rather successfully camouflaged this shift until 1938. There were a number of reasons for the secretiveness shrouding Nazi foreign policy. For one thing, Hitler took a dual approach in pursuing his policy. He showed an apparent willingness to negotiate and sought to win international recognition while simultaneously threatening, making surprise moves, and revealing *faits accomplis*. His strategy resulted in the widespread belief that, up until 1938, Hitler pursued a moderate, reasonable course toward revision of the Treaty of Versailles. The policy of appeasement practiced by the Western powers up to the very moment of the outbreak of war rested on the disastrous belief that National Socialist Germany's desire for foreign expansion could be peacefully contained. Just as Hitler's right-wing allies in 1929–33 trusted that the responsibilities of power would domesticate Hitler, so France and especially Britain thought that a just reformation of Germany's position in Europe would conciliate Hitler and check the ideological dynamism of National Socialism. Hitler, for his part, undeviatingly followed a course that, step by step, won him freedom to maneuver toward complete revision of the Versailles Treaty and then to expand German territory.

Hitler pursued this policy as far as he could through peaceful means from 1935 to 1938. He succeeded in remilitarizing the Rhineland, effecting the Anschluss with Austria, "peacefully" annexing the Sudetenland, and bringing about the consequent collapse of the Czechoslovak Republic. The ingenious turnabout in foreign policy marked by the nonaggression pact with the Soviet Union gave him a free hand to deal with Poland, even though the Western powers threatened to support Polish territorial integrity. In occupying the western sections of Poland, Germany gained yet another piece of territory immensely valuable in Hitler's plans for eastward expansion. The available evidence sustains little doubt that the idea of further eastward expansion continued to preoccupy Hitler throughout the autumn and winter of 1939. Yet he also appreciated that a future invasion of Russia could be contemplated only if he had his back secure in the West. The problem on this front was less France than Britain. Although Hitler saw the advantages of incorporating France and Belgium into a German-dominated European economy, both the means and the results of conquering Britain were less clear. Hitler knew he had to remove the threat of Britain on the continent, but how seriously he considered invading the island and the amount of materiel and the number of troops he planned to consign to this endeavor are still open questions. The feelers he put out to entice Britain into a cease-fire after the fall of France indicated that his thoughts were focused not on Britain but on his eastern borders. Only when Britain had rejected these overtures did some of Hitler's advisers urge him to attack the island, and only then were plans for Operation Sea Lion developed. The Battle of Britain in September 1940 merely strengthened the Führer's resolve not to continue the war in the West but to turn his full might once more to his primary objective. By November, preparations for the largest military campaign in history, the invasion of the Soviet Union, were in full swing.

The attack on Russia finally came on June 22, 1941. By late fall, German troops stood before Moscow. But then things changed. For the first time, Hitler was unable to counter the warnings of his military experts through an immediate success. The long-hoped-for goal of destroying Soviet power within three months turned out to be beyond his grasp. Planned as another lightning war, which had so overwhelmed first Poland, the smaller states of the West, and then France, the invasion of Russia became a very different kind of campaign. The active front no longer covered a mere few hundred miles; it now spread over three thousand miles, and the territory behind the lines was not to be enveloped by a swift set of maneuvers. Whereas a blitzkrieg required a quick display of force over a limited geographical area, the geography of Russia demanded a full-scale, heavy-infantry campaign. Initially, hundreds of thousands of Red Army soldiers were captured in huge encirclement battles, but although the rapidly advancing Wehrmacht covered thousands of miles, the Russians still continued to fight. The German lines became overextended; logistical support failed to keep up with the need for ammunition, gasoline, and food. The rainy season came, and mechanized units were mired in the mud of the primitive Russian roads. In the spring of 1942 the Wehrmacht made another gigantic effort to drive the Soviet Union out of the war, but the thrust of this southeastern offensive toward the Caucasus and its vast oil resources failed. Yet it provides a clue to the crisis that had begun to hit the Third Reich in 1941–42. The Russian campaign was not only a full-scale land operation; it was also a long-drawn-out war of attrition. Neither militarily and economically nor spiritually and psychologically was Germany prepared to wage such a campaign. By September 1942, victory was out of the question. Even Hitler finally admitted that he could not win such a protracted war.

Both the inception and the conduct of the war against Russia were the consequences of ideological obsession. By 1942, after years of success, the reverse side of the unrestrained dictatorship was becoming evident. In contrast to Germany's strategically advantageous position in 1939, the situation in 1942 presented war on many fronts; in place of isolated enemies, a powerful anti-Hitler coalition, both within and without occupied countries, had arisen. Moreover, the expansion of German Lebensraum into the vast territories of the East did not bring the expected benefits. On the contrary, Nazi expansionism and ideological rigidity proved detrimental, both to the conduct of the war and to the "new order." Occupied Russia became a great laboratory for the experiment of translating National Socialist ideology into reality. Even more so than in Germany proper, the SS state employed the policy of economic exploitation and the terror and machinery of extermination consciously, unrestrictedly, and with relentless logic. Unlike the rule by military administrations in the conquered countries of the West, from the outset of occupation a confusing multiplicity of party and SS officers controlled Russia. Racist, dogmatic, and ideologically bound policies squandered the material advantages won in conquest, turning the Russian people, imbued with hopes of liberation from Soviet domination, into recruits for the Russian army and partisan fighters against the Germans. The ideological policies of the Führer as much as his delusions and poor strategy caused the gross failures on the eastern front.

ideology to blame [handwritten margin note]

Hitler blamed the failure of the Russian campaign on his generals. One after another fell from power as scapegoats for the collapse of the ill-conceived invasion. The conflicts between Hitler and his generals, which now became endemic, did not induce military experts to hold their ground against the mistaken aims of the stubborn Führer. The successes of the first two years of the war riveted Hitler to a strategy that had to fail under the completely different conditions of the Russian war. Here, too, the reverse side of the *Führerprinzip*, which did away with consultation and permitted neither coordination of committee work nor judicious planning of the war effort, was evident. With everything subordinated to the erratic "genius" of Führer, to his idolized improvisational talents and intuitive genius, the generals resignedly accepted the role of administrative aides or limited apolitical specialists.

79. The Hossbach Memorandum

At a conference of top Nazi military officials held at the Reich chancellery building on November 5, 1937, Hitler outlined his plans for securing *Lebensraum* for the German people. The goal of territorial expansion was not new but rather reiterated the essence of the plans stated in *Mein Kampf*. Blomberg and Fritsch voiced their concerns about the practicability of Hitler's scheme, and both found themselves removed from their posts soon afterward. All those in attendance were sworn to secrecy. Hitler's adjutant, Colonel Friedrich Hossbach, took notes at this meeting. Historians refer to these notes as the Hossbach Memorandum.

Berlin, 10 Nov 1937

NOTES ON THE CONFERENCE IN THE REICHSKANZLEI
ON 5 NOV 37 FROM 1615–2030 HOURS

Present: The Führer and Reich Chancellor
The Reichsminister for War, Generalfeldmarschall v.
BLOMBERG

From U.S. Chief of Counsel for the Prosecution of Axis Criminality, *Nazi Conspiracy and Aggression* (Washington, D.C.: U.S. Government Printing Office, 1946), vol. 3, doc. no. 386-PS, pp. 295–305.

The C-in-C Army, General Freiherr von FRITSCH
The C-in-C Navy, Admiral Dr. h. c. RAEDER
The C-in-C Luftwaffe, General GOERING
The Reich Minister for Foreign Affairs Freiherr v. NEURATH
Colonel HOSSBACH

The Führer stated initially that the subject matter of today's conference was of such high importance, that its further detailed discussion would probably take place in Cabinet sessions. However, he, the Führer, had decided NOT to discuss this matter in the larger circle of the Reich Cabinet, because of its importance. His subsequent statements were the result of detailed deliberations and of the experiences of his 4½ years in Government; he desired to explain to those present his fundamental ideas on the possibilities and necessities of expanding our foreign policy and in the interests of a far-sighted policy he requested that his statements be looked upon in the case of his death as his last will and testament.

The Führer then stated:

The aim of German policy is the security and the preservation of the nation, and its propagation. This is, consequently, a problem of space.

The German nation is composed of 85 million people, which, because of the number of individuals and the compactness of habitation, form a homogeneous European racial body which cannot be found in any other country. On the other hand, it justifies the demand for larger living space more than for any other nation. If no political body exists in space, corresponding to the German racial body, then that is the consequence of several centuries of historical development, and should this political condition continue to exist, it will represent the greatest danger to the preservation of the German nation [Volkstum] at its present high level. An arrest of the deterioration of the German element in Austria and Czechoslovakia is just as little possible as the preservation of the present state in Germany itself. Instead of growth, sterility will be introduced, and as a consequence, tensions of a social nature will appear after a number of years, because political and philosophical ideas are of a permanent nature only as long as they are able to produce the basis for the realization of the actual claim of existence of a nation. The German future is therefore dependent exclusively on the solution of the need for living space. Such a solution can be sought naturally only for a limited period, about 1–3 generations.

[margin note: Need for living Space]

Before touching upon the question of solving the need for living space, it must be decided whether a solution of the German position with a good future can be attained, either by way of an autarchy or by way of an increased share in universal commerce and industry.

Autarchy: Execution will be possible only with strict National-Socialist State policy, which is the basis; assuming this can be achieved the results are as follows:

A. In the sphere of raw materials, only limited, but NOT total autarchy can be attained:

1. Wherever coal can be used for the extraction of raw materials autarchy is feasible.

2. In the case of ores the position is much more difficult. Requirements in iron and light metals can be covered by ourselves. Copper and tin, however, can NOT.

3. Cellular materials can be covered by ourselves as long as sufficient wood supplies exist. A permanent solution is not possible.

4. Edible fats — possible.

B. In the case of foods, the question of an autarchy must be answered with a definite "NO."

The general increase of living standards, compared with 30–40 years ago, brought about a simultaneous increase of the demand for an increase of personal consumption even among the producers, the farmers, themselves. The proceeds from the production increase in agriculture have been used for covering the increase in demands, therefore they represent no absolute increase in production. A further increase in production by making greater demands on the soil is *not* possible because it already shows signs of deterioration due to the use of artificial fertilizers, and it is therefore certain that, even with the greatest possible increase in production, participation in the world market could NOT be avoided.

The considerable expenditure of foreign currency to secure food by import, even in periods when harvests are good, increases catastrophically when the harvest is really poor. The possibility of this catastrophe increases correspondingly to the increase in population, and the annual 560,000 excess in births would bring about an increased consumption in bread, because the child is a greater bread eater than the adult.

Permanently to counter the difficulties of food supplies by lowering the standard of living and by rationalization is impossible in a continent which had developed an approximately equivalent standard of living. As the solving of the unemployment problem has brought into effect the complete power of consumption, some small corrections in our agricultural home production will be possible, but NOT a wholesale alteration of the standard of food consumption. Consequently autarchy becomes impossible, specifically in the sphere of food supplies as well as generally.

PARTICIPATION IN WORLD ECONOMY

There are limits to this which we are unable to transgress. The market fluctuations would be an obstacle to a secure foundation of the German position; international commercial agreements do NOT offer any guarantee for practical execution. It must be considered on principle that since the World War (1914–18) an industrialization has taken place in countries which formerly exported food. We live in a period of economic empires, in which the tendency to colonize again approaches the condition which originally motivated colonization; in Japan and Italy economic motives are the basis of their will to expand, the economic need will also drive Germany to it. Countries outside the great economic empires have special difficulties in expanding economically.

The upward tendency, which has been caused in world economy, due to armament competition, can never form a permanent basis for an economic settlement, and this latter is also hampered by the economic disruption caused by Bolshevism. It is a pronounced military weakness of those States who base their existence on export. As our exports and imports are carried out over those sea lanes which are ruled by Britain, it is more a question of security of transport rather than one of foreign currency, and this explains the great weakness in our food situation in wartime. The only way out, and one which may appear imaginary, is the securing of greater living space, an endeavor which at all times has been the cause of the formation of states and of movements of nations. It is explicable that this tendency finds no interest in Geneva and in satisfied States. Should the security of our food position be our foremost thought, then the space required for this can only be sought in Europe, but we will not copy liberal capitalist policies which rely on exploiting colonies. It is NOT a case of conquering people, but of conquering agriculturally useful space. It would also be more to the purpose to seek raw material producing territory in Europe directly adjoining the Reich and not overseas, and this solution would have to be brought into effect in one or two generations. What would be required at a later date over and above this must be left to subsequent generations. The development of great world-wide national bodies is naturally a slow process and the German people, with its strong racial root, has for this purpose the most favorable foundations in the heart of the European Continent. The history of all times — Roman Empire, British Empire — has proved that every space expansion can only be effected by breaking resistance and taking risks. Even setbacks are unavoidable; neither formerly nor today has space been found without an owner; the attacker always comes up against the proprietor.

The question for Germany is where the greatest possible conquest could be made at lowest cost.

German politics must reckon with its two hateful enemies, England and France, to whom a strong German colossus in the center of Europe would be intolerable. Both these states would oppose a further reinforcement of Germany, both in Europe and overseas, and in this opposition they would have the support of all parties. Both countries would view the building of German military strongpoints overseas as a threat to their overseas communications, as a security measure for German commerce, and retrospectively a strengthening of the German position in Europe.

England is NOT in a position to cede any of her colonial possessions to us owing to the resistance which she experiences in the Dominions.

After the loss of prestige which England has suffered owing to the transfer of Abyssinia to Italian ownership, a return of East Africa can no longer be expected. Any resistance on England's part would at best consist in the readiness to satisfy our colonial claims by taking away colonies which at the present moment are NOT in British hands, e.g. Angola. French favors would probably be of the same nature.

A serious discussion regarding the return of colonies to us could be considered only at a time when England is in a state of emergency and the German Reich is strong and well-armed. The Führer does not share the opinion that the Empire is unshakable. Resistance against the Empire is to be found less in conquered territories than amongst its competitors. The British Empire and the Roman Empire cannot be compared with one another in regard to durability; since the Punic Wars the latter did not have a serious political enemy. Only the dissolving effects which originated in Christendom, and the signs of age which creep into all states, made it possible for the Ancient Germans to subjugate Ancient Rome.

Alongside the British Empire today a number of States exist which are stronger than it. The British Mother Country is able to defend its colonial possessions only allied with other States and NOT by its own power. How could England alone, for example, defend Canada against an attack by America or its Far Eastern interests against an attack by Japan?

The singling out of the British Crown as the bearer of Empire unity is in itself an admission that the universal empire cannot be maintained permanently by power politics. The following are significant pointers in this respect.

a. Ireland's tendency for independence.
b. Constitutional disputes in India where England, by her half-measures, left the door open for Indians at a later date to utilize the nonfulfillment of constitutional promises as a weapon against Britain.
c. The weakening of the British position in the Far East by Japan.
d. The opposition in the Mediterranean to Italy which — by virtue of its history, driven by necessity and led by a genius — expands its power position and must consequently infringe British interests to an increasing extent. The outcome of the Abyssinian War is a loss of prestige for Britain which Italy is endeavoring to increase by stirring up discontent in the Mohammedan world.

It must be established in conclusion that the Empire cannot be held permanently by power politics by 45 million Britons, in spite of all the solidity of her ideals. The proportion of the populations in the Empire, compared with that of the Motherland is $9:1$, and it should act as a warning to us that if we expand in space, we must NOT allow the level of our population to become too low.

France's position is more favorable than that of England. The French

Empire is better placed geographically, the population of its colonial possessions represents a potential military increase. But France is faced with difficulties of internal politics. At the present time only 10 percent approximately of the nations have parliamentary governments whereas 90 percent of them have totalitarian governments. Nevertheless we have to take the following into our political considerations as power factors:

BRITAIN, FRANCE, RUSSIA AND THE ADJOINING SMALLER STATES

The German question can be solved only by way of force, and this is never without risk. The battles of Frederick the Great for Silesia, and Bismarck's wars against Austria and France had been a tremendous risk and the speed of Prussian action in 1870 had prevented Austria from participating in the war. If we place the decision to apply force with risk at the head of the following expositions, then we are left to reply to the questions "when" and "how." In this regard we have to decide upon three different cases.

Case 1. Period 1943–45. After this we can only expect a change for the worse. The re-arming of the Army, the Navy and the Air Force, as well as the formation of the Officers' Corps, are practically concluded. Our material equipment and armaments are modern, with further delay the danger of their becoming out-of-date will increase. In particular the secrecy of "special weapons" cannot always be safeguarded. Enlistment of reserves would be limited to the current recruiting age group and an addition from older untrained groups would be no longer available.

In comparison with the re-armament, which will have been carried out at that time by the other nations, we shall decrease in relative power. Should we not act until 1943/45, then, dependent on the absence of reserves, any year could bring about the food crisis, for the countering of which we do NOT possess the necessary foreign currency. This must be considered as a "point of weakness in the regime." Over and above that, the world will anticipate our action and will increase counter-measures yearly. Whilst other nations isolate themselves we should be forced on the offensive.

What the actual position would be in the years 1943–45 no one knows today. It is certain, however, that we can wait no longer.

On the one side the large armed forces, with the necessity for securing their upkeep, the aging of the Nazi movement and of its leaders, and on the other side the prospect of a lowering of the standard of living and a drop in the birth rate, leaves us no other choice than to act. If the Führer is still living, then it will be his irrevocable decision to solve the German space problem no later than 1943–45. The necessity for action before 1943–45 will come under consideration in cases 2 and 3.

must act now

345

Case 2. Should the social tensions in France lead to an internal political crisis of such dimensions that it absorbs the French Army and thus renders it incapable for employment in war against Germany, then the time for action against Czechoslovakia has come.

Case 3. It would be equally possible to act against Czechoslovakia if France should be so tied up by a war against another State, that it cannot "proceed" against Germany.

For the improvement of our military political position it must be our first aim, in every case of entanglement by war, to conquer Czechoslovakia and Austria simultaneously, in order to remove any threat from the flanks in case of a possible advance Westwards. In the case of a conflict with France it would hardly be necessary to assume that Czechoslovakia would declare war on the same day as France. However, Czechoslovakia's desire to participate in the war will increase proportionally to the degree to which we are being weakened. Its actual participation could make itself felt by an attack on Silesia, either towards the North or the West.

Once Czechoslovakia is conquered — and a mutual frontier, Germany-Hungary is obtained — then a neutral attitude by Poland in a German-French conflict could more easily be relied upon. Our agreements with Poland remain valid only as long as Germany's strength remains unshakeable; should Germany have any setbacks then an attack by Poland against East Prussia, perhaps also against Pomerania, and Silesia, must be taken into account.

Assuming a development of the situation, which would lead to a planned attack on our part in the years 1943–45, then the behavior of France, Poland and Russia would probably have to be judged in the following manner:

The Führer believes personally that in all probability England and perhaps also France have already silently written off Czechoslovakia, and that they have got used to the idea that this question would one day be cleaned up by Germany. The difficulties in the British Empire and the prospect of being entangled in another long-drawn-out European War, were decisive factors in the non-participation of England in a war against Germany. The British attitude would certainly NOT remain without influence on France's attitude. An attack by France without British support is hardly probable assuming that its offensive would stagnate along our Western fortifications. Without England's support, it would also NOT be necessary to take into consideration a march by France through Belgium and Holland, and this would also not have to be reckoned with by us in case of a conflict with France, as in every case it would have as consequence the enmity of Great Britain. Naturally, we should in every case have to bar our frontier during the operation of our attacks against Czechoslovakia and Austria. It must be taken into consideration here that Czechoslovakia's defense measures will increase in strength from year to year, and that a consolidation of the inside values of the Austrian army will also be effected in the course of years. Although the population of Czechoslovakia in the first place is not a thin one, the embodiment of Czechoslovakia and Austria would nevertheless constitute the conquest of food for 5–6 million people, on the basis that a compulsory emigration of 2 million from Czechoslovakia and of 1 million from Austria could be carried out. The annexation of the two States to Germany militarily and politically would constitute a considerable relief, owing to shorter and better frontiers, the freeing of fighting personnel for other purposes and the possibility of re-constituting new armies up to a strength of about 12 Divisions, representing a new division per 1 million population.

No opposition to the removal of Czechoslovakia is expected on the part of Italy; however, it cannot be judged today what would be her attitude in the Austrian question since it would depend largely on whether the Duce was alive at the time or not.

The measure and speed of our action would decide Poland's attitude. Poland will have little inclination to enter the war against a victorious Germany, with Russia in its rear.

Military participation by Russia must be countered by the speed of our operations; it is a question whether this need be taken into consideration at all in view of Japan's attitude.

Should Case 2 occur — paralyzation of France by a Civil War — then the situation should be utilized *at any time* for operations against Czechoslovakia, as Germany's most dangerous enemy would be eliminated.

The Führer sees Case 3 looming nearer; it could develop from the existing tensions in the Mediterranean, and should it occur he has firmly decided to make use of it any time, perhaps even as early as 1938.

Following recent experiences in the course of the events of the war in Spain, the Führer does NOT see an early end to hostilities there. Taking into consideration the time required for past offensives by Franco, a further three years duration of war is within the bounds of possibility. On the other hand, from the German point of view a 100 per cent victory by Franco is not desirable; we are more interested in a continuation of the war and preservation of the tensions in the Mediterranean. Should Franco be in sole possession of the Spanish Peninsula it would mean the end of Italian intervention and the presence of Italy on the Balearic Isles. As our interests are directed towards continuing the war in Spain, it must be the task of our future policy to strengthen Italy in her fight to hold on to the Balearic Isles. However, a solidification of Italian positions on the Balearic Isles can NOT be tolerated either by France or by England and could lead to a war by France and England against Italy, in which case Spain, if entirely in white (i.e. Franco's) hands, could participate on the side of Italy's enemies. A subjugation of Italy in such a war appears very unlikely. Additional raw materials could be brought to Italy via Germany. The Führer believes that Italy's military strategy would be to remain on the defensive against France on the Western frontier and carry out operations against France from Libya against North African French colonial possessions.

As a landing of French-British troops on the Italian coast can be discounted, and as a French offensive via the Alps to Upper Italy would be extremely difficult and would probably stagnate before the strong Italian fortifications, French lines of communication by the Italian fleet will to a great extent paralyze the transport of fighting personnel from North Africa to France, so that at its frontiers with Italy and Germany France will have at its disposal solely the metropolitan fighting forces.

If Germany profits from this war by disposing of the Czechoslovakian and the Austrian questions, the probability must be assumed that England — being at war with Italy — would not decide to commence operations against Germany. Without British support a warlike action by France against Germany is not to be anticipated.

The date of our attack on Czechoslovakia and Austria must be made dependent on the course of the Italian-English-French war and would not be simultaneous with the commencement of military agreements with Italy, but of full independence and, by exploiting this unique favorable opportunity he wishes to begin to carry out operations against Czechoslovakia. The attack on Czechoslovakia would have to take place with the "speed of lightning" [blitzartig schnell].

Field Marshal von Blomberg and General von Fritsch in giving their estimate on the situation, repeatedly pointed out that England and France must not appear as our enemies, and they stated that the war with Italy would NOT bind the French army to such an extent that it would NOT be in a position to commence operations on our Western frontier with superior forces. General von Fritsch estimated the French forces which would presumably be employed on the Alpine frontier against Italy to be in the region of 20 divisions, so that a strong French superiority would still remain on our Western frontier. The French would, according to German reasoning, attempt to advance into the Rhineland. We should consider the lead which France has got in mobilization, and quite apart from the very small value of our then existing fortifications — which was pointed out particularly by Field Marshal von Blomberg — the four motorized divisions which had been laid down for the West would be more or less incapable of movement. With regard to our offensive in a South-Easterly direction, Field Marshal von Blomberg draws special attention to the strength of the Czechoslovakian fortifications, the building of which had assumed the character of a Maginot line and which would present extreme difficulties to our attack.

General von Fritsch mentioned that it was the purpose of a study which he had laid on for this winter to investigate the possibilities of carrying out operations against Czechoslovakia with special consideration of the conquest of the Czechoslovakian system of fortifications; the General also stated that owing to the prevailing conditions he would have to relinquish his leave abroad, which was to begin on 10 November. This intention was countermanded by the Führer who gave as a reason that the possibility of the conflict was not to be regarded as being so imminent. In reply to the remark by the Minister for Foreign Affairs, that an Italian-English-French conflict be not as near as the Führer appeared to assume, the Führer stated that the date which appeared to him to be a possibility was summer 1938. In reply to statements by Field Marshal von Blomberg and General von Fritsch regarding England and France's attitude, the Führer repeated his previous statements and said that he was convinced of Britain's non-participation and that consequently he did not believe in military action by France against Germany. Should the Mediterranean conflict already mentioned lead to a general mobilization in Europe, then we should have to commence operations against Czechoslovakia immediately. If, however, the powers who are not participating in the war should declare their disinterestedness, then Germany would, for the time being, have to side with this attitude.

In view of the information given by the Führer, General Goering considered it imperative to think of a reduction or abandonment of our military undertaking in Spain. The Führer agreed to this in so far as he believed this decision should be postponed for a suitable date.

The second part of the discussion concerned materiel armament questions.

[signed] Hossbach

80. The Annexation of Austria in the Eyes of the German Public

Hitler's annexation of Austria caused the mood of the German people to run the gamut of emotions. The assessment of the situation in March 1938 by the outlawed Social Democrats pointed to public depression and a general fear of imminent war with the Western powers, to relief once tensions were relaxed, and ultimately to an increased admiration for Hitler, who had achieved a diplomatic coup.

The effect of the Austrian developments on the German public was quite varied. The following reports evidence that it can hardly be said that the entire nation was caught up in an ecstasy of joy. In addition to the loud enthusiasm, many secretly feared that war would come. Often this fear

From *Deutschland-Berichte der Sozialdemokratischen Partei Deutschlands (Sopade), 1934–1940* (Frankfurt: Verlag Petra Nettelbeck, 1980), 5 (March 1938): 256–57, 259–60. Translated by Dieter Kuntz.

was the initial reaction, which then gave way to muscle-flexing when it became evident that the Western powers would go no further than to protest on paper. Our agents observed this everywhere, and in almost all reports a bitterness comes through over the fact that these same Western powers who had blocked the republic's union with Austria were now backing down against this application of brute force.

Indeed, this contradictory behavior of the Western powers brings with it great psychological danger. The peace-loving segment of the population will lose its faith in the politics of international reconciliation and will gain the impression that force is necessary to achieve anything. Consequently, people will be more inclined to accept Hitler's power tactics. The more hawkish segment of the population will come to believe that the Western powers are afraid and will in the future continue to back down, so that Germany will have free rein. . . .

A report from Bavaria: "Hitler's speech of February 20 was followed by all with great interest. Contrary to other occasions, this time there was no indifference. All were anxiously awaiting what Hitler would have to say regarding Austria. [Austrian chancellor] Schuschnigg's speech had aroused the hopes of the middle-class opposition. People were convinced that Hitler had suffered a defeat and that Austria would defend itself. . . . [Hitler's speech] was a disappointment because no one could figure out just what exactly he wanted. No one had expected that Hitler would make a speech threatening war without making every possible attempt to placate the Western powers. Consequently this speech was to have the effect of heightening the fear of war. The public's mood became more depressed with every new day."

A second Bavarian report: "The entry of German troops into Austria stirred all feelings. On Saturday morning the prevailing opinion was that war was inevitable. People thought that France would march into Spain, that Czechoslovakia would mobilize, and that Russia would come to the aid of Czechoslovakia, and so on. . . . In summation, one can say that the mood of the people was one of deep depression. It was quite unlike 1914. . . ."

"By Saturday evening, when the radio transmitted Hitler's reception in Linz [Austria], the mood began to change. A noticeable relaxation of tension set in. Now there would be no war after all; sons [in the military] would come home again; no enemy planes would appear; Austria was now part of Germany; Hitler had done it after all. The Nazis were back on top. 'Without firing a shot, that is an accomplishment; and the others simply fell over! And then the *Gleichschaltung* of Austria. This tempo, this pace — no one expected this. Hitler is a master politician; yes, he really is a great statesman; greater than Napoleon, because he is conquering the world without waging war.' These were the opinions that were expressed. . . ."

81. The Nonaggression Pact with the Soviet Union

On August 23, 1939, Germany and the Soviet Union shocked the world by entering into a pact stating that the two countries would not go to war against each other. This treaty had dire consequences for the state of Poland, caught between the two powers. A secret protocol between the two states divided northeastern Europe "in the event of a territorial restructuring" into separate spheres of interest. The pact gave Hitler a free hand to attack Poland. The text of the agreement is reprinted below.

Guided by the desire to strengthen the cause of peace between Germany and the Union of Soviet Socialist Republics, and basing themselves on the fundamental stipulations of the Neutrality Agreement concluded between Germany and the Union of Soviet Socialist Republics in April, 1926, the German Government and the Government of the Union of Soviet Socialist Republics have come to the following agreement:

ARTICLE 1.

The two contracting parties undertake to refrain from any act of force, any aggressive act, and any attacks against each other undertaken either singly or in conjunction with any other Powers.

ARTICLE 2.

If one of the contracting parties should become the object of war-like action on the part of a third Power, the other contracting party will in no way support the third Power.

ARTICLE 3.

The Governments of the two contracting parties will in future remain in consultation with one another in order to inform each other about questions which touch their common interests.

ARTICLE 4.

Neither of the two contracting parties will join any group of Powers which is directed, mediately or immediately, against the other party.

From German Library of Information, *Documents on the Events Preceding the Outbreak of War,* compiled and published by the German Foreign Office (Berlin, 1939; New York, 1940), pp. 370–71. The secret protocol is from Hans-Adolf Jacobsen and Werner Jochmann, eds., *Ausgewählte Dokumente zur Geschichte des Nationalsozialismus, 1933–1945* (Bielefeld, Germany: Neue Gesellschaft GmbH, 1960), Document 23. VIII. 1939. Translated by Dieter Kuntz.

ARTICLE 5.

In case disputes or conflicts on questions of any kind should arise between the two contracting parties, the two partners will solve these disputes or conflicts exclusively by friendly exchange of views or if necessary by arbitration commissions.

ARTICLE 6.

The present agreement is concluded for the duration of ten years with the stipulation that unless one of the contracting partners denounces it one year before its expiration, it will automatically be prolonged by five years.

ARTICLE 7.

The present agreement shall be ratified in the shortest possible time. The instruments of ratification are to be exchanged in Berlin. The treaty comes into force immediately after it has been signed.

Done in two original documents in the German and Russian languages, respectively.

Moscow, August 23, 1939

For the German Government
RIBBENTROP

*As plenipotentiary of the Government
of the Union of Soviet
Socialist Republics*
MOLOTOV

SECRET ADDITIONAL PROTOCOL

On the occasion of the signing of the Nonaggression Pact between the German Reich and the Union of Soviet Socialist Republics, the undersigned plenipotentiaries of the two parties discussed, during strictly confidential talks, the question of the demarcation of their respective spheres of interest in eastern Europe. The talks led to the following result:

1. In the event of a territorial-political restructuring in the territories belonging to the Baltic States (Finland, Estonia, Latvia and Lithuania), the northern border of Lithuania shall also constitute the border of the spheres of interest between Germany and the USSR. In this connection the interest of Lithuania in the Vilna district is recognized by both sides.

2. In the event of a territorial-political restructuring of the territories belonging to the Polish state, the spheres of interest of the USSR and Germany shall be defined approximately by the line of the rivers Pissa, Narew,

Weichsel and San.[1] The question of whether the interests of both sides make the maintenance of an independent Polish state appear desirable, and how this state's borders should be defined, can ultimately be determined only in the course of further political developments. In any case, the two governments will resolve this question by way of amicable agreement.

3. In regard to southeastern Europe, the Soviet side emphasizes that it has interests in Bessarabia. The German side declares that it has no political interest at all in these territories.

4. This protocol is to be treated as top secret by both sides.

Moscow, August 23, 1939   [signed]   VON RIBBENTROP
                                                         W. MOLOTOV

82. Winter on the Russian Front

For German soldiers, the most terrifying aspect of fighting on the eastern front was the prospect of having to deal with the extremely harsh Russian winter. The Soviets had not been brought to their knees by the end of 1941, as Hitler had hoped. As the Russian winter settled in, German fortunes began to fade. Hitler suspended his offensive in December, and the German army, ill prepared for a winter campaign, attempted to hold the positions that had been won. The fear of winter fighting is expressed in this soldier's letter, which pleads for additional support from the home front.

November 5, 1941

Dear family C. F. D———:

A group of us Schleswig-Holstein infantrymen, after hard fighting in the Russian campaign, are still engaged in battle and are ever vigilant of our stubborn, cunning enemy, the Bolsheviks. We all hope with burning hearts that we will have conquered this enemy before the onset of the fierce Russian winter. But even then, after the victory, the conquered territory will have to be secured by German troops. We infantrymen know that after countless attacks against Russian bunkers and field fortifications, we will have the additional difficult task of keeping guard in the East.

From *Nationalsozialistische deutsche Arbeiter-Partei, Hauptarchiv 1919–45* (Stanford, CA: Hoover Institution on War, Revolution, and Peace), H. A. reel 50, folder 1180 (District President's Report, Schleswig-Holstein, 1942). Translated by Dieter Kuntz.

---

[1] These were the German names for the rivers. The demarcation can be traced approximately along the line formed by the rivers Vistula, Narew, and San.

As leader of my unit I have a great concern: how am I to bring these valiant men through the Russian winter? We are, of course, officially being taken care of from high up; all do their utmost — our superiors and our relatives back home. But I do have one group of soldiers whose parents or relatives have sent few or no packages at all from home. Again and again I have to witness how on mail days these men await the calling of their names with great anticipation, and how they gloomily steal away because no one at home has thought of them.

By making inquiries among my soldiers, I was able to collect a number of addresses of businesses and families who would like to, and are in a position to, gladden the hearts of my valiant infantrymen by sending any kind of gifts for this winter — but especially for Christmas. This is why I have turned to you with a heartfelt plea for your support of my endeavor, to the best of your ability. Soldiers are in need of everything. The most urgent need, however, is for long socks, gloves, wrist warmers, earmuffs, support bandages, pullovers, and shawls. Desirable items include books, magazines, playing cards, games of all sorts, harmonicas, and the like.

Candies and sweetmeats are fondly received, especially at Christmas.

83. Life on the Home Front

The war brought with it many hardships for Germans on the home front. Deprivation, uncertainty, and insecurity caused by dislocation and family separation as well as the overriding fear of physical danger were only a few of the tremendous psychological ramifications of four and a half years of warfare. The following recollections of those years by a German woman who grew up during the war chronicle these experiences and emotions. Her story describes the evacuation of civilians from border towns prior to the onset of hostilities and vividly portrays the exhaustion brought on by scurrying to air raid shelters each night during the later stages of the war.

The erection of the "West Wall" (Siegfried Line) in 1938–39 started the rumors that we would be in a state of war with France before the end of 1939. Living close to the French border (Lorraine) made everyone aware that our lives and homes would be in danger, and the possibility of an evacuation was the topic of neighborhood conversations. Women practiced packing essentials in suitcases, pillowcases, et cetera. The lucky ones with relatives [eastward] across the Rhine River made contact and plans for quarters. In other words, it came as no surprise when evacuation plans became reality.

From Louise Willbourn (formerly of Zweibrücken, Germany), personal interview, December 27, 1990, and January 10, 1991. Reprinted by permission of Louise Willbourn.

Burned into my memory are the early morning hours of Friday, September 1, 1939. I was nine years old. We were aroused from sleep by a neighbor yelling to his daughter-in-law next door, "Total mobilization! Total mobilization!" Those words fell like a bombshell. My father and mother jumped out of bed, my mother crying, my dad saying, "Well, this means war." I had visions of all good things coming to an end, maybe even dying. Not long after we were informed by local officials that we had to evacuate. Women and children were told to leave first and were instructed to pack what they could carry and assemble at the soccer stadium near the train station. Mother and I and hundreds of others sat at the stadium on our suitcases and waited for several hours. Everything seemed total chaos. We could see trains going by across the river with evacuees from Saarbrücken and other towns of the Saarland. No train was available for us. As the day grew longer my father came and said, "Your first destination is Kaiserslautern and I will take you there by car." My aunt and uncle went with us. We spent a night in a big hall at the designated school, sleeping on straw pallets with many other people from the border towns. In the morning we were fed and loaded onto a train for our destination in Bavaria. At noon the train stopped and we went out on the platform of the station, where Red Cross Workers gave us *Eintopf* [stew]. Late afternoon we reached Lichtenfels, in Bavaria. Farmers with horse-drawn wagons were waiting and the wagon we boarded took us to a little village. At the village we were driven to the local *Gasthaus* and sat outside in the beer garden waiting for the local residents to come and choose their boarders. Most of these people were farmers and were looking for people to help with chores. My aunt and uncle had a hard time finding quarters as they were in their late fifties and not in good health. Mother and I were lucky; a prosperous farmer took us in. Mother insisted that she would not go anywhere without Aunt and Uncle, so room was made for them too. On Sunday, September 3, France and England declared war. That day normally would have been the day of our hometown fair. Mother started crying because she was worried about my two brothers, who were in the infantry and navy. She worried also about our home, which in our absence served as quarters for German soldiers defending the western border. Our host tried to calm mother down and said, "Don't worry, the war will be over in six weeks — it will be a blitzkrieg." That was the first time that we heard that expression.

After a few days we were informed by the local Nazi party leader that we had to move on and make room for evacuees from Saarbrücken. It never made sense to us why they couldn't have moved the Saarbrücken people to other destinations. After a tearful goodbye we were again loaded into a train and landed in another small town. Just as before, Aunt and Uncle were again clinging to us so that a place for them could be found. Mother did not like our new place because of the mice in the bedroom.

We were evacuated until June of 1940; by then German troops had overrun the French and we were allowed to return to our homes.

I remember when the bombing raids started in 1940. Cologne and Hamburg were the first cities to be bombed, and we heard it on the radio. I was ten years old, in the fifth grade. Scores of Allied airplanes had to pass over our territory with cities like Ludwigshafen, Mannheim, Augsburg, Frankfurt, Schweinfurt, Stuttgart, and Munich as targets. I will never forget the humming sound of hundreds of airplanes above — the town in total blackout, not even a cigarette aglow for fear some pilot might unload his bombs early.

In 1940 Zweibrücken was bombed twice. Only a few bombs fell, but they were incendiary ones, so a few buildings caught fire. No one knew why the bombs fell, but everyone came to see where they had hit. From 1941 to 1944, our town was relatively quiet — a few incidents of trains being shot at from marauding daylight airplanes — and we felt fortunate to live in a small town that had no industry which might have been targeted. Usually we went to bed at nine or ten P.M.; an hour or two later the sirens would go off, alerting the population that enemy airplanes were headed our way. The pre-alarm was a sound with long wails. This gave the people enough time to prepare for cover. Often there was no pre-alarm and the sirens would sound their urgent wailing in very short intervals. We would jump into our clothes, which were ready at the bedside, grab our packed bags, and run to the nearest air raid shelters as fast as our legs could carry us. Older men — all the young ones were gone — would periodically go outside to see if it was all clear. When the planes came back, one, two, or three hours later, their motors sounded quieter. They had dropped the excess weight of bombs they earlier had on board.

As the years of war went on, the sirens sounded more often and we had to leave our warm beds almost every night. For a school kid that was very tiring, and I was longing for peace. To sleep through a whole night without fear and interruption would have been like heaven on earth.

My school attendance continued with only occasional interruptions (even while we were evacuated) until December of 1944, when the war made it impossible to continue school. School did not begin again until June of 1945. During school we also often ran to air raid shelters. We had designated areas because the school basements were not safe enough. Primary school children were assigned to collect scrap metal and newspapers once a week. On certain days we also had to go in groups to the meadows and snip nettles, et cetera, to be used in medicine or go into the potato fields to pick the potato beetles, which were destroying the crops. We also had to collect clothing for soldiers on the Russian front during the hard winter months. Food was rationed, but we were lucky because we lived in a small town and were able to plant a garden and had some chickens. We traded things with other people.

By June of 1944, as the Allied troops came closer to the German border, we could hear the thunder of the cannons. In November–December 1944, our town was teeming with German troops, mainly Waffen SS and Panzer divisions. We knew something of importance was going on. By now we spent every night in an air raid shelter, which was an old converted potato cellar. The town was almost totally evacuated, but we preferred to take our chances at home. Soldiers would come to our house to listen to the news on the radio. They were mostly military police and Waffen SS. By January they were all gone, and news came from the front that a ferocious battle was raging in the Eiffel Forest. Later we found out it was the last German offensive. After this the thunder of the cannons came closer. From January to March 14, 1945, we spent most of our time running between our house and the air raid shelter. We timed ourselves to running between "pfiffs" [whistlings] of the cannon balls. My father said when you can hear the whistle, that's when they shoot past you. Maybe that was why we did not get hit, but we did have a few close encounters. Once when Mother and I were collecting kindling wood in the forest, a small enemy plane suddenly appeared above us and sent bullets flying through the bushes.

On March 14, 1945, at seven or eight o'clock P.M., we heard an enemy reconnaissance plane persistently flying over our area. We heard the plane for several days, and nicknamed it Victor. That night the noise was so persistent that my father went outside to check. He came running back in the house, yelling "Run, run for your life, this is it!" Mother and I grabbed our bags and ran out of the house. The night had been transformed into bright daylight. Our 750-year-old town was leveled that night, and the city center totally destroyed. We had made it to the shelter, but we found out later that around 500 to 750 people lost their lives. A small number, thanks to the evacuation. My father opened the heavy outer door of the shelter, and we could see that the houses across the street were still standing. Eventually we made it back to our house that night, packed a few more things, and headed for the bunker in the forest. The bunker was very crowded when we got there. We had thermos bottles with water, dried bread, and salamis, which allowed us to live in the bunker for a while. On the seventeenth of March, 1945, German SS troops came and cleared the bunker. They did not care where the people would find shelter.

We went back to our house, got a bicycle and a hand cart, loaded both with our few belongings, and headed for the hills about twenty kilometers away.

On our way to the hills [Sickingerhöhe] we saw dead people on the side of the road. We also saw German troops in flight, gunfire and swooping planes, and then there was silence. On March 21, we saw the first American soldiers. On March 22, I was at last able to again sleep through an entire night.

84. Berlin: The Last Year of the War

The following excerpts from the diary of a woman journalist depicts life in Berlin during the last year of the war. Depression, pessimism, resignation, and an incredible war weariness marked the mood of the city.

Berlin, 31 May 1944

Pessimism is increasing. The Russian front is drawing closer. Where should my flight take me, I often ask myself, because I am prepared to flee. But for the time being we are still dancing on a stage that grows smaller and smaller and is surrounded by an abyss.

Spent the day before yesterday with Ulrich Dörtenbach in the Rose Theater. [Saw] Lessing's *Miss Sara Simpson,* starring Inge of Austria. This theater in the eastern section of the city, in the midst of the destroyed but, even in earlier times, desolate Frankfurter Allee, is one of the cheeriest showplaces in Berlin. Workers, craftsmen, housewives, and the businessmen who live in this section have had season tickets for decades. Here one is able to find a piece of the Berlin of old, no "class-conscious proletarians," no KdF [*Kraft durch Frende,* Strength Through Joy] functions, no termites, only individual human beings. Hauptmann, Ibsen, Schiller, Shakespeare, and good old burlesque are on the program. Never trash and never hokum. In the refreshment room — a well-proportioned room with mirrors built in 1877 — a small orchestra played during intermission. I could have caressed them all, musicians as well as audience; these people, with their tired faces and stooping posture, who in spite of difficult conditions, poor nourishment, and the constant threat of air raids, come here to find release from tension.

6 June 1944

It began tonight. The invasion. Excitement among the editorial staff. We have received instructions to write rejoicingly about this long-desired event. Hurrah, the time is finally here; now we will show them how we will chase them out again. Finally, we are moving toward the ultimate victory!

However, all 'round [there is] only skepticism and fear of air raids. Great doubt if the Atlantic fortifications will hold.

10 June 1944

As a substitute [for the editor] I was charged with composing the front page, and had to carry a photograph from the *Times* which showed the invasion. Incredible that it was cleared by the censors. It is a frightening

From Ursula von Kardorff, *Berliner Aufzeichnungen* (Munich: Biederstein Verlag, 1962), pp. 156–60, 163, 262. Translated by Dieter Kuntz. Reprinted by permission of Biederstein Verlag, Munich.

sight — hundreds of little dots, paratroopers and tiny boats; it looks like a swarm of grasshoppers attacking the coast. The defense appears meager. In any case, they have gotten a foothold, and "Fortress Europe" is now besieged from two sides as well as by air. Maybe now things will move rapidly.

Berlin is in a curious mood. A mixture of apathy and inordinate pleasure-seeking. The janitor's wife, who cleans at my place, warningly raises her index finger [and proclaims]: "So, soon it'll be over with little Adolf, maybe it'll go fast." No one saves these days. . . . Witnessed ordinary soldiers leaving gratuities as high as half a month's pay. The waiter at a small pub at the Gendarme Market bought himself a small farm — purely from the tips he received by procuring a bottle of Mosel [wine]. Money flows through hands like water.

16 June 1944

I arrive at the editor's office, Willy looks at me, he seems disturbed. In front of him lies the blue page containing the secret news reports: the apocalypse has begun, we are shooting at London with long-distance weapons that are supposed to destroy the city. The new weapon is called V-I. By noon the reports are publicly aired. According to Goebbels, V-II, V-III, and V-IV are soon to follow. The whole world will blow up by the time V-V rolls around.

In all the pubs, places where usually no one speaks his mind, there is much talk of vengeance, Allied vengeance, that is. A soldier who boasted that soon we would have the war won was contradicted. It is hard to fool Berliners. Goebbels has it nowhere so tough as here. Lately everyone speaks of gas warfare. That would really crown all of this horror.

During warm evenings when friends come over, we sit with them on the roof, which is flat. Several benches are up there, covered with dust. . . . All 'round one sees burned-out houses without roofs and lofts.

85. The Bombing of Dresden

During February 1945 the city of Dresden in Saxony was devastated by a massive air attack by British incendiary bombs and American explosive bombs. A "fire storm" engulfed what remained of the city, increasing the death toll to as many as a hundred thousand people. Götz Bergander, a radio journalist who was born in 1927 and who lived in Dresden during the bombardment, survived the attack and later recalled the terror of those days.

There had been two American daylight attacks on Dresden, one in October 1944, one in January 1945. The latter was somewhat heavier and we

From Johannes Steinhoff, Peter Pechel, and Dennis Showalter, *Voices from the Third Reich* (Washington, D.C.: Regnery Gateway, 1989), pp. 227–31.

knew that Dresden wasn't going to come out of it untouched. Nevertheless, we had no idea what we were in for; we didn't have the experience they had in Hamburg, Berlin, Kassel, or the Ruhrgebiet.

I got myself a grid map of Germany. You could listen in on a radio channel — we called it the flak channel but it actually came from the headquarters near Berlin — which transmitted coded air intelligence. Whenever I was home I listened to this channel and marked the flight paths on the large map which I'd covered with onionskin paper. I still have this map.

And that's how it was on the evening of February 13, which happened to be Mardi Gras. You could determine the approach of a massive raid far into central Germany, beyond Leipzig. When the alarm sounded, it was approximately 20 minutes before 10:00 P.M.

The city was already filled with refugees; everything was a dull, war gray. The train stations were bursting with people. I had already participated in some so-called refugee aid there. We received refugees from Silesia and tried to get them and their baggage out of the city as quickly as possible. They were taken to old dance halls, ballrooms, and cinemas in the suburbs, but some always remained in the city center — those who'd just arrived and had not yet been accommodated.

According to certain city documents, Dresden had approximately 640,000 inhabitants, and I'd estimate that there were perhaps a million people in the city, so there were about 300,000 refugees. There were no bunkers at all — not one public air raid shelter. At Dresden's main train station, luggage storage rooms and basements had been set up as shelters.

People thought Dresden would be spared. There were rumors that the British thought a great deal of Dresden as a cultural center. The story also went around that an aunt of Churchill's lived in Dresden, and in 1945 the rumor circulated that the Allies intended to use Dresden as their capital. Even by then, we expected partition; we thought the Russians would occupy the eastern half and the others the western half. Finally, people said, Dresden is full of hospitals.

All of this was wrong. All these claims, including the one that Dresden was protected because it was a "hospital" city, were false. Dresden was completely unprotected. The flak had been withdrawn during the winter. Half the guns were sent to the Ruhr to strengthen the air defense there, only to be lost when the Americans overran the area. It was ridiculous. The Dresden anti-aircraft troops weren't killed in Dresden, but died fighting against the Americans.

As I listened to the flak channel, I had a feeling of ever-increasing dread, but layered with excitement. You could compare it to what every soldier feels before he has to leave the trench. You're afraid, yet at the same time very excited, wondering what's going to happen. Talk about butterflies! I took my radio down to the air raid shelter and tried to tune into the flak channel. Our shelter warden was outside.

While I was still fiddling with the radio dial he came running down into the cellar and called, "It's getting light, it's getting light, it's bright as day outside! They're coming, they're coming, the dive bombers are here!" I told him: "But that's impossible, dive bombers can't fly at night." He said: "I saw them, they came right over the Friedrichstadt hospital." After the war we found out that he had really seen Mosquitos come down with target flares. They dropped the target markers about 500 yards from where we lived, and the markers exploded in the air before they hit the ground. The so-called "Christmas trees" came down by parachute. Everything was quiet for awhile, until we heard the bombers and the first explosions.

It was as if a huge noisy conveyor belt was rolling over us, a noise punctuated with detonations and tremors. It lasted for about 25 minutes before it gradually ceased. Then there was absolute quiet.

I had tuned in to the local air raid broadcasts, and their last announcement had been, "Attention! Attention! This is your local air defense office. Bombs in the city area. Citizens, keep sand and water ready." Then it was cut off.

I went outside after this first attack because our warden told us we had to look for incendiaries. We didn't find any, but coming out of the cellar was unforgettable: the night sky was illuminated with pink and red. The houses were black silhouettes, and a red cloud of smoke hovered over everything. I left our courtyard and climbed onto the roof of the factory next door with my camera. I thought, "You have to take a picture of this."

People ran toward us totally distraught, smeared with ash, and with wet blankets wrapped around their heads. These people made it out of the burning areas without too much difficulty, because the firestorm only developed about half an hour to an hour after the first of the two night attacks. All we heard was, "Everything's gone, everything's on fire."

In the meantime, many people had gathered in our courtyard. They had all come to our house because it was still intact. Everyone talked at once until someone yelled, "They're coming back, they're coming back!" Sure enough, through the general confusion we heard the alarm sirens go off again. The alarm system in the city had ceased to function, but we could hear the sirens from the neighboring villages warning of a second attack. That's when I was overcome with panic, and I'm also speaking for the rest of my family and those who lived in our house. It was sheer panic! We thought this couldn't be possible, that they wouldn't do such a thing. They wouldn't drop more bombs on a city that was already an inferno. We were a target not even the worst shot could miss. We rushed into the cellar, and the second attack began just like the first one.

The first raid was flown by the famous 5th Bomber Group which had been specially preselected for the initial incendiary attack. The rest of the bomber groups came in for the second attack. The British really put everything they had into the air that night, though not all of it was used against Dresden. Approximately 800 planes were deployed against Dresden, and another 300 went against a refinery near Leipzig.

This attack left exhaustion and tension in its wake, a feeling of utter helplessness and terror. Since high-explosive bombs came down in our immediate vicinity, we had no idea of what it looked like outside. Neither did we hear the slapping sound of incendiaries. There was an indescribable roar in the air: the fire. The thundering fire reminded me of the biblical catastrophes I had heard about in my education in the humanities. I was aghast. I can't describe seeing this city burn in any other way. The color had changed as well. It was no longer pinkish-red. The fire had become a furious white and yellow, and the sky was just one massive mountain of cloud. The blaze roared, with intermittent blasts of either delayed-action bombs or unexploded bombs which were engulfed by the flames.

In the morning I turned on my radio and listened to the BBC. On the seven o'clock news, the BBC reported: "Last night, Dresden, one of the few German cities thus far to be spared, was attacked by RAF bombers with great success."

Later, people arrived from the inner city asking if we still had water. We said yes and opened the hydrants. Several of them settled into our house, but many others told us, "Out, out, get out of the city. Get away from here," and went on. Some were speechless with horror. They only said, "My home and everything in it are gone."

Since the factory supplied its own power and water, it could be kept running. My father, who was the manager, had to decide whether work should continue. We produced yeast for baked goods. My father said that food was important, so we'd have to keep operating. And the workers showed up too. I don't know if anyone can work like the Germans. It was amazing. Some even came on their bicycles between the two night raids. I still remember one of them pedalling up and my father asking him, "What are you doing here?" And he replied, "I just had to see if the shop's still in one piece."

The city was absolutely quiet. The sound of the fires had died out. The rising smoke created a dirty, gray pall which hung over the entire city. The wind had calmed, but a slight breeze was blowing westward, away from us. That's how, standing in the courtyard, I suddenly thought I could hear sirens again. And sure enough, there they were. I shouted, and by then we could already hear the distant whine of engines. We rushed down into the cellar. The roar of the engines grew louder and louder, and the daylight attack began. This was the American 8th Air Force, and their attack came right down on our heads.

Normally, there were only 20 to 25 of us down in the cellar. But now, with many people off the street, including those who'd stopped over at our house, there were about 100 of us. Nevertheless, no one panicked — we were too numb and demoralized from the night before. We just sat there. The attack rolled closer, and then a bomb hit. It was like a bowling ball that bounced, or jumped perhaps, and at that moment the lights went out. The whole basement filled with dust. When the bomb carpet reached us, I crouched in a squatting position, my head between my legs. The air pressure was immense, but only for a moment. The rubber seals on the windows and the steel doors probably helped to absorb some of the impact. Someone screamed, and then it was quiet. Then a voice shouted, "It's all right, nothing's happened." It was the shelter warden.

Someone turned on a flashlight. We could see again, and that meant a lot. If it had remained dark, I don't know if the people wouldn't have jumped up and screamed to get out. However, after this flashlight went on everyone relaxed, and in spite of the loud crash that made me think the whole house was caving in on top of us, a loud voice shouted, "Calm down, calm down, nothing's happened." Although the drone of the bombers faded away, we heard another load of bombs explode in the distance. The entire episode lasted about 15 minutes.

We listened for it to become quiet again. The deathly silence that ensued was a stark contrast to the previous minutes. Our house was still standing, a true miracle. There were no more windows and the entire roof had been torn off and strewn about the street. In front of the house there was such an enormous crater that I thought, my God, it's not even 20 yards away, how did this house ever make it through as well as it did?

After a while, we began to clear the rubble out of our apartment. It was one big junk pile. We were so preoccupied with ourselves and the thought that we might be the next to go up in flames, it never occurred to us to go immediately into the city to help dig people out. Compared to those people still trapped in their cellars twelve hours after the night raids, waiting for someone to get them out, our problems were laughable.

86. Criticism on the Home Front, 1943

Military reverses in Russia and North Africa, as well as increased Allied air-raids on German cities, gave rise to public pessimism and criticism of the Nazi regime. The increasingly cynical mood on the home front, which even afflicted some Party members, is reflected in this spring 1943 summary of German *Gauleiter* reports, which had been submitted to Party headquarters in Munich.

From *Nationalsozialistische Deutsche Arbeiter-Partei, Hauptarchiv 1919–45* (Stanford, CA: Hoover Institution on War, Revolution and Peace), H.A. reel 50, folder 1181, Munich, (*Gauleiter* Report, March 19, April 2, 1943). Translated by Dieter Kuntz.

The rumormongers are still with us, or more correctly, [they] are busier than ever. Rumors of an impending monetary devaluation are persistently holding on. There is talk of a "taxing-away of savings accounts." From the districts of Pomerania, Hesse, southern and northern Westphalia, Mosel, Berlin, Saxony, and others, the following rumors and political "jokes" have been reported:

> The clock goes tictac and the hands move forward, Rommel goes backward but that is called tactic.

> The book of the Germans, *Mein Kampf,* can now be purchased with coupons, that is, with the spinning yarn rationing cards.

> The Führer supposedly is mentally ill and is tearing pictures and curtains from the walls.

> There is no need to fear the Bolsheviks because it is the English and the Americans who will march into the Mosel area.

> There are so few anti-aircraft devices set up in the Rhineland because this is where the most Catholics live, and the state has very little concern for them.

An especially dangerous aspect of this situation is the fact that some people are openly risking criticism of the Führer himself, attacking him in the most hateful, vulgar manner. These rumors and political jokes are finding an all too eager ear among certain elements of our people. Unfortunately, too many of our countrymen blabber and repeat everything they are told, without contradiction, because they like to cause sensation, like to boast, or are indifferent. They do not consider that they are becoming the carriers of enemy propaganda!

Again and again the sad observation has to be made that our party members often exhibit an unbelievable indolence and laxity: they witness subversive enemy propaganda but seldom muster the courage to strike a blow. If one asks one of these "insignia wearers" who has just "indignantly" reported such an incident what his reaction was, the answer given is rarely what one should expect. This is attributable to a lack of the courage of conviction, or possibly to cowardice, but often it is indolence or fear of trouble with the police.

The increasingly heavy and continuing air raids on German cities, especially Berlin, Essen, Stuttgart, Nuremberg, and Munich, have left an extraordinarily strong impression on the public. It is these air attacks that are currently causing our people grievous concern, especially insofar as we apparently are unable to counter with anything in kind — so that we are "powerless in the face of this threat". . . . One hears more and more debate about our defenses. The *Gau* leadership of Westphalia-North repeatedly points to the attack on the city of Hamm as an example of the inadequacies of German defenses. "As is now known, on March 4, seventeen American bombers made their way toward the city, and under cloudless skies and completely undisturbed — as though they were on maneuvers — dropped their bombs that morning on the city and its raid station. Because everyone in the beginning assumed they were German planes, the death toll was rather high. The populace has been shaken by the lack of sufficient antiaircraft guns, as well as by the unhindered appearance of [enemy] planes over one of Germany's most important raid stations, which is hundreds of kilometers from the English coast". . . .

The report from the *Gau* Halle-Merseburg from March 11 is noteworthy: "Among good National Socialist-minded circles — which are tolerant of justified criticism — an antipathy toward the so-called Goebbels technique is making itself felt. People have grown distrustful of National Socialist propaganda because of the great shifts within the space of a few weeks from one extreme to the other. Because of this, people are distrustful of any new adjustments. People dissect and criticize the minister's every statement in order to detect alternative possibilities. The contradiction that is often apparent between reality as expressed by attitudes and moods and the propaganda pretense that the press and radio engages in — apparently for the benefit of foreign countries — is occasionally so obvious and so blatant that people angrily turn away from it". . . .

The figures [cited by the regime] of those who have fallen at the front are increasingly being criticized as not corresponding to the facts! . . . From Posen: "As far as the officially publicized figure of 542,000 casualties is concerned — hardly anyone believes it. Even if one were to subtract the numbers of those missing in action at Stalingrad — about which we are awaiting further information — one would have to arrive at a higher total. Even old Party members are saying that it is a shame that the Führer, whose image has suffered in the last few months, especially since Stalingrad, publicly announced such a [casualty] figure, because now future speeches will generate even greater misgivings."

Heinrich Himmler reviews the ranks of his SS in January 1939, on the tenth anniversary of his appointment as Reichsführer. By this time, Himmler had absolute control over all of the police forces in Germany.

Police state? What is role of police vs. traditional role of police? — How have they changed? What does it say ab

Himmler and the SS Imperium, 1938–1945

Himmler did not receive all police powers within the state in 1933; he gradually consolidated his position in the 1930s and then greatly expanded them in 1939 and throughout the war years. Undermining the established police forces, however, began early. The Reichstag Fire Decree of February 1933, which furnished a pseudolegal basis for the state of emergency, and the Enabling Act of the following month, which established the dictatorship, had initiated extralegal activities and the overt use of coercion and terror. Even in this period, the circumvention of the courts and the state bureaucracy and the development of a police force responsible only to the Führer was undertaken. As early as March 1933 Goering placed the old political police of Prussia under the chief of the police group of the Ministry of the Interior, Rudolf Diels, and gave it very broad powers. At the end of April he formed the Gestapo, the Secret State Police, which carried out many hidden activities legally assigned to the Ministry of the Interior. More and more, under Goering's jurisdiction, the Gestapo became independent of the Prussian administration. In Bavaria Himmler had been made police president of Munich on March 9, 1933; a week later he took over the entire political police of Bavaria. Within months Himmler gained control over the political police of all the German principalities except Prussia, where he was still formally subordinate to Goering.

The union of the now-centralized Gestapo and Himmler's SS, officially separated from the SA from 1934 on, formed the power base of the SS state. Though jurisdictional conflicts with state administrations continued for years, particularly in Prussia, the Gestapo had authority "to root out and fight all pernicious efforts throughout the country," and its activities were not subject to court review. These developments culminated in the investing of the Reichsführer SS with the newly created office of chief of the German police through the Führer's decree of June 17, 1936. This action resulted in the centralization of all police power, which hitherto had been under the jurisdiction of the individual states, and the transfer of the police from governmental to SS control. Himmler's subordination to the minister of the interior was purely nominal; in practice he was given cabinet rank and himself claimed some of the powers of the interior ministry long before he formalized his powerful position and the preeminence of the SS by taking over the ministry in 1943. Himmler declined to become part of the civil service structure, thereby affirming his independence. But although this independence obviously hindered the process of *Gleichschaltung*, it freed Himmler from the machinery of the traditional bureaucracy and enabled him to work in an unencumbered manner. His position outside the civil government was the key to the development of the antistatist, totalitarian SS imperium. Even before 1939, Himmler clearly had more power than the head of the interior ministry. As supreme chief of the SS he derived his authority directly from Hitler.

The fusion of SS and police control allowed Himmler to restructure his organization to meet his and Hitler's specific designs. In June 1936, Himmler ordered the division of the police into two main departments: the Order Police (Ordnungspolizei, or Orpo) under Kurt Daluege as general of police and the Security Police (*Sicherheitspolizei,* or *Sipo*) under Reinhard Heydrich. Orpo comprised the urban and rural constabularies and the municipal police, whereas Sipo consisted of the Secret State Police (Geheime Staatspolizei, or Gestapo) and the Criminal Police (Kriminalpolizei, or Kripo). Heydrich also continued on as SS group leader and as chief of the Security Service (Sicherheitsdienst or *SD*) of the SS in charge of intelligence and ideological control, thereby amassing an astonishing amount of power in his hands. The fact that the criminal police became part of the Gestapo was of major importance. The divisions of the political police from 1938 on within the framework of the Central Office for Reich Security (Reichssicherheitshaupamt or *RSHA*) indicate the large number of groups, organizations, and political spheres Heydrich had under constant surveillance. These included sections IIA, communist and other Marxist groups; IIB, churches, sects, émigrés, Jews, ideological camps; IIC, reaction, opposition, Austrian affairs; IID, protective custody, concentration camps; IIE, economic, agrarian, and sociopolitical affairs and organizations; IIG, broadcasting; IIH, Party affairs, Nazi groups and auxiliary organizations; IIJ, foreign political police; IIBer, situation reports; IIP, press; IIS, opposition to homosexuality and abortion; III, intelligence. Beyond these areas, a separate "political administration" was created alongside and above the state administration. Before its demise, the Security Police had departments for all political areas and for the infiltration of the Wehrmacht.

Shortly after the beginning of the war (September 27, 1939), the Security Police and the Security Service (SD) were coordinated with the Central Office for Reich Security. This formally and decisively amalgamated the *Sipo* and the SD into one organization and thereby institutionalized the personal union forged under

Heydrich. In addition to the Secret State Police under Heinrich Müller and the Criminal Police under Arthur Nebe, the Central Office for Reich Security also took over the SD offices for "enemy research" under Professor Franz Six, German "living areas" under Otto Ohlendorf, and foreign intelligence under Heinz Jost. As the central agency of the SS state, the RSHA not only grew enormously in the course of wartime expansion but was also repeatedly reorganized. First a department for the "greater German area of influence" was set up, then departments for occupation and extermination policies, divided into such "subject" areas as left- and right-wing opposition, antisabotage efforts, antiespionage, Jews and churches, special tasks, and protective custody, were created. That the organization could, as needed, appear as a governmental, police, or SS agency was both vital and typical; one or another guise made possible tactical camouflage and the mobility required for measures of terror and extermination as well as the policies of Hitler, which were above the state. The traditional structures and functions of the state, which the SS could rescind or change at will and which had, in reality, long since become obsolete, provided purely formal legalization of the regime's policies. Thus was the police power of the Third Reich divorced from the government to emerge as an independent organization. Hitler's leadership position after 1938 stemmed less from his having taken over and enveloped the more traditional units of the state than from a process of "degovernmentalization" in which governmental authority over the police was gradually diluted and eventually obliterated. In addition, the institutions concerned with political activity took precedence over administrative authority.

The SS grew to encompass all the areas it brought under its control, and its organizational shape changed as it absorbed these new areas. To ensure the racial quality of SS recruits and also to lay the groundwork for Germany's future racial policies, Himmler in 1931 set up the Central Office for Race and Resettlement (RuSHA), which had as its primary function the physical and racial screening of prospective SS candidates. After the promulgation of Himmler's Betrothal and Marriage Order of December 31, 1931, the RuSHA also investigated the racial genealogy of the prospective brides of SS members. Himmler's SS grew rapidly from about fifty thousand members in 1933 to a quarter of a million by 1939. Most members belonged to the *Allgemeine* SS (General SS), which came to be organized into thirty regional divisions.

The *Allgemeine* SS spun off two other organizations: the *Verfügungstruppe* (Special Duty Troops) and the *Totenkopfverbände* (Death's Head Units). The *Verfügungstruppe,* independent of but in a tension-filled relationship with both the police forces and the Wehrmacht, was a permanent armed formation of the NSDAP exclusively at Hitler's and Himmler's disposal, to be used for "internal political tasks." By a law of August 17, 1938, it could also be used by the commander in chief of the army for military purposes. The *Totenkopfverbände* originated from the guard unit of Dachau, the first concentration camp. By March 1935 there were seven camps, with a population of ten thousand. The guard units were enlarged, organized in battalions, and designated *Totenkopfverbände*. By the end of 1937, such units had five thousand men in three formations, but unlike the *Verfügungstruppe,* they were never incorporated into the regular army except through being reconstituted as *Verfügungstruppe.* In mid-1940 these two formations were redesignated the Waffen SS.

This giant SS apparatus was tested outside Germany for the first time in the occupation of Austria and Czechoslovakia. Here the *Einsatzstäbe* and *Einsatzgruppen* (special task groups and commandos) made their first appearance to effect the "safeguarding of political life." Such units were to play a crucial role in the occupation and annihilation policies of the future. Each regular army unit was supplemented with an *Einsatz* commando with orders to "fight all anti-Reich and anti-German elements in the rear of the fighting troops." By the time war broke out, the SS was fully organized and ready to expand to institute National Socialist policies for occupation and extermination. During the war itself the constituent organizations of Himmler's empire grew with unparalleled rapidity, concomitantly becoming ever more unrestrained in their use of power.

Members of the SS were not simply acting on orders from above; rather, they were prepared to do anything for the sake of the ideology, putting obedience to the Führer before all else. The ideological goals of the totalitarian system furnished the foundation for the unbridled use of violence. SS "morality," seeking the individual's victory over the self as the advance guard of the *Volksgemeinschaft,* protected National Socialist "ideals," thereby carrying out commands for which neither the machinery of the state nor the majority of the population was ready. Only with its ideal of pursuing goals of supreme difficulty and making the ultimate sacrifice could the SS glorify the extermination of the Jews as a "historical task" that had to be "gotten over with" bravely. Himmler again and again reminded his men not to recoil from the most brutal consequences of the mass execution of defenseless individuals. Since the German people could not themselves shoulder such a task, the SS should, in Himmler's words, "carry the burden for our people . . . take the responsibility on ourselves . . . carry the secret with us to the grave." Here another inner contradiction within National Socialism arises: Although seen as supremely honorable, this act of sacrifice was to be kept absolutely secret. Whereas the highest values of a society are usually the focus of public acclamation, in the *Volksgemeinschaft* of Nazi Germany secrecy was the hallmark of honor.

87. The Nature and Purpose of the SS

By June 1936 Himmler had gained control of the political and criminal police forces throughout the Reich, having added to his position as Reichsführer SS that of chief

From International Military Tribunal, *Trial of the Major War Criminals, Nuremberg, 1945–46* (Nuremberg: International Military Tribunal, 1948), vol. 29, pp. 210–12, 216–33. Translated by Dieter Kuntz.

of the Gestapo. He discussed the nature and purpose of the SS in the following lecture to officers of the armed forces in January 1937, providing a brief sketch of the history of the SS, detailing its organizational structure, and then explaining its vital role as guarantor of internal security. He furthermore justified the establishment and maintenance of concentration camps whose inmates were imprisoned solely on the basis of their racial heredity, claiming that "no one has been sent there unjustly . . . there you will find people with hydrocephalus, people who are cross-eyed, deformed, half Jewish, and are racially inferior products."

Today — and with this I am bringing the question of selection to a close – today we are accepting the young man eighteen years of age. We already know him from his involvement in the Hitler Youth and have watched him for a few years so that we are sure to get the best man. He comes to us as a candidate when he is eighteen. He will be tested and retested tremendously. Of 100 men we can use only an average of 10 or 15, not more. . . .

I now turn to the organization of the SS. Within the SS, there are several classifications to be differentiated. First is the General SS, which will have a strength of roughly 190,000 men. This General SS consists entirely of those in civilian occupations except for the higher leader–corps, which serves full-time, namely, from *Sturmbannführer* [major] on up. . . .

Aside from the General SS there are the *Verfügungstruppen* [Special Duty Troops]. Moreover, there are the Death's Head units, the Security Service and the Race and Resettlement Office. I will deal with the individual divisions in somewhat more detail. . . .

I now turn to the Death's Head Units. The utilization and task of the Special Duty Troops I will discuss later, in conjunction with the topic of police. The Death's Head Units developed out of concentration camp guard troops. I will cite some numbers concerning the concentration camps. Today in Germany we still have the following concentration camps – and I can say right now that I do not believe that the number will diminish, but that instead for certain cases, I am of the opinion that they must grow: (1) Dachau near Munich, (2) Sachsenhausen near Berlin. This is the former camp Esterwege in the Emsland area. I phased-out this camp in Emsland on the recommendation of Reich Labor Leader Hierl who, as did the judiciary, pointed out that it was wrong to say to one person that service in the marshes, making the land arable again, is an honorable service, while we send another there as a prisoner and tell him: old chap, I am going to teach you some manners, I am going to send you to the marshes. That is indeed illogical, and after one-half or three-fourths of a year I closed the camp in Esterwege and relocated it to Sachsenhausen, near Oranienburg. There is also a camp in Lichtenburg, near Torgau, and a camp in Sachsenburg, near Chemnitz, as well as a few smaller camps. The number of those in protective custody is approximately 8,000. Allow me to explain to you why we need to have so many, and why we must have even more. In earlier years there was an excellently organized KPD [Communist Party of Germany]. The KPD was crushed in the year 1933. A segment of the functionaries went to foreign countries. We caught another segment, which was included among the very high number of those in protective custody in 1933. Because of my accurate and detailed knowledge of Bolshevism, I was always opposed to the release of these people from the camps. We must realize that the broad masses of the proletariat are positively willing to listen to National Socialism and are amenable to the state of today, as long as they are not dissuaded by these precisely instructed, carefully prepared and monetarily well supported functionaries. This much is clear: Everyone who actually was a Communist for years, is susceptible to Communism, even if he belonged only for the best of reasons. There is no danger as long as there is no functionary in his block of houses or in the suburbs who can regularly supply him with subversive material. In 1933, because of ministerial pressure, we released a large number from protective custody in Prussia and other German states. Only I, in Bavaria, did not give in and did not release my prisoners. In subsequent years, Bavaria had a much smaller number of KPD incidents than all other states. This is only natural. If I allow the leading cadres to leave, they will always be active. The result of the release was that these functionaries were not cavaliers, as we had thought, and did not say: That was decent of this National Socialist state; how easy it would have been to simply shoot us; we would have done that in Russia, in any case, if the situation had been reversed. It is decent that they did not shoot us, so now we will be thankful and fall in line. No thought of that. Most of these functionaries went to Russia where they were in the Lenin School in Moscow. They were retrained for new tactics – illegal tactics using wireless radio and technical devices, trade-union opposition and the building of popular fronts. They were issued new passports, of which I must say this: These passports are fake, but are real passports. They had earlier taken such a large number of passports, and other identification material from the Police Presidency, that these are actually real passports which have merely been altered to a new name. They then returned with new names. Now the functionary who earlier had been in Thuringia, and was probably known to every city policeman in Gotha, reappeared not in Thuringia but in East Prussia, and the one from Mecklenburg reappeared in Bavaria. It was a real drudgery to again track down these individuals and to prove: You are not the person you represent yourself as being, but you are actually someone else. When I took over the Secret State Police in 1934, I abandoned the tactics of my predecessor Ministerial Councillor Diels. I did not write much about the illegal KPD in the newspapers, because I am of the opinion that the activity of the police must proceed quietly, even though this may be difficult for some men who never get any recognition because their work is not seen. I think it best to do these things quietly, rather than to elaborate on it in the newspapers. During 1936 we raided the national headquarters of the KPD two times. You did not read about this in the newspaper. The activity [of the KPD] is, however, very lively, absolutely lively, there is no denying that, because on the other side the Russian Comintern has made an unheard of sum of money available for this activity. The GPU, from whom this propaganda emanates, has a budget of 1.3 billion *Goldmark*. Not a bad budget! These people, and these masses are constantly being let loose upon Europe. The centers from which these things emanate are in foreign countries. We are surrounded by states which allow Communist activity, who do not intervene, and by taking this position actually encourage it. We are situated in the heart of Europe. On one hand this is a plus for our situation, and is of great importance in terms of world history because as such we are really the heart of the human race; but on the other hand, this central location is a great weakness in many ways.

With the approval of the Führer, I have little by little begun to once again arrest a large number of functionaries, insofar as we are able to locate them, so that we can restore order. We will increase the number [to be arrested] in consideration of the international dangers, so that we will actually be able to guarantee that it will not be possible for them to establish a new illegal organization due to a lack of functionaries and leaders.

Furthermore, it would be extremely instructive for everyone – I could give the opportunity to some members of the armed forces – to inspect such a concentration camp. Once you have seen it, you will be convinced of the fact that no one has been sent there unjustly; that it is the offal of criminals and freaks. No better demonstration of the laws of inheritance and race, as set forth by Dr. Gütt, exists than such a concentration camp. There you can find people with hydrocephalus, people who are cross-eyed, deformed, half Jewish, and are racially inferior products. All of that is assembled there. Of course, we distinguish those inmates who are only there for a few months for the purpose of education from those who are to stay for a long time. On the whole, education consists only of discipline, never of any kind of instruction on an ideological basis, for the prisoners have, for the most part, slave-like souls and only very few people of real character can be found there. . . . Education thus means order. The order begins with these people living in clean barracks. Such a thing can really be accomplished only by Germans; hardly another nation would be as humane as we are. The laundry is frequently changed. The people are taught to wash themselves twice daily and to use a toothbrush, a thing with which most of them have been unfamiliar. . . .

The Death's Head Units guard these concentration camps. It is not possible to use married men, as was once suggested, for this guard duty because no state can pay for this. It is, furthermore, necessary to use a relatively high number of these guard troops—3,500 men are engaged in guard duty in Germany – because no duty is as awful or as strenuous for a troop as is the guarding of scoundrels and criminals. . . .

The camps are fenced in with electrified barbed wire. It goes without saying that if someone sets foot in a forbidden zone or treads on a forbidden path, we will shoot. If someone, while working, let's say in the marshes or building streets or elsewhere, even starts to escape, we will shoot. If someone is insolent and obstructive, and that does happen occasionally, we will at least make an endeavour. He will receive either solitary confinement or dark confinement with bread and water, or in extreme cases, receive 25 lashes. I beg you not to be shocked, because I have [merely] adopted the old Prussian penitentiary methods from the years 1914 to 1918. Cruelties and sadistic things, as the foreign press has frequently reported, are totally impossible. First of all, punishment can be meted out only by the inspector of the various camps, not by the camp commandant. Secondly, the punishment is administered in front of a guard company, so that there is always a platoon of 20 to 24 people present. Finally, a physician and a secretary are present during the punishment. One cannot be more punctilious.

Here, too, I would like to say: These things are necessary, because otherwise it would not be possible to keep these criminals in check. In case of a war, we must be clear on the fact that we will have to put a considerable number of undesirable customers in there if we don't want to create a hotbed for undesirable developments. . . .

I now come to the Security Service; it is the great ideological intelligence service of the Party and, in the long run, also that of the State. During the time of struggle for power it was only the intelligence service of the SS. At that time we had, for quite natural reasons, an intelligence service with the regiments, battalions and companies. We had to know what was going on on the opponent's side, whether the Communists intended to hold up a meeting today or not, whether our people were to be suddenly attacked or not, and similar things. In 1931 I had already separated this service from the troops, from the units of the General SS, because I considered it to be wrong. For one thing, secrecy is endangered; the individual men, or even the companies, are too likely to discuss everyday political problems. This was the maxim of the SS from the beginning: Everyday problems did not interest us; every leader who was appointed by the Führer will be protected by us, every leader dismissed by the Führer will be forcefully removed if it is necessary, because what matters is only the command of the Führer. . . .

The Security Service was already separated from the troops in 1931 and separately organized. Its higher headquarters coincide today with the *Oberabschnitte* [Upper Sections] and *Abschnitte* [Sections], and it has also field offices, its own organization of officials, and a great many

[handwritten margin notes: loyalty to papacy, Catholic enemy of the State]

command posts, approximately 3,000 to 4,000 men strong, at least when it is built up. The areas it handles include foremost, Communism, Judaism, Freemasonry, Ultramontanism, the activities of politically active denominations, and reaction. . . . What interests us is: What sort of big plans does the Comintern have for the coming year; in which country does it plan to develop these plans; what influence does Bolshevism have in foreign free-masonry circles; who is pulling the wires; what is the destination of the important emissaries? For example, 800 emissaries were recently sent to Austria. They arrived there three or four months ago, and now we desperately want to know: What is going to happen in Austria? Or what plans, what large-scale organizational plans do they have for Germany; which angle will they pursue; how is it that Bolshevism, for example, is hooking-up with the Confessional Front; and, given the fact that it is an atheistic movement and is now supporting these pious parsons – how is it that this is suddenly possible? Or, we are also interested in: What influence – from a large-scale perspective – can the Jews exercise in terms of economic throttling, sabotage, and foreign currency manipulations? These are things which are scientifically and thoroughly studied there, sometimes taking years, while we, on the other hand, are only in the beginning stages of our work on most of these points.

After the Security Service, we come to the last pillar, the Race and Resettlement Organization. We have, then, the General SS, which forms the greater part of the SS, of the Order; we have the Special Duty Troops which have the specific function of providing internal security in the state; we have the Death's Head Units which also provide internal security; we have the Security Service, which is the Intelligence Service of the party and state; and finally, we have the Race and Resettlement Organization, whose task is one of ideological instruction, in the positive sense – as opposed to the Security Service, which has the negative duty of spying-out the enemy. The Race and Resettlement Office processes marriage applications. For four or five years now we have had the marriage decree: No SS man can marry without the permission of the Reichsführer SS [Himmler]. For this we require a physical examination of the bride and sponsors who will vouch for her in ideological and human aspects. In doing so, we are not interested in whether or not the woman has property. We require merely a declaration stating whether or not she has debts. All the better if the girls are rich, or if they bring into the marriage what they themselves have accumulated, or their dowry. Furthermore, we demand of both of them the genealogical tree dating back to 1750, a certificate that both are of healthy racial stock, and various other matters and things of interest to the police. This is a huge undertaking, especially now, as marriages are taking place in disproportionately large numbers; we are very eager to ensure that our men do marry. We would like them to marry

[handwritten margin notes: marriage decree; Not done in practice; racial purity]

by the age of 26, so that we will really have young marriages which are capable of producing children.

Additionally, the Central Office for Race and Resettlement handles the matter of the resettlement of SS men who are to become farmers; moreover [it handles] the entire ideological training. The Race and Resettlement Office is, for all practical purposes, the scientific agency in charge of matters relating to [archaeological] excavations, and prehistoric things – with which we are very much involved. We are also actively participating in excavations, such as those in East Prussia. There, near Altchristburg, we excavated a large fortification of some 30 acres. This excavation is politically important and useful. That is why we became involved. The enemy on the other side of the border is forever contending that this land in the East is Slavic and therefore rightfully belongs to him. Consequently they are engaged in excavations on the other side of the German border, in the East, but are only digging in the Slavic strata. But when they come across a Germanic layer, they simply fill in the cavity and state: There is only Slavic material here. . . . These things interest us because they are of the greatest importance in the ideological and political battle. . . . Why? That is very simple: We want to make it clear to our men, and to the German people, that we do not have a past of only roughly 1,000 years, that we were not a barbaric people that had no culture of its own, but who had to acquire it from others. We want to make our people proud again of our history. We want to make it clear that Germany is more eternal than Rome, which is only 2,000 years old! . . .

I will now discuss the police force and its development. The police are today divided into constabulary forces and Security Police; the constabulary force wears a uniform. The Security Police is made up of a criminal investigation department and the Secret State Police. In the year 1933, we took over a complete muddle, we can honestly say that it was a police force whose decent elements were humbled; a police force whose officers had been stripped of their swords only to be given a rubber truncheon; a police force saturated with previously convicted people and absolute Communists; a police force which really did not dare to pursue crime, because the League for Human Rights, the Society for Peace, and similar societies intervened immediately, and because an absolute glorification of crime was the usual thing. This was the path of a systematic Bolshevization of mentality.

Goering took over the police in Prussia, restored order to the uniformed police, and created a state police which was incorporated into the army in 1935/36; a similar development occurred in Bavaria. From my position in the SS, I was first of all concerned only with the Secret State Police, with the Political Police of the various states, and with the Secret State Police in Prussia. Because I, myself, was the Political Police commander for all German states and was at the same time Deputy Chief of the Secret State Police in Prussia, the reins of the Secret State Police gradually fell into one hand. I am going to skip over its further development, if I may. On the 17th of June of last year, I became Chief of the German Police; that is, of the entire German Police with all its auxiliary organizations. Allow me to demonstrate how I envisioned, and still do view my duty.

First of all: I want to, once and for all, create an actual national police force from these 16 different state police forces, because the Reich Police is one of the strongest braces that a state can have. We now have a Reich Police for the first time in German history. . . .

Within the constabulary – here, too, I must give you the picture – there are three categories: first of all there is the city police, which, for example, we see on the streets of Berlin; secondly, there is the rural police, and also the country constables; third, there is the municipal police. This force is found in smaller cities, with populations of 10,000 or 15,000 inhabitants. They have a strength of up to 20 men, and have a different uniform. We are going to standardize this force too. . . .

Much depends on the uniformed police in case of a war, such as, for example, the entire civil air defense of the state. The police is the organization responsible for the civil air defense; all other organizations merely aid their effort. But for this I need people who are versatile, and who really have an understanding of this and the know-how.

I am going to replenish the man-power supply of the police, as far as I am able to, from discharged men of the SS Special Duty Troops, and from the Death's Head Units. I will replenish the police officer's corps with SS leaders who have been to the leadership schools at Tölz and Braunschweig, and who have served in the Special Duty Troops. Herein I come to an important point: I am struggling to keep the police officer's corps from becoming a second-rate officer's corps. A police officer's corps can too easily become that, and that is what it previously was.

How this relates to the entire system brings me to the main point: internal security and the task of the police during war. In a future war we will have not only the front of the land army, the front of the navy at sea, the front of the air force in the air space over Germany, but we will have a fourth war zone as well: Internal Germany! This is the sub-structure which must be kept healthy, by hook or by crook – otherwise the other three, the fighting elements of Germany, will again be stabbed in the back.

We must be fully aware that the enemy in time of war is not only an enemy in the military sense, but is also an ideological enemy. When I speak of an enemy, it goes without saying that I am referring to our natural enemy – Bolshevism, which is led by international Jewish-Freemasonry. The stronghold of Bolshevism is of course Russia. But that does not mean that the danger of a Bolshevistic attack threatens to come only from Russia. We must always reckon with a threat from that direction, as Jewish

Bolshevism has secured the decisive influence for itself there. It is therefore inevitable, that the states or races which are under the leadership of Jewish-Freemasonry Bolshevistic elements, or are at least strongly influenced by such, will be hostile toward Germany.

We must therefore constantly ask ourselves the question: In case of a war, who would come into consideration as an opponent, who is the ideological enemy, that is, who is influenced by Jewish-Freemasonry Bolshevism? We must be fully aware that Bolshevism is an organization of subhuman brutes, it forms the underpinning of Jewish power, and is the exact opposite of all that is dear, valued, and cherished by an Aryan race. . . .

The entire movement is therefore directed against the white man, and is today primarily directed against a revived Germany – which was thought to have gone to pieces, that it was done for. If we want to become immune to the poison of destruction within our nation, we must bolster our lives with social prosperity, social order, and social purity. We are working to achieve these things. . . .

With this I come back to what I said in the beginning about the race question. We are more valuable than the others, who outnumber us. We are more valuable because our blood enables us to invent more than others, it enables us to lead our people better, it enables us to be better soldiers, and better statesman, and it enables us to attain higher culture and better character. We have better quality. . . .

I spoke [earlier] of the ideological penetration of the entire nation in case of a war. Should this war come sooner than any of us expect, or wish, then we must be aware of the fact that among the German people there will always be a bottom sediment of society which will form the starting point for the Comintern. The Comintern actually has it quite easy because they have people who are political agitators and military spies at the same time. Every Communist is simultaneously a military spy who will reveal every industrial and military secret for the benefit of his imaginary Fatherland, Moscow, and who will engage in political agitation and subversion with the same conviction in order to bring the revolution into full gear. If a war should come early, the danger would be all the greater. If it should come later, then the danger would be less, as more generations of [German] youths will have had time to mature. The danger could return only if the German people stray from the path we are taking today. In any event, we must be prepared for this danger, for this internal theater of war, and we must be aware that every war can lead to disaster if the internal theater of war is neglected. . . .

If we are ever to pass a severe test, an appreciation for this totally new kind of organization must be pervasive, as must be the appreciation for the internal theater of war – which will mean either life or death for Germany. It is the task of the SS and the police to find a positive solution to the problem of internal security. This is the mission the Führer has entrusted to us. We are approaching this task in all seriousness and are thoroughly convinced that only through the best ideological training, and through racial selection, will we one day be able to accomplish this mission. . . .

88. The Function of the Police

The *Völkischer Beobachter* printed the following article in June 1936 as a response to foreign criticism of the Gestapo. It provides a sketch of the development, purpose, and functions of the Gestapo, which had been under the control of Himmler since the spring of 1934.

The German Secret State Police was created in the aftermath of the National Socialist revolution. It was organized simultaneously in all German states and came into being because of an urgent political necessity. Its creator in Prussia was Minister-President Goering, who today is still head of the German Secret Police. In Bavaria, the Bavarian Political Police was organized by Reichsführer SS Himmler, who also directed the development of the political police in the other non-Prussian states. The various political police forces received organizational unity in the spring of 1934, when Minister-President Goering appointed the Reichsführer SS to the position of deputy chief of the Prussian Secret State Police. Unified leadership and uniform development of the political police of all the states was thereby guaranteed.

The Secret State Police is an official criminal investigation department given the special assignment of pursuing offenses against the state, treasonous acts in particular. It is the task of the Secret State Police to clear up these offenses, to apprehend the perpetrators, and to bring them to trial. The number of treason cases continually pending before the People's Court is the result of this police activity. In addition to this, the Secret State Police has as its second major assignment the preventive combating of all danger to the state and its leadership. Because all open struggle against the state and against state leadership has been prohibited since the National Socialist revolution, the Secret State Police, as a preventive fighting force against state-threatening dangers, is inseparably linked to the National Socialist leadership [i.e., authoritarian] state. The opponents of National Socialism have not been eliminated through prohibition of their organizations and newspapers, for they have relied on different forms of opposition to the state. That is why the National Socialist state must

From *Völkischer Beobachter*, 22 June 1936. Translated by Dieter Kuntz.

ferret out, monitor, and render harmless those opponents illegally organized in underground movements, in camouflaged associations, within associations of well-intentioned countrymen, and even within our own party and state organizations before they have reached the point where they are able to actually undertake an action that is contrary to the best interests of the state. No leadership state will be spared the necessity of waging an all-out battle against the secret enemies of the state because the forces hostile to the state, operating from foreign headquarters, will always find one person or another who will serve their purposes and who will conduct an underground campaign against the state.

The preventive responsibility of the Secret State Police consists primarily of extensive surveillance of all enemies of the state within the Reich. The Secret State Police is, in view of the other duties incumbent upon it, not able to carry out this surveillance of state enemies to the degree required. Therefore, the Security Service of the SS, which the deputy to the Führer had constituted as the intelligence service of the movement, has been assigned duties that supplement the role of the Secret State Police. This commits a large segment of the movement's forces, mobilized by the deputy Führer, into state security service. On the basis of surveillance findings, the Secret State Police takes appropriate preventive measures. The most effective preventive measure is doubtlessly the deprivation of freedom. "Protective custody" is imposed if there is a possibility that freedom of action by a person could in some way endanger state security. The utilization of this protective custody is governed by guidelines of the Reich and the Prussian Ministry of the Interior as well as by special arrest examination procedures of the Secret State Police. These guidelines – insofar as the task of preventive measures against state enemies is concerned – contain sufficient guarantees against the misuse of protective custody. Short-term custody is spent in the jails of the police and the courts. The concentration camps, which are under the jurisdiction of the Secret State Police, house those prisoners who must be kept out of public circulation for longer periods of time. The largest group of concentration camp inmates consists of communists and other Marxist functionaries who, according to our experience, immediately return to their struggle against the state once they are free. Further police preventive measures against movements hostile to the state include breaking up associations, prohibiting and breaking up meetings and gatherings, and prohibiting publications. As the party and its leaders are especially protected by provisions of the law, it is also the duty of the Secret State Police to pursue those committing offenses against these laws as well as to safeguard the party and its leaders through preventive measures.

89. Selective Breeding

With the establishment of the Lebensborn (Spring of Life) program, Himmler intended to further his idea of selective breeding. Planned mating between racially pure stock was encouraged, and twelve special maternity centers were created which catered to the needs of "racially, biologically, and hereditarily valuable pregnant women" (SS wives and unmarried women). Himmler informed SS leaders of the founding of the organization with a memorandum on September 13, 1936, reminding all that they must fulfill their "duty."

As early as December 13, 1934, I wrote to all SS leaders and declared that we have fought in vain if political victory was not to be followed by victory of births of good blood. The question of multiplicity of children is not a private affair of the individual, but his duty towards his ancestors and our people.

The SS has taken the first step in this direction long ago with the engagement and marriage decree of December 1931. However, the existence of sound marriage is futile if it does not result in the creation of numerous descendants.

I expect that here, too, the SS and especially the SS leader corps, will serve as a guiding example.

The minimum amount of children for a good sound marriage is four. Should unfortunate circumstances deny a married couple their own children, then every SS leader should adopt racially and hereditarily valuable children, educate them in the spirit of National Socialism, let them have education corresponding to their abilities.

The organization "Lebensborn eingetragener Verein [Spring of Life, registered society]" serves the SS leaders in the selection and adoption of qualified children. The organization "Lebensborn e.V." is under my personal direction, is part of the Central Office for Race and Resettlement bureau of the SS, and has the following obligations:

1. Support racially, biologically, and hereditarily valuable families with many children.
2. Place and care for racially and biologically and hereditarily valuable pregnant women, who, after thorough examination of their and the progenitor's families by the Central Office for Race and Resettlement central bureau of the SS, can be expected to produce equally valuable children.
3. Care for the children.
4. Care for the children's mothers.

From U.S. Chief of Counsel for the Prosecution of Axis Criminality, *Nazi Conspiracy and Aggression* (Washington, D.C.: U.S. Government Printing Office, 1946), vol. 5, doc. no. 2825-PS, pp. 465–66.

It is the honorable duty of all leaders of the central office to become members of the organization "Lebensborn e. V." The application for admission must be filed prior to September 23, 1936.

The dues of the SS leaders of the central office, from the Hauptsturmfuehrer [rank of captain] on are determined in the enclosed tables.

I shall personally keep myself informed of the success of my appeal.

Let me remind every SS leader once more that only sacrifices of a personal and material nature have brought us success in the times of the battle, and that the further construction of Germany, to last hundreds and thousands of years, will not be possible unless each and every one of us is ready to keep doing his share in the fulfillment of his obvious duty.

Reichsführer SS
[signed] H. Himmler

90. Colonization of the Eastern Territories

The German invasion of the Soviet Union brought Hitler closer to his vision of *Lebensraum* for the German people. The Führer was confident that the Russian campaign would have a victorious conclusion that would allow the realization of his plans, plans in which the SS would play an important role. Hitler personally directed the military operations in the East. Evenings at headquarters such as Wolfschanze found the Führer holding long off-the-record monologues on a variety of subjects. These talks were recorded in shorthand by associates who were present. On several occasions during late 1941 and early 1942, Hitler turned to the topic of colonization of the East.

The essential thing, for the moment, is to conquer. After that everything will be simply a question of organisation.

When one contemplates this primitive world, one is convinced that nothing will drag it out of its indolence unless one compels the people to work. The Slavs are a mass of born slaves, who feel the need of a master. As far as we are concerned, we may think that the Bolsheviks did us a great service. They began by distributing the land to the peasants, and we know what a frightful famine resulted. So they were obliged, of course, to re-establish a sort of feudal régime, to the benefit of the State. But there was this difference, that, whereas the old-style landlord knew something about farming, the political commissar, on the other hand, was entirely ignorant

From *Hitler's Secret Conversations, 1941–1944* (New York: Octagon Books, 1976), pp. 28–30, 56–57, 343–45. Translated by Norman Cameron and R. H. Stevens. Reprinted with permission of the publisher.

of such matters. So the Russians were just beginning to give their commissars appropriate instruction.

If the English were to be driven out of India, India would perish. Our rôle in Russia will be analogous to that of England in India.

Even in Hungary, National Socialism could not be exported. In the mass, the Hungarian is as lazy as the Russian. He's by nature a man of the steppe. From this point of view, Horthy[1] is right in thinking that if he abandoned the system of great estates, production would rapidly decline.

Slavs are lazy, no good

It's the same in Spain. If the great domains disappeared there, famine would prevail.

The German peasant is moved by a liking for progress. He thinks of his children. The Ukrainian peasant has no notion of duty.

There is a peasantry comparable to ours in Holland, and also in Italy, where every inch of ground is zealously exploited – also, to a certain extent, in France.

The Russian space is our India. Like the English, we shall rule this empire with a handful of men.

It would be a mistake to claim to educate the native. All that we could give him would be a half-knowledge – just what's needed to conduct a revolution!

It's not a mere chance that the inventor of anarchism was a Russian. Unless other peoples, beginning with the Vikings, had imported some rudiments of organisation into Russian humanity, the Russians would still be living like rabbits. One cannot change rabbits into bees or ants. These insects have the faculty of living in a state of society – but rabbits haven't.

If left to himself, the Slav would never have emerged from the narrowest of family communities.

The Germanic race created the notion of the State. It incarnated this notion in reality, by compelling the individual to be a part of a whole. It's our duty continually to arouse the forces that slumber in our people's blood.

The Slav peoples are not destined to live a cleanly life. They know it, and we would be wrong to persuade them of the contrary. It was we who, in 1918, created the Baltic countries and the Ukraine. But nowadays we have no interest in maintaining Baltic States, any more than in creating an independent Ukraine. We must likewise prevent them from returning to Christianity. That would be a grave fault, for it would be giving them a form of organisation.

---

[1] Admiral Miklos Horthy was head of state in Hungary from 1920 to 1944. Horthy was a convinced anticommunist who established an authoritarian system in Hungary and collaborated with Hitler after 1933 in the hope of revising the harsh territorial settlement of the Treaty of Trianon, which was concluded between Hungary and the Allies in 1920.

I am not a partisan, either, of a university at Kiev. It's better not to teach them to read. They won't love us for tormenting them with schools. Even to give them a locomotive to drive would be a mistake. And what stupidity it would be on our part to proceed to a distribution of land! In spite of that, we'll see to it that the natives live better than they've lived hitherto. We'll find amongst them the human material that's indispensable for tilling the soil.

We'll supply grain to all in Europe who need it. The Crimea will give us its citrus fruits, cotton and rubber (100,000 acres of plantation would be enough to ensure our independence).

The Pripet marshes will keep us supplied with reeds.

We'll supply the Ukrainians with scarves, glass beads and everything that colonial peoples like.

The Germans – this is essential – will have to constitute amongst themselves a closed society, like a fortress. The least of our stable-lads must be superior to any native.

For German youth, this will be a magnificent field of experiment. We'll attract to the Ukraine Danes, Dutch, Norwegians, Swedes. The army will find areas for manoeuvres there, and our aviation will have the space it needs.

Let's avoid repeating the mistakes committed in the colonies before 1914. Apart from the *Kolonialgesellschaft,* which represented the interests of the State, only the silver interests had any chance of raising their heads there.

The Germans must acquire the feeling for the great, open spaces. We must arrange things so that every German can realise for himself what they mean. We'll take them on trips to the Crimea and the Caucasus. There's a big difference between seeing these countries on the map and actually having visited them.

The railways will serve for the transport of goods, but the roads are what will open the country for us.

Today everybody is dreaming of a world peace conference. For my part, I prefer to wage war for another ten years rather than be cheated thus of the spoils of victory. In any case, my demands are not exorbitant. I'm only interested, when all is said, in territories where Germans have lived before.

The German people will raise itself to the level of this empire.

In comparison with the beauties accumulated in Central Germany, the new territories in the East seem to us like a desert. Flanders, too, is only a plain – but of what beauty! This Russian desert, we shall populate it. The immense spaces of the Eastern Front will have been the field of the greatest battles in history. We'll give this country a past.

We'll take away its character of an Asiatic steppe, we'll Europeanise it. With this object, we have undertaken the construction of roads that will lead to the southernmost point of the Crimea and to the Caucasus. These roads will be studded along their whole length with German towns, and around these towns our colonists will settle.

As for the two or three million men whom we need to accomplish this task, we'll find them quicker than we think. They'll come from Germany, Scandinavia, the Western countries and America. I shall no longer be here to see all that, but in twenty years the Ukraine will already be a home for twenty million inhabitants besides the natives. In three hundred years, the country will be one of the loveliest gardens in the world.

As for the natives, we'll have to screen them carefully. The Jew, that destroyer, we shall drive out. As far as the population is concerned, I get a better impression in White Russia than in the Ukraine.

We shan't settle in the Russian towns, and we'll let them fall to pieces without intervening. And, above all, no remorse on this subject! We're not going to play at children's nurses; we're absolutely without obligations as far as these people are concerned. To struggle against the hovels, chase away the fleas, provide German teachers, bring out newspapers – very little of that for us! We'll confine ourselves, perhaps, to setting up a radio transmitter, under our control. For the rest, let them know just enough to understand our highway signs, so that they won't get themselves run over by our vehicles!

For them the word "liberty" means the right to wash on feast days. If we arrive bringing soft soap, we'll obtain no sympathy. These are views that will have to be completely readjusted. There's only one duty: to Germanize this country by the immigration of Germans, and to look upon the natives as Redskins. If these people had defeated us, Heaven have mercy! But we don't hate them. That sentiment is unknown to us. We are guided only by reason. They, on the other hand, have an inferiority complex. They have a real hatred towards a conqueror whose crushing superiority they can feel. The *intelligentsia?* We have too many of them at home.

All those who have the feeling for Europe can join in our work.

In this business I shall go straight ahead, cold-bloodedly. What they may think about me, at this juncture, is to me a matter of complete indifference. I don't see why a German who eats a piece of bread should torment himself with the idea that the soil that produces this bread has been won by the sword. When we eat wheat from Canada, we don't think about the despoiled Indians.

In order to retain our domination over the people in the territories we have conquered to the east of the Reich, we must therefore meet, to the best of our ability, any and every desire for individual liberty which they may express, and by so doing deprive them of any form of State organisation and consequently keep them on as low a cultural level as possible.

[margin note: people exist for economic]

Our guiding principle must be that these people have but one justification for existence – to be of use to us economically. We must concentrate on extracting from these territories everything that it is possible to extract. As an incentive to them to deliver their agricultural produce to us, and to work in our mines and armament factories, we will open shops all over the country at which they will be able to purchase such manufactured articles as they want.

If we started bothering about the well-being of each individual, we should have to set up a State organisation on the lines of our own State administration – and all we should achieve would be to earn the hatred of the masses. In reality, the more primitive a people is, the more it resents as an intolerable restraint any limitation of the liberty of the individual. The other great disadvantage of an organised society is, from our point of view, that it would fuse them into a single entity and would give them a cohesive power which they would use against us. As an administrative organisation, the most we can concede to them is a form of communal administration, and that only in so far as it may be necessary for the maintenance of the labour potential, that is to say for the maintenance of the elementary basic needs of the individual.

[margin note: encourage discussion & schism]

Even these village communities must be organised in a manner which precludes any possibility of fusion with neighbouring communities; for example, we must avoid having one solitary church to satisfy the religious needs of large districts, and each village must be made into an independent sect, worshipping God in its own fashion. If some villages as a result wish to practice black magic, after the fashion of negroes or Indians, we should do nothing to hinder them. In short, our policy in the wide Russian spaces should be to encourage any and every form of dissension and schism.

It will be the duty of our Commissars alone to supervise and direct the economy of the captured territories, and what I have just said applies equally to every form of organisation. Above all, we don't want a horde of schoolmasters to descend suddenly on these territories and force education down the throats of subject races. To teach the Russians, the Ukrainians and the Kirghiz to read and write will eventually be to our own disadvantage; education will give the more intelligent among them an opportunity to study history, to acquire an historical sense and hence to develop political ideas which cannot but be harmful to our interests. A loudspeaker should be installed in each village, to provide them with odd items of news and, above all, to afford distraction. What possible use to them would a knowledge of politics or economics be? There is also no point in broadcasting any of their past history – all the villagers require is music, music and plenty of it. Cheerful music is a great incentive to hard work; give them plenty of opportunities to dance, and the villagers will be grateful to us. The soundness of these views is proved by our experience at home during the time of the Weimar Republic.

[margin note: don't educate them, leads to dissent]

One thing which it is essential to organise in the Russian territories is an efficient system of communications, which is vital both to the rational economic exploitation of the country and to the maintenance of control and order. The local inhabitants must be taught our highway code, but beyond that I really do not see the need for any further instruction.

In the field of public health there is no need whatsoever to extend to the subject races the benefits of our own knowledge. This would result only in an enormous increase in local populations, and I absolutely forbid the organisation of any sort of hygiene or cleanliness crusades in these territories. Compulsory vaccination will be confined to Germans alone, and the doctors in the German colonies will be there solely for the purpose of looking after the German colonists. It is stupid to thrust happiness upon people against their wishes. Dentistry, too, should remain a closed book to them; but in all these things prudence and commonsense must be the deciding factors, and if some local inhabitant has a violent tooth-ache and insists on seeing a dentist – well, an exception must be made in his particular case!

The most foolish mistake we could possibly make would be to allow the subject races to possess arms. History shows that all conquerors who have allowed their subject races to carry arms have prepared their own downfall by so doing. Indeed, I would go so far as to say that the underdog is a *sine qua non* for the overthrow of any sovereignty. So let's not have any native militia or police. German troops alone will bear the sole responsibility for the maintenance of law and order throughout the occupied Russian territories, and a system of military strong-points must be evolved to cover the entire occupied country.

All Germans living in territories must remain in personal contact with these strong-points. The whole must be most carefully organised to conform with the long-term policy of German colonisation, and our colonising penetration must be constantly progressive, until it reaches the stage where our own colonists far outnumber the local inhabitants.

91. The *Einsatzgruppen*

The primary duty of the *Einsatzgruppen* (special task groups), who were recruited from the ranks of the SS, was to establish security in occupied areas by suppressing all opposition. Their activities included campaigns against partisans as well as rounding up Jews, communists, and other political opponents and undesirables. The units literally had free reign to liquidate anyone deemed dangerous and may have killed as many as two million people. The following extract evidences

From U.S. Chief of Counsel for the Prosecution of Axis Criminality, *Nazi Conspiracy and Aggression* (Washington, D.C.: U.S. Government Printing Office, 1946), vol. 8, Affidavit B, pp. 598–603.

the brutality of their measures. At the Nuremberg war crimes trial Otto Ohlendorf, commander of Group D, testified on January 3, 1946, that he was responsible for the liquidation of ninety thousand Jews.

A few weeks before the beginning of the Russian campaign an agreement was reached between the OKW [Oberkommando der Wehrmacht, or High Command of the Armed Forces], OKH [Oberkommando des Heeres, or High Command of the Army] and the Chief of the Security Police and SD [Sicherheitsdienst, or Security Service] (Heydrich) according to which integral units of the Security Police and the SD were attached to the Army Groups and the units subordinated to them. The official title of the Chief of the units of the Security Police and SD was Beauftragter (Commissioner and Deputy of the Security Police and SD) of the Chief of the Security Police and SD, attached to, for example, Army Group "X." The unit was called "Einsatz Group" and was subdivided into Einsatz Commandos and Special Commandos. The Special Commandos were in turn subdivided as the need arose into small units. According to the agreement, the professional work of the Security Police and the SD was basically under the jurisdiction of the Chief of the Security Police and the SD. The Army Groups and the units subordinate to them respectively were in charge of "Marsch" and foods supply. The order for the "Marsch" controls area and place into which the Einsatz Group or the Commandos had to move, the strength of the Commandos, and the time when the Commandos were to move into any area or place, and the length of stay. The Army Groups or the units subordinate to them respectively assigned additional tasks to the Einsatz Groups and their subsections. A precise line of demarkation was not fixed as between the directives by the Chief of the Security Police and SD and the right to issue directives of the Army Groups and the units subordinate to them respectively. The Army therefore issued directives covering the most varied spheres, for instance, the Army entrusted the units of the Einsatz Groups with gathering the harvest in Transsinistria, the units were called upon to perform guard and control duties at bridges. The units were also used for operational Army tasks. When the first large-scale executions took place the Army in Nikolajev ordered that liquidations were not to be carried out within 200 Km of the site of Army Headquarters. In my capacity as Chief of Einsatz Group D, I was entrusted with the task to recruit Tartars in the Crimea for the Army. The Army intended furthermore to transfer to me the leadership of the operation against the Partisans on the Crimea. Einsatz Group D did not accept this task as I was able to explain to the Army the unsuitability of the Einsatz Group for this task. If, however, the Army had insisted upon this operation on the basis of military necessity, I would have been unable to decline. The liaison between the Einsatz Group and the Army Groups and the Army respectively were effected in general by a liaison chief on the part of the Einsatz Groups. Besides, regular conferences took place with the I C or I C AO's respectively as the main competent parties. The Chiefs of the Einsatz Groups had discussions at intervals with the Chiefs of Staff or the Commanders in Chief of the Army Groups or the Army respectively. In their activities the Chiefs of the Einsatz Groups had to take into consideration that the Commander in Chief of the Army was the supreme legal authority in the operational area (master over life and death). In individual cases, the Commander in Chief of the 11th Army made use of this authority, for instance, the Army removed the proceedings against a Ukrainian member of the Simferopol City Council from the competent Einsatz Commando of the Security Police and SD in Simferopol, and finished the proceedings under its own jurisdiction.

For the Russian campaign, four commissioners of the Chief of the Security Police and SD were appointed and consequently four Einsatz Groups were established. The Einsatz Group A (Chief, Stahlecker, formerly Inspector of the Security Police and SD, last department head in the foreign office); the Einsatz Group B (Chief, Nebe, Head of the Reich Criminal Police Department, AMT V of the RSHA [Reichssicherheitshauptamt, or Central Office for Reich Security])[1]; Einsatz Group C (Chief, first Rasch or Rasche, last inspector of the Security Police and SD in Königsberg, later Thomas, last Commander of the Security Police and the SD in Paris) was attached to the three Army Groups in the East. The Einsatz Group D (Chief, Ohlendorf, later Bierkamp, last inspector of the Security Police and the SD in Hamburg) was attached to the 11th Army, Commander in Chief, first von Schoeber, later von Manstein.

The framework of the Einsatz Groups and Einsatz Commandos was formed by members of the Security Police and SD. In addition, the Einsatz Groups were supplied with units from the Order Police and the Waffen SS. The Einsatz Group D consisted of approximately 400 to 500 men and had at its disposal about 170 vehicles. There was courier service and radio communication between the Chief of the Security Police and the SD and the Einsatz Groups.

I had about four weeks advance notice of the planned war against Russia through Heydrich. The Einsatz Groups were staged in Pretz, Saxony, and vicinity. After designated leaders of the Einsatz Groups and Einsatz Commandos were gathered at Pretz [, they] were informed of their tasks on the occasion of the presence of the Chief of AMT I of the RSHA, Streckenbach, by order of Heydrich. In the course of conference, the Einsatz Groups and Commandos were given also the task of liquidating in the Russian territories Jewish and Communist functionaries in

---

[1] AMT V (the fifth branch) of the Central Office for Reich Security, was responsible for the criminal police (Kripo), headed by Arthur Nebe from 1939 to 1945. In 1941 Nebe was given command of *Einsatzgruppe* B, and directed the execution of 46,000 people.

addition to the regular tasks of the Security Police and the SD. According to a communication from Himmler, the Chiefs of the Army Groups and Armies had been informed by Hitler about this mission and ordered to aid in its accomplishment. When Himmler in the late summer of 1941 spoke to the Commanders and men of the Einsatz Group D and their Commandos in Nikolajev, he repeated this order and added that neither the leaders nor the men who were to execute the liquidation would bear responsibility of their own. Rather, he himself, together with the Führer, would bear the full responsibility for this order and its execution. The Führer was mentioned almost parenthetically, whereas Himmler stressed his own responsibility.

The Einsatz Group D marched on or about 21 June 1941 from Duebin, Saxony, to its readiness position at Piatra Neamst, Rumania, through Hungary. Upon arrival in Piatra Neamst orders by the 11th Army were ready for the departure of the first Special Commandos. The northern and eastern boundary of the Einsatz space of the Einsatz Group D is marked by the following cities: Tschernowitz, Mogilew-Podolsk, Jampol, Ananjew, Nikolajev, Melitopol, Mariopol, Taganrog, Rostov. The space expanded to the south to Odessa over Cherson and included all of Crimea.

During the one year while I was Chief of the Einsatz Group D, the Einsatz Commandos and Special Commandos reported to have liquidated 90,000 men, women and children. The vast majority of the liquidated were Jews but there were also some Communist functionaries. It may be that in connection with liquidations in Simferopol, there were also gypsies among the liquidated or members of another tribe who were considered as Jews. The liquidations were executed by the Commandos within the space into which they had moved in accordance with orders given them by the Army. For the preparation of liquidations in cities, leading Jewish inhabitants were as a rule assigned to effect the registration of the Jews. Upon registration the Jews were gathered at a place under the pretext that they were to be resettled in another town. Prior to the liquidations the Jews had to surrender their valuables to the Commandos. Those selected for liquidation were either driven or led to the place of execution. The graves were in general either antitank ditches or natural crevices. In the Einsatz Group D the mass executions took place regularly in the form of shooting by details. The shooting by individuals was forbidden in Einsatz Group D, so that the men who were to perform the executions were not faced with the task of making personal decisions. The persons designated for liquidation were either shot while kneeling or standing upright. Only the head of units or specifically designated persons were permitted to give the coup de grace to those persons who were not killed at once. These directives were issued because I learned from members of Einsatz Groups from other areas that in those areas mass executions were performed by individuals who shot those persons designated for liquidation through the rear of the neck while lying or standing upright. With this method emotional upsets could not be avoided, however, either on the part of the victims or on the part of those who performed the executions. I, therefore, disapproved of this method. Immediately prior to the liquidation the victims had to rid themselves of their outer clothing. The complete undressing, which was partially customary in other areas, was likewise forbidden in Einsatz Group D.

Whereas the Army in general did not exert any influence in the liquidations, the Army had at Simferopol requested acceleration of the liquidations and rendered corresponding assistance in that it furnished trucks. Also, the Army officially did not make available liquidation commandos from its own units, however, almost everywhere individual execution commandos, for example, of the SHD or OT, participated in the executions.

Army was somewhat involved

While at first the clothes were distributed to the population, in the winter of 1941–42, a delegation of the NSV [Nationalsoziatistische Volkswohlfahrt, or National Socialist People's Welfare Organization] arrived in Simferopol which took over the clothes of the victims and disposed of them according to their own regulations. The gold and silver which was surrendered, was confiscated for the State and sent to the Reich Ministry of Finance. Such objects as could be used immediately in the operational area were so used. For instance, in Simferopol watches were requisitioned by the Army and were made accessible through the Army to the combat troops.

In spring of 1942 two or three gas vans were sent to the Einsatz Group D by the Chief of the Security Police and SD in Berlin. These vans were furnished by AMT II of the RSHA. The gas vans were not included in the vehicle park of the group, but allocated as a separate unit to Einsatz Group D, under the leadership of Second Lieutenant Becker. In regard to the vans, an order existed by the Reichsführer SS to the effect that in the future the killing of women and children was to be effected solely by gas vans. When a sufficient number of victims were rounded up, Commandos requested a gas van. The gas vans were brought to the collecting points before the liquidation took place. The victims were induced to enter the gas vans under the pretext that they were to be relocated. After closing the doors, gas was turned into the van by starting the engine. The victims died in ten to fifteen minutes without being conscious of the process. The commandos made use of the gas vans only reluctantly as they regarded their use an additional emotional burden upon the people who partook in the executions. I estimate that during my presence with Einsatz Group D only a few hundred were killed by means of gas vans.

I have been shown the letter . . . written by Becker to Rauff, the Head of the Technical Department in AMT II of RSHA, concerning the operations of the gas vans. I knew both of these men personally and I believe it to be an authentic document.

I have seen the report of Stahlecker, Chief of Einsatz Group A . . . about the activities of Einsatz Group A. It is stated in this report that Einsatz Group A during the first four months of the Einsatz action, had killed over 135,000 Jews and Communists. I knew Stahlecker and his way of reporting and, therefore, I am of the opinion that the document is authentic.

The above statement under oath, including Appendix "A," has been dictated, re-read and signed by me voluntarily and without compulsion.

Subscribed and sworn to before me on the 20 November 1945, at Nuremberg, Germany.

/s/ OTTO OHLENDORF

92. The SS Follows Orders

In a speech to SS leaders made during a three-day conference in Posen in October of 1943, Himmler spoke of the duty of the SS and of the necessity of following orders – even if those orders were unpleasant.

I also want to talk to you, quite frankly, on a very grave matter. Among ourselves it should be mentioned quite frankly, and yet we will never speak of it publicly. Just as we did not hesitate on June 30th, 1934 to do the duty we were bidden, and stand comrades who had lapsed, up against the wall and shoot them, so we have never spoken about it and will never speak of it. It was that tact which is a matter of course and which I am glad to say, is inherent in us, that made us never discuss it among ourselves, never to speak of it. It appalled everyone, and yet everyone was certain that he would do it the next time if such orders are issued and if it is necessary.

I mean the clearing out of the Jews, the extermination of the Jewish race. It's one of those things it is easy to talk about – "The Jewish race is being exterminated," says one party member, "that's quite clear, it's in our program – elimination of the Jews, and we're doing it, exterminating them." And then they come, 80 million worthy Germans, and each one has his decent Jew. Of course the others are vermin, but this one is an A-1 Jew. Not one of all those who talk this way has witnessed it, not one of them has been through it. Most of *you* must know what it means when

From U.S. Chief of Counsel for the Prosecution of Axis Criminality, *Nazi Conspiracy and Aggression* (Washington, D.C.: U.S. Government Printing Office, 1946), vol. 4, doc. no. 1919-PS, pp. 563–64.

100 corpses are lying side by side, or 500 or 1,000. To have stuck it out and at the same time – apart from exceptions caused by human weakness – to have remained decent fellows, that is what has made us hard. This is a page of glory in our history which has never been written and is never to be written, for we know how difficult we should have made it for ourselves, if – with the bombing raids, the burdens and the deprivations of war – we still had Jews today in every town as secret saboteurs, agitators and trouble-mongers. We would now probably have reached the 1916/17 stage when the Jews were still in the German national body.

We have taken from them what wealth they had. I have issued a strict order, which SS-Lieutenant General Pohl has carried out, that this wealth should, as a matter of course, be handed over to the Reich without reserve. We have taken none of it for ourselves. Individual men who have lapsed will be punished in accordance with an order I issued at the beginning, which gave this warning: Whoever takes so much as a mark of it, is a dead man. A number of SS men – there are not very many of them – have fallen short, and they will die, without mercy. We had the moral right, we had the duty to our people, to destroy this people which wanted to destroy us. But we have not the right to enrich ourselves with so much as a fur, a watch, a mark, or a cigarette or anything else. Because we have exterminated a bacterium we do not want, in the end, to be infected by the bacterium and die of it. I will not see so much as a small area of sepsis appear here or gain a hold. Wherever it may form, we will cauterize it. Altogether, however, we can say, that we have fulfilled this most difficult duty for the love of our people. And our spirit, our soul, our character has not suffered injury from it.

93. The SS Eliminates Other "Antisocial" Elements

Despite the fact that some defendants at the Nuremberg trials attempted to deny personal responsibility for Nazi murders and to distance themselves from the actual process of extermination at the camps, evidence presented during the trials revealed otherwise. Franz Ziereis, the commander of the Mauthausen concentration camp in Austria, was one of the most brutal of SS commanders. He and his subordinates took relish in devising innovative means of murdering prisoners, including literally working prisoners to death in stone quarries. Mauthausen inmates included large numbers of political prisoners as well as common criminals, who

From U.S. Chief of Counsel for the Prosecution of Axis Criminality, *Nazi Conspiracy and Aggression* (Washington, D.C.: U.S. Government Printing Office, 1946), vol. 6, doc. no. 3870-PS, pp. 790–92.

were categorized as antisocial elements and as such were of little value to the state. A 1937 decree had already stipulated that all antisocial elements – that is, those considered a burden to the *Volksgemeinschaft* – were to be put to work in concentration or labor camps. The list included beggars, pimps, Gypsies, and criminals. A former clerk in the Mauthausen camp gave the following testimony during the Nuremberg trials.

I, Hans Marsalek, after first being duly sworn, declare as follows:

I was born on 19 July 1914 in Vienna, and was in Concentration Camp Mauthausen from 29 September 1942 until my liberation. I had the function of second clerk in this camp. My present occupation is with the Directorate of Police in Vienna as the Director of Department IV. Counter-Intelligence Service of the State Police [Staatspolizeilicher Abwehrdienst], and my present address is: Vienna 19, Grinzingerstrasse 12.

On 22 May 1945, the Commandant of the Concentration Camp Mauthausen, Franz Ziereis, was shot while escaping by American soldiers and was taken to the branch camp of Gusen. Frank Ziereis was interrogated by me in the presence of the Commander of the 11th Armored Division (American Armored Division) Seibel; the former prisoner and physician Dr. Koszeinski; and in the presence of another Polish citizen, name unknown, for a period of six to eight hours. The interrogation was effected in the night from 22 May to 23 May 1945. Franz Ziereis was seriously wounded – his body had been penetrated by three bullets – and knew that he would die shortly and told me the following:

I joined the SS on 30 September 1936 as a training specialist with the rank of Obersturmführer (Lieutenant). I was assigned to the 4th SS Regt at Oranienburg and was transferred to Mauthausen on 17 February 1939, with the rank of Hauptsturmführer (Captain) and as successor to the former Commandant of the camp, SS Führer Saurer. My rapid and extraordinary career is due to the fact that I volunteered frequently for the Front. By orders of the Reichsführer SS Himmler I was forced to remain in Mauthausen. The SS complement in Mauthasen had the following organization:

There was one SS man for ten prisoners. The highest number of prisoners was about 17,000 (seventeen thousand), with the exception of the branch camps. The highest number in Camp Mauthausen, the branch camps included, was about 90,000 (ninety thousand).

The total number of prisoners who died was 65,000 (sixty-five thousand). The complement was made up of Totenkopf units, strength of 5,000 (five thousand) men, which were made up of guards and the command staff.

Later, 6,000 (six thousand) men came from the Army and the Air Forces [Wehrmacht and Luftwaffe] for guard duty and they were put into SS uniforms. Moreover, there were many "Racial Germans" [Volks Deutsche] who had been conscripted into the Wehrmacht. The recruitment of former prisoners into the SS was done on orders of Himmler.

These were to fight against the enemy, particularly the Bolsheviks. For the greater part they were to be recruited as volunteers.

I have personally killed about 4,000 (four thousand) prisoners by assigning them to the Penal Company. The formation of Penal Companies was done by order of Berlin to effect a more rapid extermination of prisoners through hard labor. I always took part personally in the executions.

By order of Dr. Lohnauer, incorrigible professional criminals were transferred to Hartheim near Linz as mentally deficient, where they were exterminated by a special system of SS Captain Krebsbach. The greatest number of murdered prisoners goes to the account of Bachmeyer. Chemielskwy and Seidler in Gusen had human skin specially tanned on which there were tattoos. From this leather they had books bound, and they had lampshades and leather cases made.

According to an order by Himmler, I was to liquidate all prisoners on behalf of SS Lieutenant General Dr. Kaltenbrunner; the prisoners were to be led into the tunnels of the factory Bergkristall and only one entrance was to be left open. Then this entrance was to be blown up by the use of explosives and the death of the prisoners was to be effected in this manner. I refused to carry out this order. This matter was the extermination of the prisoners of the so-called Mother camp, Mauthausen, and of the camps Gusen I and Gusen II. Details of this are known to Herr Wolfram and SS Lieutenant Eckermann.

A gassing plant was built in Concentration Camp Mauthausen by order of the former garrison doctor, Dr. Krebsbach, camouflaged as a bathroom. Prisoners were gassed in this camouflaged bathroom. Apart from that a specially built automobile commuted between Mauthausen and Gusen, in which prisoners were gassed while travelling. The idea for the construction of this automobile was Dr. Wasicki's, SS Untersturmfuehrer and pharmacist. I, myself, never put any gas into this automobile, I only drove it, but I knew that prisoners were being gassed. The gassing of the prisoners was done on the urging of SS Captain Dr. Krebsbach.

Everything that we carried out was ordered by the Central Office for Reich Security [Reichssicherheitshauptamt], furthermore, by SS Lieutenant General Mueller or Dr. Kaltenbrunner, the latter being Chief of the Security Police.

SS Lieutenant General Pohl gave the order that prisoners were to be driven into the woods because they were weak and had had no food, in order to pick berries there and to eat buds. The above-mentioned shortened the daily ration from 750 grms per day to 350 grms per day through the administration. SS Major General Gluecks gave the order to classify weak prisoners as mentally deranged and to kill them by a gas plant which existed in the Castle Hartheim near Linz. . . .

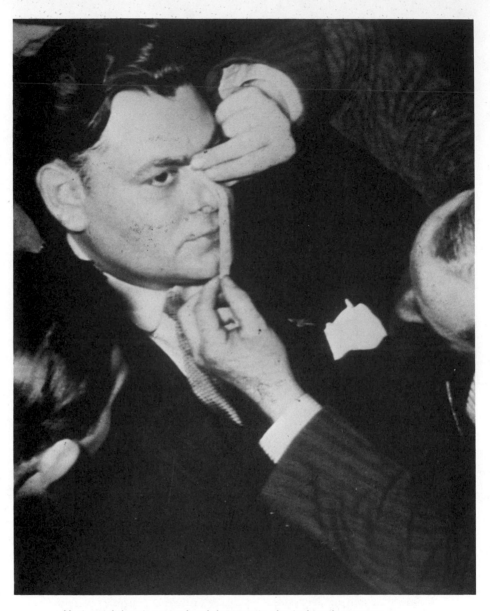

Nazi racial theories postulated that certain physical attributes were characteristic of each race. Nazi "experts" claimed that by measuring skull proportions and facial features it was possible to determine racial type.

Chapter
13

The Solutions to the "Jewish Problem," 1933–1941

Nazi policy toward the Jews evolved in definite stages. After early episodes of SA and SS violence and the organized boycott of Jewish businesses, the government turned to legislation aimed at eliminating Jews from public life. On April 7, 1933, the Law for the Restoration of the Professional Civil Service provided for the dismissal of "non-Aryans" from the state bureaucracy, including the university faculties. The importance of the law lies in a subsequent definition of "non-Aryan" propounded on April 11, by which a person who had at least one Jewish parent or one Jewish grandparent was now identified as of "non-Aryan" descent. Not only did the law undermine the principle of equality before the law so essential to modern society, but it also instituted a "biological" foundation in law and thus the legal constitution of society. The racial definition of society removed citizenship from the domain of free choice and moral action and placed it on a dubious basis determined by "blood."

A series of similar anti-Jewish legislation followed. Between April and October 1933 Jews were excluded from such occupations as assessor, juror, and commercial judge. A law of April 25 limited the number of Jewish students in institutions of higher education to 1.5 percent of new admissions. In September, with the establishment of the Reich Chamber of Culture, Jews were entirely excluded from educational and entertainment activities. They were barred from studying German literature, from performing in the theater or in films, and from engaging in creative activity in the arts. The National Press Law of October 4 excluded Jews from working on newspapers and journals. Jews were also forbidden to own farmland, and on July 14, all Jews who had recently obtained German citizenship were deprived of that status.

These various legal exclusions culminated in the Nuremberg Laws, which provided for the legal redefinition of German Jews within the Third Reich. These laws of September and November 1935 denied full citizenship to Jews: Jews could not vote or hold office, and marriage and even extramarital relations between Jews and "nationals of German and kindred blood" were forbidden. The Jews were reduced to the legal status of "subject," a position comparable to that of resident alien. A subject was defined as anyone who enjoyed the protection of the Reich and was therefore obligated to it but who possessed no political rights; a Reich "citizen," on the other hand, was a person with "German or cognate blood" and was thus entitled to a "Reich certificate of citizenship." The Reich Citizenship Law marked a major break from the idea of individual rights on which the legal relationship between citizens and the state in Western countries was based. Citizenship was no longer grounded on the equal participation of citizens under the law. To the National Socialists, the notion of the equality of all citizens did not recognize either the inequality among men and women or their racial and national differences. Differences in rights and obligations derived from racial differences. Consequently citizenship was not a matter of individual rights but stemmed from membership in the racially defined *Volk*. Although many German Jews and non-Jews alike may have thought that the Nuremberg Laws represented only a temporary state of affairs, the biological definition of citizenship became the basis and provided a psychological foundation for further persecution.

The almost uninterrupted flow of amendments to the Nuremberg Laws between 1935 and 1938 catalogues the progress of institutionalized discrimination by which Jews were almost completely shut out of German life. They were not admitted to public offices, hospitals, pharmacies, restaurants, schools, and universities, and they were not eligible for any governmental tax aid. Beginning in mid-1938, Jews had to carry identification cards and passports and add the stereotypical first name Israel or Sarah to their given names. The first "solution" to the "Jewish Problem" was complete by 1938. The Jews had been successfully eliminated from all aspects of public life.

These early phases of antisemitic activity culminated in *Kristallnacht*, the night of November 9–10, 1938, on which the level of violence against the Jews dramatically increased and became more systematic. Although large-scale violence against the Jews had tapered off by 1934 (minor acts of violence of course continued), open season was declared again in 1938 and marked a still-greater intensification of official anti-Jewish activity. On *Kristallnacht*, a pogrom against the Jews was conducted throughout Germany in which stores were looted, synagogues destroyed, and people killed. Over seven thousand Jewish businesses were ruined; approximately ninety Jews were killed and thousands more subjected to torture. About thirty to fifty thousand "prosperous" Jews were arrested and sent to concentration camps before being forced into exile, leaving everything they owned behind. The pogrom had a twofold purpose: to intensify the combative mood of the German people and to exclude Jews from economic life. But as with the

398

boycott of 1933, the organizers of the pogrom wanted it to appear as an unplanned uprising. When an opportune incident occurred — the assassination of a German diplomat in Paris by a Jewish youth — Goebbels spurred a gathering of party members and SS leaders to violence but did not give exact orders to destroy Jewish businesses and places of worship. Thus the violence was the "spontaneous reaction of the German people."

The real reasons for *Kristallnacht* were more mercenary than merely an outburst of antisemitic hatred on the part of the Nazi leadership. Toward the end of 1937, Goering was looking for the means to finance the rearmament program. In October 1938, he hit upon the Jews, declaring that they "must be driven out of the economy." The government's anti-Jewish policies therefore had a strong financial motive, as became clear the day after the pogrom when it was announced that Jews were to pay for the repair of the damage they had incited the German people "to inflict upon them." They were also fined one billion marks and had their insurance compensation confiscated. On November 12, 1938, Goering moved to "Aryanize" all Jewish businesses and industry. In its net result, *Kristallnacht* destroyed Jewish economic life in Germany. No longer could individual Jews make a living, since the professions were closed to them and their businesses were forfeited to the state. They had to live either off their capital or through relief, or when neither of these sufficed, to emigrate. On the heels of the violence of November 1938 followed more discriminatory legislation. Jews were to be completely excluded from German schools and universities. Theaters, concerts, museums, athletic fields, and public baths were barred to Jews. They were not allowed to drive automobiles or own telephones or radios. They could not possess gold or silver items. They were to move into designated "Jewish houses," and forced labor was introduced for the first time.

As legal exclusion continued and officially sanctioned violence increased, the government launched a policy of "resettlement," a euphemism for the forced expulsion of the Jews from Germany and the expropriation of their property. Beginning in 1938, the Central Office for Jewish Emigration under Adolf Eichmann began negotiating to remove all Jews from Germany. Wealthy Jews who wanted to leave were obliged to sacrifice part of their assets in order to provide foreign currency; all else was confiscated. Because other countries did not wish to admit indigent Jews from Germany and because Jews were not allowed to transfer funds outside the country, the program never seriously got under way. Eichmann even arranged with the International Committee for Refugee Problems to send a large number of Jews to Palestine. Deportation schemes continued to be a feature of National Socialist policy until 1941. By the Second Reich Citizenship Law of July 1939, all Jews were ordered to join the Reich Union of German Jews, the aim of which was to promote emigration. The most fantastic emigration project was the so-called Madagascar Plan. After the fall of France in 1940 and with the possibility of French colonies falling into German hands, the Reich Foreign Office considered evacuating four million Jews from Europe and sending them to Madagascar, a

French possession off the southeast coast of Africa. A Jewish satellite state was to be set up under Himmler's control. Many obstacles blocked the realization of this project, not least of which was the problem of shipping millions of people during wartime, with the British navy in control of the Atlantic. The Reich Foreign Office may well have proposed this wild scheme to cloak more extreme forms of elimination then being prepared. A year later the regime declared the Madagascar Plan "obsolete."

The next "solution" was concentration, the physical separation and social isolation of the Jewish community from the *Volksgemeinschaft,* which included measures placing the government of the Jewish community under German command. Henceforth, in the Reich as well as in newly conquered territories, the Germans would employ Jewish leaders for housing segregation, personal-property confiscation, forced labor, and even deportations. Concentration of the Jewish population had been contemplated even before the beginning of the war when, in the wake of the violence and arrests of November 1938, Goering and several others discussed whether to form ghettos inside Germany for Jewish subjects. The proposal was shelved when Heydrich objected, arguing that so long as Jews were not segregated but remained in sight, every German could act as an auxiliary policeman over the activities of these second-rate members of the Reich.

A number of ghettos were set up almost immediately after the occupation of Poland. The largest were those of Warsaw and Lodz, but hundreds of smaller ones also existed. These concentration centers were established not only for the Jews of Poland but more especially for the Jews of Germany. On September 21, 1939, Heydrich ordered the deportation of German Jews to Poland and provided for "councils of Jewish elders" to administer the communities. By December, evacuations of roughly one million Jews eastward had started. The plan worked extremely well until Hans Frank, the governor of occupied Poland, protested, mainly for economic reasons. Frank complained to Berlin that he had not been informed of the new Jewish policy and that he did not want any more Jews dumped in the area under his control. Frank won out; forced Jewish emigration to Poland ceased.

With the failure of concentration, a new plan had to be devised. The emigration and ghetto-organization programs already signaled that nothing less than complete evacuation of the Jews would do; no special legislation, no disenfranchisement, and no separate communities within Germany would suffice. Because there existed no territory to which Hitler and those in charge of Jewish affairs could "evacuate" the Jews, only one "solution" remained: extermination. The date on which the policy of *Endlösung,* the Final Solution, was reached is hard to determine exactly. One thing is certain; the order to go ahead with it coincided with the invasion of the Soviet Union. On July 31, 1941, just six weeks after the invasion began, Goering sent Heydrich an order instructing him to prepare "the general solution of the Jewish question within the area of German influence in Europe" and to submit "a general proposal for the implementation of the desired final solution of the Jewish question." Goering was acting as chairman of the Ministerial Defense

Council, and the order must have come from the highest echelons of the Third Reich — ultimately, from Hitler. Whoever was responsible for the order, it sealed the fate of Europe's Jews. Although it suggested no specific methods to be employed and called for no definite timetable, the order conveyed a sense of finality and irreversibility. But Goering's order did not set the Final Solution into operation. Hitler had already verbally given the order to Himmler no later than March 1941, when he expressed the wish that the *Einsatzgruppen* shoot all Soviet commissars, undesirables, and Jews they met in pacifying conquered Russian territory (the so-called Commissar Order). The Final Solution thus probably matured with the development of affairs on the eastern front. That Hitler was moving in the direction of exterminating the Jews seems clear from at least the beginning of 1939, when he confronted the inevitability of a European war. In his Reichstag address of January 30, 1939, Hitler proclaimed the goal of the "extermination of the Jewish race in Europe." Goering's order of the summer of 1941 only gave these wishes and verbal commands a legal status through governmental sanction.

94. Hitler Explains His Antisemitism to Hindenburg

President Paul von Hindenburg had reservations about the sweeping effect of Nazi antisemitic policies. In particular, he was concerned about those Jews who had served Germany loyally in World War I. In this letter of April 1933 the Führer explains his position to Hindenburg.

April 5, 1933

Honorable Herr Reich President:

The resistance of the German people to the inundation of certain professions by Jews is based on two considerations:

First of all, an obvious injustice exists in that the dominant German people are being outrageously slighted. At present there is a whole series of learned professions, such as lawyers and doctors, which in individual localities of the nation — in Berlin and other cities — are staffed by Jews to the extent that they occupy up to 80 percent or more of all positions. At the same time there are hundreds of thousands of German intellectuals, including countless war veterans, who are on welfare or find themselves holding down some kind of entirely demoralizing subordinate position.

Second, a serious blow to the authority of the state is being created by the fact that here an alien body, which has never entirely fused with

[handwritten margin note: over-represent of Jews]

From Herbert Michaelis and Ernst Schraepler, eds., *Ursachen und Folgen vom deutschen Zusammenbruch 1918 und 1945,* vol. 9 (Berlin: Dokumenten-Verlag Dr. Herbert Wendler und Co., 1958), pp. 393–95. Translated by Dieter Kuntz.

the German people and whose abilities lie mainly in the field of business, is pushing into governmental positions and is thereby sowing the seed of corruption the extent of which no one today has any adequate appreciation. The integrity of the old Prussian state was in no small measure dependent on the fact that Jews had only very limited access to the civil service. The officers' corps kept itself almost entirely pure of them. The great majority of the German people have also intuitively recognized this harm and have had to suffer from its effects. The present-day defensive measures against this were precipitated only by the entirely unjustified attack mounted by the Jews through international atrocity and boycott agitation.

It is clear that these defensive measures in this muddled situation entail serious consequences for the individual. Unemployment, however, is no more difficult for a Jewish intellectual than the unemployment that has affected millions of our own people. They have been affected by general conditions, for which they bear no blame, but which were caused by those forces that, even before November 1918 but especially since then, have pursued the systematic destruction of the Reich.

Herr Field Marshal, you are humanely and generously taking up the cause on behalf of the Jewish people who once, because of the general conscription, were forced to perform war service. I fully understand your noble, humane sentiment, Herr Field Marshal. Yet please allow me to respectfully point out that the members and supporters of my movement, who were Germans, were for years forced out of all government positions without regard for wife and child and without regard for the war services they had rendered. The National Socialist Party formerly had the highest percentage of war veterans among the members of its Reichstag delegation. All types were represented, ranging from generals and officers who had won the Pour le Merite down to the lowest private. This was true also of the party's members and supporters. Nonetheless, the members of this largest movement of millions of the German people, whose main goal in the struggle was the reestablishment of the German armed forces, were not allowed to work in government service even as workers or as civil servants. Those responsible for these atrocities were the same Jewish parties who today are complaining when their supporters, with a thousand times more justification, are barred access to government positions in which they are of little use but can possibly do unlimited damage. It was only through your intervention, Herr Field Marshal, that this ostracism of the members of my movement was done away with, initially in individual cases and then finally in general. I respect the noble motives of your sentiment, Herr Field Marshal, but I have already discussed with Minister of the Interior Frick the preparation of a law that will remove the solution of the questions from arbitrary individual action and legally regulate them in general. In this connection I have pointed out to the minister of the interior those cases which you, Herr Field Marshal, would like to see excepted. This Law [for the Restoration of the Professional Civil Service] was previously discussed at the end of last week during the first consultation conference, and will take into consideration those Jews who either performed war service themselves, or suffered war injuries, or who are otherwise deserving, or who during long terms in office never gave cause for complaint. In general, the first goal of this cleansing process is intended to be the restoration of a certain healthy and natural relationship; and second, to remove from specified positions important to the state those elements that cannot be entrusted with the life or death of the Reich. Because in the coming years we will inevitably have to take precautions to ensure that certain events that cannot be disclosed to the rest of the world for higher reasons of state really remain secret. This can only be guaranteed through an internal homogeneity of the administrative authorities in question.

Please be assured, Herr President, that I shall attempt to take your noble sentiments into consideration as far as possible. I understand your inner motivations, as I myself often suffer from the harshness of a fate that forces one to reach decisions which for humane reasons one would rather avoid a thousand times.

The law under consideration will be drafted as soon as possible, and I am certain that this question too will then have found the best solution possible.

In sincere and deep respect, yours,

ADOLF HITLER

95. Anti-Jewish Legislation: The Nuremberg Laws

The first phase of the regime's antisemitic legislation prior to the beginning of the war was initiated not long after the seizure of power. The laws enacted during the period from April to October 1933 aimed to eliminate Jews from civil service positions and professional occupations such as law, medicine, and teaching. The Law for the Restoration of the Professional Civil Service (see Chapter 4) included paragraphs dealing with "non-Aryans."

Following a brief respite, further anti-Jewish legislation was enacted in 1935, known collectively as the Nuremberg laws. The Reich Citizenship Law stripped

From U.S. Chief of Counsel for the Prosecution of Axis Criminality, *Nazi Conspiracy and Aggression* (Washington, D.C.: U.S. Government Printing Office, 1946), vol. 4, doc. no. 1416-PS, pp. 7–8; doc. no. 1417-PS, pp. 8–10; doc. no. 2000-PS, pp. 636–38.

Jews of their citizenship if they did not meet the requirement of having "German or kindred blood," whereas the Law for the Protection of German Blood and Honor prohibited Jews from marrying Aryan Germans. These laws effected the political and social exclusion of Jews from the rest of German society, prompting many Jews to emigrate from Germany.

THE REICH CITIZENSHIP LAW OF 15 SEPT. 1935

The Reichstag had adopted unananimously, the following law, which is herewith promulgated.

ARTICLE 1.

1. A subject of the State is a person, who belongs to the protective union of the German Reich, and who, therefore, has particular obligations towards the Reich.

2. The status of the subject is acquired in accordance with the provisions of the Reich- and State Law of Citizenship.

ARTICLE 2.

1. A citizen of the Reich is only that subject, who is of German or kindred blood and who, through his conduct, shows that he is both desirous and fit to serve faithfully the German people and Reich.

2. The right to citizenship is acquired by the granting of Reich citizenship papers.

3. Only the citizen of the Reich enjoys full political rights in accordance with the provision of the laws.

ARTICLE 3.

The Reich Minister of the Interior in conjunction with the Deputy of the Führer will issue the necessary legal and administrative decrees for the carrying out and supplementing of this law.

Nuremberg, 15 Sept 1935 at the Reichsparteitag of Liberty

The Führer and Reichs Chancellor
ADOLF HITLER
The Reich Minister of the Interior
FRICK

FIRST REGULATION TO THE REICHS CITIZENSHIP LAW OF 14 NOV. 1935

On the basis of Article 3, Reichs Citizenship Law, of 15 Sept. 1935 . . . the following is ordered:

ARTICLE 1.

1. Until further issue of regulations regarding citizenship papers, all subjects of German or kindred blood, who possessed the right to vote in the Reichstag elections, at the time the Citizenship Law came into effect, shall, for the time being, possess the rights of Reich citizens. The same shall be true of those whom the Reich Minister of the Interior, in conjunction with the Deputy of the Führer, has given the preliminary citizenship.

2. The Reich Minister of the Interior, in conjunction with the Deputy of the Führer, can withdraw the preliminary citizenship.

ARTICLE 2.

1. The regulations in Article 1 are also valid for Reich subjects of mixed, Jewish blood.

2. An individual of mixed Jewish blood, is one who descended from one or two grandparents who were racially full Jews, insofar as [he or she] does not count as a Jew according to Article 5, paragraph 2. One grandparent shall be considered as full-blooded if he or she belonged to the Jewish religious community.

ARTICLE 3.

Only the Reich citizen, as bearer of full political rights, exercises the right to vote in political affairs, and can hold a public office. The Reich Minister of the Interior, or any agency empowered by him, can make exceptions during the transition period, with regard to occupying public offices. The affairs of religious organizations will not be touched upon.

ARTICLE 4.

1. A Jew cannot be a citizen of the Reich. He has no right to vote in political affairs, he cannot occupy a public office.

2. Jewish officials will retire as of 31 December 1935. If these officials served at the front in the World War, either for Germany or her allies, they will receive in full, until they reach the age limit, the pension to which they were entitled according to last received wages; they will, however, not advance in seniority. After reaching the age limit, their pension will be calculated anew, according to the last received salary, on the basis of which their pension was computed.

3. The affairs of religious organizations will not be touched upon.

4. The conditions of service of teachers in Jewish public schools remain unchanged, until new regulations of the Jewish school systems are issued.

ARTICLE 5.

1. A Jew is anyone who descended from at least three grandparents who were racially full Jews. Article 2, par. 2, second sentence will apply.

2. A Jew is also one who descended from two full Jewish parents, if: (a) he belonged to the Jewish religious community at the time this law was issued, or who joined the community later; (b) he was married to a Jewish person, at the time the law was issued, or married one subsequently; (c) he is the offspring from a marriage with a Jew, in the sense of Section 1, which was contracted after the Law for the Protection of German Blood and German Honor became effective . . . ; (d) he is the offspring of an extramarital relationship, with a Jew, according to Section 1, and will be born out of wedlock after July 31, 1936.

ARTICLE 6.

1. As far as demands are concerned for the pureness of blood as laid down in Reich law or in orders of the NSDAP and its echelons — not covered in Article 5 — they will not be touched upon.

2. Any other demands on pureness of blood, not covered in Article 5, can only be made with permission from the Reich Minister of the Interior and the Deputy of the Führer. If any such demands have been made, they will be void as of 1 Jan 1936, if they have not been requested from the Reich Minister of the Interior in agreement with the Deputy of the Führer. These requests must be made from the Reich Minister of the Interior.

ARTICLE 7.

The Führer and Reichs Chancellor can grant exemptions from the regulations laid down in the law.

Berlin, 14 November 1935   *The Führer and Reichs Chancellor*
                                                              ADOLF HITLER
                                                The Reich Minister of the Interior
                                                                         FRICK
                                                      The Deputy of the Führer
                                                                      R. HESS
                                                (Reich Minister without Portfolio)

LAW FOR THE PROTECTION OF GERMAN BLOOD AND GERMAN HONOR OF 15 SEPTEMBER 1935

Thoroughly convinced by the knowledge that the purity of German blood is essential for the further existence of the German people and animated by the inflexible will to safe-guard the German nation for the entire future, the Reichstag has resolved upon the following law unanimously, which is promulgated herewith:

SECTION 1

intermarriage is forbidden

1. Marriages between Jews and nationals of German or kindred blood are forbidden. Marriages concluded in defiance of this law are void, even if, for the purpose of evading this law, they are concluded abroad.

2. Proceedings for annulment may be initiated only by the Public Prosecutor.

SECTION 2

Relation outside marriage between Jews and nationals of German or kindred blood are forbidden.

SECTION 3

Jews will not be permitted to employ female nationals of German or kindred blood in their household.

SECTION 4

1. Jews are forbidden to hoist the Reich and national flag and to present the colors of the Reich.

2. On the other hand they are permitted to present the Jewish colors. The exercise of this authority is protected by the State.

SECTION 5

1. A person who acts contrary to the prohibition of section 1 will be punished with hard labor.

2. A person who acts contrary to the prohibition of section 2 will be punished with imprisonment or with hard labor.

3. A person who acts contrary to the provisions of sections 3 or 4 will be punished with imprisonment up to a year and with a fine or with one of these penalties.

SECTION 6

The Reich Minister of the Interior in agreement with the Deputy of the Führer and the Reich Minister of Justice will issue the legal and administrative regulations which are required for the implementation and supplementation of this law.

SECTION 7

The law will become effective on the day after the promulgation, section 3 however only on 1 January 1936.

Nuremberg, the 15 September 1935 at the Reich Party Rally of freedom

The Führer and Reich Chancellor
ADOLF HITLER
The Reich Minister of Interior
FRICK
The Reich Minister of Justice
DR. GÜRTNER
The Deputy of the Führer
R. HESS
(Reich Minister without Portfolio)

96. The Boycott of Jewish Businesses

In March 1935, Hitler charged Goebbels with undertaking a campaign of economic boycott against Jewish enterprises. No business was to be conducted with Jewish firms, no services received from Jewish professionals, and stores, homes and offices of Jews were to be marked with special signs. Simultaneously, at the local and regional level, the Nazis enacted ordinances that further restricted the freedom of movement of Jews and limited their activities by excluding them from movie theaters, swimming pools, and other public recreational places. Not all Germans, however, adhered to the boycott, as the following district council president's memorandum of June 1935 indicates. The lack of success during this phase of Nazi policy did, however, prompt local officials to take an even harsher approach. The subsequent report filed by the Gestapo shows that by the fall of 1935, after the passage of the first Nuremberg Law, Jews were beginning to suffer economically and increasing numbers were contemplating emigration.

REPORT OF DISTRICT COUNCIL PRESIDENT, BAD KREUZNACH, JUNE 1935

. . . The boycott measures have not had the intended effect. Segments of the population which condemn such measures on principle tend to pity the Jews — who then, of course, take advantage of these feelings. The sales receipts of Jewish businesses have not fallen off. This is especially true of the rural areas. . . .

From Anton Doll, ed., *Nationalsozialismus im Alltag: Quellen zur Geschichte der NS-Herrschaft im Gebiet des Landes Rheinland-Pfalz* (Speyer: Landesarchiv, 1983), pp. 137, 138, 140–41. Translated by Dieter Kuntz. Reprinted by permission of Landesarchiv, Rheinland-Pfalz.

RESOLUTION OF A MUNICIPAL COUNCIL IN THE BERNKASTEL DISTRICT, AUGUST 13, 1935

Judaism, which has brought such misfortune on our German Fatherland, is today once again rearing its head more boldly than ever. These parasites on the German body politic underestimate our sense of decency and are again making themselves at home within National Socialist Germany, which they hate so much, and are again pouring out their Jewish impudence and vulgarity.

In recognizing this situation, we have resolved to act accordingly:

- All city exits will be fitted with signs bearing the inscription: JEWS NOT WANTED HERE.
- The journal *Der Stürmer,* on display in the newspaper display box in the town center, will be recommended to all citizens.
- No craftsman, businessman, or any other countryman will receive work contracts from the community and will immediately forfeit entitlement to the use and enjoyment of communal property if he or members of his family continue to traffic with Jews; that is, if he supports their businesses.
- Making purchases from Jews, employing Jewish physicians or lawyers is tantamount to committing a traitorous act against the German people and nation.
- Given the fact that the race question holds the key to our freedom, those who break these fundamental principles are to be scorned and outlawed.

SITUATION REPORT FROM GESTAPO OFFICES, KOBLENZ, OCTOBER 1935

increased emigration

The legal resolution of the Jewish question is gradually having the effect of prompting increasing numbers of Jewish families to emigrate. The exclusion of Jews from economic life continues to make progress. The Jewish influence over the livestock trade has almost totally ceased. In retail trade Jews have also continued to lose ground. The closing down of Jewish shops is proceeding at a rapid rate. Agricultural and developed sections of land have increasingly been put up for sale recently. It looks as though the Jewish question will be resolved in the near future in rural districts through the migration of Jews to large cities.

Emigration to Palestine is being heavily promoted by the Zionist organization. This organization has lately received a great influx of new members. . . . Since the promulgation of the [Nuremberg] Jewish laws, Jews no longer believe in the possibility of remaining in Germany and estimate that within ten years the last Jew will have left Germany. Since the implementation statutes of the Jewish laws have not yet been made public, Jews are somewhat uneasy. They maintain that the treatment and abuse they have been subjected to has made them so emotionally worn out that they simply cannot endure any further ill treatment. They would be thankful if the uncertainty of their situation were settled by being told that they must leave Germany within six months.

97. Intimidation of the Jewish Population

Inflammatory anti-Jewish pronouncements by Nazi officials became commonplace during 1935. During the week of September 8–14, top Nazi officials met in Nuremberg to discuss legislation defining the status of Germany's Jewish community. Rumors of impending legal action against Jews prompted local party officials to encourage further acts of intimidation against Jews.

A police-interrogation transcript of a suspect involved in vandalism at a Jewish cemetery in the Rhineland demonstrates the effect of the party's sanctioning of harassment of Jews. The document also evidences public disapproval of these random acts of violence.

On that evening I met [friends] Gross and Remle in the tavern Keller in Hassloch. Gross told me that I was to go with him. When I asked what was going on, he told me that a couple of Jews would be strung up. He said he had read a directive from S.S. leader Strubel which had declared that Jews were to be considered fair game. I hurriedly went home to eat dinner and later, after dark, met Gross and Remle in the Adolf Hitler Street. Gross then led the way, while Remle and I followed. We first went to the courtyard gate of the butcher Paul Heene. Gross began kicking the door, which prompted Heene's dog to begin barking. We then cursed all Jews and headed for the property of the livestock dealer Heinrich Heene. Here Gross kicked against the locked courtyard gate like some kind of animal, trying with all his strength to break it down. The gate held, however, and Gross then began to yell things like, "Out with you, you pack of Jews. Tonight I'm going to slit your throats." I, too, took part in abusing the Jews.

A large number of people had soon collected. They did not join us, however, because they are all still friends of the Jews. Once the racket had gotten louder, the Jew Roos appeared in the window and told Gross to go away, because his wife was a maternity case, and had delivered a child only four days before. Gross then yelled: "I'm going to bring that Jewish bitch down here, and then I'm going to kill the little Jewish bastard and throw him in the river. I'm going to cut all your Jewish heads off and

From Anton Doll, ed., *Nationalsozialismus im Alltag: Quellen zur Geschichte der NS-Herrschaft im Gebiet des Landes Rheinland-Pfalz* (Speyer: Landesarchiv, 1983), p. 139. Translated by Dieter Kuntz. Reprinted by permission of Landesarchiv, Rheinland-Pfalz.

make mincemeat out of you." When Gross saw, however, that the assembled crowd did not support him, he yelled at them, "So, you call yourselves men, but you don't help me bring this pack of Jews out." He then tried with great force to break down the door, kicking against it wilder than ever. The crowd, however, was not in favor of Gross's deed, and one could hear voices growing louder with disapproval — that this was not just. Only then did policeman Seither appear, ordering Gross to keep quiet. Remle and I tried to talk Gross into going home with us. Gross, however, went to the tavern Keller, intending to go back to the house of the Jew Heene later. I don't know who stopped him. The whole affair took about half an hour. I was not involved in the incident at the Jewish cemetery. Later I found out from [Nazi] Party local chairman Damian that the propaganda campaign against the Jews would be suspended. . . .

98. Anti-Jewish Legislation: The *Kristallnacht* Decrees

The regime relaxed its anti-Jewish policies in order to improve its image for the Olympic Games held in Berlin in 1936. Following this brief respite, however, Nazi antisemitism grew more virulent than ever. Beginning in the summer of 1938, Jews were required to carry identification cards and violent acts against Jews by the SA and SS increased. In the fall of 1938, however, this phase of the regime's policies dramatically culminated in a general pogrom. During the night of November 9–10, Goebbels and Heydrich, head of the Security Service, organized a campaign of violence that resulted in the destruction of many synagogues and thousands of Jewish businesses. This pogrom took its name, *Kristallnacht*, (crystal night — "night of the broken glass") from the broken windows of stores and synagogues.

This attack on the Jews was followed by measures designed to rob them of their economic base, in order to benefit the government's coffers and to accelerate their emigration through terror. On November 12, 1938, Goering presided over a large meeting of Party officials called together to consider future policy in the aftermath of the pogrom. Goering, who headed the Reich's Four-Year Plan, had persuaded Hitler to assign execution of Jewish policy to his jurisdiction as well. Discussed during the meeting were the financial ramifications of Kristallnacht. Participants formulated three decrees that held German Jews responsible for all damages, providing for the levying of fines, the confiscation of property, and the further restriction of Jewish freedom.

From U.S. Chief of Counsel for the Prosecution of Axis Criminality, *Nazi Conspiracy and Aggression* (Washington, D.C.: U.S. Government Printing Office, 1946); vol. 5, doc. no. 3051-PS, pp. 799–800; vol. 4, doc. no. 1816-PS, pp. 425–29, 431–33, 450–51, 454.

COPY OF TELETYPE FROM MUNICH, 10 NOVEMBER 1938, 1:20 A.M.

To all Headquarters and Stations of the State Police.
To all Districts and Sub-districts of the SD [Sicherheitsdienst, or Security Service]
Urgent! Submit immediately to the Chief or his deputy!

Re: Measures against Jews tonight.

Because of the attempt on the life of the Secretary of the Legation vom Rath in Paris tonight, 9–10 November 1938, demonstrations against Jews are to be expected throughout the Reich. The following instructions are given on how to treat these events:

1. The Chiefs of the State Police, or their deputies, must get in telephonic contact with the political leaders [Gauleitung oder Kreisleitung] who have jurisdiction over their districts and have to arrange a joint meeting with the appropriate inspector or commander of the Order Police [Ordnungspolizei] to discuss the organization of the demonstrations. At these discussions the political leaders have to be informed that the German Police has received from the Reichsführer SS and Chief of the German Police the following instructions, in accordance with which the political leaders should adjust their own measures.

a. Only such measures should be taken which do not involve danger to German life or property. (For instance synagogues are to be burned down only when there is no danger of fire to the surroundings.)

b. Business and private apartments of Jews may be destroyed but not looted. The police is instructed to supervise the execution of this order and to arrest looters.

c. On business streets, particular care is to be taken that non-Jewish business should be protected from damage.

d. Foreigners, even Jews, are not to be molested.

2. The demonstrations which are going to take place should not be hindered by the police provided that the instructions quoted above in section 1 are carried out. The police has only to supervise compliance with the instructions.

3. Upon receipt of this telegram, in all synagogues and offices of the Jewish communities the available archives should be seized by the police, to forestall destruction during the demonstrations. This refers only to valuable historical material, not to new lists of taxes, etc. The archives are to be turned over to the competent SD offices.

4. The direction of the measures of the Security Police [Sicherheitspolizei] concerning the demonstrations against Jews is vested with the organs of the State Police, inasmuch as the inspectors of the Security Police are not issuing their own orders. In order to carry out the measures of the

Security Police, officials of the Criminal Police as well as members of the SD of the Special Duty and the general SS may be used.

5. Inasmuch as in the course of the events of this night the employment of officials used for this purpose would be possible, in all districts as many Jews, especially rich ones, are to be arrested as can be accommodated in the existing prisons [Hafträumen]. For the time being only healthy men not too old are to be arrested. Upon their arrest, the appropriate concentration camps should be contacted immediately, in order to confine them in these camps as fast as possible. Special care should be taken that the Jews arrested in accordance with these instructions are not mistreated.

6. The contents of this order are to be forwarded to the appropriate inspectors and commanders of the Ordnungspolizei and to the districts of the SD [SD-Oberabschnitte und SD-Unterabschnitte], adding that the Reichsführer SS and Chief of the German Police ordered this police measure. The Chief of the Ordnungspolizei, has given the necessary instructions to the Ordnungspolizei, including the fire brigade. In carrying out the ordered measures, the closest harmony should be assured between the Sicherheitspolizei and the Ordnungspolizei.

The receipt of this telegram is to be confirmed by the Chiefs of the State Police or their deputies by telegram to the Gestapo, care of SS Lieutenant Colonel Mueller.

SS Major General
/s/ HEYDRICH

STENOGRAPHIC REPORT OF THE MEETING ON "THE JEWISH QUESTION" UNDER THE CHAIRMANSHIP OF FIELD MARSHAL GOERING IN THE REICHS AIR FORCE (12 November 1938 — 11 o'clock)

PART I

Goering: Gentlemen! Today's meeting is of a decisive nature. I have received a letter written on the Führer's orders by the Stabsleiter [staff leader] of the Führer's deputy Bormann, requesting that the Jewish question be now, once and for all, coordinated and solved one way or another. And yesterday once again did the Führer request by phone for me to take coordinated action in the matter.

Since the problem is mainly an economic one, it is from the economic angle that it shall have to be tackled. Naturally a number of legal measures shall have to be taken which fall into the sphere of the Minister for Justice and into that of the Minister of the Interior; and certain propaganda measures shall be taken care of by the Minister for Propaganda. The Minister for Finance and the Minister for Economic Affairs shall take care of problems falling in their respective resorts.

In the meeting, in which we first talked about this question and came to the decision to aryanize German economy, to take the Jew out of it, and put him into our debit ledger, was one in which, to our shame, we only made pretty plans, which were executed very slowly. We then had a demonstration, right here in Berlin, we told the people that something decisive would be done, but again nothing happened. We have had this affair in Paris now, more demonstrations followed and this time something decisive must be done!

Because, gentlemen, I have enough of these demonstrations! They don't harm the Jew but me, who is the last authority for coordinating the German economy.

If today, a Jewish shop is destroyed, if goods are thrown into the street, the insurance company will pay for the damages, which the Jew does not even have; and furthermore goods of the consumer goods belonging to the people, are destroyed. If in the future, demonstrations which are necessary, occur, then, I pray that they be directed, so as not to hurt us.

Because it's insane to clean out and burn a Jewish warehouse then have a German insurance company make good the loss. And the goods which I need desperately, whole bales of clothing and what-not, are being burned; and I miss them everywhere.

I may as well burn the raw materials before they arrive. The people, of course, do not understand that; therefore we must make laws which will show the people once and for all, that something is being done.

I should appreciate it very much if for once, our propaganda would make it clear that it is unfortunately not the Jew who has to suffer in all this, but the German insurance companies.

I am not going to tolerate a situation in which the insurance companies are the ones who suffer. Under the authority invested in me, I shall issue a decree, and I am, of course, requesting the support of the competent Government agencies, so that everything shall be processed through the right channels and the insurance companies will not be the ones who suffer. . . .

I should not want to leave any doubt, gentlemen, as to the aim of today's meeting. We have not come together merely to talk again, but to make decisions, and I implore the competent agencies to take all measures for the elimination of the Jew from German economy and to submit them to me, as far as it is necessary.

The fundamental idea in this program of elimination of the Jew from the German economy is first, the Jew being ejected from the Economy transfers his property to the State. He will be compensated. The compensation is to be listed in the debit ledger and shall bring a certain percentage of interest. The Jew shall have to live out of this interest. It is a foregone conclusion, that this aryanizing, if it is to be done quickly, cannot be made in the Ministry for Economy in Berlin. That way, we would never finish.

On the other hand, it is very necessary to have safety precautions so that the lower echelons, Statthalter [governor], and Gauleiter will not do things unreasonably. One must issue correction directives, immediately.

The aryanizing of all the larger establishments, naturally, is to be my lot — the Ministry for Economy will designate, which and how many there are — it must not be done by a Statthalter or his lower echelons, since these things reach into the export trade, and cause great problems, which the Statthalter can neither observe, nor solve from his place.

It is my lot, so that the damage will not be greater than the profit, which we are striving for.

It is obvious gentlemen, that the Jewish stores are for the people, and not the stores. Therefore, we must begin here, according to the rules previously laid down.

The Minister for Economic Affairs shall announce which stores he'll want to close altogether. These stores are excluded from aryanizing at once. Their stocks are to be made available for sale in other stores; what cannot be sold, shall be processed through the "Winterhilfe" [Winter Relief, an annual charity collection] or taken care of otherwise. However, the sales values of these articles shall always be considered, since the State is not to suffer but should profit through this transformation. For the chain and department stores — I speak now only of that, what can be seen, certain categories have to be established, according to the importance of the various branches.

The trustee of the State will estimate the value of the property and decide what amount the Jew shall receive. Naturally, this amount is to be set as low as possible. The representative of the State shall then turn the establishment over to the "Aryan" proprietor, that is, the property shall be sold according to its real value.

There begins the difficulties. It is easily understood that strong attempts will be made to get all these stores to party-members and to let them have some kind of compensations. I have witnessed terrible things in the past; little chauffeurs of Gauleiters have profited so much by these transactions that they have now about half a million. You, gentlemen, know it. Is that correct? (*Assent*.) . . .

The transfer of stores and establishments shall have to be executed by the lower echelons, not through Berlin but through the Gaue and through the Reichstatthalterschaft [governors' administration]. Therein shall be the seat of the members of the Board of Trustees, even if it consists of a few people only. The Statthalter and his people cannot do this job; the trustees will have to tackle it. But the Statthalter shall be the authority which supervises, according to the regulations given him, the trustees, particularly in dealings such as the transfer to party-members.

Naturally, these establishments cannot disappear all at once but we'll have to start by Monday, in a manner that shall make it obvious that a change has begun to materialize. Besides that, certain stores could be closed which will make things here easier.

Another point! I have noticed that Aryans took over a Jewish store and were then so clever to keep the name of the Jewish store as "formerly," or kept it altogether. That must not be; I cannot permit it. Because it may happen — what has just happened — stores were looted because their signboards bore Jewish names — because they had once been Jewish, but had been "aryanized" a long time ago. Names of former Jewish firms shall have to disappear completely, and the German shall have to come forward with his or his firm's name. I ask you to carry this out quite definitely. That much then regarding aryanizing of stores and wholesale establishments, particularly in regard to signboards and of all that is obvious!

Of the consequences resulting from this for the Jew, I shall speak later, because this is connected with other things.

Now for the factories. As for the smaller and medium ones, two things shall have to be made clear.

1. Which factories do I not need at all — which are the ones where productions could be suspended? Could they not be put to another use? If not, the factories will be razed immediately.

2. In case the factory should be needed, it will be turned over to Aryans in the same manner as the stores. All these measures have to be taken quickly, since Aryan employees are concerned everywhere. I'd like to say right now that Aryan employees shall have to be given employment immediately after the Jewish factory is closed. Considering the amount of labor we need these days, it should be a trifle to keep these people, even in their own branches. As I have just said; if the factory is necessary, it will be aryanized. If there is no need for it, it being abandoned shall be part of the procedure of transforming establishments not essential, for our national welfare into one that is essential for it — a procedure that shall take place within the next few weeks. For it, I shall still need very much space and very many factories. . . .

Goebbels: In almost all German cities synagogues are burned. Now, various possibilities exist to utilize the space where the synagogues stood. Some cities want to build parks in their place, others want to put up new buildings.

Goering: How many synagogues were actually burned?

Heydrich: Altogether there are 101 synagogues destroyed by fire; 76 synagogues demolished; and 7,500 stores ruined in the Reich.

Goering: What do you mean "destroyed by fire"?

Heydrich: Partly, they are razed, and partly gutted.

Goebbels: I am of the opinion that this is our chance to dissolve the synagogues. All these not completely intact, shall be razed by the Jews. The Jews shall pay for it. There in Berlin, the Jews are ready to do that. The synagogues which burned in Berlin are being leveled by the Jews themselves. We shall build parking lots in their places or new buildings. That ought to be the criterion for the whole country, the Jews shall have to remove the damaged or burned synagogues, and shall have to provide us with ready free space.

I deem it necessary to issue a decree forbidding the Jews to enter German theaters, movie houses, and circuses. I have already issued such a decree under the authority of the law of the chamber for culture. Considering the present situation of the theaters, I believe we can afford that. Our theaters are overcrowded, we have hardly any room. I am of the opinion that it is not possible to have Jews sitting next to Germans in movies and theaters. One might consider, later on, to let the Jews have one or two movie houses here in Berlin, where they may see Jewish movies. But in German theaters they have no business anymore.

Furthermore, I advocate that the Jews be eliminated from all positions in public life in which they may prove to be provocative. It is still possible today that a Jew shares a compartment in a sleeping car with a German. Therefore, we need a decree by the Reich Ministry for Communications stating that separate compartments for Jews shall be available; in cases where compartments are filled up, Jews cannot claim a seat. They shall be given a separate compartment only after all Germans have secured seats. They shall not mix with Germans, and if there is no more room, they shall have to stand in the corridor.

Goering: In that case, I think it would make more sense to give them separate compartments.

Goebbels: Not if the train is overcrowded!

Goering: Just a moment. There'll be only one Jewish coach. If that is filled up, the other Jews will have to stay at home.

Goebbels: Suppose, though, there won't be many Jews going on the express train to Munich, suppose there would be two Jews in the train and the other compartments would be overcrowded. These two Jews would then have a compartment all themselves. Therefore, Jews may claim a seat only after all Germans have secured a seat.

Goering: I'd give the Jews one coach or one compartment. And should a case like you mention arise and the train be overcrowded, believe me, we won't need a law. We'll kick him out and he'll have to sit all alone in the toilet all the way!

Goebbels: I don't agree. I don't believe in this. There ought to be a law.

Furthermore, there ought to be a decree barring Jews from German beaches and resorts.

Goering: Particularly here in the Admiralspalast very disgusting things have happened lately.

Goebbels: Also at the Wannsee beach. A law which definitely forbids the Jews to visit German resorts!

Goering: We could give them their own.

Goebbels: It would have to be considered whether we'd give them their own or whether we should turn a few German resorts over to them, but not the finest and best, so we cannot say the Jews go there for recreation.

It'll also have to be considered if it might not become necessary to forbid the Jews to enter the German forests. In the Grunewald, whole herds of them are running around. It is a constant provocation and we are having incidents all the time. The behavior of the Jews is so inciting and provocative that brawls are a daily routine.

Goering: We shall give the Jews a certain part of the forest, and the Alpers shall take care of it that various animals that look damned much like Jews — the Elk has such a crooked nose, — get there also and become acclimated.

Goebbels: I think this behavior is provocative. Furthermore, Jews should not be allowed to sit around in German parks. I am thinking of the whispering campaign on the part of Jewish women in the public gardens at Fehrbelliner Platz. They go and sit with German mothers and their children and begin to gossip and incite.

Goebbels: I see in this a particularly grave danger. I think it is imperative to give the Jews certain public parks, not the best ones — and tell them: "You may sit on these benches" these benches shall be marked "For Jews only." Besides that they have no business in German parks. Furthermore, Jewish children are still allowed in German schools. That's impossible. It is out of the question that any boy should sit beside a Jewish boy in a German gymnasium [high school] and receive lessons in German history. . . .

Goering: . . . Of course, I too am of the opinion that these economic measures ought to be strengthened by a number of Police-action-Propaganda-measures and cultural displays so that everything shall be fixed now and the Jewry will be slapped this week right and left.

Heydrich: In spite of the elimination of the Jew from the economic life, the main problem, namely to kick the Jew out of Germany, remains. May I make a few proposals to that effect?

Following a suggestion by the Commissioner of the Reich, we have set up a center for the Emigration of Jews in Vienna, and that way we have eliminated 50,000 Jews from Austria while from the Reich only 19,000 Jews were eliminated during the same period of time; we were so successful because of the cooperation on the part of the competent

Ministry for Economic Affairs and of the foreign charitable organizations.

Heydrich: At least 45,000 Jews were made to leave the country by legal
measures.

Goering: How was that possible?

Heydrich: Through the Jewish Kulturgemeinde,[1] we extracted a certain
amount of money from the rich Jews who wanted to emigrate. By
paying this amount, and an additional sum in foreign currency, they
made it possible for a number of poor Jews to leave. The problem was
not to make the rich Jew leave but to get rid of the Jewish mob.

Goering: But children, did you ever think this through? It doesn't help
us to extract hundreds of thousands from the Jewish mob. Have you
ever thought of it that this procedure may cost us so much foreign
currency that in the end we won't be able to hold out?

Heydrich: Only what the Jew has had in foreign currency. (*Goering:*
"Agreed") This way. May I propose that we set up a similar procedure
for the Reich, with the cooperation of the competent government agencies, and that we then find a solution for the Reich, based on our
experiences, after having corrected the mistakes, the General Field Marshal has so rightly pointed out to us. (*Goering:* "Agreed") As another
means of getting the Jews out, measures for Emigration ought to be
taken in the rest of the Reich for the next 8 to 10 years. . . .

Heydrich: As an additional measure, I'd propose to withdraw from the
Jews all personal papers such as permits and drivers licenses. No Jew
should be allowed to own a car, neither should he be permitted to drive
because that way he'd endanger German life. By not being permitted
to live in certain districts, he should be furthermore restricted to move
about so freely. I'd say the Royal Square in Munich, the Reichsweihe-
stätte, is not to be entered any more within a certain radius by Jews. The
same would go for establishments of culture, border fences, military
installations. Furthermore, like Minister Dr. Goebbels has said before,
exclusion of the Jews from public theaters, movie houses, etc. As for
cultural activities, I'd like to say this; cultural activities in holiday resorts
may be considered an additional feature, not absolutely necessary for
the individual. Many German *Volksgenossen* [fellow Germans] are unable to improve their health through a stay at a resort town. I don't see
why the Jew should go to these places at all. . . .

---

[1] Heydrich here is possibly referring to the Kulturbund (Culture Association), an
organization of Jewish entertainers, formed in 1933 after they had been deprived of their
jobs. The Kulturbund enabled Jewish entertainers to perform exclusively for the Jewish
community, thus providing a means of livelihood. It is also possible that Heydrich is
referring to the Reichsvertretung, the national Jewish association of all communities and
organizations.

99. Public Reaction to *Kristallnacht*

The pogrom of November 9–10, 1938, resulted not only in the destruction of many synagogues as well as Jewish private property but also targeted over thirty thousand Jews for arrest and incarceration in camps such as Dachau and Buchenwald. The public disapproved of this Party-orchestrated action against the Jewish community, however. The underground Social Democratic network reported that most Germans were critical of these Nazi excesses and that many individuals were attempting to aid the Jews. Public criticism did not, of course, abet the interests of a regime that was preparing for war. The Social Democrats also reported that the Gestapo had undertaken strong measures to curb this dissent, fearing that it could present a source of opposition. The pogrom certainly succeeded in terrorizing Jews, but it also led to further intimidation of the non-Jewish public as well.

All reports confirm that the steps [taken against Jews] have been heavily criticized by the majority of Germans. During the first few days of the pogrom there were arrests of hundreds of Aryans throughout the Reich because they had publicly expressed their indignation. One can often hear people asking: "Who will be next after the Jews?" One thing is clear, however, no matter how great the indignation may have been — the brutality of the pogrom has added to the intimidation of the public in general, and has solidified the feeling that any resistance to the unrestricted National Socialist might is useless.

A report from Bavaria: "All the information we have been able to gather points to the fact that most of the populace took no part in the activities of the Nazis. . . . On the contrary, there are many examples of people opposing these acts. . . . Many people are taking care of Jewish women and children. Women are buying groceries for Jews because it is illegal to sell these things to them. It is also true that the severity of the acts varied considerably from town to town. In especially small towns it all depended on the disposition of the local party chairman or SS leader. There were towns where nothing at all happened, and Jews were arrested only later. . . .

A fact too often overlooked from abroad is that a large-scale campaign against "enemies of the state" has been initiated in the wake of the pogrom. Trustworthy NSDAP members were instructed to remove party insignia and mingle with the people, and immediately report anyone to the police or SS who made even the slightest derogatory remark about the campaign

From *Deutschland-Berichte der Sozialdemokratischen Partei Deutschlands (Sopade), 1934–1940* (Frankfurt: Verlag Petra Nettelbeck, 1980), 5 (November 1938): 1204–7. Translated by Dieter Kuntz.

against the Jews. This led to arrests in the streets in unheard-of numbers. . . . Most were released once their credentials had been established, but the overall result of this was an increased intimidation of the public. Many had believed that it was impossible to catch all dissenters and grumblers because there were simply too many, but now it was evident that the Nazis were prepared to proceed quite brutally against all opposition. Public grumbling did indeed lessen. People are more hesitant to speak out. It has become clear to all that the Nazis hold control."

100. Resettlement of German Jews

In the aftermath of Kristallnacht, Nazi policy toward the Jews underwent a significant change. A new solution to the Jewish Problem was introduced with the establishment in January 1939 of the Central Office for Jewish Emigration, headed by Reinhard Heydrich (chief of the Security Service of the SS). Nazi policy began to focus on the forced emigration of Jews from Germany. During this period, however, Jews found it exceedingly difficult to emigrate because of the tight immigration restrictions of many countries. Nonetheless, the Gestapo attempted to effect the departure of Jews from the Reich by any means possible, as can be seen in this Social Democrat underground report of February 1939, which illustrates Nazi attempts to push Jews across the French border. The incident described took place in western Germany, close to the French border.

Quite by accident did I come upon the square where Jews had been herded together. They had been rounded up in the city or taken from their homes. I'll never forget this scene for the rest of my life. SA, SS, and police had requisitioned private cars and by and by were dragging their prisoners in — men, old people, women, and even children. Every time a Jew stepped out of a car a howling would ensue among the youths and several hysterical women. One could recognize well-known businessmen, workers, doctors, and old and disabled people. The sight of a well-known and previously very respected person of well over 70 years of age made a particularly moving impression on the assembled onlookers. The women and children were locked into a room, while the men were made to stand in the open square without receiving anything to eat. Only toward evening were they transported to the border. The next day they were returned, however, because the French would not let them through. They then had to stand anew before the assembled crowd until they were transported to Dachau.

From *Deutschland-Berichte der Sozialdemokratischen Partei Deutschlands (Sopade), 1934–1940* (Frankfurt: Verlag Petra Nettelbeck, 1980), 6 (February 1939): 219. Translated by Dieter Kuntz.

Most of the older people who accidentally came upon this scene could not hide their indignation over this spectacle. Words were exchanged with people who wanted to defend the measures against the Jews. People said: "They [the Jews] are no worse than other businessmen; and those who took over their businesses are more expensive and have poorer quality goods." The excitement was so great that nothing could be undertaken [by the authorities] against these dissidents. A large segment of those previously transported are here again, and have been received kindly by the public. People ask them sympathetically if they have no possibilities of emigrating. Some answer that they are trying, and others point to the great difficulties. Now it has reached the point where children confront Jews and demand money. Some give it to them and create the impression that they themselves have become childish.

101. The Effect of the War on Germany's Jews

Once the war was under way, the Nazis began to deport German Jews to ghettos that had been established in occupied Poland. There they were sealed off in barbed-wire enclosures and forced to live under extremely harsh, overcrowded, and unsanitary conditions, which frequently led to starvation and death through disease.

The Jews who had not yet been removed from Germany also faced harsh conditions, although for a time some were able to remain in their homes. A Social Democratic report of April 1940 sheds light on the plight of those Jews remaining in the Reich. Nazi policy toward these Jews centered on depriving them of the most basic comforts.

The main act of this gruesome drama is being played out on Polish territory. Within the Reich itself we receive only sparse accounts of the fate of the Jews. It does appear, however, as though the main weapons against those Jews who have not been transported are hunger and cold. The Jews are basically being discriminated against in the distribution of foodstuffs, coal, and all other rationed articles.

Report from Berlin: "The fate of Jewish families is very harsh; it really is only a question mainly of old people and children. Jews are only sparsely supplied with nutritional needs. They rarely get meat, and then only in small quantities. They receive no fish, poultry, milk, or butter. Even getting hold of simple fare such as legumes and potatoes is quite difficult for them because they can shop at only certain times. They are allowed

From *Deutschland-Berichte der Sozialdemokratischen Partei Deutschlands (Sopade), 1934–1940* (Frankfurt: Verlag Petra Nettelbeck, 1980), 7 (April 1940): 257–58. Translated by Dieter Kuntz.

into the stores only just prior to closing time when all the good-quality items are already gone and only the waste remains. Their food ration cards are stamped with a 'J.' They get none of the special rations that are sometimes doled out.

"Those who during the coldest weather still had a few coals were not certain of being allowed to keep them. Many Jews had their heating devices simply 'requisitioned.' You already know that Jews can get no clothing rationing cards. In order to keep what they have in repair, they are given a small roll of sewing-cotton every three months. 'Jewish' shoes are not allowed to be resoled, and linen cannot be replaced. Worst of all, however, is the suffering of the old people in the bitter cold. Luckily some still have Aryan friends who fearlessly provide some needed things for these ill-fated people."

102. The "Evacuation" of German Jews

Immediately after the Wannsee Conference, the Nazis put their extermination plans in motion. Adolf Eichmann, chief of the Jewish Office of the Gestapo, sent instructions to all state police stations explaining that a major operation against the Jews was planned, and that they were to collect precise data about the Jews still remaining in the Reich. Eichmann's directives established strict procedural guidelines, defining categories of Jews to be excluded from deportation because of age, nationality, or contribution to the war effort. Directives issued in June 1942 provided detailed instructions for the "evacuation" (a euphemism for "transportation to a death camp") of Jews to the East.

INSTRUCTIONAL PAMPHLET FOR OFFICIALS ENGAGED IN THE EVACUATION SCHEDULED FOR JUNE 11, 1942, FRANKFURT AM MAIN

Jews will be evacuated from the state police district and transported to the East. You have been designated to carry out this project, and you must accordingly follow the instructions contained in this pamphlet as well as the orally communicated instructions. I expect you to carry out this order with the necessary toughness, correctness, and accuracy. Only full-blooded Jews will be expelled. Stateless Jews are basically to be treated like German Jews. The Jews will attempt to soften you through pleas or threats or they may be obstinate. You must not allow yourself to be influenced in any way and you must not allow anything to interfere with the performance of your duty. . . .

From Johannes Simmert, ed., *Die Nationalsozialistische Judenverfolgung in Rheinland-Pfalz, 1933–1945* (Koblenz: Veröffentlichungen der Landesarchivverwaltung Rheinland-Pfalz, 1974), pp. 237–40. Translated by Dieter Kuntz. Reprinted by permission of Landesarchiv, Rheinland-Pfalz.

You are to proceed accordingly:

1. At the designated hour you are to go to the home of the Jews you are assigned to. Should the Jews refuse to let you in or refuse to open the door, one of you must stay there while the other immediately notifies the closest police station. Once inside the Jewish apartment you are to call all members of the family together and read aloud the state police decree you received along with these instructions. The Jews are from then on to remain in one room, which you will select. A second official will remain with the family members the entire time. In the meantime you will deal with the head of the household.

2. You will accompany the head of the household through the residence. If heating stoves are in operation, no more coal is to be put on the fire. If there are slow-combustion stoves in use (such as Dutch tiled stoves or something similar), you must unscrew the oven door in order for the fire to die out while you are still in the apartment. The fire must be put out before you leave the residence.

3. Then you and the head of the household will proceed to pack a suitcase or knapsack. Care must be taken to include only that which is allowed under the provisions of the state police decree. You are responsible for ensuring that valuables, which, according to the decree, are not to be taken along, are not packed in the suitcase. The suitcase is then secured by you with sealing tape. If it is necessary to check with other family members, you will accompany the head of the household back to the room where the other Jews are waiting and then let them tell you what they want to have packed. If necessary you can let the head of the household remain in the room with the others and accompany the wife of the Jew or another family member to continue the packing.

4. Woolen blankets that you are allowed to take along must be rolled up or folded so as to facilitate their transportation.

5. Accompany the head of the household through the residence (including cellars and attics) to determine what (perishable) foodstuffs and livestock are on hand. You and the head of the household are to gather these items, if possible, and deposit them in the entry hall. You then inform the NSV [Nationalsozialistische Volkswohlfahrt, National Socialist People's Welfare Organization] and have these items removed.

6. Valuables, savings account books, securities, and cash sums exceeding the allowed amount are to be collected by the Jew. These items or valuables are to be accepted by the officials, listed in an inventory, and packed in a bag or envelope. This container is to be sealed and marked with the name and address of the owner. The inventory is to be checked for completeness by the official and the Jew and acknowledged by signature.

STATE POLICE DECREE CONCERNING THE EVACUATION OF JEWS:
[to be read to Jews by the police]

You are hereby notified that you are to vacate your residence within two hours. The officials in charge are obliged to remain with you until you have packed your suitcases and put your residence in order, and then they will escort you to the collecting point. You are asked to leave keys in various boxes and cabinets and to leave the inner door keys as well. If you have these keys on a certain key chain, they are to be removed and placed in their respective locks. The house and corridor keys are to be tied with a small ribbon along with a piece of cardboard listing your name, address, and identity number. These keys you will turn over to the official in charge. Before you leave your residence you must hand in the statement of assets, which is to be carefully filled out and signed.

You are to take the following with you:

1. Currency of 50 marks.
2. A knapsack or handbag with linen and utensils necessary for basic daily needs.
3. A complete set of clothes (two coats and a double set of underwear may be worn).
4. Food supply for several days, cutlery, plate, bowl, drinking cup, bottle.
5. Passport, identity card, work permit and other identity papers as well as food ration stamps, potato and coal ration cards. These are not to be packed but are to be carried on one's person.

You are not allowed to bring: Securities, foreign currency, savings account books, and so on, as well as valuables of any kind (gold, silver, platinum), nor any livestock. Wedding bands and a plain watch may be brought. Valuables and precious metals are to be placed in a bag or envelope and handed over to the official. . . . The baggage that can be taken along is to have an identifying tag. . . . Each person is also to wear a nameplate around the neck listing name, birth date, and identity number. . . .

Prisoners are lined up for roll call in the concentration camp
Sachsenhausen near Berlin during 1941. Each barrack bears one word of
the sardonic camp slogan "There is one road to freedom. Its milestones are
obedience, diligence, honesty, order, cleanliness, sobriety, truthfulness,
self-sacrifice, and love for the Fatherland."

Chapter
14

The Death Camps, 1941–1945

As early as 1933, the Nazis set up concentration camps to incarcerate their political opponents, but the regime redefined the purpose of the camps in 1938. After having declined in the mid-1930s, the inmate population increased with the prohibition of a wide-ranging set of "crimes" including "antisocial parasitical" and "work-shy" elements, homosexuals, and Jehovah's Witnesses. The justification for expansion rested above all on the claim that the concentration camps also served as state reformation and labor camps. War was clearly on the horizon, and the SS prepared by organizing forced labor in SS-owned industries. Able-bodied prisoners were in demand, and camps were set up near quarries and building-materials plants. Prisoners from the territories acquired in 1938 and those arrested in the pogrom of November 9, 1938, brought about thirty-five thousand Jews into the camps. In the first two years of the war, despite a high death rate, the number grew to hundreds of thousands and later to millions.

The Final Solution meant converting some existing camps and constructing new ones with the sole purpose of extermination. The Nazi policy of mass extermination had been already put into practice in 1939 with the policy of euthanasia applied to the mentally and physically handicapped. Approximately five thousand "racially valueless" children and one hundred thousand "incurably sick" persons were gassed under this program. Increasingly put under the control of the SS, the euthanasia policy provided the model for the Final Solution. Himmler charged Odilo Globocnik personally with the extermination of the Jews of Poland in an operation given the code name Reinhard conducted at a series of camps. In the summer of 1941 the SS ordered Rudolf Hoess, the commander of Auschwitz, to expand the camp and prepare it for extermination operations. By 1942 five other death camps were established at Chelmno, Belzec, Sobibor, Majdanek, and Treblinka. Belzec had been a labor camp, but Sobibor and Treblinka were established purely for extermination purposes. Majdanek and Auschwitz functioned as extermination and concentration camps in which prisoners were utilized as a labor force. The goal of the Final Solution, however, was never the mere exploitation of slave labor.

Practical considerations connected with the need for labor played only a minor role, and ultimately they, too, were overshadowed by the Final Solution. The theory and methods of mass murder revealed the racist ideology of National Socialism as an end in itself. In rapid order, extermination sites at which serial mass murder was perfected were set up in Poland. As early as December 1941, an SS special commando unit in Chelmno poisoned more than 150,000 Jews in camouflaged gas vans. Here as elsewhere the job was done by Jewish work commandos who were subsequently shot. The largest extermination installation was at Auschwitz-Birkenau, to which Jews from all over Europe were brought and either immediately gassed or forced to work for a time and subsequently gassed. By November 2, 1944, besides Poles, Gypsies, and Soviet prisoners of war, approximately 2 million Jews had been killed following the "successful experiments" of Hoess and his camp leader, Karl Fritzsch, with the prussic acid derivative Zyklon B, which, as Hoess reported, "was used in the camp as an insecticide and of which there was always a stock on hand." Countless others were shot, injected with phenolic acid, and subjected to "medical" experiments.

Expenditures for the upkeep of inmates were of course minuscule. Living quarters were extremely primitive. In the fall of 1942, for example, many of the twenty-two barracks at Majdanek were unfinished, with cardboard roofs and no windows. At Auschwitz only every third or fourth barracks had washing and toilet facilities, and the latrines consisted of open holes. The overcrowding in the barracks was a constant strain on inmates. There was seemingly no limit to the number of people who could be jammed into them. Inmates slept without blankets or pillows on crude wooden planks. Fifteen prisoners might occupy a "bed" meant for five. The clothing situation was even worse. Jews arriving in camps were deprived of all their belongings, including their clothes. Striped prisoners' clothing was initially issued to all inmates, but on February 26, 1943, shortages made this clothing unavailable. Prisoners thereafter wore rags, and by 1944 conditions were such that many thousands had no clothes whatsoever. Food usually consisted of a watery turnip soup, supplemented by an evening meal of bread made with sawdust. The living conditions in the killing centers produced sickness and epidemics — dysentery, typhus, and skin diseases of all kinds. Hospital facilities were almost nonexistent. The prisoners nevertheless scrambled to survive, working out a few compensatory mechanisms such as black markets in food and clothing.

Aside from the technical problems of conducting mass exterminations, the most serious task confronting the directors of the camps was maintaining order. Camp commanders assumed that individual prisoners, reasoning that nothing is ever certain, not even death, would not resist on their own. Organized resistance,

How Camps prevented resistance

however, would seriously threaten order. Commanders kept constant vigil to prevent such united resistance from developing and uprisings from occurring. To this end they made use of inmate spies and instituted a bureaucracy and a system of privileges among prisoners, taking advantage of the social divisions that existed in the camps.

Even within the concentration camps, racial distinctions formed the primary divisions. An established hierarchy determined the distribution of power and privilege among inmates. This hierarchy comprised two parts, one in charge of quarters and the other in charge of work parties. In quarters, the hierarchy was *Lagerältester* (highest in camp), *Blockältester* (in charge of block), and *Stubendienst* (in charge of barracks). In work parties the hierarchical levels were *Oberkapo, Kapo,* and *Vorarbeiter.* In Auschwitz and Majdanek German prisoners filled the top echelons of the inmate bureaucracy. Not only did Germans hold the most important positions, but they also enjoyed the most extensive privileges of concentration camp life: they could receive packages, they were issued supplementary food rations and bed linen in camp hospitals, and their barracks were less crowded. Far less privileged and much worse off were Poles, Czechs, and other Slavs. At the bottom were the Jews. Between the Jewish and the German inmates lay an unbridgeable gulf. The Germans were entitled to exist, and they had at least a modicum of resources to fight for survival. The Jews were simply doomed.

Despite internal measures and the construction of more secure facilities by an order of Himmler in February 1943, armed guards were essential to deal with any suspicion of resistance. Surprisingly, however, these camps, in which more than 3 million people were killed, were rather sparsely guarded. In all, about 6,000 to 7,000 men may have manned the killing centers at any one time — about 10,000 to 12,000 if rotation is taken into account. Auschwitz had about 3,000 guards. Majdanek had a battalion; Treblinka may have had about 700 men; Chelmno was run by a *Sonderkommando* (special detail) of 150 to 180 men. Little is known about the guard forces of Belzec and Sobibor except that they numbered in the hundreds. The inmate-guard ratio in Auschwitz during 1943–44 ranged from about 20 : 1 to 35 : 1. In Treblinka the ratio was about 1 : 1 (700 inmates to 700 guards).

Even under these conditions, resistance hardly ever materialized. No mass break was ever attempted from Auschwitz, where only new inmates occasionally managed to overcome informers, barbed wire, and guards. Most escapees were captured and brought back. At times the guards indulged in a ghastly joke, propping up the corpse of an escaped prisoner on a chair with a sign reading HERE I AM. Only a handful made good their escape. In two of the smaller camps, Treblinka and Sobibor, mass uprisings did occur. Unlike Auschwitz, which had a very large inmate population, Treblinka kept only a few work parties (all Jews) for maintenance and other purposes. Precisely because there were only 700 men in Treblinka, the inmates knew they faced certain death. The outbreak plan was very simple. A locksmith made a duplicate key to the arsenal, and a former captain of the Polish army, Dr. Julian Chorazyski, worked out the simple plan of escape. Chorazyski was killed just before the uprising was to occur, but his place was taken by a new inmate, the physician Dr. Leichert, also a former officer. On August 2, 1943, twenty hand grenades, twenty rifles, and several revolvers were secretly removed from the arsenal. At 3:00 P.M. the prisoners rushed the guards. Of 700 men in the camp, almost half got out. Hunted down one by one, not many survived. There is uncertainty about the precise number of people who made it out of Treblinka, with estimates ranging from twelve to forty. On October 14, 1943, about 300 inmates of Sobibor attemped a similar breakout; here, too, less than 50 survived.

The primary reason for keeping an inmate population alive for any length of time was to exploit prison labor. Using Jews for construction projects and in industry, however, was always seen as secondary to killing them. As in decreeing life or death itself, the SS made all decisions about who should work and who should not. Among the doomed Jews, those strong enough to work were to donate their remaining days so that the SS might develop an industrial base and exercise economic power. Only this supply of forced labor enabled the SS to undertake any major tasks at all at a time when the labor supply began to grow short in occupied Europe.

After the decision on life and death had been made when prisoners entered the camps, they were divided into four work groups: one dealt with camp maintenance, another worked on the construction of concentration camps, a third worked in SS-owned and -directed industries, and the last was hired out to private industries. Economically and administratively, the four groups of employers were not identical. The camp administration did not have to apply for allocations or pay for labor. The SS industries and private plants obtained labor by applying for it from a central SS office and paying for it. Employed inmates were organized in labor parties (*Kommandos*) and were placed under the supervision of inmates in the prison work hierarchy. Two types of maintenance *Kommandos* reflected the dual purpose of the killing center: one type engaged in ordinary maintenance tasks (such as staffing kitchens, attending patients in sick bay, and the like) and the other was itself involved in the killing operations (the *Transportkommandos* cleaned freight cars after unloading; the *Kommandos* in the *Effektenkammer* sorted valuables; and most important, the *Sonderkommandos* worked in the crematoria). Besides the camp itself there were two other SS employers: *Amtsgruppe C* and the SS industries. *Amtsgruppe C* took charge of building camp installations. The SS industries that tapped labor from the camps were not, for the most part, heavy manufacturing. Because of limited financial resources, the SS confined itself to production that, besides being suited to the exploitation of slave labor, did not require great capital outlay. Such industries made cement and other construction materials, food products, and wood products like brushes, baskets, and wooden shoes. Because the SS insisted on increasing workers' output as time went on, Jewish inmates serving in SS *Kommandos* did not live long.

Unlike the SS, private firms moved into the concentration camps with large amounts of capital and made them a factor in war production. For a long time the SS attempted to lure industry into the camps. I.G. Farben (Interessen Gemeinschaft Farbenindustrie Aktiengesellschaft, or Community of Interests of Dye Industries, Incorporated) officials were invited to Dachau as early as 1935, but they did not then find camp labor suitable for industrial purposes. Although it was certainly cheap, the use of prison workers had several drawbacks. Either a plant had to be built within a camp or the camp extended to incorporate the plant. The camp also had to have enough available labor to justify the construction of a work hall or building. Last, the firm had to bring in key labor and, to some extent, skilled labor. Even when these requirements were met, the concentration camp routine did not promote labor efficiency, and Himmler was unable to find any clients for some time. The SS obtained its first major customer only after offering special inducements to outweigh disadvantages of camp operations. The first company to move in on a big scale was I.G. Farben. In close association with the SS, Farben opened two plants in Auschwitz in the spring of 1941, a synthetic rubber plant (Buna) and an acetic acid plant. The SS provided guards and the company added factory police. Plant managers requested punishments for inmates who violated its rules, and the SS administered the punishments. The SS fed inmates the standard Auschwitz diet, adding some "Buna soup" to ensure work output. About twenty-five thousand inmates who worked for Farben in the camps died. The life expectancy of a Jewish inmate working for Farben was three or four months; in the auxiliary coal fields it was one month.

The success of Farben's plant at Auschwitz led to plans for setting up other manufacturing industries at the camps. The SS began to think of taking over whole sections of German industry and transferring them to concentration camps. These vast plans broke down, however, when the question of allotting the production of important war-industry materials to the camps arose. Albert Speer, then in charge of the armaments industry, did not believe that the camps could serve as efficient centers of production. Nevertheless, several other private companies followed I.G. Farben into Auschwitz. On March 5, 1943, the Krupp fuse plant in Essen was bombed out, and by March 17 the SS had laid plans to move the remaining machinery to Auschwitz. At the same time the ubiquitous Hermann Goering Works (coal mines), Siemens-Schuckert, and a number of other firms drew on the labor resources of the auxiliary camps around Auschwitz which spread out for miles from the killing center. The number of inmates used by these industries totaled about forty thousand.

Despite the exploitation of Jewish labor in the camps, the main purpose of the extermination centers was death. Arriving Jews encountered a standard proce- dure. At camps maintaining labor installations, such as Auschwitz, 10 percent of the arrivals — those who looked fittest — were selected for work. The remainder were consigned to the gas chambers. They were instructed to undress, and women and girls had their hair cut. Told they were going to take showers, they were marched between files of police, usually not SS guards but auxiliaries from areas like the Ukraine, who hurried them along with whips, sticks, or guns to the gas chambers. The Jews were crammed in, one per square foot. The gassing itself lasted from ten to thirty minutes, depending on the facilities and the techniques used. At Belzec, according to eyewitness accounts, it took thirty-two minutes until "finally, all were dead, like pillars of basalt, still erect, not having any space to fall." To make room for the next load the bodies were tossed out right away. Later the bodies were burned, either in the open air or in crematoria. Himmler complained about the slowness of the proceedings, but no quicker or more secret method could be found.

The statistics of the death camps are only approximations. At Auschwitz, the largest mass-killing installation, many transports of deportees went directly from the detraining ramps to the gas chambers, the individual prisoners never even counted. The camps took the following tolls: Auschwitz, 2,000,000; Belzec, 600,000; Chelmno, 340,000; Majdanek, 1,380,000; Sobibor, 250,000; Treblinka, 800,000. Although the overwhelming number of those killed in this systematic manner were Jews, other groups also suffered under the Nazi program of forced labor and planned extermination. Roughly four hundred thousand of Europe's 1 million Gypsies, who were placed in the same racial category as Jews, were eliminated by the Nazis. In addition, numerous Poles, Ukrainians, and Belorussians, though not seen by the National Socialists as destroyers of culture like the Jews and the Gypsies but only as racial inferiors, were enslaved in the camps. About 4 million of them died of exhaustion. The Nazis also allowed approximately 2 to 3 million Soviet prisoners of war to die in captivity. The total number of people who were killed under the National Socialists (not including those who died as a result of combat) is, to say the least, staggering. Besides the 5 to 6 million Jews who lost their lives in the camps, members of other ethnic groups who were exterminated or died from overwork must include another 9 to 10 million. These stark figures evidence the only achieved goal of National Socialist ideology and policy, indicating the chilling historical significance of the National Socialist phenomenon.

103. The Final Solution

Nazi solutions to the Jewish problem took a more radical turn once Germany was embroiled in war. The "resettlement" of Jews in Poland had worked for some time, but this policy ended when Hans Frank, the Nazi governor of occupied Poland, refused to admit more Jews into his area. Consequently, a new and "final" solution had to be found. In 1941, Goering commissioned Heydrich, the chief of the Security Service, to formulate a plan. The Final Solution was presented at the Wannsee Conference in Berlin on January 20, 1942.

From Leon Poliakov and Josef Wulf, *Das Dritte Reich und die Juden* (Berlin: Arani Verlag, 1955); pp. 116–26. Translated by Dieter Kuntz. Reprinted by permission of Arani Verlag, Germany.

Berlin: July 31, 1941

MARSHALL OF THE GREATER GERMAN REICH
PLENIPOTENTIARY FOR THE FOUR-YEAR PLAN
CHAIRMAN OF THE MINISTERIAL COUNCIL FOR THE DEFENSE OF THE REICH

To: Chief of the Security Police and the SD [Sicherheitsdienst, or Security Service]
SS Major General Heydrich, Berlin:

In addition to the task entrusted to you in the decree dated January 24, 1939, of solving the Jewish question by emigration and evacuation in the most favorable way possible, given current conditions, I hereby charge you with carrying out all necessary preparations vis-a-vis organizational, technical and economic matters for a complete solution of the Jewish question in the German sphere of influence in Europe.

Insofar as the competencies of other central organizations are hereby affected, these are to be involved.

I further charge you to submit to me soon an overall plan showing the preliminary organizational, technical, and economic measures for the execution of the intended Final Solution of the Jewish question.

[Signed] GOERING

MINUTES OF THE WANNSEE CONFERENCE
JANUARY 20, 1942

SECRET REICH BUSINESS!

PROTOCOL OF CONFERENCE

I. The following took part in the conference on the final solution of the Jewish question held on January 20, 1942, in Berlin, Am Grossen Wannsee 56–58:

Gauleiter Dr. Meyer and Reich Office Director Dr. Leibbrandt	Reich Ministry for the Occupied Eastern Territories
Secretary of State Dr. Stuckart	Reich Ministry of the Interior
Secretary of State Neumann	Plenipotentiary for the Four-Year Plan
Secretary of State Dr. Freisler	Reich Ministry of Justice
Secretary of State Dr. Bühler	Office of the Governor General
Undersecretary of State Luther	Foreign Office
SS Oberführer [Colonel] Klopfer	Party Chancellery

Ministerial Director Kritzinger	Reich Chancellery
SS Gruppenführer [Major General] Hofmann	Central Office for Race and Resettlement [RuSHA]
SS Gruppenführer Müller	Central Office for Reich Security [RSHA]
SS Obersturmbannführer [Major] Eichmann	
SS Oberführer Dr. Schöngrath, Commander of the Security Police and the SD in the General Government [occupied Poland]	Security Police and SD
SS Sturmbannführer [Captain] Dr. Lange, Commander of the Security Police and the SD in the General District of Latvia, as representative of the Commander of the Security Police and the SD for the Reich Commissariat for the Ostland	Security Police and SD

II. The chief of the Security Police and the SD, SS Lieutenant General Heydrich, announced at the beginning of the meeting that he had been appointed by the Reich marshal as Plenipotentiary for the Preparation of the Final Solution of the European Jewish Question, and pointed out that this conference had been called to clarify fundamental questions. The Reich Marshal's request to have a draft submitted to him on the organizational, factual, and economic matters of the final solution of the European Jewish question necessitates prior joint consideration by all central agencies directly concerned with these questions, with a view to keeping policy lines parallel.

Control of the preparation of the final solution of the Jewish question was to lie centrally, regardless of geographical boundaries, with the Reichsführer SS and the chief of the German Police (chief of the Security Police and the SD).

The chief of the Security Police and the SD then gave a brief overview of the struggle waged up to now against this enemy. The most important elements are

a. forcing the Jews out of the various areas of life of the German people;

b. forcing the Jews out of the living space of the German people. In carrying out these efforts, the acceleration of the emigration of the Jews from Reich territory was intensified and systematically undertaken, since this was the sole possible provisional solution.

By order of the Reich marshal, a Central Office for Jewish Emigration was set up in January 1939, and its direction was entrusted to the chief of the Security Police and the SD. In particular it had these tasks:

a. to take all measures toward preparation of an intensified Jewish emigration;
b. to direct the stream of emigration; and
c. to hasten emigration in individual cases.

The goal of these tasks was to cleanse the German living space of Jews in a legal manner.

All authorities were quite clear as to the disadvantages entailed by such a forced emigration. These disadvantages, however, had to be accepted for the time being, given the absence of other possible solutions.

In the following period the handling of emigration was not only a German problem but also a problem with which the authorities of the countries of destination or immigration had to deal. Financial difficulties, such as increases foreign governments stipulated in terms of the amount of money immigrants were required to bring into a country, as well as debarkation fees, a lack of steamship berths, and continually intensified restrictions or bans on immigration, all hampered emigration efforts enormously. Yet in spite of these difficulties a total of approximately 537,000 Jews have been induced to emigrate between the assumption of power and the date of October 31, 1941. These consist of the following:

since 30 January 1933, from Germany [proper] — approx. 360,000
since 15 March 1938, from [former] Austria — approx. 147,000
since 15 March 1939, from the Protectorate of Bohemia and Moravia — approx. 30,000.

Financing of the emigration was handled by the Jews or by Jewish political organizations themselves. To avoid having the proletarianized Jews remain behind, we followed the principle that wealthy Jews had to finance the emigration of destitute Jews. What we did here was decree a special assessment or emigration tax which was prorated according to property levels. The amounts collected were then used to meet financial obligations in connection with the emigration of destitute Jews.

In addition to the funds collected in German marks, foreign currency was needed for the debarkation fees and for the requisite sums immigrants had to bring into a country. In order to conserve the German supply of foreign currency, Jewish financial institutions abroad were induced by the Jewish organizations in this country to see to it that appropriate funds in foreign currencies were obtained. In this way, foreign Jews made available by way of gifts a total of approximately $9,500,000 up to October 30, 1941.

Since then, in view of the dangers of emigration during wartime and in view of the possibilities in the East, the Reichsführer SS and chief of the German Police has forbidden the emigration of Jews.

III. In accordance with previous authorization, emigration has now been replaced by evacuation of the Jews to the East as a further possible solution.

These actions, however, are to be regarded merely as provisional options; nonetheless, practical experience is being gained which is of major significance in view of the coming final solution of the Jewish question.

In connection with this final solution of the European Jewish question, approximately 11 million Jews will be affected. These are distributed among individual countries as follows:

Country		Number
A.	Altreich [prewar Germany]	131,800
	Ostmark [Austria]	43,700
	Eastern Territories	420,000
	General Government [occupied Poland]	2,284,000
	Bialystok	400,000
	Protectorate of Bohemia and Moravia	74,200
	Estonia	FREE OF JEWS
	Latvia	3,500
	Lithuania	34,000
	Belgium	43,000
	Denmark	5,600
	France: Occupied territory	165,000
	Unoccupied territory	700,000
	Greece	69,600
	The Netherlands	160,800
	Norway	1,300
B.	Bulgaria	48,000
	England	330,000
	Finland	2,300
	Ireland	4,000
	Italy, including Sardinia	58,000
	Albania	200
	Croatia	40,000
	Portugal	3,000
	Rumania, including Bessarabia	342,000
	Sweden	8,000
	Switzerland	18,000
	Serbia	10,000
	Slovakia	88,000
	Spain	6,000
	Turkey (European part)	55,500
	Hungary	742,800
	U.S.S.R.	5,000,000
	Ukraine	2,994,684
	White Russia, excluding Bialystok	446,484
	TOTAL over	11,000,000

The numbers of Jews listed for the various foreign states reflects, however, only those of the Jewish faith, since definitions of Jews according to racial principles are still in part lacking there. The handling of the problem in the individual countries will meet with certain difficulties due to prevailing attitudes; this is especially true of Hungary and Romania. As an example, a Jew in Romania today can for money obtain appropriate documents that officially confirm his citizenship of some foreign country.

The influence of the Jews on all areas of the U.S.S.R. is well known. About five million live in the European area, in the Asian territory barely a half million.

The occupational breakdown of Jews residing in the European area of the U.S.S.R. was approximately as follows:

In agriculture	9.1%
Urban workers	14.8%
In commerce	20.0%
Employed as government workers	23.4%
In the professions — medicine, the press, theater, etc.	32.7%

Under appropriate direction the Jews are to be suitably assigned to labor in the East during the course of the final solution. In large labor groups, with the sexes separated, Jews capable of work will be brought to these territories and put to work building roads, whereby a large part will undoubtedly disappear through natural diminution.

The remaining remnant, which undoubtedly will constitute the segment most capable of resistance, will have to be appropriately dealt with since it represents a natural selection and in the event of release must be regarded as the germ cell of a Jewish reconstruction. (Look at the experience of history.)

In the course of the practical implementation of the final solution, Europe will be thoroughly combed from west to east. The Reich territory, including the Protectorate of Bohemia and Moravia, will have to be dealt with beforehand, if only because of housing problems and other sociopolitical necessities.

The evacuated Jews will first be brought, group by group, into so-called transit ghettos, to be transported from there farther east.

SS Lieutenant General Heydrich explained further that an important prerequisite for the implementation of the evacuation on the whole is the exact determination of the category of persons who will be affected.

The intent is not to evacuate Jews over the age of 65 but to assign them instead to a ghetto for the aged. Theresienstadt is under consideration.

Along with these age groups (of the approximately 280,000 Jews who on October 31, 1941, were in Germany proper and Austria, approximately 30 percent were over the age of 65), Jews with serious war disabilities and Jews with war decorations (Iron Cross, First Class) will be taken into the

Jewish old-age ghettos. With this expedient solution, the many interventions [requests for exceptions] will be eliminated with one stroke.

The beginning of each of the larger evacuation actions will much depend on military developments. With regard to the handling of the final solution in the European areas occupied by us and under our influence, it was proposed that qualified specialists from the Foreign Office confer with the officials who have jurisdiction within the Security Police and the SD.

In Slovakia and Croatia this matter is no longer too difficult since the central issues on that score have already been solved there. In Romania, likewise, the government has in the meantime appointed a commissioner for Jewish affairs. In order to settle the problem in Hungary it will be necessary in the near future to impose upon the Hungarian government an adviser on Jewish problems.

With regard to beginning preparations for the settling of the problem in Italy, SS Lieutenant General Heydrich considers communication with the police chief to be appropriate in these matters.

In occupied and unoccupied France, the roundup of Jews for evacuation has in all probability taken place without great difficulties.

On this point, Undersecretary of State Luther informed us that an intensive handling of this problem would create difficulties in a few countries such as in the Nordic states, and that it would therefore be advisable to set these countries aside for the time being. In consideration of the small numbers of Jews affected there, this postponement does not constitute any appreciable curtailment. But then the Foreign Office foresees no great difficulties in the southeast and west of Europe.

SS Major General Hofmann intends to have a specialist from the Central Office for Race and Resettlement sent along to Hungary for general orientation once the matter is taken up there by the chief of the Security Police and the SD. It was decided that this specialist from the Race and Resettlement Office, who is not to be active, should be temporarily assigned an official capacity as assistant to the police attaché.

IV. The Nuremberg Laws are to provide the underlying foundation in the implementation of the final solution plan, and in doing so, solving the questions concerning mixed marriages and *Mischlinge* [mixed offspring of Germans and Jews] will be a precondition for the complete settlement of the problem.

In connection with a letter from the chief of the Reich chancellery, the chief of the Security Police and the SD discusses the following points, on a theoretical basis for the time being:

1. *Treatment of first-degree* Mischlinge. *Mischlinge* of the first degree are deemed to be equal to Jews as far as the final solution of the Jewish question is concerned. The following are to be exempt from this treatment:

    a. First-degree *Mischlinge* married to persons of German blood, from whose marriages children (second-degree *Mischlinge*) have been born. These second-degree *Mischlinge* are deemed essentially equal to Germans.

    b. First-degree *Mischlinge* for whom exceptions were previously granted, in whatever area of life, by the highest authority of the Party and the state. Each individual case must be reexamined, whereby it cannot be ruled out that the decision may once again prove to be unfavorable for the *Mischling*.

The basis for granting an exception must always be the fundamental merits of the particular *Mischling* himself. (Not the merits of the parents or spouse of German blood.)

    The first-degree *Mischling* who is to be exempted from evacuation is to be sterilized in order to prevent any offspring and to settle the *Mischling* problem once and for all. Sterilization will be done on a voluntary basis. It is, however, the condition for remaining in the Reich. The sterilized *Mischling* will in the following period be freed from all restrictive regulations to which he was previously subject.

2. *Treatment of second-degree* Mischlinge. *Mischlinge* of the second degree are normally classed with persons of German blood, with the exceptions of the following cases, in which second-degree *Mischlinge* are deemed equal to Jews.

    a. Descent of the second-degree *Mischling* from a bastard marriage (both spouses being *Mischlinge*).

    b. Especially unfavorable appearance, in racial terms, of the second-degree *Mischling* which identifies him as a Jew simply by the features of his exterior.

    c. Especially poor police and political assessment of the second-degree *Mischling,* giving evidence that he feels and conducts himself like a Jew.

But even in these cases exceptions should not be made if the second-degree *Mischling* is married to a person of German blood.

3. *Marriages between full Jews and persons of German blood.* In these situations it must be decided from case to case whether the Jewish spouse will be evacuated or whether, in consideration of the effect of such a measure on the German relatives of the mixed couple, the spouse is to be assigned to an old-age ghetto.

4. *Marriages between first-degree* Mischlinge *and persons of German blood.*

    a. *Without children:* If no children resulted from the marriage, the first-degree *Mischling* will be evacuated or assigned to an old-age ghetto.

(The same treatment as in the case of marriages between full Jews and persons of German blood, item 3.)

   b. *With children:* If children were born to the marriage (second-degree *Mischlinge*), and if they are deemed equal to Jews, they are to be evacuated or assigned to a ghetto. Insofar as such children are deemed equal to Germans (routine cases), they are to be exempted from evacuation, and with that also from first-degree *Mischling*.

5. *Marriages between first-degree* Mischlinge *and first-degree* Mischlinge *or Jews*. In these marriages (including children), all parties are treated like Jews and are therefore evacuated or assigned to an old-age ghetto.
6. *Marriages between first-degree* Mischlinge *and second-degree* Mischlinge. Both spouses, regardless of whether or not there are children, are to be evacuated or assigned to an old-age ghetto, since any children of such marriages normally evidence a greater share of Jewish blood in their racial makeup than do second-degree Jewish *Mischlinge*.

SS Major General Hofmann takes the position that extensive use must be made of sterilization, particularly since the *Mischling,* when given the choice of being evacuated or sterilized, would prefer to undergo sterilization.

Secretary of State Stuckart states that the practical implementation of the possible solutions just communicated for settling the problems of mixed marriages as well as those of the *Mischling* in the way proposed would entail endless administrative labor. Therefore, in order to take biological realities fully into account, Secretary of State Dr. Stuckart suggested that compulsory sterilization be undertaken.

In order to simplify the mixed-marriage problem, he felt that further possibilities must be considered, with the objective being to have the legislator say something like: "These marriages are dissolved."

As to the question of the effect the evacuation of Jews may have on economic life, Secretary of State Neumann stated that those Jews employed in essential war industries could not be evacuated for the present as long as no replacements were available.

SS Lieutenant General Heydrich pointed out that these Jews would not be evacuated anyway under the directives approved by him for the implementation of current evacuation actions.

Secretary of State Dr. Bühler stated that the General Government would welcome it if the final solution of this problem were begun in the General Government, because here the transport problem plays no major role and labor supply considerations would not hinder the course of this project. Jews needed to be removed as quickly as possible from the territory of the General Government, he said, because here especially the Jew represents a marked danger as a carrier of epidemics, and also because through his constant black market dealings he brings disorder into the economic structure of the country. Moreover, of the approximately two and a half million Jews in question, the majority of cases were not fit for work.

Secretary of State Dr. Bühler further states that the solution of the Jewish question in the General Government is primarily the responsibility of the chief of the Security Police and the SD and that his efforts would be supported by the agencies of the General Government. He had only one request, and that was that the Jewish question in this territory be solved as quickly as possible.

In conclusion, the various kinds of possible solutions were discussed, whereby Gauleiter Dr. Meyer and Secretary of State Dr. Bühler both took the position that certain preparatory tasks connected with the final solution should be carried out in the territories concerned, but that in the course of doing so any alarm among the population must be avoided.

With the request by the chief of the Security Police and the SD to the conference participants that they support him appropriately in carrying out the tasks connected with the solution, the conference was concluded.

104. The Extermination Process

In this excerpt from his autobiography, Rudolf Hoess, the commandant of the Auschwitz death camp, discusses the actual process of extermination. Various methods were tested at Auschwitz, but gassing the victims with Cyclon (Zyklon) B proved to be the most efficient "solution." The SS attempted to dispose of the evidence of the killings afterward.

Cyclon B gas was supplied by the firm of Tesch & Stabenow and was constantly used in Auschwitz for the destruction of vermin, and there was consequently always a supply of these tins of gas on hand. In the beginning, this poisonous gas, which was a preparation of prussic acid, was only handled by employees of Tesch & Stabenow under rigid safety precautions, but later some members of the Medical Service were trained by the firm in its use and thereafter the destruction of vermin and disinfection were carried out by them.

During Eichmann's next visit I told him about this use of Cyclon B and we decided to employ it for the mass extermination operation.

The killing by Cyclon B gas of the Russian prisoners of war transported to Auschwitz was continued, but no longer in block II, since after the gassing the whole building had to be ventilated for at least two days.

From Rudolf Hoess, *Commandant of Auschwitz,* trans. Constantine FitzGibbon (New York: Weidenfeld and Nicolson, 1959), pp. 208–11. Reprinted by permission of the Comite Internationale D'Auschwitz. Reprinted by permission of the Comite Internationale D'Auschwitz.

The mortuary of the crematorium next to the hospital block was therefore used as a gassing room, after the door had been made gasproof and some holes had been pierced in the ceiling through which the gas could be discharged.

I can however only recall one transport consisting of nine hundred Russian prisoners being gassed there and I remember that it took several days to cremate their corpses. Russians were not gassed in the peasant farmstead which had now been converted for the extermination of the Jews.

I cannot say on what date the extermination of the Jews began. Probably it was in September 1941, but it may not have been until January 1942. The Jews from Upper Silesia were the first to be dealt with. These Jews were arrested by the Kattowitz Police Unit and taken in drafts by train to a siding on the west side of the Auschwitz-Dziedzice railroad line where they were unloaded. So far as I can remember, these drafts never consisted of more than 1,000 prisoners.

On the platform the Jews were taken over from the police by a detachment from the camp and were brought by the commander of the protective custody camp in two sections to the bunker, as the extermination building was called.

Their luggage was left on the platform, whence it was taken to the sorting office called Canada situated between the DAW[1] and the lumberyard.

The Jews were made to undress near the bunker, after they had been told that they had to go into the rooms (as they were also called) in order to be deloused.

All the rooms, there were five of them, were filled at the same time, the gasproof doors were then screwed up and the contents of the gas containers discharged into the rooms through special vents.

After half an hour the doors were reopened (there were two doors in each room), the dead bodies were taken out, and brought to the pits in small trolleys which ran on rails.

The victims' clothing was taken in trucks to the sorting office. The whole operation, including assistance given during undressing, the filling of the bunker, the emptying of the bunker, the removal of the corpses, as well as the preparation and filling up of the mass graves, was carried out by a special detachment of Jews, who were separately accommodated and who, in accordance with Eichmann's orders, were themselves liquidated after every big action.

---

[1] After Auschwitz had been built, the German Armaments Works (DAW) built a branch factory inside the camp, where a labor force of up to 2,500 prisoners was employed.

While the first transports were being disposed of, Eichmann arrived with an order from the Reichsführer SS stating that the gold teeth were to be removed from the corpses and the hair cut from the women. This job was also undertaken by the Special Detachment.

The extermination process was at that time carried out under the supervision of the commander of the protective custody camp or the Rapportführer. Those who were too ill to be brought into the gas chambers were shot in the back of the neck with a small-caliber weapon.

An SS doctor also had to be present. The trained disinfectors (SDG's) were responsible for discharging the gas into the gas chamber.

During the spring of 1942 the actions were comparatively small, but the transports increased in the summer, and we were compelled to construct a further extermination building. The peasant farmstead west of the future site of crematoriums III and IV was selected and made ready. Two huts near bunker 1 and three near bunker II were erected, in which the victims undressed. Bunker II was the larger and could hold about 1,200 people.

During the summer of 1942 the bodies were still being placed in the mass graves. Toward the end of the summer, however, we started to burn them; at first on wood pyres bearing some 2,000 corpses, and later in pits together with bodies previously buried. In the early days oil refuse was poured on the bodies, but later methanol was used. Bodies were burned in pits, day and night, continuously.

By the end of November all the mass graves had been emptied. The number of corpses in the mass graves amounted to 107,000. This figure not only included the transports of Jews gassed up to the time when cremation was first employed, but also the bodies of those prisoners in Auschwitz who died during the winter of 1941–42, when the crematorium near the hospital building was out of action for a considerable time. It also included all the prisoners who died in the Birkenau camp.

During his visit to the camp in the summer of 1942, the Reichsführer SS watched every detail of the whole process of destruction from the time when the prisoners were unloaded to the emptying of bunker II. At that time the bodies were not being burned.

He had no criticisms to make, nor did he discuss the matter. Gauleiter Bracht and the Obergruppenführer Schmauser were present with him.

Shortly after the visit of the Reichsführer SS, Standartenführer Blobel arrived from Eichmann's office with an order from the Reichsführer SS stating that all the mass graves were to be opened and the corpses burned. In addition the ashes were to be disposed of in such a way that it would be impossible at some future time to calculate the number of corpses burned.

Blobel had already experimented with different methods of cremation in Kulmhof and Eichmann had authorized him to show me the apparatus he used.

Hössler and I went to Kulmhof on a tour of inspection. Blobel had had various makeshift ovens constructed, which were fired with wood and oil refuse. He had also attempted to dispose of the bodies with explosives, but their destruction had been very incomplete. The ashes were distributed over the neighboring countryside after first being ground to a powder in a bone mill.

Standartenführer Blobel had been authorized to seek out and obliterate all the mass graves in the whole of the eastern districts. His department was given the code number "1005." The work itself was carried out by a special detachment of Jews who were shot after each section of the work had been completed. Auschwitz concentration camp was continuously called upon to provide Jews for department "1005."

On my visit to Kulmhof I was also shown the extermination apparatus constructed out of trucks, which was designed to kill by using the exhaust gases from the engines. The officer in charge there, however, described this method as being extremely unreliable, for the density of the gas varied considerably and was often insufficient to be lethal.

How many bodies lay in the mass graves at Kulmhof or how many had already been cremated, I was unable to ascertain.

Standartenführer Blobel had a fairly exact knowledge of the number of mass graves in the eastern districts, but he was sworn to the greatest secrecy in the matter.

105. Commandant of Auschwitz

On March 11, 1946, Rudolf Hoess, the commandant of the Auschwitz extermination camp, was arrested by British military police near Flensburg in Schleswig-Holstein. On March 29, 1947, he was condemned to death by a Polish court and was executed shortly thereafter at Auschwitz. During his time as camp commander he directed the extermination of 2.5 million camp inmates. In this excerpt from his autobiography, written while he was awaiting trial, Hoess reflected on his grisly "duty" and the effect of his job on his family life.

Like many other autobiographical accounts by Nazi officials, Hoess's story of his involvement in the regime's atrocities is apologetic in nature. Hoess sought to justify his actions on the grounds that his sense of duty compelled him to carry out Hitler's orders, despite his "innermost doubts" and the "great pity" he claimed to feel for the victims.

This mass extermination, with all its attendant circumstances, did not, as I know, fail to affect those who took a part in it. With very few exceptions,

From Rudolf Hoess, *Commandant of Auschwitz,* trans. Constantine FitzGibbon (New York: Weidenfeld and Nicolson, 1959), pp. 169–74. Reprinted by permission of the Comite Internationale D'Auschwitz.

nearly all of those detailed to do this monstrous "work," this "service," and who, like myself, have given sufficient thought to the matter, have been deeply marked by these events.

Many of the men involved approached me as I went my rounds through the extermination buildings, and poured out their anxieties and impressions to me, in the hope that I could allay them.

Again and again during these confidential conversations I was asked: is it necessary that we do all this? Is it necessary that hundreds of thousands of women and children be destroyed? And I, who in my innermost being had on countless occasions asked myself exactly this question, could only fob them off and attempt to console them by repeating that it was done on Hitler's order. I had to tell them that this extermination of Jewry had to be, so that Germany and our posterity might be freed forever from their relentless adversaries.

There was no doubt in the mind of any of us that Hitler's order had to be obeyed regardless, and that it was the duty of the SS to carry it out. Nevertheless we were all tormented by secret doubts.

I myself dared not admit to such doubts. In order to make my subordinates carry on with their task, it was psychologically essential that I myself appear convinced of the necessity for this gruesomely harsh order.

Everyone watched me. They observed the impression produced upon me by the kind of scenes that I have described above and my reactions. Every word I said on the subject was discussed. I had to exercise intense self-control in order to prevent my innermost doubts and feelings of oppression from becoming apparent.

I had to appear cold and indifferent to events that must have wrung the heart of anyone possessed of human feelings. I might not even look away when afraid lest my natural emotions got the upper hand. I had to watch coldly, while the mothers with laughing or crying children went into the gas chambers.

On one occasion two small children were so absorbed in some game that they quite refused to let their mother tear them away from it. Even the Jews of the Special Detachment were reluctant to pick the children up. The imploring look in the eyes of the mother, who certainly knew what was happening, is something I shall never forget. The people were already in the gas chamber and becoming restive, and I had to act. Everyone was looking at me. I nodded to the junior noncommissioned officer on duty and he picked up the screaming, struggling children in his arms and carried them into the gas chamber, accompanied by their mother who was weeping in the most heart-rending fashion. My pity was so great that I longed to vanish from the scene; yet I might not show the slightest trace of emotion.

I had to see everything. I had to watch hour after hour, by day and by night, the removal and burning of the bodies, the extraction of the teeth, the cutting of the hair, the whole grisly, interminable business. I had to stand for hours on end in the ghastly stench, while the mass graves were being opened and the bodies dragged out and burned.

I had to look through the peephole of the gas chambers and watch the process of death itself, because the doctors wanted me to see it.

I had to do all this because I was the one to whom everyone looked, because I had to show them all that I did not merely issue the orders and make the regulations but was also prepared myself to be present at whatever task I had assigned to my subordinates.

The Reichsführer SS sent various high-ranking Party leaders and SS officers to Auschwitz so that they might see for themselves the process of extermination of the Jews. They were all deeply impressed by what they saw. Some who had previously spoken most loudly about the necessity for this extermination fell silent once they had actually seen the "final solution of the Jewish question." I was repeatedly asked how I and my men could go on watching these operations, and how we were able to stand it.

My invariable answer was that the iron determination with which we must carry out Hitler's orders could only be obtained by a stifling of all human emotions. Each of these gentlemen declared that he was glad the job had not been given to him.

Even Mildner[1] and Eichmann, who were certainly tough enough, had no wish to change places with me. This was one job which nobody envied me.

I had many detailed discussions with Eichmann concerning all matters connected with the "final solution of the Jewish question," but without ever disclosing my inner anxieties. I tried in every way to discover Eichmann's innermost and real convictions about this "solution."

Yes, every way. Yet even when we were quite alone together and the drink had been flowing freely so that he was in his most expansive mood, he showed that he was completely obsessed with the idea of destroying every single Jew that he could lay his hands on. Without pity and in cold blood we must complete this extermination as rapidly as possible. Any compromise, even the slightest, would have to be paid for bitterly at a later date.

In the face of such grim determination I was forced to bury all my human considerations as deeply as possible.

Indeed, I must freely confess that after these conversations with Eichmann I almost came to regard such emotions as a betrayal of the Führer.

There was no escape for me from this dilemma.

I had to go on with this process of extermination. I had to continue

---

[1] Head of the Gestapo office for the Kattowitz district, in which Auschwitz was located.

this mass murder and coldly to watch it, without regard for the doubts that were seething deep inside me.

I had to observe every happening with a cold indifference. Even those petty incidents that others might not notice I found hard to forget. In Auschwitz I truly had no reason to complain that I was bored.

If I was deeply affected by some incident, I found it impossible to go back to my home and my family. I would mount my horse and ride, until I had chased the terrible picture away. Often, at night, I would walk through the stables and seek relief among my beloved animals.

It would often happen, when at home, that my thoughts suddenly turned to incidents that had occurred during the extermination. I then had to go out. I could no longer bear to be in my homely family circle. When I saw my children happily playing, or observed my wife's delight over our youngest, the thought would often come to me: how long will our happiness last? My wife could never understand these gloomy moods of mine, and ascribed them to some annoyance connected with my work.

When at night I stood out there beside the transports or by the gas chambers or the fires, I was often compelled to think of my wife and children, without, however, allowing myself to connect them closely with all that was happening.

It was the same with the married men who worked in the crematoriums or at the fire pits.

When they saw the women and children going into the gas chambers, their thoughts instinctively turned to their own families.

I was no longer happy in Auschwitz once the mass exterminations had begun.

I had become dissatisfied with myself. To this must be added that I was worried because of anxiety about my principal task, the never-ending work, and the untrustworthiness of my colleagues.

Then the refusal to understand, or even to listen to me, on the part of my superiors. It was in truth not a happy or desirable state of affairs. Yet everyone in Auschwitz believed that the commandant lived a wonderful life.

My family, to be sure, were well provided for in Auschwitz. Every wish that my wife or children expressed was granted them. The children could live a free and untrammeled life. My wife's garden was a paradise of flowers. The prisoners never missed an opportunity for doing some little act of kindness to my wife or children and thus attracting their attention.

No former prisoner can ever say that he was in any way or at any time badly treated in our house. My wife's greatest pleasure would have been to give a present to every prisoner who was in any way connected with our household.

The children were perpetually begging me for cigarettes for the prisoners. They were particularly fond of the ones who worked in the garden.

My whole family displayed an intense love of agriculture and particularly for animals of all sorts. Every Sunday I had to walk them all across the fields, and visit the stables, and we might never miss the kennels where the dogs were kept. Our two horses and the foal were especially beloved.

The children always kept animals in the garden, creatures the prisoners were forever bringing them. Tortoises, martens, cats, lizards: there was always something new and interesting to be seen there. In summer they splashed in the wading pool in the garden, or in the Sola.[2] But their greatest joy was when Daddy bathed with them. He had, however, so little time for all these childish pleasures. Today I deeply regret that I did not devote more time to my family. I always felt that I had to be on duty the whole time. This exaggerated sense of duty has always made life more difficult for me than it actually need have been. Again and again my wife reproached me and said: "You must think not only of the service always, but of your family too."

106. Escape from Treblinka

Resistance in the concentration camps was rare and extremely difficult for Jews, yet it did occur on several occasions. Mass revolts took place at Sobibor and Treblinka, while a smaller uprising occurred at Auschwitz. These revolts aimed at opening up opportunities for escape. Organizing a mass escape was no easy task, and even then, escape did not guarantee survival. The Nazis relentlessly pursued fugitives, who faced the staggering difficulties of trying to survive in a country where all Jews had been rounded up and where little help could be expected from the local population.

In a rebellion at Treblinka (in what was formerly Poland) on August 2, 1943, over 150 Jews escaped, but only about 40 survived. One of those survivors was Samuel Willenberg who, born in Częstochowa in 1923, was deported to Treblinka in 1942, where he soon became active in the underground that initiated the rebellion. He was wounded during the uprising, but managed to escape into the woods and eventually reached Warsaw. The excerpts below are from his memoirs, *I Survived Treblinka*, written in 1945.

Underground activity began in the camp almost as soon as the camp had been set up. At first the underground group consisted of only a few people.

From Samuel Willenberg, "I Survived Treblinka," in Alexander Donat, ed. *The Death Camp Treblinka: A Documentary* (New York: Holocaust Library, 1979), pp. 196–98, 207–13. Reprinted by permission of Holocaust Publications.

---

[2] The river Sola, which flows into the Vistula a few miles north of Auschwitz, formed the eastern boundary of the Auschwitz camp area.

These were monomaniacs whose plans were the fruit of imaginings and visions completely divorced from reality. It is truly unbelievable, but that group decided to purchase arms from the Ukrainian camp guards and even made contact with them for this purpose. These contacts bore no fruit whatever. The shrewd Ukrainians would take the money but did not supply the weapons. We had to employ other means of organizing the underground. For the time being, therefore, the men contented themselves with reading underground publications and listening to clandestine radio broadcasts. Later, the group decided to execute the traitors, spies and informers among the inmates. The men of the underground achieved significant results in carrying out this task. The executions would be carried out cautiously, secretly and without arousing any suspicion. The frequent cases of suicide among the prisoners helped camouflage the executions. Almost every one of us had a dose of cyanide or some other poison on hand [for ourselves] in case of trouble. Many people in the camp committed suicide by hanging themselves, but then cases of suicide in a state of nervous collapse were common even among people who were free and lived in relatively good conditions. Therefore the underground employed a unique stratagem: they would give the execution of an informer the appearance of a case of suicide, and as a rule the SS men did not realize what had happened. The executions were carried out only after a rigorous investigation of the activities of the traitor or informer. We had to be convinced beyond the shadow of a doubt that the accused was indeed guilty as charged. In many cases the traitor was first warned and given a chance to turn over a new leaf. If the warning did not help, a court was convened and meted out the death sentence. Thanks to the liquidation of such informers, the lives of many prisoners were saved, and a certain solidarity was preserved among the inmate population. I recall the case of a certain Hermann, a stooge of the Germans who for a long time had been informing the camp authorities of everything that was going on among the inmates. He gathered around him a group of petty informers and talebearers. Either directly or through these individuals he was informed about who owned gold or silver, who was planning to escape, who was engaging in barter or organizing the smuggling of food into the camp. Due to Hermann's informing, many prisoners lost their lives. Among his victims was a Jew from Częstochowa, Dzialoszynski, a very worthwhile person and an excellent comrade.

We had no pity on suspected informers during the famine period, when we would distribute equal shares of the foodstuffs obtained from various sources. We did not help them in their hard labor and paid no attention to them during punishment drills. The traitors were abandoned and isolated. One of our kapos, a man named Rakowski, knew very well that we were liquidating the informers, and he secretly gave his consent to this. It also happened that the doctors in the *Revier* [dispensary] played a certain part in the liquidation of dangerous characters. If one of the traitors fell ill, camp headquarters were notified of that fact, and he would be ordered killed by a bullet or by an injection of poison.

In the course of time the underground developed considerably. In every block and barrack, groups were organized which constituted cells of the underground. Each group numbered from five to ten members; the total number of cells was ten. Nearly everyone in the *Kommandos* [labor details] belonged to the underground, and each group comprised from 15 to 25 men. The kapo Rakowski aided the conspirators. He got us accustomed to long marches, for he was planning a revolt and hoped to lead us all out into the woods, to the partisans. During the famine period the conspirators organized a commune. Everyone contributed money to a common treasury with which to purchase foods. Afterwards we would divide up the food which had been smuggled in. Those of our comrades who could not afford to pay were not forgotten; they received their share. This form of self-help helped many to survive this difficult period. More than once dramatic conflicts broke out which posed a grave threat to the conspirators. I remember the case of a journalist whose name was Kronenberg or Korenberg. Wanting to save his life, we had spirited him out of a transport. But the journalist's body had wasted away and his mind had become unhinged. He deteriorated until he finally caught dysentery. In the course of his illness he relieved himself in his bunk. We could not hide this fact, and the SS men dragged him off to the *lazaret* [infirmary or hospital]. At the sight of the rifle aimed at him he broke down completely and, getting down on his knees, he begged for mercy. He promised his executioners that if they would let him live he would turn over to them, as a gesture of gratitude, the names of 100 prisoners who belonged to the underground. The Germans heard this and hesitated momentarily, but the day was saved by [the kapo Zev] Kurland, who made a circle with his finger on his forehead, implying to the Germans that the poor fellow had gone out of his mind. A shot rang out, and thanks to it 100 other men were saved from sure death. . . .

The conspiracy cells finally worked out the plan down to its smallest details. Every conspirator knew exactly what his assigned task would be, what place he had to attack, on whom he could rely for help, whom he should help and what weapons would be available to him. The date for the destruction of the camp had been set several times, only to be postponed for a few days and canceled at the last minute. This aroused great resentment in us. It was hard to restrain us. As we chopped down the bushes around the fence we felt ready for any mad act, and as we worked we would position ourselves in such a fashion that each guard would be surrounded by several prisoners armed with axes. Our foreman, Kleinbaum, tried to hold us back and cool our zeal. The earnest looks he gave us struck the weapons from our hands; his arguments convinced us. For the idea of our revolt was to liberate all the prisoners, not just the workers at the Treblinka camp proper but also those employed in the

Death Camp. We were forbidden entry there, and only rarely did we set foot in the *Totenlager* [death camp]. Although the two portions of the camp constituted one integral unit, their workers constituted separate *Kommandos*. In our section life lasted a little longer, while the hell in the *Totenlager* was of relatively short duration. Very rarely was one of the workers from the *Totenlager* put to work with us. One such exception in the final period of the camp's existence was a carpenter named [Jankiel] Wiernik. This man would be brought under guard each day to our section of the camp. He would do certain work there and would be taken back to his camp in the evening. We were unable to draw him into the conspiracy because we were forbidden any contact with him. But Wiernik was saved nevertheless, since at the time of the revolt he happened to be in our part of the camp.

Our confidence in ultimate success grew from day to day. We would pat each other's shoulders and encourage each other with the words: "All right then! We shall see!" . . .

And then came the unforgettable day, August 2, 1943. We arose from our bunks, excited and tense. Thousands of thoughts raced about in our brains which burned with the fever of anticipation. None of us reflected on the fact that he was eating his last breakfast, that he was reporting to the roll call square for his last roll call, that he was going out for the last time to do a day's work. Quiet reigned all around us, the everyday, regular and tedious routine. In the watchtowers, the sentries whom we knew stood at their posts and started with indifferent eyes at the doings of the prisoners below. On the grounds the SS men strolled around as they had the day before, and the day before that, the week, and the month before. There was nothing to indicate any change. Routine dominated the surroundings and misled our enemies. Our hearts were overflowing with hatred and with the desire for revenge. With great difficulty we managed to put on a vague smile whenever we encountered one of our executioners. The smoke billowed forth as usual from the chimneys, the din of conversation was no different than at any other time. But the blows of axes on the stumps of trees, our shouts, every sound held a sort of shocking announcement, and it was strange that the all-knowing Germans did not notice a thing, that they did not sense what was about to happen in another brief moment.

For the few weeks that had gone before, relative calm had prevailed in the camp. The executioners had left us alone. No one had been shot. But we feared that very silence, that absence of cruelty, the rest taken by the Angel of Death.

The time of the revolt had been set for the afternoon. The signal agreed upon was a rifle shot. We were divided into groups, each of which was assigned a specific task. Some had instructions to kill the sentries in the watchtowers, others to storm the barracks with hand grenades, and still others to fall upon the SS men who walked about in the camp. We had not forgotten a single detail or person. We had planned to cut the telephone lines, to set afire the gasoline dump and other inflammable materials, to loot the arsenal. . . .

Until noon we worked as usual in the camp area. No mishaps occurred, no one committed any offenses or fell into the hands of the murderers. And then the conversations, the confessions, the whispers died down. And the sun blazed all the more fiercely.

It began shortly after three o'clock in the afternoon. Two prisoners, young boys who performed courier duties for the Germans, were given the key to the arsenal, which was held by the conspirators. They immediately took several buckets, and a stretcher which had been used for hauling garbage and rags, and slipped into the arsenal unnoticed. It was an ideal hour for this operation. The guards and SS men were tired from the heat of the day and paid no attention to what was going on around them. The boys were allowed to walk around near the Germans' barracks, for their duties required this. The entrance to the arsenal was not guarded, for several reasons. First of all, it was well-sealed by iron doors and a barred window which faced the rear of the building. Secondly, there were construction workers busy alongside the arsenal putting up a water-boiler. Thirdly, the guards in the watchtowers were supposed to keep an eye only on what was going on in the area, not on what was happening inside the buildings.

The boys locked themselves in the arsenal and began to pass out rifles, ammunition and hand grenades through the bars of the window to the construction workers, who were in on the conspiracy. Afterwards, they slipped outside, walked around the building and carried the arms to the center of the camp on the stretcher, which was covered with rags. The grenades were taken in buckets covered with rags. Everything was placed beneath piles of potatoes, which served as the location at which the weapons were distributed. Slowly the rifles and bullets were removed. Everyone who knew how to use a hand grenade received grenades. We also had several revolvers. Additional weapons were supplied us by the storekeeper, a young, very ugly man from Warsaw whom we nicknamed "The Ape." It was he who that morning had distributed to the conspirators a larger number of axes and wire-cutters than usual and several pairs of pliers. Many of us had hammers, knives, clubs, gasoline cans. . . .

But meanwhile, something happened on the grounds which had a telling effect upon the success of our carefully detailed plan. Each of us had prepared a little silver and gold before escaping. Actually, "little" was a relative concept, for there was a lot of gold in the camp, so much so that two "mere" canteenfuls were considered a trifle.

It was close to four o'clock when one of the prisoners crossed the camp in a run and dropped a gold twenty-dollar coin on the way. Unfortunately for him this was noticed by Chaskel, who stopped the man and turned him over to "Kiewe." The investigation did not last long. "Kiewe" simply dragged the captured man off to the *lazaret* and, as usual in such cases, shot him.

This was the shot we had heard, and which we had taken for the prearranged signal to start the revolt.

That moment is well preserved in my memory. I remember the picture of the camp in all its details: there was much movement all around. I was at work chopping trees with my comrades. The heat was extraordinary. We worked clad only in shirts or half-naked. The SS man [Franz] Suchomel passed by on his bicycle and gaily shouted something to the prisoners who were busy working. Weary guards had dozed off in the watchtowers. Near the gate to the vegetable garden, which was our handiwork, one of the SS men was strolling around. When I heard the shot I started to make a run for the barracks and take my jacket, in which I had hidden the gold intended for my escape, but at that moment a shout of "Hurrah!" rang out, which turned my feet in an entirely different direction.

The assault had begun.

Shots rained down on the guards in their watchtowers. The roar of an explosion shook the air. One, a second, a third. . . . Our comrades lobbed hand grenades into the barracks and buildings of the camp. Prisoners came running from everywhere, formed into groups which kept growing larger, and with a shout fell upon the sentries, the Ukrainians, the SS men. We heard a loud and long shout, which grew stronger by the moment and faded out into a distant echo in the woods. Somewhere hand grenades cut the telephone lines and the barbed wire fences. A commotion was created which cannot be described in words. One of the wooden barracks, dried out by the sun and the heat, caught fire. Among the dense crowd of people I noticed several Germans running panic-stricken in the grounds, taking cover behind trees and forming into a group at the other end of the camp.

Two Jewish drivers, one a Pole and the other a Czech, set the gasoline and oil pools afire. The flames flared up; clouds of black smoke covered the sky. Rifle and machine gun fire burst from the six watchtowers. . . . They were answered by single shots from our side. The Ukrainian who stood at the entrance to the vegetable garden turned at the sound of the shots and the shouts, made a movement as if he was about to run for his life, but he was mowed down by a bullet. The Ukrainian arched backward and collapsed on the ground. His face had contorted with the fear which precedes death; it was a sort of mad, satanic grin. As he lay there on the ground, he still twitched as if he was having a bothersome coughing fit. One prisoner ran by him, then a second, and a third. A whole group followed in their wake. And suddenly the group was hit by machine gun fire. Many were mowed down by the bullets. The crowd retreated in panic. A cry of fear was heard, but above the sounds of fear and terror there rose a mighty shout: "Hurrah! Hurrah! . . ."

Someone sets fire to the pine branches which serve as palings for the fence wires. The dried wood burns with a bright, explosive flame, spreading farther and farther. Now the barracks are on fire, the garages, the shops, the warehouses, the building that contained the gas chambers. . . . The flames grow more intense everywhere, the heat strikes our faces, and prisoners come and assemble from every part of the camp.

The machine gun from the nearby watchtower spews forth burst after burst of fire. The bullets strike our men, thinning out our ranks. The situation in this sector is becoming dangerous. Nearby, one man is holding a rifle but does not fire. . . . I grab his weapon, aim calmly and at length, and finally squeeze the trigger once, twice, a third time. . . . The dim silhouette collapses on the railing, the machine gun falls silent. . . . From here on in the way is wide open.

"Hit! Hit! Kill!" someone shouts into my ear.

"Move back! The fences have been cut! Slow! Don't push!"

The sound of Polish commands mixed with Jewish curses, someone praying in a language unknown to me, one man calling out to God in Hebrew and another in Yiddish. . . . The smoke sears the eyes and fills the lungs; the bullets whistle and ring past our ears like cut strings from musical instruments. . . .

At the other end of the camp the Germans get organized, but their firing is still sporadic. For the time being, panic and surprise keep them from sizing up the situation and making an efficient response. They hide like rats in the corners of burning buildings and advance with caution. The arms and ammunition we have are not enough. That cursed Chaskel! Had we been able to complete our preparations, our situation would be entirely different now.

And again the rat-tat-tat of a machine gun. It forces us to make a slow retreat. We jump from tree to tree in the direction of the fence. The cut wires dangle loosely.

Now we must run across the 50 meters of open space to the barbed wire entanglements and anti-tank barriers. The machine gun steps up its fire. Behind my back tragedies are taking place. The brave climb the steel-and-wire entanglements, and there the bullets catch up with them. They collapse with cries of despair. Their bodies hang on the wires, spilling streams of blood onto the ground. No one pays any attention to them. Other prisoners who have just arrived leap over the quivering bodies. And they, too, are mowed down and collapse, their madness-stricken eyes looking at the camp, which now looks like one gigantic torch.

"Onward! Onward! Onward!" a voice booms out nearby.

"The inferno is behind us!" I shout like a madman. "The inferno is behind us!" These words infuse me with strength, bring me back to my senses, force me to behave with caution.

And now I crawl along in the exposed area and reach the barriers. I look around. Behind me the dead have created a sort of bridge over which another fleeing prisoner passes every moment. Behind the barriers are the redeeming woods — freedom.

And again the thought troubles me: if we had been able to complete our preparations, we would have been able to get weapons to every part of the camp. At the prearranged signal, our gunfire would have hit all the SS men and sentries. We would have neutralized all the watchtower guards simultaneously and wiped out all the nests of German resistance. When "Kiewe's" shot rang out [which we had taken for our own signal] there still were lots of weapons hidden beneath the piles of potatoes; many of the hand grenades had not yet reached the hands of the conspirators. Now many prisoners were forced to run from the fences to the center of the camp in order to pull out the rifles, and afterwards they had to retreat under withering gunfire. Under the circumstances, it is no surprise that so many of our men were killed. If the plans had succeeded in full, we would have been in possession of two armored cars and we would have been able to cross the Bug River in close ranks to join the partisans.

Again I lift my head cautiously and inspect the goings-on around me. The machine gun is still firing away, but we can no longer remain here. With one leap I ascend the bridge of corpses. I hear a shot, feel a blow, but one more jump and I am at the edge of the woods. In front of me, beside me and behind me, men are running. It is difficult today to figure out how many were saved. I presume that about 200 men broke out by the route along which I escaped. On another side, about 150 escaped.

Now I am running with all my might among the trees. I feel a pain in my leg. I am wearing boots, and I feel blood filling up my right boot. The woods come to an end. I cross a highway and am once again swallowed up in a thick and damp forest.

Warmth and pleasant odors are all around me. Night falls.

Map by Yad Vashem, from Leni Yahil, *The Holocaust: The Fate of European Jewry, 1932–1945* (New York: Oxford University Press, 1990), pp. 358–59. Reprinted with the permission of Schochen Publishing House, Israel.

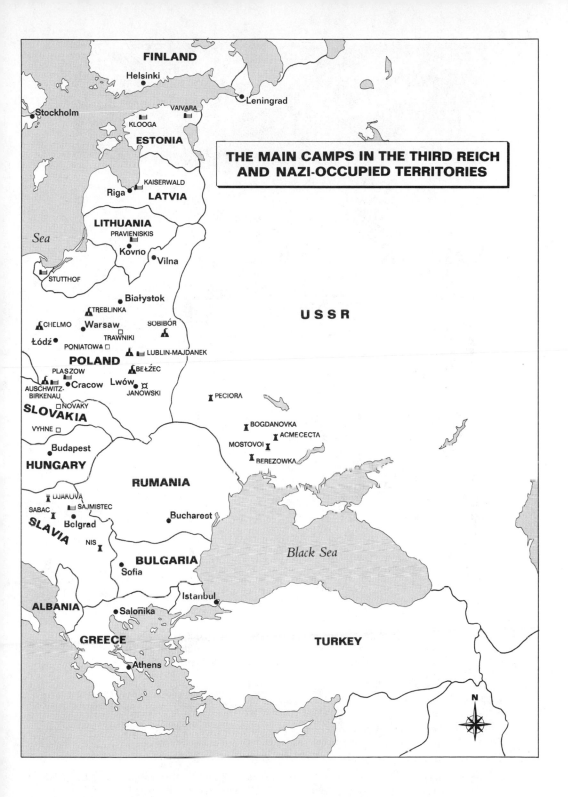

THE MAIN CAMPS IN THE THIRD REICH
AND NAZI-OCCUPIED TERRITORIES

FINLAND
Helsinki
Leningrad
Stockholm
VAIVARA
KLOOGA
ESTONIA
Riga
KAISERWALD
LATVIA
LITHUANIA
Sea
PRAVIENISKIS
Kovno
Vilna
STUTTHOF
Białystok
TREBLINKA
CHELMO
Warsaw
SOBIBÓR
Łódź
TRAWNIKI
PONIATOWA
LUBLIN-MAJDANEK
POLAND
PLASZOW
BEŁŻEC
AUSCHWITZ-
BIRKENAU
Cracow
Lwów
JANOWSKI
NOVAKY
SLOVAKIA
VYHNE
USSR
PECIORA
BOGDANOVKA
ACMECECTA
MOSTOVOI
BEREZOWKA
Budapest
HUNGARY
RUMANIA
DJAKOVA
SABAC
SAJMISTEC
Belgrad
Bucharest
SLAVIA
NIS
BULGARIA
Black Sea
Sofia
Istanbul
ALBANIA
Salonika
GREECE
TURKEY
Athens

N

The aftermath of the attempt to assassinate Hitler on July 20, 1944, at his headquarters in East Prussia. Hitler survived the bomb blast, the effects of which are examined here by Goering (in the light uniform).

Chapter

15

Criticism, Opposition, and Active Resistance

Opposition to the regime continued after the seizure of power in 1933, especially from the Social Democrats and the Communists. Because of the increasing expansion of the powers of the police and the opening of the concentration camps, this opposition proved to have little effect. Opposition also surfaced through the activities of individual members of the government, such as Papen and Schacht, who openly voiced their condemnation of certain aspects of Nazi rule, but their sporadic, isolated objections also had no influence on the regime. Even the resistance within military circles was, for all intents and purposes, overcome by 1938, with the notable exception of General Beck and his followers. The fact that Hitler came to power under the guise of constitutional forms and that the members of the army had personally sworn loyalty to the Führer dissuaded many from resorting to outright acts of disloyalty.

The most long-lived opposition group inside Hitler's Germany was known as the Kreisau Circle. Founded in 1933 and named after the estate of the leader of the organization, Count Helmuth von Moltke, this group included younger members of the traditional elites — members of the nobility, university faculties, the diplomatic corps, the civil service, and the military. Joined by members of the underground Social Democratic Party, by Catholics like the Jesuit Alfred Delp, and by such Protestants as the Lutheran minister Eugen Gerstenmaier, the group laid plans for a new Germany after the Nazis had been expelled from power. These ideas, expressed in 1943 as "Principles for the New Order in Germany" combined proposals for a re-Christianization of Germany and the development of a spirit of internationalism. The Nazis arrested Moltke in January 1944 and eventually executed him, and the Kreisau Circle dissolved.

459

The most sustained resistance to the Nazis came from the churches of Germany or, to be more exact, from scattered individual members of the clergy and Christian groups. Michael Cardinal Faulhaber, despite his earlier support for the regime, ultimately came to resist the Nazis. And although the vast majority of Protestant clergymen (like their Catholic counterparts) remained silent on many policies of the regime, a few raised their voices in opposition. Dr. Martin Niemöller and Pastor Dietrich Bonhoeffer, for instance, formed the Bekenntniskirche, the Confessional church, dedicated to defending Protestant principles against the intrusions of National Socialist ideology. Christian resistance to the regime intensified after 1940, centering on objection to the policy of euthanasia for inmates of insane asylums. The Protestant minister Friedrich von Bodelschwingh refused to hand retarded children under his care over to authorities from the SS, and the Catholic bishop of Münster, Clemens von Galen, delivered and later had published a powerful sermon condemning euthanasia. Popular response swelled this resistance. In August 1941 the regime quietly ended its euthanasia program in one of the few instances in which opposition and popular feeling led the regime to change its policy.

Especially after the onset of the war, the universities formed another source of opposition. In collaboration with a number of fellow students and Professor Kurt Huber at the University of Munich, Hans Scholl, a former Hitler Youth member who had also fought on the eastern front, began in 1941 to publish pamphlets critical of the leaders of the regime and of the "stupid Führer followers." By the winter of 1942–43 the White Rose, the symbol Scholl's organization had adopted to indicate its purity of motives, established contact with students at other universities throughout Germany. Scholl, his sister, and other members of the White Rose were eventually arrested and executed in 1943.

Effective resistance only materialized after the military situation turned against the Third Reich in 1942. The loosely organized opposition comprised military leaders such as General Ludwig Beck and General Henning von Tresckow, diplomats such as Ulrich von Hassell and Adam von Trott zu Solz, and politicians such as Carl Friedrich Goerdeler, the former mayor of Leipzig, and Julius Leber, a former Social Democratic member of the Reichstag. Members of the Kreisau Circle also joined. By March of 1943, Tresckow and his junior officer, Lieutenant von Schlabrendorff, decided that only the assassination of Hitler would lead to the overthrow of the regime.

Several attempts on Hitler's life failed in the course of 1943 and 1944. Early in 1944 Colonel Claus von Stauffenberg took the leadership of the anti-Nazi conspiracy, enlisting the support of retired field marshal Erwin von Witzleben to conduct the military operations necessary for the success of a coup. Following the beginning of the Allied invasion of Normandy on D-Day and the enrollment of the popular commander Erwin Rommel in the plot, Stauffenberg acted in the summer of 1944. After two failed attempts, he managed to smuggle a bomb inside Hitler's military headquarters in East Prussia on July 20. The explosion shattered the

Führer's eardrums, injured his hand, and inflicted several burns on parts of his body, but he was not killed. Believing they had been successful, however, the conspirators took over the War Ministry in Berlin and ordered the arrest of all major Nazi officials and SS officers. Yet before the day was over, the plot failed. Several of those who had taken part in the attempted coup were arrested immediately and shot; others were rounded up by the Gestapo, tried in the People's Court, and executed. Hitler's vengeance was severe. Over five thousand people lost their lives as a result of the July 20 plot. As was true of other opposition groups within the Third Reich, the conspirators, forming small and isolated cadres of the discontented, did not have a cohesive enough organization to be successful.

107. Public Passivity

During the years 1933–39, the Nazi regime faced no serious opposition because of the very effective system of coercion and terror the police state had established. Additionally, potential resistance had been weakened by the arrests of leftist political leaders and the breakup of political organizations. The underground Social Democratic organization also pointed in the spring of 1934 to public attitudes its reporter characterized as "cautious, passive, tolerant, and reserved" as indicative of the inner weakness of the opposition. The Social Democrats were also quick to criticize the middle class and the agricultural community, whose attitudes they saw as being shaped by a fear of bolshevism.

> Grumble yes, but to go beyond that and actively resist the regime is another matter — most are not yet prepared to go that far. An example of the cautious and tolerant reserve of the populace is an incident that transpired during the May Day festivities in Hamburg: "After Hitler's speech came the song 'Horst-Wessel,' whereupon many participants refused to offer the Hitler salute. A worker was questioned because of his attitude, was beaten and then ordered to leave the square. He was not arrested, but on the following day his unemployment money was cut off. The incident evoked only indifference among those present. There was no sympathy for the worker; instead, people said: 'Well, he should at least have saluted!' . . ."
>
> Gloating over the regime's problems and passive resistance are characteristic of public attitudes and shed much light on the inner weakness of the opposition to the regime. This inner weakness is underscored by the following report from Baden:

From *Deutschland-Berichte der Sozialdemokratischen Partei Deutschlands (Sopade)*, *1934–1940* (Frankfurt: Verlag Petra Nettelbeck, 1980), 1 (May/June 1934): 118–19, 171–72. Translated by Dieter Kuntz.

"When one questions the critics as to how they envision a change in the political situation, one receives only a shrugging of the shoulders in response. People hope an economic boycott can be realized or that the army will act. In any case, no one seems to have a concrete formula, choosing instead to wait for some kind of a political accident to occur. . . . Aside from the army, the Saar question had been a hope for some — particularly the reaction of France. . . . Now, however, people are more receptive to the idea that change can come about only through action within Germany itself. In this regard, however, people are inclined to believe that if this is the case it could take years for the present system to collapse."

The weakness of its opponents is a strength of the regime. Its opponents are ideologically and organizationally weak. They are ideologically weak because the masses consist only of dissatisfied people, only grumblers; their dissatisfaction is based solely upon economic reasons. This is especially true of the middle class and farmers. These classes are the most vocal critics today, but their criticism stems from only narrow personal interests. These classes are the least willing to earnestly fight against the regime because they know the least about the need to fight. . . . Many fear that the collapse of Hitler would bring about a chaotic situation, allowing bolshevism to come to the fore, and that those who would most immediately be affected would be the middle class and the farmers. The regime's policy toward the masses is based on this fact.

The opponents of the regime are organizationally weak because it is in the nature of the fascist system to prohibit any organizational gathering of its opponents. The forces of the "reaction" are extraordinarily splintered. Among dedicated groups there are at least five that are monarchist-oriented. The workers' movement continues to be split into socialists and communists, while within these two main orientations there are countless subgroups. . . . The attitude of the church-based opponents of the regime is not uniform. . . .

108. Negative Attitudes Toward the Regime

The Gestapo carefully monitored public opinion in order to detect any form of dissent or opposition to the regime. In this report of August 1935 the police outlined the source and nature of dissatisfaction in the Reich. "Public uneasiness" and even "dejection" among segments of the population were noted to have been caused by economic factors. The public's perception of the incompetency of lower-ranking party officials who held government posts, according to the report, had led to a loss of confidence in these offices."

From Herbert Michaelis and Ernst Schraepler, eds., *Ursachen und Folgen vom deutschen Zusammenbruch 1918 und 1945* (Berlin: Dokumenten-Verlag Dr. Herbert Wendler, 1958), vol. 11, pp. 51–55. Translated by Dieter Kuntz.

SPECIAL REPORT OF THE STATE POLICE, HANNOVER, TO THE DEPUTY CHIEF AND INSPECTOR OF THE PRUSSIAN SECRET STATE POLICE [GESTAPO], SS LIEUTENANT GENERAL HEYDRICH

TOP SECRET!

Hannover, August 18, 1935

Since the populace in general is timid and takes great care not to express its opinion publicly, it is becoming more and more difficult to observe and assess the public's attitude. Unmistakable, however, is the fact that the internal political situation has lately been considerably tense, which has adversely affected attitudes. Even though trade and industry are apparently being conducted smoothly, a certain public uneasiness and dejection can be observed which manifests itself in varying degrees among various occupational strata. As to the size of the circle so affected, it must be said openly that its extent is much greater than the limits assigned to it by [National Socialist] Party offices, the Party press, and propaganda. It includes not only reactionary segments of the population and those elements subject to their influence, but this deep dissatisfaction reaches also into the Party and to its oldest members — which gives cause for serious concern.

The causes of this attitude, insofar as economic factors are not involved, . . . can be traced to the conduct of a segment of the lower-ranking leadership of NS organizations. This is especially true of the political officeholders. This has largely contributed to a loss of public confidence in these offices. Hence it is repeatedly said that Party offices continue to be staffed by men who, according to their past and present activities, are not suited for their positions. These men lack all sense of responsibility. Their life-styles and attitudes give rise to criticism, and they simply ignore directives from higher Party offices. The end result is that they undermine the authority and discipline within the Party itself. The general public does not understand that these individuals are not publicly taken to task for their mistakes. The public has the impression that such cases are purposely hushed-up, and that state government officials who feel compelled to take measures out of a sense of duty are being prevented from acting because of pressure being exerted by Party offices. This then inevitably leads to the assumption that the state is powerless. This undermines the authority of the state government. . . . The Party, especially the political branch, can maintain or improve its image with the public if in future only impeccable, unpretentious, and ideologically and morally schooled Party members are appointed to leading positions. . . .

Another matter that has attracted considerable adverse criticism is the conduct of the press. Large segments of the population harbor the opinion that freedom of the press is being restricted and suppressed, and consequently that the truth is not being reported. Even Party members are critical when unpleasant incidents and punishments for mistakes are not publicized. It goes without saying that enemies of the Party and state are here especially vocal. I feel that it is imperative that change is brought about as soon as possible to remedy this situation. It is obvious that the public's attitude is being influenced by increased reactionary activity, much of which emanates from circles that include political Catholicism, the Confessional church, and from citizens who refuse to be reeducated and who continue to mask themselves. Periodically even monarchist sentiments are expressed. The reintroduction of compulsory military service is giving rise to the hope of a "fourth Reich" in which the armed forces will exercise authority to the exclusion of the Party. . . .

As far as individual occupational strata are concerned, one can point to economic factors as a cause for negative attitudes. In this regard the situation of the working class merits special attention in that wage rates are creating increased bitter resentment. . . . The increase in the cost of foodstuffs required on a daily basis, such as potatoes, vegetables, fruit, milk, eggs, and butter, has heightened the dissatisfaction among workers. They maintain that they have never seen such [high] prices. . . . Additionally, workers are loudly complaining about the excessive membership dues payments to the Labor Front. The organization Strength Through Joy is still accepted by a segment [of the workers], although a larger segment contends that the advantages of the organization are worthless if a worker is not in position even to basically support his family. . . .

As far as the agricultural community is concerned, it seems to be the case that peasants naturally tend to be dissatisfied. . . . Discordance has been caused by the increase in membership dues payments to the National Food Ministry, especially when the peasant compares these payments to those made in earlier days to the Chamber of Agriculture, the Farmers' League, or other earlier agricultural associations. Among craftsmen, complaints are heard about a lack of work and competition from department stores, cooperative stores, and Jewish businesses. Time and time again it is said that the Party program has not been adhered to in this matter.

In closing I might add that the mood of the populace, in regard to foreign policy developments, can be seen as a positive one. The naval agreement that has been reached with England,[1] the continued friendly German-Polish relations, the preoccupation of the erstwhile enemy alliance with the Abyssinian conflict, and the reconciliation of German and

---

[1] In June 1935, Germany and Britain concluded a naval agreement by which the British agreed to German naval rearmament, but which limited the size of its navy to 35 percent of the size of the British navy. This agreement was a diplomatic blunder on the part of the British, because it recognized Hitler's right to rearm.

English veterans has cleared away the previous war panic that was felt by all segments of the population. There is now a new feeling of optimism that Germany can gradually free itself from its international encirclement. . . .

109. Political Jokes

For Germans opposed to the regime who did not belong to organized resistance groups, it was still possible to show displeasure with National Socialism or at least to evidence a disapproving attitude. Some refused to give the "German greeting" ("*Heil Hitler*"), others might make disparaging remarks about the conduct of the war, and still others might secretly listen to radio broadcasts from the BBC in London. Political jokes frequently made the rounds in non-Nazi circles, many of which revolved around the physical attributes of Goering or Goebbels. As the war turned sour for Germany, the Führer himself became the butt of jokes. The following document, compiled in April 1943 by the Nazi Party organizational leadership, is based on reports submitted by the *Gauleiter* of the various regions. The date is important since by 1943 Germany was on the defensive on the Russian front and Hitler was beginning to suffer a series of reversals in the fortunes of war. "Popular" dissent of the type suggested increased proportionately with the severity of the war situation.

The enemy is using all sorts of measures in the attempt to shake the mood and attitude of the populace and its trust in the country's leadership. Therefore no rumor is too stupid, and no joke is too abusive. There will always be fools — aside from those elements who basically have a negative attitude — who will find a grain of truth in this. Many districts report unanimously that, lately, political jokes that *deal with the person of the Führer himself* have increased tremendously! From among the abundance of jokes, a few have been selected as examples and follow below:

The difference between the sun and Hitler: The sun "rises" in the East, while Hitler "sinks" in the East.

The difference between India and Germany: In India one person starves himself for all, while in Germany all starve for one person.

Young Max tells at school that his cat at home gave birth to kittens. He composed a short rhyme about it: "Our cat had a litter, five in all, four meowed 'Heil Hitler,' while one said nothing at all." Several weeks later

From *Nationalsozialistische Deutsche Arbeiter-Partei, Hauptarchiv 1919–45,* Stanford, CA: (Hoover Institution on War, Revolution, and Peace) H.A. reel 50, folder 1181a (Gauleiter Report, April 16, 1943). Translated by Dieter Kuntz.

the principal came to visit the classroom and, calling on Max, said: "Not long ago you composed such a nice rhyme about your cat, please recite it again." Upon which little Max began: "Our cat had a litter, five in all, four meowed 'Heil Moscow,' while one said nothing at all." This shocked the teacher, who then demanded to know why the text had suddenly changed. Max answered that it was because four weeks ago the kittens were blind, but now four of them have had their eyes opened.

The Führer, Goering, and Mussolini are in a plane above Munich. They are discussing how they can best make themselves popular with the people of Munich. Goering decides that he is going to throw down lard ration coupons. The Führer decides he will throw down meat ration coupons. Mussolini goes up to the cockpit, pats the pilot on the shoulder, and says: "Give me some advice. I don't have any lard or meat ration coupons to throw down; what can I do to become popular with the people of Munich?" The pilot advised him to throw the other two passengers down.

110. Opposition from Youth Gangs

During the early years of the Nazi regime many members of the Hitler Youth undoubtedly enjoyed the opportunities to engage in the leisure activities offered by the organization. In the 1940s, however, youths increasingly began to turn away from the Hitler Youth in reaction to its stricter disciplinary measures and overall regimentation brought about by the war. Boys between the ages of fourteen and eighteen from working-class backgrounds were not eager to give their loyalty to the National Socialist regime, resisting assimilation into a homogeneous national youth movement. One such group that began to form during the late 1930s was known as the Edelweiss Pirates. These loosely organized bands of young men were most prominent in the working-class neighborhoods of large cities in western Germany such as Essen and Düsseldorf. Their activities included meetings in the surrounding countryside or in more distant areas like the Black Forest, where various gangs would hike, camp, and sing Hitler Youth songs with the lyrics changed. Frequently the Edelweiss Pirates attacked and roughed up Hitler Youth patrols, which suggests that more than a passive resistance to Nazism was at the base of their opposition to the regime. It does not appear, however, that these groups went much beyond minor acts of defiance, although some did cooperate with the Communist Party underground. Nonetheless, the regime was concerned by their activities and regarded them as a subversive element. The Gestapo attempted repeatedly to break them up during the war years, culminating in a public hanging of Edelweiss Pirate leaders in Cologne in 1944.

From Detlev Peukert, *Die Edelweiss Piraten* (Cologne: Bund-Verlag, 1983), pp. 123–26. Translated by Dieter Kuntz. Reprinted by permission of Bund-Verlag GmbH.

The following document consists of a memorandum written by Himmler in 1944 detailing the activities of oppositional youth groups. It reflects a last attempt by the regime to combat and prosecute these movements.

Berlin, October 25, 1944

HIGHLY CONFIDENTIAL!

To SD [Sicherheitsdienst, Security Service] and other police offices

In all parts of the Reich, especially in the larger cities, associations of youths (gangs) have lately been forming in increased numbers. In part these exhibit criminal, antisocial, or political-oppositional tendencies and therefore require intensified surveillance, especially in view of the absence due to the war of many fathers, Hitler Youth leaders, and educators.

All associations of youths must be watched closely and steps must be taken against them accordingly. . . .

I. VARIETY AND APPEARANCE OF GANGS

1. Gangs are associations of youths who are not in the Hitler Youth, and who lead a separate and extraordinary existence based on principles not in accordance with National Socialist ideology. They all share a rejection of or disinterest toward their obligations within the *Volksgemeinschaft* or the Hitler Youth; this is especially evidenced by their wanting volition to conform to the exigencies of the war.

2. These gangs have made their appearance under a variety of names (clique, mob, gang, pack, the Platters, the Shufflers, the Edelweiss Pirates, and so on). A centralized organization does not, in general, exist. Outward association is often only very loose and irregular. Occasionally they wear special identifying insignia (for example, Edelweiss emblem, death's head rings, colored pins, and the like). Membership dues are usually not collected, but in some cases identification insignia are issued. The gangs more or less have their regular meeting places and operating territories; they often go on outings together. Between certain gangs cross-communication does exist. This can be of a friendly or of an antagonistic nature. It is primarily young lads who belong to these gangs, but there are a few girls as well.

3. Formation of a gang usually involves common affiliation in factory, school, some other organization, or simply residing in the same district. Initially such associations can be quite harmless (street friendships, standing at corners together, and so forth); later, however, depending on prevailing convictions and goals, ominous developments can ensue. It is not unusual to be able to trace this activity back to a single antisocial or criminally inclined fellow who knows how to bring the others to heel and can direct their harmless desire for adventure instead toward dangerous avenues. Generally three different basic forms of behavior can be deter-

mined, although it must be noted that few gangs exhibit only one of these basic characteristics in pronounced form. Moreover, activity of one particular kind most often leads to activity of another kind. We have isolated the following:

a. Groups of an *antisocial* orientation. This is characterized by acts of minor to serious criminal offenses (mischief, brawling, violations of police directives, larceny, morality [sex] offenses — especially involving members of the same sex and so on.). . . .

b. Gangs of a *political-oppositional* orientation, although not always with a well-defined program of opposition. Their orientation is marked by generally seditious behavior, rejection of the Hitler Youth and other community obligations, indifference toward the conduct of the war, engaging in disruptions of youth service obligations, attacks on Hitler Youth members, listening to foreign radio broadcasts, dissemination of rumors, maintaining the traditions, song repertoire, and the like, of the prohibited federated [youth] groups or of other groups. Youths of this orientation frequently attempt to infiltrate [Nazi] Party organizations in order to provide a screen for themselves or in order to have the possibility for subversive actions.

c. Cliques of a liberal-individualistic orientation, characterized by a predilection for English ideals, language, demeanor, dress (English-casual), cultivation of jazz [*Hottmusik*] and swing dance, and so on. The members of these gangs come primarily from the "upper middle class" and want to pursue their own pleasure and sexual or other excesses. They thereby soon conflict sharply with National Socialist ideology. They resist directives from the Hitler Youth, Labor Service, and military service, and acquire the behavioral characteristics listed under item (b).

4. The members of gangs can be differentiated, based on the degree of their participation, into leaders, active participants, and nominal members [hangers-on].

Leaders of the gangs (ringleaders) are — not that a solid leadership authority always exists — one or more people, often even adults or foreigners, who have asserted themselves through exceptional intelligence, initiative, or brutality. Some have previous criminal records, some are former members of earlier federated [youth] or other political-oppositional circles. They are only seldom members of the Hitler Youth. If, however, they are Hitler Youth members, they do not do their duties, do them only reluctantly, or have already withdrawn from the Hitler Youth due to certain offenses or loss of interest. Cases have been documented, however, where they have performed their duties flawlessly in order not to arouse any outward suspicion.

Some of the active members and hangers-on of the gangs also have previous criminal records or come from disorderly family circumstances and antisocial clans. Others, however, come from respectable families and are themselves basically still decent. In many cases they were moved to join because of negligent parents (neglect of educational and supervisory responsibilities) or because of a misguided craving for adventure, romantic conceptions, or for other puberty-related reasons.

The members of a gang frequently exhibit identical styles of clothing, hair fashions, and behavior, and often have nicknames derived from the images of their perceived world or from their approved stock of ideas. Because of the war, many youths have been left largely to their own devices. Gangs therefore exert a strong attraction on these youths and for that matter even on decent young people.

111. The Swing Youth

Youths from upper middle-class family backgrounds who rejected National Socialist ideological precepts, particularly the behavioral norms for German youth as envisioned under the ideal of the *Volksgemeinschaft,* came to be regarded as subversive groups by the regime. Particularly distressing to Nazi police agents assigned to surveillance duties were individuals who were part of the so-called Swing Youth cliques and loose associations. Although such groups were not opposed to National Socialism on political grounds, their "resistance" manifested itself in nonconformity, which in itself typified generational rebellion common to many societies. The Swing Youth, however, represented a threat to the Nazi regime because they deviated from the role assigned to youth by Adolf Hitler These groups generally harbored attitudes of apathy toward Hitler Youth activities, seeking instead to identify themselves with non-Nazi culture and accordingly Idealizing the cultural trends of Germany's enemies, England and America. Youths from families with money and social position engaged in such "countercultural" activities as dancing to American jazz ("Negro music") and wearing English clothing fashions. Concentrations of Swing Youth were found primarily in large German cities such as Hamburg, Berlin, and Frankfurt. The following excerpt from a memorandum written in September 1942 by the National Socialist Reich Youth Leadership illustrates not only the type of activities the Swing Youth engaged in but also evidences the Nazi Party's reaction to such nonconformism. Attributing their anti-Nazi behavior to innate moral corruption, the Party was all too eager to label these cultural deviants as enemies of the state.

The most striking phenomenon among the current "deviant groups" is presented by the so-called Swing Youth. Reports about this group are coming in from all parts of the Reich, but the most detailed report has

From Detlev Peukert, *Die Edelweiss Piraten* (Cologne: Bund-Verlag, 1983), pp. 201–6. Translated by Dieter Kuntz. Reprinted by permission of Bund-Verlag GmbH.

been sent in by Hamburg. This report (from the summer of 1941) provides an exhaustive portrait of the manifestations of the Swing Youth, which for the most part are representative of their appearance in other parts of the Reich. Excerpts of the report follow below:

"Since the seizure of power, it has been observed that again and again attempts have been made by youth circles antagonistic to the Hitler Youth to join together in particular gangs. This has been especially pronounced in the larger cities. . . . A special position is occupied by club-type youth associations which are especially heavily represented in northwestern Germany, and which in mental attitude and life-style are oriented toward the English model. A typical example of such an illegal association of youths established on such a 'social basis,' is the Swing Youth of Hamburg, which after years of surveillance and diverse seizures we were able to study and subdue."

"During the winter of 1937–38, young lads and girls of Hamburg, many from higher social echelons, joined together during ice skating to form the so-called Ice Rink Gang. Many were already acquainted through secondary school or knew each other from membership in exclusive sports clubs. They frequented the same taverns, wore eccentric clothing, and enthused about English music and English dance. At the turn of the year 1939–40 the Flottbeck gang founded an amateur dance band and staged several private dance parties, to which a few classes of secondary students and members of the finest Hamburg sport clubs were invited. The first of these dance parties, in February of 1940, was attended by 500 to 600 youths, and resulted in an uninhibited swing-activity and was the subject of conversation for weeks among Hamburg youth. Following are excerpts from a report about this party:"

". . . For the dance only English and American music was played. Only Swing and 'hot' [jitterbug] dancing was engaged in. At the entrance to the hall was posted a sign upon which the inscription had been altered from SWING VERBOTEN [PROHIBITED]! to SWING ERBETEN [REQUESTED]! The participants accompanied the dances and songs without exception by singing along with the English words. Moreover, throughout the entire evening they attempted to speak only English, except for a few tables where they even spoke French. The sight of those dancing was appalling. Not a single couple danced in a normal fashion; they all did the "swing" in the most vile manner. Sometimes two boys would dance with one girl, while sometimes several couples would form a circle and others would cut in and then hop around in a manner whereby they would slap each other's hands and even roll the backs of their heads together. Then in bent-over position they would let their upper bodies hang limply downward, their long hair wildly covering the face, knees half bent while legs are swung to and fro. When the band struck up a rumba, the dancers fell into a wild ecstasy. All ran around quite wildly and babbled the English refrain. The band played increasingly wilder music. None of those in the band remained seated, all jitterbugged about the stage wildly. Numerous boys danced with each other, all of them with two cigarettes in their mouths — one in each corner of their mouths. . . ."

"A subsequent dance party was prohibited by the police; thereupon the gangs dispensed with large crowd affairs and met only in small groups, such as at parties at home, and so forth. They would frequent small taverns in groups of 20 to 30 youths and dance to English music. . . . In October of 1940, the Security Police took steps against the members of the Swing Youth, as a result of which 63 youths were arrested. Four of their number were between the ages of 14 and 16, and 22 were between 16 and 18 years old. The investigation found the Swing Youth to be an illegal association of youths opposed to the Party and state, and which on a wholesale level practiced English life-styles while rejecting the German life-style. . . . In order to be considered a full member, every boy and girl had to acquire the mannerisms, clothing styles, and insignia of the Swing Youth. In order for males to legitimize their membership they wore long hair reaching down to the collar . . . checkered English business suits, shoes with thick, light-colored crepe soles, conspicuous scarfs, diplomat-style hats, umbrellas on the arm (regardless of the weather), and serving as a piece of identifying insignia, a colorful gem or stone protruding from a dress-shirt buttonhole."

"The girls too preferred to wear their hair in long wavy locks. Eyebrows were penciled, lips glossed, and fingernails were painted. . . .

"Very much characteristic of the Swing-Youth is their form of expression. They address each other as "Swing-Boys," "Swing-Girls," or "Old-hot-Boy." Letters are concluded with "Swing Heil.""

". . . . Record players and the continual acquisition of newly released dance records are items of necessity to any member of the Swing Youth. The record disk takes the place of books. . . . There was a similar fondness for English/American movies. The laxity in attitude and life-style presented in these movies had such an appeal for these youths that, by their own admission, they deliberately strove to create a dissolute impression. "American" attitudes and behavior constituted an ideal. Accordingly, the attitude of Swing Youth members toward today's Germany and its politics, the Party and its organizations, the Hitler Youth, the Labor Service, and military service, inclusive of the war, is one of rejection or at the best disinterest. They perceive the National Socialist orientation to be one of "mass coercion." The great accomplishments of our time do not stir them; the opposite is true, "they enthusiastically embrace all that is not German, but is instead English." The greeting "Heil Hitler" is rejected. On the occasion of the formation of a new gang, in the clubroom of a tavern, the picture of the Führer hanging on the wall was inverted, face to the wall. This was accompanied by the hooting of all participants."

471

". . . . Immoral activity occurred primarily during home parties, but sometimes also during the frequenting of taverns, during excursions, and during air raid night watch shifts that some youths had to participate in for their employing firms. Frequently a youth who had watch duty for his firm would invite numerous boys and girls to join him. Inevitably, alcohol was brought by all the participants. Often during these night-watches immoral conduct and sexual intercourse would occur. . . . However, the most vile excesses took place during home parties, at times when youths were not supervised by their parents. Favorite activities during home parties were the so-called forfeit games, in which an article of clothing had to be forfeited, with the result that by game's end all the participants would be totally disrobed. . . . Homosexuality also plays a role within these slovenly gangs. Among these youths, girls included, it was openly discussed that within the group there were several who were of a 'different orientation.' . . . In accordance with the general attitude of the Swing Youth, approximately ten half-Jews and Jewesses were allowed membership of the swing gangs. Male gang members even maintained friendly and in part intimate relationships with five full-blooded Jewesses (between the ages of fifteen and eighteen), even though they were aware of their racial identities. . . ."

112. The White Rose

During 1942, a group of students at the University of Munich formed an organization whose intent was to oppose the Nazi regime. Calling itself the White Rose, the group chose its name to symbolize the beautiful and noble German Christian spirit in contrast to the will-to-power of the Nazi regime. They rejected the Nazis' simplistically appropriated versions of Friedrich Nietzsche's philosophical ideal "superman," who sought only power and strength and was contemptuous of other men and their laws and religions. The White Rose established contacts with student resistance groups at other universities. Initially, the activities of the White Rose were of a clandestine nature, consisting of the distribution of literature espousing opposition to the regime within university circles. The group, led by the students Hans and Sophie Scholl, later engaged in public campaigns, circulating leaflets denouncing Nazi "subhumanity" and participating in a student demonstration against the regime — a unique event in the Third Reich. The Scholls were arrested, interrogated, tortured, and ultimately executed in February of 1943. The document that follows consists of an excerpt from a leaflet distributed by the White Rose in 1942.

Reprinted from *The White Rose: Munich, 1942–1943* [first published as *Students Against Tyranny (Middletown, CT: Wesleyan University Press, 1970)*, by Inge Scholl], pp. 85–86. Copyright 1983 by Inge Aicher-Scholl. Translated from the German by Arthur Schultz. Reprinted by permission of University Press of New England.

There is an ancient maxim that we repeat to our children: "He who won't listen will have to feel." But a wise child will not burn his fingers the second time on a hot stove. In the past weeks Hitler has chalked up successes in Africa and in Russia. In consequence, optimism on the one hand and distress and pessimism on the other have grown within the German people with a rapidity quite inconsistent with traditional German apathy. On all sides one hears among Hitler's opponents — the better segments of the population — exclamations of despair, words of disappointment and discouragement, often ending with the question: "Will Hitler now, after all . . . ?"

Meanwhile the German offensive against Egypt has ground to a halt. Rommel has to bide his time in a dangerously exposed position. But the push into the East proceeds. This apparent success has been purchased at the most horrible expense of human life, and so it can no longer be counted an advantage. Therefore we must warn against *all* optimism.

Neither Hitler nor Goebbels can have counted the dead. In Russia thousands are lost daily. It is the time of the harvest, and the reaper cuts into the ripe grain with wide strokes. Mourning takes up her abode in the country cottages, and there is no one to dry the tears of the mothers. Yet Hitler feeds with lies those people whose most precious belongings he has stolen and whom he has driven to a meaningless death.

Every word that comes from Hitler's mouth is a lie. When he says peace, he means war, and when he blasphemously uses the name of the Almighty, he means the power of evil, the fallen angel, Satan. His mouth is the foul-smelling maw of Hell, and his might is at bottom accursed. True, we must conduct the struggle against the National Socialist terrorist state with rational means; but whoever today still doubts the reality, the existence of demonic powers, has failed by a wide margin to understand the metaphysical background of this war. Behind the concrete, the visible events, behind all objective, logical considerations, we find the irrational element: the struggle against the demon, against the servants of the Anti-Christ. Everywhere and at all times demons have been lurking in the dark, waiting for the moment when man is weak; when of his own volition he leaves his place in the order of Creation as founded for him by God in freedom: when he yields to the force of evil, separates himself from the powers of a higher order; and, after voluntarily taking the first step, he is driven on to the next and the next at a furiously accelerating rate. Everywhere and at all times of greatest trial men have appeared, prophets and saints who cherished their freedom, who preached the One God and who with His help brought the people to a reversal of their downward course. Man is free, to be sure, but without the true God he is defenseless against the principle of evil. He is like a rudderless ship, at the mercy of the storm, an infant without his mother, a cloud dissolving into thin air.

I ask you, you as a Christian wrestling for the preservation of your greatest treasure, whether you hesitate, whether you incline toward intrigue, calculation, or procrastination in the hope that someone else will raise his arm in your defense? Has God not given you the strength, the will to fight? We *must* attack evil where it is strongest, and it is strongest in the power of Hitler. . . .

113. Social Democratic Opposition

Hitler officially banned the Social Democratic Party on June 22, 1933, but many of its leaders had already been arrested or had fled abroad before that date. The leaders of the organization who went abroad established an executive committee "in exile" in Prague, Czechoslovakia, moving their headquarters to Paris in 1938, where they stayed until 1940. Loyal members who remained in Germany acted as informants for the exiled leadership, sending reports of conditions in Germany to the executive committee. In 1934 the Sopade (Social Democratic Party of Germany in Exile) defined the nature of its actions and the task it had established for itself.

Our activities to date have been predicated on the following considerations: We are not content to await the collapse of the dictatorship in Germany from abroad. We are not counting on luck or chance. We know that the gathering and activation of the working class is the fundamental requirement in the fight to remove this dictatorship. The emphasis of our work was, accordingly, from the beginning within Germany itself.

In the beginning, we had great difficulties to overcome. Everything was in shambles. All workers' organizations — political, trade unionist, and cultural — had been crushed or taken over by the enemy. Most of our supporters, who since September 1930 had sacrificed and had waged a tough, exemplary struggle against the fascist threat, and who had shown admirable loyalty to the [Social Democratic] party during the terrorized elections of March 5, 1933, were in a great state of depression and almost completely paralyzed. . . . Some of the party officials refused to recognize that the task of rebuilding the movement could be accomplished only through underground activity. In the first few months we began by establishing contacts with individuals who were prepared to work with us, and with small, locally active groups of young members of the party and the Reichsbanner.[1] Only in isolated cases were we able to reestablish

From *Deutschland-Berichte der Sozialdemokratischen Partei Deutschlands (Sopade) 1934–1940* (Frankfurt: Verlag Petra Nettelbeck, 1980), 1 (August/September 1934): 456–57, 459–65. Translated by Dieter Kuntz.

---

[1] The *Reichsbanner* was the paramilitary formation of the Social Democrats, and was composed mainly of former soldiers.

the connections with the people and apparatus of the old organization. At the time it seemed as though fascism had succeeded in crushing not only the organization but also the spirit and soul of German Social Democracy. . . . Today the picture has changed considerably. When compared with the party's membership figures prior to January 30, 1933, the number of active groups and individual supporters is still relatively small. Our chance for success, however, has increased considerably. This is because the organized working class has largely survived depression and lethargy. . . .

Our relationship to the communists has been shaped by organizational and political motives and is based on principle. The immense danger of underground activity makes it necessary to maintain a distance from other illegal groups and individuals. . . . Communist activity is characterized by a disregard for the safety of their people. They recklessly sacrifice their underground agents even if the reward is only a momentary propaganda victory. The Communist party of Germany demands underground activity even from their imperiled people. Our position, on the other hand, is that underground activity should be conducted only if the utmost has been done to protect the freedom and the lives of the agents. Never should the active forces of the movement be risked for only a trivial momentary success. Cooperative work with the communists, even on a local level, is rejected by about all Social Democratic groups because the danger to informants is so great and any joint activities would almost automatically endanger our comrades. . . . Aside from this, there are still great ideological differences between Communists and Social Democrats. . . .

Besides the headquarters of the Sopade in Prague, we have established a network of bureaus at all German borders. . . . The organizational form of our underground movement is as diverse as are the underground activities. The differences reflect the varied situations within German regions. There are areas where terror and political pressure precludes the establishment of a solid organizational network; where only small circles of our members can be entrusted with informational materials, while in other districts Social Democrats are hardly bothered and where criticism of the regime has progressed to the point where the distribution of our materials is silently tolerated. . . .

Whereas in the beginning we limited our work essentially to the distribution of the Sozialistischen Aktion [Socialist Action], we now have largely moved to the publication of general propaganda material. . . . It can generally be said that the distribution of these materials has shaken the myth so eagerly propagated by the Propaganda Ministry that only the communists were involved in underground activity. We have also strengthened the self-confidence of our supporters, who previously were not cognizant of the activities of underground groups. The distribution of these materials verifies the vitality of our movement. There has been a great increase in the production of recruitment and informational leaflets within Germany.

Aside from the general distribution of materials, we have also given attention to the education of our co-workers. The dictatorship has made it impossible to disseminate political information safely, as it has made impossible political instruction of the type we formerly employed. The underground activist of today, however, must be thoroughly informed about the situation in Germany, the international situation, the differences within the socialist camp in Germany and abroad. Since the appearance of our *Zeitschrift für Sozialismus* [*Socialist Journal*] we have also distributed a covert, shortened edition of the journal which focuses on the most important news. It is not intended for mass distribution in Germany but is only meant to be distributed amongst our co-activists. We have also issued small numbers of brochures that are important to political discussion within underground groups. These include "Revolution gegen Hitler" ["Revolution Against Hitler"], and "Neu beginnen" [A New Beginning]. For the past three months we have supplemented our reports from Germany with a special section B, which includes analyses of internal and foreign politics. These [reports] are primarily intended to serve as educational material for our functionaries in Germany. . . .

114. Communist Opposition

Most political opposition to the Nazi regime during the years prior to the war came from Social Democrats and Communists. Ideological animosity, however, prevented these left-wing groups from effectively opposing the regime. Of the two, probably the Communists more actively engaged in subversive activities, although the efforts of neither group were particularly successful. The Gestapo was extremely adept at infiltrating these underground organizations and arrested many Communists and Social Democrats during the early years of the regime, forcing the remnants to conduct mostly small-scale, clandestine campaigns of circulating leaflets and painting slogans. The following document, issued by resistance leaders to the members of Communist conspiratorial organizations, instructed groups and individuals on how best to avoid detection by the ever-watchful Gestapo.

From *Nationalsozialistische Deutsche Arbeiter-Partei, Hauptarchiv 1919–45,* (Stanford, CA: Hoover Institution on War, Revolution and Peace) H.A. reel 84, folder 1722 (Communist Resistance Guidelines). Translated by Dieter Kuntz.

HOW A COMMUNIST MUST CONDUCT HIMSELF WHEN ENGAGING IN UNDERGROUND ACTIVITIES — QUESTIONS PERTAINING TO CONSPIRACY

1. You are no longer to have a good, reliable friend or acquaintance with whom you can discuss your activity.
2. Therefore, do not tell anything to someone who might know; instead tell only him who must know.
3. It is not necessary for a friend to know more about personal and internal organizational matters than is absolutely necessary in order to do one's work.
4. If when walking you slouch and shuffle along, behave conspicuously on the street, and talk a lot with your hands, you will give police an opportunity to describe you quickly and ultimately track you down.
5. The shortest way is not always the best; that is, arrange to meet your friends with whom you are working so that on the way there you will have enough time to shake possible pursuers. Allow enough time for the next rendezvous, and set an example by being punctual.
6. It is best not to talk at all about our activities in public places, public transportation, or taverns; but if you do, do it in the form of an everyday conversation.
7. At our meetings, remember to agree beforehand what you will say if the Gestapo raids the meeting.
8. Carry potential evidence on your person only if it cannot be avoided, and then only for as brief a time as possible. Keep your apartment devoid of evidence.
9. Carefully check all apartments, operative meeting places, and addresses necessary in carrying out your work.
10. No matter what, all contacts gone awry should be broken off. Make arrangements with your associates beforehand so that you will find each other again later, even without knowing names or each other's place of residence.
11. Organize the exchange of informational materials on short notice and between only two individuals. Therefore, consider well beforehand the distribution numbers and the locations.
12. Terminate normal relationships with each other. As a private person you should also have nothing to do with other friends, even if you know that they can be trusted. This is precisely why you should not burden them needlessly. If you should happen to meet on the street, walk past each other. No one but the Gestapo is interested in whether or not you are acquainted.
13. Do not make [an] habitual haunt out of any one tavern, cinema, or park. You do not need to be known to more people than necessary.
14. Fight hard and with conviction against rumors and general feelings of panic on certain occasions. No one is to pass on unverified messages.

Everyone must immediately attempt to determine the author of such things. . . .

15. Remember, carelessness is not synonymous with courage. Our work requires skill, so that by applying all measures of caution and paying heed to the smallest detail we can be maximally effective in our work for the masses. Through the proper distribution of energy and application of flexible tactics we can succeed. . . .

It is obvious that in conspiratorial matters new situations and variations will always present themselves. Therefore, you should periodically discuss the methods of the opponent and determine your own course of action accordingly. That way you will have the advantage of always being one step ahead, because in the meantime the opponent must first adjust to our tactics. Ruthlessly, but in a comradely spirit, make the guilty party accountable if the rules are broken. Through truly solid political activity you can establish the basis of such mass support that, regardless of how bloody the terror is, it will not be capable of harming you.

Let these words of Lenin guide you in your organizational activity: "Whosoever, during this period of illegality, breaches Bolshevik discipline even ever so slightly — he aids, willingly or not, our enemy, the bourgeoisie."

115. Surveillance of Left-wing Opposition

The following document, dealing with the activities of left-wing opposition groups, the Social Democrats and the Communists, exemplifies the vigilance of the regime's surveillance agencies.

In a report of November 1933 from Frankenthal (in southwestern Germany) police observed important regional variations in the scope of illegal activity that these underground organizations engaged in, noting the passivity of the Communist Party while the Social Democratic Party, which had been strong in the area prior to the seizure of power, was still deemed to be a threat. The report further suggested that the opposition was severely hampered by a lack of leadership since many Social Democratic and Communist leaders had been arrested by the Gestapo. Interestingly, the report urged the adoption of more "broad-minded" policies toward the opposition in order to integrate former enemies into the *Volksgemeinschaft*.

From Anton Doll, ed., *Nationalsozialismus im Alltag: Quellen zur Geschichte der NS-Herrschaft im Gebiet des Landes Rheinland-Pfalz* (Speyer: Landesarchiv, 1983), pp. 74–75. Translated by Dieter Kuntz. Reprinted by permission of Landesarchiv, Rheinland-Pfalz.

Frankenthal, November 6, 1933

To: District Government Office Frankenthal

BIMONTHLY REPORT — INTERNAL POLITICAL MATTERS

1. Prohibited organizations: Insofar as the local jurisdictional district is concerned, it can be said that the prohibited organizations are complying with the ban. In spite of continued surveillance, no evidence of any kind was collected which would indicate that they continue to exist in any shape or form.

Of KPD [Communist party] members it can be said that they have reconciled themselves to the new situation more readily than their like-minded political compatriots, the SPD [Social Democratic party]. In general it can be said that KPD members in our region were not as fanatic as, for instance, those in north or middle Germany. This also explains their guarded public attitude. They have apparently come to terms with existing circumstances. This might not have happened so quickly if they had had adequate leadership. None of their leaders in this area was convincing, however, much less inspiring. Their main propaganda tool was communist reading material. Since this indoctrination by correspondence has been broken off, everything has gradually withered away.

Of the SPD it can be said that reconciliation with existing circumstances has not made much progress. There are still old die-hard party members who cannot face the facts. Many will never be inwardly acquiescent, although externally they may put on a different face.

Here it can openly be said that the Führer's offer to welcome any who have good intentions must be put into practice more effectively by local lower-level leadership than it has until now. One must bear in mind that many [leftists] had been misled and were full of hate, and that the average worker believed prior to the [National Socialist] revolution that only the SPD or KPD was interested in his well-being. The idea of *class distinctions* and *class hatred* had to permeate the soul of the average person deeply. By continually hurting and pushing back the otherwise decent worker we are not doing what the Führer wants; we are not consolidating the national family — we are only dividing it.

That class hatred still lives on in the inner life of the individual worker is clearly seen by the still-heard remarks of various misguided individuals who charge that as long as the NSDAP continues to have aristocrats and officers in positions of leadership, one cannot call it a workers' party.

From this it becomes evident that many still have not in the least accepted the idea of the *Volksgemeinschaft*. It is precisely in this regard that the lower-level leader has much to make up for. He must first of all himself understand the concept of the *Volksgemeinschaft* in order to fruitfully influence others.

For the present it is possible to be admitted into the nationalistic associations. Many are receptive to this. If one or another individual is, because of his prior convictions, not yet worthy or qualified for admission, one should not allow him to slip through the net. The former SPD, KPD, or Center party supporter can, in my opinion, be reeducated in the spirit of the German *Volksgemeinschaft* and good fellowship only if he is among the old or older members of the nationalistic associations. Here he will be under surveillance, as far as the police is concerned. If, however, he is excluded and stands on the sidelines, he will feel that he is not part of the German family, and surveillance will be more difficult if not impossible. Precisely because of this, one should be broad-minded and farsighted.

2. Nonprohibited associations and clubs: Nothing substantial to report here.

3. Other reports: The popular mood is positive and optimistic. Several narrow-minded farmers who are anything but imbued with the German communal spirit, and who instead continue to be possessed by the spirit of the old German liberalism, feel that they must make known their inner attitudes by being critical of the regime's policies. The Hereditary Farm Law and its possible effect does not appeal to them. Educational work is imperative in this case.

District Police Commissioner

116. Isolating the Individual

The Social Democratic underground analyzed the effect of *Gleichschaltung* upon individual initiative in a report of November 1935. The report concluded that the Nazi regime aimed to isolate the individual and rob the working class, especially, of a sense of solidarity by denying the formation of any non-Nazi associations. The Social Democrats' observation that workers were not in a mood for collective action but were content simply to be employed again demonstrates the effectiveness of this Nazi tactic.

The aim of all National Socialist mass organization is the same, no matter if it is Strength Through Joy or the Hitler Youth. These organizations are all attempting to "collect" or "look after" all citizens while actually taking away their independence and keeping them from coming to their senses. . . . Ley recently admitted in public that the "citizen" should no

From *Deutschland-Berichte der Sozialdemokratischen Partei Deutschlands (Sopade), 1934–1940* (Frankfurt: Verlag Petra Nettelbeck, 1980), 2 (November 1935): 1375–76. Translated by Dieter Kuntz.

longer have a private life; that he should give up his private bowling club. This monopolizing of organizations is attempting to take away all independence; to squelch initiatives to form even simple associations; to keep like-minded people apart; to isolate the individual and at the same time bind him to the state's organization. . . .

. . . The National Socialists know quite well that a sense of solidarity is the main source of strength for the working class, and that is why all measures directed toward workers are attempting to kill this sense of a need to act as one body. All changes for the worse which they are heaping upon the workers in terms of wages, taxes, and social insurance are set up so as never to affect large groups simultaneously. Otherwise a general deterioration of conditions could create a general resistance movement. These policies of the National Socialists have had serious consequences, in part because the sense of solidarity had already begun to decline during the years of economic crisis. This crisis has brought workers to the point where they disregard the most important success of united action — the standard wage; instead they now seek work at any price. . . .

117. The Rejection of "Positive Christianity"

The Nazis subjected German expressions of religious faith, along with all other spheres of public and private life, to "coordination" with the goals of the regime. Traditional Protestant and Catholic practices were to be replaced by a "positive Christianity" that fused belief in Christ with Nazi racial theories and pagan Nordic rituals. As the following document, a Security Service report of 1943, makes clear, however, on the whole the populace resisted the Nazis' attempts to phase out traditional religious ceremonies and beliefs.

Berlin, August 9, 1943

COMMENTS ON THE CONSTRUCTION OF LIFE CELEBRATIONS [*LEBENSFEIERN*] — THEIR SHAPE AND THEIR ACCEPTANCE AMONG THE POPULACE

As the reports from the entire Reich have shown, the development of confessional ceremonies and the construction of the ceremonies for the

From Heinz Boberach, ed., *Berichte des SD und der Gestapo über Kirchen und Kirchenvolk in Deutschland, 1934–44* (Mainz: Matthias-Grünewald Verlag, 1971), pp. 844–45. Translated by Dieter Kuntz. Reprinted by permission of Matthias-Grünewald Verlag GmbH.

Party's Life Celebrations, have been thoroughly dissimilar: whereas church ceremonies have increased extraordinarily in numbers, National Socialist marriage, birth, and funeral ceremonies have seen a further decrease in their numbers — which even during peacetime were relatively few.

The implementation of the Life Celebrations in the various regions is very diverse, as the preconditions for systematic execution of such ceremonies is not uniform due to the diversity in attitudes of the population and the diversity of activity of the responsible organizers in the individual regions of the Reich. In general, what is undoubtedly required is extensive work and countless experiments and attempts to construct the ceremonies in such a fashion that they will everywhere convince and appeal to the innermost needs of our people, so that then they will be able to compete with the religious ceremonies of the churches. Given that today the large majority of the population still regards as foreign the idea of the National Socialist Life Celebrations, and indeed, continually even rejects them outright, the following reasons, among others, can be seen as responsible:

1. The Life Celebrations are still regarded by the population as an internal Party matter.
2. The propagation of the idea of the National Socialist Life Celebrations is today still almost completely neglected by such national German agencies as the press, radio, and film.
3. There is a lack of appropriate festival halls (or public halls) that can turn the celebrations into truly community affairs, as the churches have succeeded in doing.
4. The celebrations still suffer from the failure to clearly define their form and content, whereas the churches can call on several centuries of tradition.
5. National Socialist weddings or funerals have everywhere been rejected by the populace owing to the completely one-sided perception created by unsuccessful ceremonies, while on the other hand such misgivings do not exist in the public's perception of religious ceremonial functions.
6. A certain natural resistance to new structures and form exists which is especially pronounced in rural areas, where there are strong ties to traditional religious ceremonies.

. . . As is evident from the reports, the number of ceremonies previously held within the entire Reich is exceedingly low. . . . Only in exceptional cases are National Socialist ceremonials requested by the populace for their circle of family and friends. . . .

118. The Confessional Church

Protestant theologians who opposed the *Gleichschaltung* of German religious institutions (Catholic as well as Protestant) as well as the neopagan Nazi cult of "positive Christianity" organized the Confessional church in 1934. One of the leading figures in forming the church, the Berlin pastor Martin Niemöller, who had originally supported the Nazis but became disillusioned by the regime's plans to restructure the German Evangelical (that is, Lutheran) church. The Confessional church claimed to be the sole legitimate Protestant church in Germany, and the church's other leading member, Dietrich Bonhoeffer, preached sermons for the first three years after its establishment that Hitler considered subversive. Many of the pastors who joined the church were persecuted. Niemöller too was arrested in 1937, tried, and found guilty of attacks against the state. The court, however, gave Niemöller a very light sentence of seven months in jail. On his release, Hitler ordered him rearrested and kept him confined under "protective custody" in various concentration camps until the Allied liberation in 1945.

The SD (Security Service), which maintained a surveillance network designed to root out all enemies of the regime, compiled reports on suspected subversive elements. The following document is a Security Service assessment of the activities of the Confessional church during 1938. The report also contains guidelines issued by the national Security Service headquarters that instruct local agents in information-gathering activities.

I. OVERVIEW

The Confessional Front [church] is split on the issue of its relationship to the state as a political system. The radical or reformed wing (Pastor Niemöller) rejects any encroachment by the state in the internal or external affairs of the church, while the moderate wing (Lutheran, led by state bishop Marahrens) has, in the interest of the church . . . , avoided a similar hostile position toward the state. The Confessional Front includes by far the large majority of Protestant theologians as well as the majority of devout [Protestant] churchgoers. Similar to Catholicism, with which it maintains close personal and clerical/religious ties, Protestantism today also is attempting to gain influence over the lives of individuals. . . . Currently the main aim of Protestantism is to ensure the continued existence of the Confessional schools and to foster the training of lay persons as religious instructors. . . . The Protestant church has its greatest influence over people through its involvement in welfare work. Especially noteworthy is the missionary activity of the church within the army, Labor Service,

From Heinz Boberach, ed., *Berichte des SD und der Gestapo über Kirchen und Kirchenvolk in Deutschland, 1934–44* (Mainz: Matthias-Grünewald Verlag, 1971), pp. 920–21. Translated by Dieter Kuntz. Reprinted by permission of Matthias-Grünewald Verlag GmbH.

Agricultural Youth Service, national highway construction camps, and so on. . . .

II. OPERATIONAL INSTRUCTIONS

1. The east branch [of the Security Service] must attempt, through confidence men, to infiltrate into the ranks of the provisional church leadership and into the ranks of the Lutheran council.
2. It is the task to place confidence men in all associations and clubs of the church at the state and provincial level.
3. The [Security Service] must be informed at all times about all state and provincial church appointments.
4. The strength of individual groups is to be determined, if possible, through numerical count.
5. Through occasional check of church service participation numbers it will be possible to numerically determine the extent of popular participation in religious activities.
6. All [Security Service] sections must be in possession of church address books. . . .
7. Individuals of the theology faculty must be sounded out to determine their views on church politics, and their degree of influence on professional ranks, and their views on party and state.
8. Radio, theater, and film must be monitored for possible influence attempts by Protestantism.
9. All sections must keep informed on church institutions and associations within their districts. Possible unhygienic conditions in [Protestant] hospitals should be uncovered in joint cooperation with the NSV [National Socialist People's Welfare Organization].
10. Theological seminaries, student hostels, seminaries of the Confessional Church (see church address book) and Evangelical boarding school must be sounded out for their political views.
11. The church's methods for attracting members of the Labor Service must be monitored.

119. Catholic Opposition

Leaders of the Catholic church, which had concluded a concordat with the Nazis in 1933, hoped that the new regime would guarantee freedom of religion, protect church institutions, and allow the church to maintain its system of

From Heinz Boberach, ed., *Berichte des SD und der Gestapo über Kirchen und Kirchenvolk in Deutschland, 1934–44* (Mainz: Matthias-Grünewald Verlag, 1971), pp.927–28. Translated by Dieter Kuntz. Reprinted by permission of Matthias-Grünewald Verlag GmbH.

schools. Catholics soon learned, however, that the Nazis intended to "coordinate" the church as fully as possible. The regime attacked Catholic organizations; maintained surveillance over priests known to harbor anti-Nazi sentiments, harassing and intimidating many; pressured young Catholics to join the Hitler Youth; and arrested and murdered leaders of Catholic youth organizations during the Blood Purge of 1934.

In 1937, Pope Pius XI issued an encyclical, entitled "With Deep Anxiety," which denounced the Nazis' persecution of the Catholic church in Germany and accused the regime of violating the concordat of 1933. The pope's message, though it did not deter the Nazis, did increase the regime's distrust of the church. The following Security Service report of 1938 evidences Nazi surveillance to detect illegal resistance activity by members of the church hierarchy.

As a consequence of the steadily increasing intensity of struggle between church and state, Catholicism in Germany found it necessary to turn to illegal activity in order to reach its goals. This was reinforced by the prohibition of the papal encyclical "With Deep Anxiety." . . . The concept of illegality, which is employed in all of these reports, is to be understood to embrace not only the violation of state laws or contraventions of the agreements reached under the concordat, but includes as well all plans and measures the church can employ without penalty within its own domain, but which, were they carried out in public life, would be prohibited on the basis of the ideological principles of the NSDAP. . . .

Since it has largely been made impossible for Catholicism to influence public opinion through the press, through official gazettes, and the like, the clergy is using verbal, private, or public means rather than the printed word to attain influence. Slanderous verbiage is to be expected more frequently from the pulpit in future. A systematic monitoring of sermons must be implemented accordingly. It is more difficult to determine to what extent the pastors are engaging in direct verbal propaganda. In this case, attested testimony of witnesses should be collected if at all possible. This testimony should reflect the content of the conversations.

In the case of slanderous agitation from the pulpit, experience has shown that only rarely is it the spontaneous action of a single person but usually has been engineered by an authoritative church office and is usually done for a specific reason. . . .

Both higher- and lower-ranking clergy are receiving information and guidelines through secret messengers. A secret courier service delivers communications not only between bishops, but also communication with the subordinate clergy. If we succeed in detecting the courier channels and in finding out who the couriers themselves are, then we will be in position to neutralize their instructions. . . .

120. Opposition from the Archbishop of Münster

A formidable opponent of the Nazis was the cardinal-archbishop of Münster, Count Clemens August von Galen. He had opposed the regime's interference in church affairs in 1933 and continued his opposition by criticizing Nazi racial doctrines that he regarded as contrary to Christian teaching. In 1941 he denounced the Nazi policy of euthanasia as a program of murder. This attack on the regime prompted the Nazis to curtail aspects of the program, because they were not prepared for a full-scale confrontation with the Catholic church while Germany was at war. Hitler, however, planned retribution after the war's conclusion. The seriousness of the challenge Galen posed is evident from the correspondence of August 1941 between top Party officials.

Berlin, 12 August 1941

Division Chief — Propaganda
To the Reich Minister for Propaganda and Popular Enlightenment
Concerning: Catholic Action

At the end of July and the beginning of August several meetings of a rather select committee of the Bishops' Conference of Fulda took place. It was decided at those meetings to continue the line of increasingly sharp opposition. The execution of those decisions becomes evident in three pastoral letters of the Bishop Count von Galen of Münster. In the pastoral letters of 13 and 20 July the bishop attacked the Gestapo with harsh words because of the closing of several Jesuit houses and convents of the Mission Sisters of the Immaculate Conception; he calls the officials of the Gestapo thieves and robbers. Then he connects those confiscations with several bombings of the city of Münster and calls them just punishment from heaven for the misdeeds of the Gestapo. In these pastoral letters he glorifies Pastor Niemoeller and attempts to disprove the charge of disturbing the unity of the people by claiming that it is only the Gestapo which is destroying the unity of the people.

After such attacks against official organs of the state, stronger in form and tenor than the earlier mentioned, more hidden accusations, the Bishop of Münster on 3 August in a sermon to his diocesans came out with the most severe attack against the leadership of the German government ever

From U.S. Chief of Counsel for the Prosecution of Axis Criminality, *Nazi Conspiracy and Aggression* (Washington, D.C.: U.S. Government Printing Office, 1946), vol. 6, doc. no. 3701-PS, pp. 405–10.

made during the past decades. After first dealing again with the closing of those religious houses and convents he turns against the execution of measures concerning Euthanasia for incurable cases of feeblemindedness. He first sets forth the argument against Euthanasia and then goes so far as to claim the following:

"Yes, citizens of Muenster, wounded soldiers are being killed recklessly, since they are, productively, of no more use to the state. Mother, your boy will be killed too, if he comes back home from the front wounded." He closes with the remark that the inhabitants of Münster had not understood God's vengeance which came in the form of English air attacks and he incites the faithful to open opposition, even if they should have to die for it.

For your information I enclose the original text of the sermon.

The allegation of the Bishop of Münster that wounded soldiers are threatened by measures of Euthanasia was spread by several broadcasts of the London radio. The attitude of the bishop is treason of a definite quality.

It is to be feared that this sermon and the utterances of the bishop will get around by propaganda of mouth and will be believed in wide circles of the Reich, especially among the Catholic population. Moreover it is to be feared that those treasonable accusations will find their way to the Protestant population, especially among families who have relatives at the front.

Measures taken by the state police against the bishop can hardly be successful, because in case of an arrest and judgment the bishop would be made a martyr by the Church, and other bishops and priest would repeat his claims anew. The most suitable measure would be the enlightenment of the population concerning our measures in reference to Euthanasia; I realized, however, that the present times are very unfit for that. The manner and the means by which the bishop prepared this action makes one fear that he will not relax with his attacks, unless we effect a fundamental change of attitude particularly in the Catholic population.

I inquired at the Reich Ministry for Church Affairs as to how they regard this matter over there. I was answered that the authentic text of the sermon unfortunately was not yet known in that Department. The sermon was on 3 August.

I beg the Reich Minister to decide whether or not the Führer shall be asked by group leader Bormann whether the camouflage of Euthanasia thus far in practice ought to be modified so that a defense against the treasonable claims of the Bishop of Münster can be inaugurated by launching a campaign of popular enlightenment.

Heil Hitler!

Enclosure

Berlin, 13 August 1941
Ti/Hu–

SECRET PROPOSAL FOR REICHSLEITER BORMANN

Concerning: Sermon of the Bishop of Münster

After the conference of Ministers, Dr. Goebbels discussed with me the sermon of the Bishop of Münster. He could not say what effective measures could be taken at the moment.

I explained to him that in my opinion there could be only one effective measure, namely, to hang the bishop and that I already had informed Reichsleiter Bormann accordingly.

Thereupon Dr. Goebbels said that this was a measure upon which the Führer alone could decide. He feared, however, that the population of Münster could be regarded as lost during the war, if anything were done against the bishop, and in that fear one safely could include the whole of Westphalia.

I pointed out to him that it would only be necessary to expose properly that very vulgar lie through propaganda channels. In that way it ought to be possible not only to bring the population there to an understanding of that measure but to create among them rebellion against the bishop.

To that Dr. Goebbels answered again that the Führer himself would certainly come to a decision in that question.

After that he observed that it would have been wiser, in his opinion, not to challenge the Church during the war but to try only to steer them according to our interests as far as possible. For that reason he had ordered the interview with party comrade Gutterer. But then he had not followed up the matter in this way because the Chancery of the Party had chosen the way of uncompromising refusal and open breach. As much as it was for him — (in contrast to other Reich's Leaders) — a matter of course to suppress the press of the Church, because in that regard he had proof and excuse concerning the Church. This preserved appearances. He maintained the stand, however, that it would have been better during the war to preserve appearances as far as the Church is concerned. It is permissible always to attack an opponent only if one is in a position to answer properly at the decisive counterattack of that opponent. But this was extraordinarily difficult in the case of the counterattack of the Church during the war, yes, nearly impossible. One should not enjoy a revenge with heat but coldly. In politics one should know how to wait. This the Führer clearly and distinctly had proved again in the case of Russia. If he would have had his way one would have pretended during the war as if [the following line at end of page is missing].

I explained to him that the procedure employed so far had nevertheless accomplished this much, that the Church had opened up and in doing so played into our hands by documents valuable after the war for the struggle against it.

Dr. Goebbels said that in his opinion those measures would have been possible after the war, even without the documents, whereas the effect of the Church documents on the attitude of the people was extraordinarily troublesome now. In any case it is necessary now to establish an absolute and clear rule as to the road to be followed. In the deliberations which have to take place in this connection we should not allow ourselves to be guided by the heart but by completely cold logic.

I personally retain the viewpoint that, if the Führer should agree with my proposal to hang the bishop, we could safely still continue along the lines used so far. However, should the Führer reject this proposal and postpone a reckoning, and defer action in the present case also, until after the war, I herewith request that it be considered whether Dr. Goebbels should not try, as far as might be possible, to pursue the course he suggested.

TIESSLER

Headquarters of the Fuehrer, 13 August 1941
Bo/Fu

DOCUMENTARY REMARK FOR PARTY COMRADE WALTER TIESSLER, LEADER OF THE REICHSRING FOR NATIONAL SOCIALIST PROPAGANDA AND POPULAR ENLIGHTENMENT, BERLIN W. 8, HOTEL KAISERHOF, ROOM 117

The several speeches of Bishop Count Galen are known to me. Also the Führer has been given an over-all picture on the attitude of the bishop. He ordered me to undertake first an exact investigation of the bishop's complaints concerning the closing of cloisters in favor of the NSDAP. This was done; but so far I have not been able to report to the Führer. Concerning the effects of the speeches of the Bishop I am being continuously informed through the Gau Leader as well as by the Secret State Police.

What kind of steps the Führer will take against the bishop, however, is yet to be decided. A death sentence certainly would be appropriate; considering the state of the war, however, the Führer hardly will order such a measure.

The Führer also will have to decide whether enlightenment concerning the Euthanasia matters should be started. So far the Führer has declined to adopt this measure.

In your proposal for Reich Minister Dr. Goebbels a decision is requested whether or not the Führer should be asked by one of the adjutants if the camouflage of Euthanasia so far in effect could be modified. I request you to clarify in your office that questions of this kind are not reported to the Führer by the adjutants but through me as the Leader of the Chancery of the Party. This too is precisely one of the reasons, why I should accompany the Führer steadily, in order that all such matters may be reported to the Führer through me.

BORMANN

PROPOSAL FOR REICHSLEITER BORMANN!

In consequence of your documentary remark of 13 August I informed the Propaganda Division that questions of that kind will not be reported to the Fuehrer through the adjutants but through you. The office thereupon gave me the information that there had been a regrettable misunderstanding. It was Group Leader Bormann, yourself, they meant, not the adjutant. I have been asked by the office to beg your pardon on their behalf.

TIESSLER

Berlin, 16 August 1941
Ti/Hu

121. Combating Catholic Opposition

Pressure from the Catholic church did much to prompt the Nazis to curtail the euthanasia program, but the regime was not willing to tolerate continued public opposition from the church and continued to monitor church activities closely. A Security Service report of September 1941 suggests that the Nazis were intent on reducing the influence of the church through continued intimidation of church leaders. The Security Service developed special measures to inhibit and suppress the activities of "agitator priests."

Aachen, 26 September 1941

REPORT OF REGIERUNGSRAT ROTH'S SPEECH BEFORE CONFERENCE DATED 26 SEPTEMBER 1941 SICHERHEITSPOLIZEI [SECURITY POLICE] MEASURES FOR COMBATING CHURCH POLITICS AND SECTS

While describing the aim and methods of the Political Church in its oppositional activities, the executive measures which, in accordance with the Concordat, are at the disposal of the Stapo, were discussed.

From U.S. Chief of Counsel for the Prosecution of Axis Criminality, *Nazi Conspiracy and Aggression* (Washington, D.C.: U.S. Government Printing Office, 1946), vol. 4, doc. no. 1815-PS, pp. 419–21.

a) Punishable offences and infringements of the law by members of the Church are to be submitted to the Kripo for processing. Nachrichtendienst [intelligence] evaluation, and the compiling of evidence for a final breakdown is the responsibility of the Stapo.

b) It has been demonstrated that it is impracticable to deal with political offences (malicious) under normal legal procedure. Owing to the lack of political perception which still prevails among the legal authorities, suspension of this procedure must be reckoned with. The so-called "Agitator-Priests" must therefore be dealt with in future by Stapo measures, and, if the occasion arises, be removed to a Concentration Camp, if agreed upon by the RSHA.

c) Offences and crimes against the "Sammlungsgesetz" [Order to contribute to Party Funds] and the "Flaggenerlass" [Order to beflag Churches etc.] come under normal procedure. [A penciled note states that this is not always so, and that it depends on the case in question.]

d) The necessary executive measures are to be decided upon according to local conditions, the status of the person accused, and the seriousness of the case — as follows:

1. Warnung (Warning)
2. Sicherungsgeld (Fine)
3. Redeverbot (Forbidden to preach)
4. Aufenthaltsverbot (Forbidden to remain in parish)
5. Betätigungsverbot (Forbidden all activities as a Priest)
6. Kurzfristige Festnahme (Short-term arrest)
7. Schutzhaft (Protective custody)

The instructions for the application of individual measures are known. The following points must be remembered:

The Aufenthaltsverbot (Forbidden to remain in parish) is very much feared by all the clergy. In one case a Vicar-General appealed to the RSHA [Reichssicherheitshauptamt, or Central Office for Reich Security] for the lifting of the ban, and begged that they would rather place the priest under short-term arrest. The "Aufenthaltsverbot" is to be enforced in any case where the continued stay of the priest in his former parish is likely to bring about dissension and for disquiet among the population. It should be applied, for instance, in the event of a priest returning from arrest, in order to prevent him from being feted as a martyr. Care must be taken that the measure is only enforced where really expedient (encumbering of another Stapostelle [State Police station, or Gestapo office]).

Redeverbot (Forbidden to preach) is intended chiefly as a measure against itinerant preachers, and will only be brought against residential ones when they exceed their normal offices as priests, and preach much injurious matter.

Betätigungsverbot (Forbidden all activities as a priest) has not yet been applied, but is possible.

Schutzshaft (Protective custody). As already stated, in accordance with the Order issued by the RSHA on 24.8.36 the "Agitator Priest" is to be taken into long-term imprisonment. The technical execution of this lies in the hands of the Referat IV C 2, while it is IV B I's responsibility to present the charges.

Actions against societies are not at the moment possible as a widespread State measure. However, in cases where the Society has been involved in anti-state activity, or appears superfluous or undesirable, local measures may be applied. Small funds/properties may be liquidated. Funds may also be handed over to the NSV. In cases of activities against the State the only method is confiscation of funds. Proposals for "Declaration of Enmity to People and State" with the object of confiscation of property, are principally to be directed to the RSHA, which works nonexecutively, and directs the necessary negotiations with the MdI.

Monasteries/Convents. It is not expected at the present that they will be declared as hostile to the State. During the process of "Dissolution" it should be remembered that the Law of 10.2.36 suffices as a legal basis for the disposal. It is not essential that the Order of 28.2.33 should be quoted, and it will only be brought up if the Stapo measures are to come under "legal justification" (Betätigungsverbot 4).

Actions against Monasteries/Convents. About 100 monasteries in the Reich have been dissolved. Various incidents which may be traced back to bad tactical procedure by Stapo officials, have led to disagreeable consequences. Should the inmates of the monasteries put questions to the appointed officials, those officials must refer them to the Aktionsleiter [officer in charge of the proceedings].

Churches are to be seized at the same time, but, if possible, should not be closed. As long as the confiscation is not absolute any action which interferes with property, or causes any alteration to it should be avoided. The principle to be followed during the period of "Sicherstellung" [Safeguarding] is that life should go on within the framework of an ordered administration.

Further points made were:

Retreats, recreational organizations, etc., may now be forbidden on grounds of industrial war-needs, whereas formerly only a worldly activity could be given as a basis.

Youth camps, recreational camps are to be forbidden on principle. Church organizations in the evening may be prevented on grounds of the black-out regulations.

Processions, pilgrimages abroad are to be forbidden by reason of the overburdened transport conditions. For local events too technical traffic troubles and the danger of air attack may serve as grounds for their prohibition (one Referent forbade a procession, on the grounds of it wearing out shoe leather).

There are no new regulations regarding the despatch of Confessional literature to the troops, and the restrictions on Confessional publications.

Visas are always to be denied where the applicant cannot offer the excuse that he will dedicate himself unreservedly to working for the Fatherland while abroad. There are, however, possible exceptions. In principle the intention still holds good, that no foreign priest should enter the Reich, and that no German priest should travel abroad, above all, not to the "Aufbaugebiet."

In the meantime the Church Ministry had adopted the view of the RSHA, in which it was decided that Polish civilian workers and prisoners-of-war must definitely be separated at services.

The RSHA requests that questions of policy should be submitted to them, but that, on the other hand, they should not be bothered with unnecessary inquiries. Above all, definite proposals on how to handle the case in question should always be given, and not just requests for direction or decision.

The immediate aim: The Church must not regain one inch of the ground it has lost.

The ultimate aim: Destruction of the Confessional Churches to be brought about by the collection of all material obtained through Nachrichtendienst activities, which will, at a given time, be produced as evidence for the charge of treasonable activities during the German fight for existence.

Kriminal-Kommissar zur [of] Prussia
Signed: HAMMES

122. Catholic Reaction to War and Genocide

The Catholic church initially supported the war, but continued Nazi attempts to diminish its power and prestige engendered increased oppositional activity from leading Catholic officials. Although the church did not bring the same pressure to bear on the Nazis to end the killing of Jews as it did in the euthanasia issue, many Catholic priests did publicly protest against the inhuman extermination of Europe's Jews.

Reports of the week of 6–12 June 1943 from regional party leaders indicate heightened opposition to the conduct of the war. *Gauleiter* in several regions noted the growing popular appeal of the church in traditionally Catholic areas and reported that priests were expressing horror and outrage over Nazi policies of genocide.

From *Nationalsozialistische Deutsche Arbeiter-Partei, Hauptarchiv 1919–45* (Stanford, CA: Hoover Institution on War, Revolution and Peace) H.A. reel 50, folder 1181a (*Gauleiter Reports*: June 1943). Translated by Dieter Kuntz.

The war, with all its sorrow and anguish, has driven some families back into the arms of priests and the church. This is especially the case in those families who in times past had leaned toward our ideological views but whose menfolk are now serving at the front. This, after all, is in the nature of things and does not need to be viewed as a great tragedy. The situation is different, however, in the case of party members from whom one really should be able to expect somewhat more backbone, at least in ideological matters. Unfortunately this is not always the case, as can be observed from the following weekly report from the Upper Silesian district leadership:

> The majority of our Party members can be counted as regular churchgoers. Even old Party members, who for years have distanced themselves from the church, have now once again become avid and pious church visitors, regularly receiving the sacraments. . . .

The districts unanimously report that the church of both confessional orientations is engaging in exceptionally heavy activity. In comparison to the party, the church today still has much manpower at its disposal.

The church continues to focus its attention on youth. The clergy is urgently exhorting parents to encourage children to attend scripture lessons. The church backs up this recruiting effort through home visits and furthermore sends out requests and invitations to attend religious functions. According to the Düsseldorf district, these efforts appear to have met with success. . . .

The "Congregation of Maria," "New Germany," and other similar prohibited confessional youth organizations have also become more active recently. They have especially used theater, films, and other cultural events to strengthen their influence over youth. An ever-increasing spiritual pressure is being exerted on parents as well as children. The ministers repeatedly send word to the parents if the children fail to attend religious instruction. It is pointed out to parents that multiple absences from religious instruction, confession, and communion lessons can lead to excommunication. This approach is guaranteed of success, especially in the small communities. It is interesting to find out that the church dares to send informational material even to totally uninterested party members. There has also been noted a more intensified approach by ministers and lay helpers toward membership of N.S. organizations; in particular, the women's organization. . . .

A special device that has appeared lately, and which is to bring people into the church, is the holding of memorial church services for those who have fallen at the front or are reported missing. In this case, the church is bringing a certain amount of pressure to bear on immediate family members, relatives, or acquaintances. . . . Similar reports have come in from all districts and have been corroborated. . . .

In their weekly reports, the party regional organizations have repeatedly emphasized that the churches of both confessions — but especially the Catholic church — are in today's fateful struggle *one of the main pillars of negative influence* upon public morale. The current changeable war situation, of course, gives the church a special starting point for propaganda and gives it opportunity to influence public opinion. The church takes advantage of every opportunity to present itself as the indispensable comforter and caretaker of the people. This is done, naturally, not without more or less openly insidious agitation against National Socialism. This is unanimously reported by all the districts, excerpts from which follow below, and which serve to underscore the above-mentioned findings.

[From Upper Silesia:] "In closing, I point to the fact that the church knowingly ignores the difference between the races. Priests speak for, and pray for 'Catholics of different languages.' . . . In two districts of the old Reich, the clergy attempted to have their German congregation sing old Polish hymns with a German text. A mass was said by a German congregation for Poles who perished in a concentration camp. All of the above-mentioned cases have been transmitted to the state police authorities, who will conduct inquiries."

The churches have remained silent on the Katyn [forest] incident,[1] as the churches are noncommital regarding bolshevism. In districts of solid church loyalty this is manifesting itself in people whispering to each other that everything that has been written about the Katyn incident or broadcast over the airwaves is nothing more than National Socialist propaganda. The church is in this situation, as usual, working with its proven, clever tactics, so that one cannot lay a hand on them.

Reactions by the clergy [of Westphalia] to the gruesome news of the murders in the Katyn Forest: "The National Socialists have no right to express alarm over this bestial slaughter. In the campaign against Jews in the East the SS used similar slaughter methods. This heinous and inhuman treatment of the Jews at the hands of the SS demands of God that he punish our nation. If we don't pay the penalty for these murders, then divine justice no longer exists! The German people has taken upon itself such a blood-guiltiness, that it cannot expect mercy and forgiveness. . . ."

---

[1] Refers to the Nazi discovery in April 1943 of a mass grave of over four thousand Polish officers in the Katyn Forest. The Nazis claimed they had been murdered by the Soviet Secret Police. Recent evidence has, in fact, substantiated the Nazi claim.

123. The Kreisau Circle

A group of prominent Germans opposed to the Nazis met in Silesia in 1933 at the estate of the Berlin lawyer Count Helmut von Moltke in Kreisau. Led by Moltke and Count Peter Yorck von Wartenburg, a landowner and administrative official, the twenty members of the Kreisau Circle, including army officers, theologians, teachers, diplomats, and civil servants, saw their main task as not so much the violent overthrow of Hitler and the Nazis but rather the preparation for the new order to be implemented once the regime had been ousted. The group's plans for the re-Christianization of Germany and its political and social reorganization were predicated on the establishment of a society in which class distinctions and religious and political differences were to be overcome. Their ultimate aim was to revitalize social life in Germany by emphasizing the primacy of the family and the role of the individual within small communities.

In August of 1943, the Kreisau Circle outlined its objectives in the document reprinted here, entitled "Gundsätze für die Neuordnung in Deutschland" ("Principles for the New Order in Germany"). In the aftermath of the plot to assassinate Hitler in July 1944, Moltke and others in the group were arrested, charged with treason, and executed.

The Government of the German Reich sees in Christianity the basis for the ethical and religious revival of our people, for the conquest of hatred and lies, for the creation anew of the European community of people.

The starting point lies in the pre-ordained contemplation by the human being of the divine order which yields to him his inner and outer existence. Only if there is success in making this order the measure of the relations between individuals and communities can the disorder of our time be overcome and a real condition of peace be achieved. The inner reorganization of the Reich is the basis for the carrying-through of a just and permanent peace.

In the collapse of a power formation which is without roots and is based exclusively on the mastery of technique, European humanity is faced with a common task. The way to its solution lies in the decisive and active implementation of the Christian substance of life. The government of the Reich is therefore determined to realize the following goals, which cannot be renounced either inwardly or outwardly, with all the means at its disposal:

    1. Justice, fallen and trampled, must be restored, and must be made

From Hans-Adolf Jacobsen, ed., *Germans Against Hitler, July 20, 1944* (Bonn: Press and Information Office of the Federal Government of Germany, 1969), pp. 39–40.

supreme over all orders of human life. This justice, under the protection of conscientious, independent judges who are free from fear of men, will be the basis for the future moulding of peace.

2. Freedom of faith and conscience is guaranteed. Existing laws and regulations which offend against these principles are at once abolished.

3. The casting away of the totalitarian restraints on conscience and the recognition of the inviolable dignity of the human being are foundations of the law and of the desired peaceful order of things. Everyone cooperates with full responsibility in the various social, political and international spheres of life. The right of work and property stands under public protection without regard to race, nationality or creed.

4. The basic unit of peaceful community life is the family. It stands under public protection, which shall ensure, along with education, the tangible goods of life; food, clothing, a home, a garden and health.

5. Work must be arranged in such a way that it fosters rather than stunts the enjoyment of personal responsibility. To this belongs, besides the shaping of the material conditions of work and the improvement of education in professional training, an effective co-responsibility of each person in the enterprise and beyond that in the general economic relations to which his work contributes. Thus he may cooperate in the creation of a healthy and lasting order of life, which will enable the individual, his family and the communities to achieve their organic fulfilment within balanced spheres of economic activity. The ordering of the economy must ensure that these basic requirements are met.

6. The personal political responsibility of everyone requires his co-determining participation in the self-administration of the small and sur-veyable communities, which are to be revived. Rooted firmly in them, his co-determination in the state and in the community at large must be secured by self-elected representatives, and thus there must be conveyed to him a living conviction of his co-responsibility for political events in general.

7. The special responsibility and faithfulness which each individual owes to his national origin, his language, the spiritual and historical tradition of his people has to be respected and protected. However, it must not be misused for the accumulation of political power, for the degradation, persecution and suppression of foreign peoples. The free and peaceful development of national culture can no longer be made consonant with the maintenance of an individual state's absolute sover-eignty. Peace demands the creation of an order which encompasses the individual states. As soon as the free agreement of all peoples involved is guaranteed, the supporters of this order must also have the right to demand from each individual obedience, respect, if necessary also the risking of life and property, for the highest political authority of the community of peoples.

124. Ulrich von Hassel and the Conspiracy Against Hitler

Ulrich von Hassel, the ambassador to Rome from 1932 to 1937, became an opponent of the Nazis before the outbreak of war and contributed his expertise on foreign affairs to the German resistance. Hassel was convinced that Hitler's foreign policy would be disastrous for Germany. Along with Carl Goerdeler, General Ludwig Beck, and others, Hassel drew up plans in 1940 for a government based on a temporary military dictatorship that would guide Germany through the emergency situations following the projected overthrow of the Nazis. Hassel envisioned a German state (to include Austria) headed by the restored Hohenzollern monarchy. His diaries, excerpts of which are reprinted below, provide a fascinating glimpse into the activities of the conspirators in the plot of July 1944 to remove Hitler. Hassel knew he was under surveillance by the Gestapo as early as 1942 but nevertheless continued to take part in the conspiracy. He was arrested and executed following the failure of the plot. The diaries, which had been hidden in a tea chest and buried in the garden of Hassel's Bavarian home, were published posthumously in 1948.

DECEMBER 5, 1939

I had let Goerdeler know that I was coming to Berlin and would be glad to let him have further information concerning his Bosch business in the North. Hardly had I arrived at the Adlon when he entered my room. Although normally a man of great initiative, he was in utter despair. Incidentally, he often reminds me of Kapp. Let us hope that nomen is not omen. By his account, all opposition to the German invasion of Western Europe has collapsed on the part of the military leaders; even though Brauchitsch[1] and Halder,[2] just as all others, are convinced that the results will be disastrous. He said that they nevertheless believed they must obey orders. Goering, he informed me, was against it, as he had always been, but could not induce himself to offer any other resistance than a sort of sabotage based on the weather, which is causing widespread flooding in northern and central Germany, as I myself observed on the journey, and also in Holland. The worst of it is that there is not the slightest cooperation

From Hans-Adolf Jacobsen, ed., *Germans Against Hitler, July 20, 1944* (Bonn: Press and Information Office of the Federal Government of Germany, 1969), pp. 49–54.

---

[1] Walter von Brauchitsch, field marshal in the German armed forces, was aware of the conspiracy against Hitler, but felt bound by his oath of loyalty to the Führer.

[2] General Franz Halder led the first military conspiracy to remove Hitler from power prior to the outbreak of the war. He unsuccessfully tried to recruit Brauchitsch. Halder was removed from his post in 1942 and imprisoned in 1944, following the July Plot.

between Brauchitsch and Goering. Goering dislikes Brauchitsch, and he, in turn, as most of the generals, is mistrustful of Goering's character in the highest degree. On the other hand, Brauchitsch, it seems, as many others, is under Hitler's spell. . . .

The question I discussed with Goerdeler, then in the evening with Wilmowsky, is (1) whether something can still be done to influence the generals. (2) How, without prejudicing Germany's tactical position, the generals could be given a measure of assurance that, now, we could still bring about a reasonable peace, but not after the invasion.

Goerdeler was, as I have said, rather pessimistic. It seems that Hitler addressed the generals (Thursday, November 25) with wild, lawyer-like eloquence for three full hours. This impressed the harmless soldiers, but the more intelligent among them gained the impression of a raging Genghis Khan. Hitler said, in so many words, that humanity was an invention of the 19th Century. Neutrality, he said, was nothing, and if he were to meet his ruin in the enterprise, Germany would have to accompany him into the abyss. . . .

DECEMBER 30, 1939

I arrived in Berlin on the 27th, an hour and a half late, and first of all went to look for Popitz.[3] He judged the situation considerably more optimistically than the last time, because the terror régime of the SS in the East and the arrogance of these men towards the army were gradually opening the eyes of the soldiers to this disgrace to Germany and this brigand state within a state. . . . The idea is now that a few divisions should be halted in Berlin "on the way from the West to the East." Then Witzleben should appear in Berlin and mop up the SS. Thereupon Beck should travel to Zossen and relieve Brauchitsch's weak hands of the High Command. Hitler should be certified medically unfit to govern and be locked up. Then an appeal to the nation, with a promise to prevent any further atrocities by the SS, to continue the war, but in readiness to accept a peace on a reasonable basis.

BERLIN, FROM MAY 24 TO 27, 1940

A reshaping of the face of Europe according to Hitler's ideas now seems inevitable. Its outward manifestation will be a peace that coincides with his broad objectives. The annulment of the Peace of Westphalia is already being prepared in Münster and Osnabrück. It is as yet open whether the reduction of France's power to nil combined, as it now seems, with a certain tolerance of England overseas, is to remain the order of the day,

---

[3] Johannes Popitz was a Prussian minister of finance and a leading civilian member of the resistance movement. He was hanged in the aftermath of the 1944 July Plot.

or the complete destruction of the British Empire is to form the main emphasis. The inner manifestation will be the rise to power of Socialism as Hitler sees it, the breaking up of the upper classes, the reduction of the churches to insignificant sects, and so on. Since National Socialism, as it has developed, lacks any semblance of a soul and has force as its only ideal, we shall have a Nature without God, a Germany with neither soul nor culture and perhaps also a Europe raw and without conscience. . . .

JUNE 24, 1940

I found Y., who had turned very critical after the attack on Belgium and Holland, completely shaken by the vast military successes. He did not express a political opinion. Z., on the other hand, was obviously inclined to believe from the religious point of view that a man who could bring off such successes must have God on his side. — I am convinced that Hitler and, in quite a different way, Goering, have really played a great part in the successes, although the achievements of the military leaders, the qualities that the new army has inherited from the old, and the contributions by such men as Gessler, Seeckt, Beck and Fritsch are being shamelessly suppressed. No one can deny the magnitude of Hitler's successes. But that does not alter the real character of his acts and the dreadful dangers to which all higher values are now exposed. A demoniac Spartacus can have only a destructive effect if he is not counteracted in time. The tragic burden of not being able to rejoice at the successes is enough to drive one to despair. And among the people, stupendous, obtuse indifference holds sway, as a result of their having been subjected for seven years to a barrage of loudspeaker orations. . . .

EBENHAUSEN, DECEMBER 21, 1941 (CONTINUED)

I have been concerned and worried in the last weeks chiefly about various talks on the basic problems of a change of regime. One of the chief difficulties is Pfaff (Goerdeler), who is sanguine, sees things always as he wishes they were, and is in many ways really "reactionary," although his other characteristics are exemplary. However, we finally reached agreement on the main points.

EBENHAUSEN, NOVEMBER 26, 1942

Further drop in the barometer. Stalingrad has begun to play a part like that of Verdun. The prospects of a new winter campaign with the enemy suffering heavy damages and battling against great difficulties are becoming more and more certain. However, the air raids are getting heavier, now also in Munich. . . .

. . . There is absolutely no help to be expected from the alleged temper of the people (fury against Hitler). We are the oddest mixture of heroes and slaves. The latter applies particularly to the generals, who have succeeded absolutely brilliantly in reducing their own authority to nil, particularly towards Hitler. After the failures in the East he raged like a madman, for, of course, when things go wrong, it is not "the greatest strategical genius of all time" that is in command, but "the generals." Sauerbruch,[4] who visited him recently, thought him old and wasted. He apparently interspersed the conversation with strange unconnected mutterings (as: "I must go to India," or, "For every dead German, ten of the enemy must die."). Sauerbruch was convinced that he is now undoubtedly insane. . . .

BERLIN, JANUARY 22, 1943

If the *Josephs* (generals) have been holding back their intervention until it should become obvious that the "corporal" is leading us into the abyss, he has now complied with their wishes. The worst of it is that our confident predictions have proved true: that it will come too late and that any new regime will have to be a liquidation commission. It is probably not possible to say with certainty that the war is lost, but it is certain that it can no longer be won, and there is precious little hope of inducing the other side to make an acceptable peace now. The result is that the recognition that something must be done has gained ground among the *Josephs* (generals), while at the same time so has the weakness of the external and internal front. . . .

EBENHAUSEN, MARCH 6, 1943

The serious crises I mentioned at the beginning of my last entry unfortunately did not bring about the famous, bitterly necessary, long hoped-for thunderstorm to clear the air, that is, the change of regime. Only this could bring us at least the possibility of a tolerable peace, an internal recovery and the return to health of Europe. Failure has crowned every attempt to put a bit of backbone into the men who, with their instrument of power, are lending their support to a half-insane, half-criminal policy. This in spite of the military events, the irresponsible leadership of this wanton and megalomaniac corporal. This ought to have given them the final impetus, if the domestic disintegration and destruction were not enough to do so. . . .

EBENHAUSEN, APRIL 20, 1943

The longer the war lasts, the lower my esteem for the generals sinks. Admittedly, they have professional ability and physical courage, but little moral courage, absolutely no over-all or international view. Nor have

---

[4] Ferdinand Sauerbruch was a famous surgeon in Germany who joined the resistance movement.

they the least spiritual or intellectual independence or resistance based on true culture. They are accordingly unable to deal with a man like Hitler and absolutely at his mercy. In addition, the majority regard career in the worst sense, money and the field marshal's baton, as more important than the great principles and moral values that are at stake. All those on whom hopes had been set have proved worthless. And in the most miserable fashion: They agree to everything one says to them and join in the wildest plans, but cannot summon up the courage to act. . . .

EBENHAUSEN, DECEMBER 27, 1943

But more important than all this was the fact that in the week before Christmas, according to all assurances, there was, for the first time, a real prospect of reaching the goal. How often this has been claimed; and my belief in the report was weak enough. But the assertion of serious people sounded so convinced and convincing that I really began to take the matter seriously. A few days before my departure, the set-back came: "Postponed until January." Reason: "Because Hitler had taken off somewhere." In the decisive days, Pfaff (Goerdeler) was with me repeatedly and was in an understandable fury after the thing had been called off. The *Josephs* (the generals) would never make up their minds, but would first let things come to a full catastrophe. After a two-day-long wait in vain with Wuffi, I had a long satisfactory talk with Sophie's nephew (Schwerin) on December 15, 1943, who again made a good impression on me, and who is very active. . . .

EBENHAUSEN, JULY 10, 1944

The catastrophe shapes up ever more clearly on the horizon. Until now all signs were pointing toward a rather long duration, but now the indications are increasing that a quick end is possible. . . .

125. The July 20, 1944, Plot

The pivotal figure in the plot of July 20, 1944, was Count Claus von Stauffenberg, a colonel on the German General Staff and chief of staff to the commander of the reserve army. Stauffenberg had been a monarchist who initially hoped for a renewed German empire. He did not become anti-Nazi until he witnessed the excesses of the SS during the invasion of the Soviet Union, after which he became closely connected with the Kreisau Circle. Hitler's ideal of the *Volksgemeinschaft*, in Stauffenberg's view, was founded on a false egalitarianism; by contrast, the

From Hans-Adolf Jacobsen, ed., *Germans Against Hitler, July 20, 1944* (Bonn: Press and Information Office of the Federal Government of Germany, 1969), pp. 118–27.

government of post-Nazi Germany, which was to be based on Christian morality as well as socialist values, would be led by the well-educated, intellectual elite, the highest of society's natural "ranks."

Stauffenberg was chosen for the task of assassinating Hitler because he was the only conspirator who had access to Hitler without being searched. In July 1944 Stauffenberg placed a bomb hidden in a briefcase in the Führer's headquarters in east Prussia. Hitler survived the explosion, and Stauffenberg and many of his co-conspirators were arrested and executed in the aftermath of the incident.

The following document is excerpted from the memoirs of Fabian von Schlabrendorff, a co-conspirator who had also taken part in an abortive plot to kill Hitler in 1943, and who escaped the Nazis while on trial in 1945. Schlabrendorff here reconstructs the events leading up to the attempted assassination in 1944.

The person who was to plant the bomb had to be gotten into Hitler's headquarters. That limited the selection at the outset to a relatively small group of persons, since the great majority of the conspirators had no admission privileges there, or could only be brought there by some pretext, and with difficulty. In order to clarify the preliminary question of the possibilities in Hitler's headquarters, I went there twice by plane, and talked over necessary details with Lieut. Col. Dietrich von Bose, who was familiar with the place.

Through him I got hold of an exact outline of Hitler's daily schedule. Hitler had a servant wake him at 10 o'clock in the morning. At the same hour, breakfast was sent to the bedroom by elevator. With breakfast, excerpts from foreign newspapers, selected by Ribbentrop, were placed before Hitler. As he read no foreign language, the excerpts were translated into German. All items of writing that were presented to him were typed on a special typewriter that had unusually big letters. Hitler was nearsighted. Everything had to be written in such large characters that he could read it without spectacles. Nobody was to find out from the way he held the material that he had eye trouble. To look at a map, he used a magnifying glass or spectacles. It was strictly forbidden to photograph him with his glasses on. Hitler felt that a dictator wearing spectacles would lose authority.

At 11 A.M. he received his chief adjutant, who reported mainly on personnel matters. At noon the briefing began. During the briefing, various reports on the situation were made by the chief of the general staffs of the armed forces and the army. Other officers were called in as needed. On this occasion Hitler made military decisions personally. At 2 P.M. luncheon began. It dragged out until 4 P.M. because of the monologues that Hitler directed to the company. Then Hitler lay down for his afternoon nap, from which he arose between 6 and 7 P.M. After that, he granted audiences of a "representation" character. Dinner began at 8 P.M. and lasted until 10 P.M. Afterward Hitler surrounded himself with a circle of persons selected by himself. He talked with them until 4 A.M., usually leading the discussion himself. It was in these night hours that he developed his "fortunate for the people" ideas in the company of his faithful.

Then, at 4 A.M., he went to bed. His two secretaries participated in his night-time discussions; otherwise he had no women who were close to him at his headquarters. These women, however, had access to the Obersalzberg. Only in very urgent cases was something changed in his daily schedule. While he was sleeping he was not to be awakened under any circumstances.

The only persons who had a chance to perform the assassination were those who succeeded in procuring an invitation to the nightly circle, or who had access to the briefing session. SS men who were constantly in the room with Hitler or near-by made it almost impossible to use a pistol to kill Hitler. Anyone who has used a weapon knows how difficult it is to shoot a man dead from the wrist. If on the other hand the killing is represented as an unpremeditated act, the difficulty is much less than if a frankly calculated attempt is made on the victim's life. Moreover, the stalker is seized by hunting fever when he sees the desired game within reach of his gun. How much greater this inner excitement is likely to be if one takes up arms after overcoming a thousandfold difficulties! And the tension is redoubled by the fact that one is risking one's life, with incalculable danger of failure, to carry out a deed the success or failure of which affects the destiny of millions.

Upon consideration of those who might be capable of the deed, it developed that some who had repeatedly proved their bravery in combat freely admitted that they did not consider themselves up to the task. Thus the 30-year-old lieutenant colonel, Baron Georg von Boeselager, who had been decorated with the Knight's Cross with Oak Leaves and Swords for conspicuous gallantry, rejected the proposal. He said he could not do such a thing; but that he believed he would be able to take possession of Hitler's headquarters with the regiment under his command. Boeselager's regiment, however, was located in Russia. We attempted its transfer to East Prussia, but did not succeed.

Another individual, 1st Lt. von Haeften, Stauffenberg's orderly, felt because of his Christian convictions that he could not take the responsibility of perhaps killing persons around Hitler by a plot against Hitler himself. A young captain, Axel von dem Busche, who had conquered all such scruples in himself, was heavily wounded, was laid up in the military hospital for a long time, and thus was excluded from the conspirators who were open for consideration. Finally, General Stieff with his two aides, Major Kuhn and 1st Lt. von Hagen, offered to carry out the plot. After some consideration, Stieff decided it was impossible to bring the explosive undetected into the conference room.

After consultation with General Wagner of the artillery, he agreed on the following plan: At that time the introduction of a new uniform was being contemplated. This uniform would be modelled for Hitler. The occasion of the modelling would be the occasion of the assassination, to be carried out by an officer willing to sacrifice himself. That officer would carry the bomb on his person, pull the ignition, leap toward Hitler, embrace him, and blow himself up together with Hitler. The showing of the uniform was scheduled repeatedly. Hitler called it off again and again — almost as if he had an inkling about the plot. Finally, in November 1943, the showing of the uniform was scheduled again. At that time all preparations for the plot were made. The prospect even existed that Hitler would really show up this time. And then a bombing raid destroyed all preparations the day before the scheduled attempt, and the showing of the uniform had to be called off.

Tresckow also declared himself ready for a new attempt. But his plan was tied to the condition that he could meet with Hitler somewhere. To accomplish that would have meant to put Tresckow into a position from which he could have reached Hitler without attracting attention. Tresckow tried to arrange this in two different ways. He took pains to convince General Schmundt that a new position should be created under Schmundt. The new post was to have the aim of transmitting directly to higher authorities various psychological and political experiences among the front forces, in order to make use of them. Although Schmundt was interested in the proposal, he did not bring it into actuality. Possibly he became suspicious of it, or possibly he had a logical reason against it. Later, a further possibility arose when General Heusinger, at that time chief of the operations department in the Army high command, was to begin a long leave, and a substitute was required. It was being considered whether his substitute should also succeed him. In various ways, attempts were made to put Tresckow into this position, always in vain.

Now Tresckow approached Heusinger himself. Heusinger was a non-Nazi. The time was the late winter of 1943. We were located in a small village in the Pripet marshes. Tresckow wrote a letter to Heusinger, urging the latter to propose him as Heusinger's substitute during the approaching leave. At the same time, Tresckow wrote a second letter, this one to Stieff. He explained to Stieff, since the bomb and the ignition apparatus were being left with him, which precautions had to be taken to eliminate every possible technical slip-up in setting off the bomb. I took these two letters and flew to Minsk in the *Storch* airplane and made connection there with a courier plane of the Army high command. First I reported to Heusinger and gave him the letter from Tresckow. Heusinger read it right away, and said, without a flicker of expression: "It needs no answer." I had the impression that Heusinger saw through Tresckow's intention, and sought to express his refusal by not replying.

From Heusinger, I went to Stieff, who received me with the non-chalance and cheerfulness that was habitual with him, tore open Tresckow's letter, skimmed it, burst into approving laughter, and then tore up the letter into little pieces. As he was about to throw the scraps of paper into the waste-paper basket, I took the liberty of stopping him. At the same time I asked him to let me have the bits so I could destroy them. He complied immediately, and thanked me for the good advice.

At the time, Stauffenberg was not thought of as the potential assassin. The consideration that he had only one eye and three fingers, and that he was indispensable in a key role in Berlin on the day of the overthrow, seemed to rule him out. Instead, we came to still another decision. Another attempt was to be made to have Hitler pay a visit to the middle army group. Then several of us were to use pistols, not dynamite, in a common attempt on Hitler's life. Although we figured that not all the bullets would hit the mark, we also thought that half of them would do so, and that these would suffice. The fact that there were several of us, we figured, should make it psychologically easier to carry the burden that must press on any human being when he is on the verge of such a deed. All the preparations were made, in Smolensk as well as in Orsha and again somewhat later in Minsk. But nothing and nobody could move Hitler to repeat his earlier visit to the middle army group. . . .

Stauffenberg himself had become chief of staff with General Fromm, the commander of the reserve army, as of July 1. He had received this appointment by virtue of his outstanding organizational capacities. When General Fromm informed him that he had been selected for this key position, Graf Stauffenberg refused, pointing out that he, Stauffenberg, no longer believed that the war could be won. He added that the guilt for the defeat, however, ought to rest on nobody else than Hitler. Fromm listened to this without contradicting, and then said that his, Fromm's, opinion was not very much different from that of Stauffenberg. Stauffenberg had the courage to put up the same objections with the chief of the general staff of the army, General Zeitzler. He, too, listened quietly to the protest, and then commented that he valued a subordinate who had the courage of his convictions and spoke his thoughts frankly. . . .

Hitler's headquarters in East Prussia was surrounded by three restricted areas. These could be traversed only with difficulty, for a special pass was necessary at each barrier. The same difficulty was involved in leaving the headquarters. When Stauffenberg had reached the inner restricted area on July 20, 1944, shortly before noon, he noticed to his surprise that the briefing was not taking place in the concrete bunker, as usual, but in the so-called tea-house, the floor and ceiling of which were without solid stone covering. The conference room was located on the long corridor. In the room itself was a big table. Along its long side, there was room for five persons.

Hitler was present. With the exception of Himmler and Goering, who were absent, the usual circle of persons was there. Stauffenberg's seat was immediately to the right of Hitler on the long side of the table. After the report about the troop-replacement situation was finished, Stauffenberg made the excuse of a pretended telephone call in order to leave the room. He threw the ignition of the time bomb in his briefcase, put it beside the leg of the table which separated his chair from Hitler's, and went out of the room.

The time bomb exploded as Hitler stood at his place, bending over a map on the table. Because there was no stone frame around the building, the pressure from the explosion blasted its way out through the wall. Most of those present were hurled through the wall that gave way, and thus escaped with their lives. Four were killed: Hitler's stenographer, Berger, Hitler's chief adjutant, General Schmundt,[1] the first general staff officer of the operations department in the army high command, Col. Brandt, and the chief of the general staff of the air force, General Korten.

Hitler himself was hurled out of the room. Besides bruises and burns, he suffered only an injury to his right hand. In the wake of the explosion, the scene was terrible to contemplate. It appeared as if the persons who had been present in the room were lying dead, or dying, in their blood. Stauffenberg had stayed nearby. He waited until the explosion interrupted the silence of headquarters with its earsplitting crash. He saw that the participants of the conference — Hitler among them — were hurled from the room, and were lying there, bloody, their clothes in tatters. In the firm belief that the bomb had done its intended work, Stauffenberg headed back. But the alarm had already been sounded. The barriers were closed. With luck and cunning, however, Stauffenberg succeeded nevertheless in getting out of headquarters. He drove to the airport, flew to Berlin, and took over the leadership there. . . .

While all this was happening in the Führer's headquarters, a scene unfolded in Berlin, in the Bendlerstrasse, with one of the main participants General Fromm, the commander of the reserves. The story is known to me from Fromm's lips and from details given in his subsequent indictment.

In the early afternoon of July 20, 1944, General Olbricht had entered Fromm's room and said he had to make a report to him in private. Thereupon Fromm interrupted the military report that he was receiving just at that moment. Olbricht then reported that Hitler had been assassinated. Fromm asked: "Who told you that?" Olbricht replied that the news originated from General Fellgiebfl, who had passed it on personally from his office to the central signal office of the reserve army.

Olbricht continued: "Under these circumstances, I propose that the password for domestic unrest should be given out, and the executive power be taken over." Fromm declared that he could take such far-going measures only if he himself could make certain about Hitler's death. He would telephone Field Marshal Keitel and ask about it. Now Olbricht

---

[1] He died of his injuries only on October 1, 1944.

himself picked up the receiver in Fromm's office and asked for a *"blitz"* telephone connection with Field Marshal Keitel. After the connection was established, Fromm asked Keitel what was going on at headquarters; there were wild rumors in Berlin, he added. "What should be the matter at headquarters? Everything is all right," Keitel replied. Fromm said, "It was just now reported to me that the Führer had been assassinated." Keitel came back: "That is nonsense. An assassination attempt has taken place, that is true, but luckily it failed. The Führer is alive and only superficially hurt. And where is your chief of staff, Graf Stauffenberg?" Fromm replied: "Colonel Stauffenberg has not yet come back to my office." This conversation was listened in on by Olbricht. On the strength of Keitel's words, Fromm decided that the password for domestic unrest should not be given to the deputy general commands for the time being.

After some time General Olbricht appeared in Fromm's office again, accompanied by Colonel Stauffenberg. Olbricht told Fromm that Stauffenberg had confirmed Hitler's death to him. Fromm replied: "But that is impossible; Keitel assured me of the opposite." Said Stauffenberg: "Field Marshal Keitel is lying, as usual; I myself saw how Hitler was carried out, dead."

At this point Olbricht told Fromm: "In view of this development, we have given out the password for domestic unrest to the deputy general commands." Hearing the words, Fromm jumped up, pounded his fist on the desk, and shouted: "That is sheer disobedience! What does 'we' mean? Who has given the order?" Olbricht replied: "My chief of staff, Col. Merz von Quirnheim." Fromm told Olbricht to get von Quirnheim right away. The colonel appeared, and when Fromm asked him, he admitted that he had given the deputy general commands, without Fromm's permission, the password for domestic unrest. Whereupon Fromm, standing, declared: "You are under arrest. Further developments remain to be seen."

At that moment, Col. Stauffenberg rose, and declared with icy coldness: "General, I myself ignited the bomb in Hitler's briefing session. There was an explosion as if a 15-centimeter shell had struck. Nobody in that room can be alive any longer." Fromm replied: "Graf Stauffenberg, the assassination failed; you'll have to shoot yourself immediately." Said Graf Stauffenberg: "No, that I will not do."

Again Olbricht entered the discussion, turning to Fromm and saying: "General, the moment for action has come. If we don't strike now, our fatherland will be ruined forever by Hitler." Fromm said: "Then you, Olbricht, have a share in this coup d'état, too?" Replied Olbricht: "Yes, but I personally am only standing at the rim of this circle that will take over the power in Germany." Fromm said: "Herewith I declare all three of you under arrest." Olbricht responded: "You cannot arrest us; you deceive yourself about the true balance of power. We arrest you."

After that a scuffle ensued between Fromm and Olbricht, with Merz and Stauffenberg intervening. Fromm was overpowered. An officer with pistol drawn entered the room. Fromm was kept from leaving the room. At the same time he was informed that his telephone was switched off. General Fromm yielded to this arrest until evening. However, two generals succeeded in coming into his office that afternoon. They told him that the rumor about the failure of the assassination had spread with the speed of lightning. The officer corps and officials at the headquarters of the commander of the replacement army were not willing to participate in the coup d'état. There would be an attempt to fetch troops and arrest the insurgents. Towards evening, Fromm asked to be allowed to go to his official residence within the same building. This was permitted him. After his arrest, Fromm was visited first by General Hoepner, who had been expelled from the armed forces since 1941. Hoepner said he regretted Fromm's personal misfortune, but could tell him that nothing would happen to him. Authority as commander of the replacement army, said Hoepner, was hereby passing over to himself, while Field Marshal von Witzleben had taken over the top military command. He said General Beck was in the building, too, and that Beck was the new head of the German Reich, designated by the insurgents. For them, he added, Hitler was dead, even if Keitel denied it. Meanwhile the first measures were taken in Vienna, Prague, Paris and Kassel. At the same time, those sections of the army that were stationed in the vicinity of Berlin marched towards the city. The commanding general of Berlin and of the March of Brandenburg, who was known as a Hitler adherent, was asked to come to the war ministry, and was arrested there. General von Thüngen was appointed his successor.

By order of the commandant of Berlin, General von Hase, the first urgent measures were now undertaken. He gave the order to blockade the government quarters. The commander of the Berlin guard battalion received the order and carried it out. The raiding patrols assigned to arrest Goebbels and to occupy the Berlin radio station gathered in the Unter den Linden arsenal. Then an unlucky accident happened. The National Socialist guidance officer of the guard battalion urged that Goebbels should be asked what was the matter. This was done. Goebbels sent for the commander himself, and in his presence had a call put through to Hitler. The Führer told the young commander that the orders that had been given to him involved making a revolution. Hitler's voice made its mark. The Berlin guard battalion could no longer be lined up for the purposes of the resistance movement. But none of this would have caused the failure of the coup d'état. The weapons-school units were still marching towards Berlin. However, meanwhile the report spread in the war ministry that the assassination had failed and that Hitler was alive. This news created immense confusion. Many officers wavered, others fell out, and still others who up to now had stayed in the background prepared for a counter-stroke. Shots fell. SS units and part of the guard battalion approached. They occupied the war ministry and freed Fromm. . . .

After his release, Fromm appointed a court-martial consisting of three generals. They sentenced the leaders of the coup d'état to death. With the sentence, Fromm went to his office, where Beck, Olbricht, Stauffenberg, Merz von Quirnheim, Haeften, Hoepner and others were together. Fromm declared them all arrested, and read the death sentence to them.

Thereupon Hoepner asked Fromm to hold up the execution in his case, as he hoped to be able to justify himself. Fromm acceded to this request, and had Hoepner led off. Olbricht asked Fromm only for the opportunity to be permitted to write a few lines to his wife. Fromm granted this request, too.

Fromm then asked for the weapons of the other gentlemen. Beck rose and said: "You won't want to give this order to me, your old superior officer. For I am going to take the consequences of this bungled situation for myself." Fromm indicated consent. Then Beck sat down in an arm-chair, drew a pistol, and tried to kill himself by shooting at his head. But the bullet only grazed his scalp. Then as Beck was about to try a second time, Graf Stauffenberg supported him as he sat there in the arm-chair. Although the second shot was a fatal hit, so that the pistol dropped out of Beck's hand, it did not end his life immediately. After that, Fromm had Olbricht, Stauffenberg, Merz and Haeften shot according to martial law, each individually, by a command of soldiers. Before the volley was fired, Graf Stauffenberg shouted "Long live our blessed Germany!"

Later, when Fromm asked an officer whether Beck had died in the meantime, and the answer was no, Fromm gave the order to spare him further suffering.

In February 1945 General Fromm was sentenced to death by the people's court — for cowardice. The sentence hit him hard. He had not expected it. On March 19, 1945, Fromm was shot in the penitentiary in Brandenburg by the officials there. He died with the cry: "Heil Hitler!"

126. Hitler's Political Testament

Before committing suicide, Hitler dictated his last will and political testament to his secretary. In the political testament, reprinted below, he defended his career and blamed the war on "international Jewry." In this same document Hitler expelled certain "traitors" from the Party.

From U.S. Chief of Counsel for the Prosecution of Axis Criminality, *Nazi Conspiracy and Aggression* (Washington, D.C.: U.S. Government Printing Office, 1946), vol. 6, doc. no. 3569-PS, pp. 260–63.

FIRST PART OF THE POLITICAL TESTAMENT

More than thirty years have now passed since I in 1914 made my modest contribution as a volunteer in the First World War that was forced upon the Reich.

In these three decades I have been actuated solely by love and loyalty to my people in all my thoughts, acts, and life. They gave me the strength to make the most difficult decisions which have ever confronted mortal man. I have spent my time, my working strength, and my health in these three decades.

It is untrue that I or anyone else in Germany wanted the war in 1939. It was desired and instigated exclusively by those international statesmen who were either of Jewish descent or worked for Jewish interests. I have made too many offers for the control and limitation of armaments, which posterity will not for all time be able to disregard for the responsibility for the outbreak of this war to be laid on me. I have further never wished that after the first fatal World War a second against England, or even against America, should break out. Centuries will pass away, but out of the ruins of our towns and monuments the hatred against those finally responsible whom we have to thank for everything, International Jewry and its helpers, will grow.

Three days before the outbreak of the German–Polish war I again proposed to the British ambassador in Berlin a solution to the German–Polish problem — similar to that in the case of the Saar district, under international control. This offer also cannot be denied. It was only rejected because the leading circles in English politics wanted the war, partly on account of the business hoped for and partly under influence of propaganda organized by International Jewry.

I have also made it quite plain that, if the nations of Europe are again to be regarded as mere shares to be bought and sold by these international conspirators in money and finance, then that race, Jewry, which is the real criminal of this murderous struggle, will be saddled with the responsibility. I further left no one in doubt that this time not only would millions of children of Europe's Aryan people die of hunger, not only would millions of grown men suffer death, and not only hundreds of thousands of women and children be burnt and bombed to death in the towns, without the real criminal having to atone for this guilt, even if by more humane means.

After six years of war, which in spite of all setbacks, will go down one day in history as the most glorious and valiant demonstration of a nation's life purpose, I cannot forsake the city which is the capital of this Reich. As the forces are too small to make any further stand against the enemy attack at this place and our resistance is gradually being weakened by men who are as deluded as they are lacking in initiative, I should like, by remaining in this town, to share my fate with those, the millions of others, who have also taken upon themselves to do so. Moreover I do not wish to fall into the hands of an enemy who requires a new spectacle organized by the Jews for the amusement of their hysterical masses.

I have decided therefore to remain in Berlin and there of my own free will to choose death at the moment when I believe the position of the Führer and Chancellor itself can no longer be held.

I die with a happy heart, aware of the immeasurable deeds and achievements of our soldiers at the front, our women at home, the achievements of our farmers and workers and the work, unique in history, of our youth who bear my name.

That from the bottom of my heart I express my thanks to you all, is just as self-evident as my wish that you should, because of that, on no account give up the struggle, but rather continue it against the enemies of the Fatherland, no matter where, true to the creed of a great Clausewitz. From the sacrifice of our soldiers and from my own unity with them unto death, will in any case spring up in the history of Germany, the seed of a radiant renaissance of the National Socialist movement and thus of the realization of a true community of nations.

Many of the most courageous men and women have decided to unite their lives with mine until the very last. I have begged and finally ordered them not to do this, but to take part in the further battle of the Nation. I beg the heads of the Armies, the Navy and the Air Force to strengthen by all possible means the spirit of resistance of our soldiers in the National Socialist sense, with special reference to the fact that also I myself, as founder and creator of this movement, have preferred death to cowardly abdication or even capitulation.

May it, at some future time, become part of the code of honor of the German officer — as is already the case in our Navy — that the surrender of a district or of a town is impossible, and that above all the leaders here must march ahead as shining examples, faithfully fulfilling their duty unto death.

SECOND PART OF THE POLITICAL TESTAMENT

Before my death, I expel the former Reichsmarschall Hermann Goering from the party and deprive him of all rights which he may enjoy by virtue of the decree of June 29th, 1941; and also by virtue of my statement in the Reichstag on September 1st, 1939. I appoint in his place Grossadmiral Doenitz, President of the Reich and Supreme Commander of the Armed Forces.

Before my death I expel the former Reichsfuehrer-*SS* and Minister of the Interior Heinrich Himmler, from the party and from all offices of State. In his stead I appoint Gauleiter Karl Hanke as Reichsfuehrer-*SS* and Chief of the German Police, and Gauleiter Paul Giesler as Reich Minister of the Interior.

Goering and Himmler, quite apart from their disloyalty to my person, have done immeasurable harm to the country and the whole nation by secret negotiations with the enemy, which they have conducted without my knowledge and against my wishes, and by illegally attempting to seize power in the State for themselves. . . .

Although a number of men, such as Martin Bormann, Dr. Goebbels, etc., together with their wives, have joined me of their own free will and did not wish to leave the capital of the Reich under any circumstances, but were willing to perish with me here, I must nevertheless ask them to obey my request, and in this case set the interests of the nation above their own feelings. By their work and loyalty as comrades they will be just as close to me after death, as I hope that my spirit will linger among them and always go with them. Let them be hard but never unjust, but above all let them never allow fear to influence their actions, and set the honor of the nation above everything in the world. Finally, let them be conscious of the fact that our task, that of continuing the building of a National Socialist State, represents the work of the coming centuries, which places every single person under an obligation always to serve the common interest and to subordinate his own advantage to this end. I demand of all Germans, all National Socialists, men, women and all the men of the Armed Forces, that they be faithful and obedient unto death to the new government and its President.

Above all I charge the leaders of the nation and those under them to scrupulous observance of the laws of race and to merciless opposition to the universal poisoner of all peoples, International Jewry.

Given in Berlin, this 29th day of April 1945. 4:00 A.M.

ADOLF HITLER

[*Witnesses*]
DR. JOSEPH GOEBBELS
MARTIN BORMANN
WILHELM BURGDORF
HANS KREBS

Conclusion

Why was opposition to the totalitarian regime of National Socialist Germany so limited and ultimately so ineffective? To respond to this question, we must understand the reasons why the great majority of the German people accepted domination by the Nazis for twelve years. This domination, it should not be forgotten, came to an end not through a popular uprising but because of military defeat and complete surrender. The question of the lack of opposition to National Socialism, in other words, leads to an evaluation of the popularity of the regime.

One pervasive reason for the continued support for the National Socialist regime was the widespread longing among Germans for a strong state. The readiness to obey an authoritarian state had traditionally been a value of the German people, one they upheld even at the expense of individual rights and constituted forms, and which the Nazis manipulated and finally subverted for their own ends. In the face of dramatic diplomatic and military undertakings and under cover of continual propaganda campaigns, the regime carried out a policy of disenfranchisement and even persecution of certain sections of the population that undermined all constitutional controls and personal rights. Not only in coercion and terror but also in this passive acceptance lies part of the explanation for the apparent support for the regime.

It can also be asked how widespread active support for the Nazi regime and its policies was. How enthusiastic were Germans, for instance, for the various rounds of Nazi celebrations, or for the all-inclusive policies of *Gleichschaltung* or the creation of the *Volksgemeinschaft*? The answers to these questions vary from one social group to another and even from one individual to another. Nazi leaders themselves had difficulty assessing popular reaction to the regime. Even though the SS and the Security Service devoted much time and effort to the attempt to gauge public opinion, they were unable to make accurate evaluations. In general, however, there seems to have been considerable support for Hitler during the 1930s and even in the first years of the war, which one would expect, given the early domestic and foreign policy successes of the regime.

National Socialism found widespread support among several sectors of the population. Women and young people, in particular, were apparently enthusiastic about the new regime. Much of this support was associated with the personality of Hitler himself. The Führer became the focus of adoration that rose above the squabbles within the Party and the problems of daily life. An unending barrage of propaganda, which resulted from the constant need to legitimize the dictatorship and continue the "permanent revolution," promoted this personality cult. The cult also dissipated opposition. What criticism did emerge was directed not at Hitler but at lesser Party leaders or the Party itself.

Responses to the regime from other segments of society were at best ambivalent and varied with economic, rather than political, conditions. German workers, whose former allegiance to the Social Democrats and the Communists made them potential opponents of National Socialism, clearly displayed large-scale indifference to Nazi rule. Initially, the jobs that opened up after the world economic crisis of the early 1930s kept them content enough. But even later, when the regime demanded longer working hours, dissatisfaction was expressed only on an individual basis and never aroused organized opposition. Farmers, too, though they objected to certain National Socialist farm policies, were not entirely unhappy with the regime. Compared to the fluctuating markets and prices of agricultural goods during the Weimar years, the economic situation of Germany in the Third Reich was marked by stability and security.

Yet because the police powers of the state, especially as exercised by the SS, were so extensive, many Germans were afraid of expressing their opinions openly. Legislation against criticizing the government, such as the Law Against Malicious Attack, brought the power of the state to bear upon both actual and potential opposition. The criticism that was expressed, however morally just, tended to be trivial and ineffective. Aside from the threat of the SS, the policies aimed at reshaping German society and integrating both state and society also blunted concerted opposition. By realigning traditional social and professional groupings, *Gleichschaltung* brought individuals under the direct control of the Party, whereas the construction of the *Volksgemeinschaft* often left those disaffected with the regime isolated and ineffective. These factors left little room for individuals to initiate independent action or organize groups critical of National Socialism. Opposition therefore tended to be passive rather than active, and open resistance either fragmented into small secret groups or, when organized — as with the churches and the remnants of the political Left — was prevented from allying with other such groups.

The question of organized opposition becomes acute when we consider the problem of the public's response to policies toward the Jews. Although most Germans probably did not know about the extermination policies of the last years of Nazi rule since the SS kept its program of genocide relatively secret, still the earlier "solutions" to the "Jewish Problem" as well as the rounding up of Jews for deportation had to have been common knowledge. The public tended to dismiss these actions, as well as the consequences of other aspects of the regime, as mere by-products of the revolutionary-totalitarian component of the authoritarian order most Germans favored after the failure of the Weimar Republic.

Before the disfranchisement of the Jews, antisemitic terror "from below" intermeshed with official sanctions from above. Although the government's Jewish policy was by no means generally popular, its pseudolegal trappings accorded with the inclination of an unpolitical populace to accept the measures as a "necessary evil'' and to shut its eyes to the disfranchisement, segregation, and eventually the destruction of a segment of their fellow citizens. In this sense, the acceptance of the state's Jewish policy and tacit agreement to it, by the German people made them accomplices in this system of injustice.

Perhaps the most lasting significance of the German experience of 1933—45 is revealed in this passive acceptance on the part of the German people of the state's policies toward the Jews, for in it lies a stark warning to the modern world. To the extent that nostalgia for a sense of communal unity (a wistfulness based in all likelihood on a false historical understanding) and notions that good citizenship entails uncritical acceptance of all activities undertaken by a state persist in our world, totalitarian ideologies like National Socialism retain a lingering appeal.

The history of National Socialism therefore raises the question of the meaning of the Third Reich, not only in the context of German history but also in relation to world developments in the twentieth century. As the rise of similar movements in many European countries indicated, fascism was of course not limited to Germany alone. Although the relationship between National Socialism and other forms of fascism has not been explored here, this study of the Nazi phenomenon in all its specificity and ambiguities points to a set of circumstances that are part of a common twentieth-century experience. National Socialism was fraught with inherent contradictions. It was a revolutionary force that came to power through constitutional means, it proclaimed a forward-looking ideology while at the same time it harked back to the simplicities of the past; it established a military power that proved itself most successfully in destroying a section of its own society. Yet these contradictions may best be understood as attempts to create a stable political, military, social, and even ideological world in the face of the tensions and chaos associated with the modern condition. However misguided and destructive they proved to be, National Socialist ideology and state policies attempted to eliminate or control the threats posed by the industrialization and urbanization of society.

Although this aim and even some of the ideological tenets of National Socialism — such as the desire to reconstitute the community and strengthen the family — are quite understandable, given the conditions of the modern world, their consequences are not. Why these goals led to both war and genocide is the abiding question that must be posed of the National Socialist phenomenon. Why the rebuilding of community was attempted only by denying the essence of individual freedom and by basing social coherence on a racial foundation is the question that raises the Nazi phenomenon above a merely national context within German history, above a sociological context of the analysis of mass movements, to a more general and even universal context. The complexities of modern life are so great that we find such simple solutions appealing even when they require denying both the reality of our present-day historical situation and the racial, ethnic, and individual diversity in which we find our common humanity.

Suggestions for Further Reading

I. Politics, Diplomacy, and War

Bracher, Karl Dietrich. *The German Dictatorship: The Origins, Structure, and Effects of National Socialism.* New York: Holt, Rinehart and Winston, 1970.

Broszat, Martin. *German National Socialism, 1919–1945.* Santa Barbara, Calif.: Clio, 1966.

———. *The Hitler State.* London: Longmans, 1981.

Carr, William. *Arms, Autarchy, and Aggression: A Study in German Foreign Policy.* New York: Norton, 1972.

———. *Poland to Pearl Harbor: The Making of the Second World War.* New York: Norton, 1985.

Carsten, F. L. *The Reichswehr and Politics, 1918–1933.* New York: Oxford University Press, 1966.

Deist, Wilhelm. *The Wehrmacht and German Rearmament.* Toronto: University of Toronto Press, 1981.

Gordon, Harold J. *The Reichswehr and the German Republic, 1919–1926.* Princeton: Princeton University Press, 1957.

Hildebrand, Klaus. *The Foreign Policy of the Third Reich.* Berkeley: University of California Press, 1974.

Hoffmann, Peter. *The History of German Resistance, 1933–1945.* Cambridge: Harvard University Press, 1977.

Klein, Burton H. *Germany's Economic Preparation for War.* Cambridge: Harvard University Press, 1959.

Nyomarkay, Joseph L. *Charisma and Factionalism in the Nazi Party.* Minneapolis: University of Minnesota Press, 1967.

O'Neill, Robert J. *The German Army and the Nazi Party, 1933–1939.* London: Cassell, 1966.

Orlow, Dietrich. *The History of the Nazi Party, 1919–1933.* 2 vols. Pittsburgh: University of Pittsburgh Press, 1969–73.

Peterson, Edward N. *The Limits of Hitler's Power.* Princeton: Princeton University Press, 1969.

Robertson, E. M. *Hitler's Pre-War Policy and Military Plans, 1933–1939.* New York: Citadel, 1967.

Waite, Robert G. L. *Vanguard of Nazism: The Freecorps Movement in Postwar Germany, 1918–1923.* Cambridge: Harvard University Press, 1952.

Weinberg, Gerhard L., *The Foreign Policy of Hitler's Germany: Diplomatic Revolution in Europe 1933–36.* Chicago: University of Chicago Press, 1970.

———. *The Foreign Policy of Hitler's Germany: Starting World War II.* Chicago: University of Chicago Press, 1980.

II. Hitler: Life and Personality

Bullock, Alan. *Hitler: A Study in Tyranny.* Rev. ed. New York: Harper and Row, 1964.

Carr, William. *Hitler: A Study in Personality and Politics.* New York: St. Martin's, 1979.

Fest, Joachim C. *Hitler.* New York: Harcourt Brace Jovanovich, 1974.

Gordon, Harold J. *Hitler and the Beer Hall Putsch.* Princeton: Princeton University Press, 1972.

Jäckel, Eberhard. *Hitler in History.* Hanover, NH: University Press of New England, 1989.

————. *Hitler's Weltanschauung: A Blueprint for Power.* Middletown, Conn.: Wesleyan University Press, 1972.

Kershaw, Ian. *The "Hitler Myth": Image and Reality in the Third Reich.* Oxford: Oxford University Press, 1987.

III. Social, Economic, and Cultural Life in Nazi Germany

Bessel, Richard, ed. *Life in the Third Reich.* Oxford: Oxford University Press, 1987.

Beyerchen, Alan D. *Scientists Under Hitler: Politics and the Physics Community in the Third Reich.* 2nd ed. New Haven: Yale University Press, 1985.

Blackburn, Gilmer W. *Education in the Third Reich.* Albany: State University of New York Press, 1985.

Conway, John S. *The Nazi Persecution of the Churches Under Hitler.* Detroit: Wayne State University Press, 1979.

Dahrendorf, Ralf. *Society and Democracy in Germany.* New York: Doubleday, 1967.

Farquharson, John E. *The Plough and the Swastika: The NSDAP and Agriculture in Germany, 1928–1945.* London and Beverly Hills: Sage, 1976.

Giles, Geoffrey. *Students and National Socialism in Germany.* Princeton: Princeton University Press, 1985.

Grosshans, Henry. *Hitler and the Artists.* New York: Holmes and Meier, 1983.

Grunberger, Richard. *A Social History of the Third Reich.* London: Weidenfeld and Nicolson, 1971.

Helmreich, Ernst Christian. *The German Churches Under Hitler.* Detroit: Wayne State University Press, 1979.

Kele, Max H. *Nazis and Workers: National Socialist Appeals to German Labor 1919–1933.* Chapel Hill, NC: University of North Carolina Press, 1972.

Koonz, Claudia. *Mothers in the Fatherland: Woman, the Family, and Nazi Politics.* New York: St. Martin's Press, 1987.

Laqueur, Walter Z. *Young Germany: A History of the German Youth Movement.* New York: Basic Books, 1962.

Lewy, Guenter. *The Catholic Church and Nazi Germany.* New York: McGraw-Hill, 1964.

Milward, Alan S. *The German Economy at War.* London: Athlone Press, 1965.

Schoenbaum, David. *Hitler's Social Revolution.* New York: Doubleday, 1966.

Stephenson, Jill. *Women in Nazi Society.* London: Barnes and Noble Books, 1975.

Strachura, Peter D. *Nazi Youth in the Weimar Republic.* Santa Barbara, CA: Clio Books, 1975.

Tilton, Timothy. *Nazism, Neo-Nazism, and the Peasantry.* Bloomington, IN: Indiana University Press, 1975.

Turner, Henry Ashby Jr. *German Big Business and the Rise of Hitler.* New York: Oxford University Press, 1985.

Welch, David. *Propaganda and the German Cinema.* New York: Oxford University Press, 1985.

Zahn, Gordon C. *German Catholics and Hitler's Wars.* New York: Sheed and Ward, 1962.

IV. The Final Solution

Fleming, Gerald. *Hitler and the Final Solution.* Berkeley: University of California Press, 1984.

Gilbert, Martin. *The Holocaust: The History of Jews in Europe During the Second World War.* New York: Holt, Rinehart and Winston, 1985.

Gordon, Sarah. *Hitler, Germans and the "Jewish Question."* Princeton: Princeton University Press, 1984.

Hilberg, Raoul. *The Destruction of the European Jews.* Chicago: Quadrangle Books, 1961.

Hirschfeld, Gerhard, ed. *The Policies of Genocide: Jews and Soviet Prisoners of War in Nazi Germany.* Cambridge, MA: Unwin Hyman, 1986.

Maier, Charles S. *The Unmasterable Past: History, Holocaust, and German National Identity.* Cambridge: Harvard University Press, 1988.

Marrus, Michael. *The Holocaust in History.* Hanover, NH: University Press of New England, 1987.

Peukert, Detlev. *Inside Nazi Germany: Conformity, Opposition, and Racism in Everyday Life.* New Haven: Yale University Press, 1987.

Pulzer, Peter C. *The Rise of Political Anti-Semitism in Germany and Austria.* New York: Wiley, 1964.

Schleunes, Karl A. *The Twisted Road to Auschwitz: Nazi Policy Toward German Jews, 1933–1939*. Urbana: University of Illinois Press, 1970.

Yahil, Leni. *The Holocaust: The Fate of European Jewry, 1932–1945*. New York: Oxford University Press, 1990.